Ref KF 8742 .H37 2012 vol.1
Leiter, Richard A.
Landmark Supreme Court cases

P9-BIO-085

P91698

South Puget Sound Community College

LIBRARY-MEDIA CENTER
SOUTH PUGET SOUND COMM. COLLEGE
2011 MOTTMAN RD SW
OLYMPIA WA 98512-6292

REFERENCE

80025 75540

REFERENCE

Landmark Supreme Court Cases

*The Most Influential Decisions
of the Supreme Court of the United States*

Second Edition

Volume I

Abortion to Death Penalty

Richard A. Leiter
Roy M. Mersky

Facts On File
An Infobase Learning Company

LIBRARY-MEDIA CENTER
SOUTH PUGET SOUND COMM. COLLEGE
2011 MOTTMAN RD SW
OLYMPIA WA 98512-6292

Landmark Supreme Court Cases: The Most Influential Decisions of the Supreme Court of the United States, Second Edition

Copyright © 2012 by Richard A. Leiter and Roy M. Mersky
Copyright © 2004 by Gary Hartman and Roy M. Mersky

All rights reserved. No part of this book may be reproduced or utilized in any form or by any means, electronic or mechanical, including photocopying, recording, or by any information storage or retrieval systems, without permission in writing from the publisher. For information contact:

Facts On File, Inc.
An imprint of Infobase Learning
132 West 31st Street
New York NY 10001

Library of Congress Cataloging-in-Publication Data
Leiter, Richard A.
   Landmark Supreme Court Cases : the most influential decisions of the Supreme Court of the United States / Richard A. Leiter, Roy M. Mersky.—2nd ed.
      p. cm.
   Rev. ed. of: Landmark Supreme Court cases / Gary Hartman, Roy M. Mersky, and Cindy L. Tate. c2004.
   Includes bibliographical references and index.
   ISBN 978-0-8160-6957-6 (alk. paper)
   1. United States. Supreme Court. 2. Law—United States—Cases. I. Mersky, Roy M. II. Hartman, Gary R. Landmark Supreme Court cases. III. United States. Supreme Court. IV. Title.
   KF8742.H37 2011
   347.73'26—dc22   2010048195

Facts On File books are available at special discounts when purchased in bulk quantities for businesses, associations, institutions, or sales promotions. Please call our Special Sales Department in New York at (212) 967-8800 or (800) 322-8755.

You can find Facts On File on the World Wide Web at http://www.infobaselearning.com

Excerpts included herewith have been reprinted by permission of the copyright holders; the authors have made every effort to contact copyright holders. The publisher will be glad to rectify, in future editions, any errors or omissions brought to their notice.

Text design by Erik Lindstrom
Composition by Hermitage Publishing Services
Cover printed by Yurchak Printing, Inc., Landisville, Pa.
Book printed and bound by Yurchak Printing, Inc., Landisville, Pa.
Date printed: December 2011
Printed in the United States of America

10 9 8 7 6 5 4 3 2 1

This book is printed on acid-free paper.

LIBRARY-MEDIA CENTER
SOUTH PUGET SOUND COMM. COLLEGE
2011 MOTTMAN RD SW
OLYMPIA WA 98512-6292

P91698

CONTENTS

LIST OF ENTRIES BY SUBJECT

TAXATION

ADDITIONAL CASES

PREFACE AND ACKNOWLEDGMENTS

First, a debt of gratitude must be paid to the wonderful reference sources consulted in preparing this book. The original versions of the decisions for all cases discussed were used. Today, the true definition of *original version* nearly defies description. All U.S. Supreme Court opinions are officially published by the Government Printing Office, in the *United States Reports*. There are, in addition, several commercial sources of the official versions of decisions of the Court: *Supreme Court Reporter* (West Publishing), *United States Reports, Lawyers' Edition* (Lexis Law Publishing), and Westlaw, Lexis, and a host of other Web sites, including ones maintained by the Government Printing Office and the Court itself. Ironically, the official source of Supreme Court decisions, the *United States Supreme Court Reports,* is several years behind in releasing opinions of decided cases, and lawyers routinely rely on other sources in order to obtain the most recent opinions of the Court. (As of this writing, in August 2010, bound volumes of the *United States Supreme Court Reports* have been published through 2006, with advance sheets covering the period through May 2008.) There is an excellent webpage on the Court's Web site (http://www.supremecourt.gov/opinions; click on the "Information about Opinions" link at the bottom of the page) that describes in detail how opinions are published.

Many outstanding reference works were consulted by the army of research assistants who performed much of the grunt work in compiling this book. Kermit Hall's outstanding *The Oxford Companion to the Supreme Court of the United States* (2d ed., Oxford University Press, 2005), *The Constitution of the United States of America, Analysis and Interpretation* (Congressional Research Service, Library of Congress, GPO, 2004), and the numerous other almanacs and handbooks on the Supreme Court were regularly consulted for initial background research on case histories and legacies. Where appropriate, online resources were used. The Internet and the World Wide Web offer tools and an atmosphere that have created an amazing array of rich sources of information. Legal blogs, including those maintained by practitioners, academics, and various political or nonprofit organizations that represent causes or professional organizations, offer the researcher a dizzying store of material from which to gather information about a particular case. I am not ashamed to admit, after having used and tested it to produce the articles and summaries included in this book, that we consulted Wikipedia frequently. Its accuracy and useful information are a credit to those students and scholars, professional and amateur alike, who edit, update, and correct articles found on its webpages. Wikipedia was used with caution, however, and only when the information it presents was verified against other sources.

Two online resources deserve special mention. Oyez! (oyez.org) is a Chicago-based operation that had its start in the early 1990s as a "Hitchhiker's Guide to the Supreme Court," dedicated to making everything related to the Court accessible to everyone. At present, it provides access to opinions, audio recordings of oral arguments, summaries, access to briefs, and statutes or other rules at issue in a case. It is a well-organized and intuitive Web site and is recommended for anyone interested in any detail or aspect of the Court.

Another Web site that we valued, used frequently, and can recommend highly is Justia's U.S. Supreme Court Center (supreme.justia.com). This resource brings together all the major online resources in one place. It is a reliable one-stop resource for conducting meaningful online research on Supreme Court opinions.

This edition contains a number of innovations to the previous edition that we hope are improvements. First, we arranged the cases in chronological order within each chapter. This allows the reader to follow the development of the law in each subject area. We have also added to the case summaries a new section that includes a citation to the statute at issue in the case. If the reader wants to consult the text of that statute, using the citation provided, it will be relatively easy to look it up at a library or in any of the many sites on the World Wide Web that provide access to the United States Code, state statutes, or other regulations or treatises. We have also added a new appendix that contains the U.S. Constitution.

Some innovations to this edition have rendered parts of the former edition irrelevant. For example, because the cases are arranged chronologically, the appendix that listed cases chronologically by topic in the former edition has been eliminated. In addition, we have added a few new chapters that cover topics not dealt with fully before, such as Native American law, the death penalty, intellectual property, and sovereign immunity. In some instances, the cases that make up these new chapters are entirely new additions, and sometimes cases formerly covered were reorganized as new ones were added to a chapter, to give the reader a more focused view of the development of the law on that topic.

A book such as this cannot be written without the effort of many people. In the case of this project, it involved not only blood and sweat but tears and dedication as well.

Above all, I must recognize and thank my lead research assistant, Elizabeth "Betty" Hurst. Her passion, her careful editing, and her supreme organizational skills made the book everything it is. She not only was able to execute the work at hand but had many important ideas that contributed to the end result. Betty, thank you for your hard work and for hanging in there, even when we took those two steps back. We have, however, made three steps forward and succeeded in the end.

I also must thank the late Professor Roy M. Mersky, primary editor of the first edition of this book. Roy was my mentor in this profession and brought me in to help him complete the second edition. At the time, Roy was very ill; terminally so, it turns out. I thank him for giving me the opportunity to complete this valuable reference work, for his guidance over the years, and for his friendship.

Many research assistants worked on this book over the years. Mere mention of their names cannot possibly do justice to the work that they put into summarizing, digesting, and annotating the cases gathered herein. But, aside from the wages and gold stars that they earned, I can do little more than offer them the satisfaction of seeing their names in print. (Their names are listed alphabetically below.) Superstars among this group are Tom Freeman, Brandie Iovino, Shannon Palmer, and Ryan Stover. These individuals worked on at least 10 cases each, while Tom and Brandie researched many more. Kalyn Byers, Kelley Ekeler, Peter Haugen, Heather Hogan, and Danielle Vander Geeten also contributed to this project with distinction. Thank you all for your hard, and sometimes tedious, work:

Jamie Anderson
Nikki Bohl
Kalyn Byers
Branden Collingsworth
Kelly Ekeler
Ben Fabrikant
Tom Freeman
Peter Haugen
Heather Hogan
Brandie Iovino
Nathan Jaggers

Tara King
Tobe Leibert
Stephanie Mikesh
Jane O'Connell
Shannon Palmer
Austin Relph
Ryan Stover
Danielle Vander Geeten

I also called on some of my colleagues at the University of Nebraska College of Law for help in culling cases worthy of being deemed "landmark" from the recent docket of the Supreme Court. The constitutional law professors (and distinguished scholars) Eric Berger, Rick Duncan, and Jo Potuto each annotated lists of cases. Their combined input was extremely helpful as I tried to cull the most important cases from the last few terms of the Court.

The volume of the material contained in the book meant that nearly everyone in my life who was within reach was called upon to lend a hand. For the most part, they responded positively. My nephew Alex Haskell took three weeks from his round-the-world tour to enjoy a Lincoln, Nebraska, summer and contribute a few case summaries. In fall of that same year, he began law school at the University of Southern California and did quite well. I take some of the credit for his success; this work prepared him for the rigors of reading complex cases and distilling their essence. My daughter, Annie, and her fiancé (now husband), Matt Avery, also contributed substantially to editing the material. Annie's eagle eye caught formatting inconsistencies and errors in grammar like a sharpshooter. Matt's gift of clear prose helped to make the chapter introductions consistent and clear. Thanks, Annie and Matt, for your hard work during the "lost summer." Thanks also to my very patient wife, Wendy, who put in a fair share of effort (unpaid), editing and proofreading various parts of the book while planning two weddings. From the bottom of my heart, thank you, Wendy—for everything.

INTRODUCTION

The Supreme Court of the United States is a remarkable component of our democracy. The other two branches of government, the executive and the congressional, are democratically elected to discrete terms. Although the office of the president is technically composed of a single individual, the entire executive branch is composed of dozens of individuals, from cabinet level secretaries and heads of federal agencies to midlevel presidential appointments to career staff members, from professional to clerical levels. In the case of the Supreme Court, however, there are nine justices appointed by the president for life. Even compared with Congress, with its more than 550 elected representatives, the Court's nine justices constitute a tiny branch of government that wields outsize and enduring power.

The reasons for lifetime appointments to it and for the Court's relatively small size were debated at length during the country's formative era and represent an ingenious innovation in democratic, representational government. Lifetime appointments offer the justices independence and freedom from threats of reappraisal for decisions they make that may be contrary to the interests of particular citizens, businesses, or other branches, offices, or departments of government in any jurisdiction under the Court's purview.

This independence has, over the years, allowed the Court to make rulings of broad, sometimes revolutionary, import. Many legal positions taken for granted today were the result of bold decision making by a relatively small group of men and women. Decisions such as the right of a citizen of color to vote, of people of different races to marry, of women to obtain contra-

ceptive devices or medicines, even the right of an accused to an attorney in criminal cases reflect principles U.S. citizens take for granted today but were suppressed before the Supreme Court upheld them.

The great power that the Court wields entails great responsibility. And even that understates the magnitude of both the power and the responsibility associated with the office. The men and women who have been chosen to assume the office of justice of the Supreme Court, or of chief justice, have all, to a number, been people of remarkable intelligence. While pundits rail against this or that justice for being "ignorant" or "stupid" or what-have-you, the fact is that those accusers usually disagree with the opinions or legal philosophy of the justice in question. For every detractor that a justice has, s/he has as many fans or supporters who regard him or her as brilliant or insightful. What is surprising are the presidents and senators who seem to be continually baffled by their appointees. A president may appoint a justice whose decisions and rulings suggest liberal legal bias but who turns out to hold utterly conservative views on some issues, or vice versa. Occasionally, nominees have turned out to be more liberal than predicted, owing to the nature of the cases before the Court.

The fact that the Supreme Court drives the engine of legal evolution while being part of the engine itself, propelling our legal system through increasingly unchartered waters, should not surprise students of the Court. If one thinks about the Constitution and our entire legal system as a static system of values, morals, and ethics, it follows that humanity will be continuously testing its limits. It is human nature. And, as we test the limits of the law, we are capable of finding the gray areas that the law does not address. As people confront the gray areas, we are, not surprisingly, finding that what was wrong yesterday is not considered so today, at least to an extent. One of the fundamental principles behind our modern legal system is that it is evolving; it serves us, not the reverse. And so the law continuously and incrementally accommodates nuanced pushes to modify social and legal norms. And the justices, once installed on the Supreme Court, collectively at least, apply the law in such a way that serves to move our legal system toward social, economic, and philosophical progress.

Even though individuals on the Court may be liberal or conservative when they assume office, they end up forging a collective character and judgment of right and wrong that is nearly immutable over time. It is the Court that keeps Congress and the states moving in an orderly fashion toward progress and preserving our nation's freedoms and liberties. The Supreme Court of the United States is well worth studying in all its aspects—the justices, the legal history, and the history of the Court itself—for to understand the Court is in some ways akin to understanding ourselves and our nation and to anticipating our future.

This book provides the reader with concise summaries of the many significant Supreme Court decisions that are considered landmark cases, that is, cases that are recognized as having either defined new principles discovered in the Constitution or that significantly elaborated established ones.

LANDMARK SUPREME COURT CASES

ABORTION

Abortion is one of the most contentious issues of the modern era. It has become a social issue that has significantly contributed to the definition of the women's rights movement, a legal issue that has pitched states against the Supreme Court, and a political issue that has changed the careers of many a politician. While the public and political debate about abortion has focused on the morality of the procedure itself, the legal issues surrounding it tend to be very different and are frequently misunderstood.

Abortion is a crime in virtually every state. Its legal definition is the killing of a fetus, a form of murder; about this, there is no debate. The legal issue is whether, and under what circumstances, the right to privacy trumps the state's interest in preventing this crime. The original debate raised the question of whether a state has the right to declare an act an unlawful killing of something that is not yet "alive." Women's rights activists argued that the state may not declare abortion a crime before a fetus is alive and that doing so was an unlawful invasion of privacy, because, since the fetus was not yet alive, or "viable," terminating it was merely a personal choice regarding a biological function.

A woman is free to terminate a pregnancy in every state, as long as it is done within a protected time frame after she becomes pregnant and before a state's law prohibits it. Within that protected time period, generally the first trimester of the pregnancy, it is seen as a matter of the woman's right to privacy. The great debate regarding abortion is not, contrary to public debate, one of whether fetuses may be aborted with impunity (it is generally perceived as a criminal act), rather it is a debate over the right of a state to invade a personal right of privacy.

As one traces the development of the Supreme Court's rulings regarding abortion, one is struck by an important fact: Many states are opposed to the Court's position regarding access to abortion. This is evidenced by the fact that virtually no state has repealed its laws that make abortion a crime, and many states have passed laws that aim to restrict, in some fashion, access to and availability of abortions. The Supreme Court has never ruled that state laws making abortion a crime are illegal; they have simply declared that before the second trimester, or legal viability of the fetus, abortion is a private matter to be decided by a woman and her doctor. States interested in preventing abortions have adjusted to the Court's rulings by passing laws that limit the procedure in a variety of ways, for example, by requiring parental permission, by requiring waiting periods, or by requiring doctors to provide women with educational information intended to influence women considering abortion to change their minds.

Abortion is an issue that does not directly affect most of the population, yet its impact on politics is immense. Few Supreme Court rulings have generated as much public debate and protest, and it is not likely that the controversy will fade anytime soon.

Case Title: *Roe v. Wade*

Legal Citation: 410 U.S. 113

Year of Decision: 1973

KEY ISSUE

May a state constitutionally make it a crime to procure an abortion except to save the mother's life?

HISTORY OF THE CASE

Three reasons have been advanced to explain historically the enactment of criminal abortion laws in the 19th century and to justify their continued existence: It has been argued that (1) these laws were the product of a Victorian social concern to discourage illicit sexual conduct; (2) the laws expressed concern with abortion as a medical procedure, because when most criminal abortion laws were first enacted, the procedure was hazardous to the woman; (3) the state has an interest in protecting prenatal life.

An unmarried pregnant woman who wished to terminate her pregnancy by abortion instituted an action in the U.S. District Court for the Northern District of Texas, seeking a judgment that the Texas criminal abortion statutes, which prohibited abortions except for the medical purpose of saving the mother's life, were unconstitutional. She also sought an injunction against their continued enforcement. A physician, who alleged that he had been previously arrested for violations of the Texas statutes and that two prosecutions were presently pending against him in the state courts, sought and was granted permission to intervene. A separate action, similar to that filed by the unmarried pregnant woman, was filed by a married childless couple, who alleged that should the wife become pregnant at some future date, they would wish to terminate the pregnancy by abortion. The two actions were consolidated and heard together by a three-judge district court, which held that (1) the unmarried

pregnant woman and the physician had standing to sue; (2) the married childless couple's complaint should be dismissed because they lacked standing to sue; (3) abstention was not warranted with respect to a declaratory judgment; (4) the right to choose whether to have children was protected by the Ninth Amendment through the Fourteenth Amendment; (5) the Texas criminal abortion statutes were unconstitutionally vague and overbroad; and (6) the application for injunctive relief should be denied under the abstention doctrine. All parties appealed to the U.S. Court of Appeals for the Fifth Circuit to preserve their arguments, which court ordered the appeals be suspended pending decision on the appeal taken by all parties to the U.S. Supreme Court from the district court's denial of injunctive relief.

SUMMARY OF ARGUMENTS

Roe alleged that she was unmarried and pregnant; that she wished to terminate her pregnancy by an abortion "performed by a competent, licensed physician, under safe, clinical conditions"; that she was unable to have a "legal" abortion in Texas because her life did not appear to be threatened by the continuation of her pregnancy; and that she could not afford to travel to another jurisdiction in order to secure a legal abortion under safe conditions. She claimed that the Texas statutes were unconstitutionally vague and that they abridged her right of personal privacy protected by the First, Fourth, Fifth, Ninth, and Fourteenth Amendments. By an amendment to her complaint, Roe purported to sue "on behalf of herself and all other women" in her situation.

James Hubert Hallford, a licensed physician, alleged that he had been arrested previously for violations of the Texas abortion statutes. He described conditions of patients who went to him seeking abortions, and he claimed that for many cases he, as a physician, was unable to determine whether they fell within or outside the exception recognized by the state law—to save the life of the mother. He alleged that, as a consequence, the statutes were vague and uncertain, in violation of the Fourteenth Amendment, and that they violated his own and his patients' rights to privacy in the doctor-patient relationship and his own right to practice medicine, rights he claimed were guaranteed by the First, Fourth, Fifth, Ninth, and Fourteenth Amendments.

John and Mary Doe, a married couple, filed a companion complaint. The Does alleged that they were a childless couple because Mrs. Doe suffered from a "neural-chemical" disorder and was advised to "avoid pregnancy until such time as her condition has materially improved." Also on medical advice, Mrs. Doe was advised to discontinue use of her birth control pills. The Does stated that if Mrs. Doe should become pregnant, she would want to terminate the pregnancy by an abortion performed by a competent licensed physician under safe clinical conditions. By an amendment to their complaint, the Does purported to sue "on behalf of themselves and all couples similarly situated."

DECISION

On appeal, the U.S. Supreme Court dismissed the physician's complaint but affirmed the district court's judgment in all other respects. In an opinion by Justice Blackmun, expressing the views of seven members of the Court, it was held that (1) the pregnant unmarried woman had standing to sue; (2) the complaint of the childless married couple presented no actual justiciable case or controversy and had been properly dismissed; (3) states have legitimate interests in seeing that abortions are performed under circumstances that ensure maximum safety for the patient; (4) the right to privacy encompasses a woman's decision whether or not to terminate her pregnancy; (5) a woman's right to terminate her pregnancy is not absolute and may to some extent be limited by the state's legitimate interests in safeguarding the woman's health, in maintaining proper medical standards, and in protecting potential human life; (6) the unborn are not included within the definition of "person" as used in the Fourteenth Amendment; (7) prior to the end of the first trimester of pregnancy, the state may not interfere with or regulate an attending physician's decision, reached in consultation with a patient, that the patient's pregnancy should be terminated; (8)

from and after the end of the first trimester, and until the time when the fetus becomes viable (able to survive outside the mother's body), the state may regulate the abortion procedure only to the extent that such regulation relates to the preservation and protection of maternal health; (9) from and after the time when the fetus becomes viable, the state may prohibit abortions altogether, except those necessary to preserve the life or health of the mother; and (10) the state may proscribe the performance of all abortions except those performed by physicians currently licensed by the state; and, expressing the view of six members of the Court, it was held that the physician's complaint should be dismissed and he should return to the pending state court proceeding and the remedies available there.

AFTERMATH

The *Roe v. Wade* majority opinion appeared to establish a rigid "trimester" structure for the judicial examination of abortion regulations. Virtually no regulations would be upheld that related to first trimester abortions; any regulation of abortions performed between the end of the first trimester and the time when the fetus was viable (as determined by an attending physician) would be upheld only if the regulation was narrowly tailored to protect the health of the woman. Abortions could be outlawed after the fetus was viable, although the ban on post-viability abortions, and all other abortion regulations, would have to include an exception for abortions performed to protect the life or health of the woman. In the late 1970s and throughout the 1980s, the Supreme Court's rulings, though not its opinions, appeared to adopt a test of "reasonableness" for abortion regulations. State abortion regulations that were reasonably related to protecting the pregnant woman or were reasonably related to protecting the health or existence of a viable fetus would be upheld. An abortion regulation would be invalidated if a majority of justices believed that the regulation merely deterred abortions and was not a reasonable means of protecting a pregnant woman or a viable fetus. In 1989, in *Webster v. Reproductive Health Services*, a majority of justices on the Supreme Court appeared to reject the

Roe v. Wade formal "trimester" analytical structure, although they did not at that time replace the *Roe* analysis with any new test for the judicial review of abortion regulations.

In *Planned Parenthood of Southeastern Pennsylvania v. Casey* (1992), the Court reviewed Pennsylvania abortion law. This required informed consent and a 24-hour waiting period prior to the procedure. A minor seeking an abortion required the consent of one parent (the law allowed for a judicial bypass procedure that would allow the minor to obtain court approval instead of parental consent). A married woman seeking an abortion had to indicate that she notified her husband of her intention to abort the fetus. In a bitter 5-4 decision, the Court again reaffirmed *Roe,* but it upheld most of the Pennsylvania provisions. For the first time, the justices imposed a new standard to determine the validity of laws restricting abortions. The new standard asks whether a state abortion regulation has the purpose or effect of imposing an "undue burden," which is defined as a "substantial obstacle in the path of a woman seeking an abortion before the fetus attains viability." Under this standard, the only provision to fail the undue-burden test was the husband notification requirement.

SIGNIFICANCE

The Court held that a woman's right to an abortion fell within the right to privacy (recognized in *Griswold v. Connecticut*) protected by the Fourteenth Amendment. The decision gave a woman total autonomy over the pregnancy during the first trimester and defined different levels of state interest for the second and third trimesters. As a result, the laws of 46 states were affected by the Court's ruling.

RELATED CASES

Baker v. Carr, 396 U.S. 186, 204 (1962)

Griswold v. Connecticut, 381 U.S. 479 (1965)

Webster v. Reproductive Health Services, 492 U.S. 490 (1989)

Planned Parenthood of Southeastern Pennsylvania v. Casey, 505 U.S. 833 (1992)

Republic National Bank of Miami v. United States, 506 U.S. 80 (1992)

Bray v. Alexandria Women's Health Clinic, 506 U.S. 263 (1993)

Stenberg v. Carhart, 530 U.S. 914 (2000)

Gonzales v. Carhart, 550 U.S. 124 (2007)

STATUTES AT ISSUE

Texas Penal Code Articles 1191–1194 and 1196 (1973)

RECOMMENDED READING

Balkin, J. M., ed. *What* Roe v. Wade *Should Have Said: The Nation's Top Legal Experts Rewrite America's Most Controversial Decision.* New York: New York University Press, 2005.

John Hart Ely, *The Wages of Crying Wolf: A Comment on* Roe v. Wade, 82 Yale Law Journal 920 (April–July 1973).

Faux, Marian. *Roe v. Wade.* New York: Macmillan, 1980.

Glendon, Mary Ann. *Abortion and Divorce in Western Law.* Cambridge, Mass.: Harvard University Press, 1987.

Hoffer, Peter Charles. Roe v. Wade: *The Abortion Rights Controversy in American History.* Lawrence: University Press of Kansas, 2001.

Horan, Dennis, et al., eds. *Abortion and the Constitution: Reversing* Roe v. Wade *through the Courts.* Washington, D.C.: Georgetown University Press, 1987.

Keynes, Edward, with Randall K. Miller. *The Courts vs. Congress: Prayer, Busing and Abortion.* Durham, N.C.: Duke University Press, 1989.

Rabin, Eva R. *Abortion, Politics and the Courts:* Roe v. Wade *and Its Aftermath.* New York: Greenwood Press, 1987.

Schwartz, Bernard. *The Ascent of Pragmatism: The Burger Court in Action.* New York: Addison-Wesley, 1990.

Case Title: *Planned Parenthood of Central Missouri v. Danforth*

Legal Citation: 428 U.S. 52

Year of Decision: 1976

KEY ISSUES

Are certain provisions of Missouri House Bill No. 1211, which, among other things, regulates certain abortion procedures and requires parental or spousal consent for nonemergency abortions, unconstitutional?

HISTORY OF THE CASE

In June 1974, Missouri passed a law setting forth conditions and limitations on abortions. The statute, House Bill No. 1211, also established criminal offenses for noncompliance with the various conditions and limitations. Within three days, several physicians and Planned Parenthood of Central Missouri challenged the constitutionality of the act in the U.S. District Court for the Eastern District of Missouri. Suit was brought against John C. Danforth, the attorney general of Missouri.

The physicians and Planned Parenthood attacked seven provisions of the act. In summary, they were (1) a provision defining "viability" as that stage of fetal development when the life of the unborn child may be continued indefinitely outside the womb by natural or artificial life-supportive systems; for purposes that any abortion not necessary to preserve the life or health of the mother should not be performed unless the attending physician would certify with reasonable medical certainty that the fetus is not viable; (2) a provision requiring that a woman, prior to submitting to an abortion during the first 12 weeks of pregnancy, must certify in writing her consent to the procedure and certify that her consent is informed, freely given, and not the result of coercion; (3) a provision requiring the prior written consent of the spouse of a woman seeking an abortion during the first 12 weeks of pregnancy,

unless the abortion were certified by a physician to be necessary for preservation of the mother's life; (4) a provision, with respect to the first 12 weeks of pregnancy when the pregnant woman is unmarried and under 18 years of age, for the written consent of a parent or legal guardian unless the abortion were certified by a physician as necessary for preservation of the mother's life; (5) a provision prohibiting the saline amniocentesis technique of abortion, in which the amniotic fluid is withdrawn and a saline or other fluid is inserted into the amniotic sac, after the first 12 weeks of pregnancy; (6) record keeping and reporting provisions, imposing requirements upon health facilities and physicians concerned with abortions, irrespective of the pregnancy stage; and (7) a standard of care provision, declaring, in its first sentence, that no person who performs or induces an abortion shall fail to exercise that degree of professional skill, care, and diligence to preserve the life and health of the fetus that such person would be required to exercise in order to preserve the life and health of any fetus intended to be born and not aborted, and providing, in its second sentence, that any physician or person assisting in an abortion who failed to take such measures to encourage or sustain the life of the child would be deemed guilty of manslaughter if the child's death resulted.

The district court upheld the constitutionality of the challenged provisions of the statute with the exception of the first sentence of the standard of care provision. The physicians and Planned Parenthood appealed to the Supreme Court.

SUMMARY OF ARGUMENTS

The complaint charged that certain provisions of the bill were invalid in that they deprived doctors and patients of various alleged constitutional rights, including the privacy of the doctor-patient relationship, the physician's right to the free exercise of medical practice, the right of a woman to determine whether to bear children, the right to life of their patients, and the right to receive adequate medical treatment, all in violation of the First, Fourth, Fifth, Eighth, Ninth, and Fourteenth Amendments to the U.S. Constitution. The petition further alleged that the legislation violated the rights of due process and equal protection guaranteed physicians and their patients under the Constitution, imposing cruel and unusual punishment upon women by forcing them to bear pregnancies that they conceive.

Danforth argued that the provisions were constitutionally in line with the decision in *Roe v. Wade*. He also challenged the lower court's ruling on the unconstitutionality of the standard of care provision, arguing that it did not require physicians to utilize techniques during an abortion generally reserved for live births.

DECISION

On direct appeal from the decision of the three-judge district court, the U.S. Supreme Court affirmed in part, reversed in part, and remanded. In an opinion by Justice Blackmun, it was held, expressing the unanimous view of the Court, that (1) the viability definition provision, which reflected the fact that the determination of viability, varying with each pregnancy, was a matter for the judgment of the responsible attending physician, was not unconstitutional, since it did not circumvent the permissible limitations on state regulation of abortions; (2) the pregnant woman's consent provision was not unconstitutional since the state could validly require a pregnant woman's prior written consent for an abortion to assure awareness of the abortion decision and its significance; and (3) the record keeping and reporting provisions were not constitutionally offensive in themselves and imposed no legally significant impact or consequence on the abortion decision or on the physician-patient relationship; expressing the view of six members of the Court, that (4) the spousal consent provision was unconstitutional, since the state, being unable to regulate or proscribe abortions during the first stage of pregnancy when a physician and patient make such decision, could not delegate authority to any particular person, even a pregnant woman's spouse, to prevent abortion during the first stage of pregnancy; (5) the first sentence of the standard of care provision was unconstitutional, since it impermissibly required a physician to preserve the life and health of a fetus, whatever the stage of the pregnancy, and this provision was not severable

from the rest of the standard of care provision; and expressing the view of five members of the Court, that (6) the parental consent provision was unconstitutional, since the state did not have the constitutional authority to give a third party an absolute, and possibly arbitrary, veto over the decision of a physician and patient to terminate the patient's pregnancy, regardless of the reason for withholding the consent; and (7) the saline amniocentesis prohibition provision was unconstitutional since it failed as a reasonable regulation for the protection of maternal health, being instead an unreasonable or arbitrary regulation designed to inhibit the vast majority of abortions after the first 12 weeks of pregnancy.

AFTERMATH

The ad hoc nature of the strict scrutiny test used to examine governmental regulations of abortion procedures was well demonstrated on a single day in 1983 when the Supreme Court decided three separate cases involving several different types of abortion regulations: *Akron v. Akron Center for Reproductive Health, Inc.* (1983), *Planned Parenthood Assn. of Kansas City v. Ashcroft* (1983), and *Simopoulos v. Virginia* (1983). In the decisions, six justices required that government regulations of pre-viability abortions comply with the principles set forth in *Roe v. Wade*. These regulations must be reasonably related to the "compelling" interest in protecting the health of the woman. The justices wished to use this approach to protect the *Roe v. Wade* principle that a woman has a fundamental right to choose to have an abortion free from interference by the state with her decision or the professional judgment of her attending physician. In contrast, three justices called into question the legitimacy of judicial control of abortion regulations (although they did not advocate, at this time, a direct overruling of *Roe*), because they believed that courts should uphold any government regulation of abortion that was not totally arbitrary.

A majority of the justices on the Supreme Court, throughout the 1980s, believed that the right of privacy only protected a woman's ability to choose to have an abortion without certain types of government interference and did not give women a right to have an abortion at government expense. Thus, in *Webster v. Reproductive Health Services* (1989), the Supreme Court upheld a state law prohibition against the use of public facilities or public funds for abortion services.

SIGNIFICANCE

The decision in *Danforth* further refines *Roe* by allowing and disallowing certain medical and procedural restrictions on the woman's right to receive an abortion.

RELATED CASES

Akron v. Akron Center for Reproductive Health, Inc., 462 U.S. 416 (1983)

Planned Parenthood Assn. of Kansas City v. Ashcroft, 462 U.S. 476 (1983)

Simopoulos v. Virginia, 462 U.S. 506 (1983)

Webster v. Reproductive Health Services, 492 U.S. 490 (1989)

Ohio v. Akron Center for Reproductive Health, 497 U.S. 502 (1990)

Rust v. Sullivan, 500 U.S. 173 (1991)

Planned Parenthood of Southeastern Pennsylvania v. Casey, 505 U.S. 833 (1992)

STATUTE AT ISSUE

Missouri House Bill No. 1211 (1974)

RECOMMENDED READING

Ruth H. Axelrod, *Whose Womb Is It Anyway: Are Paternal Rights Alive and Well Despite* Danforth?, 11 Cardozo Law Review 685 (1990).

Keynes, Edward, with Randall K. Miller. *The Courts vs. Congress: Prayer, Busing and Abortion.* Durham, N.C.: Duke University Press, 1989.

David A. J. Richard, *The Individual, the Family and the Constitution: A Jurisprudential Perspective,* 55 New York University Law Review 1 (1980).

John Siliciano, *The Minor's Right to Privacy: Limitations on State Action after* Danforth *and* Carey, 77 Columbia Law Review 1216 (1977).

Case Title: *Maher, Commissioner of Social Services v. Roe*

Legal Citation: 432 U.S. 464

Year of Decision: 1977

KEY ISSUE

Does a Connecticut statute prohibiting the use of Medicaid funds in payment of abortions that are not medically necessary violate the equal protection clause of the Fourteenth Amendment?

HISTORY OF THE CASE

Under the Connecticut statute, for a patient to have an abortion in the first three months of pregnancy (first trimester) paid for with public funds (Medicaid), the medical facility must submit a certificate from the patient's physician stating that the abortion is medically necessary. The two persons involved in this case were unable to obtain certification and brought this suit in federal district court claiming violation of the due process and equal protection clauses of the Fourteenth Amendment. The district court held that the Fourteenth Amendment forbids exclusion of nontherapeutic abortions from a state welfare program that covers medical expenses that are part of pregnancy and childbirth.

SUMMARY OF ARGUMENTS

Maher, the commissioner of social services of Connecticut, argued that the Connecticut statute did not violate the equal protection and due process clauses of the Fourteenth Amendment.

Susan Roe argued that the Connecticut statute violated the equal protection and due process clauses of the Fourteenth Amendment. Roe argued that Connecticut must treat abortion and childbirth equally.

DECISION

Justice Powell delivered the opinion of the Court. The Court framed the equal protection question by noting that "the Constitution imposes no obligation on the States to pay the pregnancy-related medical expenses of indigent women, or indeed to pay any of the medical expenses of indigents. But when a State decides to alleviate some of the hardships of poverty by providing medical care, the manner in which it dispenses benefits is subject to constitutional limitations." The Court then reviewed its decision in *Roe* and contrasted the issues in *Roe* to the Connecticut regulation, focusing on the fact that "the Connecticut regulation places no obstacles—absolute or otherwise—in the pregnant woman's path to an abortion. An indigent woman who desires an abortion suffers no disadvantage as a consequence of Connecticut's decision to fund childbirth; she continues as before to be dependent on private sources for the service she desires." The Court held that the Connecticut regulation did not impinge upon the fundamental right recognized in *Roe*.

Chief Justice Burger concurred in the opinion, noting: "The Court's holdings in *Roe v. Wade*, 410 U.S. 113 (1973), and *Doe v. Bolton*, 410 U.S. 179 (1973), simply require that a State not create an absolute barrier to a woman's decision to have an abortion. These precedents do not suggest that the State is constitutionally required to assist her in procuring it."

Justice Brennan, joined by Justices Blackmun and Marshall, dissented, arguing that the decision of the majority allowed states to interfere indirectly with the privacy right, thereby protecting the rich but not the poor.

AFTERMATH

This decision had its major impact on persons dependent on public health care who sought reimbursement for abortion, while funding at greater expense the persons who carried their pregnancies to term.

SIGNIFICANCE

This case shows the evolution of the concept of medical privacy. Several other states also have restricted the use of public funds for elective abortions.

RELATED CASES

Bellotti v. Baird, 428 U.S. 132 (1976)

Poelker v. Doe, 432 U.S. 519 (1977)

Harris v. McRae, 448 U.S. 297 (1980)

Williams v. Zbaraz, 448 U.S. 358 (1980)

Akron v. Akron Center for Reproductive Health, 462 U.S. 416 (1983)

Planned Parenthood Assn. of Kansas City v. Ashcroft, 462 U.S. 476 (1983)

Selective Service System v. MPIRG, 468 U.S. 841 (1984)

Hodgson v. Minnesota, 497 U.S. 417 (1990)

Ohio v. Akron Center for Reproductive Health, 497 U.S. 502 (1990)

Planned Parenthood of Southeastern Pennsylvania v. Casey, 505 U.S. 833 (1992)

RECOMMENDED READING

Bobbitt, Philip. *Constitutional Fate: Theory of the Constitution.* New York: Oxford University Press, 1982.

Samuel Estreicher, *Congressional Power and Congressional Rights: Reflections on Proposed "Human Life" Legislation,* 68 Virginia Law Review 333 (1982).

Case Title: *Colautti v. Franklin*

Legal Citation: 439 U.S. 379

Year of Decision: 1979

KEY ISSUE

Is section 5(a) of the Pennsylvania Abortion Control Act, which mandates a standard of care for the protection of a viable unborn fetus when the abortion procedure is performed after viability, constitutional under *Roe v. Wade*?

HISTORY OF THE CASE

The Pennsylvania legislature passed the Pennsylvania Abortion Control Act in 1974, in reaction to the 1973 Supreme Court decision in *Roe v. Wade*. The *Roe* decision struck down a Texas statute as unconstitutionally infringing upon a woman's right to have an abortion but had recognized that a state had an interest in protecting potential life at the point of viability of the fetus. The Abortion Control Act had numerous provisions, including the following sections:

- Section 3(a)—Prohibited the performance of an abortion without the informed consent of the woman,
- Section 3(b)—Prohibited the performance of an abortion in the absence of consent of the woman's spouse,
- Section 4—Made it an offense of murder in the second degree to take the life of a premature infant aborted alive,
- Section 5(a)—Required physicians to adopt the abortion technique providing the best opportunity for the fetus to be aborted alive so long as a different technique was not necessary in order to preserve the life and health of the mother,
- Section 6(b)—Prohibited abortions during the post-viability stage of the pregnancy, and
- Section 7—Prohibited the use of public funds for abortion in the absence of a certificate stating that the abortion was necessary in order to preserve the life and health of the mother.

The Abortion Control Act had an effective date of October 10, 1974. Prior to its implementation, the physician John Franklin and several other organizations opposed to the legislation filed a complaint in the U.S. District Court for the Eastern District of Pennsylvania. The original defendants in the action were the district attorney of Philadelphia County and the secretary of welfare of the Commonwealth of Pennsylvania, Aldo Colautti. (By the time the case reached the Supreme Court, Frank Beal had replaced Aldo Colautti as the secretary of welfare of the Commonwealth of Pennsylvania, as reflected in court documents.) The suit challenged the majority of the act's provisions as being invalid on federal constitutional grounds. A trial was held in front of a three-judge panel of the district court. The court ruled that certain provisions of the act were valid but other sections were invalid.

The Supreme Court's decisions in *Roe v. Wade* (1973), *Doe v. Bolton* (1973), and *Planned Parenthood of Central Missouri v. Danforth* (1976) addressed nearly all of the questions in *Colautti*. The remaining issue for review was whether section 5(a) of the act was valid. The viability determination was thus the central issue when the case was presented to the Court.

SUMMARY OF ARGUMENTS

Colautti argued that, under *Roe v. Wade*, the state had a legitimate interest in protecting the life of a "viable" fetus, and that section 5(a) of the act was reasonably drafted to that end.

Franklin argued that the language in section 5(a) was too vague, leaving readers to guess at the statute's meaning. Franklin challenged the statute as too ambiguous and, therefore, void under the void for vagueness doctrine. This doctrine requires that legislative policies regarding criminal law are written in a precise manner. If a statute is indefinite on the person(s) regulated, the prohibited conduct, or the imposed punishment, then the law is unconstitutionally vague.

DECISION

The Court upheld the district court's decision that the section 5(a) viability determination was void for vagueness, as was the standard of care provision of that section. Justice Blackmun delivered the majority opinion for the court.

The opinion began by acknowledging that three previous Supreme Court decisions were essential for determining the outcome in the *Franklin* case. These cases were *Roe v. Wade* (1973), *Doe v. Bolton* (1973), and *Planned Parenthood of Central Missouri v. Danforth* (1976). Viability is a key concept in the legal status of abortion laws, as the *Roe* case held that the state's interest in the potential life of the fetus became "compelling" at the stage of viability. This compelling interest thus gave the state grounds for protecting the viable fetus and regulating abortion at that point.

The Court then stated its standard of how it would analyze any statute that purported to define the concept of viability in relation to an abortion procedure:

> In these three cases, then, this Court has stressed viability, has declared its determination to be a matter for medical judgment, and has recognized that differing legal consequences ensue upon the near and far sides of that point in the human gestation period. We reaffirm these principles. Viability is reached when, in the judgment of the attending physician on the particular facts of the case before him, there is a reasonable likelihood of the fetus' sustained survival outside the womb, with or without artificial support. Because this point may differ with each pregnancy, neither the legislature nor the courts may proclaim one of the elements entering into the ascertainment of viability—be it weeks of gestation or fetal weight or any other single factor—as the determinant of when the State has a compelling interest in the life or health of the fetus.

Upon arriving at an applied standard, the Court turned its attention to the provision in the Abortion Control Act in question, specifically section 5(a). Franklin wielded two attacks on this section. He argued that both the viability-determination requirement and the stated standard of care provision of that section were unconstitutional for vagueness. It is an established matter of due process that any criminal statute that fails to give a person of ordinary intelligence fair notice that the contemplated conduct is forbidden by the statute, or is so indefinite that it encourages arbitrary arrests, is void for vagueness.

The Court found a "double ambiguity" in the language of section 5(a) concerning the viability determination. "First, it is unclear whether the statute imports a purely subjective standard, or

whether it imposes a mixed subjective and objective standard. Second, it is uncertain whether the phrase 'may be viable' simply refers to viability, as that term has been defined in *Roe* and in *Planned Parenthood,* or whether it refers to an undefined penumbral or 'gray' area prior to the stage of viability." Thus, the Court held this section of the act void for vagueness.

Looking next at the standard of care provision in section 5(a) of the act, the Court also found that portion of the statute void. This provision called for the physician performing the abortion to use the degree of care necessary to preserve the life of a fetus determined to be viable, while also considering the life and health of the mother. The Court reviewed testimony from medical experts in the trial stage of the case and emphasized that there was considerable difference of opinion as to the abortion procedure best suited to protecting survival of the fetus. Given the conflicting expert testimony, the Court believed that compliance with this portion of the statute would be difficult for any physician.

The dissenting opinion, filed by Justices White, Burger, and Rehnquist, objected to what they viewed as the majority opinion's disregard for the state's right to protect fetal life.

AFTERMATH

Colautti was one in a series of cases between 1973 and 1986 that struck down state responses to the decision in *Roe.* The states drafted statutes making it more difficult for women to obtain abortions, which the Supreme Court deemed unconstitutional. In the 1980s, however, the Supreme Court began weakening *Roe* in many respects, as state legislatures continued to pass legislation attempting to regulate and restrict access to abortions.

SIGNIFICANCE

Critics viewed *Colautti* as a roadblock to the states' ability to regulate abortions, even in the third trimester. The Court's decision appeared contrary to the ruling in *Roe,* which determined that states had a compelling interest in fetal life at that stage.

RELATED CASES

Roe v. Wade, 410 U.S. 113 (1973)

Doe v. Bolton, 410 U.S. 179 (1973)

Planned Parenthood of Central Missouri v. Danforth, 428 U.S. 52 (1976)

Webster v. Reproductive Health Services, 492 U.S. 490 (1989)

STATUTE AT ISSUE

Pennsylvania Abortion Control Act, 1974 Pa. Laws, Act No. 209

RECOMMENDED READING

Allen Bartleman, Colautti v. Franklin: *The Court Questions the Use of Viability in Abortion Statutes,* 6 Western State University Law Review 311 (1979).

Robert H. Blank, *Judicial Decision Making and Biological Fact:* Roe v. Wade *and the Unresolved Question of Fetal Viability,* 37 Western Political Quarterly 584 (1984).

Bruce Ching, *Inverting the Viability Test for Abortion Law,* 22 Women's Rights Law Reporter 37 (2000).

Stephen G. Gilles, *Roe's Life-or-Health Exception: Self-Defense or Relative Safety?,* 85 Notre Dame Law Review 525 (2010).

E. Griffin, *Viability and Fetal Life in State Criminal Abortion Laws,* 72 Journal of Criminal Law and Criminology 324 (1981).

Mersky, Roy M. *A Documentary History of the Legal Aspects of Abortion in the United States:* Colautti v. Franklin. Littleton, Colo.: Fred B. Rothman, 2000.

Schroedel, Jean Reith. *Is the Fetus a Person? A Comparison of Policies across the Fifty States.* Ithaca, N.Y.: Cornell University Press, 2000.

Solinger, Rickie. *Pregnancy and Power: A Short History on Reproductive Politics in America.* New York: New York University Press, 2005.

Rachel Warren, *Pro [Whose?] Choice: How the Growing Recognition of a Fetus' Right to Life Takes the Constitutionality Out of* Roe, 13 Chapman Law Review 221 (2009).

Mary Anne Wood and Lisa Bolin Hawkins, *State Regulation of Late Abortion and the Physician's Duty to the Viable Fetus,* 45 Missouri Law Review 394 (1980).

Case Title: *Harris v. McRae*

Legal Citation: 448 U.S. 297

Year of Decision: 1980

KEY ISSUES

Does it violate the equal protection clause of the Fifth Amendment or the establishment clause of the First Amendment to limit federal funds to reimburse the cost of an abortion under a Medicaid program?

HISTORY OF THE CASE

In 1965, Title XIX of the Social Security Act established the Medicaid program, providing federal financial assistance to states that reimburse medical treatment costs for needy persons. In 1976, Congress passed the Hyde Amendment, which banned the use of federal funds to reimburse the costs of an abortion under a Medicaid program. Later versions of the Hyde Amendment allowed some exceptions. Actions were brought in federal district court by indigent women who sued on behalf of similarly situated women; the New York City Health and Hospitals Corporation, which provided abortion services; and officers of the Women's Division of the Board of Global Ministries of the United Methodist Church, which sought to enjoin enforcement of the Hyde Amendment on the grounds that it violated the due process clause of the Fifth Amendment, the free exercise clause of the First Amendment, and the obligation under Title XIX to provide funds for all medically necessary abortions.

SUMMARY OF ARGUMENTS

The plaintiffs argued that the Hyde Amendment was unconstitutional in that it severely limited the rights of poor women to gain access to an abortion, in violation of the due process clause of the Fifth Amendment and the free exercise and establishment clauses of the First Amendment.

DECISION

Justice Stewart wrote the opinion. He held that Title XIX of the Social Security Act does not require a state to pay for a medically necessary abortion. He noted that nothing in the legislative history revealed that Congress intended to require participating states to assume the full costs of providing any medical service in its plan. The purpose of Congress in enacting Title XIX was to provide federal assistance for all legitimate state expenditures under an approved Medicaid plan. In addition, the legislative history of the Hyde Amendment does not reveal that Congress intended the states to continue to fund medically necessary abortion even when federal funding was withdrawn.

In addition, he wrote that the funding restrictions in the Hyde Amendment do not violate the "liberty" interest identified in *Roe v. Wade* as including the freedom to decide whether to terminate a pregnancy. The reasons for this are that the Hyde Amendment does not place a government obstacle in the path of women who choose to terminate a pregnancy; there is no constitutional entitlement to funds for the full range of protected reproductive choices; to read such a requirement into the Constitution would require that Congress subsidize such procedures even when it had not enacted a medical program such as Medicaid to subsidize other medically necessary services.

He continued that although the amendment may coincide with the tenets of the Roman Catholic Church, this fact does not indicate the government's aid of or preference for the Catholic religion and make the amendment a violation of the establishment clause. He also held that the petitioners lacked standing to assert the challenge to the Hyde Amendment. The named parties for the indigent women did not allege or prove that they "sought an abortion under compulsion of religious belief." The officers of the Women's Division of the Board of Global Ministries of the United Methodist Church failed to allege that they are or expect to be pregnant, or that they are eligible for Medicaid. They therefore lacked a personal interest in the complaint that is needed to confer standing. The Women's Division as an organization fails to meet the requirement of standing because the claim is of the type "that required participation of the individual members for a proper understanding and resolution of their free exercise claims."

According to the opinion, the Hyde Amendment did not violate the Fifth Amendment equal protection provision because the government neither invaded a substantive constitutional right or freedom nor acted with the purpose of treating a suspect class in a detrimental manner. The requirement of the equal protection provision is that a purposefully detrimental action be directed at a suspect class. The Court held that the amendment was rationally related to the legitimate state interest of protecting potential life by encouraging childbirth.

Justice White wrote a concurring opinion in which he noted that in *Maher, Commissioner of Social Services v. Roe* (1977) the Court held that allowing costs for childbirth and defraying costs for nontherapeutic abortions violated the equal protection provision of the Fifth Amendment. He argued that the *Maher* case was indistinguishable from the one at issue. He reasoned that the Court in *Maher* held that the government is not required to fund nontherapeutic abortions if doing so furthered the legitimate state interest in normal childbirth.

Justice Brennan wrote a dissenting opinion in which Justices Blackmun and Marshall joined. He reasoned that through its refusal to subsidize abortions, the Hyde Amendment effectively removed an indigent woman's right to choose abortion over childbirth.

Justice Marshall wrote a dissenting opinion, in which he argued that the case was different from the case in *Maher*. He reasoned that the petitioners in *Harris* were seeking a benefit that was available to nonindigent women in a similar situation. In *Maher*, the Court held that the denial of funding for nontherapeutic abortions was not a denial of equal protection because the Medicaid funding was available only for medically necessary procedures.

Justice Stevens wrote a dissenting opinion in which he argued, similarly to Justice Marshall, that the petitioners in this case were not in the same situation as those in *Maher*. They were objecting to their exclusion from a benefit that was available to all other women who had the means to pay for an abortion. In addition, he argued that in *Roe v. Wade* it was decided that even after the fetus was viable, a state could not prohibit an abortion to protect the health of the mother. Conceding this, he said the exercise of the right to protect one's own health could not be the basis for denying an abortion to which a woman would otherwise be entitled were she not indigent. He said it was misleading of the Court to focus on the legitimate state interest, when in cases where that interest conflicts with the health of the mother the Court has conceded that the state's interest must yield.

AFTERMATH

In *Poelker v. Doe* (1977), the Court upheld a policy that prohibited abortions in public hospitals except in cases in which there was a threat of grave physiological injury or death. In *Beal v. Doe* (1977), the Court held that the Social Security Act does not require states to fund nontherapeutic abortions for participation in the Medicaid program. In *Webster v. Reproductive Health Services* (1989), the Court sustained a Missouri law that made it unlawful for any public facility to perform abortions other than to save the life of the mother. In abandoning the trimester approach to determining viability, it strengthened the antiabortion position on the Court. In later decisions, the Court has upheld the constitutionality of parental notification requirements.

SIGNIFICANCE

This case addresses direct payment to a woman or her doctor to subsidize abortion. Together with *Maher* it has provided the Court with the power to prohibit abortions in public hospitals, even in cases in which a woman does not seek state aid. In providing that the state may legitimately withhold funds to poor women seeking nontherapeutic abortions, the Court restricted the availability of choice provided by Roe and set the stage for further restrictions on the right to an abortion. It set the stage for such cases as *Webster*, which further restricted the right provided by *Roe*.

RELATED CASES

Roe v. Wade, 410 U.S. 113 (1973)

Planned Parenthood of Central Missouri v. Danforth, 428 U.S. 52 (1976)

Beal v. Doe, 432 U.S. 438 (1977)

Maher, Commissioner of Social Services v. Roe, 432 U.S. 464 (1977)

Poelker v. Doe, 432 U.S. 519 (1977)

Bellotti v. Baird, 443 U.S. 622 (1979)

Akron v. Akron Center for Reproductive Health, Inc., 462 U.S. 416 (1983)

Webster v. Reproductive Health Services, 492 U.S. 490 (1989)

STATUTE AT ISSUE

The Hyde Amendment: Pub.L. 96-123 § 109; 93 Stat. 926 (1980)

RECOMMENDED READING

Carole I. Chervin, *The Title X Family Planning Gag Rule: Can the Government Buy Up Constitutional Rights?*, 41 Stanford Law Review 401 (1989).

William J. Curran, *The Constitutional Right to Health Care: Denial in the Court*, 320 New England Journal of Medicine 788 (1989).

David J. Garrow. *Liberty & Sexuality: The Right to Privacy and the Making of Roe v. Wade*. New York: Macmillan, 1994.

Michael J. Perry, *Why the Supreme Court Was Plainly Wrong in the Hyde Amendment Case: A Brief Comment on* Harris v. McRae, 32 Stanford Law Review 1113 (1980).

Tribe, Laurence H. *Abortion: The Clash of Absolutes.* New York: Norton, 1992.

———. *Constitutional Choices.* Cambridge, Mass.: Harvard University Press, 1985.

Tushnet, Mark V. *Abortion.* New York: Facts On File, 1996.

Peter Westen, *Correspondence,* 33 Stanford Law Review 1187 (1981).

Peter Westen and Michael J. Perry, *Regarding Perry,* "Why the Supreme Court Was Plainly Wrong in the Hyde Amendment Case: A Brief Comment on Harris v. McRae," *32 Stanford L. Rev. 1113 (1980),* 33 Stanford Law Review 1187 (1981).

Case Title: *Thornburgh v. American College of Obstetricians and Gynecologists*

Legal Citation: 476 U.S. 747

Year of Decision: 1986

KEY ISSUE

Does a Pennsylvania statute regulating abortions unconstitutionally restrict the fundamental right to privacy?

HISTORY OF THE CASE

In 1974, the Pennsylvania General Assembly enacted the state's first Abortion Control Act. The Abortion Control Act contained provisions regarding the information a woman was required to receive prior to consenting to an abortion, the reporting requirements imposed upon physicians, and the procedures to be followed when faced with post-viability abortions. After five years of litigation, many provisions of this act were struck down as unconstitutional. In 1978 and 1981, the Pennsylvania legislature revised the law and imposed restrictions upon both the physician per-

forming and the woman seeking an abortion. Before the law took effect, the American College of Obstetricians and Gynecologists (ACOG) and others sued, alleging the act remained unconstitutional and seeking a preliminary injunction. The federal district court denied the motion almost entirely, finding a single provision of the act invalid.

ACOG appealed, and the U.S. Court of Appeals eventually held in favor of ACOG. The court found numerous provisions that unconstitutionally invaded a woman's fundamental right to privacy and remanded the case to the trial court. The Pennsylvania attorney general, Richard Thornburgh, appealed to the Supreme Court.

SUMMARY OF ARGUMENTS

ACOG argued that U.S. law prevented the Supreme Court from reviewing the Court of Appeals' decision since the case had been remanded to the trial court. Procedurally, the case had not yet obtained a final judgment. ACOG also argued that the Court of Appeals' review standard was appropriate in its decision to reverse the district court's injunction denial. ACOG argued that the Court of Appeals applied the correct principles when assessing the state law's constitutionality.

Attorney General Thornburgh argued that the Supreme Court was allowed to review a non-final appellate court decision holding a state statute unconstitutional. Second, Thornburgh asserted that the Court of Appeals exceeded its proper scope of review in considering the constitutionality of the act. Rather than simply determining whether the trial court had abused its discretion in denying the request for a preliminary motion, the Court of Appeals had reviewed the constitutionality of the statute. Third, and most relevant to the privacy issue, Thornburgh maintained that the Pennsylvania abortion act was constitutional, contrary to the appellate court's decision. He claimed that it was consistent with prior Supreme Court decisions.

DECISION

The Court agreed with ACOG that a federal law prevented the Supreme Court from reviewing a case on appeal before the Court of Appeals' final decision was carried out. Nevertheless, the Supreme Court accepted the case for review based on the facts in evidence, stating, "We have concluded that it is time that this undecided issue be resolved." In the 5-4 decision written by Justice Blackmun, the Court held that the Court of Appeals did have jurisdiction to evaluate the constitutionality of the state statute. Furthermore, the Court found six provisions of the Pennsylvania Abortion Control Act violated the right to privacy and were unconstitutional.

With regard to whether the Court of Appeals exceeded its authority in deciding the issues before it from the trial level, the Court ruled it did not. The Blackmun opinion noted that appropriate review standards typically limit appellate review, as Thornburgh argued. This approach was not an inflexible one, however, and proceedings deviating from the stated norm were allowable given the proper legal and factual circumstances. Here, the Court decided those circumstances existed.

On the privacy issue questions, the Supreme Court invalidated six portions of the Pennsylvania abortion law. The Court ruled that six provisions in the statute unconstitutionally burdened the fundamental right to privacy. One invalidated section, which prescribed in detail the method for securing "informed consent" from the woman, was seen as an "outright attempt to . . . discourag[e] abortion in the privacy of the informed consent dialogue between the woman and her physician." The Court considered the information required by law to be communicated from doctor to patient "intimidating," "overinclusive," and "serv[ing] only to confuse and punish [the woman] and to heighten her anxiety, contrary to accepted medical practice." Other stricken provisions mandated extensive record keeping by physicians performing abortions, allowed public inspection of the potentially revealing records, and included various regulations on post-viability abortions.

AFTERMATH

How to define the nature, provenance, and legitimacy of the constitutional right to privacy continues to bedevil the Court and, on a broader level, society at large. Public discussion on the extent of this right continues with respect to abortion, as well as other politically and socially charged issues such as homosexual privacy rights.

SIGNIFICANCE

The *Thornburgh* case represents a deep doctrinal division in the Court. As Justice White wrote in his dissent, when the Supreme Court defines "fundamental" liberties not explicitly defined in the Constitution, it must act cautiously.

RELATED CASES

Roe v. Wade, 410 U.S. 113 (1973)

Planned Parenthood of Central Missouri v. Danforth, 428 U.S. 52 (1976)

Akron v. Akron Center for Reproductive Health, Inc., 462 U.S. 416 (1983)

Planned Parenthood Ass'n of Kansas City v. Ashcroft, 462 U.S. 476 (1983)

Bowers v. Hardwick, 478 U.S. 186 (1986)

Webster v. Reproductive Health Services, 492 U.S. 490 (1989)

Planned Parenthood of Southeastern Pennsylvania v. Casey, 505 U.S. 833 (1992)

STATUTE AT ISSUE

Pennsylvania Abortion Control Act, 18 Pennsylvania Consolidated Statutes § 3201 et seq. (1982)

RECOMMENDED READING

Dworkin, Ronald. *Life's Dominion: An Argument about Abortion, Euthanasia, and Individual Freedom.* New York: Knopf, 1993.

David Fernandez, Thornburgh v. American College of Obstetricians: *Return to* Roe?, 10 Harvard Journal of Law & Public Policy 711 (1987).

David A. J. Richards, *Constitutional Legitimacy and Constitutional Privacy,* 61 New York University Law Review 800 (1986).

Reva Siegel, *Reasoning from the Body: A Historical Perspective on Abortion Regulation and*

Questions of Equal Protection, 44 Stanford Law Review 261 (1992).

Tribe, Laurence H. *Abortion: The Clash of Absolutes*. New York: Norton, 1992.

Case Title: *Webster v. Reproductive Health Services*

Alternate Case Title: The Missouri Abortion Case

Legal Citation: 492 U.S. 490

Year of Decision: 1989

KEY ISSUE

Does a state law regulating and restricting public facilities and employees from providing abortion services deprive women of the right to privacy as found in the concept of personal liberty in the Fourteenth Amendment to the U.S. Constitution?

HISTORY OF THE CASE

At the time *Roe v. Wade* (1973) was decided, Missouri had regulations in place outlawing abortions, except when necessary to save the mother's life. After *Roe,* a federal court found the Missouri antiabortion statutes unconstitutional, and the Supreme Court affirmed the decision.

In 1974, Missouri enacted new regulations defining viability and requiring written consent from a woman who was to undergo the procedure, as well as consent of the spouse. If the mother was under the age of 18, she needed her parents' written consent for an abortion during the first 12 weeks of pregnancy. The practicing physician also had to "preserve the life and health of the fetus" and could be convicted of manslaughter and liable for damages if he or she failed to do this. The regulations went on to outlaw the use of the saline amniocentesis method of abortion and required certain record keeping for health facilities. The regulations were challenged.

All but the viability provision and consent requirement for the woman undergoing the procedure were found unconstitutional.

In 1979, Missouri again passed legislation limiting abortions. This time the state required that abortions conducted during the second trimester were to be performed in a hospital; all abortions required a pathology report; a second physician was to be present for abortions performed after viability; and a minor must obtain the consent of the parents or a juvenile court for an abortion. The Supreme Court struck down the provision requiring abortions during the second trimester to be performed in a hospital but upheld the rest of the legislation.

In June 1986, the Missouri legislature enacted a statute dealing with unborn children and abortions. The statute's preamble stated that life began at conception and that this constituted an interest that must be protected by the state. The preamble further stated that unborn children had the same rights, privileges, and immunities available to other citizens of Missouri. Other statutory provisions required doctors to perform tests on women more than 20 weeks pregnant to ascertain the viability of the fetus before performing an abortion. Public hospitals and public employees were further prohibited from performing nontherapeutic abortions and from providing abortion counseling unnecessary to saving the mother's life.

The nonprofit organizations Reproductive Health Services and Planned Parenthood of Kansas City filed this suit with three physicians, one nurse, and a social worker. The five health professionals employed by the state and two nonprofit corporations brought a class action in the U.S. District Court for the Western District of Missouri challenging the constitutionality of the statute. They filed the suit on their own behalf and on the behalf of other facilities and health care professionals offering abortion services and/or pregnancy counseling within Missouri and for pregnant women seeking these services. Among other things, they asserted that the legislation violated a woman's right to privacy, a woman's right to abortion, and a doctor's right to practice medicine. The District Court struck down each of the

P91698

provisions discussed and others and restrained the enforcement of the legislation. The Court of Appeals affirmed, declaring all challenged provisions unconstitutional under *Roe v. Wade*. Missouri appealed to the Supreme Court.

SUMMARY OF ARGUMENTS

On April 26, 1989, the Supreme Court convened to hear the oral arguments on the case. The case for Missouri was argued by William L. Webster, attorney general of Missouri, facing Frank Susman, an attorney for Planned Parenthood. Susman argued to uphold the right to abortion under the Fourteenth Amendment's due process clause protecting personal liberty. He also advocated that the right of contraception and the right of abortion are not distinct and separate, and that if abortion was illegal, then contraception should be illegal.

Webster argued the constitutionality of the provisions of the Missouri statute. Charles Fried, a Harvard Law School professor and formerly solicitor general under the Ronald Reagan administration, argued for the United States as a friend of the court, supporting Missouri and claiming that there is no constitutional right to abortion and that *Roe v. Wade* should be overruled. Fried's brief and that of Missouri proposed that the constitution be interpreted to contain only "rights explicitly mentioned in the text."

DECISION

Chief Justice Rehnquist announced the 5-4 judgment of the Court. He stated that it was not necessary to pass judgment on the constitutionality of the statute's preamble stating that life begins at conception since it merely reflected the legislature's value judgment. Until the provision was used to restrict abortion activities, it need not be addressed. Rehnquist went on to say that state restrictions on the use of public facilities and employees to perform nontherapeutic abortions (but allowing for payment for medical services connected to childbirth) did not conflict with previous court decisions or with the due process clause. The Fourteenth Amendment does not grant a right to government aid even when necessary to secure "life, liberty or property interest."

The provision requiring tests by doctors to determine the viability of the fetus of 20 or more weeks was upheld because it furthered the state's interest in protecting potential human life. Such tests were found to be permissive and to be used only to make viability findings based on the physician's reasonable professional judgment.

Justice Rehnquist noted that this point conflicts with the prescription in *Roe v. Wade,* which limited state involvement in second trimester abortions to those necessary to save the mother's life. The state's interest in potential future life was found to be equally compelling throughout pregnancy and not restricted to viability.

The chief justice concluded the court's opinion by stating that *Roe v. Wade* would not be overruled because its facts differed from those presented in *Webster. Roe v. Wade* dealt with a Texas statute that made all nontherapeutic abortions illegal. Missouri, on the other hand, sought only to limit abortions after the point of viability. *Roe* was, therefore, modified and limited by a new standard for review of abortion restrictions based on furthering the state's interest.

AFTERMATH

The *Webster* decision limited abortion rights without clearly defining those limits. As a result, state legislators were left with the task of drafting statutes that would pass constitutional scrutiny in future cases. For at least the near future, however, *Webster*'s legacy appears to be a renewal of abortion as a political issue on the state and local levels.

In legalizing abortion under many circumstances, *Roe v. Wade* had a profound impact on American society. Motivated by the desire to overturn *Roe v. Wade,* opponents of abortion became unprecedentedly active in the legislative and judicial arenas. *Webster* also has inspired similar activism among those who favor less stringent regulation on abortion. The *Webster* ruling left the door open to a variety of legislative approaches to the problem, which continue to be the focus of electoral and lobbying efforts. In refusing the opportunity to overrule *Roe v. Wade,* the Court in *Webster* reaffirmed the broader constitutional concept of the right to privacy and a woman's right to an abortion.

SOUTH PUGET SOUND LIBRARY

SIGNIFICANCE

The fever pitch of interest in the case was reflected in the record number of amicus (friend of the court) briefs filed with the Supreme Court. An amicus brief is composed of information about some aspect of the case submitted by someone, who is not a party in the case, to help the court reach its decision. Seventy-eight individuals, groups, and organizations—including law professors, members of Congress, health professionals, and interest groups on both sides of the issue—submitted such briefs.

This case upheld previous court decisions allowing states to restrict the use of government funding for abortion procedures and counseling. *Webster* broadened that restriction to exclude use of government employees and facilities for abortion purposes. Since women do not have a constitutional right to state-funded abortions, states can restrict the use of government resources without causing an undue burden on women who wish to obtain abortions. Though a state cannot unduly burden a woman's access to an abortion, the state can favor childbirth over abortion and has the power to use public funds to encourage this preference. The Court reasoned that denying government resources for abortions would put a woman in the same position as if the state did not operate public hospitals. Therefore, the state was not preventing any woman from obtaining an abortion. However, the Court did not address the practical effects of restricting public resources for abortion services. For example, restrictions on public funding limit the availability of abortions to indigent women who cannot afford to pay for the procedure. Critics argue that these restrictions unduly burden the ability of poor women to obtain abortions.

The Court also avoided the issue of allowing the state to determine when life begins and what rights will be afforded to a fetus. In *Roe v. Wade,* the Court found that the unborn were not included in the definition of a person under the Fourteenth Amendment's due process clause protecting life and liberty. However, the Court did not see the need to rule on the constitutionality of the preamble in the statute, which stated life began at conception. Alone, it did not regulate abortion or any medical practices for abortion. The Court read the preamble as a value judgment of the state favoring child-birth over abortion rather than using it as an opportunity to address the state's interpretation.

RELATED CASES

Griswold v. Connecticut, 381 U.S. 479 (1965)

Roe v. Wade, 410 U.S. 113 (1973)

Planned Parenthood of Central Missouri v. Danforth, 428 U.S. 52 (1976)

Maher v. Roe, 432 U.S. 464 (1977)

Colautti v. Franklin, 439 U.S. 379 (1979)

Harris v. McRae, 448 U.S. 297 (1980)

Akron v. Akron Center for Reproductive Health, Inc., 462 U.S. 416 (1983)

Thornburgh v. American College of Obstetricians and Gynecologists, 476 U.S. 747 (1986)

Planned Parenthood of Southeastern Pennsylvania v. Casey, 505 U.S. 833 (1992)

STATUTE AT ISSUE

Missouri Revised Statutes § 1.205 (1986)

RECOMMENDED READING

James Bopp, Jr., and Richard E. Coleson, *What Does* Webster *Mean?*, 138 University of Pennsylvania Law Review 157 (1989).

Lewis, Karen J. *Abortion Law in the Aftermath of Webster.* Washington, D.C.: Congressional Research Service, Library of Congress, 1991.

Jack E. Rossotti, Laura Natelson, and Raymond Tatalovich, *Nonlegal Advice: The Amicus Briefs in* Webster v. Reproductive Health Services, 81 Judicature 118 (1997).

Tushnet, Mark V. *Abortion.* New York: Facts On File, 1996.

Case Title: *Rust v. Sullivan*

Legal Citation: 500 U.S. 173

Year of Decision: 1991

SOUTH PLACE MOUND LIBRARY

KEY ISSUE

Do the Health and Human Services regulations, drafted under the Public Health Service Act, violate the First and Fifth Amendment rights of health care providers and their clients?

HISTORY OF THE CASE

In 1970, Congress enacted Title X of the Public Health Service Act (the "Act"), which provided federal funding for public and nonprofit private family-planning services. The Act authorized the secretary of health and human services to make grants and contracts with family-planning centers. However, the Act prohibited the use of federally allocated funds for programs that offered abortion as a method of family planning.

In 1982, Health and Human Services' Office of the Inspector General ("OIG"), as well as the General Accounting Office ("GAO"), audited the use of funds in 14 Title X clinics. The investigation revealed that a significant number of the programs were using the funds inappropriately. Practices included offering Title X family planning and abortion services at the same site, failing to counsel on alternatives to abortion, distributing proabortion literature, providing referrals specifically for abortion services, and lobbying for abortion activities. In response to the investigation, the secretary, pursuant to authority granted under the Act, instituted new regulations in 1988. The regulations provided grantees with strict guidelines on appropriate dispersal of Title X funds for preventive family planning services. The regulations attached three principal conditions on the grants. First, the regulations prohibited abortion counseling and referrals as a method of family planning. Second, the regulations prohibited any Title X projects from participating in activities related to the promotion or advocacy of abortion, including lobbying for prochoice legislation, providing speakers to promote abortion, and paying dues to any group that advocates abortion. Third, the regulations required that Title X projects were physically and financially separate from the prohibited activities.

After the regulations went into effect, Dr. Irving Rust and Dr. Melvin Patawer, who received and managed Title X funds, as well as other grantees, such as the state of New York and Planned Parenthood of New York City, filed suit against then-secretary of health and human services (HHS), Dr. Louis Sullivan. Rust, Patawer, and the others ("Rust") argued that the regulations were unconstitutional. Rust sought injunctive relief to prevent implementation of the regulations and was granted a preliminary injunction. However, the district court granted summary judgment to the secretary. Upon appeal, the Court of Appeals for the Second Circuit affirmed the lower court's decision. It held that the regulations did not impermissibly burden a woman's right to obtain an abortion because it did not create any legal barriers to obtaining one. Rust appealed once more, and the United States Supreme Court granted certiorari.

SUMMARY OF ARGUMENTS

Rust claimed the regulations were facially invalid, or unconstitutional, and therefore void, because they violated the First and Fifth Amendments. Rust argued that the basis on which Title X benefits were offered infringed on the recipients' freedom of speech since the regulations prevented programs from engaging in discussions on abortion options and from advocating for proabortion services. Rust further asserted that the Act violated women's Fifth Amendment rights by impeding a woman's ability to obtain an abortion.

Sullivan argued that the new regulations merely clarified what Congress had intended when Title X was originally passed in 1970: Federal funds granted under Title X should in no way subsidize abortion counseling as a means of family planning. The new regulations, Sullivan claimed, clarified the act's requirements in an effort to minimize inappropriate use of allocated funds. According to Sullivan, the regulations did not violate providers' freedom of speech since providers could still advocate for abortion and even provide abortion services when done in locations physically and financially separate from the Title X program. Sullivan further argued that the regulations did not impede a woman's access to abortion services since they did not prevent Title X grantees from informing women that post-pregnancy services were available through other providers, who may or may not accommodate abortion counseling.

DECISION

The Court held that the HSS regulations did not violate the First or Fifth Amendment. The Court found the congressional intent in enacting Title X to be ambiguous regarding abortion counseling, and thus the Court decided to defer to the HHS. Thus, the HHS was allowed to prohibit recipients of government funds from advocating, counseling, or referring patients for abortion.

Chief Justice Rehnquist wrote the opinion. The Court addressed Rust's claim that the regulations violated the First Amendment's prohibition on viewpoint discrimination. Viewpoint discrimination occurs when a regulation attacks an individual or group's message rather than the method in which the message is relayed. According to Rust, prohibiting counselors from discussing abortion-related activities effectively attacked grantees' proabortion views. Therefore, the guidelines discriminated against grantees with proabortion viewpoints. The Court found the Title X statutory prohibition against abortion counseling constitutional, citing *Maher v. Roe.* In *Maher,* the court upheld a state welfare regulation that prevented Medicaid recipients from receiving reimbursement payments for services related to nontherapeutic abortions. The Court in *Maher* determined that the government could make value judgments that favored childbirth over abortion and allocate funds accordingly. Likewise, the Court in the present case stated that the "government can, without violating the Constitution, selectively fund a program to encourage certain activities it believes to be in the public interest, without at the same time funding an alternative program which seeks to deal with the problem in another way." The Court found this was not viewpoint discrimination but rather choosing to fund one activity over another.

Next, the Court looked at whether the secretary's interpretation of the regulations was based on a permissible construction of the statute. Usually, if the agency's interpretation of the statute ally, if the agency's interpretation of the statute

or regulation is permissible and does not conflict with Congress's intent, the Court will defer to that interpretation. The Court determined that the "broad language of Title X plainly allows the Secretary's construction of the statute." Although the secretary deemed this a "revised" interpretation, the Court found that the current interpretation was determined with reasoned analysis based on reports from the GAO and the OIG. The GAO and OIG reports showed that "prior policy failed to implement properly the statute and that it was necessary to provide 'clear and operational guidance to grantees about how to preserve the distinction between Title X programs and abortion as a method of family planning.'" Additionally, the secretary's interpretation was granted deference because the newer regulations better reflected the original intent of the statute and was justified by client experience under the prior policy.

The Court then turned to "program integrity requirements" embodied in Title X that required that the facilities, personnel, and records be kept separate from anything that would give the impression that federal funds were being used to support abortion-related activities. The Court found that "the program integrity requirements are based on a permissible construction of the statute and are not inconsistent with congressional intent." The legislative history regarding the program integrity was ambiguous and offered little guidance. However, the Court stated that Congress intended to keep Title X funds separate from abortion-related activities. Accordingly, the Court found no constitutional issues regarding the program integrity requirements and deferred to the secretary's interpretation of the program.

The Court again noted the general principle that the government may choose to subsidize some speech over other speech. The government was deemed to be merely suggesting that the funds be used for their intended purpose. The regulations did not force the grantee to give up speech; rather, it required the grantee to keep those activities separate from Title X activities and thus did not restrict the activities of individuals in their private lives. If the grantee did not want to comply with the regulations, it could simply decline the Title X benefits. The regulations also did not violate a woman's Fifth Amendment right to choose whether or not to terminate her pregnancy because the government had no constitutional duty to subsidize abortions or offer resources to facilitate abortions. Accordingly, the secretary's regulations were held to be a permissible interpretation of Title X, and the decision of the Court of Appeals was affirmed.

Justice Blackmun wrote a dissenting opinion, joined in part by Justices Marshall, Stevens, and O'Connor. He argued that the regulations violated the First and Fifth Amendments. Justice Blackmun felt that the majority had upheld viewpoint discrimination and suppressed constitutionally protected speech. He argued that since the language of the statute did not speak directly to counseling, referral, and advocacy, a constitutional construction of the regulations was possible and should be used to avoid reaching the constitutional issues altogether. Justice Blackmun further argued that the secretary's reinterpretation of the statute in 1988 was not authorized under the statute because it affected speech, as opposed to only conduct, stating, "in a society that abhors censorship and in which policymakers have traditionally placed the highest value on the freedom to communicate, it is unrealistic to conclude that statutory authority to regulate conduct implicitly authorized the Executive to regulate speech."

Justice O'Connor wrote a dissenting opinion as well, arguing that the regulations placed content-based restrictions on the speech of those that received Title X funds. Unlike Justice Blackmun in his dissent, Justice O'Connor thought there was no need to reach the constitutional questions because the Court should interpret the statute to avoid them whenever another acceptable interpretation was available. Under this approach, "Congress retains the power to force the constitutional question by legislating more explicitly" because the Court "should not tell Congress what it cannot do before it has chosen to do it."

AFTERMATH

Under this decision, the HHS was allowed to prohibit recipients of government funds from advocating, counseling, or referring patients for abortion.

SIGNIFICANCE

The Court was clear in its decision that upholding Title X did not conflict with its earlier decision in *Roe v. Wade* (1973). Allowing the Department of Health and Human Services to regulate use of federal funds to promote family planning illustrated that the government can uphold a person's constitutional rights without subsidizing the means to exercise those rights.

RELATED CASES

United States ex rel. Attorney General v. Delaware & Hudson Co., 213 U.S. 366 (1909)

Maher v. Roe, 432 U.S. 464; 97 S. Ct. 2376 (1977)

Harris v. McRae, 448 U.S. 297; 100 S. Ct. 2671 (1980)

Motor Vehicle Mfrs. Assn. of United States, Inc. v. State Farm Mut. Automobile Ins. Co., 463 U.S. 29 (1983)

Chevron U.S.A. Inc. v. Natural Resources Defense Council, Inc., 467 U.S. 837 (1984)

United States v. Salerno, 481 U.S. 739 (1987)

Webster v. Reproductive Health Services, 492 U.S. 490 (1989)

STATUTE AT ISSUE

Public Health Service Act, §§ 1002, 1008, as amended; 42 U.S.C.A. § 300

RECOMMENDED READING

Michael Fitzpatrick, *Rust Corrodes: The First Amendment Implications of* Rust v. Sullivan, 45 Stanford Law Review 185 (1992).

Elena Kagan, *The Changing Faces of First Amendment Neutrality:* R.A.V. v. St. Paul, Rust v. Sullivan, *and the Problem of Content-Based Underinclusion,* Supreme Court Review 29 (1992).

G. C. Leedes, *The Discourse Ethics Alternative to* Rust v. Sullivan, 26 University of Richmond Law Review 87 (1991).

Case Title: *Planned Parenthood of Southeastern Pennsylvania v. Casey*

Legal Citation: 505 U.S. 833

Year of Decision: 1992

KEY ISSUES

Can a state require a woman who wants an abortion (1) to obtain informed consent; (2) to wait at least 24 hours before the abortion is performed; (3) if a minor, to obtain parental consent; and (4) if married, to notify her spouse of her intention to abort the fetus, without violating the woman's right to an abortion as guaranteed by *Roe v. Wade* (1973)?

HISTORY OF THE CASE

In 1988 and 1989, a Pennsylvania abortion statute was amended, requiring a woman seeking abortion to give her informed consent prior to the abortion procedure, wait at least 24 hours before the procedure is to be performed, notify her spouse, and, if a minor, receive parental consent. Before the provisions of the statute took effect, a number of abortion clinics and a class of physicians brought suit seeking declaratory and injunctive relief on the basis that each of the provisions was unconstitutional on its face. The district court held that the provisions of the statute were unconstitutional and entered a permanent injunction against Pennsylvania's enforcement of them. The U.S. Court of Appeals for the Third Circuit affirmed in part and reversed in part, holding that only the husband notification provision was unconstitutional.

SUMMARY OF ARGUMENTS

The plaintiffs challenged the constitutionality of the Pennsylvania Abortion Control Act using the decision in *Roe v. Wade*. In *Roe,* the court recognized a constitutional right to have an abortion as part of the liberty protected by the due process clause of the Fourteenth Amendment. The plaintiffs argued that the amendments to the Pennsylvania Abortion Control Act would place enormous burdens on women seeking to obtain an abortion and thus placed burdens on a woman's right to reproductive choice.

The state defended the act by claiming that none of the amendments to the act imposed an undue burden on women, and all of them furthered legitimate state interests. The state further argued that *Roe* was wrongfully decided and urged the Court to overturn the ruling. The state argued that the holding that abortion is a fundamental right has no support in the Constitution, in history, or in the Court's precedence. The state further contended that the use of trimesters and validity to determine the right to abortion is arbitrary.

DECISION

The decision in this case was written by a plurality of the court. Justices Souter, O'Connor, and Kennedy jointly wrote the plurality opinion. With respect to parts I, II, and III of the opinion, the plurality concluded that *stare decisis* required that the essential holding of *Roe* be upheld. The plurality reaffirmed the three parts of *Roe,* (1) holding that a woman has a right to choose to have an abortion before fetal viability and to obtain it without undue interference from the state, whose pre-viability interests are not strong enough to support an abortion prohibition or the imposition of substantial obstacles to the woman's effective right to elect the procedure; (2) confirming the state's power to restrict abortions after viability, if the law contains exceptions for pregnancies endangering a woman's life or health; and (3) asserting the principle that the state has legitimate interests from the outset of the pregnancy in protecting the health of the woman and the life of the fetus that may become a child.

In part IV of the opinion, the plurality upheld the "essential holding" of *Roe,* that the right to abortion is grounded in the due process clause of the Fourteenth Amendment. However, the plurality overturned the trimester formula that was used in *Roe* to weigh the woman's interest in obtaining an abortion against the state's interest in the life of the fetus. Instead, the plurality looked at changes in medical science and determined that a pre-viability/post-viability distinction would be more appropriate. The justices imposed a new standard to determine the validity of laws that restrict abortions. The new standard looks at whether or not the regulation imposes an "undue burden" on a woman's ability to obtain an abortion. The term *undue burden* is defined as a "substantial obstacle in the path of a woman seeking an abortion before the fetus attains viability."

In parts V-A and V-C of the opinion, the plurality held that only the husband notification provision constituted an undue burden and was therefore unconstitutional. In part V-E of the opinion, Justices O'Connor, Kennedy, Souter, and Stevens concluded that all of the statute's record keeping and reporting requirements, except that relating to spousal notice, were constitutional. In parts V-B and V-D of the opinion, Justices O'Connor, Kennedy, and Souter concluded that neither the informed consent nor the parental consent requirement was unconstitutional.

The chief justice wrote an opinion that was joined by Justices White, Scalia, and Thomas. Chief Justice Rehnquist concluded that the plurality's "undue burden" standard had no right in constitutional law. The chief justice concluded that in order for judges to evaluate abortion rights under the new standard, judges would have to make "subjective, unguided" determinations on whether to place substantial obstacles in the path of a woman seeking an abortion. The chief justice argued that the new standard was no more workable than the trimester framework standard founded in *Roe*. The chief justice then discussed all of the provisions of the Pennsylvania statute at issue, finding that all sections were rationally related to the state's interests.

Justices Blackmun and Stevens wrote opinions in which they approved the plurality's preservation of *Roe* and the rejection of the spousal notification law. However, the justices disagreed with the plurality's decision to uphold the other laws at issue. Justice Blackmun went on to argue that the application of the strict scrutiny standard resulted in an invalidation of all the challenged provisions of the Pennsylvania statute.

AFTERMATH

After *Planned Parenthood of Southeastern Pennsylvania v. Casey* (1992), the question moved from whether *Roe v. Wade* would be overturned to what conditions truly constituted a woman's right to a legal abortion. After *Casey,* the Supreme Court decided a number of different cases surrounding the issue of antiabortion protests, many of which made it more difficult for antiabortion groups to disrupt the operations of family planning clinics. Also, many courts have found the "undue burden" test to allow for greater state regulation of abortion versus the previous trimester framework.

SIGNIFICANCE

This case provided the first chance to overturn *Roe v. Wade* since the two liberal justices, William Brennan and Thurgood Marshall, were replaced by David Souter and Clarence Thomas, both of whom were viewed as conservative judges. However, the plurality of the Court continued to uphold the essential holding in *Roe* finding that such a holding was necessary to preserve the country's confidence in the judiciary system. *Casey* preserved a woman's right to abortion.

RELATED CASES

Roe v. Wade, 410 U.S. 113 (1973)

Akron v. Akron Center for Reproductive Health, Inc., 462 U.S. 416 (1983)

Thornburgh v. American College of Obstetricians and Gynecologists, 476 U.S. 747 (1986)

Webster v. Reproductive Health Services, 492 U.S. 490 (1989)

STATUTE AT ISSUE

Pennsylvania Abortion Control Act of 1982 (18 Pa. Cons. Stat. 1990)

RECOMMENDED READING

Joan R. Bullock, *Abortion Rights in America,* 1994 BYUL Rev 63 (1994).

Beth A. Burkstrand-Reid, *The Invisible Woman: Availability and Culpability in Reproductive Health Jurisprudence*, 81 U Colo L Rev 97 (2010).

Mark A. Graber, *The Ghost of Abortion Past: Pre-*Roe *Abortion Law in Action*, 1 Va J Soc Pol'y & L 309 (1994).

Maureen L. Rurka, *The Vagueness of Partial-Birth Abortion Bans: Deconstruction or Destruction?*, 89 J Crim L & Criminology 1233 (1999).

INTERNET RESOURCE

National Abortion Federation: www.prochoice.org/policy/courts/pp_v_casey.html

Case Title: *Stenberg v. Carhart*

Legal Citation: 530 U.S. 914

Year of Decision: 2000

KEY ISSUE

Does a Nebraskan law prohibiting partial-birth abortions violate the right of liberty inherent in the due process clause of the Fourteenth Amendment?

HISTORY OF THE CASE

LeRoy Carhart, a physician specializing in late-term abortions, brought suit against Don Stenberg, the attorney general of Nebraska, seeking a judgment that a Nebraska law banning "partial birth abortions" was a violation of the U.S. Constitution. The Nebraska statute in question defined "partial birth abortion" as any abortion in which the physician "partially delivers vaginally a living unborn child before killing the unborn child and completing the delivery." The statute went on to define "killing the unborn child" as "intentionally delivering into the vagina a living unborn child, or a substantial portion thereof, for the purpose of performing a proce-

dure that the [abortionist] knows will kill the . . . child and does kill the . . . child."

The vast majority of first trimester abortions are "suction-aspiration" abortions. Abortions conducted in the second trimester generally use a different method known as "dilation and evacuation." This second method is needed when the fetus is too large for "suction-aspiration" to work. Dr. Carhart performed a modified version of the "dilation and evacuation" method known as "dilation and extraction." In this procedure, the fetus is dismembered in parts inside the uterus before being fully extracted. This is normally only required when the pregnancy has advanced to a later stage. It is thus considered by many to be a "later" term method of abortion. The state of Nebraska maintained that Dr. Carhart's procedure was clearly in violation of the statute.

Dr. Carhart maintained that this method was safer for his patients. Moreover, Carhart argued that the right to privacy (and thus an abortion) enshrined in *Roe v. Wade* (1973) and the requirement that no "undue burden" be created in getting an abortion decided in *Planned Parenthood of Southeastern Pennsylvania v. Casey* (1992) meant that the Nebraska law was unconstitutional. Dr. Carhart prevailed both in the district court and in the Eighth Circuit Court of Appeals. The Supreme Court granted certiorari, and the case was argued in 2000.

SUMMARY OF ARGUMENTS

Dr. Carhart argued that *Planned Parenthood v. Casey* and its ruling that any "undue burden" imposed on a woman's right to an abortion was unconstitutional meant that the Nebraska statute was unconstitutional. Carhart maintained that the Nebraska law did, in fact, constitute an undue burden because it acted as a major disincentive to the performance of late-term abortions—both of the "dilation and evacuation" and of the "dilation and extraction" variety. This is because, according to Carhart, both methods involve the partial delivery (outside the womb, but still inside the mother) of a living unborn child before the abortion is completed. Carhart argued that the Nebraska law thus prohibited *all* late-term abortions. Of course, Carhart's argument ultimately rested on the decision reached in *Roe v. Wade*, in which the Court affirmed the right to an abortion as part of a constitutional right to privacy found in the due process clause.

The state of Nebraska argued that it was merely regulating a particular *type* of abortion, which the state maintained was allowed under the ruling in *Planned Parenthood v. Casey*. Nebraska argued that "dilation and extraction" was a particularly "gruesome" technique that could be banned under the normal police powers of the state that had been upheld in *Casey*. Nebraska did not question the notion that an "undue burden" was placed on abortion *if* the statute was interpreted to apply to *both* late term "dilation and evacuation" and "dilation extraction" abortions. However, the state maintained that only the "dilation and extraction" method was prohibited by the law.

DECISION

In a 5-4 decision written by Justice Breyer, the Court ruled in favor of Carhart. Breyer wrote that "Nebraska's statute criminalizing the performance of 'partial birth abortion[s]' violates the U.S. Constitution, as interpreted in Casey and Roe." The Court agreed with Carhart that the Nebraskan law banned not only the more controversial "dilation and extraction" method, but also the "dilation and evacuation" method as well. This constituted a blanket ban on late-term abortions that the Court determined placed "an undue burden upon a woman's right to make an abortion decision." Concurring opinions emphasized that the state could not force physicians to use certain medical procedures over others if those procedures were not, in the judgment of the physician, the most appropriate.

The dissents focused on two issues. First, Justice Kennedy elaborated on the idea that *Casey* had allowed for certain limitations on abortion, and that the limitations of the Nebraska law were within the purview of legal state action. Second, dissents by Justices Thomas and Scalia attacked the very foundation of a constitutional right to abortion and right to privacy. Justices Thomas and Scalia argued that *Casey* had been wrongly decided and should be overturned. In his own dissent, Justice Scalia concluded that "the notion

that the Constitution of the United States . . . prohibits the States from simply banning this visibly brutal means of eliminating our half-born posterity is quite simply absurd."

AFTERMATH

The Nebraska law was struck down along with all other statutes across the nation banning the type of "partial-birth abortion" practiced by Dr. Carhart. However, in 2003, Congress passed the Partial-Birth Abortion Ban Act. This law outlawed, in very specific terms, the "dilation and extraction" method of abortion. In 2007, the Supreme Court upheld this federal statute in *Gonzales v. Carhart* (2007).

SIGNIFICANCE

This decision did not overrule *Roe, Casey,* or the original *Carhart* case. It remained consistent with *Carhart,* as the 2003 federal law was much more narrowly tailored to a specific form of abortion, namely, "dilation and extraction." The 2003 law could not be interpreted as an outright ban on the much more vaguely defined term "partial birth abortions." *Carhart* stands as good law.

RELATED CASES

Roe v. Wade, 410 U.S. 113 (1973)

Planned Parenthood of Southeastern Pennsylvania v. Casey, 505 U.S. 833 (1992)

Gonzales v. Carhart, 550 U.S. 124 (2007)

STATUTE AT ISSUE

Nebraska Revised Statute 28-328. Partial-birth abortion; prohibition; violation; penalties

RECOMMENDED READING

Mersky, Roy. *A Documentary History of the Legal Aspects of Abortion in the United States.* Buffalo, N.Y.: William S. Hein, 2000.

David Smolin, *Fourteenth Amendment Unenumerated Rights Jurisprudence: An Essay in Response to* Stenberg v. Carhart, 24 Harvard Journal of Law and Public Policy 815 (2000).

Case Title: *Ayotte v. Planned Parenthood of Northern New England*

Legal Citation: 546 U.S. 320

Year of Decision: 2006

KEY ISSUE

Did the courts err in invalidating the Parental Notification Prior to Abortion Act in its entirety because it lacks an exception for the preservation of pregnant minors' health?

HISTORY OF THE CASE

In 2003, New Hampshire enacted the Parental Notification Prior to Abortion Act. The act prohibited physicians from performing an abortion on a pregnant minor until 48 hours after written notice of the pending abortion is delivered to her parent or guardian.

The act allowed for three circumstances in which a physician could perform an abortion without notifying the minor's parent. First, notice was not required if the abortion provider certified that the abortion was necessary to prevent the minor's death and there was insufficient time to provide parental notice. Second, a person entitled to receive notice could certify he or she had already been notified. Third, under the judicial bypass provision, a minor could petition a judge to authorize an abortion without parental consent if the judge found the minor was mature and capable of giving informed consent or that abortion without notification was in the minor's best interest.

Planned Parenthood of New England, a physician, and several other clinics offering reproductive health services ("the Providers") challenged the act, bringing suit against then–New Hampshire attorney general Peter Heed. The U.S. District Court for the District of New Hampshire declared the act unconstitutional and issued an injunction against its enforcement. The Court of Appeals for the First Circuit affirmed the decision.

Attorney General Heed's successor, Kelly Ayotte, appealed the case to the Supreme Court, which granted certiorari.

SUMMARY OF ARGUMENTS

The Providers alleged that the act was unconstitutional because it failed to allow a physician to provide a prompt abortion to a minor whose health would be endangered by delays inherent in the act. They also challenged the adequacy of the act's life exception and of the judicial bypass's confidentiality provision.

New Hampshire argued that the act was not unconstitutional for lack of a health exception because in most, if not all cases, the act's judicial bypass and the state's "competing harms" statute should protect both physician and patient when a minor needs an immediate abortion. The competing harms statute provided that conduct that the actor believes to be necessary to avoid harm to himself or another is justifiable if the desirability and urgency of avoiding such harm outweigh, according to ordinary standards of reasonableness, the harm sought to be prevented by the statute defining the offense charged. New Hampshire conceded that it would be unconstitutional to apply the act in a manner that subjected minors to significant health risks.

DECISION

The Court vacated the lower court's decision and remanded the case to the lower courts to determine whether (1) the New Hampshire legislature intended the statute to be invalidated in total if a provision were found unconstitutional or whether it would accept the statute minus the unconstitutional applications and (2) whether an injunction was the proper remedy for application of a provision deemed unconstitutional.

Justice O'Connor wrote for a unanimous Court. The Court began the opinion affirming three propositions. First, states unquestionably have the right to require parental involvement when a minor considers terminating her pregnancy because of their "strong and legitimate interest in the welfare of their young citizens, whose immaturity, inexperience, and lack of judgment may sometimes impair their ability to exercise their rights wisely." Second, New Hampshire did not dispute, and the Court's precedent holds, that a state may not restrict access to abortions that are "necessary, in appropriate medical judgment, for the preservation of the life or health of the mother." Third, New Hampshire has not taken real issue with the factual basis of the litigation, that in some very small percentage of cases, pregnant minors, like adult women, need immediate abortions to avert serious and often irreversible damage to their health.

The Court then turned to the question of the proper judicial remedy when a statute could be applied in a manner that harms women's health. The Court articulated three principles that informed its approach to remedies. First, the Supreme Court tries not to nullify more of a legislature's work than is necessary so as not to frustrate the intent of the elected representative of the people. Thus, the normal rule is that partial, rather than facial, invalidation is the required course. Second, the Court restrains itself from rewriting state law to conform to constitutional requirements, even as it tries to salvage it. Third, the touchstone for any decision about remedy is legislative intent, for a court cannot use its remedial powers to circumvent the intent of the legislature. The court must ask itself whether the legislature would have preferred what is left of the statute or no statute at all.

In this case, the Court held that invalidating the statute entirely is not always necessary or justified, for lower courts may be able to render narrower declaratory and injunctive relief. Because only a few applications of the act would present a constitutional problem, the lower courts could issue a declaratory judgment and an injunction prohibiting the statute's unconstitutional application.

AFTERMATH

The Parental Notification Act was repealed in 2007. Subsequently, a rehearing of the case at the district level was no longer relevant. The Supreme Court has not addressed the constitutionality of requiring parental consent since its decision in *Ayotte.*

SIGNIFICANCE

Ayotte clearly set forth the Supreme Court's stance on the required role of parents in minors' abortion procedures. Though the majority of states require parental notification or consent before a minor can obtain an abortion, most states do not require parental involvement when a woman under the age of 18 chooses to place her child for adoption. Critics argue that this delineation has coercive affects, restricting a minor's decisions regarding unplanned pregnancies.

RELATED CASES

Webster v. Reproductive Health Services, 492 U.S. 490 (1989)

Planned Parenthood of Southeastern Pennsylvania v. Casey, 505 U.S. 833 (1992)

RECOMMENDED READING

Teresa Stanton Collett, *Judicial Modesty and Abortion,* 59 South Carolina Law Review 701 (2008).

David H. Gans, *Severability as Judicial Lawmaking,* 76 George Washington Law Review 639 (2008).

Robert J. Pushaw, Jr., *Partial-Birth Abortion and the Perils of Constitutional Common Law,* 31 Harvard Journal of Law & Public Policy 519 (2008).

Case Title: *Gonzales v. Carhart*

Legal Citation: 550 U.S. 124

Year of Decision: 2007

KEY ISSUE

Does the lack of an exception for the mother's health make the Partial-Birth Abortion Ban Act of 2003 unconstitutional?

HISTORY OF THE CASE

In 2003, Congress passed the Partial-Birth Abortion Ban Act. The act prohibited an abortion procedure known as intact dilation and extraction, which involves the fetus's being partially removed from the mother and then destroyed. The act was based on the findings of Congress that it was an inhumane procedure, never medically necessary, and that it was disfavored among the medical community. The act was challenged in the Northern District of California, the District of Nebraska (by Dr. LeRoy Carhart), and the Southern District of New York. These decisions were affirmed by the Second, Eighth, and Ninth Circuit Courts of Appeals, respectively.

The Supreme Court consolidated U.S. Attorney General Alberto Gonzales's appeals of *Gonzales v. Carhart* and *Gonzales v. Planned Parenthood* into a single appeal.

SUMMARY OF ARGUMENTS

The attorney general argued that the act did not place any undue burden on a woman's access to abortion. Although there was no health exception in the act, in passing the statute, Congress found that a partial-birth abortion was never medically necessary. Gonzales further claimed that there was a state interest in clearly delineating abortions from infanticide. The act was neither ambiguous nor vague, according to Gonzales, and, as such, should be deemed constitutional.

The challengers of the act argued that prior precedents of the Court in cases such as *Stenberg v. Carhart* required that laws regulating access to abortions contain exceptions where necessary for the health and safety of the mother. Under this standard, Carhart claimed, the statute was unconstitutional. Carhart also argued that the act was overbroad since the definition of partial-birth abortion would include nonintact dilation and extraction.

DECISION

The Supreme Court upheld the Partial-Birth Abortion Ban Act, deciding that the act was not vague and did not place an undue burden on a woman's access to abortion. Addressing the issue of ambiguity, the Court decided that the intent requirements and the anatomical landmarks provided in the statute offered clear guidelines to physicians performing abortions.

In addressing the issue of whether the act should fail on the basis that it did not include an exception to preserve the health of the mother, the Court concluded that evidence that a partial-birth abortion may be necessary in a small fraction of cases is insufficient to invalidate the act as a whole. While noting that the findings of Congress as to whether a partial-birth abortion would ever be medically necessary could not be deferred to in light of the contradicting evidence, the Court rejected the argument that the act should be invalidated. Such a situation would need to affect a substantial number of women for the lack of a health exception to create an undue burden. Where an individual woman's health would be better preserved by a partial-birth abortion, she could challenge the constitutionality of the law as applied to her.

The dissent would have held that the absence of the health exception made the act unconstitutional. They found the testimony that there are circumstances where partial-birth abortion would be in the best interests of the mother's health convincing and worthy of mandating a health exception.

AFTERMATH

The decision of the Supreme Court, although outwardly affirming previous decisions regarding abortions, was a small victory for the antiabortion movement. This decision also prompted concerns from the medical community. Many questioned the wisdom of allowing the judgment of Congress to substitute for that of the patient's physician.

SIGNIFICANCE

The Supreme Court seemed to back away from its previous ruling in *Stenberg v. Carhart,* where a Nebraska statute banning partial-birth abortion was struck down. The majority opinion focused more on morality and suggested a stronger interest in fetal life than previous Supreme Court abortion decisions.

RELATED CASES

Roe v. Wade, 410 U.S. 113 (1973)

Planned Parenthood of Southeastern Pennsylvania v. Casey, 505 U.S. 833 (1992)

Stenberg v. Carhart, 530 U.S. 914 (2000)

RECOMMENDED READING

Steven G. Calabresi, *How to Reverse Government Imposition of Immorality: A Strategy for Eroding* Roe v. Wade, 31 Harvard Journal of Law and Public Policy 85 (2008).

Caron, Simone M. *Who Chooses?: American Reproductive History since 1830*. Gainesville: University Press of Florida, 2008.

Martha K. Plante, *"Protecting" Women's Health: How* Gonzales v. Carhart *Endangers Women's Health and Women's Equal Right to Personhood under the Constitution*, 16 American University Journal of Gender, Social Policy & the Law 387 (2008).

Judith G. Waxman, *Privacy and Reproductive Rights: Where We've Been and Where We're Going*, 68 Montana Law Review 299 (2007).

ANTITRUST AND COMPETITION

Constitutional guaranteed rights to freedom and liberty do not only apply to human citizens of the United States; within a very carefully defined set of principles, they apply to businesses and corporations as well. One of the fundamental values of our democracy is a free market, in which hard work, talent, and good business judgment are rewarded by financial success and the accumulation of wealth. However, there has long been a tension between the protection of the rights of business to succeed and prosper and the good of society. Greed and self-serving ambition have been known to turn enterprises that exist—at least partly—for the benefit of society into enterprises that work against the public good.

Congress and the states have, over the years, enacted many important laws that seek to control businesses that engage in practices that work against society. This frequently plays out when corporations, through the people who manage them, become involved in activities that stifle competition and, as a result, can be detrimental to consumers. Consumers can be hurt through artificial price inflation or as a result of a lack of choices for products or services. This lack of choice of providers for goods or services may affect consumers by stifling innovation or by providing them with substandard quality of products.

The mechanisms by which Congress and the states combat unfair, anticompetitive, or monopolistic practices are known as antitrust laws. Antitrust laws forbid corporations, through their managers, from engaging in activities such as conspiring to fix prices, dividing markets, or using any other unfair practices that prevent competitors from entering the market.

Of course, our free market capitalist system also rewards good business judgment and shrewd business practices. Competition among businesses has resulted in some of our society's greatest innovations and has contributed in positive ways to our modern way of life. The trick for regulators—Congress and states that pass laws and the government agencies and offices charged with enforcing those laws—is to encourage competition, and hence, innovation, while protecting consumers by keeping the products and services provided by businesses affordable, available, and safe.

At the end of the 19th century and the beginning of the 20th century, during the birth of the Industrial Revolution, Congress passed a series of laws called antitrust laws that forbade corporations and their managers to engage in anticompetitive and monopolistic practices. The laws provide several remedies for violations of the antitrust laws: Corporate managers may be found guilty of crimes for violating the laws; state or federal governments, through attorneys general or agencies such as the Federal Trade Commission or the Justice Department, may sue corporations through civil actions in federal court; and even private citizens may bring civil action in federal court. In all of these cases, the courts are charged with the responsibility for balancing the harm to consumers and society with corporations' right to engage in the competitive business practices of a free market.

The result of antitrust laws is a complex web of analyses of business practices that often requires detailed study of economics. Over the years, as corporations have grown in size and diversity, not to mention growing internationally, it has become extremely difficult to determine when practices result in illegal business trusts or monopolies, or when great corporations succeed simply because they are the best at what they do, or they happen to be in the right place at the right time. Two excellent modern examples of corporations that have come under the scrutiny of the antitrust laws are Microsoft, which was sued by the Justice Department in the 1990s, and AT&T, the great telephone monopoly that was broken up by the same agency in the 1980s. Microsoft was found guilty of anticompetitive practices against its Web browser competitor Netscape, and AT&T's nationwide monopoly of telephone service was broken up into several "baby bells."

Antitrust laws may be quite technical and difficult to understand, but their effect is far reaching and touches our lives every day.

Sherman Antitrust Act, 15 U.S.C. § 1

Every contract, combination in the form of trust or otherwise, or conspiracy, in restraint of trade or commerce among the several States, or with foreign nations, is declared to be illegal. Every person who shall make any contract or engage in any combination or conspiracy hereby declared to be illegal shall be deemed guilty of a felony, and, on conviction thereof, shall be punished by fine not exceeding $100,000,000 if a corporation, or, if any other person, $1,000,000, or by imprisonment not exceeding 10 years, or by both said punishments, in the discretion of the court.

Sherman Antitrust Act, 15 U.S.C. § 2

Every person who shall monopolize, or attempt to monopolize, or combine or conspire with any other person or persons, to monopolize any part

of the trade or commerce among the several States, or with foreign nations, shall be deemed guilty of a felony, and, on conviction thereof, shall be punished by fine not exceeding $100,000,000 if a corporation, or, if any other person, $1,000,000, or by imprisonment not exceeding 10 years, or by both said punishments, in the discretion of the court.

Case Title: *The Butcher's Benevolent Association of New Orleans v. The Crescent City Live-Stock Landing and Slaughter-House Company; Paul Esteben, L. Ruch, J. P. Rouede, W. Maylie, S. Firmberg, B. Beaubay, William Fagan, J. D. Broderick, N. Seibel, M. Lannes, J. Gitzinger, J. P. Aycock, D. Verges, The Live-Stock Dealers' and Butchers' Association of New Orleans, and Charles Cavaroc v. The State of Louisiana, ex. rel. S. Belden, Attorney-General; The Butchers' Benevolent Association of New Orleans v. The Crescent City Live-Stock and Slaughter-House Company*

Alternate Case Title: *The Slaughterhouse Cases*

Legal Citation: 83 U.S. 36

Year of Decision: 1872

Key Issue

Do the Civil War amendments grant U.S. citizens broad protection against the actions of state governments?

History of the Case

The state of Louisiana granted a state corporation the exclusive right to operate facilities in New Orleans for the landing, keeping, and slaughter of livestock. The Butcher's Benevolent Association, a group of excluded butchers, sought an injunction against the monopoly on the grounds that they were prevented from practicing their trade unless they worked at the monopolist corporation and paid its fees. The state courts upheld the law.

SUMMARY OF ARGUMENTS

The plaintiffs' appeal was based on four grounds: (1) that the statute created an involuntary servitude forbidden by the Thirteenth Amendment; (2) that it abridged the privileges and immunities of citizens of the United States; (3) that it denied plaintiffs the equal protection of the laws; and (4) that it deprived them of their property without due proccss of law, all under the Fourteenth Amendment.

DECISION

The Court ruled that the state of Louisiana could act as it did, for the following reasons: (1) The proper interpretation of the Civil War amendments must reflect their historical setting. Thus, the meaning of "involuntary servitude" as used in the Thirteenth Amendment is restricted to personal servitude, not a servitude attached to property, as the plaintiffs claimed. (2) The Fourteenth Amendment clearly distinguishes between citizenship of the states and citizenship of the United States. Only those privileges and immunities of U.S. citizens are protected by the Fourteenth Amendment. Privileges and immunities of state citizens upon which the plaintiffs relied here are unaffected and rest for their security and protection in the power of the several states as recognized in article 4 of the U.S. Constitution. The Constitution does not control the power of the state governments over the right of their own citizens except to require that a state grant equal rights to its own citizens and citizens of other states within its jurisdiction. Therefore, the plaintiffs, as citizens of the United States, had no privilege or immunity that has been infringed by the state law. (3) The equal protection clause of the Fourteenth Amendment is intended primarily to prevent state discrimination against blacks, although Congress may extend its scope to other areas. But the plaintiffs did not claim a denial of equal justice in the state courts and therefore had no reason to have a remedy under the equal protection clause. (4) The restraint imposed by Louisiana upon the exercise of the plaintiffs' trade simply cannot be held to be a deprivation of property within the meaning of the Fourteenth Amendment. That clause should not be construed to cover such state restraint upon trade.

AFTERMATH

Justice Field in his dissent stated his belief that the Fourteenth Amendment protected those privileges and immunities "which of right belong to the citizens of all free governments." Among these privileges was the right to pursue lawful employment. The Supreme Court never did accept Justice Field's views of the Fourteenth Amendment's privileges and immunities clause, and the majority's interpretation in the *Slaughterhouse Cases* is still the accepted reading of that provision, rendering the clause inoperative as a check on state laws.

SIGNIFICANCE

This case, the first requiring interpretation of these amendments, rendered the privileges and immunities clause of the Fourteenth Amendment, which sought to equalize the advantages of citizenship among the states, ineffective in protecting individual rights against invasion by state governments. Instead, the Court looked to the due process and equal protection clauses. The plaintiffs in this case were not attacking the procedure used but instead the actual fairness of the state-approved monopoly. Although the Court rejected the notion of substantive due process in this case, the scope of the clause was unclear for many years. Gradually, the Court began to examine the substance of state legislation to determine whether it was reasonable.

RELATED CASES

Butchers' Union Co. v. Crescent City Co., 111 U.S. 746 (1884)

Hawaii Housing Authority v. Midkiff, 467 U.S. 229 (1984)

United States v. Kozminski, 487 U.S. 931 (1988)

Richmond v. J. A. Croson Co., 488 U.S. 469 (1989)

Morgan v. Illinois, 504 U.S. 719 (1992)

RECOMMENDED READING

Normand G. Benoit, *The Privileges or Immunities Clause of the Fourteenth Amendment: Can There Be Life after Death?*, 11 Suffolk University Law Review 61 (1976).

Philip B. Kurland, *The Privileges or Immunities Clause: "Its Hour Come Round at Last"?*, Washington University Law Quarterly 405 (1972).

Labbe, Ronald M., and Johathan Lurie. *The Slaughterhouse Cases: Regulation, Reconstruction, and the Fourteenth Amendment.* Lawrence: University Press of Kansas, 2003.

Case Title: *United States v. E. C. Knight Co.*

Alternate Case Title: The Sugar Case

Legal Citation: 156 U.S. 1

Year of Decision: 1895

KEY ISSUE

May Congress regulate the wholly intrastate manufacturing of sugar under its constitutional power to regulate commerce among the states?

HISTORY OF THE CASE

The American Sugar Refining Company acquired ownership of four other sugar refineries. These acquisitions created a virtual monopoly, with American Sugar in control of 98 percent of the U.S. refined-sugar market. The federal government then filed suit against American Sugar, alleging that it had violated the Sherman Antitrust Act of 1890, which provides that "every contract, combination . . . or conspiracy in restraint of trade and commerce among the several States is illegal . . . and that persons who monopolize trade among the several States shall be guilty of a misdemeanor." The government sought an injunction to set aside the acquisitions of the four refineries, but the U.S. Court of Appeals for the Third Circuit found no Sherman Act violation.

SUMMARY OF ARGUMENTS

American Sugar argued that the refining of sugar was not part of interstate commerce and not subject to the Sherman Act. It also contended it had not engaged in any monopoly actions that would have constituted a restraint of trade.

The government argued that sugar was a daily necessity in American life, that interstate commerce was indispensable to the nationwide consumption of sugar, and that Congress, therefore, had the power to eliminate the refining monopoly because of its effects on that commerce.

DECISION

The Supreme Court, in an opinion written by Chief Justice Fuller, held that the Sherman Act was inapplicable because Congress lacked the power to regulate "manufacturing." Chief Justice Fuller assumed for the sake of argument that American Sugar had a true monopoly, although he noted that the price of sugar had not risen significantly since the acquisitions. He argued that the regulation of wholly intrastate monopolies was part of each state's police power, whereas the power to control interstate commerce belonged exclusively to Congress. American Sugar had obtained a monopoly only in the manufacture of sugar; Chief Justice Fuller found this monopoly beyond Congress's power: "Commerce succeeds to manufacture, and is not a part of it." In his opinion, to find such indirect effects within the commerce power would strike a great blow to the federal system. He asserted that in many forms of manufacture, "the instrumentality of commerce [is] necessarily invoked," but only a monopoly that bore a direct relation to commerce between the states was within the reach of Congress through the Sherman Act.

Justice Harlan wrote alone in dissent. He took a much less formal view of the distinction between manufacture and commerce, which he saw as only a difference of degree. Since Congress clearly had the power to prohibit the interstate transportation of products made by a monopoly, it must also have the power to regulate "in advance of transportation." In Justice Harlan's view, the Constitution was not intended to render the federal government powerless in a time of "national emergency."

AFTERMATH

The formalistic analysis conducted by Chief Justice Fuller soon gave way to Justice Harlan's "realist" approach, and by the 1940s, Congress had the power to regulate almost any business activity through the commerce clause.

SIGNIFICANCE

This decision marked the beginning of the Court's attempt to define what activities and items were included in commerce and could be regulated. The Court focused on the activity itself and not the activity's effect.

RELATED CASES

Gibbons v. Ogden, 22 U.S. (9 Wheat.) 1 (1824)

Addyston Pipe & Steel Co. v. United States, 175 U.S. 211 (1899)

Northern Securities Co. v. United States, 193 U.S. 197 (1904)

United States v. Darby, 312 U.S. 100 (1941)

RECOMMENDED READING

Eicher, Alfred S. *The Emergence of Oligopoly: Sugar Refining as a Case Study.* Baltimore: Johns Hopkins University Press, 1969.

Richard A. Epstein, *The Proper Scope of the Commerce Power,* 73 Virginia Law Review 1387 (1987).

Josephson, Matthew. *The Robber Barons.* New York: Harcourt, 1934.

Kilgore, Carrol D. *Judicial Tyranny.* Chicago: Thomas Nelson, 1977.

Case Title: *Swift & Company v. United States*

Legal Citation: 196 U.S. 375

Year of Decision: 1905

KEY ISSUE

Does appellants' method of trade in fresh meat violate the Sherman Antitrust Act of July 2, 1890, "to protect trade and commerce against unlawful restraints and monopolies"?

HISTORY OF THE CASE

Swift & Co. bought livestock in Chicago, which they slaughtered in their respective states, creating meat for human consumption. They also sold meat to buyers in different states, shipping it by rail. Swift slaughterhouses controlled the majority of the trade in fresh meats. They did not compete with themselves. They did not bid against each other, and from time to time, they fixed prices at secret meetings. They also received a lower rate for transportation than others.

This case was an appeal from the circuit court granting an injunction against Swift for violations of the act of July 2, 1890, a law designed to protect commerce from monopolies.

SUMMARY OF ARGUMENTS

The United States argued that Swift and others were buying, selling, and shipping meat in a manner and with the intention to gain an economic advantage through control of the market. The government argued that through these acts, the companies had gained control of more than half of the trade of fresh meat.

Swift & Company argued that all of its acts were conducted in a lawful manner, and therefore, its intent was irrelevant.

DECISION

The federal government could regulate stockyards because they were acting in the stream of commerce. Justice Holmes wrote the opinion for the Court, holding that the activities of the packers involved interstate commerce: "Commerce among the States is not a technical legal conception, but a practical one, drawn from the course of business. When cattle are sent for sale from a place in one State, with the expectation that they will end their transit, after purchase, in another, and when in effect they do so, with only the interruption necessary to find a purchaser at the stockyards, and when this is a typical, constantly recurring course, the current thus existing is an arbitrary control to which the public might be subjected without regulation."

Justice Holmes also proposed that a business with the capacity to affect public interest affected commerce directly. A private business did not. Also, by accepting the concept of a "current of commerce," he hinted at bringing local business activities under the federal commerce power.

AFTERMATH

Holmes's solution of melding two concepts, a current of commerce and business affected with a public interest, was to last until the 1930s. After this case, a narrow interpretation of the commerce clause in which it was determined whether goods were in the stream of commerce was no longer used, and the Court merely looked at whether an activity had an effect on commerce.

SIGNIFICANCE

This ruling incorporated into the congressional power to regulate commerce the concept of business and the public interest. Conventional thinking would also classify this case as overruling *United States v. E. C. Knight Co.* (1895).

RELATED CASES

Munn v. Illinois, 94 U.S. 113 (1877)

United States v. E. C. Knight Co., 156 U.S. 1 (1895)

Northern Securities Co. v. United States, 193 U.S. 197 (1904)

RECOMMENDED READING

Barry Cushman, *A Stream of Legal Consciousness: The Current of Commerce Doctrine from Swift to Jones and Laughlin*, 61 Fordham Law Review 105 (1992).

Marc I. Steinberg, *SEC and Other Permanent Injunctions: Standards for the Imposition, Modification and Dissolution*, 66 Cornell Law Review 41 (1980).

Case Title: *Standard Oil Company of New Jersey v. United States*

Legal Citation: 221 U.S. 1

Year of Decision: 1911

KEY ISSUES

Did Standard Oil of New Jersey violate the Sherman Antitrust Act by conspiring "to restrain the trade and commerce in petroleum, refined oil" and other products with the intent to monopolize this commerce?

HISTORY OF THE CASE

From 1870 to 1882, Standard Oil of Ohio, a subsidiary of Standard Oil of New Jersey, entered into agreements with some 60 other companies engaged in the oil business to fix the price of oil products, limiting their production and controlling their transportation. The participating companies obtained preferential rates over their competitors from railroads, forcing competitors either to become members or to be driven out of business.

This case was brought to the Supreme Court on appeal from the U.S. District Court for the Eastern District of Missouri.

SUMMARY OF ARGUMENTS

Standard Oil argued that the development of its business resulted from the exercise of lawful competitive methods. Standard Oil also argued that the antitrust act was inapplicable as it extended congressional power beyond that which was granted by the commerce clause.

The United States argued that Standard Oil and others engaged in a conspiracy to restrain trade and commerce in petroleum, petroleum products, and oil.

DECISION

The Court held that Standard Oil Company of New Jersey and its subsidiaries constituted a monopoly in violation of the Sherman Antitrust Act of 1890. Therefore, it was ordered to dissolve and to discontinue the illegal combination between that corporation and its subsidiaries.

Chief Justice White delivered the majority opinion of the Court, saying that the statute was written because of the need to combat restraint of trade and all contracts that attempt to monopolize. Freedom to contract was "the essence of freedom from undue restraint on the right to contract." He set out a rule of reason balancing private rights with governmental rights.

Justice Harlan wrote for the dissent, saying that the Court's interpretation of the antitrust act had usurped the legislative function.

AFTERMATH

This represents the first case of trust-busting. The Supreme Court's adoption of the "rule of reason," a rule that requires review of the circumstances of a case to determine whether acts unreasonably restrain trade, represents the emergence of modern antitrust law. At first, the business community was afraid that the rule would lead to rampant involuntary dissolution; however, it was later found that other oil companies were still engaged in predatory pricing and other forms of unfair competition.

SIGNIFICANCE

The rule of reason was based on facts, using a case-by-case approach, not common law and constitutional arguments. Some felt that this new approach made little impact, and the market essentially remained the same.

RELATED CASES

United States v. E. C. Knight Co., 156 U.S. 1 (1895)

United States v. Trans-Missouri Freight Association, 166 U.S. 290 (1897)

United States v. Joint Traffic Association, 171 U.S. 505 (1898)

Swift & Co. v. United States, 196 U.S. 375 (1905)

National Cotton Oil Co. v. Texas, 197 U.S. 115 (1905)

Shawnee Compress Co. v. Anderson, 209 U.S. 423 (1908)

United States v. Reading, 226 U.S. 324 (1912)

Indiana Farmer's Guide Publishing Co. v. Prairie Farmer Publishing Co., 293 U.S. 268 (1934)

RECOMMENDED READING

Bringhurst, Bruce. *Antitrust and the Oil Monopoly: The Standard Oil Cases, 1890–1911.* Westport, Conn.: Greenwood Press, 1979.

Milton Handler, *Reforming the Antitrust Laws,* 82 Columbia Law Review 1287 (1982).

Rudolph J. Peritz, *The "Rule of Reason" in Antitrust Law: Property Logic in Restraint of Competition,* 40 Hastings Law Journal 285 (1989).

Case Title: *Nebbia v. New York*

Legal Citation: 291 U.S. 502

Year of Decision: 1934

KEY ISSUE

May a state fix the cost at which a product is sold?

HISTORY OF THE CASE

The New York legislature passed an act that established a Milk Control Board for the purpose of setting the price of milk. The board set the price for milk sold in stores at nine cents a quart. Nebbia, a store owner, sold two quarts of milk and a five-cent loaf of bread for 18 cents and was convicted for violating the board's order. Two appeals confirmed the conviction. Nebbia then appealed to the U.S. Supreme Court.

SUMMARY OF ARGUMENTS

Nebbia argued that the order of the Milk Control Board denied him equal protection of the laws and denied him due process. He showed that the order required him, if he purchased from a dealer, to pay eight cents per quart and to resell at no less than nine cents per quart. The same dealer, however, could buy his supply from a farmer at lower prices and deliver the milk to consumers for 10 cents a quart.

The state argued that the regulation would stabilize the industry for an essential food product.

DECISION

Justice Roberts wrote the majority opinion in a 5-4 decision that affirmed the conviction. He concluded that Nebbia was compelled neither to buy from dealers nor to sell at the minimum price. As a result, the difference in price on its face was not arbitrary or unreasonable as required of equal protection challenges.

Regarding the due process challenge, Justice Roberts held that the legislative means employed by the state had a real and substantial relation to the health and stability of the dairy industry. He concluded that as far as due process is concerned, a state is free to adopt whatever economic policy reasonably may be deemed to promote public welfare, in the absence of constitutional restriction.

The dissenting justices felt that the statute constituted an arbitrary interference with the rights of the "little" grocer to conduct his business in an open market. They did not believe that the legislature could destroy the rights of one group while enriching the other, even if it seems advantageous to the public.

AFTERMATH

Nebbia was the first case that indicated the Court's reluctance to accept total economic free-

dom for individuals in the wake of the New Deal, the social and economic reforms enacted to alleviate the effects of the Great Depression. In the years following this decision, the Court widely enforced economic regulation by the states.

SIGNIFICANCE

Nebbia required that economic regulation be substantially related to the objective sought to be attained. The test was essentially that of an earlier opinion, but the Court refused to impose its own views about correct economic policy on the states.

RELATED CASES

Munn v. Illinois, 94 U.S. 113 (1877)

In re Debs, 158 U.S. 564 (1895)

Northern Securities Co. v. United States, 193 U.S. 197 (1904)

Buchanan v. Warley, 245 U.S. 60 (1917)

Block v. Hirsch, 256 U.S. 135 (1921)

Adkins v. Children's Hospital, 261 U.S. 525 (1923)

Meyer v. Nebraska, 262 U.S. 399 (1923)

Near v. Minnesota, 283 U.S. 697 (1931)

West Coast Hotel Co. v. Parrish, 300 U.S. 379 (1937)

U.S. v. Carolene Products Co., 304 U.S. 144 (1938)

Williamson v. Lee Optical, 348 U.S. 483 (1955)

RECOMMENDED READING

Bork, Robert H. *The Tempting of America: The Political Seduction of the Law.* New York: Free Press, 1990.

Schwartz, Bernard. *A Commentary on the Constitution of the United States.* Part II. *The Rights of Property.* New York: Macmillan, 1985, 104–111.

Case Title: *Flood v. Kuhn*

Legal Citation: 407 U.S. 258

Year of Decision: 1972

❧

KEY ISSUE

Does the reserve system in professional baseball fall within the reach of antitrust law such that a team may trade a baseball player against his will?

HISTORY OF THE CASE

Beginning in the 1922 case *Federal Baseball Club v. National League*, organized baseball existed as an anomaly in antitrust laws, represented by the reserve system clause, allowing baseball teams to own their players in a similar manner to ownership of property. Ballplayers could be traded at will or kept on one team for the duration of their careers. Examining the bitterly disputed exception, the Court in *Toolson v. New York Yankees* affirmed the reserve system in 1953. Nearly two decades later, Curt Flood, a St. Louis Cardinals outfielder, refused to allow his contract to be traded to Philadelphia's baseball team, the Phillies. He cited St. Louis business interests and a distaste for Philadelphia. Baseball Commissioner Bowie Kuhn denied Flood's request to be made a free agent, and Flood brought suit in a federal district court under antitrust laws to prevent the trade. After dismissal and appeal, the court of appeals affirmed, and the Supreme Court granted certiorari.

SUMMARY OF ARGUMENTS

Counsel for Flood, as petitioners, argued that organized baseball in the United States should fall under federal antitrust law and the exemption be abolished. In support of their request, petitioners argued that baseball was interstate commerce, the decision in *Federal Baseball Club* should be overruled, baseball has changed significantly since previous adverse rulings, and the reserve system violates federal antitrust law. Kuhn's counsel, as respondents, argued for the exception to antitrust law as adherence to precedent formed in *Federal Baseball Club* and *Toolson*. Respondents also argued that organized baseball had relied on the prior decisions and that federal labor policy exempted the reserve system from federal antitrust law.

DECISION

Justice Blackmun, writing for a 5-3 majority, held baseball to be exempt from federal antitrust law, and the exemption represented a recognized aberration to be amended if necessary by Congress and not the judiciary. Heavily relying on stare decisis, which gives presumptive weight and respect to previously decided cases, Justice Blackmun upheld the earlier decisions in *Federal Baseball Club* and *Toolson* as binding law.

In a decision heavy with romanticism, the opinion contained much history and nostalgia for the game itself, even including a Ring Lardner poem. Justice Blackmun accorded substantial significance to the game's status as the national pastime, attributing the special exempt status to this factor.

The decision sparked interest and debate of a nonlegal nature between the justices. Justice Blackmun is reported to have done research for the case by spending time examining baseball cards in order to compile his list of 88 great players included in the opinion. After Justice Marshall objected to the list's all-white nature, Justice Blackmun added three African-American players in an unsuccessful attempt to win Justice Marshall's vote.

Ultimately, the Court's upholding of baseball's exempt status hinged on the long line of cases establishing this exception in light of the game's special status in American culture. Justices Douglas, Marshall, and Brennan joined in dissent, arguing against baseball's exempt status, stating that the *Federal Baseball Club* Court's narrow vision of commerce no longer comported with reality.

AFTERMATH

Baseball's reserve system remained untouched until the 1990s, despite formidable opposition from the players' union, the Major League Baseball Players Association. The association managed to bring collective bargaining practices into play and organized a reentry draft in 1976, effectively granting players free agent status. *Piazza v. Major League Baseball*, 831 F. Supp. 420 (E.D. Pa. 1993) restricted *Flood's* scope to solely pertaining to the reserve system, rendering the exemption almost completely without teeth. In 1998, Congress passed the Curt Flood Act, repealing the antitrust exemption.

RELATED CASES

Federal Baseball Club v. National League, 259 U.S. 200 (1922)

Toolson v. New York Yankees, 346 U.S. 356 (1953)

STATUTES AT ISSUE

A. Rule 3 of the Major League Rules

B. Rule 9 of the Major League Rules

C. Rules 3 and 9 of the Professional Baseball Rules, which contain provisions parallel to those just quoted

D. The Uniform Player's Contract

RECOMMENDED READING

Walter T. Champion, Jr., *The Baseball Antitrust Exemption Revisited: 21 Years after* Flood v. Kuhn, 19 Thurgood Marshall Law Review 573 (1994).

Joshua P. Jones, *A Congressional Swing and Miss: The Curt Flood Act, Player Control, and the National Pastime,* 33 Georgia Law Review 639 (1999).

Thomas A. Piraino, Jr., *A Proposal for the Antitrust Regulation of Professional Sports,* 79 Boston University Law Review 957 (1999).

Stephen F. Ross, *Reconsidering* Flood v. Kuhn, 12 University of Miami Entertainment & Sports Law Review 169 (1995).

Case Title: *Goldfarb v. Virginia State Bar*

Legal Citation: 421 U.S. 773

Year of Decision: 1975

KEY ISSUE

Does the fact that a bar association has members in a learned profession exempt its minimum fee schedule from antitrust laws' price-fixing prohibitions?

HISTORY OF THE CASE

Lewis Goldfarb and his wife, desiring to purchase property in Virginia, unsuccessfully attempted to find an attorney to perform a required title examination for less than the minimum fee published by the local county bar, Fairfax County Bar Association ("County Bar"), and enforced by the Virginia State Bar ("State Bar"). Goldfarb brought a class action suit against both County Bar and State Bar, alleging the minimum fee schedule constituted price fixing and thus violated Sherman Antitrust Act § 1. The district court enjoined publication of the fee schedule in a judgment against County Bar, finding State Bar immune from Sherman Act liability. The court of appeals reversed, finding County Bar also immune for lack of interstate commerce effect and holding that law is a learned profession not considered a trade and thus outside the Sherman Act's scope.

SUMMARY OF ARGUMENTS

Goldfarb argued that the "learned profession" classification of the County Bar did not exempt them from the Sherman Act, that the State Bar's price-fixing activities had a substantial effect on interstate commerce, and that the *Parker* doctrine's protections did not extend to the County Bar, immunizing them from liability.

State Bar argued that the fee schedule was advisory and did not constitute price fixing.

County Bar argued no substantial effect on interstate commerce existed to trigger the Sherman Act's anti-price-fixing provisions. County Bar also argued that its members were members of a learned profession; thus it did not engage in trade or commerce.

DECISION

Justice Burger, writing for a unanimous 8-0 court, of which only Justice Powell did not take part, ruled in favor of petitioner Goldfarb, holding that the fee schedule constituted price fixing, that neither State nor County Bar was immune from federal antitrust laws under the *Parker* doctrine of state action immunity, that the requirement of State Bar members to complete title examinations did affect interstate commerce, and that such examination was a service and thus commerce.

Regarding the minimum fee schedule, Justice Burger found it to constitute price fixing, reasoning it was not merely advisory but a fixed-price floor, enforced through prospective discipline, assurance of no underbidding by other lawyers, and compliance with professional norms.

Justice Burger refused to extend the *Parker* doctrine's protections to both respondents, reasoning that both the County Bar and State Bar were merely prompted by state law to publish and enforce the minimum fee requirements, not compelled, as *Parker* requires in order to extend immunity. No Virginia statute required respondent's activities, and thus no state action existed to provide immunity from the Sherman Act.

The Court recognized the examination of titles as providing a service in return for monetary compensation and, thus, defined it as commerce. Most importantly, Justice Burger held that learned professions were within the purview of the Sherman Act as constituting commerce. The Court reasoned that to grant learned professions an exclusion would be too broad, cutting against the heavy presumption for inclusion. Furthermore, Justice Burger reasoned that the nature of an occupation should not be determinative of whether a business aspect exists, as is the case with the bar association and other learned professions.

AFTERMATH

With the *Goldfarb* decision, federal antitrust enforcers began to take on medical groups, with varying success. The decision, though not overruled, has been heavily criticized and its abrogation recognized by several courts.

SIGNIFICANCE

Goldfarb's impact was felt most heavily by physicians because it applied antitrust law to professional services, clarifying an uncertainty as to what extent physicians and physician groups were immune from antitrust liability as not participating in a trade or commerce.

RELATED CASES

United States v. Trenton Potteries Co., 392 U.S. 273 (1927)

United States v. Socony-Vacuum Oil Co. Inc., 310 U.S. 150 (1940)

Parker v. Brown, 317 U.S. 341 (1943)

STATUTE AT ISSUE

Sherman Antitrust Act, 15 U.S.C. § 1

RECOMMENDED READING

Terry Calvani, James Langenfeld, and Gordon Shuford, *Attorney Advertising and Competition at the Bar*, 41 Vanderbilt Law Review 761 (1998).

Mark Freeman Kirschke, *Private Parties and State Action Immunity to the Sherman Anti-Trust Act after* Southern Motor Carriers Rate Conference, Inc. v. United States: *The Two-Prong Midcal Test as an Effective and Adequate Alternative to* Goldfarb's *Compulsion Requirement*, 24 Houston Law Review 311 (1987).

Kenneth Lasson, *Lawyering Askew: Excesses in the Pursuit of Fees and Justice*, 74 Boston University Law Review 723 (1994).

Thomas D. Morgan, *The Impact of Antitrust Law on the Legal Profession*, 67 Fordham Law Review 415 (1998).

Case Title: *Virginia Pharmacy Board v. Virginia Consumer Council*

Alternate Case Title: The Drug Advertising Case

Legal Citation: 425 U.S. 748

Year of Decision: 1976

~

KEY ISSUE

May a state completely prohibit the advertising of prescription drug prices?

HISTORY OF THE CASE

Virginia law prohibited anyone other than licensed pharmacists from dispensing prescription drugs. The state then enacted a statute making it unprofessional conduct for a licensed pharmacist to advertise the prices of prescription drugs, effectively prohibiting all advertising of prescription drug prices in any form. The Consumer Council, as consumers of prescription drugs, brought suit in the Federal District Court for the Eastern District of Virginia. They alleged that the prohibition on advertising violated their right to free speech under the First and Fourteenth Amendments of the U.S. Constitution. The council prevailed in the district court, and the state of Virginia appealed to the U.S. Supreme Court.

SUMMARY OF ARGUMENTS

The council argued that they had a constitutional right, as recipients of prescription drug advertising, to hear this form of speech free from government interference. They noted that prices for prescription drugs varied by as much as 1,000 percent even within the same city; thus, price advertisements would save them money because they could compare prices before purchasing.

Virginia argued that the statute involved a constitutional use of its police power because the widespread advertising of prescription medication might lead to a bargain hunting mentality that would eliminate the valuable pharmacist-customer relationship. The state also asserted an interest in protecting the reputation of the pharmacist as a professional rather than a "mere retailer of drugs."

DECISION

The Supreme Court, in an opinion written by Justice Powell, held that the Virginia statute was an unconstitutional interference with the freedom of speech. Justice Powell disagreed with Virginia's contention that the council, as recipient of the speech rather than the speaker, had no First Amendment interest: "Where a speaker exists . . . the protection accorded is to the communication, to its source and to its recipients both." He then proclaimed that "commercial speech," which previously had not been considered speech for First Amendment purposes, was indeed entitled to constitutional protection. In Justice Powell's opinion, the sentence "I will sell you X drug at Y prices" was not "so removed from the exposition of ideas" that it lacked First Amendment protection. He argued that the consumer's interest in the price of a prescription drug might be greater than his interest in any constitutionally protected political debate. Furthermore, Justice Powell found a strong societal interest in the free flow of commercial information because that information was "indispensable to the proper allocation of resources in [our] free enterprise system."

Justice Powell argued that the state's paternalistic reasons for the statute were contrary to the best interests of its citizens, who would be best served by full access to price information. He stated, "It is precisely this kind of choice, between the dangers of suppressing information and the dangers of its misuse if it is freely available, that the First Amendment makes for us." Thus, while Virginia remained free to regulate deceptive advertising or advertising of illegal products, it could not completely prohibit any form of valid product advertisement. In a footnote, Justice Powell contended that the Court's holding did not necessarily suggest that the state could not prohibit advertising by professionals such as doctors or lawyers. He argued that the state might have a different regulatory interest where the advertising involved services rather than products because the rendering of professional services involved an "enhanced possibility for confusion and deception."

Justice Rehnquist delivered the lone dissent. His argument in many ways echoed that of Justice Holmes in the infamous case of *Lochner v. New York.* He noted that Virginia did not prohibit the dissemination of drug prices over the phone, so this case did not concern access to price information. In Justice Rehnquist's opinion, the Court had simply determined that pharmacists had a right to advertise that could not be overriden by the Virginia legislature. He found this approach repugnant insofar as "there is certainly nothing in the United States Constitution which requires the Virginia Legislature to hew to the teachings of Adam Smith in its legislative decisions regulating the pharmacy profession." Justice Rehnquist did not believe that the First Amendment had been intended to protect "the decision of a particular individual as to whether to purchase one or another kind of shampoo." He argued that the Court was using the First Amendment as a tool to achieve its preferred result in much the same way it had once used economic due process for the same purpose.

AFTERMATH

Soon after the Court determined that the Constitution protected commercial speech, it ruled that laws prohibiting advertising of professional services were unconstitutional.

SIGNIFICANCE

The decision indicated that commercial speech, specifically price advertising, may find some protection under the First and Fourteenth Amendments.

RELATED CASES

Williamson v. Lee Optical Co., 348 U.S. 483 (1955)

Bates v. State Bar of Arizona, 433 U.S. 350 (1977)

Central Hudson Gas v. Public Service Commission of New York, 447 U.S. 557 (1980)

Bolger v. Youngs Drug Products Corp., 463 U.S. 60 (1983)

STATUTE AT ISSUE

Virginia Code Annotated 54–524.35 (1974)

RECOMMENDED READING

Ronald Coase, *Advertising and Free Speech,* 6 Journal of Legal Studies 1 (1977).

Thomas H. Jackson and John C. Jeffries, Jr., *Commercial Speech: Economic Due Process and the First Amendment,* 65 Virginia Law Review 1 (1979).

Dee Pridgen and Ivan L. Preston, *Enhancing the Flow of Information in the Marketplace: From Caveat Emptor to Virginia Pharmacy and Beyond at the Federal Trade Commission,* 14 Georgia Law Review 635 (1980).

Rosemarie Sbaratta, *Yes, FTC, There Is a Virginia: The Impact of Virginia State Board of Pharmacy v. Virginia Citizens Consumer Council, Inc. on the Federal Trade Commission's Regulation of Misleading Advertising,* 57 Boston University Law Review 833 (1977).

Caren Schmulen Sweetland, *The Demise of a Workable Commercial Speech Doctrine: Dangers of Extending First Amendment Protection to Commercial Disclosure Requirements,* 76 Texas Law Review 471 (1997).

Stephen G. Thompson, *Antitrust, the First Amendment, and the Communication of Price Information,* 56 Temple Law Quarterly 939 (1983).

Case Title: *City of Columbia v. Omni Outdoor Advertising, Inc.*

Legal Citation: 499 U.S. 365

Year of Decision: 1991

KEY ISSUE

Under federal antitrust law, does a conspiracy or sham exception apply to the *Noerr-Pennington* doctrine when a city ordinance banning the construction of new billboards has anticompetitive effects?

HISTORY OF THE CASE

Omni Outdoor Advertising, Inc. (Omni), a Georgia corporation, expanded its market into Columbia, South Carolina, joining its competitor

Columbia Outdoor Advertising, Inc. (COA). COA was a local business with deep roots in the community and close associations with the city's political leaders. With control of more than 95 percent of the billboard market in Columbia, COA successfully lobbied for a rezoning ordinance passed in 1982 to prohibit the construction of new billboards within the city. After a state court struck down this initial ordinance, a new one was passed, restricting size, location, and spacing of billboards. Omni, feeling the detrimental effects of the rezoning, filed suit against both COA and the city of Columbia, charging violations of sections 1 and 2 of the Sherman Antitrust Act. The trial jury awarded Omni damages of $600,000 on the section 1 claim and $400,000 on the section 2 claim. The court granted COA's motion for judgment notwithstanding the verdict, holding the activities outside the scope of the Sherman Act. The circuit court reinstated the jury verdict on appeal, and the Supreme Court granted certiorari.

Summary of Arguments

The city of Columbia and COA argued that no conspiracy exception existed to boot the city out of state immunity, and the lobbying process was substantively proper. Therefore, COA, as a private party, could not be liable under the federal antitrust laws.

Omni argued for a conspiracy exception to the *Noerr-Pennington* doctrine, which would deny the city of Columbia immunity. The *Noerr-Pennington* doctrine provides immunity to private entities that influence or attempt to influence the passage or enforcement of laws that may have anticompetitive consequences. Omni also argued that the lobbying practices of COA to achieve the rezoning ordinance were merely delay tactics and thus a sham, forcing COA to be liable as a private party.

Decision

Justice Scalia, writing for a 6-3 majority, reversed the decision of the court of appeals ruling for COA and denying Omni recovery. Under case law set forth in *Parker v. Brown,* a municipality is immune from federal antitrust liability when it is implementing state policy. The Court found that South Carolina's zoning statutes granted the city power

to regulate billboard construction. Thus, the City of Columbia had immunity in its decision to rezone, banning construction of new billboards.

The Court declined to apply a conspiracy exception to the *Parker* rule, finding reversible error in the court of appeals' decision to do so. Justice Scalia reasoned that the implementation of a lobbied desire could not be classified as conspiracy for fear that the exception would swallow the *Parker* rule and that defining conspiracy to include political practices such as lobbying would be outside the scope of the Sherman Act's trade restraint scope.

On the second issue, the Court also rejected the application of a sham exception to the *Noerr-Pennington* doctrine of immunizing private party lobbying for anticompetitive measures for similar reasons to its rejection of the conspiracy exception, that the exception would then swallow the rule. The Court found that COA was not using the lobbying process as a delay tactic but had legitimate substantive purposes for seeking to ban the construction of new billboards and thus held that *Noerr*'s immunity protection should continue to extend to COA as the lobbying private party. Justice Scalia remanded the case back to the court of appeals in order to determine questions relating to the sufficiency of the jury's original verdict regarding extraneous private antitrust actions of COA alleged by Omni and Omni's potential relief under South Carolina's Unfair Trade Practices Act.

Justice Stevens's dissenting opinion, joined by Justices White and Marshall, argued for a more inclusive Sherman Act and objected to the Court's decision to grant immunity to an agreement between municipalities and private parties that conferred an unfair economic benefit on the private party.

Aftermath

On remand to the court of appeals, Fourth Circuit judge Wilkinson affirmed the Supreme Court's holding, denying Omni relief. The Court held that Omni had waived their monopolization claims, disallowed amendment of the complaint to include a tortious interference with contractual relations cause of action, and did not allow Omni to use

South Carolina's Unfair Trade Practices Act to maintain an action.

SIGNIFICANCE

This is indicative of how the Sherman Antitrust Act affects the state's ability to regulate monopolies outside federal law.

RELATED CASES

Parker v. Brown, 317 U.S. 341 (1943)

Eastern R. Conference v. Noerr Motors, 365 U.S. 127 (1961)

California Motor Transp. Co. v. Trucking Unlimited, 404 U.S. 508 (1972)

RECOMMENDED READING

Antitrust Immunity: City of Columbia v. Omni Outdoor Advertising, Inc., 105 Harvard Law Review 360 (1991).

Donald I. Baker, *High Court Sheds Light on State Action,* 15 National Law Journal 22 (1993).

William E. Kovacic, *Reagan's Judicial Appointees and Antitrust in the 1990s,* 60 Fordham Law Review 49 (1991).

E. Thomas Sullivan and Robert B. Thompson, *The Supreme Court and Private Law: The Vanishing Importance of Securities and Antitrust,* 53 Emory Law Journal 1571 (2004).

Case Title: *Leegin Creative Leather Prods. v. PSKS, Inc.*

Legal Citation: 551 U.S. 877

Year of Decision: 2007

KEY ISSUE

Under section 1 of the Sherman Antitrust Act, is it a per se violation, or illegal regardless of the circumstances, for a manufacturer to set a minimum retail price for distributors?

HISTORY OF THE CASE

In 1911, the U.S. Supreme Court ruled in *Dr. Miles Medical Co. v. John D. Park & Sons Co.* that is was a per se violation under section 1 of the Sherman Antitrust Act for manufacturers and distributors to agree to set a minimum retail price for a manufacturer's goods. This means that setting a minimum price is illegal in and of itself, or per se illegal.

Leegin Creative Leather Products, Inc. (Leegin) designed a brand of belts, which it marketed under the name Brighton. PSKS, Inc. (PSKS) operated a store named Kay's Closet, which bought and sold the Brighton brand. In 1997, Leegin created the "Brighton Retail Pricing and Promotion Policy." The policy dictated that retailers selling the Brighton brand could not discount the merchandise below a certain minimum selling price. There was an exception to the policy if the product was not selling well, and the retailer was not going to reorder. Leegin sold the Brighton brand only to specialty stores offering higher-quality customer service. Leegin's policy intended to ensure stores selling the Brighton brand secured enough profit to continue to provide such excellent service. Leegin also feared that excessive discounting harmed the image and reputation of the Brighton brand. Kay's Closet agreed to the minimum price policy but later was found discounting the brand below the minimum price. Leegin stopped selling Brighton to Kay's Closet, hurting the store's revenue, as Brighton accounted for 40–50 percent of Kay's Closet's sales revenue.

PSKS brought suit against Leegin in district court alleging violation of antitrust laws for entering into a price fixing agreement. The district court did not allow Leegin to introduce expert testimony concerning the pro-competitive effects of its pricing policy. A jury ruled in favor of PSKS. The Court of Appeals for the Fifth Circuit affirmed, stating it was bound by the decision in *Dr. Miles.*

SUMMARY OF ARGUMENTS

PSKS argued that the price fixing imposed by Leegin's Brighton policy violated section 1 of the

Sherman Antitrust Act. It also argued that vertical price restraints, like those in the Brighton policy, should be per se unlawful for administrative convenience, allowing businesses to comprehend better what the judicial system would do with such policies. PSKS argued that these price restraints could lead to higher prices for the goods.

Leegin argued that the price maintenance policy had a positive impact on competition. It also contended that the rule of reason should have been applied in the lower courts when determining whether or not the policy created an unreasonable restraint on interstate trade and commerce. The decision in *Dr. Miles*, Leegin contended, was outdated and not applicable.

DECISION

The Court ruled 5-4 that "*Dr. Miles* should be overruled and that vertical price restraints are to be judged by the rule of reason." The Court held that the reasons relied upon in *Dr. Miles* did not justify a per se rule concerning price maintenance.

Justice Kennedy delivered the majority opinion of the Court. It determined that there was a good basis for determining that such price fixing policies had a pro-competitive justification, thus not always resulting in a restriction on competition and decrease in output. The Court rejected PSKS's argument that such policies should be per se illegal because of administrative convenience, stating that per se illegality was the exception and not the rule. Administrative convenience was not sufficient in itself to justify a per se rule. The Court also ruled that PSKS was mistaken in relying on a potential increase in price to show that the policy was anticompetitive, because prices can rise with pro-competitive policies as well as anticompetitive ones.

The Court previously ruled in *Texaco Inc. v. Dagher* (2006) that section 1 of the Sherman Antitrust Act only outlaws "unreasonable restraints" on trade or commerce among the states. To determine whether there was an unreasonable restraint, the court used the rule of reason, taking into account information about the business, the history, and nature of the restraint, and whether the restraint's effect was anticom-

petitive or stimulated competition. It was decided that a rule of reason and not a per se rule of unlawfulness was the appropriate standard by which to judge vertical price restrictions. The decision in *Dr. Miles* was overturned. The decision of the court of appeals was overturned, and this case remanded.

AFTERMATH

On remand to the district court, Leegin challenged the sufficiency of PSKS's allegations to bring a rule of reason antitrust case against Leegin. The district court ruled in favor of Leegin, stating PSKS did not have sufficient allegations, and dismissed the case.

SIGNIFICANCE

Vertical price restraints are no longer judged to be per se illegal. The rule of reason is applied to determine whether or not there is undue restriction of the trade and commerce between states.

RELATED CASES

Dr. Miles Medical Co. v. John D. Park & Sons Co., 220 U.S. 373 (1911)

Continental T. V. v. GTE Sylvania, 433 U.S. 36 (1977)

Business Electronics Corp. v. Sharp Electronics Corp., 485 U.S. 717 (1998)

Texaco Inc. v. Dagher, 547 U.S. 1 (2006)

RECOMMENDED READING

Mary Claire Butt, *Not a Surprise, per Se: The Advent of the Rule of Reason for Vertical, Minimum Resale Price Maintenance Agreements in* Leegin Creative Leather Products, Inc. v. PSKS, Inc., 61 Arkansas Law Review 531 (2008).

Crystal J. Clark, Leegin Creative Leather Products, Inc. v. PSKS, Inc.: *Loosening the Belt on Price Fixing,* 59 Mercer Law Review 767 (2008).

Alan Devlin, *On the Ramifications of* Leegin Creative Leather Products, Inc. v. PSKS, Inc.: *Are*

Tie-ins Next?, 56 Cleveland State Law Review 387 (2008).

Thomas A. Lambert, *Dr. Miles Is Dead. Now What? Structuring a Rule of Reason for Evaluating Minimum Resale Price Maintenance*, 50 William and Mary Law Review 1937 (2009).

Julie M. Olszewski, *Overruling a Nearly Century-Old Precedent: Why* Leegin *Got It Right*, 94 Iowa Law Review 375 (2008).

CIVIL RIGHTS AND EQUAL PROTECTION

Civil rights, perhaps more than any other topic within constitutional law, has had a most profound effect on our modern society. It is also the discipline that is most closely tied to our nation's constitutional principles. The Constitution and the Declaration of Independence are filled with profound statements about self-governance and the existence of the natural rights of its citizens that presuppose the existence of equal right of all citizens to the benefits and protections of our democracy.

Many of these protections have been so woven into the fabric of our society that we now take them for granted. For example, it was not until early in the 20th century that women won the right to vote, and as late as the 19th century, laws existed in some states that prevented women from practicing law or holding public office. For the first 100 years of our nation, people of races other than Caucasian were not even considered citizens; in some cases, they were actually counted as three-fifths of a citizen and were subject to severe restrictions on the ability to own property, conduct business, enter in contracts, or travel.

The specific rights and protections of persons from discrimination or violations of their civil rights are enumerated in the Bill of Rights, the first 10 amendments to the U.S. Constitution. When enacted, the Bill of Rights was intended to apply only to citizens with regard to the federal government. This caused a number of bizarre situations in which persons were deprived by states of rights that were protected by the federal govern-

ment. The Fourteenth Amendment extended these protections to persons in their capacities as citizens of their respective states by stating, in part, "No State shall make or enforce any law which shall abridge the privileges or immunities of citizens of the United States; nor shall any State deprive any person of life, liberty, or property, without due process of law; nor deny to any person within its jurisdiction the equal protection of the laws." Subsequent to its ratification, the Supreme Court was left with the challenge of determining when rights protected under the Constitution also applied to citizens of the states, and when states had an overriding interest in holding their citizens to different standards of conduct. As a result, the rulings of the Supreme Court on the issue of equal protection and civil rights have visited nearly every activity in the life of an ordinary citizen, including such matters as the right to equal pay for equal work or equal funding for men's and women's collegiate sports.

U.S. CONSTITUTION, SIXTH AMENDMENT— DUE PROCESS CLAUSE

In all criminal prosecutions, the accused shall enjoy the right to a speedy and public trial, by an impartial jury of the State and district where in the crime shall have been committed, which district shall have been previously ascertained by law, and to be informed of the nature and cause of the accusation; to be confronted with the witnesses against him; to have compulsory process for obtaining witnesses in his favor, and to have the Assistance of Counsel for his defence [*sic*].

U.S. CONSTITUTION, ELEVENTH AMENDMENT—SOVEREIGN IMMUNITY

The Judicial power of the United States shall not be construed to extend to any suit in law or equity, commenced or prosecuted against one of the United States by Citizens of another State, or by Citizens or Subjects of any Foreign State.

U.S. CONSTITUTION, THIRTEENTH AMENDMENT—ABOLISHMENT OF SLAVERY

Section 1. Neither slavery nor involuntary servitude, except as a punishment for crime whereof the party shall have been duly convicted, shall exist within the United States, or any place subject to their jurisdiction.

U.S. CONSTITUTION, FOURTEENTH AMENDMENT—EQUAL PROTECTION CLAUSE

Section 1. All persons born or naturalized in the United States, and subject to the jurisdiction thereof, are citizens of the United States and of the State wherein they reside. No State shall make or enforce any law which shall abridge the privileges or immunities of citizens of the United States; nor shall any State deprive any person of life, liberty, or property, without due process of law; nor deny to any person within its jurisdiction the equal protection of the laws.

U.S. CONSTITUTION, FIFTEENTH AMENDMENT—RIGHT TO VOTE REGARDLESS OF RACE

Section 1. The right of citizens of the United States to vote shall not be denied or abridged by the United States or by any state on account or race, color, or previous condition of servitude.
Section 2. The Congress shall have power to enforce this article by appropriate legislation.

Case Title: *United States v. The Libellants and Claimants of the Schooner* Amistad

Alternative Case Title: The *Amistad*

Legal Citation: 40 U.S. 518

Year of Decision: 1841

KEY ISSUE

Were Africans who were purchased at a slave auction in Cuba free people or property, when they had been kidnapped from their homeland, taken against their will to Cuba, and sold there as slaves in violation of laws and treaties of Spain, Great Britain, and the United States?

HISTORY OF THE CASE

Fifty-four Mendi people who had been kidnapped from their home in Mendiland, West Africa (now Sierra Leone), were taken aboard the Portuguese slave ship *Tecora* to Havana, Cuba, in 1839. There, the captives were sold under fraudulent papers that declared them to be Cuban slaves and put aboard the trading schooner *La Amistad* (friendship). The masters of the ship were the captain, Ramón Ferrer, and the Africans' purported Spanish owners, Pedro Montes and José Ruiz. Also aboard was Ferrer's Cuban-born slave, Antonio. While the ship was traveling from Havana to Puerto Principe, Cuba, the Mendians broke from captivity, killed the captain and a crewman, and took control of the vessel.

The Mendians ordered Montes and Ruiz to sail the ship back to Africa. The Spaniards sailed east during the day and turned west and north during the night. After more than 60 days, the ship arrived off Long Island, New York, where it was seized by the U.S. naval brig USS *Washington*, commanded by Lieutenant Thomas Gedney, and towed to New Haven, Connecticut. There, the Africans were taken into custody. Some speculate that the lieutenant, in the hope of claiming salvage on the Africans (who were worth $25,000 as slaves), purposely towed the ship from New York waters to port in Connecticut, where slavery was technically still legal.

The circuit court in Hartford, Connecticut, dismissed charges of mutiny and murder alleged against the Africans, ruling that it lacked jurisdiction, since the event had occurred aboard a Spanish ship in Spanish waters.

Lieutenant Gedney and his crew filed suit, claiming that the ship, its cargo, and the Africans were salvage rescued on the high seas. Henry Green and Palatiah Fordham, two men who had encountered some of the Africans foraging for water and provisions on the shore of Long Island, filed a salvage claim of their own. Montes and Ruiz denied all salvage claims and themselves sued for the return of the Africans as their rightful property. Queen Isabella II of Spain then demanded the captives be returned to Spain under the terms of Pinckney's Treaty of 1795 between Spain and the United States. The claims of Montes and Ruiz were subordinated to the claim of the Spanish government. At the request of President Martin Van Buren, the Office of the United States Attorney for the Connecticut District argued the case on behalf of the Spanish government.

The case quickly became a cause célèbre in the United States. The American abolitionist movement established the Amistad Committee to raise money for the Africans' defense. The prominent attorney Roger Sherman Baldwin argued on their behalf before the U.S. District Court for the District of Connecticut, asserting that they never had been slaves. Baldwin established that the Africans had been captured in Mendiland in violation of an 1819 treaty between Great Britain and Spain and a subsequent pronouncement from Spain that had outlawed the transatlantic slave trade. Having been seized illegally, he argued, the Mendians were hapless kidnap victims and, as such, should be freed.

The abolitionists additionally filed criminal charges of assault, kidnapping, and false imprisonment against Montes and Ruiz, who were subsequently arrested in New York. They were granted bail, and both men eventually returned to Cuba.

The district court agreed with the abolitionists, holding the Africans to be free people, and ordered they be delivered to the president to be returned to Africa at the expense of the U.S. government. This was pursuant to the terms of the Adams-Onís Treaty of 1818 between Spain and the United States, amended in 1819. The court

dismissed the claims of Green and Fordham, as well as those of Montes and Ruiz, and awarded Lieutenant Gedney and his crew salvage of one-third of the value of the vessel and its cargo. The court additionally held that Antonio was rightfully the property of Captain Ferrer's heirs in Cuba and should be returned to them. The U.S. Circuit Court for the Connecticut District affirmed the lower court's ruling. The U.S. attorney, on behalf of the government of Spain, appealed the denial of the Spanish government's claim over the ship, its cargo, and the Africans to the U.S. Supreme Court.

SUMMARY OF ARGUMENTS

Attorney General Henry Gilpin, arguing for the United States on behalf of the Spanish government, entered the papers of *La Amistad* into evidence as proof that the Africans were the property of Spain. The papers were in order, sealed with the sigil of the governor-general of Cuba, though they falsely declared the Africans to have been Cuban latino slaves. This was a common practice among slave traders and was condoned by the Spanish government. Gilpin argued that long-held tradition of international law held the evidence of such official ship's documents to be unquestionable proof of ownership. Because they were clearly Spanish property by international law, he argued, the Africans should be returned to Spain.

Baldwin and former U.S. president John Quincy Adams argued on behalf of the Mendians. Baldwin opened the argument, asserting that because the Spanish government did not appeal the ruling of the lower courts that held the Africans to be free people, its insistence on treating them as property was an attempt to manipulate the U.S. judiciary into doing the bidding of the executive branch.

In his argument, Adams also stressed that the judicial branch should maintain its independence of the executive. He further argued that Pinckney's Treaty did not apply to the case, since the Mendians never had been slaves and could not, therefore, be considered merchandise under the terms of Article IX of the treaty. He also argued that a previous decision holding that possession on board a ship was evidence of property was inapplicable, since that precedent had been established prior to the banning of the African slave trade in the United States.

DECISION

Justice Joseph Story wrote for a 7-1 majority of the Court. Justice Barbour took no part in the decision, and Justice Baldwin (no relation to the attorney Baldwin) entered a lone unwritten dissent. The majority affirmed the decision of the lower courts and declared that the Mendians were free people who never had been legal property. As free individuals, they had every right to commit insurrection against their oppressors and attempt to regain their liberty. Therefore, they were not criminals, as the U.S. Attorney General's Office had argued. The Court held that the ship's papers identifying the Africans as slaves were vitiated by fraud and, thus, could not provide "due and sufficient proof" of any valid title. Because the Mendians had never been property, the Court declared, the provision of Pinckney's Treaty concerning the return of merchandise was inapplicable to them.

The Court affirmed the order of the lower court granting salvage to Lieutenant Gedney in the amount of one-third of the appraised value of the ship and its cargo. It also affirmed the circuit court's ruling that Antonio should be returned to Ferrer's heirs in Cuba. It reversed the lower court only in that it found the Adams-Onís Treaty inapplicable to the case, since that treaty pertained only to Africans taken to the United States for illegal sale as slaves. Because *La Amistad* had entered U.S. waters under control of the Mendians, who could not have intended to sell themselves as slaves, that part of the decision had to be reversed, and the Mendians freed immediately.

AFTERMATH

Thirty-six of the 54 Mendians originally taken aboard *La Amistad* survived to regain their freedom. Eighteen died between the seizing of *La Amistad* by the USS *Washington* in 1839 and the Supreme Court's decision in 1841. Apparently, many more Mendians had died during the initial journey from Africa to Cuba aboard the *Tecora*.

The Amistad Committee, made up of Christian abolitionists, collected donations for an expedition to return the Africans to Mendiland. Meanwhile, they instructed the Africans in English and Christianity. Most of the Mendians had deserted the group by the time the Amistad Committee's missionary party reached their home country in 1842.

Captain Ferrer's slave Antonio, who had publicly declared his desire to return to Cuba, escaped to Canada immediately after the Supreme Court handed down its decision, apparently with the assistance of abolitionists. One of the former captives, Sarah Margru, returned to the United States and studied at the one-room Oberlin Heritage Center in Oberlin, Ohio. A statue of the nominal leader of the Mendians, who was known as Cinqué in the United States, stands beside the City Hall building in New Haven, Connecticut.

Spain continued for years to press its claim for indemnity, and resolutions calling for the United States to pay restitution arose in the House and the Senate on several occasions. Presidents Polk and Buchanan supported these efforts. John Quincy Adams fought against such claims in the House of Representatives until he died in 1848.

The history of the *La Amistad* was dramatized in 1997 in the Hollywood movie *Amistad*.

SIGNIFICANCE

The Court's ruling distilled the contemporary American legal dualism with respect to slavery into two fundamental tenets: that freedom is the natural-born state of humanity, and that this birthright of liberty could yet be denied by positive law.

The plight of the slaves and the subsequent highly publicized case bolstered the abolitionist movement.

RELATED CASE

Doe v. Braden, 57 U.S. 635 (1853)

TREATY AT ISSUE

Article IX of Pinckney's Treaty

RECOMMENDED READING

Barber, John Warner. *The History of the Amistad Captives.* . . . New Haven, Conn.: E. L. & J. W. Barber, 1840. Reprint, New York: Arno Press, 1969.

"Gilder-Lehman Center's *The Amistad.*" Available online. URL: www.yale.edu/glc/info/amistad.html. Accessed January 20, 2011.

Gold, Susan Dudley. United States v. Amistad: *Slave Ship Mutiny.* Marshall Cavendish, 2006.

Osagie, Iyunolu Folayan. *The Amistad Revolt: Memory, Slavery, and the Politics of Identity in the United States and Sierra Leone.* Athens: University of Georgia Press, 2003.

Case Title: *Jones v. Van Zandt*

Legal Citation: 46 U.S. 215

Year of Decision: 1847

KEY ISSUE

Does Congress have the power to create the Fugitive Slave Act, and is the Act constitutional?

HISTORY OF THE CASE

Jones, a citizen of Kentucky, owned nine slaves, who escaped his property and fled to Ohio, which happened to be the nearest adjoining free state. Once the slaves were in Ohio, the defendant Van Zandt took the slaves into his covered wagon under the cover of night. The slaves were eventually recovered, and Van Zandt was charged with harboring and concealing slaves in violation of the federal Fugitive Slave Act of 1793. Specifically, Van Zandt was charged under the Fugitive Slave Act of 1793, §§ 3 and 4 (hereinafter "the Act"). The suit was brought in the Circuit Court of the United States for the District of Ohio in June 1842, and the jury found for Jones.

The Circuit Court of the United States for the District of Ohio found that Van Zandt was guilty of harboring and concealing fugitive slaves under the Act. The judges of the district court, however, had opposing opinions on several points and differed pro forma (as a matter of form) so as to send the question directly to the U.S. Supreme Court.

SUMMARY OF ARGUMENTS

One of Van Zandt's many arguments was that the Fugitive Slave Act of 1793 was not consistent with the 1787 ordinance of Ohio that prohibited the existence of slaves in its territory among its residents. Van Zandt also argued that the Fugitive Slave Act was repugnant to the Constitution of the United States.

DECISION

The Court found the Act constitutional.

The Court began by discussing Article IV, Section 2, of the U.S. Constitution, which reads, "No person held to service or labor in one state, under the laws thereof, escaping into another, shall, in consequence of any law or regulation therein, be discharged from such service or labor, but shall be delivered up on claim of the party to whom such service or labor may be due." The Court then pointed out that in order to enforce this constitutional guarantee, four years later, Congress passed the Fugitive Slave Act of 1793. This Act contained two sections at issue in this case: Section 3 permitted slave owners to retrieve their slaves who escape across state borders, and section 4 made it illegal for anyone knowingly and willingly to obstruct another from retrieving an escaped slave.

The Court then turned to analyzing the constitutionality of the statute. The Act included a "notice" requirement regarding the knowledge of whether a person was a fugitive slave or not. In interpreting the statute, the Court concluded that notice can be given in speech or in writing, provided the defendant, Van Zandt, was clearly aware that he was concealing a fugitive from labor. The facts of this case demonstrated that Van Zandt had knowingly concealed the fugitive slaves in a covered wagon with the purpose of depriving the owner of their custody.

The Court next considered whether the Act of Congress was repugnant to the Constitution. This issue had previously been discussed in the Supreme Court's case of *Prigg v. Pennsylvania* (1842), in which the Court held that Article IV, Section 2, had created the right for slave owners to pursue and reclaim fugitive slaves, even if they had crossed into another state. This reflects the common law right for people to seek and recapture lost or stolen property. Thus, the Court deemed the Act to render effective an existing constitutional guarantee. In upholding the Act as constitutional, the Court pointed out that non-slave state laws and ordinances would be unaffected by the decision in this case. The Court also stated that slavery remained a political question for the states individually to decide, and the federal power over slavery was limited.

AFTERMATH

After the Fugitive Slave Act of 1793 was passed, many states passed "personal liberty" laws, which gave alleged escaped slaves a jury trial before they could be returned because of concern regarding the possibility that a free African American could be kidnapped into slavery under the assumption that he or she was an escaped slave. Although the U.S. Supreme Court had upheld the Fugitive Slave Law of 1793 in *Jones*, northern states were reluctant to assist in the retrieval and return of escaped slaves. Shortly after the Court's decision in *Jones*, Congress passed the Fugitive Slave Act of 1850, which declared that all runaway slaves must be returned to their owners. Then, in *Dred Scott v. Sandford* (1857), the Court held that African Americans, whether slaves or not, were not protected under the Constitution.

Eventually, however, this and other proslavery legislation and laws would be replaced by the passing of the Reconstruction Amendments that followed the Civil War: the Thirteenth, Fourteenth, and Fifteenth Amendments. The Thirteenth Amendment affirmatively abolished slavery, and the Fourteenth Amendment, among other things, grants citizens of all races due process rights as well as the privileges and immunities of U.S. citizens. These amendments overruled the

Court's decision in the *Dred Scott* case. In 1870, the Fifteenth Amendment, which prohibits the government from denying voting privileges to people on account of race, color, or previous conditions of servitude, was passed.

SIGNIFICANCE

This case was an early attempt by abolitionists to challenge the Fugitive Slave Act of 1793. However, the decision benefited those in favor of slavery because the Court upheld the Act. Although abolitionists did not see much success during the antebellum period leading up to the Civil War, after the war, the Thirteenth, Fourteenth, and Fifteenth Amendments were passed. Although the *Jones* case has never officially been overruled, the Thirteenth Amendment effectively rendered the decision in this case inapplicable.

RELATED CASES

Prigg v. Pennsylvania, 41 U.S. 539 (1842)

Dred Scott v. Sandford, 60 U.S. 393 (1857)

Abelman v. Booth, 62 U.S. 506 (1859)

Bailey v. Alabama, 219 U.S. 219 (1911)

United States v. Kozminski, 487 U.S. 931; 108 (1988)

STATUTES AT ISSUE

U.S. Constitution, Article IV, § 2

Fugitive Slave Act of 1793

RECOMMENDED READING

Paul Finkelman, *Race and Domestic International Law in the United States,* 17 National Black Law Journal 25 (2003).

Robert J. Kaczorowski, *The Tragic Irony of American Federalism: National Sovereignty versus State Sovereignty in Slavery and in Freedom,* 45 University of Kansas Law Review 1015 (1997).

Jules Lobel, *Courts as Forums for Protest,* 52 UCLA Law Review 477 (2004).

William E. Nelson, *The Impact of the Antislavery Movement upon Styles of Judicial Reasoning in Nineteenth Century America,* 87 Harvard Law Review 513 (1974).

Case Title: *Dred Scott v. Sandford*

Alternate Case Titles: The Missouri Compromise Decision; Citizenship for Blacks

Legal Citation: 60 U.S. 393

Year of Decision: 1857

KEY ISSUES

Did the black inhabitants of the United States have the right of citizenship, and was the Missouri Compromise a legal means of attempting to extend freedom to the black inhabitants of those territories north of latitude 36°30'?

HISTORY OF THE CASE

Dred Scott and his wife, Harriet, were slaves of Dr. John Emerson, an army physician who was stationed in various western posts. Dr. Emerson was billeted to Fort Snelling in what is now Minnesota and to the military post at Rock Island in the state of Illinois. Both of these military posts are north of the Missouri Compromise Line. The Missouri Compromise Line was so named because during the negotiations for Missouri's statehood, it was decided that, with the exception of Missouri, no new slave states could be admitted to the United States north of the latitude line 36°30'N. Harriet Scott was formerly owned by a Major Taliaferro, who sold her in 1835 to Dr. Emerson. In 1836, Dred and Harriet were married with the consent of Dr. Emerson. The Scotts had two children, Eliza and Lizzie. Eliza was born on the steamboat *Gipsey* on the Mississippi River above the boundary of Missouri. Lizzie was born in the state of Missouri at the military post called Jefferson Barracks.

After Dr. Emerson left military service, he returned to Missouri. After Dr. Emerson's death, Emerson's widow subsequently hired out the Scotts for labor, and at some point the Scotts acquired sufficient money to attempt to purchase their freedom. Mrs. Emerson refused, and the Scotts brought a suit to the circuit court of the state of Missouri for their freedom. The circuit judge granted them permission to sue.

In 1850, the jury found in favor of the Scotts. Counsel for Mrs. Emerson appealed to the Missouri Supreme Court. In March 1852, that Court ruled 2 to 1 against Dred Scott and his family in the case of *Scott, a Man of Color v. Emerson* (15 Mo. 576), which argued that the hiring of a slave for two days in a free state would entitle the slave to sue for freedom. Former cases held that the act of setting foot upon free soil was sufficient for freedom, and intent had no impact upon the freedom issue.

In a decision that clearly recognized the political climate, Justice William Scott wrote that it was "a humiliating spectacle to see a court of a state confiscate the property of her own citizens by the command of a foreign law." Justice Scott acknowledged the political climate and declared that it was time to end the "black vomit" that was becoming an epidemic in the Missouri Territory. Justices Scott and Ryland determined that they would not suffer to have the old laws enforced, and that it was entirely unreasonable to liberate slaves under the argument that the mere touching of soil of a free state entitled them to freedom.

The court further argued that the consequences of slavery are "more hurtful to the master than to the slaves. There is no comparison between the slave in the United States and the cruel, uncivilized Negro in Africa. When the condition of our slaves is contrasted with the state of their miserable race in Africa; when their civilization, intelligence, and instruction is considered, and the means now employed to restore them to the country from which they have been torn, bearing with them the blessings of civilized life, we are almost persuaded that their introduction amongst us was in the providence of God who makes the evil passions of men subservient to his own glory, a means of placing that unhappy race within the pale of civilized nations."

Justice Campbell in his dissent departed from the opinion of the majority of the court with regard to the freedom of Dred Scott and family. He thought that a review of the case law of Missouri and of the neighboring slave states clearly held that a slave held in servitude was entitled to freedom when setting foot upon free territory. Justice Campbell, however, objected to the taking of property, for example, the slave, by action of Congress. He believed that people outside the state of Missouri had no right to interfere with the institution of slavery or the domestic laws of the state. He agreed with the other two justices on the invalidity of the Missouri Compromise.

Thus, the state court departed from the commonly accepted principle that slaves who moved to free states became free. This shift in favor of the slave owners put strong pressure on the political moderates of both parties and served to entrench the differences between slave and free states.

Rather than appealing the state court decision directly to the Missouri Supreme Court, Scott's attorneys took a new direction. In 1851, the U.S. Supreme Court had decided the case of *Strader v. Graham*, which involved the case of slave musicians from Kentucky taken into Ohio for performances. To the Kentucky Court of Appeals, the persons who helped the slaves escape were guilty of theft of property, and the U.S. Supreme Court unanimously agreed. Thus, a federal suit for freedom was brought in the Circuit Court for St. Louis County, Missouri, alleging that Scott was a citizen of Missouri and that John Sandford, the son-in-law of Dr. Emerson, a resident of New York, was now the owner of the Scotts. Because of the question of diversity of citizenship, federal jurisdiction was alleged. As for whether a slave could be a free citizen, the lower court ruled against Scott and held that once he returned to slave soil, Scott remained a slave.

SUMMARY OF ARGUMENTS

The *Dred Scott* case was argued twice before the Supreme Court. In February 1856, Sandford's attorney dropped the bombshell argument that Scott was not free because the Missouri Compro-

mise was unconstitutional. The Court was bitterly divided about how to deal with the case and agreed to stall for time. The case was reargued in December 1856, and four days were devoted to the proceedings. Justice Benjamin Curtis's brother, George T. Curtis, argued with Montgomery Blair for Scott. Sandford employed Henry S. Geyer and Reverdy Johnson. Blair and Geyer dominated the second argument, with Blair claiming that case law declared Scott free and Geyer arguing that Congress had no authority to prevent a slaveholder from taking his property with him, and since Scott had never been a citizen, he could not sue his owner in federal court.

DECISION

The case had been appealed to the Supreme Court on the basis of an improper charge to the jury. Chief Justice Roger B. Taney stated the question of Dred Scott's citizenship simply: "Can a Negro whose ancestors were imported into this country and sold as slaves become a member of the political community which was formed and brought into existence by the Constitution of the United States?" In the opinion written by Chief Justice Taney, each state could determine who could be a citizen within its boundaries. Citizenship of a state is not coextensive with citizenship of the United States. Each state was allowed to determine, as deemed proper, the class or description of persons within its boundaries entitled to citizenship. The chief justice stated that the authors of the Declaration of Independence and the U.S. Constitution did not think that slaves were fit to associate with the white race, that all of the original thirteen colonies recognized slavery, and that the African race was a distinct form of property expressly recognized in the Constitution. The chief justice went on to review various state decisions with regard to property rights of slaves and concluded that it was not for the federal government to rule against the wishes of the states that abrogated the Articles of Confederation in forming the United States of America: Such an act would involve the taking of property without compensation. The chief justice held that there was no authority in the Constitution for Congress to draw a line such as in the Missouri Compromise, and that whether they had or had not the authority to do so, Congress had no right to determine freedom for the citizens of any state. The matters were to be left solely to the determination of the state courts.

The effect of Taney's opinion, which was joined by six other justices, was to conclude as a matter of law that slaves and free blacks were not citizens. They were consigned to an inferior legal position.

All of the justices wrote separate opinions. Justice Daniel wrote that "the African Negro race never have been acknowledged as belonging to the family of nations . . . that this race has been by all the nations of Europe regarded as subjects of capture or purchase; as subjects of commerce or traffic." The tenor of the seven members of the Court in the majority was extremely similar.

Only Justices Curtis and McLean dissented. Justice McLean wrote that all slavery has its origin in power and is against right: "A slave is not a mere chattel. He bears the impress of his Maker, and is amenable to the laws of God and man; and he is destined to an endless existence."

Justice McLean held that the prior cases of the state and English common law clearly held that the removal of a slave to a free state entitled the slave to freedom. He further found that it was appropriate for Congress to enact the Missouri Compromise Act in 1820 as a condition for acquiring land from the government of France. His opinion reflects the fact that some form of law was necessary to create the territories and implement the wishes of the United States, which had paid for the land. Thus, a public act of the Congress is entitled to be noticed and respected as much as any other law. Justice Curtis agreed that the states may exclude numerous people from the right to vote or hold office or other franchises on the basis of their age or sex or marital condition, but he found nothing to prevent a person of color from being a citizen of the United States and thus having the right to access the courts created by the Constitution.

Justice Curtis further found that the act of Dr. Emerson in consenting to the marriage of Dred and Harriet Scott in the free state of Illinois was an effectual abandonment of his right over the Scotts

as a master. Justice Curtis was not persuaded that the Missouri Compromise was invalid. Rather, he noted that the first seven presidents of the United States had all signed the Constitution and were all involved in the purchase of this Missouri Territory from the government of France.

AFTERMATH

In the *Dred Scott* decision, the Supreme Court judicially protected slavery. Dred Scott remained a slave, and it became apparent that the judicial process would do nothing to remove his condition of bondage. Scott died of tuberculosis less than two years later.

SIGNIFICANCE

The Fourteenth Amendment, adopted in 1868, provided citizenship to the newly freed slaves and overturned the Dred Scott decision. The "Black Codes" of the southern states, passed after Reconstruction ended, kept African Americans in a state only minimally above that of slavery. Not until the Civil Rights Act of 1964 was any significant effort made to give full citizenship to black Americans.

RELATED CASES

U.S. v. Reese, 92 U.S. 214 (1876)

Civil Rights Cases, 109 U.S. 3 (1883)

Plessy v. Ferguson, 163 U.S. 537 (1896)

RECOMMENDED READING

Ehrlich, W. *They Have No Rights: Dred Scott's Struggle for Freedom.* Westport, Conn.: Greenwood Press, 1979.

Fehrenbacher, D. E. *The Dred Scott Case: Its Significance in American Law and Politics.* New York: Oxford University Press, 1978.

Paul Finkelman, *The Dred Scott Case, Slavery, and the Politics of Law,* 20 Hamline Law Review 1 (1996).

———. *Dred Scott, Slavery, and Crisis.* New York: St. Martin's, 1997.

———. Dred Scott v. Sandford: *A Brief History with Documents*. Boston: Bedford Books, 1997.

Gunderson, Cory. *The Dred Scott Decision*. Edina, Minn.: Abdo, 2004.

"Landmark Supreme Court Cases—*Dred Scott v. Sandford*." Available online. URL: http://www.landmarkcases.org/dredscott/home.html. Accessed July 11, 2009.

Case Title: *Bradwell v. The State of Illinois*

Legal Citation: 83 U.S. 130; 16 Wall. 130

Year of Decision: 1872

KEY ISSUE

Is the right to practice law a privilege protected under the privileges and immunities clause of the Fourteenth Amendment?

HISTORY OF THE CASE

Myra Bradwell, a resident of Chicago, Illinois, applied to the Illinois Supreme Court for a license to practice law in the state of Illinois. Bradwell included in her application the required certificate from an inferior court of her good character, and upon examination she was found to possess the requisite qualifications. Bradwell's application was refused because Bradwell was a married woman, and therefore, her clients might not be able to enforce contracts against her; further, the profession of law was not suited for women. The Illinois Supreme Court also determined that it had the discretion to establish the rules for admission to practice in the state of Illinois subject to only two limitations: The first limitation was that the court could establish terms of admission that would promote the proper administration of justice; the second, that the court could not admit any persons or class of persons who were not intended by the legislature to be admitted, even if their exclusion was not expressly required by statute. The Supreme Court of Illinois indicated that the legislature never intended for women to be admitted to the practice of law; thus, the decision was properly within the court's discussion. The U.S. Supreme Court granted certiorari.

SUMMARY OF ARGUMENTS

Bradwell argued that as a citizen of the United States and Illinois, and a former citizen of the state of Vermont, she was entitled to any right granted to citizens of Vermont under the privileges and immunities clause of the Fourteenth Amendment, which indicates that there are certain privileges and immunities that belong to a citizen of the United States. Bradwell argued that because she would have had the right to practice law in the state of Vermont, she must also, under the Fourteenth Amendment, have the right practice law in Illinois.

DECISION

Justice Miller, writing for the Court, upheld the decision of the Illinois Supreme Court, ruling that the privileges and immunities clause of the Fourteenth Amendment did not include the right to practice a profession. The Supreme Court also held that regardless of Bradwell's state of birth, the Fourteenth Amendment declares that people are citizens of the state in which they reside; thus, Illinois's provisions applied to her application.

Justice Bradley concurred in the Court's judgment, but noted, "The natural and proper timidity and delicacy which belongs to the female sex evidently unfits it for many of the occupations of civil life. . . . The paramount destiny and mission of women are to fulfill the noble and benign offices of wife and mother. This is the law of the Creator." Justices Swayne and Field concurred in his opinion.

Chief Justice Chase was the sole dissent from the decision but did not file an opinion to explain his reasoning.

AFTERMATH

When the Supreme Court finally began to overturn gender discrimination, it did so by using the equal protection clause and not the privileges and immunities clause.

SIGNIFICANCE

This case determined that the privileges and immunities clause of the Fourteenth Amendment did not protect the right to practice a profession.

RELATED CASES

Slaughterhouse Cases, 83 U.S. 36 (1873)

RECOMMENDED READING

American Civil Liberties Union Women's Rights Project: www.aclu.org/womensrights/index.html

Wilson R. Huhn, *The Legacy of* Slaughterhouse, Bradwell, *and* Cruikshank *in Constitutional Interpretation,* 42 Akron Law Review 1051 (2009).

Gwen Hoerr Jordan, *"Horror of a Woman": Myra Bradwell, the 14th Amendment, and the Gendered Origins of Sociological Jurisprudence,* 42 Akron Law Review 1201 (2009).

Nina Morais, *Sex Discrimination and the Fourteenth Amendment: Lost History,* 97 Yale Law Journal 1153 (1988).

Debran Rowland. *Boundaries of Her Body: The Troubling History of Women's Rights in America.* Naperville, Ill.: Sphinx, 2004.

Smith, Roger M. *Civic Ideals: Conflicting Visions of Citizenship in U.S. History.* New Haven, Conn.: Yale University Press, 1999.

Case Title: *United States v. Cruikshank et al.*

Legal Citation: 92 U.S. 542

Year of Decision: 1875

KEY ISSUES

Do the First and Second Amendments protect citizens' rights only from congressional intrusion, and does the Fourteenth Amendment apply to actions of individuals?

HISTORY OF THE CASE

In 1873, an armed white militia attacked and killed more than 100 African Americans at the courthouse in Colfax, Louisiana, over the disputed gubernatorial election. This was known as the Colfax Massacre. Three members of the white mob were convicted under the Enforcement Act of 1870, which made it illegal for conspiracies to interfere with any citizen's constitutional rights. The defendants appealed on the grounds that the indictments were faulty.

SUMMARY OF ARGUMENTS

The prosecutor argued that the indictments of the 16 counts were good and sufficient law under the laws of the United States.

Cruikshank argued that the right that the conspirators intended to prevent was not one secured by the U.S. Constitution and, therefore, had not been made indictable by Congress. The right of people to assemble for lawful purposes existed before the U.S. Constitution and is, therefore, not a right granted by the Constitution. It was argued that the First Amendment was not intended to limit the powers of the state governments in respect to their own citizens but to operate upon the national government alone. In addition, the Second Amendment shall not be infringed by Congress, but again this only restricts the national government. Finally, the Fourteenth Amendment does not grant the right of suffrage; that right is granted by the state constitution, and unless there is racial discrimination, the U.S. Constitution has not secured the right.

DECISION

The rights to assembly in the First Amendment and to bear arms in the Second Amendment only protected citizens from congressional interference. The due process and equal protection clauses of the Fourteenth Amendment limited action only by the state, not by individuals. In addition, it was not shown that interference with the right to vote was due to racial discrimination; therefore, it was not an actionable offense under the U.S. Constitution.

Chief Justice Waite delivered the opinion of the Court, which explained that in order to bring this case under the operation of the statute, the right that was being conspired to prevent was one granted by the U.S. Constitution. Waite examined the rights each of the counts intended to prevent. Waite described one right as the right of the people peaceably to assemble for lawful purposes, which was a right long before the Constitution; therefore, the right was not guaranteed against individuals. Waite explained that this right "is found wherever civilization exists. It was not, therefore, a right granted to the people by the Constitution." The next issue was the right of "bearing arms for a lawful purpose." This is another right that is not granted by the Constitution and that shall not be infringed by Congress. The Fourteenth Amendment prohibits a state from depriving a citizen of these rights, but this does not show a right from one citizen to another. The deprivation against "the free exercise and enjoyment of their several right and privilege to the full and equal benefit of all laws and proceedings" was not an allegation that this right was deprived because of the race of the person; therefore, this is another equal protection of laws claim under the Fourteenth Amendment, where it has already been discussed that the amendment only protects the rights of citizens from the state. It was also argued that the right to vote was prevented; however, the right to suffrage is not a right granted by the Constitution; rather, it is a right that comes from individual states. Finally, the last allegation is that the parties were in great fear of bodily harm, injury, and oppression. Waite explained, "Certainly it will not be claimed that the United States have the power or are required to do mere police duty in the States." Waite held, "We are of the opinion that the first, second, third, fourth, sixth, seventh, ninth, tenth, eleventh, twelfth, fourteenth, and fifteenth counts do not contain charges of a criminal nature made

indictable under the laws of the United States and that consequently they are not good and sufficient in law." The last four counts were combined to determine the right to hinder and prevent them "in the several rights and privileges granted and secured to them by the constitution and laws of the Unites States." Waite explained that the particular rights included in the last counts must be explained to inform the court as well as the accused; the final counts were too vague and general to decide. In conclusion, Waite explained that none of the counts describe rights guaranteed under the U.S. Constitution that would give the Court jurisdiction over the claim.

AFTERMATH

The federal government had little power to interfere, so the African Americans in the South were left to the mercy of hostile state governments that did little to protect them. Eventually, the Democrats regained power in the 1870s, when they passed legislation making it harder for African Americans to vote. From 1890 to 1908, Confederate states passed constitutions or amendments with provisions for poll taxes, residency requirements, literacy tests, and grandfather clauses that disenfranchised most African Americans. As a result of the *Cruikshank* case, political parties were enabled to use paramilitary forces. This Supreme Court decision marked the nation's retreat from Reconstruction.

SIGNIFICANCE

The federal government could not interfere with the case, so it went to the state of Louisiana to provide punishment; however, the state was not likely to prosecute the crime. The federal government was severely limited in its ability to protect the civil rights of African Americans. All in all, the case opinion encouraged violence in the South.

RELATED CASES

United States v. Reese, 92 U.S. 214 (1876)

DeJonge v. Oregon, 299 U.S. 353 (1937)

Hague v. CIO, 301 U.S. 496 (1939)

STATUTE AT ISSUE

Enforcement Act of May 31, 1870, § 6

RECOMMENDED READING

Keith, LeeAnna. *The Colfax Massacre: The Untold Story of Black Power, White Terror and the Death of Reconstruction*. New York: Oxford University Press, 2008.

Lane, Charles. *The Day Freedom Died: The Colfax Massacre, the Supreme Court, and the Betrayal of Reconstruction*. New York: Henry Holt, 2008.

Case Title: *Strauder v. West Virginia*

Legal Citation: 100 U.S. 303

Year of Decision: 1880

KEY ISSUE

Does the Fourteenth Amendment prohibit discrimination in jury selection?

HISTORY OF THE CASE

Under West Virginia law, only white males could serve on juries. An all-white West Virginia jury convicted Taylor Strauder, a black man, of murder. The state supreme court affirmed the conviction. The U.S. Supreme Court agreed to hear the case because of the importance of the issues involved.

SUMMARY OF ARGUMENTS

Taylor Strauder argued that jury selection is a right that should be enjoyed without discrimination based on race.

West Virginia argued that the jury provision did not discriminate against Strauder as it nevertheless provided him with a trial by jury.

DECISION

Justice Strong wrote the majority opinion in the 7-2 decision reversing the state's conviction. The Court looked at the recently enacted Fourteenth Amendment and declared West Virginia's jury statute, which stated only white men were eligible to serve on a jury, a denial of equal protection. The Court limited the opinion to apply only to blacks, however, and not other "suspect" classes.

AFTERMATH

Since *Strauder*, the Supreme Court has dealt repeatedly with the issue of discrimination in the courtroom. The equal protection clause has come to protect not only blacks but all races. The Court in more recent years has also applied the Fourteenth Amendment to cases of gender exclusion. The enormous growth of the amendment's protection has virtually eliminated discrimination in the legal process.

SIGNIFICANCE

Strauder was the first case to confront racial discrimination in the courts. The Court's decision limited the application of the Fourteenth Amendment only to blacks rather than all citizens. While this interpretation was true to legislative intent, this view has been abandoned by subsequent decisions.

RELATED CASES

Ex Parte Virginia, 100 U.S. 339 (1879)

Taylor v. Louisiana, 419 U.S. 522 (1975)

Batson v. Kentucky, 476 U.S. 79 (1986)

Georgia v. McCollum, 505 U.S. 42 (1992)

J. E. B. v. Alabama ex rel. T. B., 511 U.S. 127 (1994)

RECOMMENDED READING

Currie, David P. *The Constitution in the Supreme Court, 1789–1888*. Chicago: University of Chicago Press, 1985.

Graglia, Lino A. *Disaster by Decree*. Ithaca, N.Y.: Cornell University Press, 1976.

William T. Pizzi, Batson v. Kentucky: *Curing the Disease but Killing the Patient,* Supreme Court Review 97 (1987).

❦

Case Title: *United States v. Stanley; United States v. Ryan; United States v. Nichols; United States v. Singleton;* and *Robinson v. Memphis & Charleston R. Co.*

Alternate Case Title: The *Civil Rights Cases*

Legal Citation: 109 U.S. 3

Year of Decision: 1883

∽

KEY ISSUE

Does Congress have the power under the Constitution to create the Civil Rights Act of 1875 under the Thirteenth or Fourteenth Amendment?

HISTORY OF THE CASE

The *Civil Rights Cases* are five different cases that had the same issue and were consolidated. The *Stanley* and *Nichols* cases were indictments for denying persons of color the accommodations and privileges of an inn or hotel. The *Singleton* and *Ryan* cases were for denying individuals the privileges and accommodations of a theater. The case of *Memphis & Charleston Railroad Company* was to recover a penalty of $500 due to the refusal by the conductor of the railroad company to allow a woman to ride in the ladies' car because she was African American. This case was taken to the Supreme Court by writ of error. The *Stanley, Nichols,* and *Singleton* cases went to the Supreme Court on certificates of division of opinion between the judges of the lower courts as to the constitutionality of the first and second sections of the act referred to. The case of *Ryan* went to the Supreme Court on a writ of error to the judgment of the Circuit Court for the District of California sustaining a demurrer to the information. All of the cases had the same issue of whether sections 1 and 2 of the Civil Rights Act, passed in March 1875, were constitutional.

SUMMARY OF ARGUMENTS

Solicitor General Samuel Phillips for the United States argued that the act of 1875 was constitutional and enacted to prevent the denial of public services on the basis of race. In addition, it was argued that Congress had the power to punish violators, therefore allowing the creation of the Civil Rights Act. Since this was a violation of public rights, it was not in the interest of an individual, but rather in the public interest, therefore, a state matter.

There were no appearances or briefs for the defendants.

DECISION

Justice Bradley delivered the opinion of the Court, which held that Congress was not given the power from the Thirteenth or Fourteenth Amendment to enact the Civil Rights Act of 1875. The Court held that the Thirteenth Amendment does not apply to discrimination in public accommodations. The Court explained, "An act of refusal has nothing to do with slavery or involuntary servitude. . . . It would be running the slavery argument into the ground to make it apply to every act of discrimination which a person may see fit to make as to the guests he will entertain, or as to the people he will take into his coach or cab or car, or admit to his concert or theater. . . . Mere discrimination on account of race or color were not regarded as badges of slavery."

It was also argued that the Fourteenth Amendment was not applicable, because it was intended to protect against state laws not against private individuals. The Court reasoned that under the Fourteenth Amendment, "it must necessarily be, and can only be, corrective in its character, addressed to counteract and afford relief against state regulations or proceedings." Therefore, the Fourteenth Amendment "extends its protection to races and classes and prohibits any state legislation which has the effect of denying to any race or class, or to any individual, the equal protection of the laws."

Justice Harlan criticized the majority's opinion. His dissent argued that the Court analyzed the Thirteenth and Fourteenth Amendments too narrowly. He disputed, explaining that the Thirteenth Amendment gave Congress authority to create sections 1 and 2 of the Civil Rights Act of 1875. Harlan argued that segregation in public accommodations was a "badge of slavery." Harlan argued that it was the job of the congressional legislation to facilitate that African Americans became mere citizens. However, it was extremely difficult to secure their legal rights to be treated equally. "To-day it is the colored race which is denied, by corporations and individuals wielding public authority, rights fundamental in their freedom and citizenship."

AFTERMATH

Ultimately, the dissent of Justice Harlan became the law. The Civil Rights Act of 1964 and the Supreme Court decision of *Heart of Atlanta Motel v. United States* (1964) followed Justice Harlan's opinion of the *Civil Rights Cases.*

SIGNIFICANCE

This decision greatly reduced the power of the federal government to provide protection for equal rights of African Americans, under the law. The state officials of the South took advantage of this opportunity to segregate African Americans and embody these practices in the law.

RELATED CASE

Heart of Atlanta Motel v. United States, 379 U.S. 241 (1964)

STATUTE AT ISSUE

Civil Rights Act, 1875

RECOMMENDED READING

Blackmon, Douglas A. *Slavery by Another Name: The Re-Enslavement of Black Americans from the Civil War to World War II.* New York: Anchor Books, 2009.

Kull, Andrew. "The 14th Amendment That Wasn't." *Constitution* 5 (Winter 1993): 68–75.

Westin, Andrew F. "The Case of the Prejudiced Doorkeeper: The Civil Rights Cases." In *Quarrels That Have Shaped the Constitution,* edited by John A. Garraty. New York: Harper & Row, 1987.

Case Title: *Yick Wo v. Hopkins*

Legal Citation: 118 U.S. 356

Year of Decision: 1886

KEY ISSUE

How far can a city or government go to use its police power without being discriminatory?

HISTORY OF THE CASE

Prior to the first Chinese Exclusion Act in 1882, free immigration of Chinese aliens led to a substantial increase in their concentration in California. By 1880, for example, the Chinese population constituted 10 percent of the population of the state of California. Moreover, almost half of them were concentrated in the San Francisco area. This concentration quickly became a concern for California lawmakers, who passed several restrictive laws that were clearly discriminatory against Chinese residents and aliens alike. For example, in 1876, the "Queue Ordinance" was passed in San Francisco, specifically denying Chinese residents police protection for their homes and businesses. Three years later, the California Constitution was amended to prohibit Chinese aliens from working for any government entity in the state. Soon after, the California legislature made employing Chinese workers by any corporation chartered in California a misdemeanor.

Although these measures were overtly unfair, they were less controversial than the seemingly nondiscriminatory ordinance regulating persons operating a laundry within the San Francisco city limits. Passed in 1880, this ordinance gave the Board of Supervisors authority to grant and renew licenses for operating wooden laundry facilities. Because the regulation dealt only with wooden facilities, the city claimed that its purpose of preventing fire was an appropriate exercise of its police power. Violation of the ordinance carried a penalty of a misdemeanor conviction with a jail sentence of up to six months and a fine of up to $1,000.

Although the purpose of the ordinance was legitimate, its application by the Board of Supervisors was clearly discriminatory. In 1880, 240 of 310 wooden laundries in San Francisco had Chinese owners. More than 200 Chinese owners applied for the license, but only a single permit out of the 80 licenses granted was issued to a Chinese owner, Mary Meagles. Yick Wo, a resident alien, continued to operate his laundry. He was arrested and fined $10. Because he refused to pay, he was jailed for 10 days. Upon his release, Yick Wo petitioned the California Supreme Court and was denied a writ of habeas corpus. He then appealed to the U.S. Supreme Court, naming Sheriff Hopkins in the suit and claiming that the city of San Francisco violated his due process rights under the Fourteenth Amendment.

SUMMARY OF ARGUMENTS

Yick Wo claimed that the ordinance violated his due process rights under the Fourteenth Amendment because of its unfair application by the Board of Supervisors. He supported this claim by using statistical information, stated previously, that showed that only one of more than 200 Chinese owners received a laundry license.

The city of San Francisco argued in response that it was exercising its "indestructible and inalienable" police power granted under the Constitution. The city also asserted that its police power could not be infringed upon even by the Fourteenth Amendment.

DECISION

Justice Matthews, in a unanimous opinion for the Court, held that the San Francisco fire prevention ordinance violated the due process clause of the Fourteenth Amendment and was, therefore, unconstitutional. The Court held that the guarantees given by the Fourteenth Amendment, under which the right to earn a living is included, apply to all persons, citizens and aliens alike. Specifically, San Francisco's arbitrary enforcement of the fire prevention ordinance discriminated against Chinese wooden laundry owners and violated their equal protection rights under the Fourteenth Amendment. The test used by Justice Matthews was the following: The legislation satisfied the constitutional requirements of the Fourteenth Amendment if it (1) specifically regulated health and safety practices and (2) were applied fairly. In this case, the power granted by the ordinance to the Board of Supervisors was broader than that which is given under police power. The ordinance allowed the board to use the fire prevention ordinance arbitrarily to regulate both the health and safety practices of wooden facilities and persons such as Yick Wo who operated wooden laundry facilities. This regulation was not only discriminatory but also outside the police power of the city of San Francisco. Therefore, the Court held that the San Francisco ordinance was unconstitutional, limiting the police power of local governments by expanding the Fourteenth Amendment to prevent discriminatory actions by these municipalities against all persons.

AFTERMATH

The Justice Matthews opinion revolutionized constitutional law by limiting the police power of local and state governments, prohibiting discrimination by using the due process clause and defining the coverage of the Fourteenth Amendment to include aliens. Although this opinion did not put an end to discrimination, the Supreme Court's classification of alienage as a "suspect" class 85 years later required proof of a compelling government interest for alienage discrimination to be upheld.

SIGNIFICANCE

The application of the Fourteenth Amendment outside the context of the Civil War and slavery had consequential implications. After this decision, public officials were notified that blatant discrimination against Chinese persons would no longer be acceptable to the legal system. The anti-Chinese movement across the country subsided somewhat. The Supreme Court's composition changed shortly after 1886, however. Afterward, the Fourteenth Amendment was used mainly to prevent restrictions against property rights up until the mid-20th century, when the due process clause was used to fight the persecution of blacks in the form of the "Jim Crow" laws.

RELATED CASES

Slaughterhouse Cases, 83 U.S. 36 (1873)

Civil Rights Cases, 109 U.S. 3 (1883)

Plessy v. Ferguson, 163 U.S. 537 (1896)

Truax v. Raich, 239 U.S. 33 (1915)

Missouri ex rel. Gaines v. Canada, 305 U.S. 337 (1938)

Ambach v. Norwick, 441 U.S. 68 (1979)

RECOMMENDED READING

Cheng-Tsu, W. *"Chink": A Documentary History of Anti-Chinese Prejudice in America.* New York: World, 1972.

Konuitz, M. R. *The Alien and the Asiatic in American Law.* Ithaca, N.Y.: Cornell University Press, 1946.

Saxton, A. *The Indispensible Enemy: Labor and the Anti-Chinese Movement in California.* Berkeley: University of California Press, 1971.

Case Title: *United States v. Jung Ah Lung*

Legal Citation: 124 U.S. 621

Year of Decision: 1888

KEY ISSUES

Does the Court have the power to pass judgment on refusing a Chinese laborer admittance to the United States who, upon attempting to reenter the United States, was unable to produce a certificate demonstrating his residence in California prior to the Chinese Exclusion Act of 1882? Does the Court have the right to allow the introduction of evidence other than such a certificate to determine whether the Chinese laborer was to be allowed reentry under the Chinese Exclusion Act of 1882?

HISTORY OF THE CASE

Jung Ah Lung was a Chinese laborer who resided and worked in California. He emigrated from China on November 17, 1880, and resided continuously in California until October 1883, when he returned to China. Before leaving California, Jung Ah Lung applied for a certificate of identification from the collector of the port of San Francisco, in full accordance with the Chinese Exclusion Act of 1882. While he was traveling by boat from his native city of Canton, China, Lung's certificate of identification was stolen from him by pirates in the area. No one presented the certificate to the customhouse of San Francisco, and so the certificate remained outstanding and uncanceled. Upon attempting to reenter the United States in August 1885, Lung was denied entry and detained by order of the customs authorities for the port of San Francisco, for lack of a certificate of identification. The district court of California issued a writ of habeas corpus (a legal action seeking relief from unlawful detention), ordering the release of Jung Ah Lung, after it considered the circumstances surrounding his failure to produce the certificate and determined that Jung Ah Lung matched the description of the person who was issued the certificate of identification in his name. This decision was upheld by the Circuit Court of California. The decision was appealed to the U.S. Supreme Court.

To understand this case fully, a brief look at the United States's changing immigration policies toward China during this period must be taken. At the time this case was decided, there was a growing anti-Chinese sentiment found with particular force in California. Specifically, working- and middle-class white Americans began to resent the Chinese for economic, racial, and cultural reasons. California suffered from a severe economic depression in 1873–78, and white American workers blamed their misfortunes on Chinese immigrants. A large percentage of the workforce in California was made up of Chinese immigrants, and Americans harbored resentment toward the Chinese laborers for "stealing" their jobs since they took jobs for lower wages, thus making it more difficult for non-Chinese workers to find work in California.

The rising anti-Chinese sentiment of many Americans was only exacerbated by feelings that the Chinese were an inferior race, and that their assimilation into the American way of life was impossible because of the racial and cultural differences that existed between America and China. Advocates for the Chinese Exclusion Act of 1882, legislation that was the focus of this Supreme Court decision, argued that the Chinese were a threat to the American way of life. Because China had always been ruled by "an imperial, despotic" government, the Chinese people themselves were "utterly unfit for and incapable of free or self-government." The existence of both races in the same country was believed to be impossible. These differences were considered to be a result of evolution under two completely different systems. In addition, "scientific studies" conducted in America found that the Chinese were a less intelligent race, who did not have the capacity for democratic rule. Chinese were linked to deadly diseases, and Chinese prostitutes were singled out as a special health concern in 1875.

All of these reasons led to increasing political pressure to curb, or end completely, Chinese immigration into the United States. This political pressure was not limited to Congress and was felt strongly in the courts of California.

SUMMARY OF ARGUMENTS

Jung Ah Lung argued that he had been unlawfully deprived of his liberty.

The arguments made by the state of California in this case were threefold. First, the District Court of California lacked the jurisdiction to issue a writ of habeas corpus. Second, even if the court's jurisdiction extended to a writ of habeas corpus, the Chinese Exclusion Act of 1882 removed that right and did not provide for judicial review. Therefore, the court was wrong to issue judgment. Third, production of the certificate of identification was the only proof accepted by the Exclusion Act so no other evidence should be allowed in weighing the court's decision.

The state argued that the district court did not have the authority to issue a writ of habeas corpus because Jung Ah Lung's liberty was not restrained within the meaning of the habeas cor-

pus act. The purpose of the habeas corpus act was to allow a person to seek relief from an unlawful detention by the state. The state contended that Jung Ah Lung was not being held in custody but was merely being refused entry into the United States, two very distinct situations.

Second, the state contended that the Chinese Exclusion Act took away the court's right to issue a writ of habeas corpus, because the act regulated the subject matter of the case and was necessarily exclusive. In addition, the Exclusion Act provided for only executive review: The collector of the port was charged with passing judgment over Jung Ah Lung, and others like him, and there was no indication that any sort of judicial review was to exist. If the treaty were to "work hardship upon the subjects of China," the Chinese minister could draw the matter to the attention of the U.S. secretary of state. Thus, because the act was "necessarily exclusive," the state argued that failure to allow specifically for judicial review in the act itself indicates that no judicial review should be allowed.

Finally, if the district court did indeed have jurisdiction and the right to issue a writ of habeas corpus, the state reasoned that weighing evidence other than the actual certificate of identification was in direct violation § 4 of the Chinese Exclusion Act. The fact that Jung Ah Lung's story was verifiable and that he corresponded with the description found in the port collector's record books was immaterial. He did not have the certificate, and he should not have been allowed reentry into the United States.

DECISION

The Supreme Court, in a 6-3 decision, affirmed the judgment rendered by the court below. In writing the opinion, Justice Blatchford systematically analyzed and dismissed the state's arguments.

With regard to whether the issuance of the writ of habeas corpus was proper, Justice Blatchford asked two questions: One, was Jung Ah Lung in custody, and two, was Jung Ah Lung detained by the state? The answers to both questions were affirmative. Jung Ah Lung was held in custody by the master of the ship on which Lung arrived, by order of the customs authorities of the port, under the provision of the Chinese Exclusion Act. That act was a piece of legislation enacted by Congress. Therefore, Lung was held in custody under the authority of the United States. Justice Blatchford concluded that this case was a proper one to issue a writ of habeas corpus.

Contrary to the state's belief that the Chinese Exclusion Act failed to allow for judicial review, the act clearly indicated that judicial review was not only allowed but also necessary. The act stated that a Chinese person found unlawfully within the United States could only be removed after being taken before a judicial authority of a court of the United States and found to be in the United States illegally. The act did specify that the collector of the port had the authority to pass judgment over Jung Ah Lung; however, that had no bearing on whether a court could review the decision. The Court interpreted that section as merely specifying which executive officer would enforce the act and did not exclude the court from reviewing his action.

In answering the state's third argument, it must be noted that only the Chinese Exclusion Act of 1882, and not the later act of 1884, was enforceable against Jung Ah Lung, because he had left the United States prior to its enactment. The Court looked at the exact language of the act in determining whether evidence outside the certificate of identification could be used. The act itself merely stated that production of the certificate entitled the owner to reentry into the United States; it did not state that production of the certificate was the *only* evidence admissible. In the absence of explicit language allowing only the certificate as evidence, the district court correctly weighed evidence outside the certificate of identification.

Justices Harlan, Field, and Lamar dissented from the majority opinion. Their dissent was based on their interpretation of the language of the Chinese Exclusion Act of 1882 and their view of the legislative intention of the act. The main thrust of their argument was that Congress sought to exclude Chinese laborers from entering the United States for 10 years after the passage of the act; that was why the certificate of identification was required to reenter the United States. The legislature clarified their intent by passing the act

of 1884, which provided that the certificate of identification was to be the only evidence permissible to establish a Chinese laborer's right of reentry. Justices Harlan, Field, and Lamar did not see the act of 1884 as declaring a new rule but as merely removing any ambiguity as to the legislature's intent in passing the act of 1882.

AFTERMATH

The anti-Chinese sentiment grew rapidly. After the decision of the California district court, as noted in this case, Congress responded in 1884 by passing amendments to the Chinese Exclusion Act of 1882, which tightened the requirements of the previous act. While the federal courts, as a whole, generally attempted to halt the growth of the anti-Chinese hysteria, the courts slowly succumbed to the pressure exerted by the general populace, allowing Chinese rights under American law to be severely curtailed.

SIGNIFICANCE

This case was one of several demonstrating the federal courts' attempt to defend Chinese rights in the United States, en route to surrendering to the anti-Chinese hysteria of the era. This case helps to catalog the process by which the federal courts allowed Chinese rights to be limited under American law.

RELATED CASES

Chew Heong v. United States 112 U.S. 536 (1884)

Chae Chan Ping v. United States 130 U.S. 581 (1889)

STATUTE AT ISSUE

Chinese Exclusion Act. 22 Stat. 58 (1882), an act to execute certain treaty stipulations relating to Chinese, approved May 6, 1882, as amended July 5, 1884

RECOMMENDED READING

Salyer, Lucy E. *Laws Harsh as Tigers: Chinese Immigrants and the Shaping of Modern Immigration Law.* Chapel Hill: University of North Carolina Press, 1995.

Case Title: *Chae Chan Ping v. United States*

Alternate Case Title: The Chinese Exclusion Case

Legal Citation: 130 U.S. 581

Year of Decision: 1889

KEY ISSUE

Does Congress have the power to pass an act prohibiting the reentry of Chinese laborers to the United States, when the Chinese in question left the country before its passing and had received a right of reentry under previous laws?

HISTORY OF THE CASE

Chae Chan Ping was a Chinese citizen who had resided in the United States from 1875 until June 1887, when he left for China. Before leaving, Ping had acquired a certificate of identification, in full accord with the Chinese Exclusion Acts of 1882 and 1884, allowing him reentry to the United States upon producing the certificate to the proper customs officials. However, Congress passed an amendment to the Chinese Exclusion Act of 1884, commonly known as the Scott Act, on October 1, 1888, while Chae Chan Ping was still out of the country. Chae Chan Ping returned to the United States on October 8, 1888, only to be refused entry into the United States by the port collector of San Francisco and taken into custody.

Chae Chan Ping petitioned the California district court for a writ of habeas corpus, alleging that he had been unlawfully detained and wished to be allowed to enter the United States. The district court, after issuing the writ and hearing the case, ruled against Chae Chan Ping, holding that the Scott Act was constitutional, that it applied to Ping, and that the fact that it violated treaties with China was immaterial. The decision was then appealed, ending up on the Supreme Court's docket, where the decision was affirmed.

SUMMARY OF ARGUMENTS

Chae Chan Ping makes two arguments: first, that the Scott Act of 1888 was an expulsion of Chinese laborers from the United States, which violated treaties between the United States and China and, therefore, should be unconstitutional; and, second, that the Scott Act would destroy Ping's previously vested right, under the Exclusion Acts of 1882 and 1884, to reenter the United States and, therefore, should be unconstitutional.

DECISION

Justice Field wrote the opinion for the Court, affirming the decision of the lower court. In doing so, Justice Field addressed both of Chae Chan Ping's arguments with one response: that as a sovereign nation, the United States had the right to exclude foreign immigrants, at any time, for any reason.

The lower court opinion essentially stated that international treaties and congressional acts were of equal standing. When there is a conflict between the two, the most recent law should be given authority. In this case, the Scott Act would be enforced over the prior Chinese Exclusion Acts of 1882 and 1884. Justice Field elaborated by citing *Edye v. Robertson* (1884): An international treaty "is subject to such acts as Congress may pass for its enforcement, modification, or repeal." The fact that the Scott Act was in direct violation of previous international treaties is of no consequence.

After dismissing the first of Chae Chan Ping's arguments, Justice Field moved to the second. He stated that the only other reason that the Scott Act might be invalidated would be that it was not within Congress's power to prohibit Chinese immigration. Before this case, Congress's power to regulate foreign immigration was generally attributed to the constitutional provision empowering Congress to "regulate Commerce with Foreign Nations." However, Justice Field departed from this reasoning, asserting that the very definition of a sovereign nation imbued that nation with the ability to exclude aliens from its territory; that if the United States were constrained by an international treaty, or any other source, it would act as a diminution of its sovereignty. This could not be allowed. Justice Field concluded that as a sovereign nation, the United States had the unquestioned power to exclude foreigners when the United States deemed it necessary. Because of this, "Whatever license . . . Chinese laborers may have obtained . . . to return to the United States after their departure, is held at the will of the government, revocable at any time, at its pleasure."

Aftermath

The immediate effects of the decision were devastating to the Chinese immigrants. An estimated 20,000 return certificates were declared void, leaving many Chinese immigrants unable to reenter the United States. More importantly, absolute exclusion of a people, based on race, had been legitimized by this decision.

Significance

This was the first major decision to uphold legislation prohibiting Chinese immigration and a major blow to the legal status of Chinese immigrants. Field's reasoning provided a more liberal and expansive view of the federal government's power over immigrants, one that was less heavily constrained by the Constitution. In the years to follow, the doctrine would expand, limiting immigrants' rights and the power of the courts to intervene.

Related Cases

Edye v. Robertson, 112 U.S. 580 (1884)

Whitney v. Robertson, 124 U.S. 190 (1887)

Recommended Reading

Salyer, Lucy E. *Laws Harsh as Tigers: Chinese Immigrants and the Shaping of Modern Immigration Law*. Chapel Hill: University of North Carolina Press, 1995.

Case Title: *Plessy v. Ferguson*

Alternate Case Title: The Separate but Equal Case

Legal Citation: 163 U.S. 537

Year of Decision: 1896

Key Issue

Do the states have the right to require separate accommodations in interstate commerce based on race?

History of the Case

In the late 19th century, the legislatures of many southern states passed laws imposing racial segregation. These laws, called "Jim Crow" laws, created two separate societies, one for whites and one for blacks.

Homer Plessy, a light-skinned black man, bought a first-class ticket to travel from New Orleans to Covington, Louisiana, on the East Louisiana Railroad. At this time, trains segregated their passengers, having cars specifically for whites and cars specifically designated for blacks. On June 7, 1892, he entered a car for white passengers, where he took a vacant seat. A police officer was summoned, and Mr. Plessy was forced to leave the coach. He was imprisoned in the jail of New Orleans for having violated the "Jim Crow" law of Louisiana, which separated blacks from whites on trains. Plessy was tried before the criminal district court of Orleans Parish, but before he could be fined or sentenced, he filed a petition for a writ of prohibition against Judge John H. Ferguson, the judge of the criminal district court. The Louisiana Supreme Court reviewed the petition of Mr. Plessy and found that the statute was constitutional and that Mr. Plessy, being one-eighth black, was "a member of the colored race." Plessy petitioned to the U.S. Supreme Court, and the Court accepted jurisdiction.

Summary of Arguments

Mr. Plessy's case was argued by Albion Tourgee, who affirmed that the concept of separate but equal was in theory equal and impartial, but that its object was to debase and to distinguish one race as inferior to the other. Regardless of the intent of the law, black citizens were constantly reminded of white superiority and supremacy. Tourgee uttered the famous words "Justice is pictured blind and her daughter, the law, ought at least to be colorblind."

Alexander Morse represented Judge Ferguson. Morse argued that the Louisiana legislature was at liberty to act with reference to the usage, custom, and traditions of their people, with a view to promoting their comfort and preserving the public peace in good order.

DECISION

Justice Henry Brown wrote the majority opinion. By a vote of 8-1, the Court ruled that laws permitting, and even requiring, the separation of persons by race do not imply the inferiority of either race to the other. Justice Brown further found that the distinction based on skin color has no tendency to destroy the legal equality of the races. Justice Brown also stated that laws requiring the separation of races commonly have been upheld, especially with regard to separate schools for white and black children. Brown ruled that there was a distinction between laws that interfere with political equality for "the negro" and those that require the separation of races in schools, theaters, and railroad cars:

> We consider the underlying fallacy of . . . [Plessy's] argument to consist in the assumption that the enforced separation of the two races stamps the colored race with a badge of inferiority. If this be so, it is not by reason of anything found in the act, but solely because the colored race chooses to put that construction upon it.

Justice John M. Harlan of Kentucky wrote a thundering dissent. Harlan, a former slave owner, argued that the Thirteenth and Fourteenth Amendments to the Constitution added to the dignity and glory of American citizenship by securing personal liberty to all persons born or naturalized in the United States. To that end, they "removed the race line" from our government. Justice Harlan had no trouble recognizing that the intent of this law was to interfere with the personal liberties of black citizens of Louisiana. Justice Harlan continued:

The white race deems itself to be the dominant race in this country. And so it is, in prestige, in achievements, in education, in wealth, and in power. So, I doubt not, it will continue to be for all time, if it remains true to its great heritage, and holds fast to the principles of constitutional liberty. But in view of the constitution, in the eye of the law, there is in this country no superior, dominant, ruling class of citizens. There is no caste here. Our constitution is colorblind, and neither knows nor tolerates classes among citizens. In respect of civil rights, all citizens are equal before the law. The humblest is the peer of the most powerful. The law regards man as man, and takes no account of his surroundings or his color when his civil rights as guaranteed by the supreme law of the land are involved. It is therefore to be regretted that this high tribunal, the final expositor of the fundamental law of the land, has reached the conclusion that it is competent for the state to regulate the enjoyment by citizens of their civil rights solely upon the basis of color.

In my opinion, the judgment this day rendered will, in time, prove to be quite as pernicious as the decision made by this tribunal in the Dred Scott Case.

AFTERMATH

For more than 60 years, the Supreme Court regarded "separate but equal" as an appropriate interpretation of the law with regard to the civil rights of black citizens.

SIGNIFICANCE

Plessy v. Ferguson encouraged legislators in the South to pass "Jim Crow" laws, which intensified the segregation of blacks and whites, the disenfranchisement of black voters, and other violations of the civil rights of blacks.

RELATED CASES

Strauder v. West Virginia, 100 U.S. 303 (1879)

Civil Rights Cases, 109 U.S. 3 (1883)

Yick Wo v. Hopkins, 118 U.S. 356 (1886)

Missouri ex rel. Gaines v. Canada, 305 U.S. 337 (1938)

Brown v. Board of Education of Topeka, 347 U.S. 483 (1954)

Muir v. Louisville Park Theatrical Assn., 347 U.S. 971 (1954)

Watson v. Memphis, 373 U.S. 526 (1963)

RECOMMENDED READING

Carmichael, Peter A. *The South and Segregation.* Washington, D.C.: Public Affairs Press, 1965.

Elliott, Mark Emory. *Color-Blind Justice: Albion Tourgée and the Quest for Racial Equality from the Civil War to* Plessy v. Ferguson. New York: Oxford University Press, 2006.

Failborg Tremé: The Untold Story of Black New Orleans. Dir. Dawn Logsdon. Serendipity Films, 2009.

Fireside, Harvey, and Marc H. Morial. *Separate and Unequal: Homer Plessy and the Supreme Court Decision That Legalized Racism.* New York: Carroll & Graf, 2005.

Fischer, Roger A. *The Segregation Struggle in Louisiana, 1862–1877.* Urbana: University of Illinois Press, 1974.

Medley, Keith Weldon. *We as Freemen:* Plessy v. Ferguson. Gretna, La: Pelican, 2003.

"Plessy v. Ferguson." Landmark Supreme Court Cases. Available online. URL: http://www.landmarkcases.org/plessy/home.html.

Thomas, Brook. Plessy v. Ferguson: *A Brief History with Documents.* Boston: Macmillan, 1996.

Woodward, C. Vann. *The Strange Career of Jim Crow.* 3d ed. New York: Oxford University Press, 1974.

Case Title: *United States v. Wong Kim Ark*

Legal Citation: 169 U.S. 649

Year of Decision: 1898

KEY ISSUE

Should an American-born person of Chinese ancestry be considered a naturalized citizen of the United States?

HISTORY OF THE CASE

Wong Kim Ark was born to Chinese immigrant parents in San Francisco, California, sometime between the years 1868 and 1873. Ark took several trips to China with his parents. However, upon returning to the United States in 1895, he was denied reentry because "the said Wong Kim Ark, although born in the city and county of San Francisco, state of California, United States of America, is not, under the laws of the state of California and of the United States, a citizen thereof." Part of the reason why questions as to Ark's citizenship arose was the Chinese Exclusion Act of 1882, which prohibited Chinese immigrants from entering the United States or becoming naturalized citizens. However, the Fourteenth Amendment to the U.S. Constitution stated, in relevant part, "All persons born or naturalized in the United States, and subject to the jurisdiction thereof, are citizens of the United States and of the State wherein they reside." The Supreme Court was, therefore, forced to decide whether the literal language of the Fourteenth Amendment should be applied, or whether a more expansive interpretation involving the new law was necessary.

SUMMARY OF ARGUMENTS

Solicitor General Holmes Conrad argued that English common law should not be used to determine the citizenship of a child of a noncitizen living in the United States. Instead, he argued that Roman law, in which citizenship of the child is determined by the citizenship of the parent, was the international law and, therefore, should be applied here since it superseded common law.

Wong Kim Ark argued that the literal interpretation of the Fourteenth Amendment should be read as indicating that any person born in the United States is a citizen. Under this interpretation, Wong Kim Ark argued he was a U.S. citizen and, therefore, could not be denied entry into the country.

DECISION

As noted, the Fourteenth Amendment explicitly states the requirements needed for an individual to be considered a U.S. citizen. As such, the decision should not have been a particularly difficult one for the Court. However, because of increasing anti-Chinese sentiment in the United States at the time, the Court had to reach its decision in a climate very hostile to the plaintiff.

The Court concluded that Roman law would not control in this case because at the time the Constitution was adopted and long before, England had followed the rule that "mere birth within the realm" entitled the person to the rights of a native-born citizen. The Court looked at British common law and state law to determine the citizenship of a person born within the United States. The Court looked at two traditional common law exceptions to the laws of citizenship: children born to diplomats and children born to enemy forces engaged in a country's occupation. Justice Gray, writing for the majority, noted: "The real object of the fourteenth amendment of the constitution, in qualifying the words 'all persons born in the United States' by the addition 'and subject to the jurisdiction thereof,' would appear to have been to exclude, by the fewest and fittest words . . . the two classes of cases—children born of alien enemies in hostile occupation, and children of diplomatic representatives of a foreign state." However, the Court found that neither of these two exceptions applied in this case. The Court found that "during all the time of their said residence in the United States, as domiciled residents therein, the said mother and father of said Wong Kim Ark . . . were never engaged in any diplomatic or official capacity under the emperor of China." The Court also noted that since Wong was already a U.S. citizen by the time he returned to China, the provisions of the Chinese Exclusion

Act, which forbade additional Chinese immigrants to enter the United States, did not apply since Ark was already a U.S. citizen.

The two dissenters, Justices Fuller and Harlan, argued that American law had split from its British counterpart and that citizenship should be determined from the citizenship of the parents. However, in the 6-2 decision, the majority ruled that Ark became a citizen of the United States at the time of his birth and should, therefore, not be denied entry into the United States.

AFTERMATH

The Court's decision had an immediate effect on the Chinese community, as well as the overall immigrant community at large. Any children born to immigrant parents inside U.S. borders were considered fully naturalized citizens with all benefits conferred. Recently, as immigration has risen to the forefront of political issues in the national debate, the *Wong* decision has come under increased scrutiny. In 1965, Congress passed the Immigration and Nationality Act, which allowed for very young citizens (from which the derogatory term "anchor baby" stems) to facilitate the legal residency in the United States for their non-citizen parents. For this reason, some have argued that *Wong* was wrongly decided, since it in effect provides a backdoor to residency in the United States for those fortunate enough to have had a child within its boundaries. Others have argued that the *Wong* decision only applied to the children of *legal* immigrants (which Wong's parents were) and not to illegal or undocumented immigrants. The question of whether the Court in *Wong* intended their decision to apply only to legal immigrants is up for debate, however, and it remains unlikely that the *Wong* decision will be overturned in the near future.

SIGNIFICANCE

Wong eventually became a cornerstone case in U.S. immigration law, with a multitude of cases citing its decision. The principle that anyone born in the United States is a U.S. citizen has been used to settle several other citizenship cases involving lost U.S. citizenship as a result of moving abroad and loss of citizenship by voting in a foreign election. To this day, *Wong* heavily influences the governing law concerning citizenship and naturalization.

RELATED CASES

Yick Wo v. Hopkins, 118 U.S. 356 (1886)

Strauder v. West Virginia, 100 U.S. 303 (1979)

RECOMMENDED READING

Chan, Sucheng. *Entry Denied: Exclusion and the Chinese Community in America, 1882–1943*. Philadelphia: Temple University Press, 1991.

Hoexter, Corinne. *From Canton to California*. New York: Four Winds Press, 1976.

Keller, Morton. *Affairs of State: Public Life in Late Nineteenth Century America*. Cambridge, Mass.: Belknap Press, 1977.

Case Title: *Williams v. State of Mississippi*

Legal Citation: 170 U.S. 213

Year of Decision: 1898

KEY ISSUES

Do the voter provisions of the constitution of the state of Mississippi and the laws enacted to enforce it violate the Fourteenth Amendment of the Constitution of the United States?

HISTORY OF THE CASE

Mississippi made a provision to the state constitution that set requirements for voter registration, including poll taxes and literacy tests. As a result of these requirements, most African Americans and poor Caucasians could not vote. There was, however, a grandfather clause that allowed illiterate people to vote as long as they or their grandfather had voted before a certain year. The

provision applied to all voters, although ultimately African Americans were largely affected by these new requirements because their relatives were not eligible to vote during the year that was named in the grandfather clause. In effect, the grandfather clause prohibited African Americans from voting. Only qualified voters could serve on juries, and because of the disenfranchisement of African Americans, they were excluded from jury service.

Henry Williams, an African American, was indicted for murder. He was indicted by an all-white grand jury and convicted by an all-white petit jury. He was sentenced to be hanged. The case was sent to the Supreme Court by arguing that the trial violated the equal protection clause of the Fourteenth Amendment since African Americans were excluded from jury service by the voting requirements of the Mississippi Constitution.

SUMMARY OF ARGUMENTS

Wilson argued that the indictment for murder was faulty because the trial violated the Fourteenth Amendment. The Fourteenth Amendment guarantees protection of the rights of citizens given under the U.S. Constitution. It was argued that since African Americans were excluded from jury service by state voting requirements, the state constitution discriminated against African Americans.

The state argued that the Mississippi Constitution was not a violation of the Fourteenth Amendment. The provision did not discriminate on its face, and there was no proof that the actual administration was intentional. In addition, the provision to the constitution did not discriminate against African Americans because the provision applied to every voter. Each state has the power to determine its voting laws, and the Fourteenth Amendment is not violated unless there is discrimination. Since there was not discrimination in this case, there was not a violation of the U.S. Constitution.

DECISION

The Court held that Mississippi's voting requirements did not violate the Fourteenth Amendment.

The Fourteenth Amendment did not grant rights; it only guaranteed protection of rights given under the U.S. Constitution, and voting rights are granted by *state* constitutions. The Court held that discrimination was not shown in the actual administration of the suffrage provisions, especially since the requirements applied to all voters.

Justice McKenna delivered the opinion of the Court, which explained that the plaintiff claimed that the discrimination was not based on the constitution of the state or its laws but rather was alleged by administrative officers. Although there was an allegation of discrimination to disenfranchise African-American citizens, McKenna stated, "We have no concern, unless the purpose is executed by the constitution of laws by those who administer them." The Court determined that even if the law is fair on its face, but it is applied unfairly, "the denial of equal justice is still within the prohibition of the constitution." McKenna explained that under the circumstances of this case, "They do not on their face discriminate between the races, and it has not been shown that their actual administration was evil; only that evil was possible under them."

AFTERMATH

Many southern states followed the lead of Mississippi and passed voter requirements further disenfranchising hundreds of thousands of African Americans and tens of thousands of poor Caucasians. African Americans were ultimately restricted from voting until the 1960s. The Civil Rights Act of 1964 and the Voting Rights Act of 1965 replaced the ruling in *Williams*.

SIGNIFICANCE

Williams's ruling enabled states to pass voting restrictions preventing many African Americans from voting and sitting on juries, essentially allowing the southern states to discriminate against African Americans, reversing the progress of their freedom and rights.

RELATED CASES

Neal v. State of Delaware, 203 U.S. 370 (1880)

Gibson v. State of Mississippi, 162 U.S. 565 (1896)

Ratliff v. Beale, 74 Miss. 247 (1896)

RECOMMENDED READING

Behrens, Angela, Christopher Uggen, and Jeff Manza. "Ballot Manipulation and the 'Menace of Negro Domination': Racial Threat and Felon Disenfranchisement in the United States, 1850–2002." 109 *American Journal of Sociology* 559 (2003): 559–605.

Case Title: *Cumming v. Richmond County Board of Education*

Legal Citation: 175 U.S. 528

Year of Decision: 1899

KEY ISSUES

Does the maintenance of an exclusively white school that is funded in part by African-American taxpayers constitute a denial to those citizens of the equal protection of the law or equal privileges of citizens of the United States?

HISTORY OF THE CASE

The plaintiffs filed suit against the Richmond County Board of Education when the county levied a $45,000 tax on its citizens for the funding of an all-white school. Plaintiffs asked for relief from the tax. Initially, the superior court ruled that the school board could not use any funds for the maintenance of an all-white school unless an all-"colored" school were established for the county's African-American children. The Supreme Court of Georgia overruled the lower court's decision, however, and the plaintiffs appealed to the U.S. Supreme Court.

SUMMARY OF THE ARGUMENTS

The plaintiffs argued that the county tax levy was illegal since it resulted in benefiting the white population exclusively and was, thus, a violation of the equal protection of the law, which the U.S. Constitution afforded all its citizens.

The Richmond County Board of Education, on the other hand, chose to make their argument on economic grounds, arguing that there were simply not enough funds available to the county for the education of both white and African-American children, though it did not comment on why the school could not be integrated, allowing a portion of both races' children to be educated.

DECISION

In general, the Court chose to bypass the question of whether or not discrimination had occurred, relying instead on technical and procedural arguments for denying the plaintiffs' petition. Nevertheless, the effect, if not the intent, of the Court's decision was heavily discriminatory toward the African-American population.

Justice Harlan argued that the school board faced the choice of educating 60 white children or educating no one. By doing so, the Court sidestepped the issue of segregation since it declined to state why the board could not use the tax levy to educate 30 white children and 30 African-American children or even 60 African-American children.

The Court also deferred to the Georgia state constitution, which stated in relevant part, "Schools shall be free to all children of the state, but separate schools shall be provided for the white and colored race." The Court, however, did not find the statute to be egregious enough to violate the plaintiffs' equal protection. Justice Harlan noted, "Under the circumstances disclosed, we cannot say that this action of the state court was, within the meaning of the Fourteenth Amendment, a denial by the state to the plaintiffs and to those associated with them of the equal protection of the laws . . . of the United States." This suggests that even though the justices may have viewed the tax levy as unfair, it was not egregious enough under the Court's interpretation of the Fourteenth Amendment to constitute a denial of their equal protection rights, and only such a violation, in the Court's view, would warrant its intervention. "The education of the people in schools maintained by state taxation is a matter belonging to the respective states, and any interference on the part of federal authority with the management of such schools cannot be justified except in the case of a clear and unmistakable disregard of rights secured by the supreme law of the land." The Court again sidestepped the issue of segregation by using the Georgia Constitution to settle the issue in part on a state's rights argument. The Court stated that it lacked jurisdiction to enforce the relief the plaintiffs asked for, since the management of the Georgia public schools was entirely within the realm of the state of Georgia. For the preceding reasons, the Court eventually declined to provide the relief that the plaintiffs sought.

AFTERMATH

Cumming was a landmark case in American legal history since the Supreme Court, by refusing to repudiate the Georgia Constitution on the issue of racial segregation in public schools, effectively condoned its use. The *Cumming* decision gave the southern Jim Crow states legal carte blanche in passing laws and statutes designed to separate the two races.

SIGNIFICANCE

Cumming essentially sanctioned de jure segregation in American public schools. It refused to challenge the Georgia Constitution, which provided for the creation of separate schools for African-American and white children. It was not until more than 50 years later, in *Brown vs. Board of Education*, that the Supreme Court ruled that the segregation of public schools was a violation of the equal protection clause of the Fourteenth Amendment of the Constitution, thereby overturning the *Cumming* decision as well as *Plessy v. Ferguson*. In *Brown*, the Court found the doctrine of "separate but equal" (which it established in *Plessy*) a violation of the equal protection clause of the Fourteenth Amendment, since for all practical purposes, the doctrine equated to separate but unequal facilities. As a result of *Cumming*, southern public schools continued to provide lower-quality education to African-American children, a legacy that remained in force for more than half a century.

RELATED CASES

Plessy v. Ferguson, 163 U.S. 537 (1896)

Brown v. Board of Education of Topeka, Kansas, 347 U.S. 483 (1954)

RECOMMENDED READING

Kousser, J. Morgan. *Colorblind Justice.* Chapel Hill: University of North Carolina Press, 1999.

Marshall, Gloria J. *Race, Law, and American Society: 1607 to the Present.* New York: Taylor and Francis Group, 2007.

Case Title: *Guinn and Beal v. United States*

Legal Citations: 238 U.S. 347

Year of Decision: 1915

KEY ISSUE

Does the grandfather clause of the literacy requirement for voting in an amendment in the Oklahoma Constitution violate the Fifteenth Amendment?

HISTORY OF THE CASE

The Oklahoma Constitution added an amendment requiring citizens to pass a literacy test in order to vote. There was, however, an exception to the amendment. The exception was a grandfather clause, which allowed illiterate citizens to vote as long as they or their grandfathers were entitled to vote on January 1, 1866, which was before the approval of the Fifteenth Amendment in 1870. The Fifteenth Amendment guaranteed the right to vote for all male citizens regardless of race. Therefore, the grandfather clause allowed illiterate Caucasians to vote but had the adverse effect of disenfranchisement of African Americans.

The district attorney, John Emory, brought criminal charges against two election officials,

Frank Guinn and J. J. Beal, for preventing African Americans from voting. When President William Howard Taft realized he needed the votes of African Americans for his reelection, the Justice Department started to take the case seriously. Taft lost reelection and Wilson won. The Wilson administration continued with the case. It was argued that the grandfather clause violated the Fifteenth Amendment because it infringed upon the right of African Americans to vote. The case was brought to the Supreme Court to determine the constitutionality of the grandfather clause.

SUMMARY OF ARGUMENTS

Guinn argued that the states have the power to fix standards for suffrage, and the Fifth Amendment did not take away power; power was only limited to the extent of the prohibitions that amendment established.

The United States argued that the provision of the amendment in the Oklahoma Constitution was an open repudiation of the Fifteenth Amendment and, therefore, was not valid. The United States did not contest with Guinn that the state did have the power to fix the standards of suffrage; however, the United States disputed the date of January 1, 1866, which was the voting requirement for the grandfather clause. Because of the date stated in the requirement, on the face of this provision and by result, this recreates the very condition the Fifteenth Amendment was intended to destroy.

DECISION

Justice White delivered the opinion of the Court, which held that the grandfather clause, which was part of an amendment to the Oklahoma Constitution, infringed upon the rights of African Americans to vote. The grandfather clause appeared to be an exception for all illiterate male citizens; however, it only benefited Caucasian males. The date used in the grandfather clause was before African Americans could vote; therefore, the requirements allowed Caucasians to vote and disenfranchised African Americans. The clause discriminated against African Americans and was, therefore, unconstitutional because it violated the Fifteenth Amendment.

AFTERMATH

As a result of the decision in this case, similar grandfather clause provisions were deemed unconstitutional in states including Alabama, Georgia, Louisiana, North Carolina, and Virginia. However, shortly after this decision, Oklahoma found another way to prevent equal voting rights. An election law that gave permanent registration to anyone who had voted in 1914 was passed; this law also granted African Americans a 12-day window to register to vote or face permanent disenfranchisement. Finally, in 1939, the Supreme Court struck down the replacement statutes that were used in the place of the old grandfather clause in Oklahoma.

SIGNIFICANCE

This decision was an important step for African Americans in securing their equal rights to vote. However, this was a short-lived victory in Oklahoma for the voting rights of African Americans.

RELATED CASES

Myers v. Anderson, 28 U.S. 368 (1915)

United States v. Classic, 313 U.S. 299 (1941)

STATUTE AT ISSUE

§ 5508, Revised Statutes of Oklahoma, now § 19 of the Oklahoma Penal Code

RECOMMENDED READING

Valelly, Richard M. *The Two Reconstructions: The Struggle for Black Enfranchisement.* Chicago: University of Chicago Press, 2004.

Case Title: *Buchanan v. Warley*

Legal Citation: 245 U.S. 60

Year of Decision: 1917

KEY ISSUE

Does an ordinance restricting the purchase and sale of property based solely on the race of the proposed occupant(s) violate the Fourteenth Amendment?

HISTORY OF THE CASE

Buchanan, a Caucasian male, sold his house to Warley, an African American. In the contract, there was a provision that stated the contract was only valid if the purchaser could live on the land without violating any laws. There was an ordinance in Louisville, Kentucky, that stated that to maintain public peace, a person of one race could not move into a neighborhood lived in primarily by people of a different race. The house that Buchanan sold was in a neighborhood where eight of 10 residents were Caucasians. Therefore, according to the ordinance, Warley could not live on the property because he was an African American. Buchanan brought a lawsuit against Warley to enforce the contract; however, Warley argued that because of the provision within the contract, the contract was void because he could not legally live on the property.

SUMMARY OF ARGUMENTS

Buchanan argued that the ordinance was unconstitutional because it was a violation of the Fourteenth Amendment. A man has a constitutional right to sell his property and cannot be denied that right solely because of the race of the purchaser.

Warley argued that because of the provision within the contract that stated he must be allowed to occupy the property under the laws of the state of Kentucky, the contract was not valid because of the ordinance affected the property.

DECISION

The Supreme Court held that the ordinance requiring segregation based on race in Louisville was a violation of the Fourteenth Amendment and, therefore, unconstitutional. The Court acknowledged that race hostility was a problem but that depriving citizens of their rights could not resolve the problem. The Court distinguished *Plessy v. Ferguson* by saying that a class of people had to follow certain rules, but the rules did not deny the right of that class to participate in an entitled activity.

Justice Day delivered the opinion of the court, which explained the case in the following terms:

> We think this attempt to prevent the alienation of the property in question to a person of color was not a legitimate exercise of the police power of the state, and is in direct violation of the fundamental law enacted in the Fourteenth Amendment of the Constitution preventing state interference with property rights except by due process of law. That being the case, the ordinance cannot stand.

The Court stated that there may be feelings of race hostility, but they "cannot be promoted by depriving citizens of their constitutional rights and privileges." The Court explained that although segregation may preserve peace, it should not be accomplished by ordinances that deny rights. In addition, the Court stated that African Americans could cause property value to be depreciated, but so could undesirable white neighbors.

AFTERMATH

The decision helped place limits on the segregation of African Americans. It was also shown that protection of property rights could have the effect of protecting civil rights. *Buchanan v. Warley* is seen by many as a case that led to *Brown v. Board of Education* (1954).

SIGNIFICANCE

The Court held that the racial segregation was a violation of the Fourteenth Amendment. The Court acknowledged the problem of race hostility but stated that depriving people of their fundamental rights cannot solve the problem. This decision was the first exception to *Plessy v. Ferguson* (1896). By upholding personal and property rights, this case was seen by many as a precursor to *Brown v. Board of Education*.

RELATED CASES

Plessy v. Ferguson, 163 U.S. 537 (1896)

Corrigan v. Buckley, 271 U.S. 323 (1926)

Brown v. Board of Education of Topeka, Kansas, 347 U.S. 483 (1954)

RECOMMENDED READING

James W. Ely. *Reflections on* Buchanan v. Warley, *Property Rights, and Race,* 51 Vanderbilt Law Review 953 (1998).

Nelson, Arthur C., Casey J. Dawkins, and Thomas W. Sanchez. "Urban Containment and Residential Segregation: A Preliminary Investigation." 41 *Urban Studies* 423 (2004).

Rice, Roger L. "Residential Segregation by Law, 1910–1917." 34 *Journal of Southern History* 179 (1968).

Case Title: *Corrigan v. Buckley*

Legal Citations: 271 U.S. 323

Year of Decision: 1926

KEY ISSUES

Do the Fifth, Thirteenth, and Fourteenth Amendments invalidate racially restrictive covenants in a private contract?

HISTORY OF THE CASE

In 1921, several property owners, including John J. Buckley and Irene H. Corrigan, agreed to a neighborhood covenant that prohibited them from selling their properties to African Americans. The covenant included the following clause:

> In consideration of the premises and the sum of five dollars ($5.00) each to the other in hand paid, the parties hereto do hereby mutually covenant, promise, and agree each to the other, and for their respective heirs and assigns, that no part of the land now owned by the parties hereto, a more detailed description of said prop-

erty, being given after the respective signatures hereto, shall ever be used or occupied by, or sold, conveyed, leased, rented, or given to, negroes, or any person or persons of the negro race or blood. This covenant shall run with the land and bind the respective heirs and assigns of the parties hereto for the period of twenty-one (21) years from and after the date of these presents.

One year after the covenant was executed, Corrigan entered into a contract to sell her property to Helen Curtis, an African American. Both Corrigan and Curtis were aware of the covenant. Each defendant revealed her intent to complete the contract, despite the protests of the other neighborhood property owners.

Buckley brought suit in the Supreme Court for the District of Columbia, seeking an injunction, or an order preventing the sale of the property, against Corrigan and Curtis. Corrigan and Curtis's motion to dismiss the complaint was overruled, and the court granted the injunction. Corrigan and Curtis appealed.

SUMMARY OF ARGUMENTS

Corrigan argued that the covenant was void because it was in violation of the Constitution and because it was contrary to public policy. Curtis argued that the covenant was void, since it attempted to deprive her of property without due process of law, abridged the privileges and immunities clause, and denied the defendants equal protection of the law. Therefore, it violated the Fifth, Thirteenth, and Fourteenth Amendments, as well as the laws enacted to aid those amendments. Additionally, Corrigan and Curtis argued that the decrees of the lower court deprived them of their liberty and property without due process.

Buckley argued that the sale of property would cause irreparable injury to the parties to the covenant, and they were, therefore, entitled to fulfillment of the original contract. Buckley claimed that Corrigan was prohibited from conveying the property to Curtis for the 21-year period.

DECISION

The Court dismissed the case for lack of jurisdiction, as it did not raise a constitutional or statutory claim. Justice Sanford delivered the opinion of the Court.

Corrigan and Curtis based review of this case on the fact that it involved the construction and application of the Constitution, as well as certain federal statutes, including the Civil Rights Act of 1866. However, the mere assertion that the Constitution and laws of the United States were involved was not enough to support jurisdiction. Jurisdiction is wanting if the constitutional assertions are without merit.

The Fifth Amendment did not apply because it limits the power of the general government and is not directed at individuals. The Thirteenth Amendment deals with slavery and does not protect rights in other areas. Finally, the Fourteenth Amendment applies to the actions of the States and not individuals. None of these amendments prohibited private individuals from entering into contracts regarding the disposition of their property.

The statutes referred to by Curtis guaranteed the rights of all citizens to make contracts and acquire property, but they did not invalidate contracts entered into by private citizens in respect to the control of their property.

The appellant's claim that the decree of the court below deprived them of due process does not support jurisdiction since there was a full hearing.

AFTERMATH

This was an important case in the development of fair housing ideals. Essentially, it ruled that judicial enforcement of private contracts was not state action. Later, in *Shelley v. Kraemer* (1948), the Court held that racially biased restrictive covenants were valid among individuals, but the equal protection clause prohibited judicial enforcement.

SIGNIFICANCE

This case upheld the ability of individuals to enter into racially biased contracts, which could not be overturned on Fifth, Thirteenth, or Fourteenth Amendment grounds.

RELATED CASES

Virginia v. Rives, 100 U.S. 313 (1879)

Civil Rights Cases, 109 U.S. 3 (1883)

United States v. Harris, 106 U.S. 629 (1883)

Hodges v. U.S., 203 U.S. 1 (1906)

Shelley v. Kraemer, 334 U.S. 1 (1948)

RECOMMENDED READING

Klarman, Michael J. *From Jim Crow to Civil Rights: The Supreme Court and the Struggle for Racial Equality.* New York: Oxford University Press, 2004.

George Rutherglen, *State Action, Private Action, and the Thirteenth Amendment,* 94 Virginia Law Review 1367 (2008).

Case Title: *Buck v. Bell*

Legal Citation: 274 U.S. 200

Year of Decision: 1927

KEY ISSUES

Does Virginia's sterilization law violate an individual's due process rights under the Fifth and Fourteenth Amendments and the equal protection clause of the Fourteenth Amendment?

HISTORY OF THE CASE

In 1924, Virginia passed a law that allowed for the sterilization of "mental defectives" and "feeble-minded" persons confined to certain state institutions. The law allowed the superintendent of the institution to determine what was in "the best interests of the patients and society." A Virginia state court determined 18-year-old Carrie Buck to be "feeble-minded" under the law, and she was committed to the Virginia State Colony for Epileptics and Feeble-Minded, where she was sentenced to compulsory sterilization.

Buck challenged the Virginia sterilization law in the Circuit Court of Amherst County, Virginia, where the law was upheld and Buck's sterilization order was affirmed. Buck appealed to the Virginia Supreme Court of Appeals, which also affirmed the decision.

SUMMARY OF ARGUMENTS

Buck argued that the due process clause guaranteed all adults the constitutional right to procreate and that the Virginia sterilization law violated this right. Next, Buck argued that the law violated the equal protection clause of the Fourteenth Amendment because it singled out "feeble-minded" patients and only applied to individuals confined to certain state institutions.

J. H. Bell, superintendent of the State Colony for Epileptics and Feeble Minded for the state of Virginia, argued that neither the equal protection clause nor the due process clause was designed to interfere with the police power of the state. This power allows the state to prescribe regulations that promote the health, morals, education, safety, and good order of the people.

DECISION

On May 2, 1927, the Court, in an 8-1 decision, determined that it was in the state's best interest to have Carrie Buck sterilized, thus upholding Virginia's sterilization procedures. Justice Holmes delivered the opinion of the Court. Holmes noted that once Buck was sterilized, she could be released from the institution and become a productive member of society. He thought that the Virginia sterilization law could provide widespread benefits: "It is better for the entire world, if instead of waiting to execute degenerate offspring for crime, or to let them starve for their imbecility, society can prevent those who are manifestly unfit from continuing their kind. The principle that sustains compulsory vaccination is broad enough to cover cutting the Fallopian tubes. . . . Three generations of imbeciles are enough."

With regard to the equal protection claim, Holmes stated that "so far as the [institution's] operations enable those who otherwise must be kept confined to be returned to the world, and thus open the asylum to others, the equality aimed at will be more nearly reached."

Justice Butler was the sole dissent from the decision but did not file an opinion to explain his reasoning.

AFTERMATH

Between 1927 and 1942, sterilization rates under eugenic laws continued to climb. In 1942, the Supreme Court decided *Skinner v. Oklahoma* (1942), which did not directly overturn the ruling in *Buck* but overturned a forced sterilization law on the grounds that "marriage and procreation are fundamental to the very existence and survival of the race." This decision weakened the holding in *Buck* enough that by 1963 sterilization laws were almost completely off the books. Virginia repealed its state sterilization law in 1974.

SIGNIFICANCE

This case determined that Virginia's sterilization laws did not violate the due process or equal protection clauses of the Constitution.

RELATED CASES

Jacobson v. Massachusetts, 197 U.S. 11 (1905)

Skinner v. Oklahoma, 316 U.S. 535 (1942)

STATUTE AT ISSUE

Virginia Sterilization Act, SB 281; an Act to provide for the sexual sterilization of inmates of State institutions in certain cases; approved March 20, 1924

RECOMMENDED READING

American Eugenics Movement Archive. Available online. URL: www.eugenicsarchive.org/eugenics/. Accessed July 10, 2010.

Carlson, Elof Axel. *The Unfit: A History of a Bad Idea.* Cold Spring Harbor, N.Y.: Cold Spring Harbor Laboratory Press, 2001.

Robert J. Cynkar, Buck v. Bell: *"Felt Necessities" v. Fundamental Values?,* 81 Columbia Law Review 1418 (1981).

Duster, Troy. *Backdoor to Eugenics.* New York: Routledge, 2003.

Gould, Stephen Jay. "Carrie Buck's Daughter." 91 *Natural History* (1984).

Paul A. Lombardo, *Three Generations, No Imbeciles: New Light on* Buck v. Bell, 60 New York University Law Review 30 (1995).

Case Title: *Nixon v. Herndon*

Legal Citation: 273 U.S. 536

Year of Decision: 1927

KEY ISSUES

Does a Texas statute forbidding African Americans to vote in primary elections violate the Fourteenth and Fifteenth Amendments?

HISTORY OF THE CASE

In May 1923, Texas passed legislation forbidding African Americans to participate in the Democratic Party's primary election. Dr. L. A. Nixon attempted to vote in the 1924 Democratic primary election but was denied a chance to do so because of his race. Dr. Nixon then filed suit against Herndon and the judges of elections ("Herndon"), seeking an injunction against the statute in a federal district court. The suit was dismissed, and that decision was appealed to the U.S. Supreme Court, which granted certiorari.

SUMMARY OF ARGUMENTS

Dr. Nixon argued that as a member of the Democratic Party, he was qualified to vote in the primary. All that preventing him from voting was the Texas statute at issue in this case, which he argued violated his Fourteenth and Fifteenth Amendment rights.

Herndon argued that Nixon failed to demonstrate any violation of the Constitution because the suit was "purely political" and outside the Court's jurisdiction.

DECISION

The Court found that the Texas legislation discriminated on the basis of race alone and was unconstitutional.

The Court began by first addressing Herndon's argument that the subject matter of the lawsuit was "purely political." This was deemed to be nothing more than wordplay because the Court had previously held that political action could result in recoverable damages. Thus, the Court reasoned, if a person would be entitled to recover for damages if prohibited from voting at the final election, the same rationale holds true for someone denied the right to vote at a primary election.

The Court argued that it was unnecessary to consider the Fifteenth Amendment with regard to the Texas statute because the Court found it "hard to imagine a more direct and obvious infringement of the Fourteenth." The purpose for creating the Fourteenth Amendment was to protect African Americans from discrimination against them and to prohibit states from denying U.S. citizens the equal protection of the law. The Texas statute forbidding African Americans to participate in the Democratic primary elections essentially denied them the right to vote because the winner of the Democratic primary elections so frequently won the final election. The Court found that this law discriminated on the basis of race alone, and thus, it was found to be unconstitutional. Accordingly, the decision of the lower court was reversed, and in conclusion, the Court stated that "states may do a good deal of classifying that it is difficult to believe rational, but there are limits, and it is too clear for extended argument that color cannot be made the basis of a statutory classification affecting the right set up in this case."

AFTERMATH

The state of Texas responded by enacting legislation giving authority to political parties to determine who can vote in their primaries. Nixon would challenge this statute in a later case, *Nixon v. Condon* (1932), in which the U.S. Supreme Court held that the all-white Democratic primary that resulted from the Texas legislation was unconstitutional. The Court found that the executive committee, which possessed the authority to exclude would-be members from the party, was acting under state authority. Thus, state action was found, and the Court applied the principle derived from *Herndon* that prohibits state officials to discriminate invidiously between white and black citizens.

This led the state of Texas to pass legislation that allowed political parties, which they considered to be "private," to enforce a rule requiring all voters in the primary to be white. As a result, the National Association for the Advancement of Colored Persons (NAACP) challenged this rule in *Smith v. Allwright* (1944). In that case, the Court held that the practice violated the Fourteenth and Fifteenth Amendment rights of potential voters and was, thus, unconstitutional. This was the last "white primary" case heard by the Supreme Court of the United States.

SIGNIFICANCE

The *Nixon v. Herndon* case was one of the earliest of a string of cases involving the voting rights of African Americans in the United States, many of which are classified as the "White Primary Cases." In many southern jurisdictions, nonwhite voters were prohibited to vote in primary elections. In *Herndon,* the Court struck down a Texas law that prohibited blacks to vote in the Texas Democratic primary elections.

RELATED CASES

Wiley v. Sinkler, 179 U.S. 58 (1900)

Giles v. Harris, 189 U.S. 475 (1903)

Nixon v. Condon, 286 U.S. 73 (1932)

Smith v. Allwright, 321 U.S. 649 (1944)

Shelley v. Kraemer, 334 U.S. 1 (1948)

Terry v. Adams, 345 U.S. 461 (1953)

STATUTE AT ISSUE

Vernon's Ann. Texas Civ. St. 1925, Article 3107 (law repealed)

RECOMMENDED READING

McKen Carrington, *In Struggle against Jim Crow: Lulu White and the NAACP 1900–1957*, 26 Thurgood Marshall Law Review 107 (2000).

Michael J. Klarman, *The White Primary Rulings: A Case Study in the Consequences of Supreme Court Decisionmaking*, 29 Florida State University Law Review 55 (2001).

Martin L. Levy, *The Texas White Primary Cases*, 33 Thurgood Marshall Law Review 223 (2008).

Case Title: *Grovey v. Townsend*

Legal Citation: 295 U.S. 45

Year of Decision: 1935

KEY ISSUE

Is a decision to bar African Americans from participating in the primary election at the Democratic State Convention constitutional?

HISTORY OF THE CASE

R. R. Grovey, an African American, attempted to obtain an absentee ballot for the Democratic primary election, which was to be held July 28, 1935. The county clerk refused to give him one pursuant to a resolution passed by the state Democratic Convention of Texas that stated only white citizens were eligible to be members of the Democratic Party and participate in deliberations. Grovey sued the clerk of Harris County, Texas, Albert Townsend, for damages of 10 dollars. The Justice Court of Harris County, Texas, sustained Townsend's motion to dismiss the case,

finding that there was insufficient law to support the complaint. Grovey appealed to the Supreme Court.

SUMMARY OF ARGUMENTS

Grovey argued that the primary election was held under statutory compulsion. As such, those charged with its management were denied under statute from placing qualifications on participation on the basis of race because this would be in conflict with the Fourteenth Amendment. Grovey argued that *Nixon v. Herndon* held that a black person has the same right to participate in a primary election as he does in the general election. The Constitution guarantees the right to participate in elections that determine senators and representatives. The Fifteenth Amendment gives the right to vote to African Americans in all elections where white persons have the right to vote. The Democratic State Convention, which passed the resolution, was a creature of a statute and, therefore, an instrument of the state.

Townsend and the state of Texas argued that the qualification was the result of private action and was not in any way a function of state control.

DECISION

Justice Roberts delivered the unanimous opinion of the Court, affirming the decision of the lower court. The Court distinguished *Nixon v. Herndon* (1927) and *Nixon v. Condon* (1932), finding that those cases involved state action. This case, on the other hand, involved representatives of the party voting at their convention and declaring the qualification. Therefore, it was not on its face a state action. While statutory controls were placed on the primaries, they remained a party instrument for nomination to the general election.

This case involved no action by the legislature. The state's highest court had ruled that government could legislate political parties to an extent, but their nature as voluntary associations must be respected. Under that holding, managers of primary elections could not be classified as state actors.

The Court held that Grovey confused the right to membership in a political party with the right to vote. This issue was not one of state action, no matter how the state regulated primaries, but of the will of a voluntary association of persons. Grovey did not show how this particular action of a voluntary association amounted to state action. Therefore, the judgment was affirmed.

AFTERMATH

This case was expressly overruled in *Smith v. Allwright* (1944), which held that primary elections were a state action.

SIGNIFICANCE

This case served to perpetuate discrimination against nonwhite voters on a state level.

RELATED CASES

Nixon v. Herndon, 273 U.S. 536 (1927)

Nixon v. Condon, 286 U.S. 73 (1932)

Smith v. Allwright, 321 U.S. 649 (1944)

RECOMMENDED READING

James D. Barnett, *What Is "State" Action under the Fourteenth, Fifteenth and Nineteenth Amendments of the Constitution?*, 24 Oregon Law Review 227 (1944).

Theodore Y. Blumoff, *Some Moral Implications of Finding No State Action*, 70 Notre Dame Law Review 95 (1994).

Hine, Darlene Clark. *Black Victory: The Rise and Fall of the White Primary in Texas*. Columbia: University of Missouri Press, 2003.

Michael J. Klarman, *The White Primary Rulings: A Case Study in the Consequences of Supreme Court Decision Making*, 29 Florida State University Law Review 55 (2001).

Ryan Siegel, *Why Equal Protection No Longer Protects: The Evolving Forms of Status-Enforcing State Action*, 49 Stanford Law Review 1111 (1997).

Case Title: *Norris v. Alabama*

Legal Citation: 294 U.S. 587

Year of Decision: 1935

KEY ISSUE

Does the exclusion of African Americans from jury service result in a denial of equal protection for the parties involved in the lawsuit?

HISTORY OF THE CASE

In 1931, nine southern African American youths, known as the Scottsboro Boys, were falsely accused of raping a white woman and upon conviction were sentenced to death in Alabama. On appeal, the case eventually led to the U.S. Supreme Court decision in *Powell v. Alabama* (1932), which reversed the convictions and held that defendants in capital trials must be given access to counsel upon request as part of due process. Thus, the Scottsboro Boys were given new trials, and on remand the venue was transferred to another county.

Norris motioned to quash the indictment on the ground that African Americans were excluded from the juries solely on the basis of their race in both the original trial and the new one. The state statute outlined qualifications based on honesty, intelligence, age, and landownership with disqualifiers such as disease, habitual drunkenness, and a conviction for a crime of morale turpitude. The evidence suggested that no African American had ever served on a jury in Jackson County and that at least 30 African Americans were qualified for jury service under the state statute. Both motions were denied, and the petitioner was convicted and sentenced to death. The Supreme Court of Alabama affirmed on the grounds that it was not established that race caused the omission from jury service. On appeal, the U.S. Supreme Court granted certiorari.

SUMMARY OF ARGUMENTS

Norris argued that while the law outlining jury qualifications may be fair on its face, the counties had participated in systematic discrimination against African Americans excluding them from jury service. Norris additionally argued that the names of African Americans were added to the jury rolls, which were introduced as evidence, after the jury was selected, essentially arguing that the documents were fraudulently altered.

Alabama argued that systematic discrimination was not involved. Rather, the state argued, African Americans had not met the extensive requirements for jury service.

DECISION

The Court first addressed whether the established principle that where the state, through the legislature, courts, or executive offices, excluded African Americans, solely on the basis of race, from serving on grand or petit juries violated equal protection. Even if the statute defining qualifications for jury service is fair on its face, the Constitution still offers protection against the action of the state through its administrative offices in effecting prohibited discrimination.

The Court considered the jury commission's testimony stating that no person was excluded on account of race in light of other testimony. It appeared to the Court that African Americans were excluded from jury service without any discussion of their actual qualifications under the state statute. The showing that a number of qualified jurors were excluded from the jury roll as well as the testimony that no African American had served on a jury in recent memory were enough to present a prima facie case. The Court refused to accept the sweeping generalization that no single African American in the county met the qualifications for jury service.

The Court also addressed whether the names of African Americans were, in fact, on the jury roll. Although the roll contained the names of six African Americans, the names had been entered at the end of the document. The Court made the following finding: "It appeared that after the jury roll in question had been made up, and after the new jury commission had taken office, one of the new commissioners directed the new clerk to draw lines after the names which had been placed on the roll by the preceding commission. These

lines, on the pages under consideration, were red lines, and the clerk of the old commission testified that they were not put in by him." The Court concluded that the indictment should have been quashed on the grounds that unconstitutional discrimination had occurred in the jury selection process. Accordingly, the case was reversed and remanded for further proceedings.

AFTERMATH

As mentioned previously, this case and *Powell v. Alabama* involved the Scottsboro Boys. After *Norris* was decided, on remand, five of the nine Scottsboro Boys were again convicted of the incident stemming from the original case. These cases were heavily covered by national media sources and were well documented. Recently, television, literature, and theatrical pieces have involved the Scottsboro Boys.

In recent case law developments, the U.S. Supreme Court has held that a criminal defendant has a right to a jury trial on both the question of guilt or innocence and any fact used to increase the defendant's sentence beyond the statutory limits. All of these determinations must be made by the jury and found beyond a reasonable doubt. This invalidated the practice of many courts that allowed sentencing enhancements based on a preponderance of the evidence standard to be made solely by the judge.

SIGNIFICANCE

The Court found that Alabama had systematically excluded African Americans from the jury roll, resulting in a violation of the Sixth Amendment rights of the defendant. The attorney in the Scottsboro Boys cases was Samuel Leibowitz, who adamantly fought for the defendants. It is interesting to note that during the oral arguments of this case before the Supreme Court, Chief Justice Charles Evans Hughes questioned Leibowitz about whether the jury roll had been fraudulently altered.

Although it is rare for Supreme Court justices to handle evidentiary exhibits, Leibowitz provided the documents along with a magnifying glass, and each justice observed the writing. The names of African-American jury members always appeared at the bottom of an otherwise alphabetical list in a space usually left blank. In the Court's decision in *Norris,* the unanimous Court seemed to agree with Leibowitz that the jury rolls had been fraudulently altered.

RELATED CASES

Virginia v. Rives, 100 U.S. 313 (1879)

Carter v. Texas, 177 U.S. 442 (1900)

Powell v. Alabama, 287 U.S. 45 (1932)

Gideon v. Wainright, 372 U.S. 335 (1963)

Miranda v. Arizona, 384 U.S. 436 (1966)

In re Winship, 387 U.S. 358 (1970)

Apprendi v. New Jersey, 530 U.S. 466 (2000)

Blakely v. Washington, 542 U.S. 296 (2000)

RECOMMENDED READING

Acker, James R. *Scottsboro and Its Legacy: The Cases That Challenged American Legal and Social Justice.* Westport, Conn., and London: Praeger, 2008.

Lonnie T. Brown, Jr., *Racial Discrimination in Jury Selection: Professional Misconduct, Not Legitimate Advocacy,* 22 Review of Litigation 209 (2003).

Michael J. Klarman, *The Racial Origins of Modern Criminal Procedure,* 99 Michigan Law Review 48 (2000).

Douglas O. Linder, *Without Fear or Favor: Judge James Edwin Horton and the Trial of the "Scottsboro Boys,"* 68 UMKC Law Review 549 (2000).

Charles W. Wolfram, *Scottsboro Boys in 1991: The Promise of Adequate Criminal Representation through the Years,* 1 Cornell Journal of Law and Public Policy 61 (1992).

Case Title: *Missouri ex rel. Gaines v. Canada*

Legal Citation: 305 U.S. 337

Year of Decision: 1938

KEY ISSUE

Does a state deny equal protection, in violation of the Fourteenth Amendment, when it requires a black citizen to pursue a legal education in another state, with any necessary funding provided by the home state, because no program within the state will admit black students?

HISTORY OF THE CASE

Lloyd Gaines, a citizen of Missouri, applied to attend the School of Law of the University of Missouri and was refused admission because he was black. Gaines had graduated in 1935 from Lincoln University, Missouri's state-sponsored school for the higher education of blacks. Upon rejection for admission at the University of Missouri, Gaines was directed to a state statute that allowed him to apply for aid from the state superintendent of schools so that he could attend a law school in an adjacent state.

Instead of applying to attend a law school in an adjacent state, Gaines brought an action to compel the curators of the University of Missouri to admit him. The circuit court ruled against him. The Missouri Supreme Court affirmed the circuit court's decision. Gaines then appealed to the U.S. Supreme Court.

SUMMARY OF ARGUMENTS

Gaines argued that forced attendance at a law school in an adjacent state denied him the equal protection privileges of a Missouri citizen who intends to practice law within the state. Gaines specifically noted the privileges of opportunities for the particular study of Missouri law, for the observation of the local courts, and for the prestige of the Missouri law school among the citizens of the state.

The state first argued that a separate state statute gave the curators of Lincoln University the power to organize a law school that would provide a substantially equal opportunity for African Americans to that the University of Missouri gave to students of other races. The state also argued that Gaines's action was unwarranted because, pending the establishment of such a school, the provision for the education of African Americans at schools in adjacent states, with Missouri funding, was sufficient to provide a substantially equal educational opportunity.

DECISION

Chief Justice Hughes wrote the opinion for the Court, in which Justices Brandeis, Stone, Roberts, Cardozo, Black, and Reed joined. The Court held that Missouri was itself to provide for the right to a legal education of its citizens and that its failure to do so within the boundaries of the state violated the Fourteenth Amendment.

The Court responded to Missouri's first argument—that state law provided for the organization of a law school at Lincoln University—by noting that the statute gave the curators of Lincoln University the power to establish a law school "whenever necessary and practicable in their opinion." The Court deemed this power too speculative, especially considering that Gaines had instead been counseled to obtain his legal training outside Missouri at the point of his inquiry. In response to the state's suggestion that the provision for attendance outside Missouri was a temporary condition, the Court remarked that the discretion granted to the curator of Lincoln University created the possibility that the condition could continue indefinitely and thus was insufficient to rectify the violation of Gaines's rights.

With regard to Missouri's provision for legal education outside the state, the Court observed that the U.S. system of federalism required each state to be responsible for the rights of its citizens within its own sphere of authority. The Court held that requiring an African American to attend school elsewhere "may mitigate the inconvenience of the discrimination but cannot serve to validate it." Moreover, the Court noted that evidence of limited demand for such an educational opportunity within the state of Missouri constituted an insufficient basis for the denial of Gaines's personal constitutional right to equal protection.

Justice McReynolds wrote in dissent an opinion that was joined by Justice Butler. Justice McReynolds noted that federal interference with Missouri's public policy in separating the races was not warranted, since Missouri adequately provided for Gaines's right through the option of attendance at an adjacent state law school.

AFTERMATH

Although *Gaines* fits within the "separate but equal" list of equal protection cases, the case began the Supreme Court's examination of the "equality" of separate state-sponsored graduate and professional educational opportunities. Twelve years later, the Court would hold in *Sweatt v. Painter* that separate provisions for legal education were, by themselves, not equal protection and, four years after that, held, in *Brown v. Board of Education,* that supplying separate public education opportunities was inherently unequal protection.

SIGNIFICANCE

The Court ruled that a device used by several states in observance of "Jim Crow" laws was insufficient to provide equal protection to African-American citizens. As a result, *Gaines* represents one of the earliest cases in which the Court upheld an African American's personal constitutional rights as a barrier to the imposition of segregationist policies.

RELATED CASES

Plessy v. Ferguson, 163 U.S. 537 (1896)

Pearson v. Murray, 169 Md. 478, 182 A. 590 (1936)

McLaurin v. Oklahoma State Regents, 339 U.S. 637 (1950)

Sweatt v. Painter, 339 U.S. 629 (1950)

Brown v. Board of Education of Topeka, Kansas, 349 U.S. 294 (1954)

RECOMMENDED READING

Armor, David J. *Forced Justice: School Desegregation and the Law.* New York: Oxford University Press, 1995.

Lusky, Louis. *By What Right?* Charlottesville, Va.: Michie, 1975.

———, *Minority Rights and the Public Interest,* 52 Yale Law Journal 1 (1942).

Case Title: *Lane v. Wilson*

Legal Citation: 307 U.S. 268

Year of Decision: 1939

KEY ISSUE

Do the provisions of the Oklahoma voter registration law of 1916 violate the Fifteenth Amendment by denying qualified citizens the right to vote?

HISTORY OF THE CASE

In 1915, the U.S. Supreme Court struck down discriminatory provisions of the Oklahoma voter registration law *(Guinn v. United States)*. In response, the Oklahoma legislature passed a new voter registration law in 1916. It stated that anyone who voted in the 1914 election (which had illegally excluded blacks) was automatically qualified, but that those who had been excluded in 1914, or had otherwise not voted, had a specified 12-day window in 1916 during which to register. If they failed to do so, they would permanently lose their right to vote.

W. Lane, a black citizen, had been excluded in 1914 and had not registered in 1916. When he attempted to register to vote in 1938, he was denied on the basis of the provision described. He sued in federal district court, claiming discrimination. Both that court and the court of appeals rejected his claim, stating that the law applied to both blacks and whites and was, therefore, not discriminatory.

SUMMARY OF ARGUMENTS

Lane argued that the Oklahoma statute violated his constitutional right to vote.

The county election officials, who included Wilson, argued that the Oklahoma statute was constitutional and that the proper forum for Lane's complaint was the Oklahoma state court system. The election officials also argued that Lane's assumption of the statute's invalidity meant there was no statute under which he could register, and, therefore, no denial of any right existed.

DECISION

Justice Frankfurter delivered the opinion of the Court. He held that the Oklahoma registration system that automatically granted voting rights to many white citizens but gave a narrow window to others, mostly blacks, to register was unconstitutional because it effectively denied black citizens the right to vote, a right guaranteed by the Fifteenth Amendment against all state attempts to deny it. The Court found "the Amendment nullifies sophisticated as well as simple-minded modes of discrimination." The Oklahoma statute gave black citizens too short a time to register to vote, making the law too confined to comply with the Fifteenth Amendment. The Court also found the "grandfather clause" of the 1914 election discriminatory because it covered mainly white voters. The amendment "secures freedom from discrimination on account of race in matters affecting the franchise."

AFTERMATH

The use of litigation to eliminate voting discrimination was difficult and not very effective. While this case was important in helping to ensure voting rights in Oklahoma, overall, each time a statute was overturned, states found a way to enact another law that would make it difficult for blacks to vote. It took Congress's passage of the Voting Rights Act of 1965 to ensure protection.

SIGNIFICANCE

This was one of many cases that chipped away at the attempts by states to disenfranchise black voters. It also was an example of the Court's commitment to rule not only on the language but on the practical effect of a statute when determining constitutionality.

RELATED CASES

Guinn v. United States, 238 U.S. 347 (1915)

Nixon v. Herndon, 273 U.S. 536 (1927)

Smith v. Allbright, 321 U.S. 649 (1944)

RECOMMENDED READING

Scott Gluck, *Congressional Reaction to Judicial Construction of Section 5 of the Voting Rights Act of 1965,* 29 Columbia Journal of Law and Social Problems 337 (1996).

Eric Schnapper, *Perpetuation of Past Discrimination,* 96 Harvard Law Review 828 (1983).

Case Title: *United States v. Classic*

Legal Citation: 313 U.S. 299

Year of Decision: 1941

KEY ISSUE

Does Article I, Sections 2 and 4, of the U.S. Constitution protect a voter's right to have his or her ballot counted in a primary election?

HISTORY OF THE CASE

In 1940, Patrick B. Classic and five of his associates were indicted for interfering with the right to cast ballots in the primary election for the candidate of the voter's choice and the right of candidates to run for offices of Congress, deprivation of privileges and immunities guaranteed by the Constitution by refusal to count votes cast, and alteration and false certification of votes. These violations stemmed from the Democratic primary election of 1940, particularly a seat in the Louisiana House of Representatives, and violated the federal law Conspiracy against Rights and Deprivation of Rights under Color of Law statutes, 18 U.S.C. §§ 51 and 52 (currently 18 U.S.C. §§ 241 and 242).

The District Court for the Eastern District of Louisiana sustained a demurrer in favor of Classic, ruling that sections 51 and 52 were inapplicable to the facts of this case because, relying on the U.S. Supreme Court decision in *United States v. Gradwell* (1917), the right to vote in a primary election was not secured by the Constitution within the meaning of those statutes. Upon appeal from the United States, the U.S. Supreme Court granted certiorari.

SUMMARY OF ARGUMENTS

While the United States argued the applicability of sections 51 and 52, Classic and the defendants argued that the constitutional guarantee of the right to select members of the House of Representatives by popular vote did not extend to the primary election. Classic also argued that section 52 was directed at deprivation of privileges and immunities on account of race and, therefore, did not apply in this case.

DECISION

Justice Stone delivered the opinion of the Court.

The Court began by noting that under Article I, Sections 2 and 4, wide discretion is given to the states in conducting elections for congressional seats. Louisiana chose the primary system as its own method, whereby the number of candidates in the general election is determined by party affiliation and success in the primary election. Under Louisiana law, only those successful in the primary election, those not included in the primary election who file the proper paperwork and those whose names are written into the primary election ballot, may be voted for at the general election. As a practical matter, any candidate could be written onto the ballot. However, the Court found that restrictions on the names of candidates listed imposed a serious restriction on the choice of candidate. Most importantly, the practical operation of the primary was to secure the election of the Democratic nominee at the general election. Therefore, interference with the choice of candidate at the primary was an interference with the choice of candidate at the only stage of the election that had any real significance.

The Court found the right to elect congressional representatives was secured by the Constitution and not one derived from the states. If the right is in any way connected to the states, it is only in as much as the states have authority to regulate elections. However, there remained the question of whether this right extended to primary elections. The Court argued that the right of electors to select congressional office holders should not be diminished by a state's administrative choice to move from a single step to a two-step election. Therefore, Congress has the authority to regulate the primary as well as the general election because the primary election is a necessary step in the choice of candidates and, thus, is an election within the meaning of Article I, Section 4. Furthermore, the "necessary and proper clause," Article I, Section 8, clause 18, gives Congress the power to appropriate legislation to safeguard the right of choice.

Accordingly, the Court's conclusion in *United States v. Mosley*, that conspiracy to prevent the official count of a ballot in a general election was a violation of section 51, applies equally in this case because in both cases the right infringed is one found in the Constitution. The broad and unambiguous language of the statute leaves no room for an interpretation that would exclude primary elections from its cover. The Court rejected the defendant's argument that section 52 applied only to deprivation of privileges and immunities when race was a factor. The Court read the language to conclude that the racial element applied only when there was a difference in punishment on account of race. The decision of the District Court was reversed.

Justice Douglas, joined by Justices Black and Murphy, dissented. The dissenters did not disagree with the sentiment that Article I, Section 4, would give Congress the power to regulate primaries, but there had been no express legislative exercise of that authority. The dissent also argued that there is no common law offense against the United States and that where civil liberties are deprived through the use of criminal sanction, the crime must be clearly spelled out and not implied. Thus, the right guaranteed by the Constitution and enforced through the criminal sanctions in sections 51 and 52 must be clear, and that is not the case here.

The dissenters further argued that the fact that primaries were hardly known when sections 51 and 52 were enacted, that the statutes were part of a legislative program governing general and not primary elections, and the fact that Congress has not specifically extended sections 51 and 52 to primary elections suggested that this was an improper extension of constitutional jurisdiction. Furthermore, prior precedent supported the notion that sections 51 and 52 do not apply to primary elections. In the absence of specific legislation, the assumption should be that Congress left control of primary elections to the states. The dissenters added that even more telling is the explicit refusal of Congress to legislate primary elections when it rejected a provision in the Hatch Act that would have extended the prohibition on voter intimidation to primary elections.

AFTERMATH

The right to a free choice of candidates was held to be a fundamental right of American people. The Court held that breaking down the elections into a two-part process by utilizing primary and popular elections would not be allowed to interfere with this fundamental right. However, the holding in this case is limited to states in which one political party has a stronghold on the political process, such as the facts in *Classic,* in which the winner of the Democratic primary had a 40-year history of prevailing candidates. Essentially, it applies when the winner of the primary tends to win the general election so often that the primary equates to the general election. However, the holding in *Classic* does not apply to special elections.

SIGNIFICANCE

This case was a further development of the decision in *Newberry v. United States* (1921). There, in a divided Court, four justices held that a primary election was not within the Article I, Section 4 jurisdiction, while a fifth justice concluded that a primary held under a law enacted prior to the Seventeenth Amendment was not a Section 4 election. The remaining four justices held that a primary for either a Senate or House of Representatives seat was a Section 4 election. The Court's decision in *Classic* made clear that at least some primary elections, such as the ones at issue in that case, would be deemed elections under the Constitution.

RELATED CASES

United States v. Gradwell, 243 U.S. 476 (1917)

Newberry v. United States, 256 U.S. 232 (1921)

Smith v. Allwright, 321 U.S. 649 (1944)

Terry v. Adams, 345 U.S. 461 (1953)

STATUTES AT ISSUE

United States Constitution, Article I, § § 2, and 4

RECOMMENDED READING

David M. Bixby, *The Roosevelt Court, Democratic Ideology, and Minority Rights: Another Look at* United States v. Classic, 90 Yale Law Journal 741 (1981).

Tiffany R. Jones, *Note: Re-Privatizing American Political Parties: From Private Groups to State Agencies and Back Again?,* 15 Journal of Law & Politics 221 (1999).

Case Title: *Skinner v. State of Oklahoma ex rel. Williamson, Atty. Gen. of Oklahoma*

Legal Citation: 316 U.S. 535

Year of Decision: 1942

KEY ISSUE

Does a state statute that provides for discretionary sterilization of repeat criminal offenders violate the Constitution's guarantees of equal protection and due process?

HISTORY OF THE CASE

Skinner was convicted of stealing chickens and sentenced to time in an Oklahoma reformatory. Three years later, he was convicted of robbery with a firearm and again sentenced to time in an Oklahoma reformatory. Five years later, he was again convicted of robbery with a firearm and again sentenced to time in a reformatory. A year later, the Oklahoma legislature passed a law that allowed for proceedings to be brought by the state attorney general for sterilization of habitual criminals involved in crimes of moral turpitude.

The purpose of the statute was to eradicate an undesirable genetic propensity for criminal activity. While Skinner was incarcerated for his third conviction, the attorney general brought proceedings to have him sterilized as a habitual offender. A judgment was entered, directing that a vasectomy be performed on Skinner. The judgment was affirmed by the Oklahoma Supreme Court. The U.S. Supreme Court agreed to hear the case after the Oklahoma Supreme Court decision.

SUMMARY OF ARGUMENTS

Skinner challenged the procedure as cruel and unusual punishment, a violation of his right to due process, and a denial of equal protection of the law. Since the statute did not provide the defendant (petitioner) an opportunity to be heard whether he was the potential parent of socially undesirable offspring, he argued that it could not afford him the due process and equal protection that the Constitution requires.

Oklahoma argued that the statute was an appropriate use of the police power traditionally reserved for the states. The state contended that all due process requirements were in effect under the statute and that the discretionary proceedings were constitutionally permissible because state legislatures have the right to recognize "degrees of evil."

DECISION

Justice Douglas wrote the majority opinion that the Oklahoma sterilization statute constituted a denial of equal protection. His opinion quickly dismissed Skinner's other arguments concerning cruel and unusual punishment and due process. The Court found that under the statute, some offenses of equal magnitude and otherwise identical punishments were omitted from the statute. For example, a criminal convicted of embezzling three times would not be sterilized, whereas a criminal convicted of larceny three times could be sterilized. The Court concluded that such an inconsistency in the operation of the law constituted a denial of equal protection and reversed the decision of the Oklahoma Supreme Court.

AFTERMATH

No state has attempted to provide for involuntary sterilization of criminals since the decision. Recent developments in Texas and California concerning voluntary chemical castration, however, raise issues very similar to those presented in *Skinner.*

SIGNIFICANCE

The decision in *Skinner v. State of Oklahoma ex rel. Williamson* made involuntary sterilization of criminals illegal. In recent years, however, states have begun to develop measures for criminals who wish to terminate their reproductive capabilities voluntarily. The Supreme Court has not decided a case on this new alternative sentencing concept. Should the opportunity arise, it may look to *Skinner* for answers.

RELATED CASES

State v. Feilen, 126 P. 75 (1912)

Buck v. Bell, 274 U.S. 200 (1977)

Zablocki v. Redhail, 434 U.S. 374 (1978)

Stump v. Sparkman, 435 U.S. 349 (1978)

RECOMMENDED READING

Blank, Robert, and Janna C. Merrick. *Human Reproduction, Emerging Technology and Conflicting Rights.* Washington, D.C.: Congressional Quarterly Press, 1995.

Bork, Robert H. *The Tempting of America: The Political Seduction of the Law.* New York: Free Press, 1990.

Nourse, Victoria F. *In Reckless Hands:* Skinner v. Oklahoma *and the Near-Triumph of American Eugenics.* New York: Norton, 2008.

Stacy Russell, *Castration of Repeat Sexual Offenders: An International Comparative Analysis,* 19 Houston Journal of International Law 425 (1997).

Elizabeth S. Scott, *Sterilization of Mentally Retarded Persons: Reproductive Rights and Family Privacy,* 1986 Duke Law Journal 806.

Case Title: *Hirabayashi v. United States*

Legal Citation: 320 U.S. 81

Year of Decision: 1943

KEY ISSUE

Does an order that places restrictions on all persons of Japanese ancestry violate the Fifth Amendment of the U.S. Constitution because the restrictions discriminate against only citizens of Japanese ancestry?

HISTORY OF THE CASE

After the Japanese attack on Pearl Harbor in December 1941, Congress declared war against Japan. During the war, President Franklin D. Roosevelt signed Executive Order No. 9066, which empowered the secretary of war to create "military areas," from which civilians could be excluded. General DeWitt imposed an 8:00 P.M.– 6:00 A.M. curfew for Japanese Americans and required all Japanese Americans to report to the Civil Control Station to be evacuated from the military area. Gordon Hirabayashi was a student at the University of Washington. He was born in Seattle in 1918 of Japanese parents, who immigrated to the United States from Japan and had never gone back. Hirabayashi had never been to Japan and had never had any association with Japanese residing there.

Hirabayashi was indicted on two counts. He failed to report to the Civil Control Station within the designated area, and the evidence showed that Hirabayashi broke curfew, because he was away from his place of residence after 8:00 P.M. on May 9, 1942. He admitted that he did not follow the order; however, he thought that he would waive his rights as an American citizen by doing so. The jury returned a verdict of guilty on both counts, and Hirabayashi was sentenced to three months of imprisonment for each offense, sentences to run concurrently.

SUMMARY OF ARGUMENTS

Hirabayashi argued that Congress unconstitutionally delegated its legislative power to the military commander by authorizing him to impose the regulation. He also argued that the Fifth Amendment prohibits the discrimination between citizens of Japanese descent and those of other ancestry.

The prosecutor argued that the curfew and evacuation were authorized by the Act of March 21, 1942. It was also argued that the Act of March 21, 1942, was a valid exercise of war powers and was constitutional.

DECISION

Chief Justice Stone delivered the opinion of the Court and held "that it was within the constitutional power of congress and the executive arm of the Government to prescribe this curfew order for the period under consideration and that its promulgation by the military commander involved no unlawful delegation of legislative power."

The Court explained that racial discrimination in most circumstances must be prohibited, but Congress and the executive must be able to take the relevant information into account for relevant measures of national security. The Court stated, "We cannot close our eyes to the fact, demonstrated by experience, that in time of war residents having ethnic affiliations with an invading enemy may be a greater source of danger than those of a different ancestry." Therefore, the curfew was within the boundaries of the war power. The Court explained that "the danger of espionage and sabotage to our military resources was imminent, and that the curfew order was an appropriate measure to meet it." It was determined that the second count was constitutional, and the Court found that the second count did not need to be reviewed because they ran concurrently. Therefore, Hirabayashi's conviction was affirmed.

AFTERMATH

In 1983, Hirabayashi's lawyer, along with three other men, filed petitions asking the judge to vacate the convictions. In 1986 and 1987, the U.S. District Court of Seattle and the Federal Court of Appeals overturned both of Hirabayashi's convictions. This was the first time that convictions held by the Supreme Court had been challenged in this way. The petition was called a writ of *error coram nobis,* which meant that they were asking the original trial court to correct an error and an injustice that occurred at the original trial. Through this process, the first count was vacated, and the second count was vacated shortly after.

SIGNIFICANCE

The Court determined that the implementation of the curfew on Japanese Americans was constitutional. It was held that it was acceptable to discriminate against certain ancestries during a time of war for the sake of national security. This was applied to all people of Japanese ancestry, whether they were born in the United States or in Japan.

RELATED CASES

Takao Ozawa v. United States, 260 U.S. 178 (1922)

Minoru Yasui v. United States, 320 U.S. 115 (1943)

Toyosaburo Korematsu v. United States, 319 U.S. 432 (1943)

Korematsu v. United States, 323 U.S. 214 (1944)

Adarand Constructors, Inc. v. Pena, 500 U.S. 200 (1995)

STATUTES AT ISSUE

Order No. 9066. 7 Federal Register 1407

Public Proclamation No. 3. 7 Federal Register 2543

Civilian Exclusion Order No. 57 of May 10, 1942. 7 Federal Register 3725

RECOMMENDED READING

Jonathan Justl, *Disastrously Misunderstood: Judicial Deference in the Japanese-American Cases,* 119 Yale Law Journal 270 (2009).

David Wolitz, *The Stigma of Conviction: Coram Nobis, Civil Disabilities, and the Right to Clear One's Name,* 2009 Brigham Young University Law Review 1277 (2009).

Case Title: *Korematsu v. United States*

Alternate Case Title: The Japanese Exclusion Case

Legal Citation: 323 U.S. 214

Year of Decision: 1944

KEY ISSUE

Can the dangers of war justify excluding people from their homes during wartime on the basis of race?

HISTORY OF THE CASE

On December 7, 1941, Japan bombed Pearl Harbor, which caused the United States to enter World War II. On February 19, 1942, President Franklin Roosevelt issued Executive Order No. 9066, designed to prevent espionage and sabotage aimed at American defense installations. The executive order provided that military commanders might, in their discretion, "prescribe military areas" and define their extent, "from which any or all persons may be excluded, and with respect to which the right of any person to enter, remain in, or leave shall be subject to whatever restrictions" the "Military Commander may impose in his discretion."

Lt. Gen. John DeWitt was designated as the military commander of the Western Defense Command on February 20, 1942. In his capacity as military commander, Lieutenant General DeWitt issued a series of public proclamations. Public Proclamation No. 1, issued on March 2, 1942, stated that the entire Pacific Coast was "particularly subject to attack, to attempted invasion . . . and, in connection therewith, is subject to espionage and acts of sabotage." Proclamations that followed included establishment of Military Areas Nos. 1 and 2, which encompassed all of California, Washington, Oregon, Idaho, Montana, Nevada, and Utah and part of Arizona.

Later that month, on March 18, President Roosevelt issued Executive Order No. 9102, establishing the War Relocation Authority. On March 21, 1942, Congress passed a law making it a misdemeanor for anyone to "enter, remain in, leave, or commit any act in any military area or military zone proscribed . . . by any military commander . . . contrary to the restrictions applicable to any such area." On March 24, Lieutenant General DeWitt instituted a curfew in the military areas. Three days later, the general proclaimed that it was necessary "to provide for the welfare and to insure the orderly evacuation and resettlement of Japanese." A March 29 order prohibited "all alien Japanese and persons of Japanese ancestry" to leave Military Area No. 1 until otherwise directed. General DeWitt directed otherwise on May 3, excluding those of Japanese ancestry from part of Military Area No. 1.

Fred Korematsu was an American citizen of Japanese ancestry. He had lived in Alameda County, California, his entire life. Soon after the Japanese bombed Pearl Harbor, Mr. Korematsu volunteered for military service but was rejected for health reasons. When the relocation orders were issued, Mr. Korematsu chose not to leave his home. On June 12, he was arrested, then tried and convicted for violating the exclusion order. A federal court sentenced him to five years imprisonment but immediately paroled him. Mr. Korematsu was taken to an assembly center, and then to an internment camp in Topaz, Utah.

SUMMARY OF ARGUMENTS

Mr. Korematsu appealed his conviction. He argued that the exclusion order violated his constitutional rights by discriminating against him and other Japanese Americans on the basis of their race. He argued that while the courts, in an earlier case, had upheld the constitutionality of a curfew order imposed only on Japanese Americans, excluding citizens from their homes was a much more drastic measure that could not be justified on the same grounds as a mere curfew. Additionally, he urged the Court to consider the entire military program directed at Japanese Americans, because as a practical matter, the program as a whole planned for the relocation of all Japanese Americans to concentration camps.

The U.S. government argued that Mr. Korematsu had been convicted only for remaining in the area contrary to the exclusion order, and that the Court, therefore, should not consider any other aspects of the military's program. Additionally, the United States argued that the exclusion order was justified because of the potential of an imminent Japanese invasion and the inability of the government to separate loyal Japanese Americans from potential saboteurs. The Ninth Circuit Court of Appeals rejected Mr. Korematsu's arguments and affirmed his conviction. Mr. Korematsu sought relief from the U.S. Supreme Court.

DECISION

The Supreme Court, in an opinion written by Justice Hugo L. Black, upheld the constitutionality of the exclusion order "in the light of the principles . . . announced in the *Hirabayashi* case," 323 U.S. at 217, in which the Court had upheld the constitutionality of a curfew order imposed on Japanese Americans. The Court rejected Mr. Korematsu's argument that the rationale of *Hirabayashi* did not apply because to exclude a person from one's home was a much greater deprivation of liberty than a simple curfew:

> True, exclusion from the area in which one's home is located is a far greater deprivation than constant confinement to the home from 8 P.M. to 6 A.M. Nothing short of apprehension by the proper military authorities of the gravest imminent danger to the public safety can constitutionally justify either. But exclusion from a threatened area, no less than curfew, has a definite and close relationship to the prevention of espionage and sabotage.

The perceived possibility of a Japanese invasion of the West Coast was enough for the Court's majority to justify ordering American citizens to abandon their homes and surrender to military authorities.

Similarly, the Court believed that Japanese Americans alone could be singled out as a group by the exclusion order: "Like curfew, exclusion of those of Japanese origin was deemed necessary because of the presence of an unascertained number of disloyal members of the group, most of whom we have no doubt were loyal to this country." Unfortunately for Fred Korematsu and the other American citizens of Japanese descent, the "war-making branches of the Government" believed that what disloyal Japanese Americans there were "could not readily be isolated and separately dealt with." Justice Black and his fellow justices in the majority refused to question this belief.

The Court also refused to consider the exclusion order together with the order that Japanese Americans were to report to assembly or relocation centers, and then be sent to internment camps. To do so "would be to go beyond the issues raised." The Court claimed that they could not "say either as a matter of fact or law that his presence in that center would have resulted in his detention in a relocation center." This was a separate issue that the Court deemed to be beyond the scope of Mr. Korematsu's conviction.

Justice Black ended his opinion defensively, responding to attacks by the dissenting justices. On behalf of the Court's majority, he claimed that this was "military urgency," and "to cast this case into outlines of racial prejudice, without reference to the real military dangers which were presented, merely confuses the issue." The Court also was unhappy with the dissenting justices' charges as to the nature of the assembly and relocation centers: "We deem it unjustifiable to call them concentration camps with all the ugly connotations that term implies."

Justice Felix Frankfurter concurred, emphasizing the military nature of the exclusion order. He added, "The war power of the Government is 'the power to wage war successfully.' That action is not to be stigmatized as lawless because like action in times of peace would be lawless." Justice Frankfurter ended by noting that "to find that the Constitution does not forbid the military measure now complained of does not carry with it approval of that which Congress and the Executive did. This is their business, not ours."

Three Supreme Court justices spoke out against forced removal of groups of American citizens from their homes. The first of these, Justice Owen J. Roberts, did not mince words:

This is not a case of keeping people off the streets at night as was *Kiyoshi Hirabayashi v. United States,* . . . nor a case of temporary exclusion of a citizen from an area for his own safety or that of the community, nor a case of offering him an opportunity to go temporarily out of an area where his presence might cause danger to himself or to his fellows. On the contrary, it is the case of convicting a citizen as a punishment for not submitting to imprisonment in a concentration camp, based on his ancestry, and solely because of his ancestry, without evidence or inquiry concerning his loyalty and good disposition towards the United States. If this be a correct statement of the facts disclosed by this record, and facts of which we take judicial notice, I need hardly labor the conclusion that Constitutional rights have been violated.

Justice Roberts expressed similar contempt for the Court's refusal to confront the conflicting orders to which Mr. Korematsu was subjected:

The two conflicting orders, one which commanded him to stay and the other which commanded him to go, were nothing but a cleverly devised trap to accomplish the real purpose of the military authority, which was to lock him up in a concentration camp. . . . Why should we set up a figmentary and artificial situation instead of addressing ourselves to the actualities of the case?

The second dissenter, Justice Frank Murphy, agreed with the Court's majority that the test for determining the constitutionality of military

action was "whether the deprivation is reasonably related to a public danger that is so 'immediate, imminent, and impending' as not to admit of delay and not to permit the intervention of ordinary constitutional processes to alleviate the danger." Justice Murphy did not believe, however, that the threat posed by Japanese Americans was sufficient to support "one of the most sweeping and complete deprivations of constitutional rights in the history of this nation in the absence of martial law." Justice Murphy recognized the need to allow the military to protect the country in time of war: "We must not erect too high or too meticulous standards; it is necessary only that the action have some reasonable relation to the removal of the dangers of invasion, sabotage and espionage." The exclusion, however, was inherently not reasonably related to national security demands. "That relation is lacking because the exclusion order necessarily must rely for its reasonableness upon the assumption that *all* persons of Japanese ancestry may have dangerous tendency to commit sabotage and espionage and to aid our Japanese enemy in other ways. It is difficult to believe that reason, logic or experience could be marshalled in support of such an assumption."

Justice Murphy thought that the exclusion order was based not on military dangers but on racial prejudices. He cited as evidence of this language used by General DeWitt in reports on the exclusion. For example, General DeWitt had referred to Japanese Americans as "'an enemy race' whose 'racial strains are undiluted.'" Justice Murphy thus viewed the general's supposed rationale "to be largely an accumulation of much of the misinformation, half-truths and insinuations that for years have been directed against Japanese Americans by people with racial and economic prejudices." Murphy concluded bluntly: "I dissent, therefore, from this legalization of racism. Racial discrimination in any form and in any degree has no justifiable part whatever in our democratic way of life."

The third dissenter, Justice Robert H. Jackson, argued that the military order of General DeWitt "ha[d] no place under the Constitution." However, while the exclusion order should not be required to "conform to conventional tests of constitutionality," neither should courts of law be required to enforce military expedients.

Justice Jackson began by focusing on the crime for which Mr. Korematsu was convicted and its tension with the U.S. Constitution. Mr. Korematsu was convicted of "being present in the state whereof he is a citizen, near the place where he was born, and where all his life he has lived." Jackson emphasized the arbitrary nature of the exclusion order's application: "Here is an attempt to make an otherwise innocent act a crime merely because this prisoner is the son of parents as to whom he had no choice, and belongs to a race from which there is no way to resign." He noted that the order was contrary to the important constitutional principle that guilt is personal and not inheritable because Mr. Korematsu's act was made criminal on the basis of the status of his parents.

Jackson, too, recognized that it was more important that military operations "be successful, rather than legal." Wartime measures cannot be made to fit peacetime notions of constitutionality: "Defense measures will not, and often should not, be held within the limits that bind civil authority in peace." Still, Justice Jackson would not "distort the Constitution to approve all that the military may deem expedient." He felt that the judiciary had no way by which to judge the constitutionality of the exclusion order:

> How does the Court know that these orders have a reasonable basis in necessity? No evidence whatsoever on that subject has been taken by this or any other court. . . . So the Court, having no real evidence before it, has no choice but to accept General DeWitt's own unsworn, self-serving statement, untested by any cross-examination, that what he did was reasonable. And thus it will always be when courts try to look into the reasonableness of a military order.

In Justice Jackson's eyes, courts, with their rules of evidence and procedure, were ill equipped to review military decisions such as the exclusion order. Additionally, purporting to test the consti-

tutionality of a military order could potentially be more harmful than the order itself:

> Once a judicial opinion rationalizes such an order to show that it conforms to the Constitution, or rather rationalizes the Constitution to show that the Constitution sanctions such an order, the Court for all time has validated the principle of racial discrimination in criminal procedure and of transplanting American citizens.

Thus, while Justice Jackson conceded that the military might reasonably execute an exclusion order, the courts could not be asked to enforce a military order that was unconstitutional: "The courts can exercise only the judicial power, can apply only law, and must abide by the Constitution, or they cease to be civil courts and become instruments of military policy." Because the exclusion order "ha[d] no place in law under the Constitution," Justice Jackson would have reversed Mr. Korematsu's conviction and ordered him released.

AFTERMATH

Fred Korematsu had to wait 40 years for justice. In January 1983, his case was reopened in federal district court in San Francisco. His conviction was overturned that November. In 1988, Congress passed legislation to help all victims of the internment program. Those interned were to be paid $20,000 each. *See Restitution for World War II Internment of Japanese-Americans and Aleuts,* Pub. L. 100–383, August 10, 1988, 50 U.S.C. App. 1989b–4.

SIGNIFICANCE

Ironically, *Korematsu v. United States* was the first case in which the Supreme Court used the "strict scrutiny" test to review a law that classified people on the basis of race. Since *Korematsu,* "strict scrutiny" review has afforded racial minorities significantly more protection than it did Fred Korematsu in 1944.

RELATED CASES

Hirabayashi v. United States, 320 U.S. 81 (1943)

Yasui v. United States, 320 U.S. 115 (1943)

Ex parte Endo, 323 U.S. 283 (1944)

RECOMMENDED READING

Daniels, Roger. *Concentration Camps USA: Japanese Americans and World War II.* New York: Holt, Rinehart, 1971.

Gold, Susan Dudley. *Korematsu v. United States: Japanese-American Internment.* New York: Benchmark Books, 2006.

Grodzins, Morton. *Americans Betrayed: Politics and the Japanese Evacuation.* Chicago: University of Chicago Press, 1949.

Irons, Peter, ed. *Justice Delayed: The Record of the Japanese American Internment Cases.* New York: Oxford University Press, 1989.

"Korematsu v. United States (1944)." Landmark Supreme Court Cases. Available online. URL: http://www.landmarkcases.org/korematsu/home.html. Accessed July 10, 2009.

Okihiro, Gary Y. *Whispered Silences: Japanese Americans and World War II.* Seattle: University of Washington Press, 1996.

Susan Kiyomi Serrano and Dale Minami, Korematsu v. United States: *A Constant Caution in a Time of Crisis,* 10 Asian Law Journal 37 (2003).

Smith, Page. *Democracy on Trial: The Japanese American Evacuation and Relocation in World War II.* New York: Simon & Schuster, 1995.

Tateishi, John. *And Justice for All: An Oral History of the Japanese America Detention Camps.* New York: Random House, 1984.

Case Title: *Smith v. Allwright*

Alternate Case Title: The White Primary Case

Legal Citation: 321 U.S. 649

Year of Decision: 1944

KEY ISSUES

Does a private political party's exclusion of citizens from the right to vote in a primary election because of their skin color violate the Fifteenth and Fourteenth Amendments?

HISTORY OF THE CASE

This case came before the Supreme Court from the Fifth Circuit Court of Appeals to review a claim for damages brought by a black citizen of Houston, Texas. The citizen claimed that he was refused a ballot in a primary election for the nomination of Democratic Party candidates to the U.S. House and Senate, governor of Texas, and other state officers. The refusal was based solely on the skin color of the proposed voter pursuant to a resolution adopted at a Democratic convention.

SUMMARY OF ARGUMENTS

Lonnie E. Smith argued that, by denying him the right to vote in the Democratic primary elections, the Democratic Party of Texas violated U.S.C. §§ 31 and 43 and deprived him of rights secured by Sections 2 and 4 of Article I and the Fourteenth, Fifteenth, and Seventeenth Amendments to the U.S. Constitution.

DECISION

Justice Reed wrote the opinion for the Court. He stated that the resolution of the Democratic Party of Texas is invalid because "the Fourteenth Amendment forbids a state from making or enforcing any law which abridges the privileges or immunities of citizens of the United States and the Fifteenth Amendment specifically interdicts any denial or abridgement by a state of the right of citizens to vote on account of color." The Court found that the running of primaries is a governmental function, even when the task is delegated by the state to a private political party. Thus, in this case, the Democratic Party was a "state actor" for purposes of the Fourteenth and Fifteenth Amendments.

Justice Reed cast a critical light on the discriminatory actions of the Democratic Party of Texas:

> The United States is a constitutional democracy. Its organic law grants to all citizens a right to participate in the choice of elected officials without restriction by any state because of race. This grant to the people of the opportunity for choice is not to be nullified by a state through casting its electoral process in a form which permits a private organization to practice racial discrimination in the election. Constitutional rights would be of little value if they could be thus indirectly denied.

Justice Roberts wrote the Court's dissenting opinion. He was concerned that overruling *Grovey v. Townsend*, a case upholding a rule barring blacks from the Texas Democratic primary, would start a trend of "good for this day and train only."

AFTERMATH

Black voter registration increased in the 1940s but stalled in the 1950s as states used other disenfranchising techniques, such as poll taxes and literacy tests.

SIGNIFICANCE

While the case may have ended "whites only" primaries, the number of black voters did not significantly increase as states scrambled to invent new ideas to prevent black citizens from voting. Five years after the decision, 80 percent of eligible black voters remained unregistered.

RELATED CASES

Nixon v. Herndon, 273 U.S. 536 (1927)

Grovey v. Townsend, 295 U.S. 45 (1935)

Terry v. Adams, 345 U.S. 461 (1953)

RECOMMENDED READING

Elliott, Ward E. Y. *The Rise of Guardian Democracy.* Cambridge, Mass.: Harvard University Press, 1974.

Schwartz, Bernard. *Civil Rights.* Statutory History of the United States. New York: Chelsea House, 1970.

Case Title: *Colegrove v. Green*

Alternate Case Title: The "Political Thicket" Case

Legal Citation: 328 U.S. 549

Year of Decision: 1946

KEY ISSUE

Can the courts, through judicial decisions, reapportion state legislative districts?

HISTORY OF THE CASE

Illinois had an apportionment plan that contained an unequal distribution of population among voting districts. It had not changed the boundaries of congressional districts in the state since 1901, and great discrepancies existed among the districts. Three voters brought suit for a decree declaring Illinois law governing congressional districts invalid. They wanted to compel a reapportionment under the guarantee clause regarding a state's apportionment of voters for seats in the federal House of Representatives. The district court dismissed the suit and the voters appealed.

SUMMARY OF ARGUMENTS

Plaintiffs claimed that the districts lacked approximate equality of population and were not spatially proportionate and, therefore, violated Article I and the Fourteenth Amendment of the U.S. Constitution. They also argued that the reduction in the effectiveness of their vote was the result of willful legislative discrimination against them and, therefore, amounted to a denial of the equal protection of the laws guaranteed by the Fourteenth Amendment.

DECISION

Justice Frankfurter wrote the opinion for the Court holding that reapportionment and voting dilution were political questions and, therefore, not justiciable. He declared that a suit to compel a reapportionment presented a political question and warned against involving the judiciary in the politics of the people. He also stated that the Court could not itself redistrict the state and that "it is hostile to a democratic system to involve the judiciary in the politics of the people. . . . Courts ought not to enter this political thicket." He believed that reapportioning and redistricting were the exclusive domain of the legislative branch of government.

Justice Rutledge wrote a concurring opinion stating the issue more bluntly: "There is not, and could not be except abstractly, a right of absolute equality in voting." He believed that the right to equal voting was not an absolute right and that trying to remedy it might have rendered worse results than the unequal voting itself. Justice Jackson took no part in the consideration or decision of the case.

Justice Black wrote a dissenting opinion stating that the district court had jurisdiction and that the complaint presented a justiciable case and controversy, since the facts as alleged by petitioners showed that they had been injured as individuals. He also believed that there was no adequate remedy at law for depriving them of their right to vote and thus the Court could have and should have granted relief. He believed that since no supervision over the elections was asked for, the Court could have declared the state apportionment bill invalid and enjoined state officials from enforcing it.

AFTERMATH

Until *Baker v. Carr* (1962), in which the Court rejected the rule of *Colegrove* and held that the judiciary was competent to decide issues of malapportionment, it was widely believed that even gross disparities in the populations of the legislative districts did not present justiciable controversies. The Court squarely overturned *Colegrove* in *Wesberry v. Sanders* (1964), holding that challenges to congressional apportionment plans were justiciable and that such plans must be consistent with the principle of one person, one vote.

SIGNIFICANCE

Colegrove was the first important apportionment decision in which there was a one man–one vote constitutional challenge. It showed the Court's reluctance to enter into disputes over redistricting and reapportionment, since it refused to adjudicate the constitutional claim.

RELATED CASES

Gomillion v. Lightfoot, 364 U.S. 339 (1960)

Baker v. Carr, 369 U.S. 186 (1962)

Wesberry v. Sanders, 376 U.S. 1 (1964)

Reynolds v. Sims, 377 U.S. 533 (1964)

RECOMMENDED READING

Larry Alexander, *Lost in the Political Thicket,* 41 Florida Law Review 563 (1989).

Bork, Robert H. *The Tempting of America: The Political Seduction of the Law.* New York: Free Press, 1990.

Hanson, Royce. *The Political Thicket.* Englewood Cliffs, N.J.: Prentice Hall, 1966.

Case Title: *Shelley v. Kraemer*

Legal Citation: 334 U.S. 1

Year of Decision: 1948

KEY ISSUE

Does the Fourteenth Amendment equal protection clause prohibit judicial enforcement by state courts of restrictive covenants based on race or color?

HISTORY OF THE CASE

J. D. Shelley, a black person, bought property without knowledge that it was encumbered by a restrictive agreement at the time of purchase. The covenant stated that "no part of this property shall be occupied by any person not of the Caucasian race." Shelley brought an action in state court. The court held that the covenant never became final because it was not signed by all the owners. The state supreme court reversed, holding that the agreement was effective and violated none of Shelley's constitutional rights. The Supreme Court agreed to hear the case.

SUMMARY OF ARGUMENTS

J. D. and Ethel Lee Shelley argued that restrictive covenants based on race or color were illegal and unenforceable and that state enforcement of such covenants was a violation of the Fourteenth Amendment.

Louis W. and Fern E. Kraemer argued that the restrictive covenant did not violate the Fourteenth Amendment; nor did the state's enforcement of the covenant violate the Fourteenth Amendment. The Kraemers also argued that the Shelleys were accorded due process and were not deprived of any property or civil rights.

DECISION

Chief Justice Vinson wrote the opinion, saying that private agreements to exclude persons of designated race or color from the occupancy of a residence do not violate the Fourteenth Amendment, but it does violate the equal protection clause for state courts to enforce them. Thus, in granting judicial enforcement of these agreements, the state denied Shelley the equal protection of the laws.

Participation of the state in the enforcement of restrictive covenants operates as a denial of equal protection; therefore, the action of the state courts cannot be valid. The difference between judicial enforcement and nonenforcement of a restrictive covenant "is the difference to Shelley between being denied rights of property available to other members of the community and being accorded full enjoyment of those rights on equal footing."

AFTERMATH

What is essentially a private act of discrimination may become illegal state action if the state is in any way involved in carrying out that action.

SIGNIFICANCE

Any private action that goes into court may become state action. This case became the basis for several civil rights actions.

RELATED CASES

Buchanan v. Warley, 245 U.S. 60 (1917)

Barrows v. Jackson, 346 U.S. 249 (1953)

Pennsylvania v. Board of Trusts, 353 U.S. 230 (1957)

Bell v. Maryland, 378 U.S. 226 (1964)

Jones v. Mayer, 392 U.S. 409 (1968)

RECOMMENDED READING

Darden, Joe T. "Black Residential Segregation since the 1948 *Shelley v. Kraemer* Decision." *Journal of Black Studies* 25 (1995): 680–691.

Louis Henkin, Shelley v. Kraemer, 110 University of Pennsylvania 473 (1962).

Lusky, Louis. *By What Right.* Charlottesville, Va.: Michie, 1975.

Maimon Schwarzchild, *Value Pluralism and the Constitution: In Defense of the State Action Doctrine,* Supreme Court Review 129 (1988).

Case Title: *Sweatt v. Painter*

Legal Citations: 339 U.S. 629; 70 S. Ct. 848

Year of Decision: 1950

KEY ISSUE

Does a state deny equal protection, as prescribed by the Fourteenth Amendment, when it provides separate and unequal opportunities for professional and graduate education in a state university to members of different races?

HISTORY OF THE CASE

Heman Marion Sweatt applied for admission to the University of Texas Law School in 1946, but his application was rejected solely on the basis that he was black. State law mandated the race restriction for the study of law at the school, and at the time, no law school in Texas admitted blacks. Sweatt brought suit against the appropriate school officials to compel his admission.

The state trial court recognized the equal protection violation but continued the case for six months to allow the state to supply substantially equal facilities. Thereafter, in December 1946, the court denied Sweatt's writ on the basis of an adopted order by the authorized university officials calling for the opening of a law school for blacks in February 1947. Sweatt appealed the decision and refused to register in the new school.

Upon remand from the Texas Court of Civil Appeals, the trial court found that the new school offered opportunities for the study of law that were substantially equivalent to those offered white students at the University of Texas. The new school, however, possessed no independent faculty or library and lacked accreditation. Nevertheless, the court of civil appeals subsequently affirmed the trial court's decision, and Sweatt's petition for a writ of error was denied by the Texas Supreme Court.

SUMMARY OF ARGUMENTS

Sweatt argued that the opportunities made available to him as a black man violated his right to equal protection of the laws.

The state argued that the new law school at the Texas State University for Negroes, established in the interim between the trial in the case and the Supreme Court briefings, provided the substantial equivalent of a white student's opportunities at the University of Texas Law School. The state noted that since the trial, the new law school was "on the road to full accreditation . . . has a faculty of five full-time professors . . . a library of some 16,500 volumes serviced by a full-time staff . . . a practice court and legal aid association . . . and one alumnus who has become a member of the Texas Bar."

DECISION

Chief Justice Vinson delivered the opinion of the Court. The Court held that the facilities available to Sweatt, under either the prior physical description of the proposed new school or the realized beginnings of the law school at the Texas State University for Negroes, were insufficient to constitute substantial equality with the facilities available to white students at the University of Texas Law School. The Court not only noted the differences in facilities but also pointed to distinctions in the reputation of the faculty, experience of the administration, position and influence of the alumni, standing in the community, traditions, and prestige as grounds for finding that substantial equality between the two schools did not exist. In this regard, the Court noted the University of Texas Law School's status as one of the nation's ranking law schools as a factor that was not offered in the new law school.

Furthermore, the Court recognized that opportunities of a legal career are also connected to the practice of the profession. The Court noted that the new law school excluded, on the basis of race, 85 percent of the population of the state. The Court also observed that "most of the lawyers, witnesses, jurors, judges and other officials with whom [Sweatt] will inevitably be dealing when he becomes a member of the Texas Bar" would be excluded from the permissible student body at the new law school. The Court held that exclusion of a white majority from the new law school did not equate with the exclusion of blacks from the University of Texas Law School because such supposition ignored the reality of the differences in prestige in the two institutions.

The Court held that the state violated Sweatt's personal right to equal protection under the

Fourteenth Amendment but limited its holding by refusing to overturn the raced-based rights analysis of *Plessy v. Ferguson* (1896) (the separate-but-equal doctrine).

AFTERMATH

Four years later, the Court extended the *Sweatt* rationale beyond state-sponsored professional and graduate education programs to prohibit separate facilities in all public education in *Brown v. Board of Education*. This holding has been extended so that all states must provide nonseparate opportunities, even in fields other than education, for all races.

SIGNIFICANCE

Sweatt represented one of several cases that chipped away at the "separate, but equal" doctrine of *Plessy v. Ferguson*. The Court's concern with the prestige of the law schools at issue in *Sweatt* provided the basis for its recognition in *Brown v. Board of Education* that the pejorative status placed upon a minority by maintaining separate facilities is inherently unequal and, therefore, violates the equal protection guarantees of the Fourteenth Amendment.

RELATED CASES

Plessy v. Ferguson, 163 U.S. 537 (1896)

Missouri ex rel. Gaines v. Canada, 305 U.S. 337 (1938)

Shelley v. Kraemer, 334 U.S. 1 (1948)

McLaurin v. Oklahoma State Regents, 339 U.S. 637 (1950)

Brown v. Board of Education of Topeka, Kansas, 349 U.S. 294 (1954)

RECOMMENDED READING

Dworkin, Ronald. *Taking Rights Seriously.* Cambridge, Mass.: Harvard University Press, 1977.

Meyer, Howard N. *The Amendment That Refused to Die.* Radnor, Pa.: Chilton Book, 1973.

Peter Westen, *The Empty Idea of Equality,* 95 Harvard Law Review 537 (1982).

Case Title: *Terry v. Adams*

Alternate Case Title: The White Primary Cases

Legal Citation: 345 U.S. 461

Year of Decision: 1953

KEY ISSUE

Is a private political association that excludes blacks from its pre-primary in county elections a "state actor, one acting under authorization of the state" and, therefore, subject to constitutional prohibitions against discrimination in voting rights?

HISTORY OF THE CASE

In order for a party to succeed on an allegation that its constitutional rights have been violated, the offending party must be acting under the authority of the state or government. There are very few exceptions to this basic tenet of constitutional law. The right to vote is not one of the exceptions.

The Jaybird Democratic Association was a private group of citizens that endorsed candidates for political office in Fort Bend County, Texas, elections. Before the Democratic Party primary, the association would decide which candidates to endorse by means of a "pre-primary," in which only members of the association could vote. Blacks were excluded from membership in the association and were, therefore, ineligible to vote in the pre-primary. The association's elections were not governed by state laws and did not use state elective machinery or funds. Candidates elected by the association were not certified by the association as its candidates in the Democratic primary but filed their own names as candidates. For more than 60 years, however, the association's candidates had nearly always been nominated in the Democratic Party primary and subsequently had nearly always been elected to county office. A group of black voters sued in district court to determine the legality of their being excluded from voting in the association pre-primaries. The district court held that the combined election machinery of the association and the Democratic Party deprived the petitioners of their right to vote on account of their race and color, contrary to the Fifteenth Amendment of the U.S. Constitution. It did not, however, issue an injunction, prohibiting the association's activities and forcing the inclusion of blacks, but instead retained jurisdiction, or power over the case, to grant further appropriate relief. The Court of Appeals for the Fifth Circuit reversed the decision of the district court, and the case went to the U.S. Supreme Court.

SUMMARY OF ARGUMENTS

The petitioners argued that they were effectively denied a voice in county elections because of the dominance of the Jaybird Democratic Association's pre-primary in the Democratic primary and subsequent general election. As a result, they believed that their Fifteenth Amendment rights were being circumvented by the association.

The respondent argued that it was nothing more than an association that merely put its "stamp of approval" on political candidates, much as religious groups or social action groups have.

DECISION

Although there was no majority opinion, the Court held that the Jaybird Democratic Association was a state actor and was, therefore, subject to constitutional restraints. Justice Black, joined by Justice Douglas and Justice Burton, found that the qualifications prescribed by Texas entitling electors to vote at county-operated primaries were the sole qualifications entitling electors to vote at the countywide Jaybird primaries, except that blacks were excluded. As a result, the three justices believed that the county and Jaybird elections were so closely linked that they were virtually indistinguishable. The justices held that for a state to permit the duplication of its election process is to permit a flagrant abuse of those processes to defeat the purposes of the Fifteenth Amendment. Although the state did not have any control or input in the Jaybird process, the mere effect of its existence was enough to justify placing the association in the category of a state actor.

Justice Frankfurter found that through the comprehensive "scheme" of regulation of political primaries in Texas, the county election officials were "clothed" with the authority of the state to secure its interest in "fair methods and a fair expression" of preferences in the selection of nominees for political office. By allowing the Jaybird pre-primary to exclude blacks, the state had a hand in the exclusionary practices. Although the Court could not directly tell the state to participate in and regulate the "pre-primary," it could, nevertheless, eliminate the unlawful tactic of circumscribing the regular channels of the democratic process to which all qualified citizens are a part.

Justices Clark, Reed, and Jackson concurred, finding that the Jaybird Democratic Association operated as "part and parcel" of the Democratic Party, which existed under the auspices of Texas law. They held that the association's mechanism for selecting candidates struck to the core of the electoral process in Fort Bend County, Texas. The association had taken on the attributes of government by its long-standing success in endorsing winning candidates. As a result, the Constitution's safeguards came into play.

Justice Minton was the sole dissenter. In his opinion, for there to have been state action, the wrong must have been committed by the state. He found that the record did not show any compliance by the organization with state standards or any cooperation by or with the state in any other manner. He saw the association's primary as the "concerted action of individuals" and not state action. Participation in the association was voluntary and secondary to the Democratic primary. The mere success rate of the candidates endorsed was not enough to bridge the gap between individual, lawful activity and state-endorsed, state-condoned, state-sanctioned activity. Justice Minton saw the Jaybirds as a "pressure" group similar to other special interest groups at the time that were not subject to constitutional scrutiny. Although he did not agree with the objectives of the group, he certainly did not believe that the federal government could prohibit its electoral actions under the auspices of state action.

AFTERMATH

The Court opened an otherwise closed door on equal protection challenges concerning private associations. Although the Court later withdrew from its activist role, it nevertheless has remained open to constitutional challenges brought by groups affected by private associations and clubs.

SIGNIFICANCE

Through this decision and other related decisions, the Court expanded the concept of state action to include private conduct. Some commentators have concluded that the Court could label a state actor as such because of the tenuous and scant relationships between the actors and the state. The result of such an approach could be the virtual privatization of the Constitution resting upon unconvincingly drawn lines.

RELATED CASES

United States v. Cruikshank, 92 U.S. 542 (1876)

Civil Rights Cases, 109 U.S. 3 (1883)

Guinn and Beal v. United States, 238 U.S. 347 (1915)

Nixon v. Herndon, 273 U.S. 536 (1927)

Grovey v. Townsend, 295 U.S. 45 (1935)

Smith v. Allwright, 321 U.S. 649 (1944)

Shelley v. Kraemer, 334 U.S. 1 (1948)

RECOMMENDED READING

Michael M. Burns, *The Exclusion of Women from Influential Men's Clubs: The Inner Sanctum and the Myth of Full Equality,* 18 Harvard Civil Rights–Civil Liberties Law Review 321 (1983).

Elliot, Ward E. Y. *The Rise of Guardian Democracy.* Cambridge, Mass.: Harvard University Press, 1974.

Case Title: *Brown v. Board of Education of Topeka, Kansas*

Alternate Case Titles: The Brown School Admissions Case; the School Desegregation Cases

Legal Citation: First Brown: 347 U.S. 483 (1954); Second Brown: 349 U.S. 294 (1955)

Years of Decision: 1954, 1955

KEY ISSUE

Did the practice of segregating schools by race—almost universal in southern and border states prior to the decision—deprive black children of equal protection of the law, guaranteed to all Americans regardless of race under the Fourteenth Amendment to the U.S. Constitution?

HISTORY OF THE CASE

In the states where slavery was practiced prior to the passage of the Thirteenth Amendment outlawing slavery in 1865, a variety of laws had prohibited the education of slaves on the basis of the theory that education might make them less tractable and encourage rebelliousness. In all parts of the country, public education was far from universal in the mid-19th century for children of any color, but tax-supported education was rare indeed in the agrarian South.

The federal government, during the Reconstruction period immediately following the Civil War, tried to establish a minimal system of schools for blacks in the former slave states under the auspices of the Freedmen's Bureau. When the bureau was shut down in 1870, this rudimentary system of education was largely abandoned. Reconstruction drew to a close in the South in the mid-1870s as federal troops were withdrawn and state governments fell back under the control of the local white population. Southern whites were determined to use both the law and extralegal intimidation to restore their domination over former slaves by establishing a rigid economic, political, and social caste system. By 1900, southern blacks had been effectively denied the right to vote, reduced to a condition of quasi-serfdom in most rural areas, and subjected to a system of legally mandated segregation that barred social interaction between whites and blacks in almost every arena of life, including education.

In the late 19th and early 20th centuries, state and local governments gradually accepted the responsibility of offering all children at least several years of free public education, but educational standards in the South lagged far behind those in the rest of the nation, for whites as well as blacks. The education provided southern black children was even more inferior and totally separate from that provided southern white children. In 1910, expenditures per pupil for black schools averaged less than a third of those spent per pupil white schools.

Black plaintiffs challenged legally imposed segregation in the courts, contending that state laws imposing segregation violated the rights to equal protection of the laws guaranteed them under the Fourteenth Amendment to the Constitution. In 1896, the Supreme Court by an 8-1 decision upheld a Louisiana law mandating separate but equal accommodations on passenger trains (Plessy v. Ferguson). Three years later, in Cumming v. Richmond County Board of Education, the Court unanimously upheld segregation in the public schools, declaring that education was a matter left to state jurisdiction and that federal interference could not be justified. In 1908, the Court gave further sanction to Jim Crow education when it upheld, in Berea College v. Kentucky, a state law requiring segregation in private educational institutions.

The National Association for the Advancement of Colored People (NAACP) formulated in the early and mid-1930s a strategy for legally challenging school segregation on the ground that, in practice, separate education was never equal. The organization began by challenging state universities in border states such as Missouri and Maryland that maintained law schools for whites but not for blacks. In a critical 1938 decision (Missouri ex rel. Gaines v. Canada), the Court ruled that the state of Missouri had to admit a black applicant to the state-supported law school since it had failed to provide a law school for black residents of the state.

The NAACP's goal was to abolish all forms of segregation in public education, but initially its legal drive focused on obtaining support in federal courts for "absolute equality," rather than challenging the courts to reverse the separate but equal doctrine laid down in Plessy v. Ferguson (1896). The organization's legal strategists believed that the South would find the support of two absolutely equal parallel educational systems too expensive to sustain. Pursuing this strategy, the NAACP won case after case: forcing school districts to pay teachers in black schools exactly what they paid teachers in white schools, state law schools to admit black students, and state universities to admit black undergraduates.

This strategy, while successful in individual cases, was painstakingly slow. In each case, the plaintiffs had to establish that separate educational facilities offered blacks were inferior in some way to those offered whites. Without a direct reversal of the Plessy doctrine ruling segregation inherently unequal, it would take generations to equalize the thousands of school districts in the South.

By 1950, the NAACP decided that it would have to develop cases that would force the Supreme Court to address the issue of whether segregated schools were inherently unequal and, therefore, a violation of the equal protection of the laws guaranteed all Americans regardless of race or color.

The decision known as Brown v. Board of Education dealt with not one case but five separate cases that raised similar issues and that the Court, therefore, decided to hear together and decide together.

Briggs v. Elliot was a challenge to the segregated schools of Clarendon County, South Carolina, carefully crafted by the NAACP to challenge segregation per se. In arguing the case before a special three-judge panel in federal district court in Charleston, the plaintiffs presented evidence from social scientists that segregation in the schools reduced the self-esteem of black children. Resting on the Plessy doctrine, two of the judges rejected this argument but ordered the defendants "promptly" to provide equal educational facilities to black pupils. Judge J. Waites Waring dissented, accepting the NAACP's argument that a child attending a segregated school was "poisoned by prejudice" and that segregation in education was "an evil that must be eradicated."

Brown v. Board of Education of Topeka, Kansas was a case challenging the very concept of segregation, since the facilities provided to black and white students were essentially comparable. The case was heard by a three-judge panel of district judges who decided unanimously against the plaintiffs on the basis that the Supreme Court had yet to overturn the separate-but-equal doctrine. In the "Findings of Fact" attached to the opinion, however, the judges declared: "Segregation with the sanction of law . . . has a tendency to retard the educational and mental development of Negro children and to deprive them of some of the benefits they would receive in a racially integrated school system." This statement, as one NAACP lawyer remarked, would clearly put the Supreme Court "on the spot."

Gebhart et al. v. Belton et al. was a Delaware case seeking to overturn a decision by the state's chancery court that segregation in the schools created inequality and, therefore, violated the constitutional rights of the plaintiffs.

Davis et al. v. County School Board of Prince Edward County, Virginia et al. framed the issue of whether segregation had to be eliminated despite rapid and substantial efforts by the school district to improve the quality of black schools. A three-judge district court decision declaring that segregation had "for generations been a part of the mores of her people" ruled in favor of the state of Virginia and simply ordered the Prince Edward School Board to continue to equalize its facilities for black students "with diligence and dispatch."

The fifth case, *Bolling v. Sharp*, challenged school segregation in the District of Columbia. The plaintiffs' arguments were based entirely on the issue of segregation per se, intentionally avoiding the question of inferior facilities. The U.S. District Court judge who heard the case ruled that no claim of inequality had been made, and given that the constitutionality of segregation had been upheld, there was no basis upon which relief could be granted.

During spring and summer 1952, the Supreme Court accepted jurisdiction by granting writs of certiorari (which require transfer of certified records from an inferior to a superior court) in the Kansas, South Carolina, and Virginia cases. Deciding that it should settle all the pending segregation cases together, the Court directed that the Delaware and District of Columbia cases also be argued at the same time.

SUMMARY OF ARGUMENTS

On December 9, 1952, the Supreme Court convened to hear the arguments on the five cases.

Each of the cases was argued separately. Thurgood Marshall, who in 1967 would become the first black justice appointed to the Court, represented the NAACP. He faced John W. Davis, the 1924 Democratic Party candidate for the presidency, who represented South Carolina in the *Briggs* case. The thrust of the arguments presented by Marshall and the other lawyers demanding an end to school segregation was that there was overwhelming psychological and sociological evidence demonstrating that school segregation did irreparable harm to black schoolchildren by stigmatizing them as inferior. The plaintiffs argued that "segregated schools are not equal and cannot be made equal, and that hence they [the plaintiffs] are deprived of the equal protection of the laws."

The defendants contended that segregation of the schools on an equal basis was in the best interests of the children and that as long as equal facilities were provided for black children there was no infringement of the plaintiffs' due process rights under the Fourteenth Amendment. The U.S. Justice Department filed an amicus curiae brief supporting the plaintiffs.

The arguments were concluded on December 11, 1952, and the Court began its own deliberations. After considerable internal discussion, during which it became apparent that the justices were deeply divided over many questions, the Court on June 8, 1953, unanimously restored all five cases to the docket for reargument October 12 and posed a series of questions to the litigants. Two of those questions required the plaintiffs and defendants to review the historical evidence on the intentions of Congress and the Fourteenth Amendment; two other questions asked, assuming the Court did find school segregation unlawful, how both plaintiffs and defendants would propose the Court go about ending it.

As both sides were preparing to reargue the cases, Chief Justice Fred Vinson died of a heart attack on September 8, 1953. President Dwight Eisenhower appointed the California governor, Earl Warren, to replace Vinson. With Warren presiding as acting chief justice, as he was still awaiting Senate confirmation, the Court convened for three days of reargument on December 7. The NAACP's basic argument was that the Fourteenth Amendment involved a flat prohibition on discriminatory actions by the states.

Davis argued for the defense that the framers of the Fourteenth Amendment had not regarded segregation per se as a denial of due process and that the Supreme Court had ruled seven times in favor of the separate-but-equal doctrine, making it a matter of settled law that should not be disturbed.

Assistant Attorney General J. Lee Rankin, appearing to present the Justice Department's brief as a friend of the Court, declared that "segregation in public schools cannot be maintained under the 14th Amendment" and that the Court should send the cases back down to the district courts with the instruction that the lower courts oversee a desegregation process to be carried out "with deliberate speed."

DECISION

In the deliberations that followed the arguments, Justice Warren convinced his colleagues that the sensitivity of the issue almost demanded that the Court speak with a single, resolute voice and settle the issue once and forever. He assigned himself the responsibility of writing a majority opinion. It would express the compromise formula to which the justices had agreed in order to overturn *Plessy v. Ferguson*—that is, to rule segregation in the schools an unconstitutional denial of equal protection of the laws but to hold over the cases for reargument during the next term as to how the decision should be implemented.

Justice Warren read the Court's firm but brief and low-key opinion on May 17, 1954. He began by stating that the Court found the circumstances surrounding the adoption of the Fourteenth Amendment as "at best . . . inconclusive." He then traced the Court's interpretation of the amendment, noting that the "separate but equal" doctrine developed 20 years after the Court's first rulings. Declaring that public education had become "perhaps the most important function of state and local government," he said that the critical issue raised by the cases was "Does segregation of children in public schools solely on the basis of race . . . deprive the children of the minority group of equal educational opportunities?" Justice Warren answered the question in his next sentence: "We believe that it does."

"Segregation," he went on, quoting from the findings of fact in the *Brown* case, "of white and colored children in public schools has a detrimental effect upon the colored children. The impact is greater when it has the sanction of the law; for the policy of segregating the races is usually interpreted as denoting the inferiority of the Negro group. A sense of inferiority affects the motivation of a child to learn." Justice Warren then declared that this "finding is amply supported by modern authority. Any language in *Plessy v. Ferguson* contrary to this finding is rejected." To this paragraph, Justice Warren added a footnote citing a number of scholarly sources, concluding the footnote by saying, "And see generally Myrdal, *An American Dilemma*." This reference to Gunnar Myrdal provoked considerable outrage in the South, since Myrdal, a Swedish socialist, had castigated the region for its ubiquitous racism. Justice Warren continued:

> We conclude that in the field of education the doctrine of "separate but equal" has no place. Separate educational facilities are inherently unequal. Therefore, we hold that the plaintiffs and others similarly situated . . . are, by reason of the segregation complained of, deprived of the equal protection of the laws guaranteed by the Fourteenth Amendment.

Justice Warren concluded by requesting that the parties present further arguments in fall 1954 on how the Court's decision should be implemented.

The Court postponed arguments until April 11, 1955, at which time Marshall argued strenuously for decisive action to end segregation by setting a fixed date by which segregation would have to end throughout the South. The defendants argued, for the most part, that no fixed timetable should be imposed and that too rapid desegregation might destroy the system of public education in many areas of the South. Speaking as a friend of the Court for the government of the United States, Solicitor General Simon E. Sobeloff urged the justices to instruct the district courts to direct the segregated school districts to make a prompt start on the process of integration and complete it "as speedily as feasible."

Finally, on May 31, 1955, Justice Warren delivered a unanimous seven-paragraph opinion on the implementation of the *Brown* decision directing the district courts to monitor the "good faith" of local school boards in planning and implementing desegregation plans. The lower courts, he said, should be guided by "equitable principles" and "a practical flexibility." In the most famous phrase of the case, he wrote that the district courts should see that the parties to the cases be admitted "to public schools on a racially nondiscriminatory basis with all deliberate speed."

AFTERMATH

The phrase "all deliberate speed" proved subject to varying interpretations. It would take nearly a quarter-century and hundreds of lower-court decisions before the Supreme Court's edict in *Brown* had been fully implemented throughout the South. Even then, in both North and South, patterns of residential segregation and concentration of blacks in urban areas and of whites in suburban areas were reflected in school enrollments.

In the immediate aftermath of the second *Brown* decision, the South sought to use tokenism to meet the letter of the law while negating the spirit. District courts frequently granted school boards long delays and accepted as adequate compliance the enrollment of handfuls of black schoolchildren in formerly white schools. The first major crisis in the desegregation process occurred in Little Rock in 1957, when the Arkansas governor, Orval Faubus, used national guardsmen to prevent the enrollment of a few blacks in the city's Central High School. After talks with Faubus led nowhere, President Eisenhower reluctantly sent U.S. Army paratroopers to enforce court orders. Some 750 school districts were desegregated—at least on a token basis—in the first four years after the *Brown* decision, but only an additional 49 were desegregated during the period 1958–60. The process of desegregation picked up speed in the early 1960s, and after the passage of the 1964 Civil Rights Act, federal authorities had more weapons in the legal battle. In 1969, Chief Justice Warren Burger wrote a short and unanimous opinion in *Alexander v. Holmes County (Mississippi) Board of Education* declaring, "The obligation of every school district is to terminate dual school systems at once." By 1972, more than 46 percent of black children in the South were attending schools in which the majority of students were white, a higher percentage than could be found in other sections of the nation.

SIGNIFICANCE

Brown v. Board of Education would be ranked by most historians as among the two or three most far-reaching and significant decisions ever handed down by an American court. Over the next decade, additional decisions wiped out legally sanctioned segregation in almost every aspect of American life, even outlawing in 1967 state laws barring interracial marriage. The decision also sparked a mass movement among blacks demanding their civil rights. Starting with the bus boycott in Montgomery, Alabama, led by Martin Luther King, Jr., in 1955 and 1956, it quickly spread across the nation, transforming the nation's political life. Although still beset by economic problems, American blacks were freed from the system of legally sanctioned discrimination within two decades of the *Brown* decision.

RELATED CASES

Strauder v. West Virginia, 100 U.S. 303 (1880)

Plessy v. Ferguson, 163 U.S. 537 (1896)

Powell v. Alabama, 287 U.S. 45 (1932)

Smith v. Allwright, 321 U.S. 649 (1944)

Sweatt v. Painter, 339 U.S. 629 (1950)

McLaurin v. Oklahoma State Regents, 339 U.S. 337 (1950)

Hernandez v. Texas, 347 U.S. 475 (1954)

Bolling v. Sharpe, 347 U.S. 497 (1954)

NAACP v. Alabama, 357 U.S. 449 (1958)

Cooper v. Aaron, 358 U.S. 1 (1958)

Boynton v. Virginia, 364 U.S. 454 (1960)

Heart of Atlanta Motel v. United States, 379 U.S. 241 (1964)

Loving v. Virginia, 388 U.S. 1 (1967)

Swann v. Charlotte Mechlenburg Bd. of Education, 402 U.S. 1 (1971)

Guey Heung Lee v. Johnson, 404 U.S. 1215 (1971)

Milliken v. Bradley, 418 U.S. 717 (1974)

Bob Jones University v. United States, 461 U.S. 574 (1983)

Parents Involved in Community Schools v. Seattle School Dist. No. 1, 551 U.S. 701 (2007)

RECOMMENDED READING

Balkin, J. M., ed. *What* Brown v. Board of Education *Should Have Said: The Nation's Top Legal Experts Rewrite America's Landmark Civil Rights Decision.* New York: New York University Press, 2002.

Bell, Derrick. *Race, Racism and American Law.* Boston: Little, Brown, 1980.

Brown v. Board of Education *and Its Legacy: A Tribute to Justice Warren Thurgood Marshall,* 61 Fordham Law Review 1 (1992).

Cottrol, Robert J., Raymond T. Diamond, and Leland Ware. Brown v. Board of Education: *Caste, Culture, and the Constitution.* Lawrence: University Press of Kansas, 2003.

Friedman, Leon, ed. *Argument: The Oral Argument before the Supreme Court in* Brown v. Board of Education, *1952–1955.* New York: Chelsea House, 1969.

Graglia, Lino. *Disaster by Decree: The Supreme Court Decisions on Race and the Schools.* Ithaca, N.Y.: Cornell University Press, 1976.

Kluger, Richard. *Simple Justice: The History of* Brown v. Board of Education *and Black America's Struggle for Equality.* New York: Knopf, 1976.

Martin, Waldo E. Brown v. Board of Education: *A Brief History with Documents.* New York: Palgrave Macmillan, 1998.

Patterson, James T. Brown v. Board of Education: *A Civil Rights Milestone and Its Troubled Legacy.* New York: Oxford University Press, 2001.

Speer, Hugh. *The Case of the Century: A Historical and Social Perspective on* Brown v. Board of Education *of Topeka, with Present and Future Implications.* Kansas City: University of Missouri Press, 1968.

Case Title: *Cooper v. Aaron*

Legal Citation: 358 U.S. 1

Year of Decision: 1958

KEY ISSUE

Are federal court orders interpreting the Constitution, in this case, ordering desegregation in public schools, binding upon the states?

HISTORY OF THE CASE

In 1954, the U.S. Supreme Court decided *Brown v. Board of Education,* which held that racial segregation in public schools is a denial of equal protection of the laws and, thus, violates the Fourteenth Amendment. One year later, in *Brown v. Board of Education,* "*Brown* II," the Court ordered a decree to effectuate their decision in

Brown. The Court stated that school systems were required to comply with the decree in good faith, including the elimination of obstacles in the way of the school systems' operating in accordance with constitutional principles. The district courts were directed to oversee that the school districts were making efforts toward compliance and to take necessary action to ensure efforts were made. Under *Brown* II, state authorities were required to make efforts that constituted good faith compliance, which could only be accomplished with a "prompt start, diligently and earnestly pursued, to eliminate racial segregation from the public schools."

Three days after the Court's decision in *Brown,* the Little Rock District School Board adopted a policy to deal with desegregation. The plan involved desegregating the schools by grade levels, beginning with the desegregation of high schools and then moving on to junior high schools. Desegregation, according to the plan, was to be accomplished by 1963. The desegregation proposal was challenged by plaintiffs who desired earlier completion of the process, but the district court upheld the school board's plan. While plans for desegregation were under way, other state authorities opposed to desegregation were trying to develop programs to perpetuate racial segregation.

The school board and the superintendant of the schools planned to carry out their preparations for desegregation, first by having nine African-American children attend Little Rock Central High School in fall 1957. One day before the students were to attend the high school, the plan was reached with drastic opposition, spurred by the governor of Arkansas, Orval Faubus. Governor Faubus had dispatched members of the Arkansas National Guard to the high school and placed the school grounds off limits to African-American students. After this dramatic event, which gained national attention, the school board asked that the African-American students not attend until the legal dispute was settled. However, the district court ordered the school board to proceed with the plan. The students attempted to attend the high school the next day but were met by national guardsmen standing shoulder to shoulder to prevent the nine students from entering, and this continued for three weeks. A district court then ordered a preliminary injunction enjoining the governor and the officers of the guard from preventing the children from attending the school. The students attended the next schoolday after the court's order; however, they were removed after large groups of demonstrators had gathered at the school. Then on September 25, 1957, President Eisenhower sent federal troops to Central High School to ensure the attendance of the nine African-American children.

In February 1958, the school board and the superintendant of schools petitioned with the district court to postpone their desegregation program because of public hostility and the difficulty in administering the program. The district court granted the petition, and the African-American respondents appealed to the Court of Appeals for the Eighth Circuit. The appeals court reversed the judgment of the district court. The U.S. Supreme Court granted certiorari for the case to be on September 11, 1958.

SUMMARY OF ARGUMENTS

In a highly unusual move, the Court convened a special summer term to review the case, beginning August 28, 1958, and heard arguments on September 11. Thurgood Marshall, later to become the first black member of the Court, argued for John Aaron and the respondents. Richard Butler represented the Little Rock School Board. The arguments of Mr. Butler raised sympathy for the school board and conditioned their request for delay on the interference of the governor and state officials with the operations of the board in the governance of their district. Marshall urged that the Court not compromise or yield to the delaying tactics of Governor Faubus or the Arkansas legislature.

DECISION

The Court held that Arkansas state officials were bound by the U.S. Supreme Court's decision in *Brown v. Board of Education* and that states in general are bound by federal court orders relying on the Constitution. Thus, judges and legislatures are not permitted to annul judgments of the

Supreme Court. The decision was guided in large part by the supremacy clause of Article VI of the Constitution and the Court's decision in *Marbury v. Madison* (1803).

The Court delivered the opinion per curiam:

The Court began its analysis by stating that "the constitutional rights of respondents are not to be sacrificed or yielded to the violence and disorder which have followed upon the action of the Governor and Legislature." The record of the case before the Court made clear that the problems in this case were created by state actors, who invoked the Fourteenth Amendment because it regarded state actions against private citizens. The Fourteenth Amendment ensures that no agency of the state, including its officers and agents, is permitted to deny any person within its jurisdiction the equal protection of the laws in that jurisdiction. With this in mind, the Court held that the "constitutional rights of children not to be discriminated against in school admission on grounds of race or color declared by this Court in the Brown case can neither be nullified openly and directly by state legislators or state executive or judicial officers, nor nullified indirectly by them through evasive schemes for segregation." Accordingly, the Court affirmed the decision of the court of appeals, which had reversed the district court's decision to allow the discontinuance of desegregation in the Little Rock School District.

In support of its decision, the Court pointed out that the supremacy clause of Article VI of the Constitution makes the Constitution the "supreme law of the land." The Court also noted the "basic principle that the federal judiciary is supreme in the exposition of the law of the constitution." Thus, the decision in *Brown* is also the supreme law of the land and is binding upon the states. The Court also noted that public officials are required to swear to uphold the Constitution, and a failure to acknowledge the Court's decision in *Brown* violated that oath. In conclusion, the Court stated that "the principles announced in [*Brown*] and the obedience of the States to them, according to the command of the Constitution, are indispensable for the protection of the freedoms guaranteed by our fundamental charter for all of us. Our constitutional ideal of equal justice under law is thus made a living truth."

Justice Frankfurter wrote a concurring opinion, noting that the problems did not arise until the state took actions to obstruct the desegregation of the schools. He stated that "while Arkansas is not a formal party in these proceedings and a decree cannot go against the State, it is legally and morally before the Court," because it had prevented the Little Rock School Board from carrying out its constitutional duty. Justice Frankfurter emphasized that public disapproval of the Court's decision in *Brown* did not justify the suspension of the desegregation program. If people oppose the decision, he suggested, they are free to use legal and political processes to change it. To hold otherwise would result in a breakdown of the rule of law.

AFTERMATH

Some critics argue that the Court's decision gave the Supreme Court too much power by making itself the final arbiter for interpreting the Constitution. However, others argue that having one branch of government interpret the Constitution allows for clarity and uniformity of the law, which makes it easier to predict what the law is.

SIGNIFICANCE

Brown v. Board of Education provided the foundation for school integration. *Cooper* provided the means for enforcement by affirming the power of the federal courts and constitutional law over the states. However, *Cooper* also showed the Court the extent of the resistance to desegregation. Implementation of school integration would be slow until the passage of the Civil Rights Act of 1964.

RELATED CASES

Marbury v. Madison, 5 U.S. 137 (1803)

Brown v. Board of Education, 347 U.S. 483 (1954)

Brown v. Board of Education ("*Brown* II"), 349 U.S. 294 (1955)

Fabus v. Aaron, 361 U.S. 197 (1959)

Green v. County School Board of New Kent County, Virginia, 391 U.S. 430 (1968)

Swann v. Charlotte Mecklenburg Board of Education, 402 U.S. 1 (1971)

RECOMMENDED READING

Edwin Meese III, *The Law of the Constitution,* 61 Tulanc Law Review 979 (1987).

Case Title: *Trop v. Dulles*

Alternate Case Title: The Denationalization Case

Legal Citation: 356 U.S. 86

Year of Decision: 1958

KEY ISSUE

May Congress denationalize soldiers who receive dishonorable discharges for desertion?

HISTORY OF THE CASE

Trop was dishonorably discharged from the U.S. Army in 1944 after he was convicted of desertion. He later sought to obtain a passport, but he was denied on the grounds that his dishonorable discharge for desertion had deprived him of his citizenship under the Nationality Act of 1940. Trop sued to stop enforcement of the act, but he was unsuccessful in both the district court and the Court of Appeals for the Second Circuit.

SUMMARY OF ARGUMENTS

Trop argued that denationalization was a punishment for desertion, and that it was unconstitutional because it was cruel and unusual in violation of the Eighth Amendment.

The government argued that the act was a reasonable exercise of Congress's war powers, that it was not "punishment" in the traditional criminal sense, and that even if it were deemed punishment, it was not cruel or unusual.

DECISION

The Court, in a narrow 5-4 decision written by Chief Justice Warren, held that the relevant portion of the act was unconstitutional. He argued that citizenship could be voluntarily relinquished or abandoned, but it could not be divested by the exercise of the powers of the national government. He also contended that while desertion or failure to pay taxes certainly "deals a dangerous blow to this country," it was not punishable by denationalization. Chief Justice Warren argued that while the death penalty would have been a constitutional form of punishment, it was cruel and unusual to denationalize a deserter. In Chief Justice Warren's opinion, denationalization was a penalty "forbidden by the principle of civilized treatment guaranteed by the Eighth Amendment." He argued that the state of perpetual uncertainty that followed denationalization was worse than execution: "It is a form of punishment more primitive than torture, for it destroys for the individual the political existence that was centuries in the development."

Justice Frankfurter, joined by three other justices, wrote a vigorous dissent. He argued that the Court's untenable view of what was cruel and unusual evinced a lack of judicial self-restraint. Justice Frankfurter acknowledged that one might disagree with the act, but "the Constitution has not authorized the judges to sit in judgment on the wisdom of what Congress and the Executive Branch do." Because desertion was a refusal to perform the "ultimate duty of citizenship," Congress had a reasonable basis for punishing deserters with the withdrawal of that citizenship. Justice Frankfurter, assailing the decision of the majority, vehemently disagreed that denationalization was unconstitutional: "Is constitutional dialectic so empty of reason that it can be seriously urged that loss of citizenship is a fate worse than death?"

AFTERMATH

In 1963, the Court held that persons who left the country to avoid military service during wartime could not be punished by banishment from the United States.

SIGNIFICANCE

Denationalizing a U.S. citizen is not an acceptable type of punishment for the crime of desertion during wartime.

RELATED CASES

Nishikawa v. Dulles, 356 U.S. 129 (1958)

Perez v. Brownwell, 356 U.S. 44 (1958)

Afroyirn v. Rusk, 387 U.S. 253 (1967)

Furman v. Georgia, 408 U.S. 238 (1972)

Gregg v. Georgia, 428 U.S. 153 (1976)

RECOMMENDED READING

Cable, John L. *Decisive Decisions of United States Citizenship.* Charlottesville, Va.: Michie, 1967.

Meltsner, Michael. *Cruel and Unusual.* New York: Random House, 1973.

Case Title: *Lassiter v. Northampton County Board of Elections*

Legal Citation: 360 U.S. 45

Year of Decision: 1959

KEY ISSUE

Does North Carolina's literacy test requirement for citizens to vote violate the Fifteenth Amendment of the U.S. Constitution?

HISTORY OF THE CASE

An African-American citizen of North Carolina sued the state in order to have the voter literacy test prescribed by the state declared unconstitutional. A three-judge panel, noting that a portion of section 4 of Article VI of the North Carolina Constitution requiring literacy tests included a grandfather clause, ruled that the literacy portion of the test would have been unconstitutional but was superseded by a 1957 act that did not contain the grandfather clause. The court then stayed its action until the state courts had interpreted the 1957 act in light of the North Carolina State Constitution. The case then began as an administrative proceeding in which Lassiter applied for registration as a voter, and the registrar denied her registration because she refused to take a literacy test, as required by the state.

Lassiter appealed to the County Board of Elections but was denied her voting rights for refusing to take the literacy test. She then appealed to and was denied her request by the superior court. Lassiter then appealed her case to the North Carolina Supreme Court, which affirmed the decision of the lower court, and the case was, thereafter, appealed to the U.S. Supreme Court.

SUMMARY OF ARGUMENTS

Lassiter argued that the North Carolina state literacy test was unconstitutional, violating the Fifteenth Amendment because it favored certain voters.

The state argued that the test applied to all voters and was not created for the purpose of discrimination.

DECISION

Justice Douglas delivered the opinion of the Court.

The Court agreed with the attorney general of North Carolina, who had filed an amicus brief, stating that the invalidity of part of Article VI of the North Carolina Constitution does not impair the remainder of Article VI. This meant that Article VI would require the same literacy test that was imposed by the 1957 statute, but without the grandfather clause, which was separable and void. Had the grandfather clause been intact, it would have favored white voters, which would violate the Fifteenth Amendment, which reads in relevant part: "The right of citizens of the United States to vote shall not be denied or abridged by the United States or by any state on account of race, color, or previous condition of servitude." The Court then turned to the issue of whether literacy tests were unconstitutional if applied to all voters, regardless of race or color.

The Court began by stating, "The states have long been held to have broad powers to determine the conditions under which the right of suffrage may be exercised, absent of course the discrimination which the Constitution condemns." The Court also stated that the suffrage conditions must not interfere with restrictions that Congress has imposed. Some examples of regulations the Court deemed permissible include residency requirements, the consideration of age, and previous criminal record. The Court reasoned that it followed that the abilities to read and write were also reasonable to ensure intelligent use of the ballot and, thus, "a State might conclude that only those who are literate should exercise the franchise." The Court noted that currently 19 states had literacy requirements for voting, with various methods being employed. Accordingly, the Court affirmed the decision of the court of appeals and held that the literacy requirement as a prerequisite to eligibility for voting, if not employed in a discriminatory manner, did not violate the Fifteenth Amendment.

The Court went on to note that if a literacy test requirement, even if fair on its face, were employed in a discriminatory manner, the Fifteenth Amendment would be violated. This is also true if other forms of prerequisites are employed in such a way that it amounts to "merely a device to make racial discrimination easy." The statute at issue was one that was deemed a "fair way of determining whether a person is literate, not a calculated scheme to lay springs for the citizen." The Court was unanimous in its decision.

AFTERMATH

The national Voting Rights Act of 1965 banned discriminatory voting practices throughout the United States. This legislation served to protect African-American and other minority voters from disenfranchisement. Thus, although *Lassiter* is still good law, it has received negative treatment and is limited under the act.

On April 30, 2009, the Supreme Court heard oral arguments for *Namudno v. Holder,* which involved the "preclearance procedure" of the Voting Rights Act of 1965. The preclearance procedure requires any change in the voting process in "covered jurisdictions" to be approved by the Department of Justice. This includes the changes in voting venue at issue in *Namudno* because Texas is a "covered jurisdiction" under the act.

SIGNIFICANCE

This case made clear that absent preconditions being administered in a discriminatory manner, literacy tests would be allowed in most cases. The Court deemed the states' interest in having an educated voting class legitimate and similar to residency and criminal record considerations concerning voter qualifications.

RELATED CASES

Guinn v. United States, 238 U.S. 347 (1915)

Northwest Austin Municipal District Number One v. Holder (2009)

RECOMMENDED READING

Anthony Ciccone, *The Right to Vote Is Not a Duty,* 23 Hamline Journal of Public Law and Policy 325 (2002).

Sandra Guerra, *Voting Rights and the Constitution: The Disenfranchisement of Non-English Speaking Citizens,* 97 Yale Law Journal 1419 (1988).

Peter M. Shane, *Voting Rights and the "Statutory Constitution,"* 56 Law and Contemporary Problems 243 (1993).

Case Title: *Gomillion v. Lightfoot*

Alternate Case Title: The Tuskegee Gerrymander Case

Legal Citation: 364 U.S. 339

Year of Decision: 1960

KEY ISSUES

Does a state legislative act that redefines a city's boundaries in such a way as to exclude almost all black citizens from the city violate the due process and equal protection clauses of the Fourteenth Amendment and the right to vote as guaranteed in the Fifteenth Amendment?

HISTORY OF THE CASE

A state redistricting measure altered the shape of Tuskegee, Alabama, from a square to a 28-sided figure, removing all but four or five of its 400 black voters and not a single white voter. Because the black population no longer resided within city limits, they no longer could vote in municipal elections.

SUMMARY OF ARGUMENTS

Appellants, black citizens of Tuskegee, Alabama, argued that the state redistricting act violated the due process and equal protection clauses of the Fourteenth Amendment and denied their right to vote in violation of the Fifteenth Amendment.

Appellees, the mayor of Tuskegee and others, argued the state had unrestricted power to define its political subdivisions and, therefore, did not violate the Fourteenth and Fifteenth Amendments.

DECISION

Justice Frankfurter delivered the opinion of the Court, saying the act constitutes discrimination against blacks in violation of the due process and equal protection clauses of the Fourteenth Amendment. The act also violated the right to vote guaranteed by the Fifteenth Amendment. Federal courts have jurisdiction over a local municipal act "when state power is used as an instrument for circumventing a federally protected right" (346), and the Court would not sanction a law that singled out a minority for discriminatory purposes.

AFTERMATH

Courts look at the intent of legislation and apply the strict scrutiny test in cases involving gerrymandering, the redistricting of political divisions

with an ulterior motive, if race is the predominant factor in drawing a district, thereby making the gerrymandering unconstitutional.

SIGNIFICANCE

This case limited state power when discrimination was the goal of state redistricting.

RELATED CASES

Hunter v. City of Pittsburgh, 207 U.S. 161 (1907)

Colegrove v. Green, 328 U.S. 549 (1946)

Baker v. Carr, 369 U.S. 186 (1962)

Reynolds v. Sims, 377 U.S. 533 (1964)

Beer v. United States, 425 U.S. 130 (1976)

Mobile v. Bolden, 446 U.S. 55 (1980)

Shaw v. Reno, 509 U.S. 630 (1993)

Miller v. Johnson, 515 U.S. 900 (1995)

RECOMMENDED READING

Elliot, Ward E. Y. *The Rise of the Guardian Democracy.* Cambridge, Mass.: Harvard University Press, 1974.

J. D. Lucas, *Dragon in the Thicket: A Perusal of Gomillion v. Lightfoot,* 1961 Supreme Court Review 194.

The Supreme Court, 1960 Term, 75 Harvard Law Review 136 (1961).

Case Title: *Burton v. Wilmington Parking Authority*

Legal Citation: 365 U.S. 715

Year of Decision: 1961

KEY ISSUE

Does the exclusion of an African-American patron on the basis of race from a privately owned and operated restaurant located in a building owned by an agent of the state of Delaware violate the equal protection clause of the Fourteenth Amendment?

HISTORY OF THE CASE

In Wilmington, Delaware, the Eagle Coffee Shoppe ("the Restaurant") was located inside an off-street-parking building. The building in which the Restaurant was located was owned and operated by the Wilmington Parking Authority ("Parking Authority"), which was an agency of the state of Delaware. All property owned or used by the authority was exempt from state taxes, and both national and state flags were hung from the rooftop of the building. The lease agreement between the Restaurant and the Parking Authority did not contain a requirement that the Restaurant's services be made available on a nondiscriminatory basis. The Restaurant refused to serve William Burton because he was African American. Because the Parking Authority leased the building to the Restaurant, Burton claimed the refusal violated his rights under the equal protection clause of the Fourteenth Amendment. The Supreme Court of Delaware held that the Restaurant was a private actor, and thus, the Fourteenth Amendment had no application to the case. The U.S. Supreme Court granted certiorari on the merits.

SUMMARY OF ARGUMENTS

The state argued that only a small percentage of the total cost of the facility was paid by public funds, that leasing the property was meant to be a way of earning revenue through the building, and that "the Authority had no original intent to place a restaurant in the building, it being only a happenstance resulting from the bidding." The Restaurant alleged that serving African Americans would hurt business.

Burton argued that, because the Restaurant was located in a building operated by the state, its actions were state actions, and refusal of service was a violation of equal protection.

DECISION

Justice Clark delivered the opinion of the Court, finding that Burton's equal protection rights were violated. Under the *Civil Rights Cases*, the principle was established that the individual rights guaranteed in the Fourteenth Amendment dealt with violations by the states, not private actors. In *Cooper v. Aaron*, the Court established that state participation could be found through "any arrangement, management, funds, or property" and other factors regarding the degree of involvement by the state. On the basis of these holdings, the main question in this case was whether state action was involved on the basis of the relationship between the Restaurant, a private actor, and the Parking Authority, an arm of the state.

The Court applied a balancing test, first acknowledging the difficulty in applying a test that dealt with "sifting facts and weighing circumstances" to determine whether "the nonobvious involvement of the State in private conduct [can] be attributed its true significance." The Court found that the land and building were publicly owned and meant for public use for government functions. The building was also maintained by the state with regard to repairs and upkeep. The state derived money from leasing to places such as the Restaurant, and mutual benefits resulted from this arrangement.

The Court stated that the state had acted unconstitutionally, regardless of whether it had acted in good faith, and its joint participation with the Restaurant was within the scope of the Fourteenth Amendment. In reversing the judgment of the Supreme Court of Delaware, the Court held that "when a State leases public property in the manner and for the purpose shown to have been the case here, the proscriptions of the Fourteenth Amendment must be complied with by the lessee as certainly as though they were binding covenants written into the agreement itself." Accordingly, the Court held that Delaware had violated Burton's equal protection rights when the Eagle Coffee Shoppe refused to serve him food and drink because of his race.

Justice Stewart wrote a concurring opinion, stating that Burton should not have been denied service because the language of the Delaware statute authorized discrimination based exclusively on race, which was a clear violation of the Fourteenth Amendment.

Justice Harlan wrote a dissenting opinion, joined by Justice Whittaker, stating that state action was probably lacking under the facts of this case, but the case should have either been remanded to the Delaware Supreme Court or held, pending application to the state court for clarification. He expressed that the time for adjudicating was not right, stating that it was "unnecessary and unwise to reach issues of such broad constitutional significance as those now decided by the Court, before the necessity for deciding them has become apparent." Justice Frankfurter also filed a dissenting opinion, expressing that the case was decided too early, and he thought the case should have been sent back to state court for clarification as to how the statute was construed.

AFTERMATH

In *Moose Lodge No. 107 v. Irvis* (1972), the Court refused to apply *Burton* where it determined that the state was not a participant in a business solely because the establishment had a liquor license issued by the state. Although questioned, the holding in *Burton* remains good law.

SIGNIFICANCE

The Court determined that where there is sufficient state participation in a business, that business may not violate the equal protection clause by refusing to serve an individual on the basis of race.

RELATED CASES

Civil Rights Cases, 109 U.S. 3 (1883)

Cooper v. Aaron, 358 U.S. 1, 4 (1958)

Moose Lodge No. 107 v. Irvis, 407 U.S. 163 (1972)

RECOMMENDED READING

Hala Ayoub, *The State Action Doctrine in State and Federal Courts,* 11 Florida State University Law Review 893 (1984).

Kevin Cole, *Federal and State "State Action": The Undercritical Embrace of a Hypercriticized Doctrine,* 24 Georgia Law Review 327 (1990).

Epstein, Lee and Thomas G. Walker. *Constitutional Law for a Changing America: Rights, Liberties, and Justice.* Washington, D.C.: Congressional Quarterly Books, 2000.

Case Title: *Hoyt v. Florida*

Legal Citation: 368 U.S. 57

Year of Decision: 1961

KEY ISSUE

Does a Florida statute that permitted females to serve on juries only on a voluntary basis and after they had registered to do so violate the equal protection clause of the Fourteenth Amendment of the U.S. Constitution?

HISTORY OF THE CASE

In 1958, Gwendolyn Hoyt was convicted of second-degree murder of her husband in Hillsborough County, Florida. At trial, the evidence showed that she had beaten her husband to death with a baseball bat during an argument over his infidelity. Hoyt was convicted by an all-male jury and sentenced to 30 years of hard labor. At the time of her conviction, section 40.01(1) of the Florida Statutes governed the impaneling of jurors in Florida. This statute provided that while both males and females could serve on Florida juries, females could serve only after having registered with the local circuit court office. In effect, this meant that Florida juries were overwhelmingly male, as few females volunteered by completing the registration process.

Also at issue in the case was section 40.10 of the Florida Statutes, which controlled the action of county jury commissioners in drawing up the annual list of qualified persons to sit on a jury. The statute required that the jury commissioners compile a list of 10,000 names of potential jurors, drawing from both the qualified male electorate and the list of females who had registered for jury service. The testimony was that only 10–12 female names were added to the list of 10,000 potential jurors each year in Hillsborough County.

After her conviction, Hoyt appealed to the Florida Supreme Court, which affirmed the conviction.

SUMMARY OF ARGUMENTS

Hoyt argued that she was denied equal protection of the laws by the operation of Florida laws that were on their face, and as applied to her particular case, discriminatory, as they prevented women from sitting on her jury. Hoyt asserted that the particular nature of her crime required the inclusion of persons of her own sex to judge her guilt or innocence properly.

The state reasoned that Section 40.01 was a constitutional provision that did not violate the defendant's rights. Also, according to the state, the trial record did not indicate that a systematic or intentional exclusion of women occurred during selection of the jury.

DECISION

The Court held that while women had made great strides in their participation in community life, a legislature could still rationally conclude that women were still to be regarded as the center of "home and family life." Jury service might interfere with these obligations. Thus, the difference in treatment between men and women under the Florida statute could be regarded as a "reasonable classification" and not a violation of the U.S. Constitution.

The mere fact that the Florida statute made it likely that all-male juries would be normal in Florida was not enough to invalidate the statute in the Court's view. The opinion, by Justice Harlan, framed the issue as follows: "Of course, these premises misconceive the scope of the right to an impartially selected jury assured by the Fourteenth Amendment. That right does not entitle one accused of crime to a jury tailored to the circumstances of the particular case, whether relating to the sex or other condition of the defendant. . . . It requires only that the jury be indiscriminately drawn from among those eligible in the community for jury service. . . . The result

of this appeal must therefore depend on whether such an exclusion of women from jury service has been shown."

The Court began by recognizing that, on its face, Section 40.01(1) did not exclude women from jury service but permitted them to serve if they so chose. The statute would be valid as long as this exemption was based on "some reasonable classification and whether the manner in which it is exercisable rests on some rational foundation."

The Court also considered Hoyt's attack on Section 40.10 of the Florida Statutes, which governed the actual selection of jurors in her particular case. The operation of this statute, too, resulted in an all-male jury, which she argued was a violation of the equal protection clause of the U.S. Constitution. The Court agreed that the jury list compiled for use in selecting jurors for Hoyt's case had a very small percentage of women, but there was no showing that this was done for any discriminatory purpose. The court distinguished Hoyt's case from cases such as *Hernandez v. Texas* (1954), where the evidence showed that Hispanic jurors were deliberately kept off juror lists, in circumstances that showed a discriminatory intent against persons of particular ethnic background.

AFTERMATH

Hoyt was effectively overruled by the 1975 Supreme Court decision in *Taylor v. Louisiana*. The Court in *Taylor* heard a challenge to a Louisiana statute very similar to the Florida statute at issue in *Hoyt,* which also excluded females from participating in juries unless they registered their willingness to do so. The *Taylor* court held that such a statute was unconstitutional as it denied a defendant the right to be tried by a jury drawn from a representative cross section of the community.

SIGNIFICANCE

This decision perpetuated legalized gender discrimination and remained good law for 14 years. When *Hoyt* was finally overturned in 1975, the decision was based on a defendant's right to a jury rather than a woman's right to participate on a jury.

RELATED CASES

Smith v. Texas, 311 U.S. 128 (1940)

Glasser v. United States, 315 U.S. 60 (1942)

Ballard v. U.S., 329 U.S. 187 (1946)

Taylor v. Louisiana, 419 U.S. 522 (1975)

STATUTES AT ISSUE

Section 40.01(1) of the Florida Statutes § 40.01(1), Fla. Stat. (1959)

Section 40.10 of the Florida Statutes § 40.10, Fla. Stat. (1959)

RECOMMENDED READING

Note, *Courts—Women Jurors—Automatic Exemption,* 36 Tulane Law Review 858 (1962).

Joanna L. Grossman, *Women's Jury Service: Right of Citizenship or Privilege of Difference?,* 46 Stanford Law Review 1115 (1994).

Case Title: *Baker v. Carr*

Alternate Case Titles: The Reapportionment Case; the Political Thicket Case

Legal Citation: 369 U.S. 186

Year of Decision: 1962

KEY ISSUE

Do federal courts have the power to hear claims by voters challenging the constitutionality of the distribution of legislative seats in a state legislature, or is this a matter that can be decided only by the voters through their elected representatives?

HISTORY OF THE CASE

The Tennessee constitution required that both houses of the state legislature be apportioned among districts "according to the number of qualified electors in each." The legislature had been reapportioned only three times: in 1881, 1891, and 1901.

By 1960, the legislative districts were grossly unequal. Rural areas had a disproportionate number of representatives in relation to their population. Senate district populations ranged from 25,000 to 132,000; thus 20 the 33 members of the Senate were elected by barely one-third of the state's population. Though urban areas had grown significantly in the 60 years since the last reapportionment, the rural areas managed to retain their political power and control of the state legislature.

Charles Baker was the mayor of Millington, Tennessee. This Memphis suburb had grown rapidly since the end of World War II. With this growth came increased financial needs. Little money, however, was forthcoming from the rural-dominated legislature.

Baker and voters in the urban counties brought suit in federal district court to compel the state legislature to reapportion the legislative districts so that the urban areas would have representation in proportion to their population. They alleged that the 1901 apportionment statute still in effect denied voters in urban areas equal protection under the Fourteenth Amendment "by virtue of the debasement of their votes." A three-judge federal court dismissed their claim, holding that the court lacked jurisdiction to hear the case and that no claim was stated upon which relief could be granted. The voters appealed.

SUMMARY OF ARGUMENTS

The appellants, who included the mayor of Nashville, argued that the state of Tennessee arbitrarily apportioned the legislative seats among the counties and subsequently failed to reapportion the seats in light of substantial population growth and redistribution in violation of the Fourteenth Amendment. The appellees, including Joe C. Carr, the secretary of state, argued that the Court lacked jurisdiction to hear the case and that the appellants failed to state a claim for which relief could be granted.

DECISION

The Supreme Court did not rule on the merits of the voters' claims but instead only grappled with the procedural issues of whether a federal court had the power to decide issues such as these. Specifically, the Court ruled on the legal issues of jurisdiction, standing, and justiciability.

Justice William J. Brennan, Jr., writing for a six-member majority, quickly determined that the federal court had the power to rule on the voters' claim. Justice Brennan wrote that if a claim arises under the Constitution, federal laws, or treaties, a federal court has jurisdiction over the claim, provided that the claim is not "so attenuated and unsubstantial as to be absolutely devoid of merit." Since this was not a meritless claim, the district court possessed jurisdiction.

Justice Brennan also quickly resolved the standing question, which asked whether the individuals who brought the suit had had their rights violated. Brennan considered whether they had "such a personal stake in the outcome." The Court held that "voters who allege facts showing disadvantage to themselves as individuals have standing to sue."

The question of whether the challenge to the state legislature's apportionment was a justiciable claim was the most difficult of the three issues addressed in *Baker v. Carr*. The state argued that the federal court could not hear a claim that challenged the apportionment of the legislature because it was a nonjusticiable "political question." The state relied on the case of *Luther v. Borden* (1849). *Luther* involved a simple trespass, complicated by the fact that Rhode Island, the state where the case arose, was in the midst of a civil dispute. Two groups claimed to be the rightful government of the state. The defendants in *Luther* responded to the claim of trespass by arguing that they were the agents of Rhode Island's government. The Supreme Court declined to rule on the case, noting that to do so would require a finding of which of the two competing groups had the rightful claim to the state's government.

One hundred years later, the state of Tennessee argued that the makeup of its legislature involved a similar "political question" that could not be resolved by federal courts.

In the lengthiest part of his opinion, Justice Brennan explained, "The mere fact that the suit seeks protection of a political right does not mean it presents a political question." Instead, the political question doctrine is "primarily a function of the separation of powers."

Tennessee's apportionment of its legislature did not present a political question because, as a state, it was not a "coequal branch" of the federal government. Justice Brennan explained that in *Luther v. Borden,* the Court had not deferred to the state of Rhode Island but instead had declined to rule to avoid conflict with the executive branch and Congress. In this case, the Court therefore directed the district court to conduct a full trial to decide the constitutionality of the apportionment of the Tennessee legislature.

Three justices wrote separate decisions concurring in the Court's decision. Justice Douglas defended the Court's decision against charges that this matter was "beyond the competence of courts." It made no difference that legislative apportionment involved complicated issues. Justice Douglas explained, "Adjudication is often perplexing and complicated."

Justice Tom C. Clark also joined in the Court's opinion, but he was unhappy that the Court had not ruled on the merits: "The Court holds that the appellants have alleged a cause of action. However, it refuses to award relief here—although the facts are undisputed—and fails to give the District Court any guidance whatever." Justice Clark affirmed "that an appropriate remedy may be formulated." Also of interest, Justice Clark stated that he believed it was constitutional for state legislatures to have one house whose representation is not exclusively based on population, as in the U.S. Senate.

Justice Stewart wrote his concurrence to emphasize the narrowness of the majority's holding. He criticized his fellow justices: "The separate writings of my dissenting and concurring Brothers stray so far from the subject of today's decision as to convey, I think, a distressingly inaccurate impression of what the Court decides." He explained that the Court decided "three things and no more: '(a) that the Court possessed jurisdiction of the subject matter; (b) that a justiciable cause of action is stated upon which appellants would be entitled to relief; and (c) that the appellants have standing to challenge the Tennessee apportionment statutes.'"

Justices Felix Frankfurter and John Marshall Harlan each wrote lengthy dissenting opinions. Justice Frankfurter warned of the dire consequences of the Court's decision. He described the holding as "a massive repudiation of the experience of our whole past." Justice Frankfurter believed the ruling, by involving itself in the political arena, would undermine the legitimacy of the U.S. Supreme Court:

> The Court's authority—possessed of neither the purse nor the sword—ultimately rests on sustained public confidence in its moral sanction. Such feeling must be nourished by the Court's complete detachment, in fact and in appearance, from political entanglements and by abstention from injecting itself into the clash of political settlements.

Justice Frankfurter then spent the next 63 pages explaining why the Court's holding involved a break with past decisions in outlining the history of the judiciary's attempts to avoid involvement in the political arena.

While Justice Frankfurter criticized the majority's opinion for ignoring the broad issues of the Court's involving itself in the political arena, Justice Harlan focused on what he perceived as a lack of harm from the abridgment of a federal right. Justice Harlan accused the majority of ignoring a simple and basic question: "Does the complaint disclose a violation of a federal constitutional right?" He wrote, "I can find nothing in the Equal Protection Clause or elsewhere in the Federal Constitution which expressly or impliedly supports the view that state legislatures must be so structured as to reflect with approximate equality the voice of every voter."

AFTERMATH

On remand, the district court gave the legislature an additional year to reformulate a different apportionment plan and implied that Tennessee possibly could have one house not based exclusively on population, as suggested by Justice Clark. This was held not to be constitutionally permissible in the 1964 Supreme Court case *Reynolds v. Sims*.

SIGNIFICANCE

The Court's ruling in *Baker* opened the door for numerous challenges to the apportionment of state legislatures. Even though the *Baker* decision did not rule on the merits of the case, the majority's opinion was interpreted by lower courts as requiring at least one house of state legislatures to be apportioned on the basis of districts of equal population. As subsequent Supreme Court cases would hold, however, this was a narrow reading of *Baker v. Carr.*

RELATED CASES

Colegrove v. Green, 328 U.S. 459 (1946)

Gray v. Sanders, 372 U.S. 368 (1963)

Reynolds v. Sims, 377 U.S. 533 (1964)

Wesberry v. Sanders, 376 U.S. 1 (1964)

RECOMMENDED READING

Cortner, Richard C. *The Apportionment Cases.* Knoxville: University of Tennessee Press, 1970.

Dixon, Robert G., Jr. *Democratic Representation: Reapportionment in Law and Politics.* New York: Oxford University Press, 1968.

Graham, Gene S. *One Man, One Vote:* Baker v. Carr *and the American Levellers.* Boston: Little, Brown, 1972.

Grofman, Bernard. *Voting Rights, Voting Wrongs: The Legacy of* Baker v. Carr. New York: Twentieth Century Fund, 1990.

Hanson, Royce. *The Political Thicket.* Englewood Cliffs, N.J.: Prentice Hall, 1966.

Hasen, Richard. *The Supreme Court and Election Law: Judging Equality from* Baker v. Carr *to* Bush v. Gore. New York: New York University Press, 2003.

Schwab, Larry M. *The Impact of Congressional Reapportionment and Redistricting.* Lanham, Md.: University Press of America, 1988.

Case Title: *Reynolds v. Sims*

Alternate Case Titles: The Reapportionment Case; the State Legislature Apportionment Case; the "One Person, One Vote" Case

Legal Citation: 377 U.S. 533

Year of Decision: 1964

KEY ISSUE

Does the equal protection clause of the Fourteenth Amendment require representatives in state legislatures to be elected from districts with the same population?

HISTORY OF THE CASE

As with many southern states in the early 1960s, the Alabama legislature gave greater representation to voters living in rural areas. The Alabama legislature consisted of a Senate with 35 members and a House of Representatives with 106 members. The 35 senators were divided among districts composed of one or more of the state's 67 counties, with no counties split between separate districts. Each of the 67 counties elected at least one member of the House of Representatives, with the remaining 39 members allocated among the counties on the basis of their population. Because the rural counties had much smaller populations than their urban counterparts, rural voters were represented disproportionately. The apportionment of seats in the Alabama legislature had been unchanged since 1903.

On August 26, 1961, voters from Jefferson County, an urban county, challenged the apportionment of the Alabama legislature in federal district court. The voters argued that "since the population growth in the state from 1900 to 1960 had been uneven, Jefferson and other counties were now the victims of serious discrimination with respect to the allocation of legislative representation."

Encouraged by the holding of *Baker v. Carr*, the voters from Jefferson County urged the fed-

eral court to enjoin the upcoming primary election, scheduled for the following month. The district court refused to stop the election. The federal court urged the legislature to take action in reapportioning its body. If the legislature failed to act, the court warned it would be under a "clear duty" to take some sort of action before the November 1962 general election.

The Alabama legislature responded to the federal court's suggestion half-heartedly. In July, the Alabama legislature adopted two reapportionment plans to take effect for the 1966 elections. One plan was a proposed constitutional amendment, and the other plan was a statutory measure, enacted as standby legislation in case the proposed amendment failed.

The proposed constitutional amendment provided for the House of Representatives to consist of 106 members, "apportioned by giving one seat to each of Alabama's counties and distributing the others according to population using an 'equal proportions' method. . . . The Senate was to be composed of 67 members, one from each county." In the statutory reapportionment plan, the Senate would have 35 members, "representing 35 senatorial districts established along county lines, and altered only a few of the former districts." The House of Representatives would have 106 members, with each county receiving one member and the remaining 39 apportioned "on a rough population basis, requiring increasingly more population to be accorded additional seats."

SUMMARY OF ARGUMENTS

On July 21, 1962, the federal district court held that both the current composition of the Alabama legislature and the two proposed plans violated the equal protection clause of the Fourteenth Amendment of the U.S. Constitution. The court cited the great disparity in the size of the legislative districts: "Only 25.1 percent of Alabama's population resided in districts represented by a majority of the members of the Senate, and only 25.7 percent lived in counties which could elect a majority of the members of the House of Representatives. Population-variance ratios of up to about 41-to-1 existed in the Senate, and up to about 16-to-1 in the House." For example, Bullock County, with a population of 13,462, had two seats in the House of Representatives, whereas Mobile County, with a population of 314,301, had only three representatives.

The district court held that the proposed plans did not adequately improve the existing disparities, and they actually made representation more unfair. The court pointed out that under the proposed constitutional amendment, "the present control of the Senate by members representing 25.1 percent of the people of Alabama would be reduced to control by members representing 19.4 percent of the people of the State." The court also rejected an argument that the allocation of at least one representative to each county in the upper house was analogous to the representation of the states in the U.S. Senate, in which each state receives two senators regardless of the state's population: "The analogy cannot survive the most superficial examination into the history of the Federal Constitution . . . nor can it survive a comparison of the different political natures of states and counties."

The district court issued an order for a temporary apportionment plan for the general election in November. In the temporary plan, the House of Representatives would follow the state's constitutional amendment plan, with 106 members, one for each county, and the remainder allocated to the counties by population, and the Senate would follow the statutory plan, with 35 senators from districts established along county lines. The district court made it clear that this was only a "'moderate action' . . . designed to break the strangle hold by the smaller counties on the Alabama Legislature and would not suffice as a permanent reapportionment."

Both the voters and the state appealed the district court's decision, and the U.S. Supreme Court agreed to resolve the issue.

DECISION

The U.S. Supreme Court agreed with the district court that both the existing and proposed apportionments of the Alabama legislature were unconstitutional. Chief Justice Earl Warren, in his opinion for the Court, began by explaining the constitutional right to vote: "The Constitution protects the right of all qualified citizens to vote, in state as well as in federal elections." The right to vote is one of the most important of rights protected by the Constitution. "Any alleged infringement of the right of citizens to vote must be carefully and meticulously scrutinized."

Chief Justice Warren then looked at the Court's decisions involving statewide primary elections and congressional elections. The Court stated that these cases held that "one person's vote must be counted equally with those of all other voters in a State." This concept applied equally to state legislatures. The argument that the apportionment respected the boundaries of counties did not excuse the unconstitutionality of Alabama's not giving equal weight to all votes. Chief Justice Warren stated it simply: "Legislators represent people, not trees or acres. Legislators are elected by voters, not farms or cities or economic interests." Thus, Alabama's legislative apportionment, based upon county lines, amounted to discrimination: "Diluting the weight of votes because of place of residence impairs basic constitutional rights under the Fourteenth Amendment just as much as invidious discriminations based upon factors such as race . . . or economic status."

In the Court's view, the allocation of two senators to each state in the U.S. Senate was "inapposite" to the composition of state legislatures. "Arising from unique historical circumstances, [the U.S. Senate's apportionment] is based on the consideration that in establishing our type of federalism a group of formerly independent States bound together under one national government." Alabama, therefore, was bound to provide equal representation for rural and urban voters alike because the Constitution required "that the seats in both houses of a bicameral state legislature must be apportioned on a population basis."

Justice Tom Clark concurred in the Court's opinion, but he would have decided the case on narrower grounds. He believed that the "federal analogy" was applicable at the state level: "In my view, if one house of the state Legislature meets the population standard, representation in the other house might include some departure from it so as to take into account, on a rational basis, other factors in order to afford some representation to the various elements of the State." Justice Potter Stewart also concurred in the majority opinion; he would have affirmed the district court's opinion on somewhat narrower grounds.

Justice Harlan strongly dissented from the Court's majority opinion, as he had in *Baker v. Carr*. He raised many compelling scholarly constitutional arguments in his lengthy dissenting opinion. Justice Harlan focused primarily on the wording and history of the Fourteenth Amendment, issues not discussed in Chief Justice Warren's opinion for the majority.

Justice Harlan began by making the unpopular statement that the Fourteenth Amendment *permits* the states to deny its citizens the right to vote. He cited the following language from Section 2 of the Fourteenth Amendment:

> But when the right to vote at any election for the choice of electors for President and Vice President of the United States, Representatives in Congress, the Executive and Judicial officers of a state, or the members of the Legislature thereof, is denied to any of the male inhabitants of such State. . . .

The wording of the amendment then continued, explaining that the state's representation in Congress would be reduced if the right to vote were denied. Justice Harlan concluded from the amendment's wording that if the denial of the right to vote were permitted, then so too, would be a "dilution" of the right.

Justice Harlan further argued that because most of the states that ratified the Fourteenth Amendment had state legislatures in which representation was not based entirely on population, it was unlikely that they intended the Fourteenth Amendment to prohibit such legislative apportionment. Justice Harlan queried: "Can it be seriously contended that the legislatures of these states, almost two-thirds of those concerned, would have ratified an amendment which might render their own States' constitutions unconstitutional?"

Last, Justice Harlan was concerned about the ramifications of the Court's decision. He saw no end to the Court's involvement in supervising legislative apportionment.

It should by now be obvious that these cases do not mark the end of reapportionment problems in the courts. Predictions once made that the courts would never have to face the problem of actually working out an apportionment have proved false. . . .

Generalities cannot obscure the cold truth that cases of this type are not amenable to the development of judicial standards.

Harlan was concerned that the majority's decision did not provide a workable standard for the lower courts to test the constitutionality of legislative apportionment. Whatever the merit of his arguments, they did not persuade his fellow justices; he was but one of nine justices on the Supreme Court who opposed the Court's holding.

AFTERMATH

Although the case was remanded to the district court, there were no further proceedings. The Alabama legislature was accordingly reapportioned so that both houses had equal population districts.

SIGNIFICANCE

With the Court's decision in *Reynolds v. Sims,* there was no longer any ambiguity that both houses of state legislatures had to be apportioned according to population. This case thus required the majority of state legislatures to be reapportioned, since most had at least one house that was not based exclusively on equal population districts.

RELATED CASES

Baker v. Carr, 369 U.S. 186 (1962)

Gray v. Sanders, 372 U.S. 368 (1963)

Wesberry v. Sanders, 376 U.S. 1 (1964)

RECOMMENDED READING

Cortner, Richard C. *The Reapportionment Cases.* Knoxville: University of Tennessee Press, 1970.

Dixon, Robert G., Jr. *Democratic Representation: Reapportionment in Law and Politics*. New York: Oxford University Press, 1968.

Hanson, Royce. *The Political Thicket*. Englewood Cliffs, N.J.: Prentice Hall, 1966.

Case Title: *Pointer v. State of Texas*

Legal Citation: 380 U.S. 400

Year of Decision: 1965

KEY ISSUE

Is the Sixth Amendment guarantee that an accused can confront the witnesses against him or her applicable to the states under the Fourteenth Amendment?

HISTORY OF THE CASE

Bob Pointer and Lloyd Earl Dillard were arrested in Texas and charged with robbing Kenneth Phillips of $375, in violation of Texas Penal Code Art. 1408. Pointer and Dillard were brought before a judge for a preliminary hearing on this charge. At the preliminary hearing, neither Pointer nor Dillard had counsel. The assistant district attorney examined Phillips as a chief witness for the state, and Phillips gave his account of what happened. Dillard attempted to cross-examine Phillips, while Pointer did not.

Phillips moved to California shortly before the case went to trial. The state introduced the testimony of Phillips against the defendant Pointer. Represented by counsel during this time, Pointer objected to the evidence, claiming that it was a denial of his right to confront witnesses against him as guaranteed in the Sixth Amendment.

SUMMARY OF ARGUMENTS

Pointer argued that the evidence of Phillips's testimony should have been inadmissible, as he was not given the proper opportunity to cross-examine the witness afforded him under the Sixth Amendment of the Constitution.

The state argued that Pointer did have the opportunity to cross-examine the witness at the preliminary hearing but chose not to attempt to cross-examine.

DECISION

The Court held that the Sixth Amendment's guarantee that an accused may confront a witness against him or her did apply to the states through the Fourteenth Amendment. The Court also held that states must enforce Sixth Amendment rights under the Fourteenth Amendment using the same standards that protect those personal rights against federal encroachment. Therefore, Pointer was entitled to a trial in accordance with the Sixth Amendment's guarantee.

The Court further held that Phillips's statement was taken under circumstances not affording Pointer, through counsel, an adequate opportunity to cross-examine the witness. Subsequently, the introduction of Phillips's statement into the federal criminal case was a denial of Pointer's Sixth Amendment privilege of confrontation. Pointer's conviction was reversed and remanded.

AFTERMATH

Since *Pointer,* defendants are guaranteed the right of confronting a witness whether they are in federal or state court.

SIGNIFICANCE

While many states recognized the Sixth Amendment right of confrontation that was guaranteed in federal trials, Texas did not. *Pointer* highlighted that upholding the right of confrontation necessitated uniformity throughout the states.

RELATED CASES

Gideon v. Wainwright, 372 U.S. 335 (1963)

Malloy v. Hogan, 378 U.S. 1 (1964)

RECOMMENDED READING

Roger W. Kirst, *The Procedural Dimension of Confrontation Doctrine,* 66 Nebraska Law Review 485 (1987).

Todd E. Pettys, *Counsel and Confrontation,* 94 Minnesota Law Review 201 (2009).

Case Title: *Harper v. Virginia State Board of Elections*

Legal Citation: 383 U.S. 663

Year of Decision: 1966

KEY ISSUE

Do poll taxes violate the equal protection clause of the Fourteenth Amendment?

HISTORY OF THE CASE

Virginia residents brought suits to have the Virginia poll tax declared unconstitutional. A three-judge district court dismissed the complaint on the basis of the holding in *Breedlove v. Suttles* (1937), which upheld a poll tax in Georgia. The plaintiffs appealed this dismissal to the Supreme Court.

The Virginia Constitution directed the General Assembly to levy an annual poll tax not to exceed $1.50 on every resident of the state above the age of 21. Payment of the poll tax was a precondition to voting. The poll tax was to be paid for three years preceding the year in which a voter registered. Those who did not pay the poll tax were disenfranchised.

SUMMARY OF ARGUMENTS

The plaintiffs argued that the poll tax worked to disenfranchise in a discriminatory manner and thus violated the equal protection clause of the Fourteenth Amendment.

The Virginia State Board of Elections argued that voting was not a First Amendment right, and the Fourteenth Amendment did not place a limit on the state's power to prescribe the qualifications of voters. The board also argued that the poll tax did not violate the equal protection clause.

DECISION

Justice Douglas, writing for six judges, held that the poll tax was unconstitutional because it was inconsistent with the equal protection clause of the Fourteenth Amendment. He noted that the right to vote in state elections is nowhere expressly protected in the Constitution and that the right to vote is implicit in the First Amendment. As a result, this right may not be conditioned upon payment of a tax or fee. In addition, he noted that once the right of suffrage was granted, it could not be made conditional on requirements inconsistent with the equal protection clause: "That is to say, the right of suffrage is subject to the imposition of state standards which are not discriminatory and which do not contravene any restriction that Congress, acting pursuant to its constitutional powers, has imposed."

He concluded that a state violates the equal protection clause when it makes affluence or a payment of any fee an electoral standard. He reasoned that, unlike literacy tests, poll taxes bear no relation to the ability of the voter to exercise his right. He continued that the case history demonstrated that the equal protection clause of the Fourteenth Amendment prohibits the state from adopting voter qualifications that work invidiously to discriminate.

Justice Black dissented on the ground that in *Breedlove v. Suttles* the Court held that a state poll tax in Georgia, which was a prerequisite to voting in state elections, was valid. The Court explicitly rejected the reasoning that the equal protection clause was violated by placing an undue burden on different groups of people according to age, sex, or the ability to pay. In addition, he noted that in *Butler v. Thompson* (1951) the Court upheld a Virginia state poll tax also challenged on equal protection grounds. He argued that the Court should adhere to the holding in those cases. By doing the opposite, he argued, the majority had given the clause a new meaning; the fact that a law has the result of treating groups differently does not by itself make the law invalid. He also thought that the Court used "the old natural-law-due-process formula" as the basis for invalidating the poll tax as a violation of the equal protection clause. This formula uses the equal protection clause to write into the Constitution what the Court considers good government policy.

Justice Harlan joined by Justice Stewart dissented on the ground that the Court's invalidation of the poll tax was an infringement on the right of the state and the federal political process. They argued that the Court, in using the equal protection clause to invalidate the Virginia state poll tax, departed from the established standard regarding the application of the clause. He reasoned that the equal protection clause prohibits the state from arbitrarily treating people differently but that the clause does not require equal treatment of all people.

He continued that poll taxes and property qualifications have been a traditional part of the political structure, and though they may not be in accord with modern notions of equity, it is not the job of the Court to invalidate these provisions. If these provisions truly do not square with the modern notion of equity, then the legislature should address this by invalidating these taxes.

AFTERMATH

In *Bullock v. Carter* (1972), the Court invalidated a Texas scheme that imposed filing fees on political candidates for state and local office. The Court reasoned that the scheme was invalid because the Texas filing fees had an impact on voters by limiting their candidate choices as a result of the candidate's or voters' lack of financial resources to support a campaign; therefore, the law must be "closely scrutinized and found reasonably necessary to the accomplishment of legitimate state objectives in order to pass constitutional muster." In *Lubin v. Panish* (1974), the Court invalidated a similar scheme in California.

SIGNIFICANCE

The decision in *Harper* was an extension of the holding in *Edwards v. California* (1941), in which the Court invalidated a law that prohibited taking a nonresident indigent into the state. The Court reasoned that the state may not qualify or limit one's right as an American citizen on the basis of his wealth.

This decision occurred two years after the passage of the Twenty-fourth Amendment, which prohibits states from imposing poll taxes as a requirement for voting in federal elections. This decision in applying strict scrutiny to the classification gauged whether wealth is a suspect classification. The decision reaffirmed a basic underpinning of the American political system: that all citizens,

regardless of wealth, should be able to participate in decision making of the government.

The case also occurred in the aftermath of other cases in which the Court addressed other infringements on the exercise of one's right to vote. In *Reynolds v. Sims* (1964), a seminal case in the area of reapportionment, the Court held that the equal protection clause required state legislatures to be apportioned on a one man–one vote basis. In *Carrington v. Rash* (1965), the Court invalidated a Texas statute that prohibited a member of the armed services who moved into the state during active duty to vote in state elections. In *Kramer v. Union Free School District No. 15* (1969), the Court invalidated a New York educational law that made otherwise eligible voters in state and federal elections ineligible to vote in school district elections if they did not meet one of the following three requirements: (1) the person was the owner or lessee of taxable real property located in the district, (2) the person was the spouse of one who owned or leased property in the district, or (3) the person was the parent or guardian of a child enrolled for a specific period in the school district during the preceding year. The Court held that the law was not narrowly enough tailored to capture only the target group of persons primarily interested in school affairs.

In *Cipriano v. City of Houma* (1969), the Court invalidated a Louisiana law that permitted only property-owning taxpayers to vote in municipal elections. A similar provision was invalidated by the Court in *City of Phoenix v. Kolodziejski*. However, in *Salyer Land Co. v. Tulare Lake Basin Water Storage District* (1973), the Court held that *Kramer*, *Cipriano*, and *Kolodziejski* did not prevent California from limiting participation in a water district election to persons and corporations that owned land in the district or from apportioning votes to the assessed value of the land. The justices reasoned that the representation afforded was in proportion to the land possessed, and therefore, the plural election requirement of *Reynolds* and its progeny were inapplicable.

RELATED CASES

Breedlove v. Suttles, 302 U.S. 277 (1937)

Edwards v. California, 314 U.S. 160 (1941)

Lassiter v. Northampton County Board of Elections, 360 U.S. 45 (1959)

Reynolds v. Sims, 377 U.S. 533 (1964)

Carrington v. Rash, 380 U.S. 89 (1965)

Cipriani v. City of Jouma, 395 U.S. 701 (1969)

City of Phoenix v. Kolodziejski, 399 U.S. 204 (1969)

Kramer v. Union Free School District No. 15, 395 U.S. 621 (1969)

Bullock v. Carter, 405 U.S. 134 (1972)

Salyer Land Co. v. Tulare Lake Bason Water Storage District, 410 U.S. 719 (1973)

Ball v. James, 451 U.S. 355 (1981)

RECOMMENDED READING

Berger, Raoul. *Government by Judiciary: The Transformation of the Fourteenth Amendment*. Cambridge, Mass.: Harvard University Press, 1977.

Sandford Levinson, *Suffrage and Community: Who Should Vote?*, 41 Florida Law Review 545 (1989).

Gerald L. Neuman, *We Are the People*, 13 Michigan Law Review 259 (1992).

William Van Alstyne, *The Fourteenth Amendment, the "Right" to Vote, and the Understanding of the Thirty-ninth Congress*, 1965 Supreme Court Review 33.

Case Title: *Katzenbach v. Morgan*

Legal Citation: 384 U.S. 641

Year of Decision: 1966

KEY ISSUES

Did Congress exceed its constitutional powers, thereby violating the Tenth Amendment, through the enactment of section 4(e) of the Voting Rights Act of 1965, which provided that the right to vote could not be denied to a person who successfully completed the sixth grade in a public or accredited private school in Puerto Rico, even if the classes were not taught in English?

HISTORY OF THE CASE

State laws in New York conditioned the right to vote on an ability to read and write English. The Supreme Court had previously held that English literacy requirements did not violate the Fourteenth and Fifteenth Amendments. In 1965, Congress enacted the Voting Rights Act pursuant to its enforcement power under section 5 of the Fourteenth Amendment. Section 4(e) gave the right to vote to Puerto Ricans who had completed the sixth grade in an accredited public school and were unable to read or write English. Under section 4(e), voting could not be conditioned on English literacy.

SUMMARY OF ARGUMENTS

Appellant Katzenbach, the U.S. attorney general, argued that section 4(e) was a proper exercise of congressional power.

Appellees, registered voters in New York City, including Morgan, argued that section 4(e) could be upheld only if the judiciary first determined that the state law was prohibited by the Fourteenth Amendment. The appellees also argued that section 4(e) was inconsistent with the letter and spirit of the Constitution.

DECISION

Justice Brennan delivered the opinion of the Court. Brennan found that Congress could enact appropriate legislation prohibiting certain actions to enforce the equal protection clause without a prior determination by the Court that the act sought to be prohibited violated the Fourteenth Amendment. Brennan found that it was within Congress's grant of legislative power to exercise its discretion in determining what legislation was necessary to protect Fourteenth Amendment guarantees. The Court restricted its determination to whether section 4(e) was a permissible enactment to enforce the equal protection clause. Specifically, Brennan found that section 4(e) constituted legislation to enforce the equal protection clause and was within congressional authority as the Court could perceive a basis for the action.

Justice Douglas joined the Court's opinion, but he reserved judgment on whether section 4(e) was consistent with the letter and spirit of the Constitution.

Justices Harlan and Stewart dissented, defining the relevant issue as whether New York's literacy test was reasonably designed to further a legitimate state interest. The justices found voting essentially to be a matter of state concern and believed it was the place of the judiciary to determine whether a state practice violated the equal protection clause. The justices would have upheld the New York literacy test. They believed that allowing Congress to override New York's literacy test allowed the Fourteenth Amendment to eclipse state authority regarding voting.

AFTERMATH

The decision enabled many New York City residents who had migrated from Puerto Rico to vote.

SIGNIFICANCE

The Court's decision in *Katzenbach v. Morgan* allowed Congress to find certain actions unconstitutional and enact legislation to remedy the violations.

RELATED CASES

South Carolina v. Katzenbach, 383 U.S. 301 (1966)

Gatson County v. United States, 395 U.S. 285 (1969)

Oregon v. Mitchell, 400 U.S. 112 (1970)

Richmond v. United States, 422 U.S. 358 (1975)

Beer v. United States, 425 U.S. 130 (1976)

Rome v. United States, 446 U.S. 156 (1980)

RECOMMENDED READING

Alexander M. Bickel, *The Voting Rights Cases,* 1966 Supreme Court Review 79 (1966).

Robert A. Burt, *Miranda and Title II: A Morganatic Marriage,* 1969 Supreme Court Review 81.

Bybee, Keith J. *Mistaken Identity: The Supreme Court and the Politics of Minority Representation.* Princeton, N.J.: Princeton University Press, 1998.

Stephen L. Carter, *The Morgan "Power" and the Forced Reconsideration of Constitutional Decisions,* 53 University of Chicago Law Review 819 (1986).

Keynes, Edward, with Randall K. Miller. *The Courts vs. Congress.* Durham, N.C.: Duke University Press, 1989.

Daniel J. Leffell, *Congressional Power to Enforce Due Process Rights,* 80 Columbia Law Review 1265 (1980).

Case Title: *Loving v. Virginia*

Legal Citation: 388 U.S. 1

Year of Decision: 1967

KEY ISSUE

Does a state antimiscegenation statute, that is, one that prohibited marriage between persons of different races, violate the equal protection clause of the Fourteenth Amendment?

HISTORY OF THE CASE

In 1967, 16 states had laws prohibiting interracial marriage: Alabama, Arkansas, Delaware, Florida, Georgia, Kentucky, Louisiana, Mississippi, Missouri, North Carolina, Oklahoma, South Carolina, Tennessee, Texas, Virginia, and West Virginia. Section 20-54 of the Virginia Code prohibited white people from marrying "colored" persons. Section 20-57 declared interracial marriages void. Section 20-58 prohibited interracial couples from leaving the state to marry and then returning to the state to cohabit as spouses. Section 20-59 declared violations of the previous sections as felonies punishable by one to five years in prison.

In 1958, Richard Loving, a white man, married Mildred Jeter, a black woman, in Washington, D.C. After the couple moved to Virginia, a grand jury indicted the Lovings for violating Virginia's ban on interracial marriages. The Lovings pleaded guilty of violating sections 20–58 of the Virginia Code. The trial judge suspended a one-year jail sentence for a 25-year period upon the condition that the Lovings leave the state and not return together for 25 years. The Lovings moved to Washington, D.C. In 1963, the Lovings moved for the state trial court to vacate the judgment and set aside the sentence on the grounds that it violated the Fourteenth Amendment to the U.S. Constitution. The trial judge denied the motion, and the Lovings appealed. The Supreme Court of Appeals of Virginia upheld the convictions.

SUMMARY OF ARGUMENTS

The Lovings argued that the Virginia statute violated the equal protection and due process clauses of the Fourteenth Amendment.

Virginia argued that equal protection merely demands that penal laws be applied equally to members of different races. Moreover, Virginia argued that the antimiscegenation statutes were applied equally among the races and were, therefore, not racially discriminatory.

DECISION

The Supreme Court rejected Virginia's argument, finding that "equal application" of a penal statute composed of racial classifications does not necessarily remove that statute from the Fourteenth Amendment's prohibition of invidious racial discrimination, discrimination unrelated to a legitimate purpose. Consequently, the Court employed a strict scrutiny analysis of the antimiscegenation statutes. Finding no legitimate state purpose that could justify the racial classifications, the Court declared Virginia's antimiscegenation statutes in violation of the equal protection clause of the Fourteenth Amendment.

AFTERMATH

After initiation of the litigation, Maryland repealed its prohibition of interracial marriage.

The Court's decision in *Loving* had the effect of invalidating other states' similar miscegenation statutes. Unfortunately, only eight years after the Court's decision, Richard Loving died.

SIGNIFICANCE

As the Court aptly stated, "There can be no doubt that restricting the freedom to marry solely because of racial classifications violates the central meaning of [equal protection]."

RELATED CASES

Pace v. Alabama, 106 U.S. 583 (1883)

Maynard v. Hill, 125 U.S. 190 (1888)

Meyer v. Nebraska, 262 U.S. 390 (1923)

Skinner v. Oklahoma, 316 U.S. 535 (1942)

Zablocki v. Redhail, 434 U.S. 374 (1978)

RECOMMENDED READING

David Orgon Collidge, *Playing the* Loving *Card: Same Sex Marriage and the Politics of Analogy,* 12 BYU Journal of Public Law 201 (1998).

Anita Kathy Foeman and Teresa Nance. "From Miscegenation to Multiculturalism: Perceptions and Stages of Interracial Relationship Development." *Journal of Black Studies* 29, no. 4 (1999): 540–557.

Mr. and Mrs. Loving. Dir. Richard Friendenberg. Hallmark Television, 1996.

Robert A. Pratt, *Crossing the Color Line: A Historical Assessment and Personal Narrative of* Loving v. Virginia, 41 Howard Law Journal 229 (1998).

W. Wadlington, *The Loving Case: Virginia's Anti-Miscegenation Statute in Historical Perspective,* 52 Virginia Law Review 1189 (1966).

Lynn D. Wardle, Loving v. Virginia *and the Constitutional Right to Marry, 1790–1990,* 41 Howard Law Journal 289 (1998).

Case Title: *Jones v. Alfred H. Mayer Co.*

Legal Citation: 392 U.S. 409

Year of Decision: 1968

KEY ISSUES

Does the Civil Rights Act of 1866 bar all racial discrimination, private as well as public, in the sale or rental of property, and is the statute a valid exercise of the power of Congress to enforce the Third Amendment?

HISTORY OF THE CASE

Jones was interested in buying a house in the Paddock Woods community of St. Louis County. However, when he called to inquire the price of the property, he was informed that the developing company did not sell houses to African Americans. On September 2, 1965, Jones brought this complaint in the District Court of the Eastern District of Missouri. The district court granted the motion to dismiss. The Court of Appeals of the Eighth Circuit affirmed. The Supreme Court granted certiorari to consider the case.

SUMMARY OF ARGUMENTS

Jones argued that the Civil Rights Act of 1866, later codified as 42 U.S.C. section 1982, prohibited racial discrimination in the sale of houses. It was also argued that section 1982 was validly reenacted by Congress under the Fourteenth Amendment.

Alfred H. Mayer Co. et al. argued that Congress did not intend to regulate discrimination of against African Americans by private individuals. It was argued that Congress only intended for the protection of discrimination by the government, because Congress was not aware of the individual discrimination, and therefore, they could not have intended to protect against it. It is also argued that Jones was not entitled to relief under the Fourteenth Amendment.

DECISION

Justice Stewart delivered the opinion of the Court, which held that section 1982 prevents discrimination by private individuals in addition to the government. The Court explained, "At the very least, the freedom that Congress is empowered to secure under the Thirteenth Amendment includes the freedom to buy whatever a white man can buy, the right to live wherever a white man can live. If Congress cannot say that being a free man means at least this much, then the Thirteenth Amendment made a promise the Nation cannot keep."

Stewart explained that one reason behind the holding was that on the face of section 1982, it appeared to prohibit all discrimination against African Americans by private individuals and public authorities. The exact wording of the section—"grants to all citizens, without regard to race or color, the same right to purchase and lease property as is enjoyed by white citizens"—it explained that the section must encompass every racially motivated action to sell or lease, including those by private individuals. In addition, if clause 1 of section 1982 did not intend to grant immunity from private individuals as well as public authority, than clause 2 of section 1982 would be irrelevant. Section 2 provided fines and prison term punishment for individuals who deprived others of their rights.

Stewart also explained that Congress had the power to create section 1982 under the Thirteenth Amendment. The enabling clause of the Thirteenth Amendment enabled Congress to "pass all laws necessary and proper for abolishing all badges and incidents of slavery in the United States." It was reasoned that discrimination against African Americans in refusing to sell houses to people on the basis of the color of their skin forced these individuals to live in ghettos and was therefore a relic of slavery. Therefore, Congress had the power to enact section 1982 to prevent discrimination by private individuals.

AFTERMATH

Jones set the stage for *Runyon v. McCrary* (1976), which was a reach of private discrimination in contracts. Together, these cases provided for a generous and broad interpretation of section

1981 and section 1982, the antidiscrimination provisions. Neither *Jones* nor *Runyon* has ever been modified, so both cases remain good law.

SIGNIFICANCE

Section 1982, which protected the rights of African Americans, was deemed constitutional and applicable to discrimination by private individuals, as well as actions by government. With this ruling, African Americans were given equal property rights to purchase and sell property anywhere. Ultimately, this was the first ruling that held that African Americans could not be denied property rights by anyone.

RELATED CASES

Civil Rights Cases, 109 U.S. 3 (1883)

Virginia v. Rives, 100 U.S. 313 (1879)

Hodges v. United States, 203 U.S. 1 (1906)

Buchanon v. Warley, 245 U.S. 60 (1917)

Corrigan v. Buckley, 271 U.S. 323 (1926)

Hurd v. Hodge, 334 U.S. 24 (1948)

Runyon v. McCrary, 427 U.S. 160 (1976)

STATUTE AT ISSUE

Civil Rights Act of 1866; 42 U.S.C. § 1982

RECOMMENDED READING

Darrell A. H. Miller, *White Cartels, the Civil Rights Act of 1866, and the History of* Jones v. Alfred H. Mayer Co., 77 Fordham Law Review 999 (2008).

Mira Tanna, Jones v. Mayer *Revisited,* 57 Cleveland State Law Review 269 (2009).

Case Title: *Kramer v. Union Free School District*

Legal Citations: 395 U.S. 621; 89 S. Ct. 1886

Year of Decision: 1969

KEY ISSUES

The New York state legislature passed a law that limited the right to vote in school board elections to the parents of school-age children or to persons who owned or leased real property. The question before the Court was whether a state law that limits the right to vote in school board elections should be subjected to "strict scrutiny" analysis.

HISTORY OF THE CASE

In 1965, Morris Kramer had no children and did not own or lease any real property. He attempted to register to vote in a local school district election. His application was rejected for the reasons stated, even though he was a U.S. citizen and registered to vote in New York state and federal elections. Kramer filed a class action suit in the U.S. district court. This court, after some procedural wrangling and an appeal to the court of appeals, dismissed his complaint. Kramer appealed directly to the Supreme Court, which accepted his case.

SUMMARY OF ARGUMENTS

The state of New York argued for the Union Free School District. The state claimed that it had the right to limit "franchise" to those primarily interested in school district elections. *Franchise* means any constitutional or statutory right or privilege; here, it involves the right to vote. The state claimed that because Kramer had no children and paid no real property taxes (monies that partly fund state schools), the often complex school system operations had little, if any, relevance to him. It argued that the law was "rationally related" to the state's legitimate goal of streamlining the electoral process by involving only those "directly affected" by school system matters.

Kramer asserted that by excluding him from participating in the district elections, the state denied him equal protection of the laws. He claimed that all members of the community have an interest in the quality of public education and that decisions taken by local school boards affect the entire population. He also pointed out that property taxes affect everyone through their impact on the prices of goods and services in the community. Because voting is such a fundamental right in our country, he argued that strict scrutiny should be given the statute.

DECISION

The Court struck down the New York law as unconstitutional. Chief Justice Warren wrote the Court's 5-3 majority opinion. The majority used strict scrutiny analysis to determine that the state law violates the equal protection clause of the Fourteenth Amendment.

The Court determined that the rational basis standard should not be used when reviewing statutes that deny some residents the right to vote. The general presumption of constitutionality afforded this type of state law and the traditional approval courts give it was not applicable in this situation.

Instead, strict scrutiny must be used when any fundamental right may be infringed by a law or regulation. The test requires the state to establish that it has a compelling interest justifying the law. Distinctions created by the law must be essential to further some governmental purpose, and the law must be "narrowly tailored" to meet the state's objective. Chief Justice Warren justified this careful examination, instead of a lesser standard, because the right to vote is a foundation of our representative society.

Using strict scrutiny, the Court did not address the compelling-interest question. It sidestepped the issue of whether a state could limit the franchise to those "primarily interested" or "primarily affected" by these school district elections. Instead, the Court said the distinctions drawn by the law did not meet the exacting precision required of statutes. The Court announced that the restrictions imposed by the law did not select for "interest" with sufficient precision to meet the strict standard of review that the Court concluded should apply when the right to vote is denied. The Supreme Court reversed the judgment of the district court and found the law unconstitutional.

AFTERMATH

In this and other similar cases, the Warren Court established the strict scrutiny standard as the cor-

rect test of legislation denying the right to vote. It used the equal protection clause to invalidate these denials of the right to vote. When the Court invokes this test, it virtually always condemns the classification.

SIGNIFICANCE

As odd as it may seem, the right to vote has no direct textual support in the Constitution. True, the Fifteenth Amendment forbids denying the right on the basis of race, and the Nineteenth Amendment forbids denial on the basis of sex; however, the Constitution itself grants no positive right to vote in general. The Supreme Court nevertheless interprets the Constitution to grant the right, using the equal protection clause as the vehicle for creation and ultimate subsidy of that particular right.

RELATED CASES

Cipriano v. City of Houman, 395 U.S. 701 (1969)

McDonald v. Board of Election Commissioners, 394 U.S. 802 (1969)

Phoenix v. Kolodziejski, 399 U.S. 204 (1970)

Hill v. Stone, 421 U.S. 289 (1975)

Ball v. James, 451 U.S. 355; 101 S. Ct. 1811 (1981)

RECOMMENDED READING

The Supreme Court, 1968 Term, 83 Harvard Law Review 77 (1969).

Case Title: *Shapiro v. Thompson*

Legal Citation: 394 U.S. 618

Year of Decision: 1969

KEY ISSUE

Does a state that creates a one-year residency requirement as a condition for receiving state welfare assistance violate the Fourteenth Amendment's guarantee of equal protection?

HISTORY OF THE CASE

Vivian Thompson, a pregnant unmarried woman with one child, was denied welfare benefits solely because she and her child had not been residents of Connecticut for a full year prior to their applications. Two similar cases were joined before the Supreme Court. In all three instances, the district courts found that the state's denial of benefits to otherwise eligible residents of less than a year constituted an invidious discrimination denying all the petitioners equal protection of the laws. Shapiro, representing Connecticut, appealed.

SUMMARY OF ARGUMENTS

Bernard Shapiro, the welfare commissioner of the state of Connecticut, argued that Connecticut had a historical right to legislate for the public welfare and that there was a legislative purpose for passing the provisions in question.

Vivian Thompson and others argued that the Connecticut statute violated the privileges and immunities clause of the Fourteenth Amendment because it infringed upon the right to travel. Thompson also argued that the statute violated the equal protection clause because it discriminated against certain persons on the basis of their wealth and created an unreasonable classification of persons.

States may not withhold welfare benefits anymore than they may withhold state services from short-term residents. Because a fundamental constitutional right is involved, the strict standard of compelling state interest must be applied. State statutes must be examined without regard to federal law, and Congress cannot authorize the states to deny equal protection.

Justice Stewart wrote a concurring opinion in which he stated that the Court has recognized an established constitutional right.

Justices Warren and Black wrote dissenting opinions, pointing out that Congress has imposed residence requirements, and since the state acted pursuant to congressional authority, the statutes should be upheld.

Justice Harlan also wrote a rather lengthy dissent, saying that the compelling interest doctrine should be applied only in racial discrimination cases and not expanded to include recent interstate travelers. Harlan also said that when a statute affects matters not in the Constitution, they should not be defined as affecting fundamental rights to which the stringent equal protection test is applied.

DECISION

The Court held that a state's denial of welfare benefits to residents of less than a year constitutes discrimination and violates the equal protection clause.

Justice Brennan delivered the opinion of the Court. He agreed that the statute preserves the fiscal integrity of state public assistance programs, but he noted that it does this only by discouraging the influx of poor families needing assistance. He held that a state purpose of inhibiting immigration by needy persons violates the Constitution as a burden on the right to travel. Any law whose "sole purpose is the chilling of the exercise of a constitutional right" is invalid. It is obvious that the statute's intent is to prevent needy people from going into the state to obtain larger benefits, thus infringing on the right to travel.

AFTERMATH

The fundamental rights approach as applied to residency requirements is limited and not expanded into other areas, such as in-state tuition or state mineral royalties. *Shapiro* was distinguishable from subsequent residency requirement cases because it involved the "basic necessities of life."

SIGNIFICANCE

Since this case, the Court has held that there is no constitutional right to receive welfare benefits.

RELATED CASES

San Antonio Independent School District v. Rodriguez, 411 U.S. 1 (1969)

Dunn v. Blumstein, 405 U.S. 330 (1972)

Memorial Hospital v. Maricopa County, 415 U.S. 250 (1974)

Sosna v. Iowa, 419 U.S. 393 (1975)

Zobel v. Williams, 457 U.S. 55 (1982)

Plyler v. Doe, 457 U.S. 202 (1982)

Attorney General v. Soto-Lopez, 476 U.S. 898 (1986)

RECOMMENDED READING

Keynes, Edward, with Randall K. Miller. *The Court v. Congress.* Durham, N.C.: Duke University Press, 1989.

Lusky, Louis. *By What Right?* Charlottesville, Va.: Michie, 1975.

Margaret K. Rosenheim, Shapiro v. Thompson: *The Beggars Are Coming to Town,* 1969 Supreme Court Review 303.

Schwartz, Bernard. *The Ascent of Pragmatism: The Burger Court in Action.* New York: Addison-Wesley, 1990.

Todd Zubler, *The Right to Migrate and Welfare Reform: Time for* Shapiro v. Thompson *to Takera Hike,* 31 Valparaiso University Law Review, 893 (1997).

Case Title: *Dandridge v. Williams*

Legal Citation: 397 U.S. 471

Year of Decision: 1970

KEY ISSUE

Does imposition of a ceiling on welfare benefits deny equal protection to large families, who receive less assistance per family member than do smaller families?

HISTORY OF THE CASE

In a series of decisions in the 1960s concerning rights to fair treatment in the criminal process,

voting rights, and ability to engage in interstate travel, opinions of the Supreme Court had indicated classifications that burden the poor were to be reviewed under an increased standard of review as suspect classifications, those based upon traits that seem to violate constitutional principles and therefore are subject to strict scrutiny. The Court had not yet squarely faced a law, however, that burdened a class of persons who lacked financial resources for the allocation of benefits that had no other constitutional recognition. The Court has never recognized the interest of an individual in government subsistence benefits as a fundamental constitutional interest.

The state of Maryland had a welfare scheme that implemented the Aid to Families with Dependent Children (AFDC) program, jointly financed by the state and federal governments. Maryland granted most eligible families their "standard of need," but Annapolis imposed a "maximum grant" limit of $250 per month per family, regardless of the family size or computed standard of need.

SUMMARY OF ARGUMENTS

Maryland argued that its maximum grant regulation was wholly free of any invidiously discriminatory purpose or effect, and that the regulation was rationally supportable because it encouraged gainful employment, maintained an equitable balance in economic status between welfare families and those supported by a wage earner, provided incentives for family planning, and allocated available public funds in such a way as fully to meet the needs of the largest possible number of families. Williams, the plaintiff, challenged the Maryland scheme as denying equal protection since large families received less aid per child than small families.

DECISION

A majority of the Court upheld the law under a rational relationship test, which requires a rational basis for enactment and a reasonable relationship to the achievement of a legitimate government objective. The Court found that the state had a legitimate interest in the economy and the provision of certain families. The majority found no basis for distinguishing this law from any other economic regulation, since all such measures to some extent involved the reallocation of resources or wealth. The majority found that the regulations constituted "economic and social welfare" legislation, which merited only the traditional standard of review. The Maryland scheme satisfied this deferential standard since it bore a rational relation to several legitimate state objectives (e.g., encouraging employment by prohibiting payments that might compare favorably with what a job would provide).

Specifically, Justice Stewart's majority opinion stated:

> [Here] we deal with state regulation in the social and economic field, not affecting freedoms guaranteed by the Bill of Rights, and claimed to violate the 14th Amendment only because the regulation results in some disparity in grants of welfare payments to the largest AFDC families. For this Court to approve the invalidation of state economic or social regulation would be far too reminiscent of an era when the Court thought the 14th Amendment gave it power to strike down state laws "because they might be unwise, improvident, or out of harmony with a particular school of thought." That era long ago passed into history.
>
> In the area of economics and social welfare, a State does not violate the Equal Protection Clause merely because the classifications made by its laws are imperfect. If the classification has some "reasonable basis," it does not offend the Constitution.
>
> The Constitution may impose certain procedural safeguards upon systems of welfare administration. But the Constitution does not empower this Court to second-guess state officials charged with the difficult responsibility of allocating limited public welfare funds among the myriad of potential recipients.

This result was reached over the strong dissent of Justice Marshall, who argued that classifications that burden poor persons in the ability to obtain the basic necessities for functioning in society should be judged by some meaningful standard of review, even if they were not subjected to the compelling interest test. Marshall conceded that strict scrutiny was not appropriate, but he also disagreed with the majority's finding that the traditional, deferential, "mere rationality" test was the correct one. Instead, he gave the first major exposition of his "sliding scale" theory: Rather than a rigid "two-tier" standard, by which all statutes are given either extreme deference or strict scrutiny, the degree of review should be adjusted along a spectrum, depending on (1) the type of classification, (2) the "relative importance to individuals in the class discriminated against of the governmental benefits that they do not receive," and (3) the strength of the interests asserted by the state in support of the classification.

When this analysis was applied to the facts of *Dandridge,* Marshall concluded that a significant degree of scrutiny should be given, since the welfare recipients' interest in the benefits was large, and, in his view, the state's asserted interest in its scheme relatively weak. The scheme was not sufficient to withstand this significant scrutiny, he contended.

AFTERMATH

This position has been followed consistently by the Court; it has held that there was no basis for using any form of strict scrutiny, or increased standard of review, to test legislation that burdens classifications of poor persons in the receipt of other forms of welfare benefits, public housing, or access to the judicial process when no fundamental right is involved.

SIGNIFICANCE

Dandridge falls squarely in line with a series of cases in which the Court rejected claims that various "necessities of life" were fundamental interests whose impairment should trigger strict scrutiny.

RELATED CASES

Shapiro v. Thompson, 394 U.S. 618 (1969)

Graham v. Richardson, 403 U.S. 365 (1971)

James v. Valtierra, 402 U.S. 137 (1971)

San Antonio Independent School District v. Rodriguez, 411 U.S. 1 (1973)

RECOMMENDED READING

Cox, Archibald. *The Court and the Constitution.* Boston: Houghton Mifflin, 1987.

The Equal Protection Clause and Exclusionary Zoning after Valtierra *and* Dandridge, 81 Yale Law Journal 61 (1971).

Schwartz, Bernard. *The Ascent of Pragmatism: The Burger Court in Action.* Reading, Mass.: Addison-Wesley, 1990.

Case Title: *Graham v. Richardson*

Legal Citations: 403 U.S. 365; 91 S. Ct. 1848

Year of Decision: 1971

KEY ISSUES

Does the equal protection clause of the Fourteenth Amendment prevent a state from conditioning welfare benefits on whether the beneficiary is a U.S. citizen or upon the number of years a noncitizen beneficiary has resided in the United States?

HISTORY OF THE CASE

This case was brought as a class action suit: There were three named plaintiffs in the action. One case arose in Arizona. The plaintiff in that case questioned the constitutionality of a state statute that restricted the benefits of general assistance to citizens of the United States and those who resided in the United States for a total of 15 or more years. The plaintiff in that case, Richardson, was a legal resident alien. She met all of the requirements for conferring benefits under this program except for the 15-year residency require-

ment. She instituted her claim in the District Court of Arizona against the commissioner of the state's Department of Public Welfare, seeking declaratory relief, an injunction against the enforcement of the statute, and an award in the amount allegedly due her. She claimed that the alien residency requirement violated the equal protection clause of the Fourteenth Amendment and the constitutional right to travel. A three-judge court upheld Richardson's motion for summary judgment.

The second claim arose in Pennsylvania. The statute challenged in that case restricted the provision of general assistance to needy persons who qualified under the federally supported assistance programs originating with the Social Security Act and partly supported by federal grants and other needy persons who are citizens of the United States. The plaintiff in that case, Leger, was a legal resident alien. For four years, she resided continually in Pennsylvania, where she worked and paid taxes. Her husband, a U.S. citizen, became ill, forcing them both to give up their employment. They both applied for public assistance. They were both ineligible under federal programs. Her husband qualified under a state program, but she was denied the state benefits because of her alienage. Leger instituted her class action in the District Court of Pennsylvania against the executive director of the Philadelphia County Board of Assistance and the Department of Public Welfare. She sought declaratory relief, an injunction against the enforcement of the statute, and a money award for back payments that had been withheld. She obtained a temporary restraining order preventing the state agents from continuing to deny her assistance.

The third claim was brought by Jervis, a legal resident alien living in Pennsylvania, who after five years of working and paying taxes became unable to work as a result of illness. She applied for aid and was denied because of alienage. Her motion for immediate relief through a temporary restraining order was denied. A three-judge court ruled that the statute violated the equal protection clause of the U.S. Constitution and prevented its further enforcement.

SUMMARY OF ARGUMENTS

The plaintiffs argued on behalf of the class that restricting benefits on the basis of alien status effects invidious discrimination in violation of the equal protection clause of the Fourteenth Amendment.

The state agents argued that consistent with the equal protection clause of the Fourteenth Amendment, a state may favor U.S. citizens over aliens in the distribution of welfare benefits. They offered that this distinction was not invidious discrimination because the states were not discriminating with respect to race or national origin.

DECISION

Justice Blackmun, writing for eight justices, held that the Fourteenth Amendment prohibition against denying equal protection of the laws encompasses resident aliens as well as citizens. He concluded that the challenged statutes thus were unconstitutional. Using traditional equal protection analysis, a state retains broad discretion to classify as long as it does so on a reasonable basis. He noted the previous decisions of the Court established that classifications based on alienage, like those based on nationality or race, are suspect classifications and subject to close judicial scrutiny. He noted that aliens as a group represent a discrete and insular minority for whom heightened judicial solicitude is appropriate.

Blackmun concluded that under this standard the state's proffered reason of preferring U.S. citizens in the assignment of benefits was insufficient: "We conclude that a State's desire to preserve limited welfare benefits for its own citizens is inadequate to justify Pennsylvania's making noncitizens ineligible for public assistance, and Arizona's restricting benefits to citizens and longtime resident aliens." He offered two reasons for this conclusion. The first reason was that special public interest doctrine upon which the state agencies grounded their argument had been refuted by the Court. The second reason was that a state may not accomplish the legitimate purpose of preserving fiscal integrity by creating invidious distinctions between classes of citizens. For equal protection purposes, both legal aliens and citizens are "persons"; therefore, the concern for fiscal integrity is not a compelling justification.

Justice Harlan concurred in the judgment and the part of the opinion that discussed federal and state relations regarding aliens and the terms of their occupancy in the United States and the refutation of Arizona's argument that the classification based on years of residency is allowed under the Social Security Act.

AFTERMATH

Shortly after this decision, the Court began to retreat from its characterization of alienage as a suspect classification. The political community exception to treating alienage classifications as inherently suspect was articulated in *Foley v. Connelie* (1978) and *Ambach v. Norwick* (1979). This exception adopted a rational basis standard in circumstances in which the classification involved participation in the processes of democratic decision making. This political community exception has been broadened to encompass not only those positions involving extensive discretionary powers but also all functions important to the concept of self-government. Since *Graham,* the Court had addressed claims distinguishing the economic and sovereign functions of the state; *Graham* addressed only the economic function of the state. This distinction supports the political community exception, which allows a state to limit participation in state government to those persons who are citizens.

In *Cabell v. Chavez-Salido* (1982), the Court established a two-part test to gauge which standard of review is appropriate in cases involving classifications based on alienage. Part one of the test requires the Court to gauge the inclusiveness of the restrictive classification. Once the Court determines whether the classification is overinclusive or underinclusive, it will determine whether the classification involves a state political function. If the Court determines that the state classification is narrowly written and involves a state political function, the rational relation test is applied. Critics of the current approach by the Court argue that the political community exception, which applies the rational basis standard, threatens to swallow the rule that classifications based on alienage are inherently suspect and subject to close judicial scrutiny.

SIGNIFICANCE

Though the Court had acknowledged in previous cases that legislation that discriminated against aliens was illegitimate, it did so on grounds that the legislation was based on an illegitimate state purpose or constituted an unjustified means to a legitimate end. *Graham* was the first time that the Court recognized aliens as a "discrete and insular" minority for the purpose of applying an equal protection standard and review to challenged legislation. This case was the first to establish that classifications based on alienage were inherently suspect and subject to close judicial scrutiny.

The Court reasoned that resident aliens contribute equally to citizens to the tax revenues, and thus the state justification of preserving tax revenues for citizens could not alone constitute a compelling state interest. This case constituted a clear rejection of the right-privilege distinction, under which government benefits were a privilege that could be taken away by the government, unlike rights. This distinction had been the basis for the special public interest doctrine used by states to justify such classifications.

RELATED CASES

Yick Wo v. Hopkins, 118 U.S. 356 (1886)

Shapiro v. Thompson, 394 U.S. 618 (1969)

Sugarman v. Dougall, 413 U.S. 634 (1973)

Mathews v. Diaz, 426 U.S. 67 (1976)

Foley v. Connelie, 435 U.S. 291 (1978)

Ambach v. Norwick, 441 U.S. 68 (1979)

Cabell v. Chavez-Salido, 454 U.S. 432 (1982)

Plyler v. Doe, 457 U.S. 321 (1983)

Martinez v. Bynum, 461 U.S. 321 (1983)

RECOMMENDED READING

Linda S. Bosniak, *Membership, Equality, and the Difference That Alienage Makes,* 69 New York University Law Review 1047 (1994).

Developments in the Law—Immigration Policy and the Rights of Aliens. VI, Discrimination against Documented Aliens. 96 Harvard Law Review 1400 (1983).

Elizabeth Hull, *Undocumented Aliens and the Equal Protection Clause: The Burger Court's Retreat from* Graham v. Richardson, 47 Brooklyn Law Review 1 (1980).

Gerald Rosberg, *The Protection of Aliens from Discriminatory Treatment by the National Government,* 1977 Supreme Court Review 275.

Case Title: *Griggs v. Duke Power Company*

Legal Citation: 401 U.S. 424

Year of Decision: 1971

KEY ISSUE

Did Duke Power Company's transfer policy, which required a high school education and the passage of two aptitude tests, violate Title VII of the Civil Rights Act of 1964?

HISTORY OF THE CASE

Duke Power Company is a power-generating facility located in Draper, North Carolina. Prior to the passage of the Civil Rights Act of 1964, the company openly discriminated against its African-American employees at its Dan River plant by segregating them into the Labor Department of the plant, which paid the lowest wages. Only whites were employed in the other four departments of the plant; the Coal Handling, Operations, Maintenance, and Laboratory and Testing Departments. The company abandoned its policy of segregation in 1965 but extended its requirement of a high school diploma to all transfers from the Labor Department to any of the other four. Also in 1965, the company added two aptitude test requirements (the Wonderlic Personnel

Test and the Bennett Mechanical Comprehension Test) for all employees not in the Labor Department. The testing requirements were aimed toward general knowledge of the work, as opposed to measuring the ability to perform a particular job.

Thirteen African-American workers filed suit in district court, alleging that Title VII prohibits employment requirements that operate in a racially discriminatory way and do not assess the skills necessary to perform certain jobs. The district court found that since the policy of segregation had been abandoned, the current policy did not violate Title VII of the Civil Rights Act of 1964. The district court also held that Title VII was not intended to remedy prior conduct, only prospective conduct. On appeal, the court of appeals used a subjective test of the employer's intent to discriminate and found no showing of discriminatory purpose in the company's requirements. However, the court of appeals reversed the decision of the district court pertaining to the scope of Title VII. The U.S. Supreme Court granted certiorari.

SUMMARY OF ARGUMENTS

The company's policy that required taking tests and a high school diploma in order to qualify for advancement within the company had a disproportionate effect of preventing hiring or advancement of African-American employees. The requirements were also unrelated to the employee's ability to perform the job but were rather imposed in order to ensure preferential hiring and promotion of white workers at the company, and as such, the requirements were a violation of Title VII of the Civil Rights Act of 1964.

DECISION

The Court held that Duke's testing policies resulted in preventing a disproportionate number of African-American employees from being hired by, and advancing in, the company. The Court found that neither the high school graduation requirement nor the aptitude tests reflected the employees' ability to learn or perform the required work.

Chief Justice Burger delivered the opinion of the Court.

The Court first looked to the language of Title VII to determine the legislative intent, finding that it was passed to "achieve equality of employment opportunities and remove barriers that have operated in the past to favor an identifiable group of white employees over other employees." Title VII was deemed to apply to facially discriminatory, as well as facially neutral, procedures that attempted to maintain the prior racially discriminatory status quo, even if no discriminatory intent was found. The Court found that Congress had created Title VII to require "the removal of artificial, arbitrary, and unnecessary barriers to employment when the barriers operate invidiously to discriminate on the basis of racial or other impermissible classification." Thus, tests and other procedures used in determining employee placement must relate to job performance. On the facts of this case, neither the tests nor the requirement of a high school diploma were deemed to show "a demonstrable relationship to successful performance of the jobs for which it was used," and no "meaningful" study was used to determine the relationship of the requirements to job performance. The Court also noted that employees who had not met the requirements performed satisfactorily at their jobs.

Acknowledging the Court of Appeals subjective intent test, the Court refused to inquire into the intent of the employer because "good intent or absence of discriminatory intent does not redeem employment procedures or testing mechanisms that operate as 'built-in headwinds' for minority groups and are unrelated to measuring job capability." Congress aimed the Civil Rights Act of 1964 at the "consequences" of employment practices, not the motivation of the employers, and placed the burden on employers to show that the requirements are related to the particular employment in question.

The Court then turned to the Company's contention that its tests are permitted under section 703 of the Civil Rights Act, which authorizes the use of professionally developed tests that are not intended to discriminate on the basis of race. The Court, noting section 703 does not apply to the diploma requirement, found that the Equal

Employment Opportunity Commission, who had the enforcement power under section 703, found the statute only applies to "job-related" tests. In interpreting the statute, the EEOC is granted great deference and was found to express the will of Congress. The Court held that the Civil Rights Act of 1964 requires "that any tests used must measure the person for the job and not the person in the abstract." Accordingly, the portion of the Court of Appeals decision pertaining to diploma and test requirements was reversed. The ruling applied only to the facts of this case, declining to determine if testing requirements for the same purposes at other facilities violated Title VII.

Aftermath

The Court found that the purpose of the education and aptitude test requirements was to maintain the company's policy of giving preference to white employees in hiring and promotions. Although the Court stated that the burden of proving the required tests are necessary was on the employer, the burden was reduced from the "necessity" requirement to a "justification" requirement in *Wards Cove Packing Co. v. Atonio* (1989).

Significance

The U.S. Supreme Court made clear that employment practices regarding hiring and job placement that disparately impact minorities must be reasonably related to the job.

Related Cases

United Steelworkers v. Weber, 443 U.S. 193 (1979)

Wards Cove Packing Co. v. Atonio, 490 U.S. 642 (1989)

Piscataway v. Taxman, 91 F.3d 1547 (3d Cir. 1996)

Ricci v. DeStefano (Heard 2009; Opinion not filed)

Recommended Reading

Barry Goldstein and Patrick O. Patterson, Ricci v. Destefano: *Does It Herald an "Evil Day," or*

Does It Lack "Staying Power"?, 40 University of Memphis Law Review 705 (2010).

Case Title: *James v. Valtierra*

Alternate Case Title: *Shaffer v. Valtierra*

Legal Citations: 402 U.S. 137; 91 S. Ct. 1331

Year of Decision: 1971

Key Issue

Does a California law that requires that low-rent housing projects be approved by a majority vote at a community election violate the equal protection clause of the Fourteenth Amendment?

History of the Case

Citizens of San Jose, California, and San Mateo County, California, filed suit in federal district court seeking a declaration that the referendum requirement for low-income housing projects (article 34) in the California Constitution violated the equal protection clause of the U.S. Constitution. As a result of a local vote, the housing authorities in their area could not apply for federal funds. A three-judge court held that article 34 denied the plaintiffs equal protection of the laws and enjoined its enforcement. Two appeals were taken from the judgment, one by the San Jose City Council and the other by a single member of the council.

Summary of Arguments

Ronald James argued that the justification for the referendum requirement was reasonable and that the equal protection clause of the Fourteenth Amendment was incorrectly applied by the trial court.

Anita Valtierra, one of the citizens opposing the referendum, argued that the referendum requirement violated the equal protection clause of the Fourteenth Amendment because it denied poor people the use of ordinary lawmaking procedures and because it encouraged a racial veto of the federal fund distribution for public housing. Valtierra also argued that the referendum requirement violated the supremacy clause because it was inconsistent with federal public housing provisions.

DECISION

The Court held that the California law requiring a local referendum on low-income housing projects did not violate the equal protection clause of the Fourteenth Amendment. The Court found no racial bias in "a law seemingly neutral on its face."

Justice Black delivered the opinion of the Court. He held that article 34 does not make any "distinctions based on race" and that "a lawmaking procedure that 'disadvantages' a particular group does not always deny equal protection." The referendum provision, Justice Black argued, demonstrates a "devotion to democracy, not to bias, discrimination, or prejudice."

Justice Thurgood Marshall disagreed. In his dissenting opinion, he stated: "The article explicitly singles out low-income persons to bear its burden. Publicly assisted housing developments designed to accommodate the aged, veterans, state employees, persons of moderate income, or any class of citizens other than the poor, need not be approved by prior referenda."

AFTERMATH

Courts have consistently refused to require local communities to construct affordable housing, even in the face of an enduring pattern of racial discrimination.

Nevertheless, where a court finds a constitutional violation in a given municipality that is aggravated by the discriminatory practices of neighboring communities, a court may conceivably order area-wide relief under *Hills v. Gautreaux* (1976). In *Hills*, a tenant of Chicago's public housing system brought suit against the Chicago Housing Authority (CHA) and the Department of Housing and Urban Development (HUD). The complaint alleged that the CHA deliberately selected housing sites in predominantly black areas to avoid placing black families in white neighborhoods. The federal district court ordered both agencies to take corrective action limited to the city of Chicago. The Supreme Court held that a remedial order beyond Chicago's geographic boundary was warranted in view of HUD's constitutional and statutory violations. Such relief is justified when there is evidence of discrimination by neighboring communities and where the disturbance to government operations caused by the order would be minimal, especially in a suit against HUD.

SIGNIFICANCE

Although local housing authorities may not discriminate on the basis of race, communities have no statutory or constitutional obligation to construct affordable housing.

RELATED CASES

Hunter v. Erickson, 393 U.S. 385 (1969)

Dandridge v. Williams, 397 U.S. 471 (1970)

RECOMMENDED READING

The Equal Protection Clause and Exclusionary Zoning after Valtierra and Dandridge, 81 Yale Law Journal 61 (1971).

Mark J. Powell, *Fair Housing in the United States: A Legal Response to Municipal Intransigence*, University of Illinois Law Review 279 (1997).

The Supreme Court, 1970 Term, 85 Harvard Law Review 122 (1971).

Case Title: *Swann v. Charlotte-Mecklenburg Board of Education et al.*

Legal Citation: 402 U.S. 1

Year of Decision: 1971

&

KEY ISSUE

Can the federal government impose court-ordered busing to promote the desegregation of schools, in order for citizens to have equal rights under the equal protection clause of the Fourteenth Amendment?

HISTORY OF THE CASE

The schools in Charlotte-Mecklenburg were segregated into separate schools for African-American and Caucasian children. After *Brown v. Board of Education* (1954), the area attempted to end segregation with a school assignment that was based on neighborhoods but also allowed voluntary transfer, a plan that the district court approved. When the plan went into effect, the majority of African-American students still attended schools made up of 99 percent or more African Americans. The National Association for the Advancement of Colored People (NAACP) Legal Defense Fund brought this case on behalf of James Swann and nine other families.

In 1965, the district court held that there was not a requirement in the Constitution purposely to increase racial integration, so the case was dropped. However, once the *Green v. County School Board* (1968) ruling came down, the case was filed in district court once again. Charlotte devised a new school board plan, but this left more than half of the African-American elementary students at schools where the majority of students were African American. The court rejected this plan and favored the Finger plan, named after Dr. John Finger. The Finger plan required busing 300 additional African-American students along with a pairing and grouping technique to achieve more integration. The U.S. Court of Appeals for the Fourth Circuit affirmed the Finger plan for older students, but it remanded the plan for students in elementary school. After the case was remanded, the district court decided to stick with the original plan for elementary students, with less integration. The case was than brought to the Supreme Court for review.

SUMMARY OF ARGUMENTS

Swann argued that the schools were racially segregated in violation of the equal protection clause of the Fourteenth Amendment, and the court of appeals should have determined that additional busing was a reasonable means to desegregate the Charlotte-Mecklenburg schools. The Fourth Circuit's new reasonableness rule made the goal of desegregation less complete and threatened to undermine *Brown v. Board of Education*. The Finger plan would create integration in the school system, and the plan was feasible, so the court should implement it. In addition, the cost would have been minimal, and the benefits the African-American children would gain would outweigh the cost.

The Charlotte-Mecklenburg Board of Education argued that the Finger plan would be too expensive to implement. In addition, the law was provided to give children the right to go to school in a system that was not segregated, and with the board's plan, the school system overall would be integrated. It was also argued that the rule of reason should be used: that if a school board makes every effort to integrate the school system, then the plan should be allowed.

DECISION

The Court held that busing students to school would be an appropriate remedy to solving segregation in schools, including the busing of the elementary students. The Court determined that this would be a good way for all students to get an equal education, and schools would become more integrated.

Justice Burger delivered the opinion of the Court, that "the remedial techniques used in the District Court's order were within that court's power to provide equitable relief; implementation of the decree is well within the capacity of the school authority." The Court argued that there was no reason why the school district should not require and employ bus transportation for the students to solve the problem of desegregation.

AFTERMATH

Later on, Charlotte created magnet schools that each had a quota of how many African-American and how many Caucasian children could attend the school. This caused problems when many Caucasian children were not able to attend the magnet schools, because there were too many Caucasian students already enrolled at the school.

In 1997, William Capacchione sued the school system because his daughter was denied entrance into a magnet school two times, based on her race. The court determined that a unitary system had been met, and the court order on mandatory busing was lifted. This decision was upheld, and eventually in Charlotte-Mecklenburg the federal order of busing was ended, allowing the city to determine the new assignment policy. The school system eventually determined a new plan, which was based on neighborhoods, and ultimately reinstated segregation. However, students were given the option to choose other schools as well. But public transportation was not given to those students who chose to attend schools farther away from their homes.

SIGNIFICANCE

The decision in this case led to extensive busing to end segregation in many school systems. However, court-imposed busing was not popular with many people. Throughout the 1970s, the Court did very little to help integrate and promote desegregation. The Court's reluctance kept some school districts segregated.

RELATED CASES

Brown v. Board of Education, 347 U.S. 483 (1954)

Brown v. Board of Education II, 349 U.S. 294 (1955)

Griffin v. County School Board of Prince Edward County et al., 377 U.S. 218 (1964)

Green v. County School Board of New Kent County, 391 U.S. 430 (1968)

Milliken v. Bradley, 433 U.S. 267 (1974)

Pasadena Board of Education v. Spangler, 427 U.S. 424 (1976)

RECOMMENDED READING

R. K. Godwin, S. M. Leland, A. D. Baxter, and S. Southworth. "Sinking Swann: Public School Choice and the Resegregation of Charlotte's Pub-

lic Schools." 23 *Review of Policy Research* 983 (2006).

Marcus, D. L. "After the Buses Stop." *U.S. News and World Report* 127, no. 23 (1999): 38–39.

Michaelson, Roslyn A. "The Incomplete Desegregation of the Charlotte-Mecklenburg County Schools and Its Consequences." In *School Resegregation: Must the South Turn Back?,* edited by John C. Boger and Gary Orfield. Chapel Hill: University of North Carolina Press, 2005.

Reid, K. S. "Color Blind." *Education Week* 23, 18 February 2004 at 44.

Smith, C. "Resegregation: When Busing Ends." *New York Times,* 18 January 2004.

Walsh, M. "High Court Closes Historic Desegregation Case." *Education Week* 21, 13 February 2002 at 31.

Case Title: *Reed v. Reed*

Legal Citation: 404 U.S. 71

Year of Decision: 1971

KEY ISSUE

Is a statute preferring men to women as administrators of estates constitutional?

HISTORY OF THE CASE

Richard Reed died without a will. His adoptive parents, then separated, filed competing petitions seeking to administer their son's estate. An Idaho statute established a scheme for the selection of the administrator of such an estate, where eligible persons were grouped into 11 categories by their relationship to the decedent. The statute further provided that when more than one person in the same category are claiming and are "equally entitled" to administer, males must be preferred to females.

On the basis of this portion of the statute, the probate court held in favor of the father. Sally Reed, the mother of the deceased, appealed to the U.S. District Court of the Fourth Judicial District of Idaho. The district court held that the challenged section violated the equal protection clause under the Fourteenth Amendment and was, therefore, void. However, Cecil Reed, the father of the deceased, took a further appeal to the Idaho Supreme Court, which reversed the district court's holding.

SUMMARY OF ARGUMENTS

The state, on behalf of Cecil Reed, argued that the statute's preference of males over females simply reduced the workload of probate courts by eliminating hearings on the merits. Therefore, the state contended that the statute was intended as "benign" legislation.

Sally Reed argued that the section of the Idaho Code violated the equal protection clause of the Fourteenth Amendment because the selection of males over equally qualified females was arbitrary. She also challenged the section as a violation of the Idaho Constitution.

DECISION

The Supreme Court reversed the judgment of the Idaho Supreme Court. Chief Justice Burger delivered the unanimous decision of the Court, holding that the arbitrary preference of males could not withstand constitutional attack. He reasoned that the equal protection clause forbids the states to legislate that different persons be placed into separate classes on the basis of criteria wholly unrelated to the objective of that legislation. He stated that such gender-based classifications must be reasonable, not arbitrary. Most important, Burger decided that the scheme's mandatory preference of males was not reasonably related to the state's objective of reducing the workload by eliminating one class of contests.

AFTERMATH

Before *Reed,* the Court had easily found that a sex-based statute was rationally related to some legitimate state objective, usually the preservation of women's "proper role." The Court, in *Reed,* overcame this traditionally weak rational basis test in holding that the state's objective was not legitimate. However, after *Reed,* the Court began to develop a higher, intermediate standard of review for gender classifications. By this level of scrutiny, the Court analyzes whether the classifications by gender serve important governmental objectives that are substantially related to the achievement of those objectives. Today, this intermediate level of review is difficult to overcome in cases involving gender-based classifications. In 1996, the Court seemed to heighten this intermediate standard of review in determining that a state must show an "exceedingly persuasive justification" for a gender-based scheme, and that the courts must give "skeptical scrutiny" to that scheme. The justification given must be genuine and not created after the fact or in response to litigation. This is a demanding burden that rests on the state.

SIGNIFICANCE

For the first time in its history, the Court rejected sex-based legislation under the equal protection clause. Although the Court declined to make gender a "suspect" classification entitling it to greater scrutiny than a "mere rationality" review, it did pave the way for later cases to elevate the standard of review.

RELATED CASES

Minor v. Happerseh, 88 U.S. 162 (1875)

Frontiero v. Richardson, 411 U.S. 677 (1973)

Craig v. Boren, 429 U.S. 190 (1976)

Michael M. v. Superior Court, 450 U.S. 464 (1981)

Mississippi University for Women v. Hogan, 458 U.S. 718 (1982)

U.S. v. Virginia, 116 S. Ct. 2264 (1996)

RECOMMENDED READING

John D. Johnson, Jr., *Sex Discrimination and the Supreme Court, 1971–1974,* 49 New York University Law Review, 617 (1974).

Kirp, David L. et al. *Gender Justice*. Chicago: University of Chicago Press, 1986.

Schwartz, Bernard. *The Ascent of Pragmatism: The Burger Court in Action*. New York: Addison-Wesley, 1990.

Case Title: *Whitcomb v. Chavis*

Legal Citation: 403 U.S. 124

Year of Decision: 1971

KEY ISSUE

Did an Indiana county's multimember district illegally minimize and cancel out the voting power of the resident black community? Multimember districts are represented by two or more legislators, whereas a single-member district is represented by only one legislator.

HISTORY OF THE CASE

A lawsuit was filed in the U.S. District Court for the Southern District of Indiana attacking Indiana's state legislative apportionment for creating a single district of Marion County for the election of eight state senators and 15 state assemblymen. The district court, after withholding judgment for two months to allow the state legislature to correct the malapportionment according to the principles enumerated by the court, (1) redistricted Marion County into single-member districts on the ground that the multimember Marion County district illegally minimized and canceled out the voting power of the cognizable racial minority in the Marion County ghetto, as evidenced by fewer legislators' having resided in the ghetto than the ghetto's proportion of the county population; and (2) redistricted the entire state into single-member districts on the ground that the state was malapportioned by population-per-senator variations of 80,496 to 106,790 and population-per-assemblyman variations of 41,449 to 53,003.

SUMMARY OF ARGUMENTS

Plaintiffs attacked the constitutionality of two statutes of the state of Indiana that provided for multimember districting at large of General Assembly seats in Marion County, Indiana. They also alleged that the two statutes invidiously diluted the force and effect of the vote of black citizens and poor persons living within certain Marion County census tracts constituting what was termed "the ghetto area." Residents of the area were alleged to have particular demographic characteristics rendering them a minority interest group with distinctive interests in specific areas of the substantive law. With single-member districting, it was said, the ghetto area would elect three members of the house and one senator, whereas, under the present districting, voters in the area "have almost no political force or control over legislators because the effect of their vote is canceled out by other contrary interest groups" in Marion County. The mechanism of political party organization and the influence of party chairs in nominating candidates were additional factors alleged to frustrate the exercise of power by residents of the ghetto area.

DECISION

On appeal, the U.S. Supreme Court reversed the decision of the lower court. Justice White announced the Court's judgment. In parts I through VI of his opinion, expressing the view of five members of the Court, he held that evidence that the ghetto has fewer resident legislators than its proportion of the county population did not prove invidious discrimination against ghetto residents. In part VII of his opinion, Justice White, joined by Chief Justice Burger and Justices Black and Blackmun, held that the district court properly ordered statewide reapportionment.

AFTERMATH

Voting districts that were purposely created to contain racial discrimination were found unconstitutional. In *White v. Regester* (1973), the Court upheld a judgment of a district court that invalidated two multimember districts, one found to discriminate against blacks, the other against

Hispanic Americans. The Court found that plaintiffs had proven that "the political processes leading to nomination and election were not equally open to participation by the group in question—that its members had less opportunity than did other residents in the district to participate in the political processes and to elect legislators of their choice."

SIGNIFICANCE

The Court has refused to overturn legislative districting that complies with the one-person, one-vote principle because the particular districting plan has a disproportionate effect on racial minorities.

RELATED CASES

Missouri v. Jenkins, 495 U.S. 33 (1990)

Spallone v. United States, 493 U.S. 265 (1990)

Chisom v. Roemer, 501 U.S. 380 (1991)

RECOMMENDED READING

Thernstrom, Abigail M. *Whose Votes Count?* Cambridge, Mass.: Harvard University Press, 1987.

Case Title: *Furman v. Georgia*

Alternate Case Title: The Death Penalty Case

Legal Citation: 408 U.S. 238

Year of Decision: 1972

KEY ISSUES

Does the death penalty constitute cruel and unusual punishment within the meaning of the Eighth and Fourteenth Amendments of the U.S. Constitution?

HISTORY OF THE CASE

William Henry Furman was convicted of murder in a shooting that occurred during the commission of a burglary. He was sentenced to death. The Supreme Court consolidated his appeal with two other cases questioning the constitutionality of the death sentence for rape. Because of the arbitrary nature of the imposition of the death sentence, the issue was whether it constituted cruel and unusual punishment.

SUMMARY OF ARGUMENTS

The petitioner, William Henry Furman, argued that his sentence of death violated the Eighth Amendment, because the death penalty violated the standards of decency and did not properly account for his mental impairment.

The state of Georgia argued that the death penalty was not cruel and unusual punishment and did not deprive Furman of his life without due process of law. Further, Georgia argued that the death penalty was an appropriate maximum punishment for murder.

Justice Douglas wrote one of the majority opinions, saying that current systems of criminal justice in the United States operate in an unpredictable and arbitrary manner and do not serve as a deterrent.

DECISION

Standardless, discretionary jury sentencing in capital cases violates the Eighth Amendment because arbitrary imposition of the death penalty is cruel and unusual punishment, as is punishment that is too severe for the crime.

AFTERMATH

This is the first Supreme Court case to hold unconstitutional a state capital punishment law, but state legislatures did not do away with capital punishment. Instead, they devised ways to administer it in a more consistent fashion. More than 600 prisoners on death row had their death sentences lifted by the *Furman* decision.

SIGNIFICANCE

The Court recognized important new rights in capital punishment law without abolishing it. The decision required that capital punishment be administered in a more organized fashion so there is some assurance that jury findings justify the imposition of the death sentence. Most states enacted death penalty statutes to preclude arbitrariness.

RELATED CASES

Yick Wo v. Hopkins, 118 U.S. 356 (1886)

Louisiana ex rel. Francis v. Resweber, 329 U.S. 459 (1947)

Reid v. Covert, 354 U.S. 1 (1957)

Trop v. Dulles, 356 U.S. 86 (1958)

Robinson v. California, 370 U.S. 660 (1962)

Gideon v. Wainwright, 372 U.S. 335 (1963)

Mallory v. Hogan, 378 U.S. 1 (1964)

Witherspoon v. Illinois, 391 U.S. 510 (1968)

Gregg v. Georgia, 428 U.S. 280 (1976)

Gardner v. Florida, 430 U.S. 349 (1977)

RECOMMENDED READING

David C. Baldus et al., *Identifying Comparatively Excessive Standards of Death: A Quantitative Approach,* 33 Stanford Law Review 1 (1980).

Masseur, Louis P. *Rites of Execution: Capital Punishment and the Transformation of American Culture.* New York: Oxford University Press, 1989.

Sheleff, Leon Shaskolsky. *Ultimate Penalties.* Columbus: Ohio State University Press, 1987, 82–87.

Stephen F. Smith, *The Supreme Court and the Politics of Death,* 94 Virginia Law Review 283 (2008).

Stefoff, Rebecca. Furman v. Georgia: *Debating the Death Penalty.* New York: Benchmark Books, 2007.

Trombley, Stephen. *The Execution Protocol: Inside America's Capital Punishment Industry.* New York: Crown, 1992.

White, Welsh S. *Life in a Balance.* Ann Arbor: University of Michigan Press, 1984.

Case Title: *Moose Lodge No. 107 v. Irvis*

Legal Citations: 407 U.S. 163; 92 S. Ct. 1965

Year of Decision: 1972

KEY ISSUE

Is a state, by virtue of the power to dispense liquor licenses, significantly involved in discrimination so as to violate the equal protection clause of the Fourteenth Amendment of the U.S. Constitution?

HISTORY OF THE CASE

Moose Lodge, a private club, refused to serve the black guest of a member. The guest contended that since the state of Pennsylvania had given the club one of a limited number of liquor licenses, the act was sufficient to render the club's discrimination attributable to state action. In *Burton v. Wilmington* (1961), a similar situation existed, but that case involved a public restaurant and a public building; Moose Lodge was a private club in a private building.

SUMMARY OF ARGUMENTS

K. Leroy Irvis argued that the club's refusal to serve him violated the equal protection clause of the Fourteenth Amendment.

The Moose Lodge argued that it was not acting under the authority of the state in its refusal; therefore, no state action and no violation existed.

DECISION

Justice Rehnquist wrote the opinion for the Court, holding that the mere fact that a state grants a license to an entity does not transform it into an action by the state for which a citizen may recover, "even where the number of licenses is limited." There was a suggestion that if the licenses were so limited that those who had them had a monopoly in dispensing liquor, the result would be different.

Justice Douglas wrote one of the dissenting opinions. He conceded that, as a general rule, activities of a private club were beyond the reach of the Constitution, but the situation here was different because there was a state-enforced scarcity of licenses that restricted the ability of blacks to obtain liquor. If someone wanted to form a club to serve blacks, he or she would have to buy an existing club license and pay a monopoly price attributable to the state.

AFTERMATH

The difference between the theories of "state action" and "under color of state law" are still unclear after *Moose Lodge.* The Court has yet to settle on one of these theories, so it refers to it as the state action theory, an uncertain area of the law. Further, even though no state action was found in *Moose Lodge,* several states attempted to use their regulation of alcoholic beverages to fight racial discrimination.

SIGNIFICANCE

State regulation of an activity does not automatically constitute "state action" that may be reviewed on constitutional grounds.

RELATED CASES

Shelley v. Kraemer, 334 U.S. 1 (1948)

Burton v. Wilmington Parking Authority, 365 U.S. 715 (1961)

Reitmann v. Mulkey, 387 U.S. 369 (1967)

Flagg Brothers v. Brooks, 436 U.S. 149 (1978)

RECOMMENDED READING

Michael M. Burns, *The Exclusion of Women from Influential Men's Clubs and the Inner Sanctum and the Myth of Full Equality,* 16 Harvard Civil Rights and Civil Liberties Law Review 321 (1983).

Lucretia I. Hollingsworth, *Sex Discrimination in Private Clubs,* 29 Hastings Law Journal 421 (1977).

Case Title: *Sugarman v. Dougall*

Legal Citation: 413 U.S. 634

Year of Decision: 1973

KEY ISSUE

Does a state statute violate the equal protection clause of the Fourteenth Amendment because it provides that only citizens may hold permanent positions in the competitive class of the state civil service?

HISTORY OF THE CASE

Nonprofit organizations that received funds through the Human Resources Administration of New York City employed Patrick Dougall, a registered resident alien, and other registered resident aliens. The organizations merged with a state agency. After the merger, all employees became employees of the city. A state law provided that only citizens could hold permanent positions in the competitive sector of the civil service. The city dismissed all alien employees from permanent positions in the competitive sector. The aliens brought a class action against Sugarman, the administrator of the New York City Human Resources Administration, and others, alleging that the statute denied them equal protection. The district court agreed and declared the statute unconstitutional. The Supreme Court agreed to hear the case because of the importance of the issue presented.

SUMMARY OF ARGUMENTS

The city argued that civil servants participate directly in the formulation and execution of government policy and should, therefore, be free of competing obligations to another power. The city believed that having loyal employees was a substantially important enough interest to warrant the citizenship requirement.

The aliens maintained that the law swept indiscriminately and was not narrowly tailored to achieve the government interest.

DECISION

Justice Blackmun wrote for the majority in the 8-1 decision invalidating the citizenship requirement. The level of scrutiny the Court applied required the city to show a "substantial state interest" in requiring citizenship for civil service workers. In addition, the challenged law must be "narrowly and precisely drawn" to achieve that end. When the Court applies this approach, the government almost always loses. This case is no exception. The Court reasoned that a resident alien may lawfully reside in New York for an extended period, pay taxes, and serve in the armed forces. In view of the breadth and imprecision of the law in the context of strict scrutiny, the Court struck it down as a violation of equal protection.

AFTERMATH

The Court has continued to examine the rights of aliens under various state and federal laws. The level of scrutiny has not diminished, yet there have been instances in which a state has a compelling enough interest in regulating aliens as such. As a result, citizenship may be important in some circumstances.

SIGNIFICANCE

Sugarman mandates that the states are constitutionally required to allow aliens to represent government entities. Aliens enjoy a vast array of privileges that U.S. citizens enjoy.

RELATED CASES

Yick Wo v. Hopkins, 118 U.S. 356 (1886)

Graham v. Richardson, 403 U.S. 365 (1971)

Examining Board of Engineers v. Flores de Otero, 426 U.S. 572 (1976)

Toll v. Moreno, 458 U.S. 1 (1982)

RECOMMENDED READING

Earl M. Maltz, *Citizenship and the Constitution: A History and Critique of the Supreme Court's Alienage Jurisprudence,* 28 Arizona State Law Journal 1135 (1996).

John E. Richards, *Public Employment Rights of Aliens,* 34 Baylor Law Review 371 (1982).

Schwartz, Bernard. *The Ascent of Pragmatism: The Burger Court in Action.* New York: Addison-Wesley, 1990.

Case Title: *Lau v. Nichols*

Legal Citation: 414 U.S. 563

Year of Decision: 1974

KEY ISSUES

Does the failure of a school system to provide English language instruction to approximately 1,800 students of Chinese ancestry who do not speak English violate the equal protection clause of the Fourteenth Amendment or section 601 of the Civil Rights Act of 1964?

HISTORY OF THE CASE

Non-English-speaking Chinese students brought a class action against officials of the San Francisco Unified School District because the school district did not teach English to all Chinese-speaking students. The petitioners did not seek any specific relief. Both the district court and the court of appeals denied relief, holding that there was no violation of the equal protection clause of the Fourteenth Amendment or of section 601 of the Civil Rights Act of 1964. The Supreme Court agreed to hear the case because of the public importance of the question presented.

SUMMARY OF ARGUMENTS

Lau argued that the exclusionary policy that denied teaching English to the Chinese-speaking students and the failure to provide for alternate instructional procedures were an outright denial of equal protection as guaranteed by the Fourteenth Amendment, as well as a violation of section 601 of the Civil Rights Act of 1964, which bans discrimination based on race, color, or national origin in any program or activity receiving federal financial assistance.

The school district argued that under the California Educational Code, it could determine when and under what circumstances instruction was to be given bilingually. Since not all Chinese-speaking students were denied the opportunity for bilingual instruction, the school system held that it was not denying equal protection to those students on the basis of their race, color, or national origin.

DECISION

Justice Douglas delivered the unanimous opinion of the Court that the denial of bilingual teaching to the 1,800 students was a violation of section 601 of the Civil Rights Act of 1964. He did not see a need to address the issue of the equal protection argument. The statute governed the issue because the school district involved in the litigation received large amounts of federal financial assistance. The Court held that the Chinese-speaking minority received fewer benefits from the school system, which denied them a meaningful opportunity to participate in the educational program of the state than the English-speaking majority. Quoting President John F. Kennedy's address to Congress on June 19, 1963, the Court concluded that simple justice requires that public funds, to which all taxpayers of all races contribute, should not be spent in any way that would encourage, entrench, subsidize, or result in racial discrimination.

Justice Blackmun stressed in a concurring opinion, joined by Chief Justice Burger, that the opinion of the Court should not be taken too broadly, as it relates to a large number of children and not merely one or two or even a small group. He did not regard the decision as conclusive on the issue of whether school districts would be required to provide special instruction to minority students. To him, numbers were at the heart of the case.

AFTERMATH

After the *Lau* decision, the Department of Health, Education and Welfare appointed a task force consisting primarily of professional educators to advise the department on implementing the decision throughout the country. A system of guidelines was developed that came to be known as the "*Lau* Remedies." These remedies required instruction in students' native language where it was practical to do so. Although there were no uniform standards for school districts to follow, the Department of Health, Education and Welfare had begun to treat the remedies as regulations. Between 1975 and 1980, nearly 500 compliance agreements were negotiated in deficient school districts. The Reagan administration withdrew a proposal to formalize the *Lau* Remedies.

SIGNIFICANCE

Since *Lau,* a number of lower courts have enforced the *Lau* Remedies and have found the requirements of the task force to be essential components of educational programs providing meaningful access to education for non-English-speaking children.

RELATED CASES

Otero v. Mesa County School District Number 51, 568 F. 2d 1312 (10th Cir. 1977)

Cintron v. Brentwood Union Free School District, 455 F. Supp. 57 (E.D.N.Y. 1978)

Guadalupe Organization, Inc. v. Tempe Elementary School District, 587 F. 2d 1022 (9th Cir. 1978)

Rios v. Read, 480 F. Supp. 14 (E.D.N.Y. 1978)

RECOMMENDED READING

Jonathan D. Haft, *Assuring Equal Educational Opportunities for Language Minority Students: Bilingual Education and the Equal Educational Opportunity Act of 1974,* 18 Columbia Journal of Law and Social Problems 209 (1983).

Betsy Levin, *An Analysis of the Federal Attempt to Regulate Bilingual Education: Protecting Civil Rights or Controlling Curriculum?,* 12 Journal of Law and Education 29 (1983).

Case Title: *Milliken v. Bradley*

Legal Citation: 418 U.S. 717

Year of Decision: 1974

KEY ISSUE

Does the district court have the power to fashion a remedy encompassing both a segregated urban school district and independent suburban school districts?

HISTORY OF THE CASE

In *Brown v. Board of Education* (1954), the Court held racial segregation in public schools unconstitutional, but in the early 1970s, the Supreme Court began to permit racial school assignments. These resulted in racial quotas (*Swann v. Charlotte-Mecklenburg Board of Education* [1971]). Quotas did not improve education. More recent cases have encouraged a color-blind interpretation of the Constitution.

A federal district court in 1971 held that the Detroit Board of Education maintained a racially segregated system. The findings showed that meaningful desegregation was impossible within the predominantly black Detroit school system, so the district court devised a new remedy. It ordered Detroit and surrounding suburbs to become one school district and ordered racial busing with the goal of eliminating the predominantly black schools.

SUMMARY OF ARGUMENTS

William G. Milliken, governor of the state of Michigan, argued that the decision of the court of appeals finding de jure segregation was without basis in fact or law and the decision of the court of appeals that a Detroit-only desegregation plan was insufficient to remedy segregation was clearly erroneous.

Bradley argued that an interdistrict desegregation plan was proper, and no constitutionally guaranteed rights of the suburban school districts had been violated.

DECISION

Chief Justice Burger, who wrote for the majority, decided that federal district courts have limited power to impose interdistrict desegregation orders, and that this issue belonged to the local school boards. Justice Burger worried about the district court's intervention into local affairs and the massive impact of its remedy. Although the district court had not found evidence of a violation in the suburban schools, its remedy included not only Detroit but 53 suburban school districts. The Court rejected the busing plan because there was no interdistrict violation. It went on to affirm the historical importance of local control over public schools. Limits for school busing were set for the first time.

Justice Douglas, in dissent, stated that the district court plan should be affirmed; in that manner, there would be no violation of the equal protection clause even if the schools were segregated and black schools were not only "separate but inferior." He thought that state actions such as choosing sites for building schools had brought about black schools and white schools, and that the majority was recommending a return to local control of school systems.

AFTERMATH

This case represented a defeat for busing in Detroit. School systems remained separate and unequal.

SIGNIFICANCE

Interdistrict remedies for segregation will not be allowed if intentional segregation exists in only one district.

RELATED CASES

Brown v. Board of Education, 347 U.S. 483 (1954)

Green v. School Board of New Kent County, 391 U.S. 432 (1968)

Swann v. Charlotte-Mecklenburg Board of Education, 402 U.S. 1 (1971)

Keyes v. School District No. 1, 413 U.S. 89 (1972)

RECOMMENDED READING

Paul Gewirtz, *Remedies and Resistance,* 92 Yale Law Journal 585 (1983).

Graglia, Lino A. *Disaster by Decree.* Ithaca, N.Y.: Cornell University Press, 1976.

Case Title: *Albemarle Paper Company v. Moody*

Legal Citation: 422 U.S. 405

Year of Decision: 1975

KEY ISSUE

What standards should a federal district court follow in deciding whether to award back pay to an employee, or former employee, who has been unlawfully discriminated against at work?

HISTORY OF THE CASE

A group of present and former African-American employees ("Employees") at a paper mill, the Albemarle Paper Company ("Albemarle"), filed a complaint with the Equal Employment Opportunity Commission (EEOC) and received a right to sue. Thereafter, this class action lawsuit was filed in a federal North Carolina district court on behalf of the Employees against Albemarle and the Employees' labor union. The Employees sought permanent injunctive relief for violations of Title VII of the 1964 Civil Rights Act, which prohibits discrimination in the workplace. The Employees claimed their rights were violated by both the seniority system and job placement tests. The Employees later added a class demand for the award of back pay.

The district court found that Albemarle's seniority system effectively segregated African-American employees from whites, locking the African Americans into low-paying jobs. That court then ordered that Albemarle implement a system of plantwide seniority; however, no back pay was awarded, and the testing program was not enjoined. The Employees appealed the district court's decision regarding the denial of back pay and the court's refusal to enjoin Albemarle's use of employment testing. The Fourth Circuit Court of Appeals reversed the judgment of the district court on both issues. On appeal, the U.S. Supreme Court granted certiorari on the issues of back pay and the use of testing in determining employment.

SUMMARY OF ARGUMENTS

The Employees argued that they should be given back pay for the loss they suffered as a result of the discriminatory procedures and that the district court erred by not awarding back pay.

Albemarle argued that the district court has the complete discretion to award or deny back pay, so there was no error of in discretion.

DECISION

The Court agreed with the court of appeals that the district court had erred in concluding that Albemarle had proved job-relatedness. The Court vacated the judgment of the court of appeals and remanded the case to the district court, providing an opportunity for the district court to reconsider denial of back pay on remand. Justice Stewart delivered the majority opinion.

The Court began with a discussion of the back pay award, determining that it should be left to the discretion of the courts to decide whether or not to award it. The Court claim to this conclusion by noting that Congress has the equitable power to award back pay to correct past wrongs of racial discrimination, in light of the objective of the guidelines of the EEOC. The Court then looked at the purpose of Title VII, which the Court had previously determined was "to achieve equality of employment opportunities and remove barriers that have operated in the past to favor an identifiable group of white employees over other employees." This purpose was deemed to have a connection to back pay because, as the Court noted, the threat of a back pay award provides an incentive to employers to self-evaluate that their employment practices avoid racial discrimination. Another purpose of Title VII, made evident in the legislative history, was to make persons wrongfully discriminated against whole, a purpose that seems to justify an award of back pay. The Court accordingly held that "back pay should be denied only for reasons which, if applied generally, would not frustrate the central statutory purpose of eradicating discrimination throughout the economy and making persons whole for injuries suffered through past discriminations." If back pay were denied, the district court must articulate its reasons.

Applying these standards to this case, the Court examined the district court's reasons for denying back pay. The Court first noted that the finding that Albemarle had not acted in bad faith was an insufficient basis to deny back pay because "if back pay were awardable only upon a showing of bad faith, the remedy would become a punishment of moral turpitude, rather than a compensation for workers' injuries." The fact that the Employees had not initially requested back pay and, thus, were denied back pay because of prejudice to Albemarle in refuting the action was also deemed insufficient to deny back pay on that basis alone. Whether Albemarle was prejudiced was left for the district court to determine on remand, and that decision would be subject to review by the court of appeals. Although the district court had denied back pay on the basis of accumulated factors, the Court gave the district court an opportunity to reconsider its position on remand.

The Court next turned to the use of preemployment tests. In *Griggs v. Duke Power Co.* (1971), the Court held that Title VII forbids discriminatory tests in employment and placed the burden of showing that the test is related to the job on the employer, upon a prima facie showing of discrimination by the plaintiff. There, the Court also held that Congress requires that any test used "must measure the person for the job and not the person in the abstract." Albemarle required two tests for its employees, the Wonderlic Test and the Beta Exam, and in consideration of the history of these testing requirements, the Court found the history to be inconclusive. The inquiry then turned to whether the EEOC guidelines were being followed regarding Albemarle's testing policies, finding that the study used by Albemarle to validate its practices was

defective, for several reasons. The Court found that the tests used by Albemarle did not involve an analysis of attributes or the skills needed to perform the jobs studied. The tests were also deemed to be based on subjective supervisorial rankings, and the Court found there was "simply no way to determine whether the criteria actually considered were sufficiently related to the Company's legitimate interest in job-specific ability to justify a testing system with a racially discriminatory impact." Thus, the Court agreed with the court of appeals that the district court had erred in concluding that Albemarle had proved job-relatedness. The Court vacated the judgment of the court of appeals and remanded the case to the district court for proceedings consistent with the following EEOC Guidelines regarding whether testing requirements are sufficiently job-related:

> If job progression structures and seniority provisions are so established that new employees will probably, within a reasonable period of time and in a great majority of cases, progress to a higher level, it may be considered that candidates are being evaluated for jobs at that higher level. However, where job progression is not so nearly automatic, or in the time span is such that higher level jobs or employees' potential may be expected to change in significant ways, it shall be considered that candidates are being evaluated for a job at or near the entry level.

Justice Marshall filed a concurring opinion, focusing primarily on the back pay analysis. He argued that the bar of laches should be difficult for Albemarle to establish because the information needed to determine the amount of back pay owed is contained in personnel records and pay schedules. However, he agreed that Albemarle was "entitled at least to an opportunity to prove that [the Employees'] delay prejudiced their defense so substantially as to make an award of compensatory relief oppressive."

Justice Blackmun also filed a concurring opinion but disagreed with Justice Stewart's conclusion "that an employer's good faith is never a sufficient reason for refusing to award back pay." He would have taken the Employer's intent into consideration and would not have followed the EEOC Guidelines as rigidly as the majority had, stating that he feared "that a too-rigid application of the EEOC Guidelines will leave the employer little choice, save an impossibly expensive and complex validation study, but to engage in a subjective quota system of employment selection."

Justice Rehnquist filed a concurring opinion, as well, arguing that difficulty in ascertainment of award does not preclude the right of recovery if the plaintiff's rights have been violated. He thought that since the injunction sought was equitable in nature, neither side was entitled to a jury trial under the Seventh Amendment. He also asserted that the determination of whether the back pay award is governed by equitable considerations or damages should be considered by the district court. Chief Justice Burger concurred in part and dissented in part. He agreed with the Court that the availability of back pay is to be determined by the discretion of the trial court. However, he disagreed with the Court's suggestion that the district court conditioned the award of back pay on a showing of bad faith. He also disagreed with the Court's review of the district court findings regarding Albemarle's testing policies, stating that it was based on a "wooden" application of the EEOC Guidelines. He argued that "slavish adherence to the EEOC Guidelines regarding test validation should not be required" The provisions are only guides in making a decision, as their name suggests.

AFTERMATH

This ruling placed a strict burden on employers to ensure that employment testing does not have a discriminatory effect and is, in fact, job-related.

SIGNIFICANCE

The holding in this case provided certainty that a back pay remedy is available to employees whose Title VII rights have been violated.

RELATED CASE

Griggs v. Duke Power Co., 401 U.S. 424 (1971)

RECOMMENDED READING

William Gordon, *The Evolution of the Disparate Impact Theory of Title VII: A Hypothetical Case Study,* 44 Harvard Journal of Legislation 529 (2007).

Hall, Ketmit L. "Albermarle Paper Co. v. Moody." In *The Oxford Companion to the Supreme Court of the United States,* 2005. Available online. URL: Encyclopedia.com. Accessed May 29, 2010.

Case Title: *Schlesinger v. Ballard*

Legal Citation: 419 U.S. 498

Year of Decision: 1975

KEY ISSUE

Does a federal statute treat male and female naval officers differently for purposes of pension retirement benefits?

HISTORY OF THE CASE

The Fourteenth Amendment directs the government to treat similarly situated persons equally. This "equal protection" guarantee governs all state actions that classify individuals for different benefits or burdens under the law. The Fifth Amendment's due process clause prohibits the federal government from engaging in unjustifiable discrimination.

The navy lieutenant Robert C. Ballard failed twice to be selected for promotion to lieutenant commander. A federal statute (10 U.S.C. § 6382 [a]) made male officers subject to mandatory discharge if they failed to be selected for promotion after nine or more years of active service. A similar statute, 10 U.S.C. § 6401, on the other hand, allowed female officers 13 years of commissioned service before a mandatory discharge for want of promotion. Ballard filed suit claiming that the difference in the two statutes unconstitutionally discriminated against him on the basis of sex in violation of his Fifth Amendment due process rights. A California federal district court upheld his claim, and the government appealed. Neither contending party challenged the preceding discrimination against women officers that barred their being assigned to positions likely to lead to promotion.

SUMMARY OF ARGUMENTS

Ballard contended that the dueling statutes treated male and female officers differently, existed for mere administrative and fiscal convenience purposes, and, therefore, were impermissibly unconstitutional. The government argued that the differing treatment accorded male and female naval officers reflected not an overboard generalization but instead the demonstrable fact that male and female officers are not similarly situated.

DECISION

The severely divided Court analyzed the issues using "rational relationship" scrutiny, as opposed to the "strict scrutiny" criterion used by the lower court. The rational relationship standard is traditionally lenient and used by courts in equal protection cases involving nonsuspect classes. The strict scrutiny test requires a narrowly tailored compelling state interest showing that the governmental classification is necessary.

The Supreme Court held Congress's motivation in enacting the two statutes legitimate under the "rational relationship" standard. The Court found that certain social policies and the fact that there were fewer positions to which women could be assigned, nearly affecting military promotional opportunities, guided the legislation. Additionally, the majority decided that the statutes were nonarbitrary and did not exist for mere administrative and fiscal convenience. The 5-4 majority reversed the trial court and held that Ballard suffered no constitutional injury, in that the statute did not violate the Fifth Amendment's due process guarantee.

AFTERMATH

The *Ballard* decision reviewed in isolation a single aspect of a large case involving pension benefits in a complicated military retirement situation. In one respect, it illustrated the problem courts encounter when asked to decide such discrete issues.

The Court's decision was viewed by some as an indication that the Court wanted to protect legislation favoring opportunities for women. Others saw the decision as emphasizing the view that women were inferior and thus needed special treatment.

SIGNIFICANCE

Prior to *Ballard*, the Supreme Court analyzed equal protection claims under one of two tiers: either a rational relationship or a strict scrutiny test. As the 1970s progressed, the courts began to apply broader levels of scrutiny to the same cases. The *Ballard* case helped pave the way to an "intermediate-level" scrutiny applied to equal protection issues. This intermediate-level standard is widely used in gender classification litigation today.

RELATED CASES

Reed v. Reed, 404 U.S. 71 (1971)

Craig v. Boren, 404 U.S. 76 (1972)

Frontiero v. Richardson, 411 U.S. 677 (1973)

Kahn v. Shevin, 416 U.S. 351 (1974)

Weinberger v. Weisenfeld, 420 U.S. 636 (1975)

Owens v. Brown, 455 F. Supp. 291 (D.D.C. 1978)

Davis v. Passman, 442 U.S. 228 (1979)

Rostker v. Goldberg, 448 U.S. 1306 (1980)

RECOMMENDED READING

The Supreme Court, 1974 Term, 89 Harvard Law Review 59 (1975).

Case Title: *Sosna v. Iowa*

Legal Citation: 419 U.S. 393

Year of Decision: 1975

KEY ISSUE

Does an Iowa provision that requires people to be a state resident for one year before they sue for divorce violate the equal protection or due process clauses of the U.S. Constitution?

HISTORY OF THE CASE

Sosna and her husband were married in Michigan in 1964. They lived together in New York from October 1967 until August 1971, when they separated: They both continued to live in New York. In August 1972, Sosna moved to Iowa and petitioned for a divorce the following month. The court dismissed the petition for lack of jurisdiction, because, according to Iowa Code provisions, one must be a resident of Iowa for one year before suing for divorce. She then took the case to the district court of Jackson County, Iowa, claiming that the code provision was unconstitutional. The district court found that the provision was constitutional, and the U.S. Supreme Court took the case. Even though Sosna met the Iowa residency requirement by the time the case reached the Supreme Court, the issue was not moot because a class of persons who did not meet the residency requirements still existed.

SUMMARY OF ARGUMENTS

Sosna contended that the provision created two classes of persons and discriminated against those who had recently traveled to Iowa, thereby violating the equal protection clause. Additionally, Sosna claimed that the provision violated the due process clause because it denied one the opportunity to prove residency by means other than the time in the state and, therefore, denies the only means of divorce.

Iowa argued that the provision merely delayed the divorce process. Iowa also contended that it had the right to regulate divorces so as to protect its judgments from collateral attacks by other states, actions with another purpose that have the effect of overturning the judgment.

DECISION

Justice Rehnquist delivered the opinion of the Court, which held that Iowa's provision requiring one year of residence in order to sue for divorce was constitutional. The Court stated that the provision delayed divorce, but it did not prevent it. Also, the residency requirement required a showing of more than just physical presence with the intent to remain in the state. Therefore, Sosna's due process rights were not violated.

Additionally, the Court found that Iowa has an interest in assuring that those seeking a divorce be attached to the state to avoid mingling in other state's affairs. This was also found to avoid collateral attacks from other states. The state had a stronger interest in not becoming a forum for countless divorces, which, combined with the fact that divorces would eventually be granted after a year of residency, was enough for the Court to hold that it did not violate the equal protection clause.

Justice White dissented on the grounds that he believed the case to be moot because Sosna had already obtained her divorce by the time the Supreme Court heard the case.

Justice Marshall and Justice Brennan dissented, stating that the provision interfered with the right to travel. They believed that strict scrutiny should be applied, not the balancing test that the majority applied. Applying the strict scrutiny test, the dissent found that Iowa did not have a compelling interest in keeping the one-year residency provision. Therefore, they believed the equal protection clause was violated.

AFTERMATH

The Court continues to follow *Sosna*, but it is quick to distinguish cases in which residency requirements penalize aliens seeking benefits available to residents. The Court also distinguishes cases in which the freedom to travel is severely impaired.

SIGNIFICANCE

Interference with the freedom to travel usually triggers strict scrutiny because it is a fundamental right. Strict scrutiny is applied to cases in which residency requirements constitute a penalty or a deterrent because that impairs the freedom to travel, but in cases where what is sought will eventually be given, the Court has applied a lesser standard. Here, the Court determined that the state's interest was stronger and that it was not penalizing Sosna, so equal protection was not violated.

RELATED CASES

Shapiro v. Thompson, 394 U.S. 618 (1969)

Dunn v. Blumstein, 405 U.S. 330 (1972)

Martinez v. Bynum, 461 U.S. 321 (1983)

RECOMMENDED READING

Radcliffe, James E. *The Case or Controversy Provision.* University Park: Pennsylvania State University Press, 1978.

The Supreme Court, 1974 Term, 89 Harvard Law Review 87 (1975).

Case Title: *Craig v. Boren*

Alternate Case Title: The "Gender-Based Discrimination" Case

Legal Citation: 429 U.S. 190

Year of Decision: 1976

KEY ISSUE

Does an Oklahoma statute that established different drinking ages for men and women violate the equal protection clause of the Fourteenth Amendment? The case was an appeal of an action that challenged the constitutionality of a state law.

HISTORY OF THE CASE

This was the third case involving the issue of gender classification to come before the Supreme Court in five years. Beginning in 1971 with *Reed v. Reed* (1971), the Court had struggled with the issue of when it is appropriate to treat men and women differently under the Constitution.

Oklahoma enacted a law establishing the legal age to purchase 3.2 percent "nonintoxicat-

ing" beer as 18 for females and 21 for males. Curtis Craig, a man then between the ages of 18 and 21, and Carolyn Whitener, a female beer vendor, challenged the law as discriminatory. The district court held that the state's statistical evidence regarding young males' drunk driving arrests and traffic injuries demonstrated that the gender-based discrimination was substantially related to the achievement of traffic safety on Oklahoma roads. The district court sustained the constitutionality of the different age limits for males and females and dismissed the action. The appellants appealed to the U.S. Supreme Court, but by the time the case was to be heard, Craig had turned 21 and no longer had standing to sue. The Court, nevertheless, agreed to hear the case on the basis of the third-party standing of Whitener, explaining that while she and other vendors were only indirectly affected by the statute, they have standing "by acting as advocates of the rights of third parties who seek access to their market."

SUMMARY OF ARGUMENTS

The appellant argued that the Oklahoma statute constituted a gender-based discrimination that denied to males 18–20 years of age the equal protection of the laws.

The appellees argued that the difference between males and females warranted the differential in age drawn by the Oklahoma statute, presenting statistics showing a much higher incidence of "drunk" driving and public intoxication among males 18–20 than females of the same age. They also argued that the provisions of the Twenty-first Amendment should override the application of equal protection standards.

DECISION

Justice Brennan wrote the opinion for the Court holding that under *Reed,* Oklahoma's 3.2 percent beer statute unfairly discriminated against males 18–20 years of age. The holding struck down the Oklahoma statute, finding that the evidence the state presented to justify the gender discrimination did not substantially advance Oklahoma's purpose of preventing traffic accidents.

Justice Brennan began his analysis referring to *Reed v. Reed,* which emphasized that statutory classifications that distinguished between males and females were "subject to scrutiny under Equal Protection Clause." Classifications by gender could withstand constitutional challenge only if they served important governmental objectives and were substantially related to the achievement of those objectives.

Justice Brennan then turned to the alleged necessity of the age differential between males and females with respect to the purchase of 3.2 percent beer. He concluded that the gender-based distinction did not closely serve the objective of enhancing traffic safety as the state purported. He believed that the statistics presented by the appellees were unpersuasive and unhelpful to the equal protection analysis. He concluded that sex did not represent a legitimate, accurate substitute for the regulation of drinking and driving.

Justice Powell wrote a concurring opinion expressing reservations about the appropriate standard for equal protection analysis and the relevance of the statistical evidence. He concluded that the gender-based classification did not bear a fair and substantial relation to the state objectives of promoting highway safety.

Justice Rehnquist wrote a dissenting opinion, objecting, among other things, to the Court's rejection of the state's statistics. He also stated that the Court's analysis was not relevant to equal protection but to due process, asking whether there were enough persons in the category who drove while drunk to justify the application of such a prohibition against all members of that group.

AFTERMATH

After *Craig,* discrimination based on gender was neither suspect nor subject to the less exacting rational basis standard; rather, it was "quasi-suspect," judged by a more flexible intermediate level of scrutiny. The test articulated in *Craig* has been employed in other areas of constitutional adjudication, such as in cases of regulations based on illegitimacy and alienage.

SIGNIFICANCE

Craig was the first case in which the Court held that equal protection challenges based on gender

classifications would be subject to an intermediate level of scrutiny. It marked the third standard concerning gender classification announced by the Court in a five-year period, and it constituted a retreat from the Court's strict level scrutiny employed three years earlier in *Frontiero v. Richardson.*

RELATED CASES

Reed v. Reed, 404 U.S. 71 (1971)

Frontiero v. Richardson, 411 U.S. 677 (1973)

Michael M. v. Superior Court of Sonoma County, 150 U.S. 464 (1981)

Mississippi Univ. for Women v. Hogan, 458 U.S. 718 (1982)

RECOMMENDED READING

Ruth Ginsburg, *Sexual Equality under the Fourteenth and Equal Rights Amendment,* 1979 Washington University Law Quarterly 161 (1979).

Kenneth Karst, *Forward: Equal Citizenship under the Fourteenth Amendment,* 91 Harvard Law Review 1 (1977).

Case Title: *Hampton v. Mow Sun Wong*

Legal Citation: 426 U.S. 88

Year of Decision: 1976

KEY ISSUE

Does a federal regulation that bars noncitizens from employment in the federal competitive civil service violate the due process of the law as set out in the Fifth Amendment?

HISTORY OF THE CASE

The Civil Service Commission had regulations barring noncitizens from employment in positions with certain federal agencies that were filled on the basis of the results of a competitive examination. Five resident aliens brought the action to challenge the policy. Each of the aliens was denied federal employment on the sole basis that he or she was not an American citizen or native of American Samoa. All were Chinese residents who qualified in all other respects for an available job.

One of the plaintiffs was terminated after 10 days of satisfactory work at the post office because his personnel record revealed that he was not a citizen. Two of the plaintiffs were denied access to the positions of janitor and file clerk, even though they had participated in the California Supplemental Training and Education Program and had other work experience that demonstrated their capabilities as workers. One plaintiff was not permitted to take an examination although she had adequate work and education experience. The last plaintiff sought a position as a clerk-typist but, because of her alienage, was not allowed to take the typing test.

The plaintiffs brought this class action on behalf of all aliens living in the United States. They named as defendants the chairman and the commissioners of the Civil Service Commission and the heads of the three agencies that denied them employment. The complaint alleged that aliens face special problems in seeking employment because of language barriers. The plaintiffs noted that although 300,000 federal jobs become available each year, noncitizens are not eligible to compete for them except when these jobs are exempted from the competitive civil service. They contended that the advantage given to citizens seeking such employment is arbitrary and violates the due process clause of the Fifth Amendment and Executive Order No. 11,478, 3 CFR 803, which forbids discrimination in federal employment on the basis of "national origin." They sought declaratory and injunctive relief.

The defendants sought to have the complaint dismissed. The district court reasoned that the prohibition against discrimination on the basis of "national origin" in the executive order prohibited discrimination among citizens on that basis, not between citizens and noncitizens. In addition, the court rejected the Civil Service Commission's argument that the regulation was inconsistent with section 502 of the Public Works for Water

Pollution Control and Power Development and Atomic Energy Commission Appropriation Act, which permitted payment to classes of persons who are made ineligible by the Civil Service Regulation. Last, the district court held that discrimination against aliens was constitutional.

Four of the plaintiffs appealed this decision. During the time the appeal was pending, the Supreme Court decided two cases, *Sugarman v. Dougall* (1973) and *In re Griffiths* (1973), in which the Court recognized the importance of protecting the employment opportunities of aliens.

The court of appeals reversed the decision. It agreed with the analysis of the nonconstitutional issues but held that the regulations violated the due process clause of the Fifth Amendment. The court concluded that the commission regulation could not be justified, considering that it protected only a small fraction of the positions covered by the rule. The court accepted the conclusion that exclusion was constitutional in positions involving policymaking or national security, but the court was unwilling to support the broad exclusion fostered by the regulation at issue.

The Supreme Court agreed to hear the case to resolve the question of "whether a regulation of the United States Civil Service Commission that bars resident aliens from employment in the federal competitive civil service is constitutional."

Summary of Arguments

The plaintiffs argued that by excluding all persons except American citizens and native American Samoans, the regulation adopted and enforced by the Civil Service Commission violated the due process clause of the Fifth Amendment and Executive Order No. 11,478, which prohibited discrimination in employment based on "national origin."

The Civil Service Commission argued that discrimination on the basis of alienage was not unconstitutional. The Public Works for Water Pollution Control and Power Development and Atomic Energy Commission Appropriations Act provided that "no part of any appropriation shall be used to pay compensation of any officer or employee of the Government . . . unless such person (1) is a citizen of the United States, (2) is a person in the service of the United States on the date of enactment of this Act, who, being eligible for citizenship, had filed a declaration of intention to become a citizen of the United States prior to such date, (3) is a person who owed allegiance to the United States." On the basis of this regulation, the commission contended that it acted permissibly in not opening up the civil service to all those whom Congress had indicated it would be willing to pay for their work. The commission additionally argued that the equal protection element of the due process clause of the Fifth Amendment did not apply to federal actions related to aliens. Therefore, there was no need to justify the regulation. In the alternative, they contended that the Fifth Amendment imposes a slight burden on the federal government to justify the exclusion of aliens and that this burden was met by several factors not considered by the lower courts.

DECISION

Justice Stevens wrote for the plurality and affirmed the opinion of the court of appeals. In refuting the contention of the commission, Justice Stevens argued that the federal government is compelled, as are the states, to govern impartially. While agreeing with the defendant's position that a justification for citizenship requirement may have importance in certain contexts, Justice Stevens did not agree with the argument that the power of the federal government in this area was so complete that it may arbitrarily subject all aliens to rules substantially different from those applied to citizens.

He went on to note that the rule adopted and enforced by the commission subjected this already disadvantaged group to disparate treatment based solely on their alienage. He noted that this deprivation infringed on the interest in liberty protected by the due process clause of the Constitution: "The added disadvantage resulting from the enforcement of the rule—ineligibility for employment in a major sector of the economy—is of sufficient significance to be characterized as a deprivation of an interest in liberty." Because the regulation had the effect of disadvantaging this group, which constituted a discrete and insular minority, they must be afforded due process of law.

In subjecting the rule to scrutiny, the Court noted that the commission identified several interests that Congress or the president might deem sufficient to justify the exclusion of noncitizens from federal service. A broad exclusion, for example, might help the president in negotiating treaties with foreign powers by enabling him to offer employment opportunities to citizens of a given foreign country in exchange for reciprocal concessions. Excluding aliens also provides an adequate incentive to qualify for naturalization.

Justice Stevens held that the problem with the cited interests was that they could not be reasonably assumed to have influenced the Civil Service Commission, the U.S. Postal Service, the General Service Administration, or the Department of Health, Education, and Welfare in the administration of their responsibilities, and particularly in relation to this case. He went on to note that neither Congress nor the president required the commission to adopt a citizenship requirement as a condition of eligibility for employment in the civil service. The policy had been in place since the commission's inception in 1883, and both Congress and the president were aware of it; therefore, Justice Stevens thought that the appropriate question was whether they acquiesced to this rule and whether this acquiescence should be given the same support as an express statutory or presidential command.

The last interest cited by the commission was that in certain positions, there is a need for undivided loyalty to the federal government. The citizenship requirement served that end while eliminating the need for the commission specifically to delineate those positions that required such loyalty. The Court held that this is a valid interest and that in situations in which the government has such an interest, it may limit access to those positions to citizens.

Justice Stevens then went on to recount the history of the Civil Service Commission. He thought that this history revealed that there was a trend to establish standards with respect to citizenship but that this was not demonstrative of whether the president would act in such a manner. He believed that this trend merely gave the commission discretion in how to formulate its standard rather than set in place obligatory commands.

It is the business of the commission to adopt regulations that will best promote the efficiency of the federal civil service. The commission's function is limited and specific: to promote an efficient federal service. Justice Stevens noted that, in general, removing unnecessary restrictions fostered this end. He continued that, with the exception of the interest served by having citizens in positions that require loyalty to the U.S. government, the interests cited by the commission are not matters properly the business of the commission.

Justice Stevens went on to note that even in light of the cited and acceptable interest of securing citizens in positions that require loyalty, the commission had a responsibility to perform its responsibilities with a level of expertise that demanded it make known the reasons for its important decisions. The commission had not made any attempt to evaluate the desirability of a general exclusionary rule and the value of enlarging the eligible applicant pool. Justice Stevens continued that the Court had no basis on which to infer that setting up categories in which citizenship would be required was an onerous task that justified such a broad exclusionary policy. He, therefore, rejected their argument of administrative convenience.

He concluded the impact of the rule adopted by the commission was the same as those state regulations rejected in the *Sugarman* case, which rejected a large group of people, all of whom were not the target of the legislation. Since the decision to admit these aliens was made by Congress and the president, the decision to exclude them from an area traditionally noted as part of an individual's liberty—economic opportunity—must be made at that same level of government. He concluded that the regulation at issue denied the class of liberty without due process of law and was, therefore, invalid.

Justice Brennan wrote a concurring opinion, in which Justice Marshall joined. He noted that there are equal protection questions that would be raised if the Congress or president were the relevant actor barring employment of aliens by the government.

Justice Rehnquist wrote a dissenting opinion, in which the chief justice, Justice White, and Justice Blackmun joined. He reasoned that the Court's holding enunciated a concept of procedural due process guaranteed by the Fifth Amendment that is out of line with the doctrine established by the previous Court decisions.

He first noted that in the areas of immigration and regulation of aliens, the power of the deferral courts is severely limited. He continued that though Congress wields broad power to prescribe the terms and conditions of entry of aliens, this power is curtailed by the requirements of complying with the due process clause of the Constitution. However, this requirement of due process does not mean that aliens have protected liberty interest in securing federal employment. He noted that in reaching their decision, the plurality overlooked this limitation.

He continued that the *Sugarman* case to which the Court referred specifically did not apply its holding to the federal government. The Court, instead of applying traditional equal protection analysis, melded together the concepts of equal protection and procedural due process. "What the Court seems to do is to engraft notions of due process onto the case law from this Court dealing with the delegation by Congress of its legislative authority to administrative agencies."

Justice Rehnquist noted that the only grounds on which the procedure may be challenged is to argue that it was an improper delegation of authority. Yet, he thought that under traditional standards governing the delegation of authority, the commission was empowered to act as it did. Congress delegated to the president the power to prescribe regulations for admission of individuals to the Civil Service and to ascertain the fitness of applicants as to age, health, character, knowledge, and ability for employment as set down in the Civil Service Act. The president, acting under this authority, promulgated Executive Order 10, 577, in which he authorized the Civil Service Commission to establish standards with respect to citizenship, age, education, residency, or other requirements that must be met before an individual may be eligible to compete for civil service employment. Under this authority, the Civil

Service Commission promulgated regulations to exclude aliens from examination for or appointment to the civil service. Thus, concluded Justice Rehnquist, Congress and the president took power they possessed and delegated it to the commission. "This is the process by which all federal regulations are promulgated, and to forbid it would be to necessarily dismantle the entire structure of the Executive Branch."

Justice Stevens then noted that the decision to exclude aliens is a political question reserved to Congress. Once it is determined that the power has been delegated appropriately, then the reason why this power is exercised is foreclosed from consideration by the judiciary. This is because the delegation is subject to the same scrutiny as if Congress had itself exercised such authority. For the Court to exercise authority in this area would transcend the bounds of its jurisdiction. He concluded that the regulation does not infringe upon any constitutional right of the class members. "I conclude therefore the Congress, in the exercise of its political judgment, could have excluded aliens from the civil service. The fact that it chose, in a separate political decision, to allow the Civil Service Commission to make this determination does not render the governmental policy any less 'political' and consequently, does not render it any more subject to judicial scrutiny."

AFTERMATH

To determine whether a federal statute is constitutionally valid, courts review the statute for congressional violations of the equal protection clause of the Fifth Amendment. For state classifications involving alienage, the Court analyzes whether the appropriate entity is making the relevant decision. This question often turns on whether the entity is authorized to act in such a manner and whether the action is congressionally sanctioned.

After this decision, President Ford issued an executive order making citizenship a condition for federal employment.

SIGNIFICANCE

The original position of the Court stated in *Detroit Bank v. United States* (1943) was that the Fifth Amendment does not contain an equal protection

clause. In *Bolling v. Sharpe,* the Court held that discrimination may be of such a degree as to be unjustifiable and, as such, violative of due process protected by the Fifth Amendment. In invalidating a gender classification in *Weinberger v. Weisenfeld* (1975), the Court later held that "this Court's approach to Fifth Amendment equal protection claims has always been the same as to equal protection claims under the Fourteenth Amendment."

On the same day as this decision, *Mathews v. Diaz* was decided. In *Mathews,* the Court reached a seemingly opposite conclusion. The Court held that a federal statute that limited participation in a federal medical insurance program to citizens and aliens who had resided continuously in the United States for five years was valid. The Court reasoned that Congress may legitimately determine that a resident's ties to the United States grow stronger the longer the residency and may condition the receipt of benefits on the stronger tie. It further reasoned that the business of regulating the conditions of entry and residence of aliens is exclusively within the dominion of the political branches of the federal government.

The basis of the reasoning in *Hampton* is that the decision to impose a deprivation of an important liberty must be made by either Congress or the executive branch, which made the decisions under which the aliens were admitted. This reasoning implies the nondelegation doctrine. The nondelegation doctrine is grounded in the separation of powers. It allocates power to perform functions by branch and views the delegation of these functions to another branch or an administrative person as invalid. The rationale for this approach includes the objectives of (1) ensuring policy choices are made by the legislature and not by the executive branch, (2) promoting reliability for those affected by regulation, and (3) working against arbitrariness or caprice of administrators because the discretion is limited. The nondelegation doctrine serves to promote the rule of law.

RELATED CASES

Detroit Bank v. United States, 317 U.S. 329 (1943)

Bolling v. Sharpe, 347 U.S. 497 (1954)

In re Griffiths, 413 U.S. 717 (1973)

Sugarman v. Dougall, 413 U.S. 634 (1973)

Weinberg v. Wiesenfeld, 420 U.S. 636 (1975)

Mathews v. Diaz, 426 U.S. 67 (1976)

Vance v. Bradley, 440 U.S. 93 (1979)

RECOMMENDED READING

David F. Levi, *The Equal Treatment of Aliens: Preemption or Equal Protection?,* 31 Stanford Law Review 1069 (1979).

Richard A. Posner, *The DeFunis Case and the Constitutionality of Preferential Treatment of Racial Minorities,* 1974 Supreme Court Review 1.

Gerald M. Rosberg, *The Protection of Aliens from Discriminatory Treatment by the National Government,* 1975 Supreme Court Review 275.

State Burdens on Resident Aliens: A New Preemption Analysis, 89 Yale Law Journal 940 (1980).

Case Title: *Pasadena City Board of Education v. Spangler*

Legal Citation: 427 U.S. 424

Year of Decision: 1976

KEY ISSUE

To what extent does a district court have to oversee the desegregation of a school district that has been found to practice segregation?

HISTORY OF THE CASE

In 1968, the Pasadena City Board of Education, which operates the Pasadena Unified School District ("PUSD"), practiced segregation in its high schools. Several students, along with their parents, sought injunctive relief in federal district court against the PUSD and several officials. The district court allowed the United States to intervene; however, it later granted a motion to strike portions of the U.S. complaint dealing with the elementary schools, junior high schools, and special schools. This motion was the subject of an interlocutory appeal to the Ninth Circuit Court of Appeals, which reversed the decision of the lower court and reinstated the federal demand of systemwide relief. Ruling on the remaining issues, the district court found that PUSD's educational policies violated the Fourteenth Amendment and ordered the PUSD to submit a plan for desegregating the schools. The district court, in its decree, retained jurisdiction over the execution of the order.

The PUSD submitted their proposal, and the district court approved it in March 1970. In 1974, the successors of the PUSD defendants (also "PUSD") in the original action filed a motion with the district court seeking relief from the 1970 decree. The PUSD sought to dissolve the court order, eliminate the requirement that no school can have a majority of minority students, terminate the district court's retained jurisdiction, and obtain approval of PUSD's proposed modifications to their plan. The district court denied all four motions, and the PUSD appealed to the Ninth Circuit Court of Appeals. That court affirmed the district court's decision, and because of the importance of the extent of a district court's authority to oversee desegregation plans, the U.S. Supreme Court granted certiorari.

SUMMARY OF ARGUMENTS

PUSD argued that it was entitled to release from regulatory jurisdiction under the standards acknowledged by the government. The petitioner also argued that the appellate court abused its discretion by rejecting the alternative desegregation plan.

The students and parents argued that despite the court order requiring the school system to desegregate, the school system had not achieved that status. Therefore, the district court should continue to hold judicial control over the district until the segregation issue was completely solved by the school system. The respondents also argued that the proposed alternative plan would cause the school to be placed back in the same segregated position it was in before the lawsuit began.

DECISION

The Supreme Court held that the PUSD's approved plan for desegregation did not have to be adjusted periodically to accommodate shifting racial balances among student bodies in their school district, provided that such change was due to factors outside the control of the school board.

Justice Rehnquist delivered the opinion of the Court. The PUSD first asserted that since the original student plaintiffs had graduated, and this was not a certified class action lawsuit pursuant to Federal Rule of Civil Procedure 23, that the case was moot. However, as the Court noted, the intervention of the United States pursuant to 42 U.S.C. § 2000h-2 authorized the United States to continue the action as the plaintiff. The Court next turned to the PUSD's request to dissolve the injunctive order regarding the requirement that no school in the district have a majority of minority students enrolled, which had been refused by the district court. The Court did not consider the validity of the original judgment, since it had not been appealed, and, instead, considered whether the district court was correct in denying the modification. The Court first noted that the parties' understanding of the decree differed from that of the district court. The district court interpreted the order to mean that a particular degree of racial balancing must be achieved in order to comply with the injunction; however, the Court had previously disapproved of this sort of reasoning in *Swann v. Charlotte-Mecklenburg Board of Education* (1971). The district court further interpreted this to mean that each year the schools had to be reevaluated to comply with the order. However, the Court found that "in enforcing its order so as to require annual readjustment of attendance zones so that there would not be a majority of any minority in any Pasadena public school, the District Court exceeded its authority."

In support of this finding, the Court argued that its decision in *Swann* had previously stated

that neither the school authorities nor the district courts were required to adjust the racial composition of the student body on a year-by-year basis once desegregation had been accomplished. The Court further found that the school district had achieved a system of determining admissions on a non–racially discriminatory basis and that there was no showing that changes in the racial composition of the schools after 1971 were caused by the school district. Rather, the changes in racial composition were attributed to people moving in and out of the PUSD school district, causing a change in the demographics of the area. The Court stated that "the District Court was not entitled to require the PUSD to rearrange its attendance zones each year so as to ensure that the racial mix desired by the court was maintained in perpetuity." The Court went on to hold that the district court had fully performed its duty of remedying the prior racially discriminatory patterns in the school district.

The Court then turned to the ambiguities in the decree, noting that violation of a decree can result in criminal or civil contempt, and thus, decrees must be "specific and reasonably detailed" to prevent misinterpretation. In *United States v. Mine Workers United* (1974), the Court held that injunctive orders of courts must be obeyed until modified or reversed, even if there are reasonable and proper objections available. In this case, the PUSD had established their entitlement to relief from the injunction regarding the "no majority of minority students" requirement. Thus, the Court thought the court of appeals should probably have reversed the district court's decision not to modify that portion of the order. However, this decision was left to the court of appeals, as the judgment of that court was vacated, and the case was remanded to that court for further proceedings consistent with this decision. The Court thought it was unnecessary to rule on the remaining issues since the case was to be remanded.

Justice Marshall wrote a dissenting opinion, joined by Justice Brennan. He did not agree with the Court's decision that the district court's refusal to modify the injunction was wrong. He thought that racial discrimination had not been eliminated in the school district, agreeing with a lower court judge that there was ample evidence to support this contention. Relying on *Swann* as well, he argued that "until such a unitary system is established, a district court may act with broad discretion which includes the adjustment of attendance zones so that the goal of a wholly unitary system might be sooner achieved." Justice Marshall further argued that the Court's decision may result in desegregation of the school district never to be achieved, "for at the point that the Pasadena system is in compliance with the aspects of the plan specifying procedures for hiring and promoting teachers and administrators, it may be that the attendance patterns within the system will be such as to once again manifest substantial aspects of a segregated system." He further argued that the district court should not have to modify the injunction until it was clear that the problem had been remedied and no longer existed.

AFTERMATH

Some schools again became segregated, because the areas around the school would change over time, and the numbers of minorities within school districts would increase or decrease, depending on the area.

SIGNIFICANCE

This case made it clear that annual reassignments were not necessary in order for school districts to comply with court orders for desegregation. Once a school board has complied with a desegregation plan, the district court no longer has power to impose a new desegregation plan.

RELATED CASES

Swann v. Charlotte-Mecklenburg Board of Education, 402 U.S. 1 (1971)

Milliken v. Bradley, 418 U.S. 717 (1974)

RECOMMENDED READING

Rosina A. Lozano, Brown's *Legacy in the West: Pasadena Unified School District's Federally Mandated Desegregation,* 36 Southwestern University Law Review 257 (2007).

Uhrich, Kevin. "Leaving No Child Behind: The Story of a Group of Local Parents Who Fought All the Way to the Supreme Court to Change Education Forever" *Pasadena Weekly,* April 5, 2007.

Case Title: *Runyon v. McCrary*

Legal Citation: 427 U.S. 160

Year of Decision: 1976

KEY ISSUE

Are private schools prohibited to deny admission to qualified black applicants solely on account of their race?

HISTORY OF THE CASE

Two Virginia private schools, supported entirely by tuition payments, denied admission to blacks. Two black students who had been denied admission brought an action in federal district court under 42 U.S.C. § 1981, which guarantees all persons the right to make and enforce contracts. Congress passed the act to forbid discrimination by private parties in making contracts. The district court found that the schools violated the act by summarily rejecting non-Caucasians. The court of appeals affirmed the district court's decision. Because of the importance of the issues presented by the case, the Supreme Court agreed to a review.

SUMMARY OF ARGUMENTS

The school district argued that the power of Congress to enact legislation under the Thirteenth Amendment is limited to ending slavery. The schools believed that even if Congress had the authority to remove "badges and incidents" of slavery, it does not have the power to regulate private citizens in their associational choices, for example, who will be allowed to attend their school. The schools maintained that the relationships between the schools and the students were not commercial contracts but merely associational relationships that had the utmost protection from governmental intrusion.

McCrary argued that the act of Congress does not compel individuals to make contracts, but it does prohibit someone who makes an offer to contract to make a condition based on race. Since the schools held themselves open to public enrollment, with the exception of blacks, they were generally within the scope of governmental regulation.

DECISION

Justice Stevens wrote for the majority in the 7-2 decision affirming the lower courts. The Court held that the Constitution has never provided affirmative protection for outright discrimination. The Court also maintained that the enabling clause of the Thirteenth Amendment gives Congress the ability to determine the badges and incidents of slavery rationally. The consequence of this ability is that any determination must be rationally translated into effective legislation. The Court believed that the act of Congress regarding contractual obligations was a rational exercise of its ability to enact such laws and was, therefore, valid.

The Court rejected the questions concerning associational freedoms because the conduct was not merely associational but commercially public in nature. The schools solicited by mailers, and one posted an advertisement in the Yellow Pages. As a result, the schools could not reasonably claim to be private in nature. The conduct prohibited by the act was related to discrimination affecting the public interest. Since the schools held themselves out to the general public and excluded blacks, the conduct was within the regulatory powers of Congress.

AFTERMATH

The Court later narrowed its view concerning the right to enter contracts under 42 U.S.C. § 1981. Private associational concerns and freedom of contract notions seem to have risen to the surface of the issue. The Court now looks to the literal meaning of the statute rather than enlarging it. As a result, discrimination after a contract is formed is not actionable under the statute because it does not affect the right to enter the contract.

SIGNIFICANCE

The Court's decision in *Runyon* prohibited racial discrimination in the private sector and was viewed as an important step toward eliminating racial discrimination.

This case opened the doors to private schools for black students but had minimal long-range effects. The case is limited yet has the potential for great expansion in the area of contractual discrimination. Since it has never been expressly overruled, it is still good law. The contract questions answered by the Court may yet prove to affect other types of contracts and associations.

RELATED CASES

Jones v. Alfred H. Mayer Co., 392 U.S. 409 (1968)

Johnson v. Railway Express Agency, 421 U.S. 454 (1975)

Patterson v. McLean Credit Union, 491 U.S. 164 (1989)

RECOMMENDED READING

John A. Bogdanski, *Section 1981 and the Thirteenth Amendment after* Runyon v. McCrary: *On the Doorsteps of Discriminatory Clubs,* 29 Standford Law Review 747 (1977).

Robert J. Kaczorowski, *The Enforcement Provisions of the Civil Rights Act of 1866: A Legislative History in Light of* Runyon v. McCrary, 98 Yale Law Journal 565 (1989).

Samuel A. Marcosson, *The Court at the Cross Roads:* Runyon, *Section 1981, and the Meaning of Precedent,* 37 Emory Law Journal 949 (1988).

James McClellan, *The Foibles and Fables of* Runyon, 67 Washington University Law Quarterly 13 (1989).

Bernard Schwartz, *Rehnquist,* Runyon, *and* Jones—*The Chief Justice, Civil Rights, and Stare Decisis,* 31 Tulsa Law Journal 251 (1995).

Case Title: *Washington v. Davis*

Alternate Case Title: The Police Admission Test Case

Legal Citation: 426 U.S. 229

Year of Decision: 1976

KEY ISSUE

May a police department base hiring decisions on written test scores when a greater percentage of black applicants than whites fail the test?

HISTORY OF THE CASE

The District of Columbia Metropolitan Police Department used a written examination, created by the U.S. Civil Service Commission for use by government agencies, as one of the standards for admission to its police training program. The exam, known as "Test 21," tested verbal ability, vocabulary, reading, and comprehension. Along with other requirements, applicants needed to answer 40 of the test's 80 questions correctly in order to gain admission to the program. Test 21 had been a useful tool in predicting training school performance, although it was not necessarily a predictor of future job performance. A higher percentage of blacks failed the test than whites. Alfred E. Davis, a black applicant who had failed the test, filed a suit against the police department and Walter E. Washington, who was then the mayor of the District of Columbia, alleging that the test deprived him of the equal protection of the law guaranteed by the Fourteenth Amendment. Washington prevailed in the district court, but the Court of Appeals for the District of Columbia Circuit reversed and directed judgment for Davis.

SUMMARY OF ARGUMENTS

Davis argued that the test was unconstitutional because (1) it did not predict job performance, (2) the number of black police officers was not proportionate to the population mix of the city, and

(3) a disproportionate percentage of blacks failed the test.

Washington argued that because Davis had not alleged that the police department had a discriminatory purpose in administering the test, the test was constitutional under rational basis review.

DECISION

The Supreme Court, in an opinion written by Justice White, held that the police department's use of Test 21 had been constitutional. Under the Court's equal protection analysis, the police department's action would be subject to rational basis review unless Davis could demonstrate that the use of Test 21 had both a racially discriminatory impact and some underlying discriminatory purpose. Justice White began by noting that there was no evidence of discriminatory purpose; in fact, 44 percent of new police recruits were black, and the "Department had systematically and affirmatively sought to enroll black officers, many of whom passed the test but failed to report for duty." Justice White argued that these factors also distinguished this case from those in which discrimination was impossible to explain on nonracial grounds. In the absence of a showing of discriminatory purpose, the Court would not subject the police department's actions to strict scrutiny. As Justice White stated: "Disproportionate impact is not irrelevant, but it is not the sole touchstone of an invidious racial discrimination forbidden by the Constitution."

Justice White then proceeded to inquire whether the police department had a rational basis for concluding that the test served a constitutionally permissible purpose. The police department had contended that the test provided insight into the applicant's oral and written communication skills, both of which are required for the job. In Justice White's view, it was "untenable that the Constitution prevents the Government from seeking modestly to upgrade the communicative abilities of its employees rather than to be satisfied with some lower level of competence." He argued that Davis's position might invalidate "a whole range of tax, welfare, public service, regulatory, and licensing statutes that may be more burdensome to the poor and to the average black than to

the more affluent white." Given these considerations, the Court was unable to say that Davis's
misfortune required a constitutional remedy.

AFTERMATH

This decision forced civil rights groups to work
harder because it compelled them to prove the
discriminatory intent behind challenged rules and
practices thought to have a racially disproportionate effect.

SIGNIFICANCE

A racially disproportionate impact by itself does
not automatically render a practice or rule
unconstitutional.

RELATED CASES

Strauder v. West Virginia, 100 U.S. 303 (1880)

Yick Wo v. Hopkins, 118 U.S. 351 (1886)

Bolling v. Sharpe, 347 U.S. 497 (1954)

Gomillion v. Lightfoot, 364 U.S. 339 (1960)

Griggs v. Duke Power Company, 401 U.S. 424
(1971)

*Personnel Administrator of Massachusetts v. Fee-
ney,* 442 U.S. 256 (1979)

RECOMMENDED READING

Robert W. Bennett, *"Mere" Rationality in Constitutional Law: Judicial Review and Democratic
Theory,* 67 California Law Review 1049 (1977).

Block, Farrell E. *Antidiscrimination Law on
Minority Employment: Recruitment Practice and
Regulatory Constraints.* Chicago: University of
Chicago Press, 1994.

John Hart Ely, *Legislative and Administrative
Motivation in Constitutional Law,* 79 Yale Law
Journal 1205 (1970).

Case Title: *Arlington Heights v. Metropolitan
Housing Development Corp.*

Legal Citation: 429 U.S. 252

Year of Decision: 1977

KEY ISSUE

Did the village's denial of the Metropolitan Housing Development Corporation's (MHDC's) proposal to rezone an 80-acre parcel from single-family
dwelling units to multifamily, low-income housing violate the Fourteenth Amendment?

HISTORY OF THE CASE

The Village of Arlington Heights (the "Village") is
a suburb of Chicago, which was zoned for single-
family homes. The Clerics of St. Viator (the
"Order") owned an 80-acre parcel in Arlington
Heights. The parcel included the Viatorian High
School and the Order's newly ordained clerics'
building, which had dormitories and a Montes-
sori school. The remaining portion of the lot was
vacant. Beginning in 1959, all the land surrounding the 80-acre parcel had been zoned for single-
family use. However, in 1970, the Order sought to
allocate some of its land to low- and moderate-
income housing with the help of a nonprofit
developer. The developer offered experience
working with federal housing subsidies under section 236 of the National Housing Act. This section allows for "interest reduction payments" for
the owners of housing projects that abide by the
act's requirements, provided that the savings are
passed on to the tenants.

The Order chose MHDC as its developer and
entered into a 99-year lease and agreement of sale
for 15 acres of the Order's property. However, the
agreement for the sale of land was contingent
upon MHDC's securing both the necessary clear-
ances with the Village and housing assistance
from the federal government. If MHDC could
not meet both of these contingencies, the lease
and the land sale contract would both lapse.
MHDC, then, petitioned with the Village for
rezoning the parcel, and a series of hearings were
held. In September 1971, the Village Board held
a public hearing and denied the rezoning of the
property.

The following June, MHDC, along with three African-American individuals, filed a lawsuit against the Village, seeking declaratory and injunctive relief. The district court ruled in favor of the Village, finding a lack of racial discrimination against low-income families. The court of appeals reversed, holding that although the Village lacked the intent to discriminate, the denial of the rezoning petition would have a disparate impact on African Americans. Looking at the historical context as well, the court of appeals also found that the Village and much of the surrounding areas experienced residential segregation, even though the population and employment opportunities had both grown rapidly. On appeal, the U.S. Supreme Court granted certiorari.

SUMMARY OF ARGUMENTS

MHDC argued that the Village wrongfully denied MHDC's rezoning petition. MHDC argued that the Village had a racially discriminatory intent to deny the petition. MHDC also argued that the denial violated the Equal Protection Clause of the Fourteenth Amendment and the Fair Housing Act.

The Village argued that it had no racially discriminatory intent to deny the petition. The Village argued that it denied the petition because the zoning had always been single-family and denying the petition would protect property values.

DECISION

The Court held that MHDC failed to demonstrate that the Village had racially discriminatory intent; however, the case was remanded to determine whether the denial of the rezoning petition resulted in a violation of MHDC's statutory claims.

Justice Powell wrote the majority opinion. The Court first addressed whether MHDC had standing to challenge the Village's decision. To demonstrate standing, the plaintiff must show a personal injury created by the challenged action of the defendant. In this case, MHDC's project was put in jeopardy by the Village's decision not to rezone the 80-acre parcel, and the Court found that it did have standing. Additionally, although

MHDC does not have a racial identity, at least one plaintiff was able to demonstrate standing because he was an African-American man who worked in Arlington Heights and had previously testified that he would move into the new housing area if it were developed. Thus, this plaintiff demonstrated an "actionable causal relationship" between his injury and the Village's zoning practices.

The Court then proceeded to the merits of the case. In *Washington v. Davis* (1976), the Court held that "disproportionate impact is not irrelevant, but it is not the sole touchstone of an invidious racial discrimination." This principle has been applied in various contexts, including schools, election districting, and jury selection, but discriminatory intent is also reviewed because impact alone is not determinative absent a stark pattern of discrimination. Although judicial deference is usually given to legislators regarding their legislation, it is not granted when a discriminatory purpose has been shown. When reviewing discriminatory purposes, the Court noted that circumstantial and direct evidence of intent are two important considerations. Additionally, the Court pointed out several other factors to be considered: the historical background of the decision not to rezone the property in order to determine whether invidious purposes can be found; the sequence of events leading up to the challenged decision; departures, especially substantive departures, from normal procedural sequences; and the legislative or administrative history of the decision, including statements by members of the decision-making body, the minutes of the meetings, and other reports.

Next, the Court applied these guidelines to this case, finding that the district court had acted properly. Although the Village's decision seemed to bear more heavily on racial minorities, the Court found little evidence regarding the sequence of events surrounding the decision to suggest discriminatory purpose. The rezoning request progressed in the same manner as other procedures, and the policy had been in place and been consistently applied since 1959. Accordingly, the case was reversed and remanded, with the Court finding that MHDC had "failed to carry their burden of proving that discriminatory purpose was a motivating factor in the Village's decision." The Court went on to note that even if it was demonstrated that the decision by the Village was motivated by a racially discriminatory intent, it would not have been dispositive, but it would have shifted the burden of proof to the Village to prove that the same results would have occurred absent the impermissible purpose.

Justice Marshall wrote a separate opinion, joined by Justice Brennan, concurring in part and dissenting in part. Justice Marshall agreed with most of the Court's opinion but would have remanded the case to the court of appeals because he found them to be better suited to reevaluate the evidence in light of the Court's decision. Justice White filed a dissenting opinion, arguing that the constitutional issue of this case (i.e., whether or not there was racial discrimination) should have been remanded and evaluated by the court of appeals. He also argued that MHDC's Fair Housing Act claim should have been remanded for determination by the court of appeals. He saw no need for the Court to address the proper inquiry in determining whether a racially discriminatory purpose could be found because the court of appeals accepted the finding of the district court that the Village had a legitimate reason for its decision, and the Court had not overturned that decision.

AFTERMATH

Although the Court determined that there was no racial discrimination by preventing the multifamily housing from being built in the center of the single-family housing, later statistics show that this may not have been the case. In 10 years, the percentage of African Americans in the Village had risen only from .04 percent to 0.4 percent, a very small increase.

SIGNIFICANCE

The Court declined to review the case under strict scrutiny and instead instituted the Disparate Impact/Purposeful Discrimination Test to determine whether the Village's zoning ordinance was intentionally racially discriminatory. Under this test, the party challenging the ordinance has the burden of showing that the official action affects a protected class disproportionately to others, and, if this is established, that the official action was intentionally discriminatory against a protected class. Factors used to determine this include the following: the historical context of the official action, the events of the particular case, decision-making processes of the officials, and the legislative history of the governmental body that authorized the official action.

RELATED CASES

Euclid v. Ambler Realty, 272 U.S. 365 (1926)

James v. Valtierra, 402 U.S. 137 (1971)

RECOMMENDED READING

R. C. Howell, Village of Arlington Heights v. Metropolitan Housing Development Corp.: *Exclusionary Zoning—Constitutional Classism and Racism,* 21 Howard Law Journal 256 (1978).

Robert J. Lotero, *The Village of Arlington Heights: Equal Protection in the Suburban Zone,* 4 Hastings Constitutional Law Quarterly 361 (1977).

Case Title: *Ballew v. Georgia*

Legal Citation: 435 U.S. 223

Year of Decision: 1978

KEY ISSUE

Is the Sixth Amendment right to a jury trial, as applied to the states through the Fourteenth Amendment, violated when courts use a five-person jury?

HISTORY OF THE CASE

Claude Davis Ballew managed the Paris Adult Theatre in Atlanta, Georgia. On November 9,

1973, two investigators viewed a motion picture at the theatre entitled *Behind the Green Door*. The investigators later obtained a warrant for and seized the motion picture and arrested Ballew and a cashier. The investigators later seized a second copy of the film, and Ballew was charged with two misdemeanor counts of distributing obscene materials, in violation of the Georgia Code. At trial, a five-member jury was impaneled, and Ballew moved that the court impanel a 12-person jury. This was denied, as well as Ballew's alternative motion for a transfer, and Ballew was found guilty on both counts. He was then sentenced to one year of incarceration and ordered to pay a $1,000 fine.

Ballew appealed to the court of appeals, contending that the film was not obscene, the evidence was insufficient to support the verdict, the lower court had improperly shifted the burden of proof, and the five-person jury violated the Sixth and Fourteenth Amendments. His contentions were rejected, and the Supreme Court of Georgia denied certiorari. Ballew then appealed to the U.S. Supreme Court and was granted certiorari.

SUMMARY OF ARGUMENTS

Ballew argued that a conviction with a five-person jury deprived him of his Sixth and Fourteenth Amendment rights.

Georgia argued that there was not a constitutionally established minimum number of jurors required.

DECISION

The Court held that the five-person jury trial at issue violated the defendant's right to a jury trial, as guaranteed by the Sixth and Fourteenth Amendments. The Court noted statistical studies suggesting that jury error was increased with small juries and thought that small juries are likely to result in poor deliberation. The Court also asserted that testimony is more difficult to remember for smaller juries, compromises are more easily made with larger juries, and larger juries are more likely to be self-critical and reflective.

Writing for the majority, Justice Blackmun delivered the opinion of the Court. The Court began with a discussion of relevant precedents. In *Duncan v. Louisiana* (1968), the Court extended the Sixth Amendment right of trial by a jury to all state, nonpetty criminal cases. Ballew's charges, thus, qualified him to trial by jury because the maximum penalty exceeded six months of imprisonment. The Court then discussed its decision in *Williams v. Florida* (1970), which held that a six-person jury was constitutional. There, the Court reserved its opinion as to whether a jury smaller than six people was constitutional, and that decision was now to be made in Ballew's case.

To analyze the impact of smaller juries, the Court relied on several studies and scholarly works on the subject. The empirical data analyzed by the Court suggested that "smaller juries are less likely to foster effective group deliberation. At some point, this decline leads to inaccurate fact-finding and incorrect application of the common sense of the community to the facts." The studies also found that in smaller groups, members were less likely to make the contributions necessary for a finding of the correct decision. Smaller juries were found not to remember as much as larger groups, a finding that suggests shortcomings because most juries are not allowed to take notes. The studies also suggested that smaller groups had trouble overcoming the biases of their members, hindering the application of common sense to the facts of the case.

Other data suggested that smaller jury panels were less accurate and, thus, were more likely to convict an innocent person. These studies found that when the size of the jury decreases, the likelihood of a wrongful conviction increases. Additionally, jury member compromises were found to be less likely with smaller juries. The presence of minority viewpoints is also diminished as jury size is lessened, resulting in a lack of meaningful community participation. Citing problems in jury member studies, the Court referenced several authors who had identified methodological problems in jury research, such as the aggregation of data, which often resulted in the masking of differences in jury size.

After analyzing these studies and scholarly works, the Court held that "the purpose and functioning of the jury in a criminal trial is seriously impaired, and to a constitutional degree, by a reduction in size to below six members." The data analyzed raised serious doubts about the reliability of jury panels smaller than six people, and the Court found that "any further reduction that promotes inaccurate and possibly biased decision-making, that causes untoward differences in verdicts, and that prevents juries from truly representing their communities, attains constitutional significance." The Court refused to accept Georgia's contention that the use of five-member juries for misdemeanor cases does not violate the Sixth and Fourteenth Amendments, because "the purpose and functions of the jury do not vary significantly with the importance of the crime." The Court could not find any state interest to justify the reduction of the jury size because it thought that the states would save little money, and none of the other justifications offered was suitable. Accordingly, the Court found that using the five-member jury had deprived Ballew of his right to a jury trial, and the decision of the court of appeals was reversed; the case was remanded for further consideration consistent with this opinion.

Justice Powell, joined by Chief Justice Burger and Justice Rehnquist, concurred in the judgment only, stating that he agreed that the use of a five-person or smaller jury brought into question the fairness of the trial. He stated that although the difference between five- and six-member juries may be difficult to discern, "a line has to be drawn somewhere if the substance of jury trial is to be preserved." Justice Powell disagreed that jury practices had to be the same in state and federal courts. He went on to express his view that the Sixth Amendment should not be fully incorporated to the states through the Fourteenth Amendment. He also stated the studies cited had methodological problems because they were not subjected to the adversarial process.

Justice Brennan also concurred in the judgment, joined by Justices Stewart and Marshall, stating that Ballew should not have been subjected to a new trial because the Georgia statute at issue was overbroad and, thus, facially unconstitutional.

AFTERMATH

This case succeeded several other decisions regarding the right to a jury trial. In *Williams v. Florida,* the Court held that although juries had traditionally been composed of 12 people, using six jurors in a state trial did not violate the Constitution. The Court later extended *Williams* to federal courts, in *Colegrove v. Battin* (1973). *Ballew* set the number of jurors at a minimum of six people.

SIGNIFICANCE

A six-person jury was constitutionally required in criminal jury trials.

RELATED CASES

Duncan v. Louisiana, 391 U.S. 145 (1968)

Baldwin v. New York, 399 U.S. 66 (1970)

Williams v. Florida, 399 U.S. 78 (1970)

Apodaca v. Oregon, 406 U.S. 404 (1972)

Johnson v. Louisiana, 406 U.S. 356; 92 (1972)

Colegrove v. Battin, 413 U.S. 149 (1973)

Paris Adult Theatre I v. Slaton, 413 U.S. 49 (1973)

Sanders v. Georgia, 424 U.S. 931 (1976)

RECOMMENDED READING

Grofman, Bernard. "Jury Decision Making Models and the Supreme Court: The Jury Cases from *Williams v. Florida* to *Ballew v. Georgia.*" *Policy Studies Journal* 8 (Spring 1980): 749–772.

Richard Owen, Lempert. *Uncovering "Nondiscernible" Differences: Empirical Research and the Jury-Size Cases,"* 73 Michigan Law Review, 643 (1975).

Saks, Michael J. *Jury Verdicts: The Role of Group Size and Social Decision Rule.* Lexington, Mass.: D. C. Heath, 1977.

Varat, J. D., et al. *Constitutional Law Cases and Materials, Concise Thirteenth Edition.* New York: Foundation Press, 2009, p. 356.

Case Title: *Foley v. Connelie, Superintendent of New York State Police, et al.*

Legal Citation: 435 U.S. 291

Year of Decision: 1978

KEY ISSUE

Does a New York statute requiring state police officers to be citizens of the United States violate the equal protection clause of the Fourteenth Amendment?

HISTORY OF THE CASE

This case was an appeal from the U.S. District Court for the Southern District of New York, where Edmund Foley, an alien lawfully in the United States as a permanent resident, applied for a position as a New York State trooper, for which an examination is required. Foley was denied the right to take the examination because he was not a U.S. citizen. Foley was an Irish citizen who had lived in the United States for four years and not yet eligible for American citizenship because of the waiting period imposed by Congress. He brought this action for declaratory judgment that New York State's exclusion of aliens from its police force violated the equal protection clause of the Fourteenth Amendment. The district court held the statute constitutional.

SUMMARY OF ARGUMENTS

The appellant, Edmund Foley, argued that the New York statute precluding aliens from being members of the state police force violated the equal protection clause of the Fourteenth Amendment.

The appellee, Connelie, the superintendent of the New York State Police, argued that police officers were state officers who participated directly in the execution of broad public policy. Therefore, the state was entitled to limit the position to persons who were U.S. citizens.

DECISION

A New York statute limiting appointment of members of the state police force to U.S. citizens does not violate the equal protection clause of the Fourteenth Amendment.

Chief Justice Warren Burger wrote for the majority, stating that a trooper in New York is a member of the police force charged with law enforcement for the benefit of the people of New York; strict scrutiny of the law is not required because it would erase all distinction between citizen and alien. An alien cannot vote and has other restrictions. A state only needs to justify its exclusionary classifications by showing a relationship between "the interest sought to be protected and the limiting classification. . . . The right to govern is reserved to citizens." The enforcement and execution of the police function bear a rational relationship to citizenship.

Justices Marshall and Stevens, in their dissents, opposed the rational basis tests. Justice Marshall favored strict scrutiny of a compelling state interest; Justice Stevens favored an individual determination of the alien's employment skills, instead of prejudgment based on characteristics that aliens as a group are supposed to have.

AFTERMATH

States have the power to exclude aliens from certain jobs in the public sector. A stricter standard of review will be applied when reviewing the exclusion of aliens from private positions, whereas a rational basis standard will apply to review of alien exclusion from positions involving democratic decision making.

SIGNIFICANCE

Foley gave meaning to the exception carved out of the application of strict scrutiny to alienage in *Sugarman v. Dougall* (1973). In *Sugarman,* the Court found that in certain circumstances, states may require citizenship as a qualification for holding a public position. The decision in *Foley* gave substance to this ruling by determining that the position of police officer could require citizenship as an employment qualification.

RELATED CASES

Graham v. Richardson, 403 U.S. 365 (1971)

Sugarman v. Dougall, 413 U.S. 634 (1973)

In re Griffiths, 413 U.S. 717 (1973)

Examining Board v. Flores de Otero, 426 U.S. 527 (1976)

Elrod v. Burns, 427 U.S. 347 (1976)

Nyquist v. Mauclet, 432 U.S. 1 (1977)

Ambach v. Norwick, 414 U.S. 68 (1979)

RECOMMENDED READING

Steven J. Casad, *Alienage and Public Employment: The Need for an Intermediate Standard in Equal Protection,* 32 Hastings Law Journal 163 (1980).

A Dual Standard for State Discrimination against Aliens, 92 Harvard Law Review 1516 (1979).

Schwartz, Bernard. *The Ascent of Pragmatism: The Burger Court in Action.* New York: Addison-Wesley, 1990.

Case Title: *Regents of the University of California v. Bakke*

Alternate Case Title: The Reverse Discrimination Case

Legal Citation: 438 U.S. 265; 98 S. Ct. 2733

Year of Decision: 1978

KEY ISSUES

Was a white male applicant denied admission to the University of California at Davis Medical School discriminated against when the admissions process held open spaces in each year's class for less qualified minority applicants?

HISTORY OF THE CASE

In 1973, the Medical School of the University of California at Davis had a class size of 100 students. The medical school had a dual admissions process; in addition to the general admissions program, a special admissions program operated with a separate committee that chose students for 16 of the 100 spaces in each class. Applicants who wished to be considered in the special admissions process indicated on the 1973 application form that they were "economically and/or educationally disadvantaged" applicants. On the 1974 application, applicants checked a box to indicate they were members of a "minority group," which the medical school considered to be "Blacks," "Chicanos," "Asians," and "American Indians." Students considered under the special admissions program were also considered under the general program for the remaining 84 spaces, but at no point did they compete with the applicants in the general program for the 16 reserved seats. Although many disadvantaged whites sought consideration under the admissions program, none received an offer for admission under the special program. Thus, under the Davis Medical School admissions process, whites competed for 84 spaces in each entering class, whereas members of the preferred "minority groups" were considered for all 100 spaces.

Allan Bakke was a white male who applied to the Davis Medical School in 1973 and in 1974. He was a graduate of the University of Minnesota, where he had received a mechanical engineering degree and earned a 3.50 GPA. Bakke had served in the Naval Reserve Officers Training Corps to pay for his education and, after college, from 1963 to 1967, served in the U.S. Marine Corps in Vietnam. During his military service, he had developed an interest in becoming a doctor. After leaving the Marine Corps, Bakke took the required prerequisites for medical school while working full-time as a National Aeronautics and Space Administration (NASA) research engineer. Bakke was twice denied admission under the general program, whereas students were admitted under the special program with lower entrance exam scores, grade-point averages, and interview scores.

After Bakke's second rejection, he filed suit in the Superior Court of California, the trial court level, to compel the medical school to admit him. He argued that the special admissions program excluded him on the basis of his race, violating his rights under the equal protection clause, Title VI of the Civil Rights Act of 1964, and the California Constitution. The university in response asked the court to determine that their admissions process was lawful. They defended the admissions process, arguing it was necessary to overcome the substantial, chronic minority underrepresentation in the medical profession. The Superior Court found that the special program operated as a racial quota because the minority applicants were rated only against one another. The trial court also declared that taking race into account when making admissions decisions violated the U.S. Constitution, the California Constitution, and Title VI of the Civil Rights Act of 1964, which prohibits discrimination on the basis of race, color, or national origin under federally funded programs.

The California Supreme Court heard the case directly on appeal from the trial court "because of the importance of the issues involved." The California high court determined that, while the aims of the medical school's special admissions program were legitimate, the program was unconstitutional because it did not use the least intrusive means of achieving those goals.

Additionally, the California Supreme Court held that the equal protection clause of the Fourteenth Amendment required that "no applicant may be rejected because of his race, in favor of another who is less qualified, as measured by standards applied without regard to race."

SUMMARY OF ARGUMENTS

The petitioner—the university—argued that its special admissions program was lawful and did not violate the equal protection clause of the Fourteenth Amendment. The university also argued that no private right of action existed under Title VI of the Civil Rights Act of 1964.

Bakke, the respondent, argued that the admissions program excluded him on the basis of his race in violation of the equal protection clause of the Fourteenth Amendment. Bakke also argued that he had a private right of action under Title VI of the Civil Rights Act of 1964.

DECISION

The U.S. Supreme Court both affirmed and reversed the ruling of the California Supreme Court. In the Court's confusing ruling, the California Supreme Court's decision ordering the Davis Medical School to admit Bakke was upheld. Only a single justice, Justice Powell, supported the opinion of the California court in its entirety. Four of the remaining nine justices agreed with the ordering of the medical school to admit Bakke but disagreed with Justice Powell's reasoning. The other four justices disagreed with compelling the medical school to admit Bakke but agreed with part of Justice Powell's opinion. While finally resolving the case at the personal level, the *Bakke* decision left the issue of the constitutionality of racial preferences in college admissions processes unsettled.

Justice Powell's opinion, which "announced the Court's judgment" and "express[ed] his views of the case," began by stating that Title VI of the Civil Rights Act of 1964, which prohibited discrimination "on the ground of race, color, or national origin" in the administering of programs funded by the federal government, prohibited the same sort of discrimination as the equal protection clause of the U.S. Constitution. Powell then analyzed the degree of constitutional protections accorded Bakke. He first concluded that "racial and ethnic distinctions of any sort are inherently suspect and thus call for the most exacting judicial examination." He also rejected the argument made by the medical school that "discrimination against members of the white 'majority' cannot be suspect if its purpose can be characterized as 'benign.'"

Justice Powell continued by stating that the university's racial criteria would only pass constitutional scrutiny if they were "'necessary . . . to the accomplishment' of its purpose or the safeguarding of its interest." The university gave four purposes for the racial classifications: (1) "reducing the historic deficit of traditionally disfavored minorities in medical schools and in the medical profession," (2) "countering the effects of societal discrimination," (3) "increasing the number of physicians who will practice in communities currently underserved," and (4) "obtaining the educational benefits that flow from an ethnically diverse student body."

Justice Powell rejected the first three of these purposes. First, Powell rejected the goal of having a certain percentage of minorities in the student body because "preferring members of any one group for no reason other than race or ethnic origin is discrimination for its own sake." Second, countering the effects of societal discrimination was not the university's job: "Its broad mission is education, not the formulation of any legislative policy or the adjudication of particular claims of illegality." Third, though Powell agreed that increasing the number of physicians serving in areas currently underserved was a laudable goal, "there is virtually no evidence in the record indicating that petitioner's special admissions program is either needed or geared to promote that goal."

Justice Powell did recognize that attaining a diverse student body was a constitutionally permissive goal. Such diversity, however, "encompasses a far broader array of qualifications and characteristics of which racial or ethnic origin is but a single though important element. Petitioner's special admissions program, focused solely on ethnic diversity, would hinder rather than further attainment of genuine diversity." Because the medical school's special admissions program focused solely on race, Bakke's constitutional rights were violated, and he was, therefore, entitled to be admitted to the Davis Medical School. The California Supreme Court's order to admit Bakke was thus affirmed. The part of the state high court's opinion that prohibited the school from ever taking race into account in their admissions process was, however, reversed. Justice Powell wrote that "the courts below failed to recognize that the State has a substantial interest that legitimately may be served by a properly devised admissions program involving the competitive consideration of ethnic origin."

Justice Stevens wrote an opinion, joined by Chief Justice Burger, Justice Stewart, and Justice Rehnquist, that agreed with the judgment to uphold the order to admit Bakke but on the narrow grounds of Title VI. Because Stevens and the justices who joined his opinion believed that the case could be resolved completely under the statute, it was unnecessary to reach the constitutional issues. "The question whether race can ever be used as a factor in an admissions decision is not an issue in this case, and that discussion of that issue is inappropriate."

Justices Brennan, White, Marshall, and Blackmun jointly wrote an opinion that dissented from the order to admit Bakke but agreed with part of Justice Powell's reasoning. These four justices agreed with Justice Powell that "Title VI goes no further in prohibiting the use of race than the Equal Protection Clause" and also agreed "that some uses of race in university admissions are permissible." They disagreed, however, with Powell that the specific use of race in the admissions process was unconstitutional. Justices Brennan, White, Marshall, and Blackmun believed that the medical school's consideration of race was constitutional because it did not act "to demean or insult any racial group, but to remedy disadvantages cast on minorities by past racial prejudice."

Justices White, Marshall, and Blackmun also wrote their own separate opinions. Justice White wrote separately to state his belief that Bakke did not have a "private cause of action under Title VI." Justice Marshall wrote to state his strong conviction that the university could constitutionally "remedy the effects of [the] legacy of discrimination." Justice Blackmun expressed his hope that a policy of affirmative action, such as the one used by the medical school, could soon be halted: "I yield to no one in my earnest hope that the time will come when an 'affirmative action' program is unnecessary and is, in truth, only a relic of the past. . . . At some time, however, beyond any period of what some would claim is only a transitory inequality, the United States must and will reach a stage of maturity where action along this line is no longer necessary."

AFTERMATH

Allan Bakke was admitted to the University of California at Davis Medical School and graduated in 1982. He interned at the Mayo Clinic in Rochester, Minnesota, where he later served as a resident in anesthesiology.

SIGNIFICANCE

The significance of the *Bakke* decision stems from what it did not do. It did not finally resolve the constitutionality of affirmative action programs. It was a complex compromise that strictly held only that Allan Bakke was to be admitted to the Davis Medical School. The U.S. Supreme Court to this day has not established a firm rule explaining how race can constitutionally be taken into account in school admissions and hiring decisions.

In 1997, California passed a law outlawing state affirmative action programs. In 2002, the U.S. Supreme Court agreed to hear two affirmative action lawsuits involving the University of Michigan, *Grutter v. Bollinger* and *Gratz v. Bollinger,* which will gave the Court the opportunity to revisit its decision in *Bakke.*

RELATED CASES

Kaiser Aluminum & Chem. Corp. v. Weber, 443 U.S. 193 (1979)

Grutler v. Bollinger, 539 U.S. 306 (2003)

RECOMMENDED READING

Ball, Howard. *The* Bakke *Case: Race, Education, and Affirmative Action.* Lawrence: University Press of Kansas, 2000.

Philip T. K. Daniel, *Diversity in University Admissions Decisions: The Continued Support of* Bakke, 32 Journal of Law and Education 69 (2003).

Dreyfus, Joel, and Charles Lawrence III. *The* Bakke *Case: The Politics of Inequality.* New York: Harcourt, 1979.

Stephen M. Kirkelie, *Higher Education Admissions and Diversity: The Continuing Vitality of* Bakke v. Regents of the University of California *and an Attempt to Reconcile Powell's and Brennan's Opinions,* 38 Willamette Law Review 615 (2002).

"Regents of the University of California v. Bakke." Landmark Supreme Court Cases. Available online. URL: http://www.landmarkcases.org/bakke/home.html. Accessed June 3, 2010.

Wilkenson, J. Harvie. *From* Brown *to* Bakke: *The Supreme Court and School Integration: 1954–1978.* New York: Oxford University Press, 1979.

Case Title: *Caban v. Mohammed*

Alternate Case Title: The "Parental Rights for Fathers" Case

Legal Citation: 441 U.S. 380

Year of Decision: 1979

KEY ISSUE

Is a New York statute constitutional that required the consent of the mother, but not the father, for the adoption of a child born out of wedlock?

HISTORY OF THE CASE

Abdiel Caban and Maria Mohammed lived together out of wedlock in New York from 1968 until the end of 1973. They had two children. Caban was identified as the father on the birth certificates. The couple separated; Mohammed took the children and married another man. During the next two years, Caban maintained contact with the children and contributed to their support.

Mohammed and her husband subsequently petitioned for adoption of the children, and Caban filed a cross-petition for the same purpose. The trial court granted Mohammed's petition under section 111 of the New York Domestic Relations Law, which permits an unwed mother, but not an unwed father, to block adoption of the child simply by withholding consent. Caban appealed, asserting that section 111 was unconstitutional. The appellate court affirmed the lower court's decision, and Caban appealed to the U.S. Supreme Court.

SUMMARY OF ARGUMENTS

Caban claimed that the distinction drawn under New York law between the adoption rights of an unwed father and those of other parents violates the equal protection clause of the Fourteenth Amendment. He further argued that the Supreme Court's decision in *Quilloin v. Walcott* (1978) recognized the due process right of natural fathers to maintain a parental relationship with their children unless a court finds that they are unfit as parents.

Mohammed and her husband argued that the statute was justified by a fundamental difference between maternal and paternal relations. They also argued that the statute served the end of promoting the adoption of illegitimate children and that unwed fathers were not treated differently under section 111 from other parents.

DECISION

Justice Powell wrote the decision for the Court joined by Justices Marshall, Brennan, White, and Blackmun. He held that the New York statute was unconstitutional because the distinction it made between the rights of unmarried mothers and the rights of unmarried fathers was not shown to be substantially related to an important state interest.

Justice Powell believed that section 111 treated unmarried parents differently according to their sex because Mohammed could block adoption of her children by withholding her consent; however, Caban could block Mohammed's adoption only by showing that it was not in the best interest of the children. When Justice Powell was unable to find a substantial relation to any important state interest, he found the sex-based distinction in section 111 between unmarried mothers and unmarried fathers in violation of the equal protection clause of the Fourteenth Amendment.

Justice Powell did not believe that maternal and paternal roles were invariably different in importance. He also did not believe that unwed fathers were more likely to oppose adoption of their children than unwed mothers. However, he stated that when the father did not participate in the child rearing, the equal protection clause did not preclude the state from withholding the privilege of blocking the adoption of that child.

Justice Stewart wrote a dissenting opinion stating that the New York Domestic Relations Law did not violate the Constitution. He reasoned that the Court underestimated the state's interest in promoting the welfare of illegitimate children. He thought that children born out of wedlock were born with certain handicaps that adoption could remove. He saw major differences in the roles of parents concerning illegitimate children, and he believed that only the mother was an indispensable party.

Justice Stewart disregarded Caban's contention that the statute violated the equal protection clause by granting rights to the unwed mother that it did not give to the unwed father. He believed that it was enough for Caban to be given the opportunity to participate in the adoption proceedings and to present evidence on whether the adoption would be in the best interest of the children. He challenged whether unwed mothers and fathers were similarly situated with respect to adoptions of newborn children and infants, because only the mother carried and gave birth to the child. The mother also is always an identifiable parent. Stewart also found the contention troublesome that the statute, in withholding from the unwed father certain rights granted to all other classes of parents, violated the equal protection and due process clauses. Justice Stewart believed that the state's interest in facilitating adoptions that were in the best interests of illegitimate children was an important state interest, and the gender-based statute fully served this goal.

Justice Stevens also wrote a dissenting opinion joined by Chief Justice Burger and Justice Rehnquist. He believed that the state's interest in facilitating adoption was strong, maybe even "compelling," when one considered the large number of children born out of wedlock and the benefits of legitimacy and life's basic necessities that adoption could provide. He further believed that the differences between natural mothers and natural fathers provided justification for treating them differently. He observed that the mother carried and had the final decision whether to bear the child. He also stressed that after birth, the mother's identity is certain while the father's may not be, and that the mother inevitably must make decisions regarding child care while the father may take no part. He argued that the differences between males and females through pregnancy and infancy were important and have a large impact on a child's destiny. Finally, Justice Stevens regarded the Court's holding as very narrow because it would not be applied retroactively and applied to only future adoptions for older children with whom the father has established a relationship.

AFTERMATH

The Court left open the question of whether the unwed father of a newborn, with whom the father has not had the opportunity to develop a relationship, had a legal interest in and the right to veto the adoption of his child. However, the New York Court of Appeals answered this question in *In re Raquel Marie X* (1990). It held that an unwed father has such a right if he is willing to assume custody of the child and promptly manifests parental responsibility using all possible means.

SIGNIFICANCE

With *Caban,* the Supreme Court expanded the sphere of fundamental rights to include an unmarried father's, granting a father some power to block the adoption of his children by others. This case was championed as giving all fathers, regardless of their past or present marital status, the ability to enjoy a fundamental right to sustain a relationship with their children.

RELATED CASES

Stanley v. Illinois, 405 U.S. 645 (1972)

Quilloin v. Walcott, 434 U.S. 246 (1978)

Lehr v. Robertson, 463 U.S. 248 (1983)

RECOMMENDED READING

Dowd, Nancy E. *Redefining Fatherhood.* New York: New York University Press, 2000.

Ann Freedman, *Sex Equality, Sex Differences, and the Supreme Court,* 92 Yale Law Journal 913 (1983).

Sylvia Law, *Rethinking Sex and the Constitution,* 132 University of Pennsylvania Law Review 955 (1984).

Lerman, Robert I., and Theodora J. Ooms, eds. *Young Unwed Fathers: Changing Roles and Emerging Policies.* Philadelphia: Temple University Press, 1995.

Christine Littleton, *Reconstructing Sexual Equality,* 75 California Law Review 1279 (1987).

Skaine, Rosemarie. *Paternity and American Law.* Jefferson, N.C.: McFarland, 2003.

Case Title: *Orr v. Orr*

Legal Citation: 440 U.S. 268

Year of Decision: 1979

KEY ISSUE

Do the Alabama alimony statutes under which only husbands may be required to pay alimony violate the equal protection clause of the Fourteenth Amendment to the U.S. Constitution?

HISTORY OF THE CASE

William and Lillian Orr were divorced in 1974. The divorce decree provided that Mr. Orr would pay Mrs. Orr alimony each month. Two years later, Mrs. Orr initiated a contempt proceeding in circuit court alleging that Mr. Orr was not obeying the decree and paying alimony. Mr. Orr defended himself with a motion that Alabama's alimony statutes be declared unconstitutional because they authorize courts to obligate husbands to pay alimony but not wives.

SUMMARY OF ARGUMENTS

The appellant, William Herbert Orr, argued that Alabama's alimony statute was based on "archaic notions" of gender roles, rather than any real difference between men and women, and the distinction in the statute did not serve any important governmental purpose.

The appellee, Lillian M. Orr, argued that the alimony law gave economic preference to women to compensate for past discrimination.

DECISION

Justice Brennan wrote the opinion for the Court. Declaring sex and gender a quasi-suspect classification, he held that the alimony statutes had to be in furtherance of an important government objective. Although it is important to remedy past discrimination against women who cannot support themselves, the courts should do so on a case-by-case basis and not make the generalization that all men can support themselves. The Court emphasized that this was a statute that perpetuated a negative stereotype against women and was based on the idea that a woman's place was in the home.

The dissent emphasized that Mr. Orr did not have standing to bring this suit. As the gender issue was not brought before a lower court, Mr. Orr should still have to pay alimony.

The Alabama alimony statutes that provide that husbands, but not wives, may be required to pay alimony on divorce violate the equal protection clause of the Fourteenth Amendment.

AFTERMATH

States are forced to amend their alimony statutes to be gender neutral in response to the decision in *Orr.*

SIGNIFICANCE

The Court analyzed the gender-based classification found in the Alabama statute by applying an intermediate standard of review that required that the classification serve an important governmental objective and be substantially related to achieving that objective.

RELATED CASES

Reed v. Reed, 404 U.S. 71 (1971)

Stanton v. Stanton, 471 U.S. 7 (1975)

Craig v. Boren, 429 U.S. 190 (1976)

Califano v. Webster, 430 U.S. 313 (1977)

RECOMMENDED READING

Mary E. Becker, *Prince Charming: Abstract Equality,* 1987 Supreme Court Review 201.

Gary D. Gilson, *Alimony Awards and Middle-Tier Equal Protection Scrutiny,* 59 Nebraska Law Review 172 (1980).

Lynn, Naomi B., ed. *Women, Politics and the Constitution.* Binghamton, N.Y.: Harrington Park Press, 1990.

Diane M. Signoracci, *A Husband's Constitutional Right Not to Pay Alimony,* 41 Ohio State Law Journal 1061 (1980).

Case Title: *Personnel Administrator of Mass. v. Feeney*

Legal Citation: 442 U.S. 256

Year of Decision: 1979

KEY ISSUE

Does a state statute that grants absolute, lifetime preference for state civil service employment to veterans of American military service deny equal protection to women?

HISTORY OF THE CASE

While working for 12 years as a state employee, Helen B. Feeney had passed numerous competitive civil service examinations for better jobs. Because a Massachusetts law granted absolute preference to military veterans, however, Feeney was ranked below male veterans who had achieved lower test scores than she had. In addition, since more than 98 percent of the veterans in Massachusetts were men, the statute overwhelmingly benefited males to the detriment of females.

Feeney brought suit in federal district court, claiming the statute discriminated against women and denied her equal protection under the Fourteenth Amendment to the U.S. Constitution. The

Fourteenth Amendment provides, in part, that no state shall "deny to any person within its jurisdiction equal protection of the laws." The federal court invalidated the law because of its severe exclusionary impact upon women. The personnel administrator of Massachusetts appealed to the U.S. Supreme Court.

SUMMARY OF ARGUMENTS

Feeney argued that the Massachusetts legislators were aware of the natural and probable consequences of the law. She maintained that when they passed the law, they knew that the absolute preference would produce an enormous statistical impact to discriminate against women. Thus, she reasoned that the legislators intentionally discriminated against women in violation of the Fourteenth Amendment.

Massachusetts contended that the purpose of the preference for veterans was to benefit veterans and not to discriminate against women. Also, because the policy did not, at face value, purposefully discriminate against women, the state argued that the statute should not be subject to the sort of special scrutiny the Court gives to such laws.

DECISION

Justice Stewart delivered the 7-2 majority opinion of the Court, which held that the statute was not purposefully gender based. Stewart reasoned that because a significant number of men were also nonveterans, they were equally affected by the law, so the statute does not intentionally prefer men over women. The Court also stressed that only when the legislature passes a law "because of" and not "in spite of" its adverse effects upon women can there be said to have been purposeful discrimination. The majority concluded that there was no proof that the Massachusetts legislature sought to disadvantage women by the policy; the fact that 50 times as many veterans were men was just one of the incidental consequences of the statute. Therefore, the statute did not violate the equal protection clause.

The dissenters believed that the state did not meet its burden of proving that sex-based considerations played no part in the adoption of the scheme. They saw no difference in previous Court decisions that invalidated laws reflecting "archaic assumptions about women's roles."

AFTERMATH

The *Feeney* requirement that the plaintiff must prove an actual discriminatory purpose has been a roadblock for pregnancy-based discrimination. The Court also has upheld seniority systems even though employers had for years excluded minorities from certain jobs; even though the seniority system had a foreseeable, discriminatory effect upon a minority's ability to obtain future promotions, it was upheld because no purposeful discrimination was proven. After losing her Supreme Court battle, Feeney later obtained a degree in gerontology.

SIGNIFICANCE

The Fourteenth Amendment's guarantee that no person shall be denied the equal protection of the laws must coexist with the practical necessity that most legislation classifies for one purpose or another. Such classifications inevitably result in disadvantages to various groups or persons. The Court has come to grips with this reality by stating that if a law neither burdens a fundamental right nor targets a class based on race, sex, national origin, alienage, or other similar trait, it will uphold the legislative classification so long as it bears a rational relation to some legitimate end. In *Feeney*, because the Court believed that women were not being targeted by the veterans preference scheme, the legislation was upheld.

RELATED CASES

Massachusetts Board of Retirement v. Murgin, 427 U.S. 307 (1976)

Washington v. Davis, 426 U.S. 229 (1976)

Arlington Heights v. Metropolitan Housing Corp.; 429 U.S. 252 (1977)

International Brotherhood of Teamsters v. United States, 431 U.S. 324 (1977)

United Jewish Organizations v. Carey, 430 U.S. 144 (1977)

Bray v. Alexandria's Women's Health Clinic, 506 U.S. 263 (1993)

RECOMMENDED READING

Gayle Binion, *"Intent" and Equal Protection: A Reconsideration,* 1983 Supreme Court Review 397–457.

Leo Kanowitz, *"Benign" Sex Discrimination: Its Troubles and Their Cure,* 31 Hastings Law Review 1379 (July 1980).

Bruce E. Rosenblum, *Discriminatory Purpose and Disproportionate Impact: An Assessment after Feeney,* 79 Columbia Law Review 1376 (1979).

Case Title: *City of Mobile, Alabama v. Bolden*

Legal Citation: 446 U.S. 55

Year of Decision: 1980

KEY ISSUES

Does a city's system of municipal elections violate the constitutional rights of the city's black voters under the Fifteenth Amendment right to vote and the equal protection clause of the Fourteenth Amendment to be free of discrimination?

HISTORY OF THE CASE

Mobile, Alabama, was governed by a commission of three members elected at large, which means the city was not divided into districts and the whole city voted on all members, who exercise all executive, legislative, and administrative power for the city. A class action brought by black residents of Mobile, including Bolden, in federal district court alleged on behalf of the black constituents of the city that this at-large election process diluted their voting strength in violation of the Fifteenth Amendment and the Fourteenth Amendment. This prevented the election of a black commissioner, who probably would have been elected if the city were divided into election districts. The blacks had "registered to vote without hindrance." The district court held the at-

large elections to be in violation of the Fifteenth Amendment and to have "invidiously discriminated" against blacks and ordered the commission to disband and be replaced with single-member districts. The court of appeals affirmed.

SUMMARY OF ARGUMENTS

The black residents of Mobile argued that the at-large election process violated their Fifteenth Amendment rights. The city and the three incumbent commissioners argued that to violate the Fifteenth Amendment, there had to be a discriminatory motive, and none existed; therefore, there was no violation of the Fifteenth Amendment.

Justice Stewart wrote for the Court, holding that Mobile's at-large electoral system did not violate the rights of black voters according to the Fifteenth Amendment. "Racially discriminatory motivation" is necessary for a violation of that amendment. The amendment prohibits only premeditated discriminatory practices related to the right to vote. Here the blacks registered to vote without any problems.

The Court held that the at-large voting system does not violate the Fourteenth Amendment because the amendment does not require proportional representation. Blacks can participate, but there is no constitutional guarantee of electoral victory.

Justice Blackmun wrote that the district court should have considered an alternative governing system to convert Mobile to a mayor-council system instead of doing away with the at-large elections. This would have given black voters equal footing with others.

Justice Stevens wrote that the standard adopted by the Court in *Gomillion v. Lightfoot* (1960) should be followed. It entails:

1. whether the political structure is traditional;
2. whether it has an adverse impact on a minority;
3. whether there is any support for the system or whether it was motivated to curtail the strength of a minority.

Under this standard, it is necessary to retain Mobile's government.

Justice White wrote a dissenting opinion, saying that the majority looked only at the invidious aspect while past decisions under these fact patterns looked at whether the electoral plan excluded the black vote.

DECISION

Mobile's at-large voting system does not violate the right to vote under the Fifteenth Amendment because there were no discriminatory activities. The blacks voted without any problems. There was no violation under the Fourteenth Amendment because there was no premeditated discrimination.

AFTERMATH

Two years later, Congress amended section 2 of the Voting Rights Act, overruling *Bolden* and making at-large elections illegal where they cause discrimination or result in discrimination.

SIGNIFICANCE

For a violation of the Fifteenth Amendment to be found, there must be a showing of discriminatory motivation.

RELATED CASES

Ex Parte Yarbrough, 110 U.S. 651 (1884)

Guinn v. United States, 238 U.S. 347 (1915)

Ashivander v. Tennessee Valley Authority, 297 U.S. 288 (1936)

Lane v. Wilson, 307 U.S. 268 (1939)

Smith v. Allwright, 321 U.S. 649 (1944)

Gomillion v. Lightfoot, 364 U.S. 339 (1960)

Wright v. Rockefeller, 376 U.S. 52 (1964)

Reynolds v. Sims, 377 U.S. 533 (1964)

Whitcomb v. Chavis, 403 U.S. 124 (1971)

Personal Administrator of Massachusetts v. Feeny, 442 U.S. 256 (1979)

RECOMMENDED READING

Gayle Binion, *Intent and Equal Protection: A Reconsideration*, 1983 Supreme Court Review 397.

Davis, Olethia. "Tenuous Interpretation: Sections 2 and 5 of the Voting Rights Act." *National Civic Review* (Fall–Winter 1995): 310.

Making the Violation Fit the Remedy: The Intent Standard and Equal Protection Law, 92 Yale Law Journal 328 (1982).

Daniel D. Polsby and Robert D. Popper, *Ugly: An Inquiry into the Problem of Racial Gerrymandering under the Voting Rights Act*, 92 Michigan Law Review 652 (1993).

Therstrom, Abigail M. *Whose Vote Counts?* Cambridge, Mass.: Harvard University Press, 1987.

Case Title: *Fullilove v. Klutznick*

Legal Citation: 448 U.S. 448

Year of Decision: 1980

KEY ISSUE

Do "minority business enterprise" provisions of the Public Works Employment Act of 1977, which require that 10 percent of federal funds for public works programs go to minority-owned companies, violate the equal protection clause of the Fourteenth Amendment?

HISTORY OF THE CASE

In 1977, Congress passed the Public Works Employment Act of 1977 ("the Act"), which amended the Local Public Works Capital Development and Investment Act of 1976. The new amendments authorized a $4 billion appropriation for federal grants to be distributed by the secretary of commerce, through the Economic Development Administration ("EDA"), to state and local governmental entities for use in public works projects. Also among the amendments was a provision, § 103(f)(2) of the Act, referred to as the "minority business enterprise" ("MBE").

MBE required that 10 percent of the funds authorized by the secretary must be expended for minority business enterprises. In October 1977, the EDA promulgated detailed instructions and information to help grantees meet the 10 percent requirement.

On November 30, 1977, the several associations of construction contractors and subcontractors, along with a firm engaged in heating, ventilation, and air-conditioning work, joined as petitioners to file a complaint in a New York federal court seeking declaratory and injunctive relief. The secretary of commerce and the state and city of New York were named as the defendants. The complaint claimed that the petitioners had sustained economic injury from the 10 percent MBE requirement and that the provision violated the equal protection clause of the Fourteenth Amendment, the due process clause of the Fifth Amendment, and several antidiscrimination provisions. The district court upheld the validity of the MBE provision and accordingly denied the petitioners injunctive relief. The U.S. Court of Appeals for the Second District affirmed, holding that the provision was a valid way to remedy past racial discrimination. On appeal, the U.S. Supreme Court granted certiorari.

SUMMARY OF ARGUMENTS

The petitioners argued that they had been economically harmed by the federal statute and that the race-conscious classification violated the "equal protection component" of the Fifth Amendment's due process clause.

DECISION

The Court held that the government program was a legitimate exercise of Congress's spending powers. The Court mentioned that the commerce clause could have also justified the spending bill provision.

Writing for the majority, Chief Justice Burger delivered the opinion of the Court. The Court began by discussing the legislative history behind the 1977 amendments to the Local Public Works Capital Development and Investment Act of 1976. Near the beginning of 1977, Congress began to consider expanding the amount of

appropriations available for the grant program, as well as addressing issues of fairness in the process of allocating funds. Through this process the MBE provision was introduced, because Congress deemed it "necessary to ensure that minority businesses were not deprived of access to the government contracting opportunities generated by the public works program," as stated by the Court. The Court considered this against the promise of equality of economic opportunity in the United States, noting that although Congress had passed legislation to assist the development of minority businesses, previous efforts had generally proven to be inadequate.

The Court then examined the administrative background of the Act. The secretary of commerce, along with guidance of the EDA, was given the authority to administer the funds. The EDA guidelines outlined the administration of applications for waiver of the MBE requirement, which was allowed to prevent subcontracting with a minority business that asked for an unreasonable price that was above competitive levels not attributed to the business's attempt to remedy present effects of discrimination. Thus, the legislative and administrative backgrounds made the purpose of the MBE provision clear: "Grantees who elect to participate would not employ procurement practices that Congress had decided might result in perpetuation of the effects of prior discrimination which had impaired or foreclosed access by minority businesses to public contracting opportunities."

Next, the Court inquired whether the objectives of the Act were within the power of Congress, determining that they were within its power. The Court found that Congress had acted pursuant to its spending power, under Article I, Section 8, Clause 1 of the Constitution. The Court had previously upheld voluntary programs, such as the MBE provision, that condition the receipt of federal money, by government and private parties alike, upon compliance with statutory and administrative directives. The Court noted that the Act could also have been enacted pursuant to Congress's commerce power, as well, because if minority businesses were unable to pursue public contracting opportunities, that inability it would have an effect on interstate commerce. The Court, then, determined whether the use of racial and ethnic criteria is a constitutionally permissible means for achieving the Act's objectives and whether it violates the equal protection component of the due process clause in the Fifth Amendment. The Court determined that the MBE objectives were within the enforcement powers of Congress under Section 5 of the Fourteenth Amendment because Congress had recognized a national problem regarding minority businesses and had acted to remedy past acts of discrimination.

The Court also determined that Congress may use racial and ethnic criteria in some circumstances, such as it had here, as a condition attached to the receipt of federal funds, provided the programs do not violate the equal protection clause. To avoid an equal protection violation, the Court stated that "any congressional program that employs racial or ethnic criteria to accomplish the objective of remedying the present effects of past discrimination is narrowly tailored to the achievement of that goal." The Court additionally stated that Congress is not required to be "color-blind" in the remedial context of fashioning legislation. Accordingly, the Court held that the 10 percent MBE program was constitutionally valid and affirmed the decision of the appeals court.

Justice Powell wrote a concurring opinion, and while he agreed with the decision of the majority, he applied a strict level of scrutiny, as previously set forth in his opinion in *Regents of the University of California v. Bakke* (1978). He argued that under this level of scrutiny, the MBE provision was "justified as a remedy that serves the compelling governmental interest in eradicating the continuing effects of past discrimination identified by Congress." Justice Marshall wrote a concurring opinion, as well, joined by Justices Brennan and Blackmun, relying on his coauthored opinion in *Bakke*. Justice Marshall argued that racial classifications are not per se invalid under the equal protection clause of the Fourteenth Amendment, and the program at issue did not violate that clause. Justice Marshall asserted that the majority opinion furthered the promise of equal opportunity by remedying past discrimination.

Justice Stewart wrote a dissenting opinion, joined by Justice Rehnquist, arguing that this decision was wrong for the same reasons that *Plessy v. Ferguson* (1896) was wrongly decided: because each case upheld practices that give preference to some citizens over others, on the basis of racial identity. Justice Stevens also wrote a dissenting opinion, arguing that the MBE provision had created a monopoly for certain investors, based on racial criteria. Justice Stevens stated that history teaches us that granting exclusive privileges based on characteristics given at birth is likely to create animosity between the classes of people. He argued that the MBE provision was not justified as a remedial measure because of the lack of evidence that minority business firms had been wrongfully discriminated against in the public contracts market.

AFTERMATH

In 1995, in the case of *Adarand Constructors, Inc. v. Pena,* the U.S. Supreme Court held that all racial classifications, whether imposed by federal, state, or local authorities, must be reviewed under strict scrutiny, as was articulated in *Bakke.* Thus, the legislation must serve a compelling governmental interest and must be narrowly tailored to further that interest. However, compensation programs related to disadvantaged people in general should be evaluated under lower equal protection standards. In *Fullilove v. Klutznick* (1980), the Court did not use one of the formulas set forth in *Bakke,* which articulated both intermediate and strict scrutiny throughout the various opinions written for that case. However, the Court in *Fullilove* stated that "the MBE provision would survive judicial review under either 'test' articulated in the several *Bakke* opinions."

SIGNIFICANCE

Pursuant to the Congress's spending power, the Court upheld a provision of the 1977 spending bill that required that 10 percent of federal funds allocated to public works programs be awarded to minority-owned companies. Thus, the Court allowed Congress to use its spending power to remedy past discrimination, including the minority set-aside program at issue in this case. The Court also held that Congress was not required to act "in a wholly 'color-blind' fashion."

RELATED CASES

Brown v. Board of Education of Topeka, Kansas, 347 U.S. 483 (1954)

Regents of the University of California v. Bakke, 438 U.S. 265 (1978)

Gratz v. Bollinger, 539 U.S. 244 (2003)

Grutter v. Bollinger, 539 U.S. 306 (2003)

Parents Involved in Community Schools v. Seattle School District No. 1, 551 U.S. 701 (2007)

RECOMMENDED READING

McWhiter, Darien A. *The End of Affirmative Action: Where Do We Go from Here?* New York: Carol Publishing Group, 1996.

Mills, Nicolaus, ed. *Debating Affirmative Action: Race, Gender, Ethnicity, and the Politics of Inclusion.* New York: Dell, 1994.

Zelnick, Bob. *Backfire: A Reporter's Look at Affirmative Action.* Washington, D.C.: Regnery, 1996.

Case Title: *Kirchberg v. Feenstra*

Alternate Case Title: The Sex Discrimination Case

Legal Citation: 450 U.S. 455

Year of Decision: 1981

KEY ISSUE

Does a superseded Louisiana statute that gave the husband the right to dispose of property without the wife's consent violate the equal protection clause of the Fourteenth Amendment?

HISTORY OF THE CASE

In 1974, Joan Feenstra filed a criminal charge against her husband. He hired an attorney to represent him and signed a $3,000 promissory note secured by a mortgage on the home Feenstra owned jointly with his wife. She had no knowledge of this mortgage, nor need she, on the basis of article 2404 of the Louisiana Civil Code, which gave a husband exclusive control over the community property. Mrs. Feenstra learned of the mortgage in 1976, when Karl Kirchberg, her husband's attorney, threatened to foreclose. She refused to pay. This action was filed in the U.S. District Court for the Eastern District of Louisiana. While Mrs. Feenstra's appeal was pending before the Fifth Circuit Court of Appeals, the Louisiana legislature revised its code relating to community property and granted spouses equal control over community property. The provisions became effective in 1980, so that the court of appeals was required to deal with the old provisions and decide whether they violated the Fourteenth Amendment.

SUMMARY OF ARGUMENTS

Kirchberg argued that Mrs. Feenstra could have prohibited her husband from executing a mortgage without her consent by using state statutory provisions. He also argued that the mortgage was valid because of the decision of the court of appeals that the state statute was prospective, not retroactive.

Mrs. Feenstra argued that the mortgage was invalid because article 2404 violated the equal protection clause of the Fourteenth Amendment and, therefore, was unconstitutional.

DECISION

Justice Marshall wrote the opinion for the Court. The court of appeals found that the old code discriminated on the basis of gender and that in order for it to be valid, there must be a strong state interest; otherwise, the statute violated the equal protection clause. The Court held that its finding was not retroactive. The Court affirmed the judgment because Kirchberg focused on what Mrs. Feenstra could do to avoid the situation and not on an important government interest. Also, Mrs. Feenstra did not appeal from the decision below and so avoided any claim that an important government objective was served by the statute. The mortgage executed on the Feenstra home by the husband without the wife's consent under an unconstitutional statute is void.

The gender allocation of managerial rights to the husband allowing him to sell or exchange community property without the wife's consent violates the equal protection clause of the Fourteenth Amendment.

SIGNIFICANCE

The Supreme Court has accepted the view that the negative stereotype of a woman does not provide constitutional grounds that denies women access to positions of power in the public sphere. A claim of citizenship is to be treated with respect and equality. In the years that followed, more and more women would serve in Congress, in the Attorney General's Office, and as heads of large corporations.

RELATED CASES

Reed v. Reed, 404 U.S. 71 (1971)

Frontiero v. Richardson, 411 U.S. 677 (1973)

Califano v. Westcott, 443 U.S. 76 (1979)

RECOMMENDED READING

Kirp, Donald. *Gender Justice.* Chicago: University of Chicago Press, 1986.

Case Title: *Michael M. v. Superior Court of Sonoma County*

Legal Citation: 450 U.S. 464

Year of Decision: 1981

KEY ISSUE

Does California's statutory rape law violate the equal protection clause of the Fourteenth Amendment?

HISTORY OF THE CASE

A complaint filed in summer 1978 in the municipal court of Sonoma County, California, alleged that a 17-year-old male had unlawful sexual intercourse with a female below the age of 18. Unlawful sexual intercourse defined under California law is "an act of sexual intercourse accomplished with a female not the wife of the perpetrator, where the female is under the age of 18." The trial court and the California court of appeals denied the request for relief and the California Supreme Court reviewed the case.

The California Supreme Court held the law to be discriminatory on the basis of sex because only females may be victims and only males may violate this law. The court further stated that the state had a compelling interest in preventing pregnancies that resulted from rape. The gender classification was necessary to identify the offender and victim. The U.S. Supreme Court agreed to hear the case.

SUMMARY OF ARGUMENTS

The petitioner argued that the California law discriminated on the basis of gender in violation of the equal protection clause of the Constitution because only men were held criminally liable under the statute. The petitioner also argued that the California statute was both over- and underinclusive and that a gender-neutral statute would have served the state's goals equally well.

California argued that the statute was justified because it sought to prevent illegitimate teenage pregnancies, and the statute did not violate the equal protection clause of the Fourteenth Amendment. California also argued that a gender-neutral statute would hinder effective enforcement of the statute.

DECISION

Justice Rehnquist delivered the opinion of the Court affirming the California Supreme Court's decision. The California statutory rape law, in which only the male participant in the sexual act is criminally liable, was upheld because it is designed to prevent illegitimate adolescent pregnancies. The statute does not violate the equal protection clause. Gender-based classifications are not inherently suspect so as to compel "strict scrutiny," but they must further the state interest. Because all significant consequences of teenage pregnancy fall on the female, the legislature is within its rights to punish the male, who suffers few consequences of his conduct. For the female also to be criminally liable would frustrate the state's interest because she would be less likely to report the rape if she would be subject to criminal prosecution. This statute protects women from sexual intercourse at a young age when the consequences are more severe. The statute is an additional deterrent for men.

Justice Brennan dissented, saying that the Court put too much emphasis on the prevention of teenage pregnancy and not enough on whether the sex-based discrimination is related to the achievement of that goal. He argued that California had not met the burden of proving there were fewer teenage pregnancies under the gender-based rape law than there would be if the law were gender neutral. California must show that it deters females more effectively than males from having sexual intercourse.

AFTERMATH

The holding furthered "traditional attitudes toward male-female relationships by making males more guilty."

SIGNIFICANCE

This case illustrated the intermediate scrutiny the Court uses to review cases of gender discrimination. Here, the state's interest in preventing unwanted teenage pregnancy outweighed the interests of male defendants to be treated equally under the law.

RELATED CASES

Reed v. Reed, 404 U.S. 71 (1971)

Kahn v. Shevin, 416 U.S. 351 (1974)

Schlesinger v. Ballard, 419 U.S. 498 (1975)

Craig v. Boren, 429 U.S. 190 (1976)

Califano v. Webster, 430 U.S. 313 (1977)

RECOMMENDED READING

Kanowitz, Leo. *Equal Rights: The Male Stake.* Albuquerque: University of New Mexico Press, 1981.

Kirp, Donald L. *Gender Justice.* Chicago: University of Chicago Press, 1986.

Leslie Landau, *Gender Based Statutory Rape Law Does Not Violate the Equal Protection Clause,* 67 Cornell Law Review 1109 (1982).

Frances Olsen, *Statutory Rape: A Feminist Critique of Rights Analysis,* 63 Texas Law Review 387 (1982).

Case Title: *Rostker v. Goldberg*

Legal Citation: 453 U.S. 57

Year of Decision: 1981

KEY ISSUE

Does mandatory draft registration for men, but not women, violate equal protection?

HISTORY OF THE CASE

This case started in 1971, when several men subject to registration for the draft filed a claim in district court stating that the registration violated due process and equal protection rights, among other things. In 1975, registration for the draft was discontinued, and the case was in limbo. The case was never dismissed, and it was resurrected in 1980, when an act providing for the registration for the draft was about to go into effect. The district court found that the act violated the due process clause of the Fifth Amendment, as well as the equal protection clause of the Fourteenth Amendment. This decision was appealed to the Third Circuit, which stayed the district court's order. The U.S. Supreme Court decided to review the case.

SUMMARY OF ARGUMENTS

The young men who were subject to draft registration contended that the act took away property without due process, imposed involuntary servitude, violated rights of free expression and assembly, and discriminated between males and females (equal protection).

Congress argued that there was no military need to draft women. Women were excluded from combat through statutes and military policy, so drafting them was unnecessary.

DECISION

Justice Rehnquist delivered the opinion of the Court, which held that the act did not violate the due process clause or the equal protection clause. The Court used a middle-level, heightened scrutiny (between strict scrutiny and rational basis) standard of *Craig v. Boren*. The Court stated that great deference should be given to Congress in military affairs, and that Congress weighed this decision carefully by conducting studies and holding hearings on the subject. Because women were unavailable for combat, Congress was justified in exempting them from the draft; it did not violate the equal protection clause. Additionally, volunteers could fill noncombat posts, so the distinction between drafting for combat versus noncombat posts was irrelevant.

Justice White dissented, stating that women could be drafted for noncombat purposes. He doubted that all of the noncombat positions could be filled by volunteers.

Justices Marshall and Brennan dissented, contending that women should be required to register for the draft even if they were not actually drafted when the time came. This would enable the military to decide at the time whether only men were needed. They believed that the need to maintain an adequate army was important, but that the male-only registration was not substantially related to that objective.

AFTERMATH

The Court has continued to give great deference to Congress in assuming the constitutionality of its decisions, especially in matters of military affairs.

SIGNIFICANCE

This case showed that the Court will give Congress the benefit of the doubt regarding the constitutionality of its legislation, and that men and women must be "similarly situated" to overcome the heightened scrutiny test in an equal opportunity challenge.

RELATED CASES

Reed v. Reed, 404 U.S. 71 (1971)

Columbia Broadcasting System v. Democratic National Committee, 412 U.S. 94 (1973)

Greer v. Spock, 424 U.S. 828 (1976)

Craig v. Boren, 429 U.S. 190 (1976)

Orr v. Orr, 440 U.S. 268 (1979)

Michael M. v. Superior Court, 450 U.S. 464 (1981)

RECOMMENDED READING

Anderson, Martin, ed. *Registration and the Draft.* Palo Alto, Calif.: Hoover, 1982.

Equal Protection, the Supreme Court, 1980 Term, 95 Harvard Law Review 162 (1981).

Kirp, Donald L., et al. *Gender Justice.* Chicago: University of Chicago Press, 1986.

Marmion, Harry A. *Selective Service: Conflict and Compromise.* New York: Wiley, 1968.

S. E. H., *Males Only Draft Registration Does Not Violate Equal Protection Component of the Fifth Amendment,* 59 Washington University Law Quarterly 1371 (1982).

Case Title: *Mississippi University for Women v. Hogan*

Legal Citations: 458 U.S. 718; 102 S. Ct. 3331

Year of Decision: 1982

~

KEY ISSUE

Does a state university's provision that reserves certain educational opportunities solely for women violate the equal protection clause of the Fourteenth Amendment?

HISTORY OF THE CASE

In 1884, the Mississippi University for Women was founded by the state legislature as the Mississippi Industrial Institute. From its beginnings, its enrollment was limited to women. In 1971, a School of Nursing was established, offering a two-year degree. Three years later, the school offered a baccalaureate program in nursing. Joe Hogan, a registered nurse, applied for admission in 1979. Although otherwise qualified, he was denied admission solely because of his sex. He filed an action in the U.S. District Court for the Northern District of Mississippi based on the single-sex admission of the school. He sought injunctive and declaratory relief and compensatory damages. Injunctive relief orders someone to reverse an injury inflicted, and declaratory relief gives a determination of the rights and status of the parties.

The district court denied the injunctive relief, saying that the same-sex policy bears a rational relationship to the state's legitimate interest in giving women an education and affording them unique benefits. The court entered summary judgment, a decision that determines a question of law and disposes of an action without a trial. The Court of Appeals for the Fifth Circuit reversed. It stated that the district court used the wrong test, and that the proper test was the state interest in providing an education for all its citizens. The state failed to show that providing a unique educational opportunity for females but not for males bears an important relationship to that interest. The Supreme Court agreed to hear the case.

SUMMARY OF ARGUMENTS

Hogan argued that the single-sex admissions policy violated his Fourteenth Amendment right to equal protection. He noted that the opportunity to study at other state-supported institutions was not equivocally the same, since he would have to give up his job to attend those schools.

Mississippi argued that the single-sex admissions policy was justified as a remedial program for prior discrimination against women in educational opportunities.

DECISION

Justice O'Connor delivered the opinion of the Court, which held that the state's policy of excluding males from the Mississippi University of Women School of Nursing violated the equal protection clause. She noted that the party seeking to uphold a statute that classifies the individual on the basis of gender has the burden of showing "exceedingly persuasive justification" for the classification. This burden is met when the classification serves "important governmental objectives and the discrimination means employed are substantially related to the achievement of those objectives."

Single-sex admission cannot be upheld on the grounds that it compensates for discrimination against women. Rather than compensating for discrimination, the school's policy tends to perpetuate a stereotype view that nursing is a woman's job. This case is inconsistent with the claim that excluding men from the School of Nursing is necessary to educational goals.

Chief Justice Burger dissented to emphasize that this finding is limited to a professional nursing school.

AFTERMATH

The case brought about intermediate scrutiny as a standard of review for gender-based classifications, a lesser standard than strict scrutiny and a higher standard than the rational basis test. Care is necessary in ascertaining whether a statute reflects stereotyped images. The Virginia Military Institute and the Citadel resisted desegregation of their all-male facilities; however, the Court's decision in *United States v. Virginia* (1996) forced the schools to admit women upon the Court's order.

SIGNIFICANCE

Prior to *Mississippi University,* the Court's focus regarding the equal protection clause had been on racial inequality. *Mississippi University* expanded the Court's focus regarding the equal protection clause to include gender. This was the Court's first ruling on education segregated by sex.

RELATED CASES

Katzenbach v. Morgan, 384 U.S. 641 (1966)

Reed v. Reed, 404 U.S. 71 (1971)

Frontiero v. Richardson, 411 U.S. 677 (1973)

Craig v. Boren, 429 U.S. 190 (1976)

Califano v. Goldfarb, 430 U.S. 199 (1977)

Califano v. Webster, 430 U.S. 313 (1977)

Orr v. Orr, 440 U.S. 268 (1979)

Kirchberg v. Feenstra, 450 U.S. 455 (1981)

RECOMMENDED READING

David H. Gans. *Stereotyping and Differences: The Future of Sex Discrimination Law,* 104 Yale Law Journal, 1875 (1995).

Keynes, Edward, with Randall Miller. *The Court versus Congress: Prayer, Busing and Abortion.* Durham, N.C.: Duke University Press, 1989.

Kirp, Donald L. *Gender Justice.* Chicago: University of Chicago Press, 1986.

Mary Ellen Shull, *Reinforcement of Middle Level Review Regarding Gender Classification,* 11 Pepperdine Law Review 421 (1984).

Case Title: *Plyler v. Doe*

Legal Citation: 457 U.S. 202

Year of Decision: 1982

KEY ISSUE

Did Texas violate the Equal Protection Clause of the Fourteenth Amendment when it denied undocumented school-age children free public education that is provided to children who are citizens of the United States?

HISTORY OF THE CASE

In May 1975, Texas revised its education laws to authorize local school districts to deny illegal immigrant children enrollment in their public schools and to withhold state funds from school districts that used the funds to educate illegal immigrants. Some school-age children of Mexican origin who resided in Smith County, Texas, who could not establish legal U.S. citizenship, filed a class action lawsuit in federal district court. The superintendent and certain members of the board of trustees of the school district were named as defendants, and the state of Texas intervened as a defendant. The district court found that the revised education law violated the equal protection clause of the Fourteenth Amendment, because the discrimination involved was not supported by a rational basis and the supremacy clause of the Constitution. Accordingly, a permanent injunction was issued against the statute. The Fifth Circuit Court of Appeals upheld the injunction; however, it held that the district court had erred in holding that the Texas statute was preempted by federal law. The U.S. Supreme Court noted probable jurisdiction.

That case was consolidated with another Texas case dealing with the education laws, *In re Alien Children Education Litigation,* 501 F. Supp 544 (1980). This case arose from several consolidated suits challenging the constitutionality of the same Texas education laws. The federal district court held that the statute violated the equal protection clause. That court also held that the deprivation of education triggers strict scrutiny, and the statute at issue did not satisfy this level of scrutiny. The state's concern for fiscal integrity was not deemed to be a compelling state interest, and the statute was not narrowly tailored to the state's interests. The court of appeals affirmed the decision of the district court, and the U.S. Supreme Court noted probable jurisdiction.

SUMMARY OF ARGUMENTS

Petitioners argued that section 21.031 was a violation of the equal protection clause of the Fourteenth Amendment. The petitioners argued that Mexican immigrants should be afforded the same rights, and the children should be allowed to attend public school free, as did other children within the state.

The defendants argued that section 21.031 was a financial measure to prevent a drain on the state's fiscal budget. The defendants argued that the increase in population due to immigration had created a problem for public schools of the state. In addition, the immigrants from Mexico had special education needs, which caused further problems.

DECISION

The Court held that Texas had violated the Fourteenth Amendment by denying undocumented school-age children free public education. The Court reasoned that all illegal aliens are people and, therefore, are granted Fourteenth Amendment protections. Texas could not prove a compelling state interest for denying these children an education.

Writing for the majority, Justice Brennan delivered the opinion of the Court. The appellants argued that illegal immigrants were not deemed "persons" for purposes of the equal protection clause because of their status and, thus, did not have the right to equal protection of Texas law. The Court rejected this argument, stating that regardless of immigration status, "an alien is surely a 'person' in any ordinary sense of that term." The Court went on to state that "the protection of the Fourteenth Amendment extends to anyone, citizen or stranger, who is subject to the laws of a State, and reaches into every corner of a State's territory." Thus, the illegal aliens, in this case were able to claim equal protection rights from the Fourteenth Amendment.

When the equal protection clause is applied to most forms of state action, rational basis scrutiny is used; that means, as the Court noted, the law must "bear some fair relationship to a legiti-mate public purpose." At times, the Court will apply a heightened form of scrutiny (i.e., intermediate or strict) if a suspect class or a fundamental right is at issue, but illegal aliens are not mentioned in the Constitution, and their status is the result of voluntary action, unlike that of members of other suspect classes. Thus, illegal aliens do not receive a heightened form of scrutiny because they are not deemed to be a suspect class.

In applying rational basis scrutiny, the Court reasoned that although benefits could be withheld from illegal aliens because they are in the United States as a result of their own unlawful conduct, the same argument does not carry the same force when dealing with their minor children. The Court believed that good citizenship has its foundation in education and stated that

> The inability to read and write will handicap the individual deprived of a basic education each and every day of his life. The estimable toll of that deprivation on the social, economic, intellectual, and psychological well-being of the individual, and the obstacle it poses to individual achievement, make it most difficult to reconcile the cost or the principle of a status-based denial of basic education with the framework of equality embodied in the Equal Protection Clause.

As well as handicapping the individual, the Court noted, the nation would suffer, as well, because without an education, the child will be unable to contribute to society. In light of the costs placed on the life of the individual and that of society, the Court found that the Texas law could not be rational unless it furthered a substantial goal of the state.

States do have some authority to legislate regarding illegal aliens, provided that they mirror a federal objective and further a legitimate state interest. The Court was unable to find any congressional policy that corresponded with the Texas law. The Court rejected the appellants' argument that the alienage classification was a test of residency, arguing that "illegal entry into the country would not, under traditional criteria, bar a person from obtaining domicile within a State." Thus, given the standards by which the state has historically tested for residency status, illegal immigrants could potentially be deemed residents. The Court also noted that although a state can protect itself from an influx in population, there was no evidence in the record suggesting that illegal immigrants overly burden the state's economy. The Court also rejected the appellants' argument that Texas has a justified interest in withholding education benefits because illegal immigrants are less likely than other residents to remain within the boundaries and have productive value for the state. The Court reasoned that this was simply too difficult to quantify. Accordingly, the denial of education to illegal immigrants was deemed unjustified because it did not further a substantial state interest, and the decision of the court of appeals was affirmed.

Justice Marshall wrote a concurring opinion, arguing, unlike the majority, that education was a fundamental interest and, thus, should be reviewed under a higher level of scrutiny than that applied by the majority. He went on to argue that denying it to illegal immigrants was a class-based denial that was incompatible with the equal protection clause. Justice Blackmun wrote a concurring opinion, as well, arguing that the "denial of an education is the analogue of denial of the right to vote: the former relegates the individual to second-class social status; the latter places him at a permanent political disadvantage." He thought that the denial of education to some while providing it to others creates class distinctions inconsistent with the equal protection clause. Justice Powell also wrote a concurring opinion, arguing that the state's power to regulate immigration and naturalization is limited because this power is reserved for federal authority. He agreed with the majority that the status of illegal immigrants did not afford them strict scrutiny.

Chief Justice Burger wrote a dissenting opinion, joined by Justices White, Rehnquist, and O'Connor. The dissenters argued that the majority's decision infringed on the separation of powers among the coordinate branches of government. They argued that it was not the duty of the judiciary to determine the outcome of this issue on the basis of the failure of the other political branches to act. In this case, the dissenters stated, Congress "bears primary responsibility for addressing the problems occasioned by the millions of illegal aliens flooding across our southern border." They further argued that Texas, as well as other states, should have the authority to differentiate between persons legally and illegally in that state.

AFTERMATH

Public schools were prohibited from adopting policies or taking actions that would deny students access to education on the basis of their immigration status. This ruling required schools to look into many other policies and be careful about how such situations were handled. Essentially, this caused schools to be more careful when dealing with the immigrant students.

SIGNIFICANCE

The Court struck down a Texas state law that denied free public education to illegal immigrant children. The Court used intermediate scrutiny to determine whether the law furthered a substantial state goal and held that it did not.

RELATED CASES

Botiller v. Dominguez, 130 U.S. 238 (1889)

Hernandez v. Texas, 347 U.S. 475 (1954)

Espinoza v. Farah Mfg. Co., 414 U.S. 86 (1973)

San Antonio Independent School District v. Rodriguez, 411 U.S. 1 (1973)

United States v. Brignoni-Ponce, 422 U.S. 873 (1975)

RECOMMENDED READING

Soltero, Carlos R. *Latinos and American Law.* Austin: University of Texas Press, 2006.

Case Title: *Rogers v. Lodge*

Legal Citation: 458 U.S. 613

Year of Decision: 1982

~

KEY ISSUE

Does an at-large election system that has the mere effect of excluding blacks from county offices violate the Fourteenth Amendment's guarantee of equal protection?

HISTORY OF THE CASE

Generally speaking, in order for a party to succeed on a claim of denial of equal protection, it must show that the unequal treatment was intentional. Upon showing this intentional or purposeful discrimination, the Court will raise its level of scrutiny in examining the facts of the case. The higher the level of scrutiny, the more likely the offended party is to succeed. The mere fact that a law is less favorable to one group than another, however, is generally not enough to warrant a finding of a denial of equal protection.

Burke County, Georgia, elected its five county commissioners in an at-large election system, one when voters are not divided into districts but all vote on all candidates. White voters constituted a marginal majority of eligible voters, and no black candidate had ever been elected to office. A class action suit was brought on behalf of all black residents of the county. The federal district court found the election system denied blacks equal protection and ordered the county divided into districts. The Court of Appeals for the Fifth Circuit affirmed. The Supreme Court agreed to hear the case because of the importance of the issues raised.

SUMMARY OF ARGUMENTS

The county argued that the election procedure was neither discriminatory in purpose nor in effect, as only 38 percent of registered voters were black. As a result, the fact that no black had ever won any election was merely a reflection of the county demographics among registered voters. The county further argued that the election procedure as adopted in 1911 was not adopted for discriminatory purposes.

The class members argued that the system diluted the power of the black vote because they were in a minority. They also maintained that past discrimination had restricted the opportunity of blacks to participate effectively in the elections.

DECISION

Justice White delivered the opinion of the Court in the 6-3 decision affirming the lower courts' findings. The Court decided that the discriminatory purpose of the election scheme could be shown by circumstantial evidence. The Court noted that the system was indeed neutral and adopted with no malignant intent. Given the discriminatory impact on black citizens, however, as well as the history of discrimination in the county, the unresponsiveness of county officials to the needs of the black community, and the fact that the state legislature maintained the system, enough circumstantial evidence was provided to support an inference of intentional discrimination.

AFTERMATH

The Court has followed a generally uniform approach to equal protection challenges. The Court does not believe that an otherwise neutral law should be struck down simply because it adversely affects a certain group. The law must still be shown to have a discriminatory purpose. Discriminatory purpose has been dealt with in a number of ways, none of which is exclusive. The Court's focus on vote dilution issues remained on the effect on the black population. The Court's concern for its effect on other minority groups was not as prevalent.

SIGNIFICANCE

Rogers effectively widened the route that may be taken in challenges based on discrimination and equal protection grounds. Circumstantial evidence is not widely looked upon as the most favorable evidence to support any given conclusion. However, the accumulation of circumstantial evidence may secure a position well enough to prove purposeful discrimination.

RELATED CASES

Yick Wo v. Hopkins, 118 U.S. 356 (1886)

Fortson v. Dorsey, 379 U.S. 433 (1965)

Burns v. Richardson, 384 U.S. 73 (1966)

Whitcomb v. Chavis, 396 U.S. 1064 (1971)

White v. Regester, 412 U.S. 755 (1973)

Richmond v. United States, 422 U.S. 358 (1975)

Arlington Heights v. Metropolitan Housing Corporation, 429 U.S. 252 (1977)

Personnel Administrator of Massachusetts v. Feeney, 445 U.S. 901 (1980)

Mobile v. Bolden, 446 U.S. 55 (1980)

Thornburgh v. Gingles, 478 U.S. 30 (1986)

RECOMMENDED READING

Davis, Olethia. "Tenuous Interpretation: Sections 2 and 5 of the Voting Rights Act." *National Civic Review* 84, no. 4 (1995): 310–322.

Timothy G. O'Rourke, *Constitutional and Statutory Challenges to Local At-Large Elections*, 17 University of Richmond Law Review 39 (1982).

The Supreme Court, 1981 Term, 96 Harvard Law Review 106 (1982).

Case Title: *Equal Employment Opportunity Commission (EEOC) v. Wyoming et al.*

Alternate Case Title: The Age Discrimination in Employment Case

Legal Citation: 460 U.S. 226

Year of Decision: 1983

KEY ISSUE

Did Congress violate state sovereignty provisions of the Tenth Amendment when it made the Age Discrimination in Employment Act of 1967 (ADEA) applicable to state and local governments?

HISTORY OF THE CASE

The ADEA makes it unlawful for an employer to discriminate against an employee between the ages of 40 and 70 on the basis of age except where age is a "bona fide occupational qualification reasonably necessary to the normal operation of the particular business." In 1974, Congress extended the definition to apply to state and local governments. A Wyoming supervisor of the Game and Fish Department was forced to retire at age 55 under Wyoming law. He filed a complaint with the EEOC, which then filed a suit in federal district court. The court dismissed the suit, holding that the ADEA violated the doctrine of Tenth Amendment immunity as set forth in *National League of Cities v. Usery* (1976).

SUMMARY OF ARGUMENTS

The appellant, the EEOC, argued that the extension of the ADEA to state and local governments did not intrude upon Wyoming's state sovereignty, as reserved by the Tenth Amendment.

The appellee, the state of Wyoming, argued that the application of the ADEA to the states was precluded by the Tenth Amendment constraints on the commerce powers of Congress.

DECISION

In a 5-4 decision, the Court held that the 1974 extension of the ADEA was a valid exercise of congressional powers under the commerce clause and not limited by the protections given states under the Tenth Amendment. Justice Brennan, writing for the majority, stated that the three-prong test to invalidate such powers had not been met. In his dissent, Chief Justice Burger disagreed, stating that Congress had intruded on state sovereignty, and the test indeed had been met.

Justice Burger concluded that the act of defining the qualifications of employees was an essential of sovereignty. He also concluded that neither the Constitution nor any of the amendments transferred the function of establishing these employment qualifications from the states to the federal government. Further, he stated, the 1974 amendment to the ADEA violated the Tenth Amendment, which states that Congress may not exercise power not delegated to it.

AFTERMATH

The courts continue to resolve issues of state autonomy on the basis of balancing the merits of congressional policy. The courts at times are reluctant to strike down an act of Congress on Congress's own authority.

SIGNIFICANCE

This decision settled the conflict between state sovereignty under the Tenth Amendment and the commerce power of Congress. The jurisdiction of the commerce clause was extended, with a major impact on early retirement laws. Further, this ruling was crucial because employment in the state and local governments was one of the fastest growing sectors of the economy.

RELATED CASES

National League of Cities v. Usery, 426 U.S. 833 (1976)

Hodel v. Virginia Mining and Reclamation Association, 452 U.S. 264 (1981)

RECOMMENDED READING

Dean Alfange, Jr., *Congressional Regulation of the States qua States: From National League of Cities to* EEOC v. Wyoming, 1983 Supreme Court Review 215.

Keyes, Edward, and Randall K. Miller. *The Court vs. Congress: Prayer, Busing and Abortion.* Durham, N.C.: Duke University Press, 1989.

Case Title: *Batson v. Kentucky*

Alternate Case Title: The "Excluded Black Jurors" Case

Legal Citations: 476 U.S. 79; 106 S. Ct. 1712

Year of Decision: 1986

KEY ISSUE

Does a prosecutor's use of peremptory challenges to exclude jurors solely on the basis of race violate a defendant's right to a fair trial and equal protection under the Sixth and Fourteenth Amendments to the Constitution?

HISTORY OF THE CASE

James Batson, a black man, was indicted in Kentucky on charges of second-degree burglary and receipt of stolen goods. On the first day of trial, the prosecutor used his peremptory challenges, those not requiring explanation, to strike all four black persons on the venire, the group of citizens from which the trial jury was to be selected. A jury composed of only white persons was selected. Defense counsel moved to discharge the jury before it was sworn and requested a hearing on his motion. The trial judge denied the motion, stating that the parties could use their peremptories to "strike anybody they wanted to." He reasoned that the cross-section requirement of the Sixth Amendment applied only to the selection of the venire, not the selection of the trial jury itself.

The jury convicted Batson on both counts. On appeal, Batson argued that although *Swain v. Alabama* (1965), a prior decision requiring a demonstration of the systematic exclusion of African Americans as jurors to sustain an equal protection action, foreclosed on any equal protection claims based solely on the prosecutor's conduct, he was still entitled to a jury drawn from a cross section of the community and that the prosecutor's use of peremptories violated his rights under the Sixth Amendment and section 11 of the Kentucky Constitution. The Supreme Court of Kentucky affirmed the convictions. It relied on *Swain* and held that a defendant alleging lack of a fair cross section must demonstrate systematic exclusion of a group of jurors from the venire. The U.S. Supreme Court granted certiorari, 471 U.S. 1052 (1985), and reversed.

SUMMARY OF ARGUMENTS

Batson's counsel argued that the prosecutor's removal of the black veniremen violated his rights under the Sixth Amendment to a jury drawn from a cross section of the community.

The state argued that the privilege of unfettered exercise of the peremptory challenge is of vital importance to the criminal justice system and should remain unchanged from the standards set out in *Swain*. They also argued that changing the current standards would cause serious administrative difficulties.

DECISION

Justice Powell wrote the opinion for the Court, in which Justices Brennan, White, Marshall, Blackmun, Stevens, and O'Connor joined. Justice Powell held that a state denies a black defendant equal protection when it puts him on trial before a jury from which members of his race have been purposefully excluded, reaffirming the principle announced in *Strauder v. West Virginia* (1860). Powell stated that the resolution of petitioner's claims turned on the application of equal protection principles and did not express a view on the merits of petitioner's Sixth Amendment claims (although Batson raised only a Sixth Amendment claim, not an equal protection claim).

Justice Powell found that a defendant does not have a right to a trial jury composed in whole or in part of members of his own race. The equal protection clause guarantees the defendant only that the state will not exclude members of his race from the jury panel on account of race, or on the false assumption that members of his race as a group are not qualified to serve as jurors. Justice Powell urged that such discrimination was not only against the defendant but also against the excluded juror and undermined public confidence in the fairness of the judicial system. He also stated that although these principles concern the selection of the venire, they also apply to the selection of the trial jury itself.

Justice Powell rejected the portion of *Swain v. Alabama* concerning the evidentiary burden placed on a defendant who claimed that he had been denied equal protection through the state's discriminatory use of peremptory challenges. *Swain* required a defendant to show proof of repeated striking of blacks over a number of cases to establish a violation of the equal protection clause—a very difficult burden of proof. Justice Powell found that a defendant may make a prima facie showing, a presentation of evidence sufficient for the case to move forward, of purposeful racial discrimination in the selection of the venire by relying solely on the facts concerning its selection at defendant's own trial. A defendant no longer had to show that the peremptory challenge system as a whole was being perverted.

Justice Powell even devised a method by which a defendant could make a prima facie showing of purposeful discrimination. First, he had to show that he was a member of a cognizable racial group and that the prosecutor had exercised peremptory challenges to remove from the venire members of the defendant's race. Then he had to show that such facts and any circumstances raised an inference that the prosecutor used peremptory challenges to exclude the veniremen from the petit jury because of their race. Once this was shown, the burden shifted to the prosecutor to state a neutral reason for challenging the black jurors. Justice Powell also directed that a prosecutor could not rebut the defendant's case by merely denying that he had a discriminatory motive or good faith in making the individual selections. Justice Powell did not believe that his decision would undermine the contribution the challenge generally makes to the administration of justice; nor would it create serious administrative difficulties.

In Justice White's concurring opinion, he stated that the practice of peremptorily eliminating blacks from petit juries in cases with black defendants remained widespread. Therefore, he agreed that an opportunity to overcome the peremptory's presumption of legitimacy should be afforded when this occurred. Justice White added that he would adhere to the rule announced in *De Stefano v. Woods* (1968), that decisions by the Court should not be applied retroactively.

In a concurring opinion, Justice Marshall stated that the Court's decision in this case would not end the racial discrimination that peremptories inject into the jury-selection process. He argued that any prosecutor could easily assert a neutral reason for striking a juror, making the Court's protection in the instant case illusory. He feared that a prosecutor's own conscious or unconscious racism might lead him to lie to himself in an effort to convince himself that his motives were legal. Justice Marshall stressed that this could lead to more racial prejudice. He believed that the only way to eliminate racial prejudice in the use of peremptories was to eliminate peremptory challenges entirely. He noted that they were not required by the Constitution, and their elimination would not impair the constitutional guarantee of impartial jury and fair trial. However, he viewed the majority decision as a step toward eliminating that practice.

Justice Stevens was joined by Justice Brennan in his concurring opinion. He believed that the Court correctly decided the issues regarding peremptories and their use in violation of the equal protection clause, even though Batson did not raise these issues. Justice Stevens based his conclusion on the respondent reliance on an equal protection argument in defense of the judgment, and on the several amici curiae, persons who are not parties to the case but have an interest in the matters at issue, which also addressed the equal protection argument. He supported his findings with specific quotes from the respondent's arguments identifying the Fourteenth Amendment as the controlling issue.

Justice O'Connor's concurrence stated that in addition to agreeing with the majority's opinion, she also believed that the decision should not apply retroactively.

Chief Justice Burger wrote a long and spirited dissent, which was joined by Justice Rehnquist. He urged that review of an equal protection argument is improper when a petitioner has not made an equal protection claim at the lower courts or the U.S. Supreme Court and can show no reason why he did not make those claims. Justice Burger criticized the reversal of the 21-year-old unanimous decision and constitutional holding in *Swain* on the basis of arguments disclaimed by petitioner, arguing without explanation that this was a departure from the Court's usual procedure. He stated that there should have been a reargument on the equal protection question, the Court should have directed the parties

to brief that issue in addition to the Sixth Amendment question, or the Court should have dismissed the petition for certiorari as improvidently granted as a result of the lack of argument regarding equal protection.

Justice Burger then gave examples of the importance of the peremptory challenge by quoting Justice White, who in his majority opinion in *Swain* traced the development of the peremptory challenge. This historical account highlighted the long and venerable tradition of peremptory challenges in England and the United States. Justice White wrote that the "peremptory challenge is 'one of the most important of the rights' in our justice system" and should not require inquiry into a party's use of it. Justice Burger stated that the majority in the instant case should have paid more attention to the history of the peremptory challenge, instead of recounting the well-established principle that intentional exclusion of racial groups from jury venires violates the equal protection clause. He criticized the Court's silence on applying the conventional equal protection framework, and on its failure to state whether there were limits to the exercise of peremptory challenges by defense counsel. He did not like the majority's middle ground requirement of a "neutral" explanation, and he believed that it would not further the ends of justice, believing that either a challenge has to be explained or it does not. He insisted that the likely results of *Batson*'s holding was to diminish confidence in the jury system and to interject racial matters into the jury-selection process. Justice Burger also saw the Court's holding as developing a newly created constitutional right. He ended by assenting to Justice White's conclusion that the decision not apply retroactively, but he still urged that this case be set for reargument.

Justice Rehnquist wrote the final dissenting opinion, in which Chief Justice Burger joined. He began by questioning whether the majority did what they set out to do: merely to reexamine the portion of *Swain* concerning the evidentiary burden placed on a criminal defendant who claims he has been denied equal protection through the state's use of peremptory challenges to exclude members of his race from the petit jury. He then showed two circumstances in which a state might legitimately use its peremptories to exclude blacks from juries in criminal cases.

He quoted *Swain,* which held that when a state uses the peremptory to exclude a black person from a particular jury on the basis of the belief that that person would be more likely to favor a black defendant, it is not a violation of equal protection. Justice Rehnquist reiterated that peremptory challenge should be used, as was done historically, upon the instincts, beliefs, and "unaccountable prejudices" of the prosecutor or defense counsel. He believed that in light of these considerations, it is not a denial of equal protection to strike black people in a particular case.

He further argued the fairness of such peremptory challenges, which state that everyone is subject to being challenged without cause. Justice Rehnquist saw nothing "unequal" about the state's using its peremptories to strike blacks from the jury in cases involving black defendants—as long as the challenges were also used to strike white jurors in cases involving white defendants, as well as with Asians, Hispanics, or any other racial or ethnic group. If it was applied across the board, he did not see an equal protection violation.

Additionally, Justice Rehnquist did not see a violation of any other constitutional interest, nor any harm to the remainder of the community or the excluded jurors. He backed the use of group affiliations as a legitimate basis for a state's use of peremptory challenges, and he felt they were helpful in eliminating persons who may be biased. He did not agree with any substantive departure from *Swain,* and he argued that the petitioner in this case did not make an appropriate showing to overcome the presumption announced in *Swain* that the state's use of peremptory challenges was related to the context of the case.

AFTERMATH

Since *Batson,* the Court has extended its doctrine to prohibit the use of racially discriminatory peremptories by criminal defendants, civil litigants, or defendants of a different race from the excluded juror and in cases of sex-based discriminatory peremptory strikes.

SIGNIFICANCE

The Court overruled the part of *Swain* that precluded a criminal defendant from making out an equal protection violation based on the exclusion by peremptory challenges for black jurors, in the defendant's particular case. As a result, *Batson* took a significant step toward eliminating racial discrimination in the selection of criminal juries.

RELATED CASES

Strauder v. West Virginia, 100 U.S. 303 (1880)

Swain v. Alabama, 380 U.S. 202 (1965)

Powers v. Ohio, 499 U.S. 400 (1991)

Edmonson v. Leesville Concrete, 500 U.S. 614 (1991)

Georgia v. McCollum, 505 U.S. 42 (1992)

J. E. B. v. Alabama, 511 U.S. 127 (1994)

Miller-El v. Dretke, 545 U.S. 231 (2005)

RECOMMENDED READING

Albert W. Alschuler, *The Supreme Court and the Jury: Voir Dire, Peremptory Challenges, and the Review of Jury Verdicts,* 56 University of Chicago Law Review 153 (1989).

Benjamin Hoorn Barton, note, *Religion-Based Peremptory Challenges after* Batson v. Kentucky *and* J. E. B. v. Alabama: *An Equal Protection and First Amendment Analysis,* 94 Michigan Law Review 191 (1995).

David F. Breck, *Peremptory Strikes after* Batson v. Kentucky, 74 ABA Journal 54 (1988).

Leonard Mandell, *Extending* Batson v. Kentucky: *Do Gender-Based Peremptory Challenges Violate the Constitutional Guarantee of Equal Protection?* 2 ABA Preview of United States Supreme Court Cases 57 (1993).

Paul Reidinger, *Rainbow Juries,* 25 ABA Journal 100 (1989).

Case Title: *Wygant v. Jackson Board of Education*

Alternate Case Title: The Teacher Seniority Case

Legal Citation: 476 U.S. 267

Year of Decision: 1986

KEY ISSUE

May a school board lay off nonminority teachers while retaining minority teachers with less seniority in order to prevent a reduction in the total percentage of minority teachers?

HISTORY OF THE CASE

The collective bargaining agreement between the school board of Jackson County, Michigan, and the local teachers union provided that in laying off teachers, those with the most seniority would be retained. However, it also contained a clause providing that at no time would there be a greater percentage of minorities laid off than the current percentage of minorities employed at the time of the layoff. The plaintiffs, including Wendy Wygant, were nonminority teachers who had been laid off. In some cases, those who had been laid off were tenured teachers, while certain minority teachers retained had been in a trial period of employment and under review to determine whether they would become permanent employees. The plaintiffs filed suit in federal district court, alleging that the minority clause violated their right to the equal protection of the laws under the Fourteenth Amendment. The district court held that the clause was constitutional as an attempt to remedy societal discrimination by providing role models for minority schoolchildren. The Court of Appeals for the Sixth Circuit affirmed the decision.

SUMMARY OF ARGUMENTS

The plaintiffs argued that the minority retention provision was a racial classification that required strict scrutiny under the equal protection clause of the Fourteenth Amendment. They claimed that strict scrutiny would require proof that the provision constituted an attempt to remedy past discrimination by the school board, and none had been shown in this case.

The board, supported by briefs filed by the attorneys general of numerous states, argued that the provision was a narrowly tailored attempt to remedy societal discrimination by providing minority teachers as role models for children. It also claimed that it had engaged in past hiring discrimination against minorities; thus, the provision was an appropriate remedial response.

DECISION

Justice Powell announced the judgment of a narrowly divided Court. Five justices agreed that the provision violated the Fourteenth Amendment, although they differed over the reason for this interpretation. Traditional equal protection analysis requires that race-based classifications be justified by a "compelling government interest," and the means chosen must be "narrowly tailored" to fulfill that purpose. Justice Powell argued that only an attempt to remedy past discrimination by the school board, and not societal discrimination in general, would serve as a compelling government interest. Justice Powell argued that the district court's role model theory, if taken to its logical conclusion, could lead to exactly the type of segregated schools rejected by the Court in its historic *Brown v. Board of Education* decision. He acknowledged the difficulties facing public school officials who were constitutionally required to take race into account in order to remedy the vestiges of discrimination while facing a duty to prevent discrimination on the basis of race. He then noted that even if the board were able to demonstrate past discrimination, the provision was unconstitutional because it was not a narrowly tailored means of fulfilling the government interest in question.

Justice Powell held that because layoffs "impose the entire burden of achieving racial equality on particular [innocent] individuals," they cannot serve as a narrowly tailored means of fulfilling even legitimate purposes. He referred to the use of hiring goals as a more acceptable means of remedying past discrimination.

Justice O'Connor's concurrence differed from the plurality in two respects. First, she did not believe that the relevant government actor—in this case, the school board—should be required to make particularized findings of past discrimination in order to enact a remedy. Justice O'Connor would have left it to the plaintiffs in any given case to prove that there had been no past discrimination by the government. Second, she did not address the general question of whether layoffs were a constitutional means to remedy past discrimination. Because the minority layoff provision, in this case, was tied to the number of minority students in the school district, not the number of qualified minority applicants in the relevant labor pool, it was clearly not narrowly tailored to remedy past discrimination.

Justice Marshall wrote a dissent joined by Justices Blackmun and Brennan. He argued that the Court had applied an overly stringent form of analysis; in his opinion, the provision constituted a constitutional attempt to preserve the benefits of a legitimate affirmative action hiring program. Justice Marshall also argued that eliminating the layoff provision would eviscerate the benefits of that hiring program. He asserted that while layoffs clearly impose a burden on any group, their effect is similar to minority hiring preferences, which are clearly constitutional.

AFTERMATH

Less than a year after the decision in *Wygant*, the Court indicated that proper uses of affirmative action were a remedy for past discrimination permitted by the Constitution.

SIGNIFICANCE

Unless past discrimination can be shown, the preference of one person over another based on race is unconstitutional as an equal protection violation.

RELATED CASES

Swann v. Charlotte-Mecklenburg Board of Education, 402 U.S. 1 (1971)

Fullilove v. Klutznick, 448 U.S. 448 (1980)

Firefighters v. Cleveland, 478 U.S. 501 (1986)

Martin v. Wilks, 490 U.S. 755 (1989)

RECOMMENDED READING

Cox, Archibald. *The Court and the Constitution.* Boston: Houghton Mifflin, 1987.

Kahlenburg, Richard D. *The Remedy: Class, Race, and Affirmative Action.* New York: Basic Books, 1996.

Joel L. Selig, *Affirmative Action in Employment: The Legacy of a Supreme Court Majority,* 63 Indiana Law Review 301 (1988).

Case Title: *Johnson v. Transportation Agency, Santa Clara County*

Legal Citations: 480 U.S. 616

Year of Decision: 1987

KEY ISSUE

Was a male employee of a county transportation agency discriminated against when he was passed over for promotion in favor of a female employee?

HISTORY OF THE CASE

In December 1978, the Santa Clara County Transit District Board of Supervisors adopted an affirmative action plan for the county Transportation Agency. The plan was adopted because "mere prohibition of discriminatory practices is not enough to remedy the effects of past practices and to permit attainment of an equitable representation of minorities, women and handicapped persons." The plan intended to achieve "a statistically measurable yearly improvement in hiring, training and promotion of minorities and women throughout the Agency in all major job classifications where they are underrepresented." As a benchmark to evaluate progress, the agency stated its long-term goal was to attain a workforce whose composition reflected the proportion of minorities and women in the area labor force. The agency's plan set aside no specific number of positions for minorities or women, but it authorized the consideration of ethnicity or sex as a factor when evaluating qualified candidates for jobs in which members of such groups were poorly represented. One such job was the road dispatcher position, the subject of the dispute in this case.

On December 12, 1979, the agency announced a vacancy for the promotional position of road dispatcher in the agency's Roads Division. Dispatchers assign road crews, equipment, and materials, and they maintain records pertaining to road maintenance jobs. Twelve employees applied for the promotion, including Diana Joyce, a woman, and Paul Johnson, the petitioner in this case. Joyce had worked for the county since 1970, serving as an account clerk until 1975. She had applied for a road dispatcher position in 1974 but was deemed ineligible because she had not served as a road maintenance worker. In 1975, Joyce transferred from a senior account clerk position to a road maintenance worker position, becoming the first woman to fill such a job. During her four years in that position, she occasionally worked as a road dispatcher.

The petitioner Johnson began work with the county in 1967 as a road yard clerk, after private employment that included working as a supervisor and dispatcher. He had also unsuccessfully applied for the road dispatcher opening in 1974. In 1977, his clerical position was downgraded, and he sought and received a transfer to the position of road maintenance worker. He also occasionally worked as a dispatcher while performing that job.

Nine of the applicants, including Joyce and Johnson, were deemed qualified for the job, and they were interviewed by a two-person board. Seven of the applicants scored above 70 on this interview, which meant that they were certified as eligible for selection by the appointing authority. The scores awarded ranged from 70 to 80. Johnson was tied for second with a score of 75 while Joyce ranked next with a score of 73. A second

interview was conducted by three agency supervisors, who ultimately recommended that Johnson be promoted. Prior to the second interview, Joyce had contacted the county's Affirmative Action Office because she feared that her application might not receive disinterested review. The office, in turn, contacted the agency's affirmative action coordinator, whom the agency's plan makes responsible for, among other things, keeping the director informed of opportunities for the agency to accomplish its objectives under the plan. At the time, the agency had never employed a woman as a road dispatcher. The coordinator recommended to the director of the agency, James Graebner, that Joyce be promoted.

Graebner, authorized to choose any of the seven persons deemed eligible, thus had the benefit of suggestions by the second interview panel and by the agency coordinator in arriving at his decision. After deliberation, Graebner concluded that the promotion should be given to Joyce. As he testified: "I tried to look at the whole picture, the combination of her qualifications and Mr. Johnson's qualifications, their test scores, their expertise, their background, affirmative action matters, things like that. . . . I believe it was a combination of all those."

Johnson filed suit in the U.S. District Court for the Northern District of California alleging that he had been denied promotion on the basis of sex in violation of Title VII of the 1964 Civil Rights Act, which makes it an unlawful employment practice to discriminate in the hiring, firing, and treatment of employees on the basis of "race, color, religion, sex or national origin." The district court found that Johnson was more qualified for the dispatcher position than Joyce, and that the sex of Joyce was the "determining factor in her selection." The court found the agency's plan invalid on the ground that the evidence did not satisfy the criterion of *Steelworkers v. Weber* (1979) that the plan be temporary. In *Weber,* the Court upheld an affirmative action plan because, among other things, it did not seek to maintain a racial balance but to eliminate a racial imbalance.

The Court of Appeals for the Ninth Circuit reversed, holding that the absence of an express termination date in the plan was not conclusive as to the plan's validity, since the plan repeatedly expressed its objective as the attainment, rather than the maintenance, of a workforce mirroring the labor force in the county. The court of appeals added that because the plan established no fixed percentage of positions for minorities or women, a relatively explicit deadline was less essential. The court held further that the agency's consideration of Joyce's sex in filling the road dispatcher position was lawful. The agency plan had been adopted, the court said, to address a conspicuous imbalance in the agency's workforce and neither unnecessarily trammeled the rights of other employees nor created an absolute bar to their advancement. After the Ninth Circuit decision denying his Title VII claim of sexual discrimination, Johnson sought review in the U.S. Supreme Court.

SUMMARY OF ARGUMENTS

Johnson argued that he had been denied promotion on the basis of sex in violation of Title VII of the 1964 Civil Rights Act.

Johnson argued that the plan could not be justified as remedial because the agency had not been guilty of past sexual discrimination, and even if the plan could be justified as remedial, it was not narrowly tailored.

The agency argued that gender was only one of the considerations taken into account when promoting a qualified person to a job in which women had not been previously employed. The agency also argued that the plan was narrowly tailored, and Johnson's Title VII rights had not been violated.

DECISION

Justice Brennan delivered the opinion of the Court. Following the Court's precedent in *Steelworkers v. Weber,* Justice Brennan used a two-part analysis to address Johnson's claim of employment discrimination. The first question in this case was whether the consideration of the sex of applicants for particular types of jobs was justified by the existence of a "manifest imbalance" that reflected underrepresentation of women in "traditionally segregated job categories." By comparing the percentage of women in the employer's workforce with the percentage in the area labor market, the Court concluded that such a "manifest imbalance" did exist. The Court also pointed out that the plan did not establish quotas and that sex was only one factor to be considered of many. The Court held that "the promotion of Joyce thus satisfies the first requirement enunciated in *Weber,* since it was undertaken to further an affirmative action plan designed to eliminate Agency work force imbalances in traditionally segregated job categories."

The next question the Court considered was whether the plan violated the rights of male employees. The Court reiterated that the plan enforced no quotas: "The plan sets aside no positions for women." The Court again noted that sex was only one factor of many: "The Plan . . . resembles the 'Harvard Plan' approvingly noted by Justice Powell in *Regents of the University of California v. Bakke,* . . . which considers race along with other criteria in determining admission to college." The Court also pointed out that "the Agency Plan requires women to compete with all other qualified applicants" and that Johnson "had no absolute entitlement to the road dispatcher position." Finally, the Court found that the goal of the plan to "attain" a balanced workforce was aspirational, not mandatory. For all of these reasons, the Court held that the plan did not violate the rights of male employees.

The Court concluded that "the Agency has sought to take a moderate, gradual approach to eliminating the imbalance in its work force, one which establishes realistic guidance for employment decisions, and which visits minimal intrusion on the legitimate expectations of other employees." The Court held that "the Agency appropriately took into account as one factor the sex of Diane Joyce in determining that she should be promoted to the road dispatcher position. . . . Such a plan is fully consistent with Title VII, for it embodies the contribution that voluntary employer action can make in eliminating the vestiges of discrimination in the workplace."

AFTERMATH

According to one commentator, employers have been unable to institute broad remedial affirmative action plans because of the focus on job skills and the difficulty of determining the existence of a manifest imbalance in job categories.

SIGNIFICANCE

This case established a two-part test for determining whether voluntary affirmative action programs are in compliance with Title VII of the 1964 Civil Rights Act. This case laid down the general rule that an employer need not suggest that it is guilty of past illegal discrimination in order to employ voluntary affirmative remedies.

The Johnson decision made it possible for public employers to institute affirmative action plans. Criticism of the decision or the lack of criticism depended on a person's view of affirmative action. In the end, Johnson retired early, and Joyce continued her work with the agency.

RELATED CASES

McDonnell Douglas Corp. v. Green, 411 U.S. 792 (1973)

Regents of University of California v. Bakke, 438 U.S. 265 (1978)

Steelworkers v. Weber, 443 U.S. 193 (1979)

Fullilove v. Klutznick, 448 U.S. 448 (1980)

Firefighters Local Union #1784 v. Stotts, 467 U.S. 561 (1984)

Wygant v. Jackson Board of Education, 476 U.S. 267 (1986)

Local #28 of the Sheet Metal Workers International v. Equal Employment Opportunity Commission, 478 U.S. 421 (1986)

Firefighters v. Cleveland, 478 U.S. 501 (1986)

RECOMMENDED READING

Bork, Robert H. *The Tempting of America: The Political Seduction of the Law.* New York: Free Press, 1990.

David D. Meyer, *Finding a "Manifest Imbalance": The Case for a Unified Statistical Test for Voluntary Affirmative Action under Title VII,* 87 Michigan Law Review 1986 (1989).

Urofsky, Melvin I. *Affirmative Action on Trial: Sex Discrimination in* Johnson v. Santa Clara. Lawrence: University Press of Kansas, 1997.

Case Title: *Turner v. Safley*

Legal Citation: 482 U.S. 78

Year of Decision: 1987

KEY ISSUES

Are prison regulations prohibiting inmates to write to inmates at other institutions and to marry without the prison superintendent's permission constitutional?

HISTORY OF THE CASE

Leonard Safley was an inmate in the Missouri Division of Corrections. The case at hand stems from his attempts to write to and marry his girlfriend, who was an inmate at a different facility with the Missouri Division of Corrections. There was a policy prohibiting unrelated inmates in different institutions to write to each other unless it was deemed to be in the best interests of the inmates to communicate, as was almost never found to be the case. A second policy required that inmates receive the prison superintendent's permission to marry; it was generally only given when there was a pregnancy or child. Safley challenged the constitutionality of these policies, and all Missouri Division of Corrections inmates were later certified as a class.

The district court found the policies to be unconstitutional, a decision that was affirmed by the Eighth Circuit Court of Appeals. As the rights at issue were considered basic, fundamental rights, both the district court and court of appeals used strict scrutiny as the standard of review.

SUMMARY OF ARGUMENTS

The Missouri Division of Corrections argued that the lower courts had applied the wrong standard of review in deciding the case. Rather than strict scrutiny, the standard of review should have been whether the policies had a rational relationship to legitimate penological goals. They contended that under this standard of review, the policies should be upheld, as communication between inmates and inmate marriage threaten to disrupt the security of the institutions.

Safley argued that the standard of review used by the lower courts was correct, as previous Supreme Court decisions had been clear that prisoners do retain their constitutional rights. The policy on the correspondence between inmates should be deemed unconstitutional because it was applied without regard to whether the communications actually posed any security threat. The finding that the marriage policy was unconstitutional should be upheld because of a lack of actual security threat posed by allowing the marriages.

DECISION

The Supreme Court decided that the policy on communications between inmates at different facilities was constitutional, and the policy on inmate marriage was unconstitutional. At the outset, the Supreme Court held that the proper standard governing constitutional challenges to prison regulations is that "the regulation is valid if it is reasonably related to legitimate penological interests." The majority believed that this standard of review was appropriate because the courts are ill equipped to rule effectively on manners of security in prisons. The determinations of the prison administrators should be given the deference due to their experience in that area.

The Supreme Court was unanimous in its determination that the marriage policy was unconstitutional. The right to marry is a fundamental right that is only altered by the reality of prison life. Those realities do not include an absolute deprivation of the right to enter into a marriage. The regulation was overly broad and did not even alleviate the problem of love triangles leading to the violence that was suggested by the Division of Corrections.

The Supreme Court was divided on the question of whether the mail policy was constitu-

tional; however, a majority decided that it was. A policy of reviewing every communication between inmates to determine whether it posed a threat to security would be overly burdensome, and the Supreme Court found that the threat posed by communications between inmates was a real one.

The dissent found the mail policy at Renz, the institution where Safley was incarcerated, to be overly restrictive. Noting that the policy at Renz was harsher than that of the rest of the institutions in the Missouri Department of Corrections, the dissent desired a showing that the heightened policy used at Renz was necessary, as opposed to the generally stated policy of the Missouri Division of Corrections.

AFTERMATH

The Supreme Court adopted a standard of review in *Turner* that is the standard of review to be used in all challenges to prison regulations. This standard, often referred to as the rational basis standard, has been criticized by advocates of prisoners' rights as being overly deferential to prison officials in practice, as courts tend to err on the side of caution and deference.

SIGNIFICANCE

Turner marked the end of an era of expansion of prisoners' rights and a return to an approach that was more deferential to prison officials. With few exceptions, the standard identified in *Turner* has been used in determining prisoners' constitutional claims.

RELATED CASES

Pocunier v. Martinez, 416 U.S. 396 (1974)

Beard v. Banks, 548 U.S. 521 (2006)

RECOMMENDED READING

Fliter, John A. *Prisoners' Rights: The Supreme Court and Evolving Standards of Decency.* Westport, Conn.: Greenwood Press, 2001.

Cheryl Dunn Giles, Turner v. Safley *and Its Progeny: A Gradual Retreat to the "Hands-Off" Doctrine?,* 35 Arizona Law Review 219 (1993).

Trevor N. McFadden, *Note: When to Turn to Turner? The Supreme Court's Schizophrenic Prison Jurisprudence,* 22 Journal of Law and Politics 135 (2006).

Jennifer M. Wimsatt, *Rendering* Turner *Toothless: The Supreme Court's Decision in* Beard v. Banks, 57 Duke Law Journal 1209 (2008).

Case Title: *City of Richmond v. J. A. Croson Co.*

Legal Citation: 488 U.S. 469

Year of Decision: 1989

KEY ISSUE

Is setting aside a quota for contracts with minority-owned businesses by the city of Richmond an unconstitutional violation of equal protection?

HISTORY OF THE CASE

The city of Richmond's city council decided to set aside 30 percent of the construction contracts to be awarded to minority-owned businesses. The decision was made because, while half of the population of Richmond is black, less than 1 percent of contracts were awarded to businesses owned by minorities. A contract would only be awarded to another company if there were not any minority-owned businesses that were able or available to take the contract. Croson, as the sole bidder for such a contract, was awarded a contract subject to the requirement that he subcontract with a minority-owned business. When Croson failed to meet that requirement, the contract was opened up to another bidding process. Croson then filed a lawsuit against the City of Richmond.

The district court determined that there were no constitutional violations and found for the City of Richmond. The court of appeals agreed with the district court initially; however, the Supreme Court granted certiorari and sent the case back to the court of appeals to be decided in accordance with *Wygant v. Jackson Board of Education* (1986). On remand, the court of appeals found that the City of Richmond's method for awarding contracts was unconstitutional. The City of Richmond appealed this decision to the Supreme Court.

SUMMARY OF ARGUMENTS

The City of Richmond argued that the court of appeals erred in relying on the plurality opinion in *Wygant* that would have required the City of Richmond to have found discriminatory practices in its own awarding of contracts to justify a quota system. It was the discrimination within the construction industry that the City of Richmond was attempting to correct, as attempts to find discrimination on the part of the government would be difficult in light of the fact that historical discriminatory practices by the construction industry largely prevented minority bids on projects.

Croson argued that the court of appeals interpreted *Wygant* correctly. The city council merely assumed discriminatory practices without evidence of discrimination in awarding contracts. Further, Croson argued that the regulations were overly broad, as there was no specific problem that it attempted to remedy.

DECISION

The Supreme Court affirmed the decision of the court of appeals and held that the precedent in *Fullilove v. Klutznick* (1980), that Congress need not make any specific findings of discrimination in creating a set-aside program, was inapplicable to state and local legislative bodies. Congress's ability to act in that way is derived from the Fourteenth Amendment, which gives Congress powers to combat discrimination that are not given to state and local governments. However, that does not mean that the City of Richmond may not combat its own discrimination or remedy discrimination in which it found had become a passive participant.

The City of Richmond's rationale behind this program was that there was a history of discrimination. The Supreme Court held that past discrimination without a finding of such present discrimination was insufficient to support a set-aside program. Although the Supreme Court recognized that past discrimination had caused minority-owned businesses to be underrepresented, the majority decided that there was no way to attribute a specific number to such past barriers. Comparisons to the racial compositions of the general population were inappropriate in situations such as this, where special skills are required to do the job.

The dissent stated that more credit should have been given to the City of Richmond's findings, as the city was in the best position to assess whether there was discrimination occurring within their city. The evidence that the City of Richmond had should have been more than sufficient to show the need for a set-aside program. Further, government actions seeking to remedy discrimination should be held to a lower standard of scrutiny than in other race-based classifications. Applying a heightened level of scrutiny impedes the ability to remedy the effects of past discrimination at a local level, an undesirable result.

AFTERMATH

After this ruling, state and local governments could not be sure that their local affirmative action programs would withstand the application of this case, should they be challenged on equal protection grounds. As a result of this holding, the quality of the disparity studies used to show the need for affirmative action programs improved drastically. Additionally, more programs became race-neutral.

SIGNIFICANCE

The Supreme Court decided that all programs that use race as a criterion would be subject to strict scrutiny, the highest level of judicial scrutiny. Even measures that were taken to remedy discrimination would be subject to this review. Further, the decision created a need for better, more

reliable data on the discrimination the programs were supposed to be remedying.

RELATED CASES

Fullilove v. Klutznick, 448 U.S. 448 (1980)

Wygant v. Jackson Board of Education, 476 U.S. 267 (1986)

Adarand Constructors, Inc. v. Pena, 515 U.S. 200 (1995)

RECOMMENDED READING

Nina Farber, *Justifying Affirmative Action after* City of Richmond v. J. A. Croson: *The Court Needs a Standard for Proving Past Discrimination*, 56 Brooklyn Law Review 975 (1990).

George R. La Noue, *The Impact of Croson on Equal Protection Law and Policy*, 61 Albany Law Review 1 (1997).

Jill B. Scott, *Will the Supreme Court Continue to Put Aside Local Government Set-Asides as Unconstitutional?: The Search for an Answer in* City of Richmond v. J. A. Croson Co., 42 Baylor Law Review 197 (1990).

Case Title: *Metro Broadcasting, Inc. v. Federal Communications Commission v. Shurberg Broadcasting of Hartford, Inc.*

Alternate Case Title: *Metro Broadcasting v. FCC*

Legal Citation: 497 U.S. 547

Year of Decision: 1990

KEY ISSUE

Do the Federal Communication Commission's (FCC's) minority preference policies violate the equal protection element of the Fifth Amendment?

HISTORY OF THE CASE

Since the broadcasting industry began, the U.S. government has made efforts to promote participation of minority businesses in it. In 1934, Congress passed the Communications Act, which granted the FCC the authority to grant licenses to people involved in operating radio and television broadcast stations in the United States. The FCC has worked to encourage minorities to become involved in the broadcast industry, and in order to do this, it has created regulations that prohibit discrimination against minorities in employment. In May 1978, the FCC adopted its Statement of Policy on Minority Ownership of Broadcasting Facilities, which made it policy to take minority ownership and participation in management into consideration during comparative proceedings for new licenses. The FCC also developed its "distress sale" policy, which was a plan to increase the number of opportunities for minorities to obtain reassigned and transferred licenses.

From these regulations arose the consolidated cases at issue in this decision. Metro Broadcasting, Inc., ("Metro") challenged the FCC's policy of preferring minority business owners to others in comparative proceedings for new licenses. This occurred after Rainbow Broadcasting ("Rainbow") was granted a license over Metro because of its larger percentage of minority ownership. On appeal, the Court of Appeals of the District of Columbia affirmed the decision of the FCC. The U.S. Supreme Court granted certiorari. In the second case, Shurberg Broadcasting of Hartford, Inc., ("Shurberg") challenged the FCC's minority distress sale policy on equal protection grounds. This challenge was denied, and Shurberg appealed to the Court of Appeals of the District of Columbia. The court of appeals invalidated the FCC's distress sale policy, and the Court granted certiorari.

SUMMARY OF ARGUMENTS

Metro argued that the FCC's "minority preference" policy was in violation of the Fifth Amendment equal protection clause.

The FCC argued that there was a relationship between minority ownership and broadcasting diversity. According to them, existence of a diverse broadcasting industry would reduce the portrayal of racial and ethnic stereotypes.

DECISION

The Court held that the "minority preference" policy used by the FCC did not violate the Fifth Amendment. The Court reasoned that the policy had a legitimate purpose of achieving diversity in FCC program options and that providing diverse programming furthered the First Amendment promise of freedom of speech.

Writing for the majority, Justice Brennan delivered the opinion of the Court. In other cases decided by the Court, such as *Fullilove v. Klutznick* (1980), Congress had been granted some deference in its policies that were aimed at minority ownership programs, like the one at issue in this case. The FCC justified its minority ownership policy by aiming it toward programming diversity. The Court agreed that this interest was an important government objective and acknowledged that the scarcity of electromagnetic frequencies made it reasonable for the government to place restraints on licensees to promote diversity.

Next, the Court reviewed the minority ownership program under an intermediate level of scrutiny, which requires a substantial relationship to the achievement of the government's stated interests. The FCC demonstrated an empirical relationship between minority ownership and broadcasting diversity, which coincided with practices under the Communications Act of 1934. The evidence suggested that a diverse broadcasting industry would produce more diversity than a racially homogeneous one. This was because the selection of news coverage and editorial viewpoint would be influenced by the minority ownership and, therefore, was likely to decrease the amount of racial and ethnic stereotypes often seen when characters portrayed minorities. Congress also had a history of supporting policies such as this and required the FCC to maintain the program without alteration. The Court acknowledged and gave great weight to the consistent findings of the FCC and government, agreeing that the evidence was based on analysis, rather than assumptions. The Court went on to state, "While we are under no illusion that members of a particular minority group share some cohesive, collective viewpoint, we believe it a legitimate inference for Congress and the [FCC] to draw that as more minorities gain ownership and policymaking roles in the media, varying perspectives will be more fairly represented on the airwaves."

The Court went on to reason that Congress and the FCC both engaged in long studies and considered many alternatives before establishing their current policy. Prior to the creation of the current policy, efforts of creating broadcasting diversity without taking minority ownership into consideration had failed to create a sufficient level of diversity in programming. In the late 1960s, the FCC developed equal employment opportunity regulations and ascertainment rules that required broadcasters to accommodate the residents of the particular broadcasting community. Only after determining that this method was also insufficient did the FCC establish their current minority ownership policy and Congress give its approval. The Court also considered other factors, such as Congress's reassessment and reevaluation of finite appropriations acts prior to reenactment.

The Court found that the minority ownership policies also did not unduly burden nonminorities because applicants were not guaranteed that their application would be granted without first being subjected to public interest factors, which include minority ownership. Additionally, nonminorities have some control over whether a distress sale will occur because those sales only occur when there are no competing applicants. Thus, to prevent the distress sale, the nonminority needed only to apply in a timely manner. In concluding, the Court held that the "commission's minority ownership policies bear the imprimatur of long-standing congressional support and direction and are substantially related to the achievement of the important governmental objective of broadcast diversity." Accordingly, the judgment of the first of the consolidated cases, which involved Metro Broadcasting, Inc., was affirmed. The judgment of the court of appeals in the case involving Shurberg Broadcasting of Hartford, Inc., was reversed. Jus-

tice Stevens wrote a concurring opinion, stressing that racial preference should only be used in limited situations, such as to promote broadcasting diversity.

Justice O'Connor wrote a dissenting opinion, joined by Chief Justice Rehnquist and Justices Scalia and Kennedy, arguing that equal protection guarantees prohibit racial classifications except those in place for the purpose of remedying past racial discrimination. She argued that racial classifications are to be reviewed under strict scrutiny, which requires that the classifications must be necessary and narrowly tailored toward achieving a compelling interest. Instead of using this standard, argued the dissenters, the majority used a standard similar to the one used to evaluate "routine" legislation. Justice O'Connor stated that "the dangers of such classifications are clear. They endorse race-based reasoning and the conception of a Nation divided into racial blocs, thus contributing to an escalation of racial hostility and conflict." Justice O'Connor also believed that diversity of viewpoints in broadcasting did not remedy past racial discrimination, as recognized by modern equal protection doctrine as a justification for race-based classifications, and was not a compelling interest and not narrowly tailored to the legislative interest.

Justice Kennedy wrote a dissenting opinion as well, joined by Justice Scalia, arguing that the decision in this case was similar to the Court's decision in *Plessy v. Ferguson* (1896), in which racial classifications were upheld, provided accommodations were "separate but equal." That case was later overturned by *Brown v. Board of Education* (1954). Justice Kennedy stated that this decision would result in the government's having to choose which races to favor and when, and that the interest in broadcast diversity was too trivial a matter to allow racial classifications. He also stated that racial and ethnic minorities not on the FCC's list are excluded from the policy, which only hinders the government's stated objective. Justice Kennedy ended with the following statement:

Perhaps the Court can succeed in its assumed role of case-by-case arbiter of when it is desirable and benign for the Government to disfavor some citizens and favor others based on the color of their skin. Perhaps the tolerance and decency to which our people aspire will let the disfavored rise above hostility and the favored escape condescension. But history suggests much peril in this enterprise, and so the Constitution forbids us to undertake it. I regret that after a century of judicial opinions we interpret the Constitution to do no more than move us from "separate but equal" to "unequal but benign."

AFTERMATH

In 1995, the U.S. Supreme Court decided *Adarand Constructors v. Pena,* a case that involved a contractor that submitted the lowest bid for a particular part of a project funded by the Department of Transportation. However, the job was awarded to the Gonzales Construction Company, a minority business, because the primary contractor was able to receive additional compensation for hiring socially and economically disadvantaged individuals. The Supreme Court held that the presumption of disadvantage based on race alone and subsequent privileges based on that classification violated the equal protection component of the Fifth Amendment, which overruled *Metro Broadcasting, Inc. v. FCC.* The Court held that all racial classifications were to be reviewed under strict scrutiny, which entails that they must serve a compelling government interest and be narrowly tailored to furthering that interest. Accordingly, the Court in *Adarand* remanded the case to be reviewed by that standard.

Although it was only decided five years after *Metro,* by the time *Adarand* was decided, four new justices had been commissioned to the Supreme Court: Justice David H. Souter replaced Justice William J. Brennan in 1990, Justice Clarence Thomas replaced Justice Thurgood Marshall in 1991, Justice Ruth Bader Ginsburg replaced Justice Byron R. White in 1993, and Justice Stephen G. Breyer replaced Justice Harry A. Blackmun in 1994. Of these justices, each voted the same as his or her predecessor, with the exception of Justice Thomas. Thus, the four dissenting jus-

tices in *Metro,* with the addition of Justice Thomas, created the majority in *Adarand.*

SIGNIFICANCE

The Court ruled that programs in which racial minorities were presumed to be disadvantaged for purposes of federal agency contracts were not required to be reviewed under strict scrutiny. However, this decision was overruled by the Supreme Court's decision in *Adarand Constructors v. Pena* (1995).

RELATED CASES

Brown v. Board of Education of Topeka, Kansas, 347 U.S. 483 (1954)

Regents of the University of California v. Bakke, 438 U.S. 265 (1978)

Fullilove v. Klutznick, 448 U.S. 448 (1980)

Adarand Constructors v. Pena, 515 U.S. 200 (1995)

Gratz v. Bollinger, 539 U.S. 244 (2003)

Grutter v. Bollinger, 539 U.S. 306 (2003)

Parents Involved in Community Schools v. Seattle School District No. 1, 551 U.S. 701 (2007)

RECOMMENDED READING

Torres, Sasha, ed. *Living Color: Race and Television in the United States.* Durham, N.C.: Duke University Press, 1998.

Case Title: *Edmonson v. Leesville Concrete Co.*

Legal Citation: 500 U.S. 614

Year of Decision: 1991

KEY ISSUE

May a litigant in a civil lawsuit use a peremptory challenge to exclude jurors on the basis of race?

HISTORY OF THE CASE

Thaddeus Donald Edmonson was a construction worker who was injured on a job site in Fort Polk, Louisiana. He sued the Leesville Concrete Company for negligence in the U.S. District Court for the Western District of Louisiana, claiming that a Leesville employee was negligent in allowing a truck to roll backward and injure him. At the stage of the trial when the attorneys were selecting the jury, counsel for Leesville used two of its three allowed peremptory strikes to remove black persons from the prospective jury. Peremptory strikes can be used by a litigant to remove a person for inclusion in a jury and can be exercised without stating a reason why the particular juror is being eliminated from consideration. A peremptory strike is to be contrasted to striking a prospective juror "for cause," as when the juror might have a demonstrated bias (e.g., being related to a party in the case). In this case, three peremptory challenges were allowed to each party under 28 U.S.C. § 1870.

Edmonson, who was black, objected to the striking of the black jurors and asked that the district court require Leesville to articulate a race-neutral explanation for striking these two jurors. This request was based upon the Supreme Court decision in *Batson v. Kentucky,* a 1986 case that held that it was impermissible for a prosecutor to use peremptory strikes to eliminate black prospective jurors in the criminal trial of a black defendant. The district court denied Edmonson's request, reasoning that the *Batson* rule applied only in criminal cases and not in a civil personal injury action.

Edmonson's case proceeded with a jury of 11 white persons and one black person, who eventually rendered a verdict in his favor. However, although the jury found Edmonson's damages to be in the amount of $90,000, they apportioned 80 percent of the fault of the accident to Edmonson, thus reducing his verdict to $18,000.

Edmonson appealed to the U.S. Fifth Circuit Court of Appeals, which ultimately affirmed the decision of the district court and held that a private litigant in a civil case could exercise peremptory challenges without being held accountable for whether a strike was racially motivated. The

Fifth Circuit reasoned that the use of a peremptory challenge by a private litigant did not constitute "state action," which is a necessary threshold to implicate constitutional guarantees.

SUMMARY OF ARGUMENTS

Edmonson, the petitioner, argued that his constitutional right of equal protection was violated by Leesville's striking of potential jurors because of their race.

Leesville, the respondent, argued that no constitutional violation could be found because there was no "state action": That is, the Constitution constrains only actions of the government, and Leesville was a private party.

DECISION

The Court held that a "state action" had indeed occurred and that Edmonson's constitutional rights had been violated.

Justice Kennedy wrote the majority opinion for the Court. Kennedy began by summarizing previous cases that held racially motivated use of peremptory strikes by a government official, such as a prosecutor, was a clear violation of equal protection guarantees. But could the same action implicate the equal protection clause when a private party in a civil lawsuit used it? It is a basic principle that protections of constitutional law extend only as against actions of the state.

The issue of what constitutes "state action" is not always clear. Kennedy's opinion explored whether the actions of Leesville's attorney in this case could be said to involve sufficient "state action" so as to bring equal protection guarantees against racial discrimination to bear. Kennedy framed the inquiry as follows: "Although the conduct of private parties lies beyond the Constitution's scope in most instances, governmental authority may dominate an activity to such an extent that its participants must be deemed to act with the authority of the government and, as a result, be subject to constitutional restraints."

The decision then recognized that the determination of whether "state action" existed would have to be determined by the two-part test set forth in the Court's earlier decision in *Lugar v. Edmondson Oil Company* (1982). The *Lugar* test required two inquires: first, whether the claimed constitutional deprivation resulted from the exercise of a right or privilege having its source in state authority; and second, whether the private party charged with the deprivation could be described in fairness as a state actor.

The first part of the *Lugar* test was clearly met in this case. The exercise of peremptory strikes was something that could not take place outside a court of law, and peremptory challenges were specifically authorized by federal statute in this instance. The second part of the *Lugar* test required much more analysis.

The Court then laid out the tests traditionally applied in answering this second inquiry: first, the extent to which the actor relies on governmental assistance and benefits; second, whether the actor is performing a traditional governmental function; and third, whether the injury caused is aggravated in a unique way by the incidents of governmental authority. The Court found that when applying these tests to the facts in the *Edmonson* case, there was no question that "state action" had occurred, and thus the protections of the U.S. Constitution applied. The Court laid out in some detail the ways that it believed that the actions of counsel in choosing a jury satisfied each part of this three-part inquiry. Essentially, the Court focused on the plain fact that the entire jury selection process takes place under the control and direction of the trial court, which is an arm of the state.

Justices O'Connor, Scalia, and Rehnquist filed a dissenting opinion. They criticized the majority opinion for its willingness to find "state action" purely because the challenged conduct "occurs in the course of a trial." The dissent argued that Leesville's use of peremptory challenges could not be fairly attributed to the government, and so no "state action" existed. Therefore, no constitutional violation should be found.

AFTERMATH

The *Edmonson* case was a significant extension of the *Batson* case. The majority decision went to great lengths to find "state action" in the acts of Leesville's counsel. The next extension of the logic

of *Batson* occurred the following year in the case of *Georgia v. McCollum*, where the Court held that criminal defendants (and not just prosecutors) could not exercise peremptory strikes in a racially discriminatory manner.

SIGNIFICANCE

The Court established that race-based peremptory challenges in jury selection violated the Constitution.

RELATED CASES

Lugar v. Edmondson Oil Company, 457 U.S. 922 (1982)

Batson v. Kentucky, 476 U.S. 79 (1986)

Powers v. Ohio, 499 U.S. 400 (1991)

Georgia v. McCollum, 505 U.S. 42 (1992)

STATUTE AT ISSUE

28 U.S.C. § 1870

RECOMMENDED READING

Michael V. Hammond, *Peremptory Challenges: Edmonson v. Leesville Concrete Co. and the Batson Motion in Civil Litigation,* 43 South Carolina Law Review 617 (1992).

Mark L. Josephs, *Fourteenth Amendment: Peremptory Challenges and the Equal Protection Clause,* 82 Journal of Criminal Law & Criminology 1000 (1992).

Barbara D. Underwood, *Ending Race Discrimination in Jury Selection: Whose Right Is It Anyway?,* 92 Columbia Law Review 725 (1992).

Case Title: *Daubert v. Merrell Dow Pharmaceuticals, Inc.*

Legal Citation: 509 U.S. 579

Year of Decision: 1993

~

KEY ISSUE

What is the standard for admitting expert scientific testimony in federal trial court?

HISTORY OF THE CASE

The parents of Jason Daubert and Eric Schuller (collectively "Plaintiffs") brought suit in the names of their children against Merrell Dow Pharmaceuticals ("Merrell") that their mothers' ingestion of Bendectin, produced by the defendant, had caused their birth defects. Bendectin was a prescription antinausea medicine often used during women's pregnancy. The case was originally brought in California state court, but the defendant removed the suit to federal court on diversity grounds. Merrill moved for summary judgment with an affidavit from an expert who found that no studies had found Bendectin capable of causing malformations in fetuses. The plaintiffs opposed the motion, calling eight experts of their own, who found that Bendectin could cause birth defects. The district court granted the motion for summary judgment, holding that expert opinion not based on epidemiological evidence was not admissible to establish causation in this case and, thus, the plaintiffs could not raise a reasonably disputable jury issue regarding causation.

The U.S. Court of Appeals for the Ninth Circuit affirmed the decision of the lower court, ruling that expert opinion must be based on "generally accepted" techniques that are seen as reliable in the scientific community. The plaintiffs' experts had not based their decision on published material that had been subjected to peer review and, thus, was viewed as generally accepted. The U.S. Supreme Court granted certiorari due to divisions among the lower courts regarding the proper standard for the admission of expert testimony.

SUMMARY OF ARGUMENTS

The plaintiffs argued that the *Frye* test was superseded by the adoption of the Federal Rules of Evidence.

Merrell argued that the *Frye* test was not superseded and should still be followed by the courts.

DECISION

The Court vacated the judgment of the court of appeals because it had based its decision on the *Frye* test, which focused on the "general acceptance" of expert procedure and methodology in making their assessments. The Court held that Federal Rules of Evidence 702 had effectively replaced the *Frye* test with a standard that gave judges wide latitude to ensure that expert testimony both rests on a reliable foundation and is relevant to the issue before the court. In general, pertinent evidence that is based on scientifically valid principles will satisfy these requirements.

Justice Blackmun delivered the opinion of the Court. The Court began by pointing out that the *Frye* test was the traditional test used to determine the admissibility of novel scientific evidence at trial. The test essentially states that information from which expert testimony is deduced must be from scientific principles or discovery that have gained general acceptance in the particular field in which it belongs. The *Frye* test was still used until this case; however, it predated the Federal Rules of Evidence. The Court noted that neither Federal Rule of Evidence 402 nor Rule 702, which governs expert testimony, mentioned the *Frye* test. Defendants offered no evidence that the rules intended to incorporate the *Frye* standard into the federal rules. The Court held that the *Frye* test was incompatible with the Federal Rules of Evidence and ruled against its use in federal trials.

Under the Federal Rules of Evidence, the judge is still allowed to screen evidence and must also ensure that all scientific testimony or evidence admitted is reliable and relevant. The Court determined that the language of Rule 702 suggests that the standard of evidentiary reliability regarding experts was that their explanations must be based on "scientific knowledge." Rule 702 also takes relevance into account by allowing any evidence or testimony that will "assist the trier of fact to understand the evidence or to determine a fact in issue." The Court held that federal trial judges have the dual duty to determine "whether the reasoning or methodology underlying the testimony is scientifically valid and of whether that reasoning or methodology properly can be applied to the facts in issue." The Court was confident that federal judges would be able to undertake this review, taking into account many factors with each case.

In general, the Court viewed Rule 702 as a flexible one, focusing on scientific validity through relevance and reliance of proposed admissions. For relevance, judges should consider whether or not the scientific evidence ties in with the facts of the case. As for reliance, the Court stated that the "focus, of course, must be solely on principles and methodologies, not on the conclusions they generate." The Court pointed out that judges will have to consider many factors, with no single one being dispositive, and acknowledged that unconventional propositions are more likely to be challenged than well-established propositions. Judges should examine whether or not theories can be tested and whether the theory or technique has been subjected to peer review and publication. The rate of error in any given test is also an important consideration. The Court also noted other rules, such as Rules 702, 702, and 403, all available safeguards to reduce the likelihood of the misuse of expert testimony. Additionally, cross-examination, careful instruction on the burden of proof, and summary judgment are available safeguards.

Chief Justice Rehnquist filed an opinion concurring in part and dissenting in part, joined by Justice Stevens. The chief justice thought that the *Frye* test did not survive the enactment of the Federal Rules of Evidence and agreed with the majority on that issue. He asserted that the majority had created a difficult test that is unlikely to be applied with uniformity. Chief Justice Rehnquist also expressed his view that this holding would require federal judges to become "amateur scientists" to perform their role.

AFTERMATH

The Court in this case created the *Daubert* test, which is a two-part test for judges to use in determining the admissibility of scientific evidence. Under the test, trial judges must evaluate expert witnesses to determine whether their testimony is relevant (whether it ties in with the facts of the case) and whether it is reliable (derived from scientific method). The Court has since expressed that the standard in *Daubert* could be applied to technical evidence, in addition to scientific evidence, although it was deemed as unreliable under the particular facts of *Kumho Tire Co. v. Carmichael* (1998).

SIGNIFICANCE

This case changed the standard required for admitting expert testimony.

RELATED CASE

Frye v. United States, 293 F. 1013 (D.C. Cir. 1923)

STATUTE AT ISSUE

Federal Rules of Evidence, Rule 702: Testimony by Experts

RECOMMENDED READING

Scott Brewer, *Scientific Expert Testimony and Intellectual Due Process*, 107 Yale Law Journal 1535 (1998).

Faigman, David L. "Is Science Different for Lawyers?" *Science* 297 (2002): 339–340.

Johnson, Lynn R., Stephen N. Six, and Patrick A. Hamilton. "Deciphering Daubert." 33 *Trial* (1997).

Adina Schwartz, *Dogmas of Empiricism Revisited:* Daubert v. Merrell Dow Pharmaceuticals, Inc. *and the Need to Resurrect the Philosophical Insight of* Frye v. United States, 10 Harvard Journal of Law & Technology 149 (1996).

Soloman, Shana M., and Edward J. Hackett. "Setting Boundaries between Science and Law: Lessons from *Daubert v. Merrell Dow Pharmaceuticals, Inc.*" *Science, Technology & Human Values* 21, no. 2 (1996): 131–156.

Case Title: *Harris v. Forklift Systems, Inc.*

Alternate Case Title: The Abusive Work Environment Case

Legal Citation: 510 U.S. 17

Year of Decision: 1993

KEY ISSUES

To be legally actionable as "abusive (or hostile) work environment" harassment, must an employer's conduct seriously affect an employee's psychological well-being or lead the employee to suffer injury?

HISTORY OF THE CASE

Title VII of the Civil Rights Act of 1964 makes it "an unlawful employment practice for an employer . . . to discriminate against any individual with respect to his compensation, terms, conditions, or privileges of employment, because of such individual's race, color, religion, sex, or national origin." In the earlier case of *Meritor Savings Bank, FSB v. Vinson* (1986), the U.S. Supreme Court held that the Title VII language "is not limited to 'economic' or 'tangible' discrimination." But, in the aftermath of *Meritor,* the various federal courts of appeals had failed to agree on a definition of conduct that would constitute an abusive or hostile work environment.

Teresa Harris worked as a manager at Forklift Systems, Inc., an equipment rental company, where, throughout her time of employment, her supervisor insulted her because of her gender and often made her the target of unwanted sexual innuendo. After two years of such treatment, Harris quit and then sued Forklift, claiming that the employer's conduct had created an abusive work environment for her because of her gender. The trial court found this treatment to be close to an abusive environment but held that the work environment was not intimidating or abusive to Harris, in part because the employer's conduct was not so severe as to be expected to affect Harris's psychological well-being seriously.

SUMMARY OF ARGUMENTS

Harris argued that her employer's behavior offended her and would have offended any reasonable woman. The trial court erred, according to Harris, in considering whether she had suffered concrete psychological harm.

The employer argued that the trial court correctly applied the *Meritor* standard in concluding that the work environment was not intimidating or abusive to Harris.

DECISION

The Court unanimously held in favor of Harris that, to be actionable as abusive work environment harassment, conduct need not seriously affect an employees's psychological well-being or lead the employee to suffer injury. In her opinion for the Court, Justice O'Connor emphasized that whether an environment is hostile or abusive can be determined only by looking at all the circumstances. Factors to be considered may include the frequency of the discriminatory conduct; its severity; whether it is physically threatening or humiliating, or a mere offensive utterance; and whether it unreasonably interferes with an employee's work performance. The effect on the employee's psychological well-being is relevant to determining whether she actually found the environment abusive. But while psychological harm may be taken into account, neither psychological harm nor any other single factor is required.

AFTERMATH

In addressing a conflict among the lower courts, the Court in the *Harris* case attempted to clarify the standard by which abusiveness in the workplace would be determined. The complaining employee is now required to prove neither psychological harm nor injury resulting from the employer's offensive conduct. Rather, juries must look at all the circumstances to decide whether sex-related conduct engaged in (or permitted by) an employer is egregious enough to warrant an award of damages.

SIGNIFICANCE

The decision in *Harris* reflected the strength of Title VII and the extent to which its values had been woven into the fabric of society over a 30-year span. Even a relatively conservative Court had little difficulty in reaching the unanimous pro-plaintiff conclusion. Yet, in crafting a resolution, the Court failed to confront some other issues lurking in the sexual harassment context. Even though the objectionable conduct in *Harris* consisted mostly of speech, the Court did not address the interplay between Title VII and the First Amendment—why speech presumably protected by the First Amendment is nevertheless actionable under Title VII. Nor did the Court explain why the burden is on the victim of sexual harassment to prove that the offensive conduct is so pervasive and unreasonable as to constitute an abusive environment—why disparate treatment of male and female employees is not itself sufficient proof of a Title VII violation. Such issues are bound to arise in future cases as the Court responds to modern workplace relationships.

RELATED CASES

Mississippi University for Women v. Hogan, 458 U.S. 718 (1982)

Meritor Savings Bank, FSB v. Vinson, 477 U.S. (1986)

RECOMMENDED READING

Cynthia L. Estlund, *The Architecture of the First Amendment and the Case of Workplace Harassment,* 72 Notre Dame Law Review 1361 (1997).

Robert D. Lee, Jr., and Paul S. Greenlaw, *The Legal Evolution of Sexual Harassment,* 55 Public Administration Review 357 (July–August 1995).

Jeffrey M. Lipman and Hugh J. Cain, *Evolution in Hostile Environment Claims since* Harris v. Forklift Systems, Inc., 47 Drake Law Review 585 (1999).

Miranda Oshige, *What's Sex Got to Do with It?,* 47 Stanford Law Review 565 (1995).

Bettina Plevan, *Harris Won't End Harassment Questions,* National Law Journal 19 (December 6, 1993).

Case Title: *Shaw v. Reno*

Alternate Case Title: The Racial Gerrymandering Case

Legal Citation: 509 U.S. 630

Year of Decision: 1993

KEY ISSUE

Does an allegation of irregularly drawn boundary lines in a voting district reapportionment plan state an equal protection claim without proof of a discriminatory effect?

HISTORY OF THE CASE

Because of the results of the 1990 census, North Carolina was entitled to one more representative in the House of Representatives. Therefore, North Carolina had to create an additional voting district in the state. North Carolina created a reapportionment plan that included one district in which the majority of the voters were black. Under the Voting Rights Act of 1965, North Carolina had to have federal authorization to change its voting districts, so North Carolina submitted its reapportionment plan to the attorney general of the United States, Janet Reno, for approval. Reno objected to the reapportionment plan, finding that North Carolina could have created a second "majority black" district. Subsequently, North Carolina revised its reapportionment plan and created a second majority black district that had extremely irregularly shaped boundaries. As a result, five white North Carolina residents, including Shaw, filed a lawsuit against the state and federal officers, including Reno, alleging that the reapportionment plan constituted unconstitutional racial gerrymandering in violation of the Fourteenth Amendment.

The district court dismissed the suit against the federal officers, finding it lacked subject matter jurisdiction. The district court also dismissed the claim against the state for failure to state an equal protection claim upon which relief could be granted. The Supreme Court noted that it had probable jurisdiction and reviewed the claims.

SUMMARY OF ARGUMENTS

Shaw and the other North Carolina residents argued that the state had created an unconstitutional racial gerrymander that violated the equal protection clause of the Fourteenth Amendment. However, the residents did not argue that the plan unconstitutionally dilated white voting strength. Rather, the segregation of a majority of black voters into two districts violated the white residents' right to participate in a "color blind electoral process." The residents argued that the redistricting was so irregular on its face that it could only be viewed as racial segregation unjustified by a compelling state interest.

The state of North Carolina argued that it had a compelling interest in creating majority black districts to comply with the Voting Rights Act and that the plan advanced the state's compelling interest in eradicating the effects of past discrimination.

DECISION

Justice O'Connor wrote the opinion for the majority, which was joined by Chief Justice Rehnquist and Justices Scalia, Kennedy, and Thomas. Justice O'Connor indicated that the district court had properly dismissed the residents' claims against the federal officers, but she found that the residents had stated an equal protection claim upon which relief could be granted.

First, Justice O'Connor found that if a racial classification appears on the face of a statute, it is not necessary to question the legislative purpose of the statute. Second, if a statute does make a distinction based upon race, the statute must be narrowly tailored to further a compelling government interest. Justice O'Connor found this strict scrutiny standard to apply to statutes, such as the North Carolina reapportionment plan, that cannot be explained on grounds other than race and

that the difficulty of proof does not reduce the amount of scrutiny such statutes should receive as compared to other statutes that make racial classifications. Therefore, Justice O'Connor found that appearances are important when analyzing reapportionment. Moreover, Justice O'Connor found that it was more likely that elected officials would believe that their primary obligation was to represent only members of the majority group in the district rather than their whole constituency. Justice O'Connor also took issue with some of the dissenters, finding that neither did the Court's case law indicate that racial and political gerrymandering had to be subjected to the same level of judicial scrutiny nor was equal protection analysis dependent upon whether the racially segregated group was benefited or burdened by the statute.

Justice White dissented, joined by Justices Blackmun and Stevens. Justice White found the Court's decision in *United Jewish Organizations of Williamsburgh, Inc. v. Carey* (1977) to be controlling. That decision rejected a claim that the creation of majority-minority districts violated the Constitution because the Court found that the white majority's influence over the political process had not been affected. Therefore, Justice White held that the appropriate question was whether the residents had been unconstitutionally denied their chance effectively to influence the political process. To prove this denial of effective influence, a group must show a "strong indicia of lack of political power" and "denial of fair representation." Justice White concluded that the residents had not stated an equal protection claim upon which relief could be granted.

Justice Blackmun wrote a separate dissent, stating that consciously using race in a reapportionment plan was not a violation of the equal protection clause unless the effect of such use denied a group equal access to the political process or reduced the group's voting strength.

Justice Stevens also wrote a separate dissent, finding that it is not a violation of the equal protection clause to reapportion voting districts in a manner to facilitate the election of a minority group member. Justice Stevens thought the issue should be whether the purpose of the reapportionment was to enhance the majority's power at the expense of the minority group. If the reapportionment was to benefit the minority, no constitutional violation would exist.

Finally, Justice Souter dissented, finding that the majority's decision had created an entirely new cause of action subject to strict scrutiny. Justice Souter distinguished electoral districting from other governmental conduct, stating that electoral districting always involves the consideration of race, whereas other governmental conduct typically considers race at the expense of a member of another race. Further, Justice Souter found that the decision of the district in which a voter was placed did not deny a right of one voter to the benefit of another—both were still entitled to vote. Moreover, no constitutional violation exists when the candidate a voter supports loses the election. Therefore, Justice Souter held that to state a claim for equal protection relief, the purpose and effect of the reapportionment must be to reduce the effectiveness of a voter.

AFTERMATH

After the decision in *Shaw,* the case was returned to the district court. The district court upheld the reapportionment plan as constitutional under the *Shaw* standard. However, the decision was appealed again to the Supreme Court. In *Shaw v. Hunt* (1996), the Supreme Court found one of the majority black districts unconstitutional.

SIGNIFICANCE

Future reapportionment plans will be subject to the *Shaw* standard; however, the states will still be subject to the Voting Rights Act, as well. Compliance with both of these laws may prove to be difficult, if not impossible, as race must be a consideration under the Voting Rights Act, yet *Shaw* essentially precludes consideration of race as the only factor in reapportioning voting districts.

RELATED CASES

Guinn v. United States, 238 U.S. 347 (1915)

Gomillion v. Lightfoot, 364 U.S. 339 (1960)

Wright v. Rockefeller, 376 U.S. 52 (1964)

Reynolds v. Sims, 377 U.S. 533 (1964)

Whitcomb v. Chavis, 403 U.S. 124 (1971)

Washington v. Davis, 426 U.S. 229 (1976)

Arlington Heights v. Metropolitan Housing Development Corp., 429 U.S. 252 (1977)

United Jewish Organizations of Williamsburgh, Inc. v. Carey, 430 U.S. 144 (1977)

Mobile v Bolden, 446 U.S. 55 (1980)

Rogers v. Lodge, 458 U.S. 613 (1982)

Davis v. Bandemer, 478 U.S. 109 (1986)

RECOMMENDED READING

T. Alexander Aleinikoff and Samuel Issacharoff, *Race and Redistricting: Drawing Constitutional Lines after* Shaw v. Reno, 92 Michigan Law Review 588 (1993).

James F. Blumstein, *Racial Gerrymandering and Vote Dilution:* Shaw v. Reno *in Doctrinal Context,* 26 Rutgers Law Journal 517 (1994).

Richard H. Pildes, *The Supreme Court, Racial Politics and the Right to Vote:* Shaw v. Reno *and the Future of the Voting Rights Act,* 44 American Law Review 1 (1994).

Yarbrough, Tinsley E. *Race and Redistricting: The* Shaw-Cromartie *Cases.* Lawrence: University Press of Kansas, 2002.

Case Title: *Wisconsin v. Mitchell*

Legal Citation: 508 U.S. 476

Year of Decision: 1993

KEY ISSUE

Does Wisconsin's "penalty enhancing" statute violate First Amendment rights?

HISTORY OF THE CASE

In October 1989, a group of African-American males, after watching the film *Mississippi Burning* (and in particular a scene in which "a white man beat a young black boy who was praying"), went outside "to move on some white people." The group saw a 14-year-old white male and assaulted him so viciously that the boy "was rendered unconscious and remained in a coma for four days."

Todd Mitchell, the ringleader of this group, was convicted of aggravated battery in the Circuit Court of Kenosha County under a Wisconsin statute that increased Mitchell's sentence because Mitchell had "intentionally selected his victim because of the boy's race." After being sentenced to four years' imprisonment (two years for the battery and an additional two years because of the sentence enhancing statute), Mitchell appealed on the grounds that Wisconsin's penalty enhancement provision violated the First Amendment by punishing "offensive thought" and, in the alternative, because it was unconstitutionally overbroad. After the Wisconsin Court of Appeals rejected Mitchell's challenge, the Wisconsin Supreme Court reversed, finding that the statute violated the First Amendment's freedom of expression as it "[criminalized] bigoted thought with which it disagrees" and that the penalty enhancement statute was unconstitutionally overbroad because, in order to show that someone selected a victim on the basis of race, "the State would often have to introduce evidence of the defendant's prior speech." The state of Wisconsin appealed this decision, and the U.S. Supreme Court granted certiorari.

SUMMARY OF ARGUMENTS

Mitchell argued that the Wisconsin penalty enhancing statute violated the First Amendment for two reasons: first, because it was targeted at one's beliefs (it criminalized "bigoted" or "offensive" thoughts); and, second, because it was unconstitutionally overbroad. He claimed it was overbroad because, in order to prove that a defendant intentionally selected a victim on the basis of race, the court would have to introduce into evidence constitutionally protected speech that the defendant uttered at some point before the act of violence took place. Thus, Mitchell argued, the Wisconsin statute would have a "chilling" effect on constitutionally protected speech.

The state of Wisconsin, meanwhile, argued that the statute did not violate the First Amendment because it did not look at one's *beliefs* but rather one's "intentional selection of the victim" on the basis of race. At oral argument at the U.S. Supreme Court, the attorney general of Wisconsin stated:

> The Wisconsin penalty enhancement statute quite simply does not punish thought and it does not punish the expression of any idea or belief. It punishes criminal conduct. Mr. Mitchell was and is free to think any thought he wants to think. . . . But when he violates the Wisconsin criminal code he subjects himself to the punishment of the State of Wisconsin, and it is perfectly appropriate for the State of Wisconsin through its legislature . . . to consider his reason for committing the crime in determining what the appropriate sentence should be.

DECISION

The U.S. Supreme Court affirmed the decision of the Wisconsin Supreme Court and held that the penalty enhancing statute did not violate Mitchell's First Amendment rights.

Justice Rehnquist delivered the opinion of the Court. Regarding Mitchell's first argument—that the Wisconsin penalty enhancing statute violated the First Amendment's right to freedom of speech because it sanctioned "offensive thought"—Rehnquist concluded that while the First Amendment would prohibit a statute aimed at preventing a belief or viewpoint, the Wisconsin statute's consideration of the defendant's motive was similar to state and federal antidiscrimination laws that had already been upheld, and the state of Wisconsin's desire to combat the social harm done through crimes such as these "[provided] an adequate explanation for the provision." In other words, Wisconsin's desire to prevent the secondary effects caused by such "hate crimes" was significant enough that, according to Justice Rehnquist, it trumped Mitchell's freedom of speech claim.

The Court also dismissed Mitchell's "overbreadth" claim. Justice Rehnquist stated that the idea of a Wisconsin citizen's "suppressing his unpopular bigoted opinions for fear that if he later commits an offense covered by the statute, these opinions will be offered at trial to establish that he selected his victim on account of the victim's protected status" was outside the "realm of rationality." The Court reasserted that the Wisconsin statute did not sanction constitutionally protected speech; rather, it punished the *action* of selecting a victim on the basis of race.

AFTERMATH

In *R. A. V. v. City of St. Paul* (1992), the Supreme Court struck down an ordinance that was specifically targeted at expression (the statute, in this case banned burning of a cross or Nazi swastika on public or private property; the Court held that it was unconstitutionally content-based as it only proscribed messages concerning specific topics). However, in *Wisconsin v. Mitchell*—involving a statute that, on its surface, might seem as content-based as the one in *R. A. V.*—the Court distinguished "expressive speech" that promoted hate-based views (such as the burning of a cross) from hate-motivated conduct. In other words, even though the Wisconsin statute was arguably "content-based," it was not struck down, because the Court found that it was not a statute that attempted to regulate speech but rather the *action* of selecting a victim on the basis of race. In the wake of *Wisconsin v. Mitchell,* Congress passed the Violent Crime Control and Law Enforcement Act of 1994, which "[increased] the penalties for hate crimes committed on the basis of the actual or perceived race, color, religion, national origin, ethnicity, gender, disability, or sexual orientation of any person."

SIGNIFICANCE

This case defined the difference between First Amendment protected speech and criminal activity based on race, religion, or related biases. The Court determined that hate crimes can be considered more dangerous and, therefore, can also be punished more severely.

RELATED CASES

United States v. O'Brien, 391 U.S. 367 (1968)

National Association for the Advancement of Colored People v. Claiborne Hardware Co., 458 U.S. 886 (1982)

Barclay v. Florida, 463 U.S. 939 (1983)

R. A. V. v. City of St. Paul, 505 U.S. 377 (1992)

RECOMMENDED READING

Alison T. Fenton, *Constitutional Law—First Amendment—Overbreadth Doctrine—Hate Crimes—Penalty Enhancement,* 32 Duquesne Law Review 939 (1993).

Frederick M. Lawrence, *The Punishment of Hate,* 93 Michigan Law Review 320 (1994).

Case Title: *Missouri v. Jenkins*

Legal Citation: 515 U.S. 70

Year of Decision: 1995

KEY ISSUES

Did the federal court exceed its authority in desegregating Missouri's schools by ordering salary increases and remedial education programs?

HISTORY OF THE CASE

After a lawsuit brought on behalf of an African-American student, K. Jenkins, in Kansas City in 1977, the federal courts had mandated desegregation. As a part of the desegregation effort, the district court ordered Missouri to raise teachers' salaries and create education programs, particularly magnet schools. The expenditures necessary to comply with these orders would be borne by the state of Missouri. The reasoning behind these orders was that they would promote desegregation and help reduce population movement to the suburbs.

The Eighth Circuit, in hearing Missouri's challenge to this order, affirmed the order, finding that it was related to the goal of desegregating the schools.

SUMMARY OF ARGUMENTS

The state of Missouri argued that it is beyond the power of the district court to order the state to fund salary increases. Missouri further argued that the court of appeals erred in ordering them to continue funding the education programs, as scholastic achievement is not one of the criteria used to determine whether segregation still exists.

Jenkins argued that the continued funding of salaries and remedial education programs is a necessary part of the desegregation plan. The inability of the school district to pay adequate salaries and disparities in scholastic achievement are among the continuing effects of segregated schools. As such, courts may order the state to continue to fund salaries and remedial education programs in order to eliminate this lingering effect.

DECISION

The Supreme Court held that the district court had exceeded its authority in ordering continued funding of the salaries and remedial programs.

The Court looked at its decision in *Milliken v. Bradley* (1977) to determine the extent of that remedial authority. First, the remedy must be related to "the condition alleged to offend the Constitution." The remedy must be remedial. It must restore the victim. Finally, it must take into account the state and local interests.

Funding the salary in this situation would be exceeding that authority in that rather than addressing the segregation within the Kansas City Metropolitan School District (KCMSD), it was designed to attract better instructors from outside the school district. The authority of the district court is only to order remedies that are limited to that school district. The educational programs suffer from the same problem, in that they are designed to attract students from outside the school district.

The dissent rejected the notion that the issue of segregation could be confined to solely that school district. Students leaving the KCMSD for the suburbs would have exacerbated the problem of segregation within the KCMSD. As such, remedying the problems of segregation in one school district may reasonably require attracting those students back to the school district.

AFTERMATH

The Supreme Court's decision greatly limits the ability of courts to impose effective remedies for segregation on the states and school districts. By eliminating the possibilities of remedies that go beyond the segregated school district, the Supreme Court forced the lower courts to deal with the uncomfortable task of desegregating a school district that primarily comprised a single race of students.

SIGNIFICANCE

Although district courts still have what little authority remains to desegregate schools, this decision represents a shift in thinking about desegregation. Rather than being imposed by a federal court, the Supreme Court believes, state and local legislators may be in a better position to remedy the lingering effects of segregation.

RELATED CASES

Milliken v. Bradley, 418 U.S. 717 (1974) *(Milliken I)*

Milliken v. Bradley, 433 U.S. 267 (1977) *(Milliken II)*

Freeman v. Pitts, 503 U.S. 467 (1992)

RECOMMENDED READING

Derek M. Black, *The Uncertain Future of School Desegregation and the Importance of Goodwill, Good Sense, and a Misguided Decision,* 57 Catholic University Law Review 947 (2008).

Dunn, Joshua M. *Complex Justice: The Case of Missouri v. Jenkins.* Chapel Hill: University of North Carolina Press, 2008.

Christina J. Nielsen, Missouri v. Jenkins: *The Uncertain Future of School Desegregation,* 64 UMKC Law Review 613 (1996).

Carter M. Steward and S. Felicita, *Torres Limiting Federal Court Power to Impose School Desegregation Remedies,* 31 Harvard Civil Rights–Civil Liberties Law Review 241 (1996).

Case Title: *Bush v. Vera*

Legal Citation: 517 U.S. 952

Year of Decision: 1996

KEY ISSUES

Does a state redistricting plan motivated by race consciousness, incumbency protection, and compliance with the Voting Rights Act violate the equal protection clause of the Fourteenth Amendment?

HISTORY OF THE CASE

The results of the 1990 census indicated that Texas experienced a rise in population and was entitled to three additional congressional seats in the House of Representatives. Therefore, Texas adopted a redistricting plan that, among other things, created two new congressional districts and reconfigured a third. One of the new districts was a majority black district, another was a majority Hispanic district, and the reconfigured district was a majority black district. Six Texas voters filed a lawsuit alleging that 24 of the 30 congressional districts in the state constituted racial gerrymanders in violation of the Fourteenth Amendment. The district court found the two new congressional districts and the reconfigured district to be unconstitutional. The governor of Texas, George W. Bush, and others appealed the decision.

SUMMARY OF ARGUMENTS

George W. Bush and the other appellants argued that the strange shape of the districts was the result of efforts to protect incumbents and unite "communities of interest." Further, appellants contended that the districts were justified as the state's attempt to comply with the Voting Rights

Act, specifically section 2, which prohibits any electoral procedure that results in hindering a person's right to vote on account of race or color. Finally, appellants argued that the districts were justified by the state's interest in remedying past racial discrimination, conceding that the districts were created to enhance the opportunity for the election of minority representatives.

The appellees, Al Vera and other Texas voters, argued that the districts constituted racial gerrymanders that were not narrowly tailored to further a compelling state interest in violation of the Fourteenth Amendment.

DECISION

The Supreme Court found the districts at issue to be unconstitutional. The Court found that the districts were subject to strict scrutiny because race was a predominant factor in drawing district lines and the traditional districting principles were subordinated to the race factor. Further, the Court found that the districts were not narrowly tailored to serve a compelling state interest.

Justice O'Connor wrote the opinion for the Court, which was joined by Chief Justice Rehnquist and Justice Kennedy. Justice O'Connor first addressed whether the districts were subject to strict scrutiny. Justice O'Connor stated that strict scrutiny applied when redistricting on its face was so irregular that it could be viewed only as a segregation of the races for voting purposes or when race was the dominant factor in drawing the district lines. While Justice O'Connor acknowledged that Texas had mixed motives for the way the district lines were drawn, she found that race was the predominant factor as there was substantial direct evidence of Texas's racial motivations. Justice O'Connor found that the creation of majority-minority districts in and of itself was not objectionable but became objectionable when traditional districting principles were subordinated to race. If the traditional districting principles had outweighed race, then strict scrutiny would have been inapplicable. Justice O'Connor reviewed each district individually and determined that no reason existed to reverse the district court's findings.

Next, Justice O'Connor looked at whether the racial classifications had been narrowly tailored to further a compelling interest of the state. While Justice O'Connor indicated that compliance with the Voting Rights Act could be a compelling state interest, it could not be a compelling interest in this situation, as traditional principles of districting were subordinated to race substantially more than necessary. She also stated that a state interest in remedying past discrimination could be a compelling interest when the discrimination sought to be remedied was specific, identified discrimination and a strong evidentiary basis indicated remedial action was necessary. However, the racial classifications were not narrowly tailored in this case.

Justice O'Connor wrote a separate concurrence in an attempt to give guidance to states on the issue of simultaneous compliance with the Court's decisions in this case, the *Shaw* decisions, and the Voting Rights Act. Justice O'Connor clearly stated that the Voting Rights Act could coexist both in principle and in practice with *Shaw* and its progeny.

Justice Kennedy also concurred, reiterating that strict scrutiny should apply to this case and that the racial classifications were not narrowly tailored to further a compelling state interest. However, Justice Kennedy indicated that he did not want to extend these determinations in a general manner so as to require this result despite varying facts of future cases.

Justice Thomas was joined by Justice Scalia in a separate concurrence indicating his view that the application of strict scrutiny to the redistricting plan was not a close question. Justice Thomas also stated his disagreement with Justice O'Connor that strict scrutiny was not automatically applicable to the intentional creation of majority-minority districts. Rather, Justice Thomas found that strict scrutiny applies to all government classifications based on race with no exception.

Justice Stevens, joined by Justices Ginsberg and Breyer, dissented. Justice Stevens found that the Court erred in finding the districts unconstitutional, in applying strict scrutiny to all the districts at issue, and concluding that none met this standard. Further, Justice Stevens found that the Court had improperly focused on the role the race factor played in redistricting decisions. However, even if strict scrutiny were applicable, Justice Stevens would have found the districts constitutional as race was only considered to the extent necessary to comply with the Voting Rights Act. Justice Stevens would have classified this case as political rather than racial gerrymandering and cautioned that states would find it difficult to avoid litigation in future redistricting. Further, Justice Stevens stated that the Court has guaranteed it will have a hand in drawing voting district lines.

Finally, Justice Souter, joined by Justices Ginsburg and Breyer, also dissented. Justice Souter found that the Court had failed to describe the necessary elements for this new cause of action for racial gerrymanders; thus, potential litigants were not adequately on notice; nor did courts have standards to enforce the Court's decision. Justice Souter felt the Court had failed to distinguish adequately between lawful and unlawful uses of race in redistricting. Justice Souter pointed out what he considered to be the problems associated with this lack of standards, only to find that any effort by the Court to define the applicable standards created more questions and confusion.

AFTERMATH

Texas continued to have problems with its voting districts after the decision in *Bush v. Vera*. After the decision, the courts provided an interim districting map that was used for elections in 1998. After the 2000 census, Texas was entitled to two additional congressional seats; however, the legislature still did not enact a redistricting plan. Because of difficulty reaching a compromise on a districting map, Texas has continued to use court-drawn maps.

SIGNIFICANCE

The decision in *Bush v. Vera* confirmed that the Court was not going to back away from its decision in the *Shaw* cases to apply strict scrutiny to cases alleging racial gerrymandering and to find redistricting plans unconstitutional if race was a predominant consideration in drawing district lines. However, *Bush v. Vera* did provide some clarification as to how states might comply with *Shaw*'s standards and the Voting Rights Act. Unfortunately, questions remain as to how to avoid redistricting litigation and create a constitutional redistricting plan.

RELATED CASES

Gomillion v. Lightfoot, 364 U.S. 339 (1960)

Davis v. Bandemar, 478 U.S. 109 (1986)

Shaw v. Reno, 509 U.S. 630 (1993)

Miller v. Johnson, 515 U.S. 900 (1995)

Shaw v. Hunt, 517 U.S. 899 (1996)

RECOMMENDED READING

Burke, Christopher M. *The Appearance of Equality: Racial Gerrymandering, Redistricting, and the Supreme Court.* Westport, Conn.: Greenwood Press, 1999.

Charles Cameron, David Epstein, and Sharyn O'Halloran, *Do Majority-Minority Districts Maximize Black Representation in Congress?,* 90 American Political Science Review 794 (1996).

Kousser, J. Morgan. *Colorblind Justice: Minority Voting Rights and the Undoing of the Second Reconstruction.* Chapel Hill: University of North Carolina Press, 1999.

Peacock, Anthony A. *Affirmative Action and Representation:* Shaw v. Reno *and the Future of Voting Rights.* Durham, N.C.: Carolina Academic Press, 1997.

Richard C. Reuben, *Heading Back to the Thicket: Voting District Cases Pose Politically and Racially Charged Questions,* 82 ABA Journal 40 (1996).

Case Title: *Jaffee v. Redmond*

Legal Citation: 518 U.S. 1

Year of Decision: 1996

KEY ISSUE

Are statements a patient made to her therapist during counseling sessions protected from compelled disclosure in a federal action brought by the family of the deceased against the therapy patient?

HISTORY OF THE CASE

On June 27, 1991, Mary Lu Redmond, a police officer at the time for the Village of Hoffman Estates in Illinois, was the first officer to respond to a fight at an apartment complex. When she arrived on the scene, two girls informed Redmond that a stabbing had taken place in one of the buildings. As Redmond approached the building, several men ran out, one wielding a pipe. The men refused to lie on the ground, and Redmond pulled out her revolver. At this time, two other men ran out of the building, one chasing the other. Redmond claimed that one of the men was holding a butcher knife and refused to drop the weapon. Upon his refusal, Redmond shot the man, believing that he was about to stab the man he was chasing. The man's name was Ricky Allen, and he died at the scene. Redmond left the police department after these events took place.

The administrator of Ricky Allen's estate ("Petitioner") filed suit in federal district court, alleging that Redmond had used excessive force during the incident. During pretrial discovery, the Petitioner learned of Redmond's participation in numerous counseling sessions with a clinical social worker named Karen Beyer, who was licensed by the state of Illinois and was employed by the Village of Hoffman Estates at the time of the incident. The Petitioner sought the notes from the sessions in order to use them in the cross-examination of Redmond. The district court judge rejected Redmond's argument for keeping the records private; however, neither Redmond nor Beyer complied with the order to disclose the notes. The jury found in favor of the Petitioner, and the case was appealed to the Seventh Circuit Court of Appeals. The court of appeals reversed the decision and remanded the case for a new trial. Because of the lack of uniformity in the appeals courts regarding a psychotherapist-patient privilege, the U.S. Supreme Court granted certiorari.

SUMMARY OF ARGUMENTS

The Petitioner argued that privileges were left to the courts to decide and that the psychotherapist-patient privilege did not exist.

The respondent argued that the court erred by forcing disclosure of the social worker's notes, because they were privileged under the psychotherapist-patient privilege.

DECISION

The Court held that since the possibility of disclosure of information may impede the confidential relationship between therapist and patient, society has an interest in protecting conversations between these people. Thus, the Court ruled that Federal Rule of Evidence 501 protects conversations between psychotherapists and patients, establishing the "psychotherapist-patient privilege."

Writing for the majority, Justice Stevens delivered the opinion of the Court. Federal Rule of Evidence 501 provides, in relevant part, that federal courts have the authorization to define new privileges by interpreting "common law principles . . . in the light of reason and experience." The Senate Report for the Federal Rules of Evidence stated that the recognition of testimonial privileges should be decided on a case-by-case basis in order to further the development of these privileges. Traditionally, the general rule with evidence has been that all should be disclosed. However, exceptions have been allowed if a public good that outweighs the principle of utilizing all means of obtaining evidence is found.

Similarly to the attorney-client and marital privileges, the need for confidence and trust is the predominant reason for having a psychotherapist-patient privilege. The Court reasoned that confidence and trust are needed because, unlike treatment by a physician, which can primarily be done through a physical examination, treatment by a psychotherapist depends on the patient's willingness to disclose all relevant "facts, emotions, memories, and fears." However, patients are often reluctant to disclose sensitive information for reasons such as embarrassment or humility, and thus, "the mere possibility of disclosure may impede development of the confidential relationship necessary for successful treatment." For these reasons, the protection of confidential communications between patients and psychotherapists serves important private interests.

However, as the Court pointed out, asserted privileges must serve public interests as well. For example, the attorney-client privilege is said to promote the public interest of observing law and the administration of justice, and the spousal privilege furthers the public interest in marital harmony. The Court reasoned that the "psychotherapist privilege serves the public interest by facilitating the provision of appropriate treatment for individuals suffering the effects of a mental or emotional problem. The mental health of our citizenry, no less than its physical health, is a public good of transcendent importance." The Court also pointed out that entire communities may suffer if police officers do not receive adequate counseling after traumatic incidents because trained officers may prematurely leave the profession or officers in need of treatment may not receive it. The benefit of denying the privilege was deemed modest by the Court because conversations between psychotherapists and patients would be chilled and, thus, not spoken at all. The Court went on to note that all 50 states and the District of Columbia have some form of psychotherapist privilege, an indication that reason and experience support such a privilege. If the privilege were not allowed in federal courts, it "would frustrate the purposes of the state legislation that was enacted to foster these confidential communications." Additionally, a psychotherapist-patient privilege was one of nine recommended by the advisory committee when it proposed privilege rules.

Accordingly, the Court held that "confidential communications between a licensed psychotherapist and her patients in the course of diagnosis or treatment are protected from compelled disclosure under Rule 501 of the Federal Rules of Evidence." As with other testimonial privileges, the patient has the right to waive the protection. The Court went on to state that social workers, who provide a substantial amount of mental health treatment, are also included in this privilege. However, the Court disagreed with the court of appeals as to whether a balancing component should be utilized, arguing that it should not. The Court found that the balancing approach would create uncertainty whether particular discussions would be protected, which would defeat the purpose of the privilege. Thus, the judgment of the court of appeals was affirmed, and the conversations between Redmond and Beyer were protected from compelled disclosure.

Justice Scalia wrote a dissenting opinion, joined by Chief Justice Rehnquist in part, arguing that the majority's decision would result in injustices because reliable, probative evidence would be excluded. The victims of these injustices, he argued, are the state and the public. Because the Court's decision created the privilege, the decision "causes the courts of law not merely to let stand a wrong, but to become themselves the instruments of wrong." Regarding the fact that defendants can now tell their psychotherapists the truth and be privileged from admitting it at trial, he stated, "It seems to me entirely fair to say that if [the defendant] wishes the benefits of telling the truth [he or she] must also accept the adverse consequences." Additionally, he urged that the new rule ignored the truth and replaced it with an ill-defined rule. A decision regarding the adoption of a social worker—psychotherapist privilege, he thought, should be left to Congress.

AFTERMATH

This ruling not only created a privilege but took this decision away from the judges in individual cases. It created an absolute privilege blocking access to the content of conversations between psychotherapists and their patients.

SIGNIFICANCE

In this case, the Court established that Federal Rule of Evidence 501 encompasses a psychotherapist-patient privilege, which encompasses confidential conversations between social workers and their patients.

RELATED CASES

Funk v. United States, 290 U.S. 371 (1933)

Wolfe v. United States, 291 U.S. 7 (1934)

United States v. Bryan, 339 U.S. 323 (1950)

Trammel v. United States, 445 U.S. 40 (1980)

Upjohn Co. v. United States, 449 U.S. 383 (1981)

RECOMMENDED READING

Dale Colledge, Frank Zeigler, Craig Hemmens, and Carl Hodge, *What's Up Doc?* Jaffee v. Redmond *and the Psychotherapeutic Privilege in Criminal Justice,* 28 Journal of Criminal Justice 1 (2000).

"The Federal Psychotherapist-Patient Privilege: History, Documents, and Opinions." Available online URL: jaffee-redmond.org/. Accessed July 20, 2010.

Anne Bowen Poulin, *The Psychotherapist-Patient Privilege after* Jaffee v. Redmond: *Where Do We Go from Here?,* 76 Washington University Law Quarterly 1341 (1998).

Case Title: *Romer v. Evans*

Legal Citation: 517 U.S. 620

Year of Decision: 1996

KEY ISSUE

Does the Colorado State Constitution's amendment 2, which forbids the extension of official protections to citizens who suffer discrimination based on sexual orientation, violate the Fourteenth Amendment's equal protection clause?

HISTORY OF THE CASE

The enactment at issue in this case was an amendment to the Colorado State Constitution known as amendment 2. Amendment 2 repealed several municipal ordinances around the state of Colorado that had prohibited discrimination on the basis of sexual orientation. Additionally, the amendment prohibited all legislative, executive, and judicial action, at any level of state and local governments, that was designed to protect such a class. Soon after the passage of Amendment 2, this action was brought by several homosexual Colorado citizens, some of whom worked for the government, in the District Court for the City and County of Denver. The plaintiffs alleged that Amendment 2 would result in immediate and substantial risk of discrimination on the basis of sexual orientation. Although the governor of Colorado, Roy Romer, had opposed the adoption of Amendment 2, he was named as the defendant in his official capacity.

The district court temporarily enjoined Amendment 2, and an appeal was heard by the Supreme Court of Colorado, which sustained the injunction and remanded the case with the order that it be reviewed under strict scrutiny under the Fourteenth Amendment. On remand, the district court enjoined the enforcement of Amendment 2, which was later affirmed by the Colorado Supreme Court. On appeal, the U.S. Supreme Court granted certiorari.

SUMMARY OF ARGUMENTS

The state of Colorado's principle argument for the enactment of Amendment 2 was to "put gays and lesbians in the same position as all other persons. So, the State says, the measure does no more than deny homosexuals special rights."

DECISION

The Court held that Amendment 2 of the Colorado State Constitution violated the equal protection clause of the Fourteenth Amendment because it denied homosexual and bisexual persons the right to seek and receive certain legal protections from discrimination. Amendment 2 was deemed to have the purpose of harming a politically unpopular group, and thus it did not advance a legitimate government interest.

The Court rejected Colorado's argument that Amendment 2 was intended to conserve resources that were to be used to counter discrimination of "suspect classes" (race, religion, gender, etc.). Amendment 2 was deemed to do more than this by imposing a disability on persons discriminated against on the basis of sexual orientation alone, as opposed to its being aimed at a more general group. The Court reasoned that gays and lesbians' only remedies were to enlist "the citizenry of Colorado to amend the State Constitution or perhaps, on the State's view, by trying to pass helpful

laws of general applicability." The Court would not allow this because it resulted in persons' being excluded from many "transactions and endeavors that constitute ordinary civic life in a free society."

The Court used a rational basis approach to analyze Amendment 2 instead of a strict scrutiny approach, as had previously been ordered to be used on remand by the court of appeals. Typically under rational basis review, if a law neither burdens a fundamental right nor targets a suspect class, the Court will uphold the law provided that it bears a rational relation to some legitimate end. However, the Court determined that amendment 2 could not survive this constitutional inquiry. The amendment was deemed "at once too narrow and too broad." It was too narrow because it was aimed at one particular classification based on sexual orientation, and it was too broad because it denied this group "protection across the board." The Court determined that the Amendment lacked a rational relationship to a legitimate state interest because it was overly broad, leading the Court to believe that it was based on animus toward gays and lesbians.

In conclusion, the Court stated that it "is not within our constitutional tradition to enact laws of this sort. Central to the idea of the rule of law and to our own Constitution's guarantee of equal protection is the principle that government and each of its parts remain open on impartial terms to all who seek its assistance." Amendment 2 was determined by the Court to be "a status-based enactment divorced from any factual context from which we could discern a relationship to legitimate state interests; it is a classification of persons undertaken for its own sake, something the Equal Protection clause does not permit." The Court held that Amendment 2 was unconstitutional because it made homosexuals unequal to other citizens, and accordingly, the judgment of the Supreme Court of Colorado was affirmed.

Justice Scalia wrote a dissenting opinion, joined by Chief Justice Rehnquist and Justice Thomas. Justice Scalia thought that Amendment 2 was an attempt by Coloradans "to preserve traditional sexual mores against the efforts of a politically powerful minority to revise those mores through use of the laws." Justice Scalia argued that Amendment 2 maintained homosexuals' access to the political process; however, as the dissent acknowledged, it did make it more difficult to enact laws in their favor. The dissenters thought that the majority's decision raised the opposition to homosexuality to the level of being as reprehensible as racial and religious biases. Additionally, they argued that since the Constitution did not mention anything about this topic, it should be left to be resolved through democratic means, such as through the ratification of a state constitution at issue here. The Supreme Court, the dissent reasoned, has no business imposing on the states their view that animosity toward homosexuals is evil and that the Court should not take part in a "culture war."

AFTERMATH

This case was considered a major victory for sexual rights advocates. However, it seemed to stand in tension with a prior Supreme Court opinion, *Bowers v. Hardwick* (1986), in which the Court upheld a Georgia sodomy law that criminalized private oral and anal sex between consenting adults. Seventeen years later, the Court heard the case of *Lawrence v. Texas* (2003), holding that a Texas statute forbidding two persons of the same sex to engage in sexual conduct was unconstitutional, overruling *Bowers.* In *Lawrence,* the Court held that the Texas statute violated the defendant's liberty rights under the due process clause of the Fourteenth Amendment.

SIGNIFICANCE

Colorado's initial reasoning for the statute, to "put gays and lesbians in the same position as all other persons," led to the enactment of state statutory schemes to counter discrimination. Colorado's state and municipal laws were examples of this, using a similar pattern to other states by enumerating persons or entities subject to a duty not to discriminate. However, this case demonstrates that discrimination based on sexual orientation is prohibited under the Fourteenth Amendment's equal protection clause. The Colorado constitutional amendment prohibiting city, town, and county legislatures from taking action

to prevent discrimination on the basis of sexual orientation clearly discriminated against homosexual and bisexual people by diminishing the remedies available to them.

RELATED CASES

Civil Rights Cases, 109 U.S. 3 (1883)

Plessy v. Ferguson, 163 U.S. 537 (1896)

Louisville Gas & Electric Company v. Coleman, 277 U.S. 32 (1928)

Department of Agriculture v. Moreno, 413 U.S. 528 (1973)

Bowers v. Hardwick, 478 U.S. 186 (1986)

Kadrmas v. Dickinson Public Schools, 487 U.S. 450 (1988)

Hurley v. Irish-American Gay, Lesbian and Bisexual Group of Boston, Inc., 515 U.S. 557 (1995)

Lawrence v. Texas, 539 U.S. 558 (2003)

RECOMMENDED READING

Marouf Hasian, Jr., and Trevor Parry-Giles, *"A Stranger to Its Laws": Freedom, Civil Rights, and the Legal Ambiguity of* Romer v. Evans, 34 Argumentation and Advocacy 27 (1997).

Murdoch, Joyce, and Deb Price. *The Constitution Neither Knows nor Tolerates Classes among Citizens: Courting Justice: Gay Men and Lesbians v. the Supreme Court.* New York: Basic Books, 2001.

Case Title: *United States v. Virginia*

Legal Citation: 518 U.S. 515

Year of Decision: 1996

KEY ISSUE

Did the Virginia Military Institute's all-male admissions policy violate the equal protection clause of the Fourteenth Amendment, in light of Virginia's creation of a comparable women-only academy?

HISTORY OF THE CASE

The Virginia Military Institute ("VMI") was founded in 1839 as one of the nation's first military colleges, and prior to this Court's decision, it was the sole single-gender school among Virginia's 15 public institutions of higher learning. VMI is a state-funded male school with an enrollment of about 1,300 cadets. The school's mission is to produce "citizen-soldiers" prepared for military service. VMI uses an "adversative method" of teaching, to develop physical and mental discipline among its cadets. To do this, rigorous physical training is required, privacy is denied, and values found desirable by the school are indoctrinated into the cadets. Upon acceptance, cadets are placed on the "rat line," which is comparable to U.S. Marine Corps boot camp, and is designed to establish bonding among cadets and, eventually, their superiors, for seven months.

In 1990, the United States sued the Commonwealth of Virginia and VMI after a female student who had been denied admission filed a complaint with the attorney general. The complaint alleged that VMI's all-male admission policy violated the equal protection clause of the Fourteenth Amendment. The district court, using an "exceedingly persuasive justification" standard, ruled in favor of VMI, finding that VMI enhanced the level of diversity because the Virginia school system was otherwise coeducational. The Court of Appeals for the Fourth Circuit reversed the judgment of the district court, and in May 1993, the U.S. Supreme Court denied certiorari.

Upon the ruling of the Fourth Circuit, VMI proposed a parallel program for women, known as Virginia Women's Institute for Leadership ("VWIL"). The school was to be located at Mary Baldwin College, which is a private liberal arts school for women and would enroll 25–30 students. According to the proposal, VWIL would adopt the same mission as VMI, to produce "citizen-soldiers"; however, it differed from VMI in academics, teaching methods, and financial resources. The district court approved the VWIL proposal, and the court of appeals affirmed, denying rehearing en banc. Upon appeal, the Supreme Court granted certiorari.

SUMMARY OF ARGUMENTS

The state of Virginia claimed that single-sex education contributed to the diversity of educational choices in the state. Virginia also argued that VMI's adversative approach would have to be significantly modified in order to admit women, resulting in drastic changes for the school.

DECISION

The Court held that Virginia Military Institute's policy of admitting only male cadets was unconstitutional. Using a standard of heightened scrutiny, the Court reasoned that the gender-based policy violated the equal protection clause of the Fourteenth Amendment because it failed to demonstrate an "exceedingly persuasive justification" for its admissions policy. The program was not aimed at educational diversity, and Virginia Women's Institute for Leadership, VMI's women-only counterpart, was not comparable to the male program.

Justice Ginsburg delivered the opinion of the Court. Justice Clarence Thomas recused himself from the opinion, presumably because his son was a recent graduate of VMI.

The Court began by stating the precedent that parties seeking to defend gender-based government action have the burden of showing an "exceedingly persuasive justification" for the action, which is a form of "heightened scrutiny." Under this analysis, the Commonwealth of Virginia must show that the policy serves "important governmental objectives," and the discriminatory policy is "substantially related to the achievement of those objectives." The Court stated that the "justification must be genuine, not hypothesized or invented post hoc in response to litigation. And it must not rely on overbroad generalizations about the different talents, capacities, preferences of males and females." This level of scrutiny is derived from the history of sex discrimination in the United States, and the Court has consistently ruled that principles of equal protection are violated when a law or public policy denies women equal opportunities simply because they are women.

Using this analysis, the Court evaluated the VMI program and its counterpart, VWIL. The commonwealth claimed that single-sex education contributed to the diversity of educational choices in the state. However, the Court reasoned that Virginia failed to demonstrate that this was a purpose for establishing or maintaining the school, stating that "'benign' justifications proffered in defense of categorical exclusions will not be accepted automatically; a tenable justification must describe actual state purposes, not rationalizations for action in fact differently grounded." The Court held that Virginia's plan to offer a unique, male-only education did not pass the "exceedingly persuasive justification" test because, as the Court noted, "however 'liberally' this plan serves the Commonwealth's sons, it makes no provision whatever for her daughters. That is not equal protection."

Virginia also argued that VMI's adversative approach would have to be significantly modified in order to admit women, resulting in drastic changes for the school. The Court reasoned that neither the goal of producing citizens-soldiers nor the program at VMI was inherently unsuitable for women. The Court followed its precedent in *Mississippi Univ. for Women* and *J. E. B.*, which required that state actors not exclude otherwise qualified individuals on the basis of "fixed notions" regarding the abilities of male and females. The fact that women had already proven to be successful in federal military academies was also a factor in the Court's decision to conclude that Virginia had not adequately justified its gender-based classification program.

Next, the Court addressed whether VMI's comparable female program, VWIL, was a sufficient remedial plan. The Court first noted that remedial decrees must closely fit the constitutional violation in order to place the persons being discriminated against in the position they would have occupied but for the discrimination. To remedy the situation properly, the plan must remedy past discriminatory effects as much as possible and prohibit the discrimination in the future. Looking at the VWIL program, the Court found

that it did not offer women an experience comparable to VMI's famous program. VWIL's program was to use a "cooperative method" of learning, as opposed to VMI's adversative approach. Unlike at VMI, students at VWIL were free to leave campus, did not wear uniforms, and did not have to eat meals together. Other differences included the course offerings, student body, faculty, facilities, alumni networking, financial resources, and prestige of VMI's 157-year history. Since many of the features that make VMI unique were not offered at VWIL, the Court concluded, "kept away from the pressures, hazards, and psychological bonding characteristic of VMI's adversative training, VWIL students will not know the 'feeling of tremendous accomplishment' commonly experienced by VMI's successful cadets." Accordingly, the Court held that VWIL did not offer women an equal opportunity to that experienced at VMI and that VMI could not deny women entrance into its school. The final judgment of the court of appeals was reversed, and the case was remanded.

Chief Justice Rehnquist wrote a concurring opinion; however, he disagreed with the Court's analysis. Instead of the majority's "exceedingly persuasive justification" test, the chief justice preferred the test offered in *Craig v. Boren* (1976), that "to withstand constitutional challenge, . . . classifications by gender must serve important governmental objectives and must be substantially related to achievement of those objectives." He believed the test from *Craig* was already firmly established, and the majority's analysis created uncertainty by using language that was not precise. Chief Justice Rehnquist also stressed his opinion that if "Virginia made a genuine effort to devote comparable public resources to a facility for women, and followed through on such a plan, it might well have avoided an equal protection violation."

Justice Scalia wrote a dissenting opinion, arguing that the majority's decision "drastically revise[d] our established standards for reviewing sex-based classifications." In his opinion, the majority's analysis seemed to apply strict scrutiny, while gender-based classifications had traditionally been evaluated under an intermediate standard of review. Justice Scalia also argued that the

Court's decision ignored the long-standing history of state and federal support for men's military colleges. He stated, "The tradition of having government-funded military schools for men is as well rooted in the traditions of this country as the tradition of sending only men into military combat," and "the assertion that either tradition has been unconstitutional through the centuries is not law, but politics smuggled into law."

AFTERMATH

As a direct result of this decision, on September 22, 1996, a divided Board of Visitors of the Virginia Military Institute voted to admit women to the school beginning with the 1997 school term by a vote of 9-8. This ended 157 years as an all-male academy and effectively rejected a proposal to forgo state funding and become a private institution. VMI was the nation's last all-male military school.

SIGNIFICANCE

The Court's decision finding VMI's male-only admission policy unconstitutional meant that similar public policies and laws, those that refuse women an equal opportunity to participate solely because they are women, were also likely to be found unconstitutional.

RELATED CASES

Reed v. Reed, 404 U.S. 71 (1971)

Frontiero v. Richardson, 411 U.S. 677 (1973)

Craig v. Boren, 429 U.S. 190 (1976)

Mississippi University for Women v. Hogan, 458 U.S. 718 (1982)

RECOMMENDED READING

David K. Bowsher, *Cracking the Code of* United States v. Virginia, 48 Duke Law Journal 2 (1998).

Catherine A. O'Neill, *Single-Sex Education after* United States v. Virginia, 23 Journal of College and University Law 489 (1997).

Heather L. Stobaugh, *The Aftermath of* United States v. Virginia: *Why Five Justices Are Pulling in the Reins on the "Exceedingly Persuasive Justification,"* 55 SMU Law Review 1755 (2002).

Case Title: *Abrams v. Johnson*

Legal Citation: 521 U.S. 74

Year of Decision: 1997

KEY ISSUE

Does the district court's redistributing plan violate the 1965 Voting Rights Act or Article I of the Constitution, guaranteeing "one person, one vote"?

HISTORY OF THE CASE

In 1990, Georgia had a population increase, which allowed the state to increase from 10 congressional seats to 11. A special session of the legislature occurred in August 1991, to determine the redistricting. Georgia is a jurisdiction that is covered by the Voting Rights Act, and section 5 of that act requires the state to obtain preclearance by the attorney general or approval by the U.S. District Court for the District of Columbia for any change in a "standard practice, or procedure with respect to voting," since "the proposed change must not have the purpose or effect 'denying or abridging the right to vote on account of race or color.'" On October 1, 1991, the legislature submitted a plan to the attorney general for preclearance. This plan contained two majority-black districts, whereas Georgia previously had only one majority-black district. However, in January 1992, the Department of Justice refused preclearance of the plan. A second plan was also denied preclearance, it also had two majority-black districts. The General Assembly attempted to create three black-majority districts to gain preclearance.

On November 4, 1992, elections were held under the new plan. All three of the black-majority districts elected African-American candidates. In

1994, five Caucasian voters, from a majority-black district, filed suit in the U.S. District Court for the Southern District of Georgia, alleging racial gerrymandering in the 11th District, which was a violation of the equal protection clause. This district was described as "a monstrosity, stretching from Atlanta to Savannah." Therefore, the defendants were trying to show that the "bizarre" shape of the district could only be explained on the basis of race. The court of appeals held that by the shape and the racial demographics of the district, it was clear the district was designed to bring in the black population. The court also held that the General Assembly was driven by a "predominant, overriding desire" to create three black-majority districts for the satisfaction of the Department of Justice. The case was remanded, and the district court gave the Georgia legislature time to draw a new congressional map. From August 14 to September 12, 1995, the governor held a special assembly to determine the new districts; however, the legislature was deadlocked. On September 13, 1995, the district court was informed that the legislature could not resolve their differences and reach a conclusion. This left the district court to determine the districts in Georgia. However, the plan that the court made had only one black-majority district. The contention here is that there is not a second or third black-majority district in Georgia.

SUMMARY OF ARGUMENTS

Petitioners argued that the plan violated the holding in *Upham v. Seamon* (1982), because the district court did not take into account the legislative preference, and that the plan did not contain two majority-black districts. It was argued that the district court abused its equitable powers. The petitioners argued that the plan was a violation of section 5 of the Voting Rights Act. Finally, it was argued that the plan did not comply with "one person, one vote" under the Constitution.

Respondents argued that the district court's order was not clearly erroneous, and it properly exercised its equitable powers to create a remedy for racial discrimination. It was argued that section 2 of the Voting Rights Act does not require an additional minority district. In addition, it was argued that the district court's plan was not retrogressive and did not require another minority district under section 5 of the Voting Rights Act. Finally, the court's plan had a small population deviation, which was better than any of the other plans.

DECISION

The Supreme Court affirmed the district court and held that the plan adopted by the district court did not violate either the Voting Rights Act or the Constitution. Justice Kennedy delivered the opinion of the Court and explained that the district court did not err in disregarding the state's legislative policy choices and in considerably changing the previous plan. Kennedy explained that it would not have been possible to draw a second black-majority district without allowing the racial consideration to predominate in the design of the districts.

Kennedy also explained that the plaintiffs had to reach three thresholds in order to prove that the court-ordered plan violated section 2 of the Voting Rights Act: first, that "the minority group is sufficiently large and geographically compact to constitute a majority in a single-member district"; second, that "the minority group is politically cohesive"; and third, that "the majority votes sufficiently as a bloc to enable it . . . to defeat the minority's preferred candidate." The Court found that the population of African Americans was not "sufficiently compact for second majority-black district." The first element was not shown; therefore, the Court invalidated the argument. Kennedy also stated that the district court's plan did not violate the Constitution under the guarantee of "one person, one vote." He explained that the legislature was not designing districts to remedy "one person, one vote" but rather to keep in mind while designing the districts that "population equality" is a dominant objective. However, the district court's plan had a lower percentage of population deviation than any of the other plans; therefore, the plan was not a violation of the Constitution.

SIGNIFICANCE

The Supreme Court upheld the district court's plan that stressed that race could not be taken into account by a state legislature or court in creating election districts, even where race is used to promote minority representation.

RELATED CASES

Upham v. Seamon, 456 U.S. 37 (1982)

Thornburg v. Gingles, 478 U.S. 30 (1986)

Shaw v. Reno, 509 U.S. 630 (1993)

Miller v. Johnson, 515 U.S. 900 (1995)

RECOMMENDED READING

America Votes! A Guide to Modern Election Law and Voting Rights. Chicago: American Bar Association, 2008.

Commerce Clearing House: Federal Election Campaign Financing Guide. Chicago: Commerce Clearing House, 1976.

Graham, Gene S. *One Man, One Vote.* Boston: Little, Brown, 1972.

Hasen, Richard L. *The Supreme Court and Election Law: Judging Equality from* Baker v. Carr *to* Bush v. Gore. New York: New York University Press, 2003.

Law and Election Politics: The Rules of the Game. Boulder, Colo.: Lynne Rienner, 2005.

Pinaire, Brian. *The Constitution of Electoral Speech Law: The Supreme Court and Freedom of Expression in Campaigns and Elections.* Stanford, Calif.: Stanford Law Books, 2008.

Case Title: *Burlington Industries, Inc. v. Ellerth*

Alternate Case Title: The Employer Liability for Sexual Harassment Case

Legal Citation: 524 U.S. 742

Year of Decision: 1998

KEY ISSUES

Can an employer be liable for the sexual harassment of an employee when the employee suffers no adverse tangible job consequences and there is a lack of evidence indicating the employer is negligent or otherwise at fault?

HISTORY OF THE CASE

Title VII of the Civil Rights Act of 1964 makes it "an unlawful employment practice for an employer . . . to discriminate against any individual with respect to his compensation, terms, conditions, or privileges of employment, because of such individual's race, color, religion, sex, or national origin." Earlier cases held that the Title VII language "is not limited to 'economic' or 'tangible' discrimination" (*Meritor Savings Bank, FSB v. Vinson*, U.S. 57, 64 [1986]) and that abusive conduct may be actionable even if it does not seriously affect the employee's psychological well-being or lead the employee to suffer injury (*Harris v. Forklift Systems, Inc.*, 510 U.S. 17 [1993]). By 1994, when Ellerth brought her suit against Burlington Industries, the courts had developed no consistent standard for holding employers liable for abusive conduct of supervisors.

Kimberly Ellerth worked for more than one year as a salesperson in one of Burlington's divisions in Chicago. During her employment, Ellerth was subjected to constant sexual harassment by one of her supervisors but did not inform anyone in authority about the supervisor's offensive conduct, despite knowing that Burlington had a policy against sexual harassment. Some months after quitting her job, Ellerth sued, alleging that Burlington engaged in sexual harassment and forced her resignation, in violation of Title VII.

The trial court found the supervisor's behavior severe and pervasive enough to create a hostile work environment but found that Burlington neither knew nor should have known about the conduct. Accordingly, the trial court dismissed Ellerth's claim. On appeal, however, Ellerth succeeded in having her claim reinstated. The appellate judges wrote eight separate opinions, reflecting no consensus for a controlling rationale.

These judges were able to agree that the issue they confronted was vicarious liability—that is, whether Burlington has liability for the supervisor's misconduct, rather than liability limited to its own negligence—but they were unable to agree whether Burlington could be held responsible for the supervisor's actions even though Burlington was not negligent. The Supreme Court decided to hear the case to resolve whether an employer has vicarious liability when a supervisor creates a hostile work environment by making explicit threats based on sex to alter a subordinate's terms or conditions of employment but does not follow through on the threats.

SUMMARY OF ARGUMENTS

The Supreme Court stated the issue of real concern as vicarious liability. Thus, the parties argued principles of agency law, since Title VII defines the term *employer* to include "agents" of the employer. Ellerth argued that, under the common law of agency, Burlington should be held liable for harm caused by the misuse of supervisory authority. Burlington argued that its own lack of negligence or of knowledge of the supervisor's actions should shield Burlington from liability.

DECISION

The Supreme Court, in its decision favoring Ellerth, held that an employer is subject to vicarious liability to a victimized employee for a hostile environment created by a supervisor with authority over the employee. The effect on employers was somewhat softened in that the Court also crafted a defense for cases where a supervisor takes no tangible employment action such as denying a promotion or raise. In such cases, the employer can avoid liability if it can prove "(a) that the employer exercised reasonable care to prevent and correct promptly any sexually harassing behavior, and (b) that the plaintiff employee either unreasonably failed to take advantage of any preventive or corrective opportunities provided by the employer or to avoid harm otherwise."

This was not an easy case, as demonstrated by the complicated reasoning in the opinion writ-

ten by Justice Kennedy for the majority. Despite the opinion's detailed discussion of agency law, the outcome ultimately flowed from Title VII's strong policy stance against sexual harassment in the workplace.

The dissent, written by Justice Thomas and joined by Justice Scalia, argued that the majority took the policy too far. Justice Thomas objected that, under the rule stated by the majority, employer liability now would be judged by different standards depending upon whether a sexually or racially hostile work environment were alleged. The standard, according to Justice Thomas, should be the same in both instances: An employer should be liable if, and only if, the plaintiff proves that the employer was negligent in permitting the supervisor's conduct to occur. Because sexual harassment is a form of employment discrimination, Justice Thomas would restore parallel treatment of employer liability for racial and sexual harassment rather than holding employers to a higher standard of liability for a sexually hostile work environment. The dissent also argued that the defense for employers is poorly articulated by the majority and provides little guidance for how employers can actually avoid vicarious liability.

AFTERMATH

Kimberly Ellerth's suit had been dismissed at trial because Burlington, neither knowing nor having reason to know of the hostile work environment created by Ellerth's supervisor, was not legally negligent. In light of the Supreme Court's decision, plaintiffs in Ellerth's position now are able to proceed to trial, and the burden shifts to the employer to prove (a) reasonable care to prevent and correct promptly any sexually harassing behavior, and (b) the plaintiff employee failed to take advantage of the preventive or corrective opportunities or otherwise to avoid harm.

SIGNIFICANCE

Much as *Harris v. Forklift Systems, Inc.*, *Burlington Industries* demonstrates the vitality of Title VII in the workplace sexual harassment context. Even a relatively conservative Supreme Court continues to expand the scope of Title VII protection against sexually motivated harassment. It is too early to assess the degree to which the holding will further "Congress's intention to promote conciliation rather than litigation in the Title VII context." In the short run, in fact, there is likely to be more litigation to clarify the applicable legal rules broadly described by the Court.

RELATED CASES

Meritor Savings Bank, FSB v. Vinson, 477 U.S. 57 (1986)

Harris v. Forklift Systems, Inc., 510 U.S. 17 (1993)

Faragher v. City of Boca Raton, 524 U.S. 775 (1998)

RECOMMENDED READING

Elizabeth M. Brama, *The Changing Burden of Employer Liability for Workplace Discrimination,* 83 Minnesota Law Review 1481 (1999).

Misty L. Gill, *The Changed Face of Liability for Hostile Work Environment Sexual Harassment: The Supreme Court Imposes Strict Liability in* Faragher v. City of Boca Raton *and* Burlington Industries, Inc. v. Ellerth, 32 Creighton Law Review 1651 (1999).

Tara Kaesebier, *Employer Liability in Supervisor Sexual Harassment Cases: The Supreme Court Finally Speaks,* 31 Arizona State Law Journal 203 (1999).

Joy Sabino Mullane, *Employer Liability for Hostile Environment Sexual Harassment Created by Supervisors under Title VII: Toward a Clearer Standard?,* 51 Florida Law Review 559 (1999).

Case Title: *Oncale v. Sundowner Offshore Services, Inc.*

Legal Citation: 523 U.S. 75

Year of Decision: 1998

KEY ISSUE

Does same-sex workplace harassment violate the prohibition against employment discrimination "because of . . . sex" found in Title VII of the Civil Rights Act of 1964?

HISTORY OF THE CASE

Joseph Oncale was employed as an oil platform worker by Sundowner Offshore Services, Inc., which operated in the Gulf of Mexico. Oncale claimed that on several occasions, he was subjected to sex-related and humiliating actions by the rest of his work crew, with the knowledge and participation of his supervisors. He was also threatened with rape and sodomized with a bar of soap.

Oncale brought suit against his employer in the U.S. District Court for the Eastern District of Louisiana. He claimed that the harassment directed against him by his male coworkers constituted "discrimination . . . because of . . . sex," which is prohibited by Title VII of the Civil Rights Act of 1964, 42 U.S.C. § 2000e-2(a)(1). The district court granted summary judgment against Oncale, and the Fifth Circuit Court of Appeals affirmed the district court's ruling, holding that same-sex sexual harassment is not actionable under Title VII. Both the district court and the Fifth Circuit concluded that the earlier Fifth Circuit case of *Garcia v. Elf Atochem North America,* 28 F.3d 446 (5th Cir. 1994) was controlling precedent and necessitated a ruling against Oncale.

SUMMARY OF ARGUMENTS

Oncale argued that discrimination on the basis of sex was broader than the traditional assumption that such discrimination must be between members of the opposite sex in order to be actionable. He argued that Title VII prohibits conduct of an employer that communicates an individual's right to continued employment is contingent upon submission to unwelcome sexual advances. A person of either sex who perceives that he or she must abandon a job to escape sexual harassment is a victim of employment discrimination as defined by Title VII. The trier must decide the question of whether the defendants' conduct was sexually harassing in nature after having heard the evidence presented.

Sundowner argued that Oncale's position was contrary to the language and legislative purpose of Title VII, which they believed to be the protection of women from their traditional subordination in the workplace. Indeed, the clear majority of precedent in the federal courts held that same-sex harassment was not actionable under this law. Sundowner also argued that recognizing liability for same-sex harassment would transform Title VII into a general civility code for the American workplace.

Decision

The Supreme Court, in a decision authored by Justice Scalia, reversed the Fifth Circuit Court of Appeals and ruled that accusations of same-sex sexual harassment could be the basis of an employment discrimination claim under Title VII of the Civil Rights Act of 1964. The court began by recognizing that Title VII's prohibition of discrimination on the basis of sex protected both men and women. The court emphasized that in earlier rulings based on allegations of racial discrimination in the workplace, the court rejected any presumption that an employer would never impermissibly discriminate against a member of his or her own race.

The Court concluded that it saw no justification in the language of the statute, or in its earlier precedents, for a rule categorically rejecting same-sex harassment claims from the scope of Title VII. While same-sex harassment was acknowledged not to be the main evil that Congress intended to combat with the passage of Title VII, the Court stated that statutory prohibitions often go beyond the principal concerns of the legislators and could cover reasonably comparable evils as well.

The Court also was not convinced by the respondents' arguments that recognizing this claim for same-sex harassment would turn Title VII into a general civility code of the workplace. The Court said that this risk was no greater for

same-sex harassment than for opposite-sex harassment, and that careful attention to the language of the statute would prevent such a development. The Court emphasized that on remand to the courts below, Oncale would still have to prove that there was discrimination against him on the basis of sex, as the statute requires.

Aftermath

The difficulty in the later applications of the holding of Oncale has been in distinguishing those situations in which the same-sex harassment is seen to be based on the sexual orientation of the employee rather than sexual in nature (for example, when a homosexual employee is harassed by other male workers or supervisors because of his sexual orientation). Currently, there is no federal statute that prohibits employment discrimination on the basis of sexual orientation.

Significance

Oncale opened the courts to same-sex harassment cases under Title VII, holding that any sexually based discrimination is actionable, regardless of whether or not it is motivated by "sexual desire," when it creates unlawful working conditions.

Related Case

Meritor Savings Bank v. Vinson, 477 U.S. 57 (1986)

Statute at Issue

42 U.S.C. § 2000e-2; Title 42—The Public Health and Welfare, Chapter 21—Civil Rights, Subchapter VI—Equal Employment Opportunities, § 2000e-2. Unlawful employment practices

Recommended Reading

Jonathan David Bible, *Same-Sex Sexual Harassment: When Does a Harasser Act "Because of Sex"?*, 53 Labor Law Journal 3 (2002).

Charles R. Calleros, *Same-Sex Harassment, Textualism, Free Speech, and Oncale: Laying the Groundwork for a Coherent and Constitutional*

Theory of Sexual Harassment Liability, 7 George Mason Law Review 1 (1998).

Paul A. Davis, *What Is "Sex"? Heterosexual-Male-on-Heterosexual-Male Sexual Harassment Actions after* Oncale v. Sundowner Offshore Services, Inc., 71 Southern California Law Review 1341 (1998).

Dabney D. Ware and Bradly R. Johnson, Oncale v. Sundowner Offshore Services, Inc.: *Perverted Behavior Leads to a Perverse Ruling,* 51 Florida Law Review 489 (1999).

Case Title: *Davis v. Monroe County Board of Education*

Alternate Case Title: The Peer Sexual Harassment in Schools Case

Legal Citation: 526 U.S. 629

Year of Decision: 1999

KEY ISSUE

May the parents of a victim of "student-on-student" harassment successfully sue a school board under the provisions of Title IX of the Educational Amendments of 1972?

HISTORY OF THE CASE

Aurelia Davis filed suit against the county school board and school officials seeking damages for the sexual harassment of her daughter LaShonda by a fifth-grade classmate. Davis alleged that the school board's deliberate indifference to the persistent sexual advances created an intimidating and abusive school environment that deprived her daughter of educational benefits guaranteed under Title IX of the Educational Amendments of 1972 (Title IX). The lower federal courts dismissed Davis's suit, finding that student-on-student harassment provides no ground for a private cause of action under Title IX. Davis appealed to the Supreme Court.

SUMMARY OF ARGUMENTS

Davis argued that the plain language of Title IX compels the conclusion that the statute is intended to prevent recipients of federal funding from permitting this form of discrimination in their programs or activities. Because the statute has its focus on the benefited class of students rather than the perpetrator of the discrimination, argues Davis, the statute must work to protect students from the discriminatory misconduct of their peers.

The school board argued that Title IX only proscribes misconduct by grant recipients (schools), not third parties (students). Moreover, contended the school board, it would be contrary to the purpose of the legislation to impose liability on a funding recipient for the misconduct of third parties, over whom recipients exercise little control.

DECISION

The Supreme Court held that a private Title IX damages action may lie against a school board in cases of student-on-student harassment, but only where the school board is deliberately indifferent to the harassment of which it has actual knowledge. Additionally, the harassment must be so severe, pervasive, and objectively offensive as to deprive the victims of access to the educational opportunities or benefits provided by the school.

In her opinion for a narrow 5-4 majority, Justice O'Connor agreed with the school board that a recipient of federal funds is liable under Title IX only for its own misconduct, not for that of third parties. However, pointing to the prolonged pattern of sexual harassment documented in the case history, Justice O'Connor concluded that the school board should be held liable for its *own* decision to remain idle in the face of known student-on-student harassment in its schools.

AFTERMATH

The immediate result of the decision merely allowed Davis her day in court. Originally, the lower courts had dismissed her suit without trial. The predictions made by Justice Kennedy in his dissent that the decision would create a flood of litigation, cripple school disciplinary powers, bankrupt school districts, and further involve the federal government in matters better left to local control have not proven true.

SIGNIFICANCE

The decision in this case reflected the continuing strength of gender discrimination laws and the degree to which their values have been absorbed into American society. It helped to open the door to relief for victims of peer harassment by finding school districts to be liable in certain well-defined situations.

RELATED CASES

Pennhurst State School and Hospital v. Halderman, 451 U.S. 1 (1981)

Gebser v. Lago Vista Independent School Dist., 524 U.S. 274 (1998)

RECOMMENDED READING

Conn, Kathleen. *Bullying & Harassment: A Legal Guide for Educators.* Alexandria, Va.: PASCD, 2004.

Daniel G. McBride, *Guidance for Student Peer Sexual Harassment? Not!,* 50 Stanford Law Review 523 (1998).

Michael W. McClain, *New Standards for Peer Sexual Harassment in the Schools: Title IX Liability under* Davis v. Monroe County Board of Education, 28 Journal of Law and Education 611 (1999).

Joanna L. Routh, *The $100,000 Kiss: What Constitutes Peer Sexual Harassment for Schoolchildren under the* Davis v. Monroe County Board of Education *Holding?,* 28 Journal of Law and Education 619 (1999).

Case Title: *National Collegiate Athletic Association v. Smith*

Legal Citation: 525 U.S. 459

Year of Decision: 1999

KEY ISSUE

Does the National Collegiate Athletic Association's (NCAA's) acceptance of membership dues from institutions receiving federal funding put them under the scope of Title IX of the Education Amendments of 1972?

HISTORY OF THE CASE

Title IX of the Education Amendments of 1972 (Title IX) was established to ensure that "any education program or activity receiving Federal financial assistance" could not discriminate on the basis of sex.

The NCAA is an association with "approximately 1,200 members, including virtually all public and private universities and 4-year colleges conducting major athletic programs in the United States." The rules of the NCAA allow postbaccalaureate students to compete in athletics only at the institution(s) they previously attended as an undergraduate. If the student wishes to participate in athletics for another institution while attending graduate school, he/she must apply for a waiver.

Renee M. Smith, the complainant in this case, graduated from St. Bonaventure. She then enrolled in the postgraduate programs at Hofstra University (1994–95) and the University of Pittsburgh (1995–96). She applied to the NCAA for a waiver through these universities to play intercollegiate volleyball. Her waiver was denied both times, and she sued the NCAA under Title IX, alleging that more waivers are granted for men than women, thus constituting discrimination on the basis of sex.

Smith argued that because "the NCAA governs the federally funded intercollegiate athletics programs of its members, that these programs are educational, and that the NCAA benefited" financially "from its members' receipt of federal funds." The district court dismissed the suit, stating there was not a strong enough connection to bring the NCAA under the scope of Title IX. The district court denied Smith's attempt to amend her claim to add Hofstra and the University of Pittsburgh as defendants and to "allege that the

NCAA receives dues from members who receive federal funds."

The Court of Appeals for the Third Circuit reversed the district court and allowed Smith to amend the complaint. With this amendment, all Smith would need to do on remand was show that the NCAA received dues from members who receive federal funds, a fact that was not contested.

SUMMARY OF ARGUMENTS

In addition to the arguments raised by Smith in the lower courts, she argued two more at the Supreme Court level: first, that the NCAA receives federal funding through the National Youth Sports Program it operates; and, second, that the NCAA assumes control over a federally funded program and should, therefore, be subject to Title IX.

The NCAA alleged that the court of appeals's decision conflicted with *Department of Transportation v. Paralyzed Veterans of America* (1986), which held that airlines were not recipients of federal funds given to airports and thus not subject to § 504 of the Rehabilitation Act of 1973, prohibiting discrimination based on disability.

DECISION

The Supreme Court chose not to rule on the two additional arguments raised by Smith concerning the funding through the National Youth Sports Program and the NCAA's control over a federally funded program, since these issues were not raised in the lower courts. The Supreme Court ruled in favor of the NCAA stating that the court of appeals erred in its interpretation of *Department of Transportation v. Paralyzed Veterans of America,* finding that Title IX coverage is not triggered when an entity does not directly receive federal funding and simply benefits financially from funding given to others. There was no way to determine whether the money that members use to pay dues to the NCAA is the same money received from federal sources.

The judgment of the Court of Appeals for the Third Circuit was vacated, and the case sent back to the court of appeals for further proceedings.

AFTERMATH

Upon remand to the Court of Appeals for the Third Circuit, Smith renewed her two arguments brought before the Supreme Court. She argued that the NCAA receives federal funding through the National Youth Sports Program it operates; and, second, that the NCAA assumes control over a federally funded program and should, therefore, be subject to Title IX. The court of appeals found that the NCAA does not control the federally funded program. They also found that the NCAA was indirectly receiving federal funding through the National Youth Sports Program and remanded the case to the district court to find out the facts surrounding this situation.

SIGNIFICANCE

This case determined that although the NCAA receives dues from members that receive federal funding, this is not a strong enough connection to put the NCAA under the scope of Title IX.

RELATED CASES

Grove City College v. Bell, 465 U.S. 555 (1984)

Department of Transportation v. Paralyzed Veterans of America, 477 U.S. 597; 106 S. Ct. 2705 (1986)

RECOMMENDED READING

Melody Harris, *Hitting 'Em Where It Hurts: Using Title IX Litigation to Bring Gender Equity to Athletics,* 72 Denver University Law Review 57 (1994).

Thomas M. Rowland, *Level the Playing Field: The NCAA Should Be Subject to Title IX,* 7 Sports Law Journal 143 (2000).

Case Title: *Saenz v. Roe*

Legal Citation: 526 U.S. 489

Year of Decision: 1999

KEY ISSUES

Does a California statute providing fewer benefits to new state residents than to state residents of more than one year violate the privileges and immunities clause of the Constitution?

HISTORY OF THE CASE

In 1992, in an attempt to reduce the state welfare budget, California enacted a statute that limited the welfare benefits new residents would receive for the first year they were living within the state of California. The law limited welfare benefits of new residents to the amount they would have received in the state of their prior residency. The result was that new residents would receive less welfare benefits than the amount other California citizens received. On December 21, 1992, three California residents who were eligible for assistance filed an action claiming the statute was unconstitutional. The district court held that the statute placed "a penalty on the decision of new residents to migrate to the State and be treated on an equal basis with existing residents." The court of appeals affirmed. The Supreme Court granted certiorari. However, the case was vacated because the Health & Human Services' approval of the statute was invalidated by the Court of Appeals for the Ninth Circuit.

In 1996, Congress enacted the Personal Responsibility and Work Opportunity Reconciliation Act, also known as PRWORA. The new statute applied to all states, including California. It removed the need for HHS approval and authorized California's program limiting benefits for the first-year residents to the same amount the previous state allowed. On April 1, 1997, the two respondents, including Brenda Roe, filed this action. They claimed that the statute was unconstitutional and challenged the constitutionality of PRWORA's approval of the durational residency requirement. The district court issued a temporary restraining order and certified the case as a class action. The court of appeals affirmed the issuance of a preliminary injunction. The Supreme Court granted certiorari because of the importance of the case.

SUMMARY OF ARGUMENTS

Rita L. Saenz, the director of the California Department of Social Services, argued that the California statute was an adjustment to the benefit level a person received, and the court should not have analyzed it by using strict scrutiny. Saenz argued that even if there were an impact on travel, the impact was so small that strict scrutiny analysis should not be used. Finally, Saenz argued that this statute was saving the state of California $10.9 million a year.

Roe argued that citizens are free to choose which state they want to reside in, and the Constitution supports this view. In addition, the Constitution protects the rights of residents and requires that the states treat all residents in the same way no matter how long they have lived within the state. The California statute discriminated against residents on the basis of the time they have lived within the state. This also prevented poor people from moving to the state. Ultimately, the state of California was discriminating against new residents, and the state did not even give a proper reason for this discrimination.

DECISION

The Court held that the statute of California to pay new residents the amount of benefits their previous state of residence supplied for the first 12 months of residence within California was unconstitutional because it violated the citizenship clause of the Fourteenth Amendment.

Justice Stevens delivered the opinion of the Court, explaining that the Court had long held that citizens are free to travel throughout the United States, "uninhibited by statutes, rules or regulations which unreasonably burden or restrict this movement." The Court further held that "imposing a penalty on the exercise of the right to travel violated the Equal Protection Clause 'unless shown to be necessary to promote a compelling governmental interest.'" The Court explained that there were circumstances when discrimination was justified, such as requiring nonresidents to pay more for a fishing license or tuition at a state college. These special circumstances did not apply to the situation at hand, in which there was discrimination between residents and nonresidents that affected the nonresidents' exercise to move to another state and become a resident of that state. In addition, the circumstances definitely did not apply when the state argued that the discrimination statute was enacted to save the state money.

The Court finally discussed the importance of the citizenship clause of the Fourteenth Amendment by describing it: "That Clause does not provide for, and does not allow for, degrees of citizenship based on length of residence." Three elements of the right to travel were described: the right to enter a state and leave another, the right to be treated as a welcome visitor rather than a hostile stranger, and, for those who want to become permanent residents, the right to be treated equally to native-born citizens. The Court stated that the length of time a person lived within a state or which state that person was from had no effect on the person's need for assistance. Ultimately, the Court reasoned that citizens have a right to choose the state in which they want to reside; however, a state does not have the right to choose the citizens it wants to reside within it.

The Court finally discussed whether Congress could authorize the statute. Since it had been determined that the statute violated the Fourteenth Amendment, Congress could not authorize the statute. Congress did not have the power to authorize statutes that violate the Fourteenth Amendment.

AFTERMATH

Saenz has not been overruled and remains good law. People have the right to move throughout the states without being discriminated against because of their previous location.

SIGNIFICANCE

States cannot discriminate against new residents to save money. Although California may have a good welfare program, that is not a justification for denying the program to new residents. Citizens have the choice to travel throughout the country and decide which state they want to live in, without any discrimination. A state cannot choose which people reside within it.

RELATED CASES

Shapiro v. Thompson, 394 U.S. 618 (1969)

Zobel v. Williams, 457 U.S. 55 (1982)

RECOMMENDED READING

Nan S. Ellis and Cheryl M. Miller, *Welfare Waiting Periods: A Public Policy Analysis of* Saenz v. Roe, 11 Sanford Law & Policy Review 343 (Spring 2000).

Case Title: *Bush v. Gore*

Alternate Case Title: The Hanging Chad Case

Legal Citation: 531 U.S. 98

Year of Decision: 2000

KEY ISSUES

Is it unconstitutional for a state supreme court to create new standards for addressing presidential election conflicts and to order a manual recount of votes without providing a uniform standard for the procedure?

HISTORY OF THE CASE

During the 2000 presidential election between George W. Bush and Albert Gore, Jr., the state of Florida encountered difficulty with its election process. After the votes had been tabulated in the various counties of the state of Florida, Bush had received more votes, but his margin of victory was less than one-half of 1 percent. Because of the small margin of victory, the Florida election rules provided for an automatic machine recount. The result of the machine recount still indicated victory for Bush, but by an even smaller margin. Gore then sought manual recounts in several counties. Because of these recounts, the Florida Supreme Court extended the deadline by which the counties had to submit their election returns to the Florida secretary of state. The U.S. Supreme Court reviewed this decision and vacated it, but upon return of the case to the Florida Supreme Court, the extended deadline was reinstated.

Bush was declared the winner of Florida's 25 electoral votes. However, Gore filed a lawsuit contesting the certification of the election results. Upon appeal, the Florida Supreme Court ordered a manual recount of all undervotes, votes that when counted by the machines did not register a vote for president.

Bush and Richard Cheney filed an application in the U.S. Supreme Court seeking to have the Florida Supreme Court's order to recount stopped. The Supreme Court granted the application and granted review of the issues.

SUMMARY OF ARGUMENTS

George W. Bush and Richard Cheney argued that the Florida Supreme Court's decision to have a manual recount violated Article II of the U.S. Constitution and conflicted with 3 U.S.C. § 5. Bush also argued that the Florida Supreme Court's decision violated the equal protection clause and the due process clause.

Albert Gore, Jr., argued that Article II of the U.S. Constitution did not give the Supreme Court a basis to override the Florida Supreme Court's decision. Gore also argued that the Florida Supreme Court's decision was consistent with 3 U.S.C. § 5. Finally, Gore argued that the Fourteenth Amendment provided no basis for the Supreme Court to disregard Florida's statutory rules and proceedings for determining the outcome of the presidential election.

DECISION

The Court indicated that individual U.S. citizens do not have a "constitutional right to vote for electors for the President of the United States unless and until the state legislature chooses a statewide election" as the way in which it will appoint the electoral college members. Article II of the Constitution provides that the state legislatures will select how electors are appointed. The states have decided that the individual citizens

will vote for the electors, making the right to vote a fundamental right.

The Court found that the Florida Supreme Court had ordered the recount to determine the intent of the voters with respect to undervotes; however, the Court found the procedures used to perform the Florida Supreme Court–ordered recount were not uniform. For example, some counties counted a punch ballot where a chad, a piece of the ballot, was merely dimpled, whereas other counties required the chad to be separated from the ballot on several corners to be counted. Therefore, an unequal evaluation of the ballots occurred in violation of the equal protection clause. The Court also found that the manual recount in some counties was extended to overvotes, ballots that contained more than one vote for president, and the Florida Supreme Court's order did not specify who was to recount the ballots. The Court found the whole recount process to be inconsistent and unable to be conducted so as to comply with equal protection and due process standards without additional standards. The Court found that any recount able to meet the December 12 deadline for appointing electors to the electoral college would not be conducted in a constitutional manner; thus, the Court reversed the Florida Supreme Court's order to recount.

Chief Justice Rehnquist, joined by Justices Scalia and Thomas, wrote a concurrence finding additional grounds on which to reverse the judgment of the Florida Supreme Court. While in most cases, the Supreme Court defers to state court decisions on state law, in this case, a federal question existed. The Florida Supreme Court's interpretation of the state's election laws, allowing the extension of the deadline for certification of votes and requiring late vote tallies to be included in the certification, created new election law, which only the state legislature can do, and thus violated Article II of the U.S. Constitution.

Justice Stevens, joined by Justices Ginsburg and Breyer, dissented. Justice Stevens found that there was no substantial federal question at issue in this case to be resolved by the Court. Justice Souter found the Florida Supreme Court's decision to be consistent with Article II's grant of authority. Further, Justice Stevens did not think the Florida Supreme Court's failure to specify uniform standards for the recount constituted a constitutional violation. Rather, he found unconstitutional the majority's decision to disenfranchise those voters whose ballots were legal votes but were rejected during the machine count. Finally, Justice Stevens found that the Florida Supreme Court had made no substantive changes to Florida election law.

Justice Souter, joined by Justice Breyer and joined in part by Justices Stevens and Ginsburg, dissented, finding that no issue presented required the U.S. Supreme Court's review. Specifically, Justice Souter found that the interpretations of Florida law by the Florida Supreme Court, such as what constituted a legal vote, raised no substantial question under Article II. Justice Souter did find evidence of an equal protection violation in the various standards used to recount ballots and determine a voter's intent; however, he thought the majority should have remanded the case to the Florida Supreme Court and given them a chance to remedy the standard inequities and attempt to count the ballots before the deadline.

Justice Ginsburg wrote a separate dissent, joined by Justice Stevens and joined in part by Justices Souter and Breyer. Justice Ginsburg found no reason to reverse the Florida Supreme Court's interpretation of Florida law, stating that rarely did the Court reject an interpretation of a state's highest court; rather, federal courts deferred to state supreme court interpretations of their state law. Further, Justice Ginsburg found that Bush did not present a substantial equal protection claim and that any concern about the December 12 deadline was irrelevant.

Justice Breyer, joined in part by Justices Stevens, Ginsburg, and Souter, dissented, finding it was wrong for the Court to review the decision of the Florida Supreme Court as the federal questions were insubstantial, except for the lack of uniform standards for the recount that implicated equal protection concerns. Justice Breyer found no justification for halting the recount, as there was no evidence that the recount could not have been completed by the established deadline.

AFTERMATH

George W. Bush ultimately was declared the winner of the 2000 presidential election.

SIGNIFICANCE

The significance of this case resides in the media attention the election received and the worldwide pause that ensued as all waited for the outcome of the election. Given the economic and foreign policy whirlwinds the Bush presidency was thrust into almost immediately, one might wonder whether the election fiasco was a sign of times to come. The Supreme Court's decision to insert itself into this dispute was unexpected and suggests that when an issue is of national importance, the Court will find a federal question so that it may control the outcome.

RELATED CASE

Bush v. Palm Beach County Canvassing Board, 531 U.S. 70 (2000)

RECOMMENDED READING

Bugliosi, Vincent. *Betrayal of America: How the Supreme Court Undermined the Constitution and Chose Our President.* New York: Thunder Mouth Press, 2001.

Dionne, E. J., and William Kristol. Bush v. Gore: *The Court Cases and the Commentary.* New York: Brooking Institution Press, 2001.

Florida State Law Review 29 (2001). (Entire volume consists of articles on *Bush v. Gore.*)

Gilman, Howard. *The Votes That Counted: How the Court Decided the 2000 Presidential Election.* Chicago: University of Chicago Press, 2001.

Spencer Overton, *Rules, Standards, and* Bush v. Gore: *Form and the Law of Democracy,* 37 Harvard Civil Rights–Civil Liberties Law Review 65 (2002).

Posner, Richard A. *Breaking the Deadlock: The 2000 Election, the Constitution and the Courts.* Princeton, N.J.: Princeton University Press, 2001.

Case Title: *Gratz v. Bollinger*

Alternate Case Title: The Case of Racial Preferences in Undergraduate Admissions

Legal Citation: 539 U.S. 244

Year of Decision: 2003

KEY ISSUES

Does a state university's use of racial preferences in its undergraduate admissions process violate the equal protection clause of the Fourteenth Amendment, Title VI of the Civil Rights Act, which states that no person may be discriminated against by a program receiving federal funding, and 42 U.S.C. § 1981, which states all persons shall be entitled to the "full and equal benefit of all laws"?

HISTORY OF THE CASE

The admissions policy for the University of Michigan changed over the years. In 1995 and 1996, the policy was to consider in the admissions process combined grade-point averages with factors including strength of high school curriculum, residency, alumni connections, and unusual circumstances pertaining to the applicant. The resulting combined score was coupled with an applicant's ACT or SAT score to determine admission. During those years, the admission of students with identical scores varied on the basis of the racial and ethnic status of the applicant. In 1997, additional points were added to applicants' scores if they were in an underrepresented minority or attended a high school populated predominantly by minorities underrepresented at the university. Beginning in 1998, the university changed to a points system that awarded an applicant a certain number of points for each admission factor considered and then set the admission decision at various numerical levels. For example, if an applicant scored between 100 and 150 points, the applicant was

automatically admitted. In 1999 and 2000, an applicant from an underrepresented minority or racial group was automatically given 20 points. However, during those years, the university also had a review committee that individually considered certain applicants who met minimum scores but who may have had qualities important to the university, including race or ethnicity.

The petitioners, Jennifer Gratz and Patrick Hamacher, were white Michigan residents who had applied for admission to the University of Michigan's College of Literature, Science, and the Arts in 1995 and 1997, respectively. Both petitioners were denied admission despite being qualified applicants. In 1997, the petitioners brought a class-action suit in the District Court for the Eastern District of Michigan alleging racial discrimination in violation of the Fourteenth Amendment, Title VI of the Civil Rights Act of 1964, and 42 U.S.C. § 1981. The district court certified the class of petitioners who had applied for admission to the university but had not been admitted and who were members of racial and ethnic groups treated less favorably by the university. Hamacher was designated as the class representative. The district court found in favor of the petitioners with regard to the admissions procedures for the years 1995 through 1998 but found for the respondents with regard to the years 1999 and 2000. Appeals were made to the Sixth Circuit Court of Appeals, but before the case was heard, Gratz and Hamacher petitioned the U.S. Supreme Court for review so the case could be heard together with *Grutter v. Bollinger,* a case challenging the admissions procedures of the university's law school.

The last time the U.S. Supreme Court had considered racial preferences in university admissions programs was in *Regents of the University of California v. Bakke* in 1978. The parties and the Court in *Gratz* relied on Justice Powell's opinion in *Bakke* that the consideration of race as a factor in admissions may in some situations serve a compelling government interest. However, the parties' interpretation of what met or violated Justice Powell's guidelines was significantly different.

SUMMARY OF ARGUMENTS

Petitioners argued that the university's use of race as an admissions factor violated the equal protection clause of the Fourteenth Amendment, Title VI of the Civil Rights Act of 1964, and 42 U.S.C. § 1981. They further argued that racial classifications could only be used to remedy identified discrimination, and, moreover, diversity was not a compelling interest to be furthered by racial preferences. Even if diversity were a compelling interest, the petitioners argued that the university had not narrowly tailored its use of race to achieve this interest.

The respondents, who included Lee Bollinger, the university's president when Hamacher applied for admission, argued that the admissions program was narrowly tailored to further the university's interest in educational diversity and provided the individualized consideration found constitutionally permissible in *Bakke*.

DECISION

The Court found that the undergraduate admissions procedures of the University of Michigan violated the equal protection clause of the Fourteenth Amendment, Title VI, and section 1981. Chief Justice Rehnquist gave the opinion of the Court. Although no party had addressed the issue of standing, the chief justice addressed this issue because Justice Stevens raised it in his dissent. The chief justice found that the petitioners had standing because Hamacher was able and willing to apply as a transfer student if race were no longer used in the admissions process. The use of race in transfer admissions and freshman admissions did not differ significantly; thus, Hamacher had a personal stake in the litigation, considering his past injury of admission denial, and a potential future injury if he reapplied to the university.

The strict scrutiny standard was applied in arriving at a decision, as all racial classifications reviewed under equal protection analysis are subject to strict scrutiny. The Court found that the procedure of awarding an automatic 20 points to every underrepresented minority applicant was not narrowly tailored to achieve the university's diversity interest. The chief justice reviewed Justice Powell's opinion in *Bakke* and determined that the university's policy did not give individualized consideration to applicants, a process found to be constitutional by Justice Powell.

Justice O'Connor concurred, also stating that the admissions process did not give applicants a meaningful individualized review. Justice O'Connor also pointed out that the points awarded for other diversity variables besides race, such as leadership and personal achievement, are significantly lower than those awarded for race.

Justice Thomas also concurred, indicating that he found the Court's decision to be a correct application of precedent, and Justice Breyer concurred with the Court's decision as well.

Justice Stevens, joined by Justice Souter, dissented, finding that the petitioners lacked standing because they were not in the process of reapplying to the university through the undergraduate admissions process at the time the suit was filed. Thus, he found the action should be dismissed. Justice Stevens sought to differentiate between the freshman admissions process and the transfer admissions process, stating that the freshman policy was at issue and only the transfer policy, which was not challenged, would have applied to Hamacher, the class representative. Justice Stevens found that the petitioners did not have a personal stake in the suit and, therefore, lacked standing.

Justice Souter, joined by Justice Ginsburg, also dissented. Justice Souter agreed with Justice Stevens that Hamacher had no standing to seek relief regarding the freshman admissions policy because he would not be harmed by it. Justice Souter also indicated that he would not find the admissions policy unconstitutional because the process was not a "quota" system, one that set a certain number of minority applicants that must be admitted, like the system struck down in *Bakke*. He found that a nonminority applicant could achieve a score that exceeded that of a minority applicant who received the automatic 20 points through points earned on other factors, such as leadership, curriculum, and test scores, and that race was not set apart from the other point-assessed considerations. Moreover, Justice

Souter did not find that the automatic 20 points "convert race into a decisive factor comparable to reserving minority places in *Bakke*." Justice Souter found the undergraduate process to accomplish the same objective, achieving a "critical mass" of minority students, as the law school process upheld in *Grutter v. Bollinger.*

Justice Ginsburg wrote a separate dissent along with Justice Souter, finding that the undergraduate admissions policy did not violate the Constitution. Justice Ginsburg reflected on the racial oppression of the past and still existing in society at large and concluded that in implementing policies of equality, there was a distinction between a policy of inclusion and one of exclusion. Specifically, denial of a benefit or imposition of a burden based on race is violative of the Constitution, but consideration of race to undo the effects of past discrimination and prevent future discrimination may not be. Justice Ginsburg clarified that any "race-conscious" measuring system should be carefully reviewed. She found no evidence that the university's policy was meant to be an exclusionary policy, one that limited a particular race's enrollment. Moreover, Justice Ginsburg praised the university's forthrightness as favorable compared to other programs that seek to accomplish the same goal but achieve it through "winks, nods and disguises."

AFTERMATH

The Court's decision was met with mixed reactions. Overall, the university was pleased that the Court found that affirmative action could be used in admissions but acknowledged it would be adjusting its admissions policy for more individualized review. While the Court's decision technically only affects public university admissions, it will probably impact admissions decisions at private institutions and hiring decisions in the business world. Additionally, the decision will be likely to make affirmative action a significant issue in future presidential elections.

SIGNIFICANCE

The decisions in this case and *Grutter v. Bollinger* marked the most significant decision on affirmative action in admissions policies in 25 years. On the basis of the decision, race may be considered in the admissions process, but institutions of higher education will have to replace numerically indexed systems of admissions with systems of individual review if they plan to include race as a factor.

RELATED CASES

Regents of the University of California v. Bakke, 438 U.S. 265 (1978)

Richmond v. J. A. Croson Co., 488 U.S. 469 (1989)

Grutter v. Bollinger, 539 U.S. 306 (2003)

RECOMMENDED READING

Beckman, James A. *Affirmative Action Now: A Guide for Students, Families, and Counselors.* Westport, Conn.: Greenwood Press, 2006.

Goodwin Liu, *The Causation Fallacy:* Bakke *and the Basic Arithmetic of Selective Admissions,* 100 Michigan Law Review 1045 (2002).

Orfield, Gary, ed. *Diversity Challenged: Evidence on the Impact of Affirmative Action.* Cambridge, Mass.: Harvard Education Publishing Group, 2001.

Orfield, Gary, and Edward Miller. *Chilling Admissions: The Affirmative Action Crisis and the Search for Alternatives.* Cambridge, Mass.: Harvard Education Publishing Group, 1998.

Perry, Barbara A. *The Michigan Affirmative Action Cases.* Lawrence: University Press of Kansas, 2007.

Case Title: *Grutter v. Bollinger*

Alternate Case Title: The Law School Admissions Case

Legal Citation: 539 U.S. 306

Year of Decision: 2003

KEY ISSUE

Is the use of race as a factor in a university's law school admissions process unlawful?

HISTORY OF THE CASE

The law school at the University of Michigan is ranked as one of the top law schools in the United States. The law school's admissions process consisted of an evaluation of each applicant, considering his or her undergraduate grade-point average, LSAT (Law School Admissions Test) score, personal statement, letters of recommendation, and essay, as well as other criteria important to the law school's objectives, one of which is to achieve diversity. The law school did not define this diversity as only racial or ethnic diversity, although it did seek to enroll a "critical mass" of minority students.

The petitioner, Barbara Grutter, applied to the school in 1996. Grutter was a white Michigan resident with a grade-point average of 3.8 and an LSAT score of 161 (of a perfect score of 180). While Grutter was initially put on the school's waiting list, she ultimately was denied admission. Grutter brought suit in the District Court for the Eastern District of Michigan. Her motion to certify a class action was granted, and it was ultimately decided that the use of race as a factor in the law school's admissions process was unlawful. The court of appeals reversed the decision, finding the law school's use of race to be narrowly tailored. The U.S. Supreme Court granted certiorari.

SUMMARY OF ARGUMENTS

The petitioner, Grutter, argued that the law school discriminated against her on the basis of race, violating the equal protection clause of the Fourteenth Amendment, Title VI of the Civil Rights Act of 1964, and 42 U.S.C. § 1981. Grutter argued that race was used as a "predominant" factor in making admissions decisions, and that the use of such a factor was not justified by any compelling interest.

The respondents, one of whom was Lee Bollinger, the university's president at the time of Grutter's application, argued that the consideration of race in the admissions process was justified because it assisted the school in attaining a diverse student body.

DECISION

Justice O'Connor wrote the opinion of the Court, which found that the law school had a "compelling interest in obtaining a diverse student body" and that its use of race was narrowly tailored to achieve this objective. She noted that the Court only had one significant holding in the decision of *Regents of the University of California v. Bakke* (1978), which was that the consideration of race in a university's admissions process could serve a substantial interest, and that Justice Powell had approved only one such interest, attaining diversity in the student body. Justice O'Connor indicated that the Court endorsed this view held by Justice Powell. The Court applied a strict scrutiny analysis, stating that all governmentally imposed racial classifications must be reviewed under this standard.

Justice O'Connor deferred to the law school's judgment that it was essential for the university to have a diverse student body and to its determination that a "critical mass" of underrepresented minority students was necessary to achieve this diverse student body. She determined that the law school's admissions program was not a quota system, a system that would not have been considered "narrowly tailored," because it did not give "bonuses" for certain races or ethnicities, but, rather, had an individualized review of each applicant's information. Moreover, Justice O'Connor found that the law school gave significant weight to diversity factors other than race. Finally, Justice O'Connor noted that all admissions programs that were conscious of race must have time limitations and indicated that the Court believed the law school's promise that it would terminate the "race-conscious" admissions procedures as soon as possible.

Justice Ginsburg, joined by Justice Breyer, concurred with the opinion of the Court, citing the perpetuation of racial bias as impeding realization of the goal of diversity and predicting progress toward nondiscrimination, which would end the need for affirmative action.

Justice Rehnquist dissented, joined by Justices Scalia, Kennedy, and Thomas, finding that the law school's consideration of race was not narrowly tailored to achieve the interest of diversity in education. Justice Rehnquist found the "critical mass" requirement to amount to racial balancing at the law school. Justice Rehnquist pointed out that the percentage of students from underrepresented minority groups admitted was closely correlated to the percentage of applicants from that same minority group. For example, if 9.7 percent of the applicants were black, approximately 9.7 percent of the students admitted were black. Justice Rehnquist also found the admissions process failed the strict scrutiny analysis because the use of race as a factor in admissions did not have a precise time limitation.

Justice Kennedy wrote a separate dissent, finding that the Court failed to apply the strict scrutiny analysis required of a governmentally imposed racial classification. He pointed to the Court's deference to the law school's definition of its diversity objective as constituting such failure. Justice Kennedy found the law school's administration of the admission process to constitute a quota system.

Justice Scalia also dissented, joined by Justice Thomas. Justice Scalia found that the statistics proved that the law school's admissions program sought to achieve a class racially proportionate to the pool of applicants. He found racial understanding not "uniquely relevant" to law school or public education, concluding that if universities could use racial discrimination to achieve this understanding, then public and private employers could also use racial discrimination to achieve racial understanding.

Finally, Justice Thomas, joined by Justice Scalia, dissented, indicating his belief that blacks did not need the interference of university administrations to succeed. Justice Thomas focused on the diversity interest the law school sought to further through its admissions process. He found that educational benefits were the interest sought by the law school, not diversity, and that in achieving this interest, the law school did not want to sacrifice its status as one of the nation's top institutions. Justice Thomas indicated that maintenance of a public law school was not a necessity, and therefore, the state of Michigan had no compelling interest in having a law school in general or an elite law school. He also found the deference of the Court to the law school to be violative of the strict scrutiny analysis.

AFTERMATH

While the decision permits the use of race as a factor in the admissions process, the challenge will be to create a policy that is narrowly tailored. Further, the decision will probably affect the hiring processes for both public and private companies.

SIGNIFICANCE

This was the first time in 25 years that the Court had reviewed the use of race in the public university admissions process. The decision affirms that race may be considered as part of the admissions process for public universities. Many public groups and individuals, including the Bush administration and a number of Fortune 500 companies, voiced their opinions on the affirmative action issue by filing briefs in the case.

RELATED CASES

Regents of the University of California v. Bakke, 438 U.S. 265 (1978)

Sheet Metal Workers v. EEOC, 478 U.S. 421 (1986)

Gratz v. Bollinger, 539 U.S. 244 (2003)

RECOMMENDED READING

Neal Devins, *Explaining* Grutter v. Bollinger, 152 University of Pennsylvania Law Review 347 (2003).

Kathleen A. Graves, *Affirmative Action in Law School Admissions: An Analysis of Why Affirmative Action Is No Longer the Answer . . . or Is It?,* 23 Southern Illinois University Law Journal 149 (1998).

Perry, Barbara A. *The Michigan Affirmative Action Cases.* Lawrence: University Press of Kansas, 2007.

Linda F. Wightman, *The Threat to Diversity in Legal Education: An Empirical Analysis of the*

Consequences of Abandoning Race as a Factor in Law School Admission Decisions, 72 New York University Law Review 1 (1997).

Joshua Wilkenfield, *Newly Compelling: Reexamining Judicial Construction of Juries in the Aftermath of* Grutter v. Bollinger, 104 Columbia Law Review 2291 (2004).

Case Title: *Lawrence v. Texas*

Legal Citation: 539 U.S. 558

Year of Decision: 2003

KEY ISSUE

Does a law that prohibits certain consensual sexual acts between persons of the same sex violate the Fourteenth Amendment?

HISTORY OF THE CASE

Houston, Texas, police officers, on a report of a weapons violation, entered the house of John Lawrence and observed him and another man, Tyron Garner, engaged in a sexual act. The men were arrested and charged pursuant to a Texas law that outlawed "deviate sexual acts" between persons of the same sex. The men were convicted by the Harris County Criminal Court, and their conviction was affirmed by the Court of Appeals for the 14th District of Texas. At both trials, the defendants asserted the unconstitutionality of the Texas law under the Fourteenth Amendment. The court of appeals cited a previous Supreme Court case, *Bowers v. Hardwick* (1986), which upheld a similar, though not identical, Georgia law in 1986. The Court granted certiorari to consider the defendants' constitutional arguments and to consider *Bowers*'s continuing validity.

SUMMARY OF THE ARGUMENTS

Lawrence argued that the law criminalizing same-sex sexual contact violated his substantive due process rights because it infringed upon his right to liberty. Alternatively, he argued that because the law treated conduct of same-sex partners differently than that of opposite-sex partners, it violates the equal protection clause of the Fourteenth Amendment.

Texas cited *Bowers v. Hardwick* for the proposition that the right to engage in homosexual conduct was not a fundamental right that would be subject to protection under the due process clause. The state also argued that though the law only criminalized homosexual behavior, it applied equally to all people and, therefore, did not violate the equal protection clause.

DECISION

Justice Kennedy, writing for a five-justice majority of the Court, held that the Texas law violated Lawrence's right to liberty under the due process clause of the Fourteenth Amendment. Specifically, the right to liberty includes the right to be free of governmental intrusion into a person's sexual relationships, provided they are private and between consenting adults.

In finding such a right, the Court, first, had to overturn the holding in *Bowers v. Hardwick.* The Court first noted that *Bowers* only asked whether the right to engage in homosexual behavior was a fundamental right deserving of due process protection. According to Justice Kennedy, this inquiry was improperly narrow because it was limited to homosexual behavior. Rather, the proper question is, Does due process allow consenting adults to be free of governmental intrusion into their private sexual relationships? The majority believed it does.

The majority next cast some factual doubt on the "ancient roots" of antihomosexuality laws that the *Bowers* court claims as a justification for its holding. The Court noted that there was no long-standing tradition in the United States of laws directed specifically against homosexual conduct. It cited academic writing and amicus briefs filed in the case as sources providing historical explanation of this issue.

Finally, Justice Kennedy cited two post-*Bowers* cases, *Planned Parenthood of Southeastern Pa. v. Casey* (1996) and *Romer v. Evans* (1992), as significantly weakening the foundations of *Bowers. Casey* stated at the heart of liberty is the right of an individual to make intimate choices relating to personal dignity and autonomy. *Romer* held that a state could not explicitly exempt homosexual persons from antidiscrimination laws. Having thus overturned *Bowers,* Justice Kennedy concluded that the Texas law improperly intruded into the intimate personal affairs of two consenting adults without furthering any legitimate governmental interest.

Justice O'Connor wrote an opinion concurring in the holding of the majority but not its reasoning. Justice O'Connor based her objection to the Texas law on the equal protection clause of the Fourteenth Amendment, not the due process clause. She would not have overturned *Bowers;* nor did she find such an expansive right to liberty as the majority. According to Justice O'Connor, the key fact is that the law criminalized conduct only for certain participants, namely, people of the same sex. Texas's argument that the law applies equally to all persons does not save it from the fact that it is directed at homosexual people as a class and is, therefore, discriminatory to that class.

In his dissent, Justice Scalia focused on comparing *Bowers* to *Roe v. Wade.* His main argument centered on the similarly weak foundation remaining in support of *Roe.* Essentially, if *Bowers* can be so easily and summarily overturned, then *Roe* can and should be similarly dismissed. Against the majority's due process argument, Justice Scalia would require that any right guaranteed protection under the due process clause be "fundamental." Against Justice O'Connor's equal protection argument, he was persuaded by Texas's argument that the law applies equally to all persons and, therefore, does not treat people differently.

AFTERMATH

As this case was recently decided, it is unclear exactly what its implications are. Some claim that *Lawrence* paves the way for recognition of other homosexual rights, such as the right to marry. *Lawrence* probably does not go far down this path because the majority expressly declined to address "whether the government must give for-

mal recognition to any relationship that homosexual persons seek to enter." In addition, the majority based its decision on the due process clause, while the most recognizable justification for recognition of gay marriage is based on the equal protection clause. Others claim that *Lawrence* will lead to the overturning of all sexual legislation, such as prohibitions on incest, obscene materials, and prostitution. Again, it is unclear exactly how far *Lawrence* goes. It is clear that laws prohibiting other forms of private consensual sexual conduct, such as laws prohibiting fornication, will be hard pressed to survive post-*Lawrence* scrutiny. However, in areas where the government can demonstrate a more tangible interest, such as promotion of marriage and protection of children, the applicability of *Lawrence* may be limited.

SIGNIFICANCE

This case acknowledged the constitutionally protected right of sexual privacy.

RELATED CASES

Griswold v. Connecticut, 381 U.S. 479 (1965)

New Jersey v. Saunders, 75 N.J. 200; 381 A.2d 333 (1977)

New York v. Onofre, 51 N.Y.2d 476; 415 N.E.2d 936 (1980)

Bowers v. Hardwick, 478 U.S. 186 (1986)

Kentucky v. Wasson, 842 S.W.2d 487 (1992)

Planned Parenthood of Southeastern Pa. v. Casey, 505 U.S. 833 (1992)

State v. Morales, 826 S.W.2d 201 (1992)

Romer v. Evans, 517 U.S. 620 (1996)

STATUTE AT ISSUE

Tex. Penal Code Ann. § 21.06(a) (2003)

RECOMMENDED READING

Mary Anne Case, *Of "This" and "That" in* Lawrence v. Texas, 2003. Supreme Court Review 75.

Katherine M. Franke, *The Domesticated Liberty of* Lawrence v. Texas, 104 Columbia Law Review 1399 (2004).

Cass R. Sunstein, *What Did* Lawrence *Hold? Of Autonomy, Desuetude, Sexuality, and Marriage,* 2003 Supreme Court Review 27.

Lawrence H. Tribe, Lawrence v. Texas: *The "Fundamental Right" That Dare Not Speak Its Name,* 117 Harvard Law Review 1893 (2004).

Case Title: *Nevada Department of Human Resources v. Hibbs*

Legal Citation: 538 U.S. 721

Year of Decision: 2003

KEY ISSUES

Can an individual sue a state for money damages in federal court for a violation of the Family and Medical Leave Act (FMLA)?

HISTORY OF THE CASE

In 1993, Congress passed the FMLA, which entitles employees who are eligible to take up to 12 workweeks of unpaid leave each year for various reasons. Under the family-care provision of the FMLA, employees could seek leave from work for, among other things, the onset of a serious health condition of an employee's spouse, child, or parent. Those eligible employees who were denied this benefit were entitled to seek both equitable relief and monetary damages against their employer in a proper federal or state court.

Robert Hibbs worked for the Department of Human Resources ("the Department"), in the Department's Welfare Division. Hibbs sought leave under the FMLA to care for his wife in April and May 1997 after she had been involved in a car accident. Hibbs was granted leave at various times between that period and August 5, 1997, when he stopped going to work. In October 1997, the Department contacted Hibbs to inform him that he had exhausted his FMLA leave and that no further leave would be granted. He was also told that he must return to work by November 12, 1997, and after failing to do so, he was terminated.

Hibbs sued the Department in the U.S. District Court for violations of the FMLA, and summary judgment was granted for the Department on the grounds that the Eleventh Amendment barred FMLA claims, and there was no Fourteenth Amendment violation. Hibbs appealed the decision to the Ninth Circuit, and the case was reversed. The U.S. Supreme Court then granted certiorari due to splits among appeals courts on the issue of whether an individual can sue a state for money damages in federal court for an FMLA violation.

SUMMARY OF ARGUMENTS

Hibbs argued that the FMLA family medical care provision was validly passed under Section 5 of the Fourteenth Amendment. Since the provision was valid legislation, states were not immune from federal lawsuits under the Eleventh Amendment.

The state of Nevada argued that the FMLA family medical care provision was not valid legislation under Section 5. Therefore, Nevada was protected from federal lawsuits related to the provision under Eleventh Amendment sovereign immunity.

DECISION

The Court held that state employees are permitted to recover money damages in federal court if the state fails to comply with FMLA's family-care provision. The Court ruled that Congress had clearly stated its intention to abrogate the state sovereign immunity and had acted properly under Section 5 of the Fourteenth Amendment. The legislation was deemed prophylactic rather than substantive, and thus, it was not deemed to redefine any constitutional rights.

Chief Justice Rehnquist delivered the opinion of the Court. The Court began by noting relevant powers possessed by Congress under the Constitution, which include the power to abrogate state sovereign immunity pursuant to a valid exercise of its power under Section 5 of the Fourteenth Amendment. Section 5 provides Congress with the power to enforce the rights granted to individual citizens under Section 1 of the Fourteenth Amendment. Through Section 5, Congress is permitted to enact "prophylactic legislation that proscribes facially constitutionally conduct, in order to prevent and deter unconstitutional conduct." One limitation is that the prophylactic legislation cannot redefine the Fourteenth Amendment right at issue. Also, the means taken to prevent or remedy an injury must be congruent and proportional to the injury, as defined in the legislation.

The Court then turned to the history of the act. When Congress enacted the FMLA, it did so in order to remedy the unequal treatment of men and women regarding employment. The aim was "to protect the right to be free from gender-based discrimination in the workplace." Since gender was at issue, the Court reasoned that "heightened scrutiny," in which the legislation is required to "serve important governmental objectives" and "the discriminatory means employed [must be] substantially related to the achievement of those objectives," would apply.

The Court first looked to the history of gender discrimination in the workplace, arguing that "the history of the many state laws limiting women's employment opportunities is chronicled in this Court's own opinions." Examples include state laws that prohibited women from practicing law and others that limited the benefits women could receive at work. The Court also noted that there was evidence before Congress when it enacted the FMLA suggesting that "states continue to rely on invalid gender stereotypes in the employment context, specifically in the administration of leave benefits." The Court thought that this discrimination justified Congress's passage of Section 5 legislation to remedy the problem.

The Court recognized that the stereotypes regarding women in the workplace caused women and men to be discriminated against because men were discouraged from taking leaves of absence for family-related issues. The Court asserted that

these "stereotypes created a self-fulfilling cycle of discrimination that forced women to continue to assume the role of primary family caregiver, and fostered employers' stereotypical views about women's commitment to work and their value as employees." Making the problem worse, the subtle discrimination was difficult to detect when viewed on a case-by-case basis.

Additionally, the Court deemed the FMLA to be congruent and proportional legislation to remedy and prevent gender discrimination in the workplace. The gender-neutral family-leave provision of the FMLA helped to ensure that employers could not evade leave obligations by hiring only men. In finding that Congress had intended to abrogate state sovereign immunity for purposes of the statute at issue, the FMLA was deemed to be "narrowly targeted at the fault-line between work and family, precisely where sex-based overgeneralization has been and remains strongest, and affects only one aspect of the employment relationship." Justice Stevens wrote a concurring opinion, stating that Congress does have the power to abrogate state sovereign immunity pursuant to the commerce clause. Thus, he thought that Nevada's sovereign immunity defense was without merit.

Justice Kennedy wrote a dissenting opinion, joined by Justices Scalia and Thomas, expressing his view that the FMLA family provision was invalid because it unconstitutionally abrogated state sovereign immunity. Justice Kennedy believed that allowing citizens to sue the state for monetary damages blurs the line of accountability for states when dealing with citizens. Additionally, he argued, there was no evidence of a pattern of unlawful conduct regarding the granting of employment leave for family or medical care. He also criticized the majority for relying on evidence of private practices, as opposed to those of state employers. Justice Kennedy also asserted that the states were already doing an adequate job of providing forms of leave for family care, as 30 states, the District of Columbia, and Puerto Rico all had programs in place prior to the enactment of the FMLA. Justice Kennedy deemed the FMLA a substantive benefit created by Congress for state employees, which was unconstitutional because Congress's powers are limited to remedial (not substantive) legislation. He determined that the "scheme enacted by the Act does not respect the States' autonomous power to design their own social benefits regime."

Justice Scalia joined Justice Kennedy's dissent and wrote his own to express his view that the prophylactic legislation should only be aimed at those states with a history of such discrimination. He stated, "There is no guilt by association, enabling the sovereignty of one State to be abridged under § 5 of the Fourteenth Amendment because of violations by another State, or by most other States, or even by 49 other States."

AFTERMATH

The equal protection clause of the Fourteenth Amendment reads as follows: "No State shall . . . deny to any person within its jurisdiction the equal protection of the laws." Accordingly, it applies only to state and public employers, not private businesses. However, Congress retains the ability to regulate private businesses through the commerce clause of Article I, § 8, clause 3, of the U.S. Constitution. Congress has enforced the FMLA through these two constitutional provisions.

SIGNIFICANCE

This case was preceded by a series of rulings that held that state governments were exempt from federal laws. These cases included *Alden v. Maine* (1999), *Florida Prepaid v. College Savings Bank* (1999), and *Kimel v. Florida Board of Regents* (2000). In this case, the Court changed course for the issue of gender discrimination in the workplace to hold that the FMLA was valid legislation even though it abrogated state sovereign immunity for violations of the act.

RELATED CASES

Hans v. Louisiana, 134 U.S. 1 (1890)

Fitzpatrick v. Bitzer, 427 U.S. 455 (1976)

City of Boerne v. Flores, 521 U.S. 507 (1997)

Alden v. Maine, 527 U.S. 706 (1999)

Florida Prepaid v. College Savings Bank, 527 U.S. 666 (1999)

Kimel v. Florida Board of Regents, 528 U.S. 62 (2000)

STATUTES AT ISSUE

U.S. Constitution, Fourteenth Amendment, § 5

29 U.S.C. § 2612(a)(1)(C)—Family Medical Leave Act: Leave Requirement

RECOMMENDED READING

Jennifer Yatskis Dukart, *Geduldig Reborn:* Hibbs *as a Success (?) of Justice Ruth Bader Ginsburg's Sex-Discrimination Strategy,* 93 California Law Review 541 (2005).

Nicole E. Grodner, *Disparate Impact Legislation and Abrogation of the States' Sovereign Immunity after* Nevada Department of Human Resources v. Hibbs *and* Tennessee v. Lane, 83 Texas Law Review 1173 (2005).

Allison K. Slagle, Nevada Department of Human Resources v. Hibbs: *Regulation or Simply Encouragement?,* 33 Capital University Law Review 869 (2005).

Jana L. Tibben, *Family Leave Policies Trump States' Rights:* Nevada Department of Human Resources v. Hibbs *and Its Impact on Sovereign Immunity Jurisprudence,* 37 John Marshall Law Review 599 (2004).

Case Title: *Blakely v. Washington*

Legal Citation: 542 U.S. 296

Year of Decision: 2004

KEY ISSUE

Can a judge impose a sentence beyond the statutory maximum on the basis of facts not brought before a jury?

HISTORY OF THE CASE

In 1998, Ralph Howard Blakely, Jr., abducted his estranged wife, Yolanda, from their home in Washington. Blakely bound her with duct tape and forced her into a wooden box at knifepoint. Blakely forced the couple's 13-year-old son to follow behind in another car and threatened to shoot Yolanda with a shotgun if he did not follow orders. Blakely drove to a friend's house in Montana, with Yolanda locked in the wooden box. Blakely's friend called the police, and Blakely was arrested. He pled guilty to second-degree kidnapping involving domestic violence and use of a firearm.

The standard range of incarceration for the charges was 49–53 months. In the state of Washington, a judge has the ability to increase the sentence from the standard range if he or she finds "substantial and compelling reasons justifying an exceptional sentence." On the basis of Yolanda's description of the kidnapping, the judge sentenced Blakely to 90 months, exceeding the statutory maximum sentence. Blakely objected to the sentence. The judge then conducted a three-day bench trial, in which he heard testimony from Yolanda, the couple's son, a police officer, and medical experts. The judge issued 32 findings of fact and concluded that Blakely acted with deliberate cruelty, thus justifying the exceptional sentence. The court of appeals affirmed, and the Washington Supreme Court denied discretionary review.

SUMMARY OF ARGUMENTS

Blakely argued that the sentencing procedure deprived him of his Sixth Amendment right to a trial by jury. The judge's finding of "deliberate cruelty" was based on facts not submitted to a jury. If a jury did not determine the facts were true beyond a reasonable doubt, then the sentence was based on information inappropriately reviewed under the Sixth Amendment.

The state argued that the guidelines in *Apprendi v. New Jersey* did not apply to the state of Washington. A court can exercise discretion for sentencing if the court finds "substantial and compelling reasons justifying an exceptional sentence." Further, the state argued that finding Blakely's sentence in violation of the Sixth Amendment would necessarily invalidate state determinate sentencing schemes.

DECISION

In a 5-4 decision, the Court found that an exceptional sentence based on a judge's determination of what constitutes "deliberate cruelty" violated Blakely's Sixth Amendment right to trial by jury. "Other than the fact of a prior conviction, any fact that increases the penalty for a crime beyond the prescribed statutory maximum must be submitted to a jury, and proved beyond a reasonable doubt." In order to impose a sentence above the standard range of 49–53 months, the facts used to support the judge's determination that Blakely had acted with "deliberate cruelty" either had to be admitted by Blakely or found by a jury.

The majority asserted that the right to a trial by jury was not just a procedural formality but a fundamental right protected under the Constitution. "The Framers would not have thought it too much to demand that, before depriving a man of three more years of his liberty, the State should suffer the modest inconvenience of submitting its accusation to 'the unanimous suffrage of twelve of his equals and neighbors' rather than a lone employee of the State."

AFTERMATH

Washington's sentencing guidelines were so similar to the standards set out in the Federal Sentencing Guidelines, which direct U.S. federal court systems, that many viewed the *Blakely* decision as a weakening force in the guidelines' validity. The U.S. Supreme Court addressed these concerns in a special summer session, reviewing *United States v. Booker* (2005) and *United States v. Fanfan* (2005). Both cases addressed the constitutionality of the Federal Sentencing Guidelines. The Court held in both cases that any imposed sentence outside the guidelines range must be based on facts reviewed by a jury.

SIGNIFICANCE

The Court firmly determined that the right to a trial by jury was not just a procedural formality but a fundamental right protected under the Constitution.

RELATED CASES

Apprendi v. New Jersey, 530 U.S. 466 (2000)

State v. Gore, 143 Wash. 2d 288 (2001)

United States v. Booker, 543 U.S. 220 (2005)

Cunningham v. California, 549 U.S. 270 (2007)

STATUTES AT ISSUE

Wash.Rev.Code Ann. § 9A.20.021. Maximum sentences for crimes committed July 1, 1984, and after

Wash.Rev.Code Ann. § 9A.40.030. Kidnapping in the second degree

RECOMMENDED READING

Douglas Berman and Steven Chanenson, *The Real (Sentencing) World: State Sentencing in the Post-Blakely Era,* 4 Ohio State Journal of Criminal Law 27 (2006).

Case Title: *Ledbetter v. Goodyear*

Alternate Case Title: *Lilly M. Ledbetter v. The Goodyear Tire & Rubber Company, Inc.*

Legal Citation: 550 U.S. 618

Year of Decision: 2007

KEY ISSUE

Can an individual bring an action for salary discrimination when the pay decision occurred within the 180-day statute of limitations period but the result of that pay discrimination occurred outside the statute of limitations?

HISTORY OF THE CASE

Title VII of the Civil Rights Act of 1964 makes it illegal to "discriminate against any individual with respect to his compensation . . . because of such individual's sex." Under 42 U.S.C.A. § 2000e-5, an action alleging such discrimination must be subsequent to filing a charge with the Equal Employment Opportunity Commission (EEOC) within 180 or 300 days (depending on the state).

Lilly Ledbetter worked for Goodyear Tire and Rubber Company ("Goodyear") from 1979 to 1998. During that time, salary increases were mainly based on supervisor evaluations. In 1998, Ledbetter filed a formal charge with the EEOC. After she took early retirement at the end of 1998, she commenced an action asserting a Title VII pay discrimination claim, stating she did not receive fair evaluations from her supervisors because of her sex. As a result of these unfair evaluations, Ledbetter's pay was not increased as much as it would have been if she had been evaluated fairly. These past incidents of discrimination affected the amount she was paid well after the pay discrimination occurred. By the time she retired, she was making significantly less than her male counterparts.

A jury at the district court level found in favor of Ledbetter. Goodyear appealed to the court of appeals, arguing that Ledbetter's claim should be time barred for all pay decisions made more than 180 days before she first contacted the EEOC about the discrimination. This eliminated all pay decisions except those made in 1997 and 1998, both of which denied Ledbetter a raise. The court of appeals ruled there was not enough evidence to establish that Ledbetter was discriminated against during either the 1997 or 1998 pay decisions and reversed the district court verdict.

SUMMARY OF ARGUMENTS

Ledbetter argued that all of the paychecks issued to her after the pay decisions as a separate act of discrimination and would all have their own 180-day statute of limitations. Alternatively, she argued that the 1998 denial of a raise was a continuation of discrimination that occurred in prior years.

Goodyear argued that any alleged pay discrimination that occurred six months prior to

Ledbetter's filing of the complaint with the EEOC was barred from inclusion in the lawsuit under Title VII. Goodyear claimed that no discrimination regarding Ledbetter's pay occurred after she had filed the complaint with the EEOC.

DECISION

The Court disagreed with Ledbetter's argument that the EEOC claim was within 180 days of the discriminatory pay decision. The critical question was whether or not a "present violation existed," and the continuing effects of the period before EEOC charges were filed did not create a present violation. Ledbetter failed to show that Goodyear intentionally discriminated against her in these instances; thus, there was no present violation shown. In a 5-4 decision, the Court affirmed the judgment of the court of appeals, finding Ledbetter barred by the 180-day statute of limitations. Citing Supreme Court precedent from *United Air Lines, Inc. v. Evans* (1977), the Court found "a discriminatory act which is not made the basis for a timely charge . . . is merely an unfortunate event in history which has no present legal consequences."

AFTERMATH

In 2009, the Lilly Ledbetter Fair Pay Act was passed by Congress and signed into law. This act allows for inclusion of pay discrimination outside the 180-day limitation period in a pay discrimination claim.

SIGNIFICANCE

This case determined that discrimination claims must be filed *before* the 180-day statute of limitations has passed. If claims are not filed in a timely manner, courts can bar otherwise valid claims unless Congress has provided an explicit exception. For example, the Lilly Ledbetter Fair Pay Act allows for claims regarding pay discrimination outside the Title VII 180-day limitation period.

RELATED CASES

United Air Lines, Inc. v. Evans, 431 U.S. 553 (1977)

Delaware State College v. Ricks, 449 U.S. 250 (1980)

Lorance v. AT&T Technologies, Inc., 490 U.S. 900 (1989)

National Railroad Passenger Corporation v. Morgan, 536 U.S. 101 (2002)

RECOMMENDED READING

Adrienne Nicole Calloway, *180 Days or No Equal Pay: Limiting Employment Discrimination Suits in* Ledbetter v. Goodyear Tire & Rubber Co., 59 Mercer Law Review 785 (2008).

Christopher S. Pieske, *What Ledbetter Means for Employees Facing Gender-Based Pay Discrimination:* Ledbetter v. Goodyear Tire & Rubber Co., 127 S. Ct. 2162 (2007), 84 North Dakota Law Review 299 (2008).

Katie Putnam, *On Lilly Ledbetter's Liberty: Why Equal Pay for Equal Work Remains an Elusive Reality,* 15 William and Mary Journal of Women and the Law 685 (2009).

Case Title: *Parents Involved in Community Schools v. Seattle School District No. 1; Meredith v. Jefferson County Board of Education*

Alternate Case Title: *Parents v. Seattle School District*

Legal Citation: 551 U.S. 701

Year of Decision: 2007

KEY ISSUES

Do the *Grutter v. Bollinger* (2003) and *Gratz v. Bollinger* (2003) decisions apply to public high school students and, if so, does racial diversity serve as a compelling interest that justifies using race in its admission policies?

HISTORY OF THE CASE

In 1998, Seattle School District No. 1 ("the School District") adopted a plan for assigning students to one of its 10 public high schools. Incoming freshmen selected the school of their choice by ranking the School District's high schools in order of preference. If one school was selected in excess of its capacity, the School District used a "tiebreaker" to determine which students would attend. The first tiebreaker admitted students who had a sibling currently enrolled in that particular school. The second tiebreaker was contingent upon the school's racial composition in contrast with the race of the student on the basis of whether the student was "white" or "nonwhite." To do this, the district used a white/nonwhite racial balancing test, and if an oversubscribed school was not within 10 percentage points of the racial balance in the district, the School District would select students whose race enabled the school to achieve the balance sought. A third tiebreaker was the geographic proximity of the school to the student's residence.

Seattle did not implement this plan to remedy past racial discrimination. In fact, the Seattle School District had never practiced segregation in its schools. The purpose of the plan was to address the racial impact of housing patterns on student assignments. Many of the white students lived in northern Seattle, whereas many of the nonwhite students lived in the southern part of the School District. For the 2000–01 school year, five schools were oversubscribed: Ballard, Nathan Hale, Roosevelt, Garfield, and Franklin. Of these, Garfield was the only oversubscribed school within the racial guidelines in the previous year. In some instances, the racial tiebreaker was used, causing some students to be denied assignment to the school of their choice on the basis of their race. The Parents Involved in Community Schools ("Parents Involved"), a nonprofit corporation made up of parents whose children were denied assignment to the school of their choice because of race, filed suit in the Western District of Washington. The suit alleged that the use of race in school assignments violated the equal protection clause of the Fourteenth Amendment.

The district court granted summary judgment in favor of the School District, reasoning that the plan was not prohibited by state law and survived strict scrutiny under the federal Constitution. The Ninth Circuit Court of Appeals, although it initially reversed and enjoined the School District's use of the racial "tiebreaker," withdrew its decision because the litigation was not likely to be resolved in time for the 2002–03 school year. That court additionally certified the state-law question to the Washington Supreme Court. The Washington Supreme Court deemed the plan "racially neutral" and returned the case to the Ninth Circuit. The Ninth Circuit again reversed the district court's decision, finding that the plan was not narrowly tailored to achieve its stated interests of achieving racial diversity and avoiding racial isolation. The Ninth Circuit then reheard the case en banc and ruled to reverse their previous decision, affirming the district court's opinion. The U.S. Supreme Court granted certiorari.

A few years later, a similar issue arose in Jefferson County, Louisville, Kentucky. Unlike the Seattle School District, the Jefferson County Public School system ("Jefferson County") had previously maintained a segregated school system. In 1975, Jefferson County was ordered by the district court to desegregate, and the order dissolved in 2000 after compliance. In 2001, Jefferson County adopted a voluntary student assignment plan, which required all "nonmagnet" schools to maintain at least 15 percent black enrollment with a maximum of 50 percent. At the elementary school level, the schools are grouped into racial clusters, and students are assigned to particular schools on the basis of their address in what are known as "resides" schools. Decisions to assign students to particular schools within the clusters must comply with the racial guidelines in order to establish a proper racial balance. Students can apply for transfers but may be denied as a result of a lack of space and impact on racial guidelines.

Crystal Meredith sought to enroll her son, Joshua McDonald, in kindergarten for the 2002–03 school year. His residential school, which was a mile from his home, was full, so Jefferson County enrolled him in another school in his cluster, which was 10 miles from his home. Meredith tried to transfer her son to another school within the cluster. However, although it had available space, Joshua was denied admission under the racial guidelines. Meredith filed suit in the Western District of Kentucky under the equal protection clause of the Fourteenth Amendment, but the district court upheld the assignment plan. The Sixth Circuit Court of Appeals affirmed, and upon appeal, the U.S. Supreme Court granted certiorari.

The cases of *Parents Involved in Community Schools v. Seattle School District No. 1* and *Meredith v. Jefferson County Board of Education* were consolidated prior to being heard by the U.S. Supreme Court.

SUMMARY OF ARGUMENTS

The parents argued that the admission policies violated the equal protection clause of the Fourteenth Amendment.

DECISION

In a narrow decision (5-4), the Court held that the racial "tiebreaker" admission policies violated the equal protection clause of the Fourteenth Amendment. The Court applied strict scrutiny and determined the policies to be unconstitutional because they lacked individual consideration for students, defined "diversity" too narrowly, and failed to demonstrate a lack of nonrace-based alternatives. The Court thought that the aim for "racial diversity" was a form of racial balancing, which was held to be unconstitutional.

Chief Justice Roberts announced the judgment of the Court and delivered the opinion of the Court for parts I, II, III-A, and III-C.

The Court began by establishing that it had jurisdiction over the case. Under the equal protection clause, race-based public systems that prejudice a plaintiff establish an injury, and in this case, the parents were afforded the right to sue on behalf of their children. Although the Seattle School District had ceased using its racial tiebreaker, the Court noted that voluntary cessation will only moot an issue if it is certain the behavior will not recur, and that certainty did not exist in this case. Jefferson County did not challenge the

Court's jurisdiction, but the Court nonetheless explained that it had jurisdiction because Meredith had suffered an injury under the equal protection clause.

The Court began its analysis by pointing out that government distributions based on racial classifications are reviewed under strict scrutiny; that means the school plans must be narrowly tailored to achieving a compelling governmental interest. Historically, as the Court pointed out, only two interests have been viewed as compelling enough to satisfy strict scrutiny analysis: as a remedy for past discrimination and in the interest of higher education diversity, as was upheld in *Grutter v. Bollinger*. Remedying past discrimination was not an interest for either school because it did not exist in the Seattle School District and Jefferson County had satisfied its desegregation decree by achieving unitary status. As for diversity, unlike the broad aspect of diversity sought in *Grutter*, the Seattle School District viewed race as "white" or "nonwhite," and Jefferson County categorized its students as "black" or "other." Both school assignment plans at issue in this case made race a decisive factor and, thus, essentially amounted to racial balancing, which the Court in *Grutter* described as "patently unconstitutional." The Court stated, "The principle that racial balancing is not permitted is one of substance, not semantics. Racial balancing is not transformed from 'patently unconstitutional' to a compelling state interest simply by labeling it 'racial diversity.'" The Court added that *Grutter* did not govern the current cases because it dealt with diversity in higher education, not school at the elementary and secondary levels.

The Seattle School District argued that it wanted to reduce racial concentration in schools, and Jefferson County argued that it wanted to create a "racially integrated" environment. The schools argued that since they seek racial diversity, they should be allowed to address that sole issue directly. However, the Court argued that the "plans are tied to each district's specific racial demographics, rather than to any pedagogic concept of the level of diversity needed to obtain the asserted educational benefits." The school districts failed to demonstrate that the level of racial diversity needed to achieve a certain degree of educational benefits could be accomplished by making school attendance coincide with the racial demographics of the school districts. The Court noted that under the schools' current plans, "as the districts' demographics shift, so too will their definition of racial diversity."

Noting the minimal effects the racial classifications actually had on students, the Court reasoned that other means probably would have been just as effective. There was no evidence that either school district had made a good-faith effort to utilize race-neutral alternatives. The Court concluded that "the way to stop discrimination on the basis of race is to stop discriminating on the basis of race." Accordingly, the judgments of the courts of appeals for both the Sixth and Ninth Circuits were reversed, and the cases were remanded for further proceedings.

Justice Kennedy wrote a concurring opinion, in which he agreed with the majority's decision but only on the particular facts of this case. He reasoned that the goal of achieving a particular level of diversity in elementary and secondary schools is a compelling state interest. He also argued that use of race-conscious assignment plans by school districts should be allowed because it helps ensure people have equal opportunities. However, Justice Kennedy stated that neither Jefferson County nor the Seattle School District narrowly tailored its plan to satisfy strict scrutiny analysis because of the existence of race-neutral alternatives. Justice Thomas also wrote a concurring opinion, primarily to refute arguments made in Justice Breyer's dissenting opinion. He argued that despite the dissenters' contention, resegregation was not occurring in either Seattle or Louisville, and he suggested that Justice Breyer's argument for allowing schools to determine their student body according to race was "reminiscent of that advocated by the segregationists in *Brown v. Board of Education*."

Justice Stevens wrote a dissenting opinion, in which he agreed with and added to Justice Breyer's dissent. He expressed his view that "a decision to exclude a member of a minority because of his race is fundamentally different from a decision to include a member of a minority for that reason." He thought the latter was constitutional and in accordance with *Brown*. As mentioned, Justice Breyer also wrote a dissenting opinion, joined by Justices Stevens, Souter, and Ginsburg. He argued that Seattle and Jefferson County's plans sought to counter resegregation by increasing student choice and that "the Constitution permits local communities to adopt desegregation plans even where it does not require them to do so." He considered the plans to be remedial, educational, and valid under the equal protection clause. Addressing the Jefferson County plan, Justice Breyer asked, "how could such a plan be lawful the day before dissolution but then become unlawful the very next day?" Additionally, Justice Breyer argued that the "holding upsets settled expectations, creates legal uncertainty, and threatens to produce considerable further litigation, aggravating race-related conflict."

AFTERMATH

Schools were no longer able to conduct admissions selection by using racial "tiebreakers."

SIGNIFICANCE

The significance of these consolidated cases is that the U.S. Supreme Court officially prohibited the practice of assigning students to public schools solely to achieve racial diversity. In reaching its conclusion, the Court reasoned that the school districts' use of racial balancing did not serve a compelling state interest. However, Justice Kennedy's concurring opinion suggests that schools are allowed to be "race conscious" when seeking diversity.

RELATED CASES

Mendez v. Westminster School District, 64 F.Supp. 544 (C.D. Cal. 1946), aff'd; 161 F.2d 774 (9th Cir. 1947) (en banc)

Brown v. Board of Education of Topeka, 347 U.S. 483 (1954)

Green v. County School Board of New Kent County, 391 U.S. 430 (1968)

Swann v. Charlotte-Mecklenburg Board of Education, 402 U.S. 1 (1971)

Regents of the University of California v. Bakke, 438 U.S. 265 (1978)

Gratz v. Bollinger, 539 U.S. 244 (2003)

Grutter v. Bollinger, 539 U.S. 306 (2003)

RECOMMENDED READING

Joel K. Goldstein, *Not Hearing History: A Critique of Chief Justice Robert's Reinterpretation of Brown*, 69 Ohio State Law Journal 791 (2008).

Case Title: *District of Columbia v. Heller*

Legal Citation: 554 U.S. 570

Year of Decision: 2008

KEY ISSUE

Does a District of Columbia law prohibiting usable handgun possession in the home violate the Second Amendment of the Constitution?

HISTORY OF THE CASE

The District of Columbia prohibited the possession of registered and unregistered handguns. The law required that no person could carry a handgun without a license, which could be granted by the chief of police for a one-year period. The District of Columbia also required lawfully owned guns, such as long guns, to be unloaded and either dissembled or with a locking device on the trigger unless lawfully being used.

Dick Heller, a policeman authorized to carry a handgun while on duty at the Federal Judicial Center, had his application for a handgun for his home denied. Heller, then, filed a lawsuit in the Federal District Court for the District of Columbia in an attempt to enjoin the city from enforcing the handgun law. The district court dismissed the complaint, and after an appeal was filed, the D.C.

Court of Appeals reversed on the ground that the ban violated the Second Amendment by not allowing operable guns in the home for the purpose of self-defense. Upon further appeal, the U.S. Supreme Court granted certiorari.

SUMMARY OF ARGUMENTS

Heller argued that the Second Amendment applies to all citizens, regardless of military affiliation.

Conversely, the District of Columbia argued that the Second Amendment is worded such that it applies only to people associated with militia services.

DECISION

The Court held that the District of Columbia handgun prohibition violated the Second Amendment of the Constitution. The Court found that, under the Second Amendment, individuals unaffiliated with the military have the right to possess a firearm and to use it for lawful purposes within the home.

Justice Scalia delivered the opinion of the Court. The Court first discussed the meaning of the Second Amendment, which reads: "A well regulated Militia, being necessary to the security of a free State, the right of the people to keep and bear Arms, shall not be infringed." The Court then began its inquiry by dividing the Second Amendment into two parts: the operative clause and the prefatory clause. The Court first inspected the operative clause, which reads "the right of the people to keep and bear arms, shall not be infringed." Rather than a collective right, the Court found the operative clause to "guarantee the individual right to possess and carry weapons in case of confrontation," regardless of military affiliation. The Court additionally found the right to bear arms to be a right that preexisted the Constitution, noting that the "very text of the Second Amendment implicitly recognizes the preexistence of the right and declares only that it 'shall not be infringed.'" The Court next turned to the prefatory clause, which reads: "A well regulated Militia, being necessary to the security of a free State." Although the Constitution explicitly grants Congress the power to create armies and navies, militia were understood to be already in existence at the time the Constitution was ratified. The Court interpreted the phrase "security of a free State" to refer to the security of a free "polity," as opposed to the security of each individual state.

Considering the relationship between the two clauses, the Court noted that "history showed that the way tyrants had eliminated a militia consisting of all the able-bodied men was not by banning the militia but simply by taking away the people's arms, enabling a select militia or standing army to suppress political opponents." The constitutional debates in which the Second Amendment was discussed, according to the Court, were not about whether the right should exist but whether it should be codified in the Constitution. The right was codified to prevent elimination of the militia by tyrants and to preserve other uses of arms, such as self-defense and hunting. Additionally, prior to the ratification of the Constitution and thereafter, states had drafted similar amendments for their respective governments. The Court also noted that several founding-era legal scholars, 19th-century case law, and post–Civil War legislation interpreted the Second Amendment as preserving an individual right to bear arms regardless of militia service.

The Court next determined whether prior Supreme Court precedents were consistent with the majority's interpretation of the Second Amendment. In *United States v. Cruikshank,* the Court stated that the amendment applies only to the federal government, thus reserving states the freedom to restrict or uphold the right under their policing powers. This was reaffirmed in *Presser v. Illinois* (1886) and *Miller v. Texas* (1894). The Court in *Miller* held that the Second Amendment applies only to certain types of weapons in "common use." The Court in *Miller* addressed which types of weapons this included; reading *Miller* "to say only that the Second Amendment does not protect those weapons not typically possessed by law-abiding citizens for lawful purposes," handguns were deemed to be in common use and used for the lawful purposes of self-defense and recreational activities. After viewing other historical precedents, the Court found nothing that foreclosed the understanding

of the Second Amendment adopted by the majority. The Court went on to add that "nothing in our opinion should be taken to cast doubt on longstanding prohibitions on the possession of firearms by felons and the mentally ill, or laws forbidding the carrying of firearms in sensitive places such as schools and government buildings, or laws imposing conditions and qualifications on the commercial sale of arms." A further limitation against carrying "dangerous and unusual weapons" was also mentioned, as it was supported by historical traditions.

Addressing the specific law at issue in this case, which was a total ban on handgun possession in the home, the Court found it to be overly broad because it "amount[ed] to a prohibition of an entire class of 'arms' that is overwhelmingly chosen by American society" for the lawful purpose of self-defense. The fact that the prohibition extended to the home, where the Court argued the need of self-defense was most prevalent, also factored into the Court's conclusion that the law would fail constitutional muster under any of the standards of scrutiny traditionally applied to constitutional rights. The Court declined to rule on the injunction sought against petitioners from enforcing the separate licensing requirement because the issuance of a license to Heller would satisfy his prayer for relief, and it was likely to be granted. In conclusion, the Court stated that although whether the Second Amendment is outdated in a society with adequate military and police forces is debatable, "what is not debatable is that it is not the role of this Court to pronounce the Second Amendment extinct." Accordingly, the judgment of the court of appeals was affirmed.

Justice Stevens wrote a dissenting opinion, joined by Justices Souter, Ginsburg, and Breyer. Justice Stevens argued that the Court's decision in *United States v. Miller* (1939), mentioned earlier, limited the right to bear arms to military purposes and that the majority should follow this precedent based on stare decisis. He argued that no new evidence had surfaced since *Miller* to justify overturning the long-standing precedent established in that case. He asserted that *Miller* did not prevent legislatures from regulating non-military use of firearms as the District of Columbia had in this case. Discussing the drafters of the Constitution, Justice Stevens noted, "specifically there is no indication that the Framers of the [Second] Amendment intended to enshrine the common-law right of self-defense in the Constitution."

Justice Breyer also wrote a dissenting opinion, joined by Justices Stevens, Souter, and Ginsberg. He pointed out two main reasons for his conclusion that the majority's decision was wrong: first, as Justice Stevens had pointed out in his dissenting opinion, the Second Amendment is related only to militia interests, and, second, the amendment is not absolute and thus can be limited legislatively. Justice Breyer thought the District of Columbia law was justifiably responsive to serious gun crime issues in that area. Thus, he argued the law advanced public interests, was limited to a particular geographic location in which the problem existed, and provided a sufficient nexus between the problem addressed (i.e., crime) and the handgun law at issue. Under these particular circumstances, Justice Beyer argued, "The District's law falls within the zone that the Second Amendment leaves open to regulation by legislatures."

AFTERMATH

Soon after the decision in *Heller,* the National Rifle Association filed a lawsuit challenging a San Francisco city gun ban in public housing in *Guy Montag Doe v. San Francisco Housing Authority.* The purpose of the lawsuit was to determine whether the Court's decision in *Heller* applied to state and local gun laws. However, this lawsuit was settled outside court.

Two parallel cases, *McDonald v. Chicago* and *NRA v. Chicago,* were granted certiorari by the Supreme Court on September 30, 2009. These cases are seeking to overturn a handgun ban and other gun regulations in Chicago, Illinois. The trial court in *McDonald* ruled in favor of the city of Chicago, and upon appeal, it was consolidated with *NRA v. Chicago.* The Seventh Circuit Court of Appeals upheld the gun regulations. The Supreme Court has yet to make its decision.

SIGNIFICANCE

This was the first case in which the U.S. Supreme Court addressed the issue of whether the Second Amendment's right to keep and bear arms is a right of individuals in addition to the firearm rights of state-regulated militias. However, this case was decided in federal court, so it is unclear whether this decision applies to state prohibitions on usable handguns within the home.

RELATED CASES

United States v. Cruikshank, 92 U.S. 542 (1876)

Presser v. Illinois, 116 U.S. 252 (1886)

Miller v. Texas, 153 U.S. 535 (1894)

United States v. Miller, 307 U.S. 174 (1939)

McDonald v. Chicago, 561 U.S. ____ (2010)

RECOMMENDED READING

Ryan L. Card, *An Opinion without Standards: The Supreme Court's Refusal to Adopt a Standard of Constitutional Review in* District of Columbia v. Heller *Will Likely Cause Headaches for Future Judicial Review of Gun-Control Regulations,* 23 BYU Journal of Public Law 259 (2009).

Ben Howell, *Come and Take It: The Status of Texas Handgun Legislation after District of Columbia v. Heller,* 61 Baylor Law Review 215 (2009).

Allen Rostron, *Protecting Gun Rights and Improving Gun Control after* District of Columbia v. Heller, 13 Lewis and Clark Law Review 383 (2009).

Lawrence B. Solum, District of Columbia v. Heller *and Originalism,* 103 Northwestern University Law Review 923 (2009).

Case Title: *Ricci v. DeStefano*

Legal Citation: 557 U.S. ____

Year of Decision: 2009

~

KEY ISSUE

Can a municipality reject civil service exams when the results prevent the promotion of minority candidates?

HISTORY OF THE CASE

The New Haven, Connecticut, Fire Department relies on objective civil service examinations to determine promotions to and within officer ranks, including lieutenant and captain positions. In 2003, 118 firefighters took the promotional examinations to determine the order in which employees would be considered for promotion over the next two years. The tests were developed by Industrial/Organizational Solutions, Inc. ("IOS"), and utilized by the New Haven Civil Service Board (the "Board") to help them determine which candidates would be placed in each position on the basis of their test scores. The firefighters absorbed both the personal and financial costs of preparing for the tests. The results of the tests demonstrated that white candidates had performed better than minority candidates, so the mayor of New Haven, along with other local politicians, held public debates to determine whether or not the test results should be retained for promotional purposes.

Both the city and the employees had arguments based on Title VII of the Civil Rights Act of 1964. On one side, a discrimination lawsuit against the city was threatened if the test results were used for their intended purpose on the basis of the disparate-*impact* provision. However, the other side also threatened a discrimination lawsuit if the tests were not used on the basis of the disparate-*treatment* provision. The city decided to throw out the test results. Several white and Hispanic firefighters, including Ricci, sued the city and some of its officials, alleging that the defendants discriminated against the plaintiffs on the basis of their race, in violation of Title VII and the equal protection clause of the Fourteenth Amendment. The district court granted summary judgment for the defendants, which was affirmed on appeal. The U.S. Supreme Court granted certiorari.

SUMMARY OF ARGUMENTS

The thrust of Ricci's argument was that an employer cannot avoid unintentional discrimination by using intentional discrimination. Title VII prohibits discrimination on the basis of race, color, religion, sex, or national origin, whether it is intentional or unintentionally has a disparate impact on the adversely affected class.

The city argued that if it had not administered the test, it would have been liable for discrimination under the Title VII disparate-impact provision. Essentially, race-conscious conduct was necessary to comply with the law.

DECISION

The Court determined that whether a municipality can reject otherwise valid civil service exams because they prevent minorities from being promoted is dependent upon the facts of each individual case. In this case, the Court found that that city of New Haven violated Title VII of the Civil Rights Act of 1964 by rejecting the exam scores. The Court further held that an employer, prior to engaging in intentional discrimination to avoid a disparate impact, must have strong evidence that it will be subject to disparate-impact liability if it fails to take such action. The city of New Haven failed to demonstrate that it would have faced liability had it not thrown out the exams.

Justice Kennedy delivered the opinion of the Court. The Court first noted that it had both statutory and constitutional issues before it. The Court chose to address the Title VII statutory claim first, because if Ricci and the firefighters prevailed on that issue, the Court would dispose of the case without needing to rule on the constitutional issue. Title VII prohibits discrimination on the basis of race, color, religion, sex, or national origin, whether it is intentional or unintentionally has a disparate impact on the adversely affected class. Originally, the Civil Rights Act of 1964 applied only to disparate treatment, but the Court in *Griggs v. Duke Power Company* interpreted the act sometimes to prohibit employer practices that appear neutral on their face but have a discriminatory impact. That case developed the standard, which was later codified in the Civil Rights Act of 1991, that employment practices that discriminate must be significantly related to job performance and consistent with business necessity. If that is demonstrated, for the plaintiff to prevail, it must show a legitimate available alternative that would discriminate less or not at all.

Ricci argued that an employer could not avoid unintentional discrimination by using intentional discrimination. The Court noted that the city had undoubtedly discriminated against its employees by throwing out the test results, and this could only be upheld by some justifiable reason. However, the purposes of Title VII, which are to free workplaces of discrimination and to eliminate race as a barrier to opportunity, apply to both provisions of the act. The Court rejected both a requirement that the employer in fact be in violation of the disparate-impact provision before it can justify using disparate treatment and a requirement that the employer need only a "good-faith" reason for throwing out the tests to prevent disparate-impact discrimination. Instead, the Court adopted a standard similar to that used in equal protection cases, particularly in *Wygant v. Jackson Board of Education,* known as the "strong basis in evidence" standard. Accordingly, the Court held, "Under Title VII, before an employer can engage in intentional discrimination for the asserted purpose of avoiding or remedying an unintentional disparate impact, the employer must have a strong basis in evidence to believe it will be subject to disparate impact liability if it fails to take race-conscious, discriminatory action."

Applying this standard, the Court noted that violating one provision in order not to violate another provision, as happened in this case, could only be justified under narrow circumstances. While analyzing the facts of this case under the "strong basis in evidence" standard, the Court noted that the firefighters had a legitimate expectation not to be judged on the basis of race. The Court also pointed out that the test takers had invested a lot of time and money in preparing for and taking the test. According to the record, the Court found the city lacked a strong basis in evidence for throwing out the test scores because evidence showed that many of the

experts questioned by the Board suggested the tests were not biased. Further, according to the Equal Employment Opportunity Commission, to implement the disparate-impact provision of Title VII, the pass rates for one racial group must be 80 percent higher than the pass rate for other groups. Here, the pass rates for minorities were only half that of whites.

The Court next turned to the issue of summary judgment, which requires that there is no dispute over an issue of genuine fact. Generally, a threshold showing of racial statistical disparity is not sufficient to establish a prima facie case of disparate-impact liability. The Court argued that "the City could be liable for disparate-impact discrimination only if the examinations were not job related and consistent with business necessity, or if there existed an equally valid, less discriminatory alternative that served the City's needs but that the City refused to adopt." There was no dispute that the examinations were job related and part of business necessity because of the steps taken by the IOS in developing the test to prevent disparities based on race. The respondents could not demonstrate an alternative, less-discriminatory remedy that the city refused to adopt, in part because, although the city offered alternatives, Title VII prohibits adjusting test scores on the basis of race, as some of the alternatives would have required. The Court held that summary judgment was appropriate for the petitioners on their disparate-treatment claim because it was clear they had been discriminated against in having their test scores thrown out.

In conclusion, the Court stated that if "after it certifies the test results, the City faces a disparate-impact suit, then in light of our holding today, it should be clear that the City would avoid disparate-impact liability based on the strong basis in evidence that, had it not certified the results, it would have been subject to disparate-treatment liability." Since the petitioners were entitled to summary judgment on their disparate-treatment claim, the Court did not decide the underlying constitutional question. Accordingly, the judgment of the court of appeals was reversed, and the case was remanded for further proceedings consistent with this opinion. Justice Scalia concurred with the majority; however, he wrote separately to emphasize the fact that the Court will eventually have to address the issue of whether the disparate-impact provisions of Title VII are consistent with the equal protection clause of the Fourteenth Amendment.

Justice Ginsburg wrote a dissenting opinion, joined by Justices Stevens, Souter, and Breyer. She argued that the tests were not thrown out because whites did better than other groups but, rather, were thrown out because of the many flaws in the examinations. The dissenters explained the long history of racial discrimination in firefighting and stated that although progress has been made, significant disparities remain in supervisory positions. Justice Ginsburg also argued that the city's decision was race-neutral because since all of the test results were discarded and no one was promoted, all of the test takers were being treated in the same way. Although the dissenters would have held that no employer should be liable under disparate-impact discrimination if there is "good cause to believe the device would not withstand examination for business necessity," the majority had already addressed this issue, stating that this would "encourage race-based action at the slightest hint of disparate impact." Justice Ginsburg also argued that the holding in this case could deter voluntary compliance with Title VII because employers may fear similar lawsuits.

Justice Alito also wrote a concurring opinion, joined by Justices Scalia and Thomas. Justice Alito wrote separately to point out key factual omissions in Justice Ginsburg's dissenting opinion. He noted the city's concern about a political backlash spurred by a controversial African-American minister, the reverend Boise Kimber, who previously had been forced to resign as chairman of the New Haven Board of Fire Commissioners because of racial slurs he had made. He argued that the city's asserted justification for throwing out the tests was "pretextual" because he thought the city threw out the tests "to please a politically important racial constituency." He concluded by stressing the amount of time and effort the firefighters spent preparing for the examination.

AFTERMATH

This case was decided just before Justice Sonia Sotomayor replaced Justice David H. Souter, a dissenter in this opinion. As a judge for the Second Circuit, the then-judge Sotomayor joined the majority opinion of that court, which was reversed in this case. Some observers believe the Court's decision may lead to uncertainty regarding whether the administration of civil service examinations is discriminatory in impact or treatment. One critical response suggested that simply throwing out discriminatory tests does not solve the problem, because the employer now has the burden of determining whether there is substantial evidence to demonstrate that a test actually discriminates against employees before it can be abandoned. Thus, employers are left with the task of determining in advance whether a promotional or entry-level exam is discriminatory. Justice Ginsburg also discussed these same views in her dissenting opinion in this case.

SIGNIFICANCE

The Court made clear in this case that after the government employer certifies test results, if the municipality faces a disparate-impact lawsuit, it can avoid disparate-*impact* liability by showing a strong basis in evidence that had the test results not been certified, it would have been subject to disparate-*treatment* liability. However, the Court did not address whether the disparate-impact provisions of Title VII are consistent with the equal protection clause of the Fourteenth Amendment because the case was disposed of without having to reach that issue. Thus, the answer to that question has yet to be determined.

RELATED CASES

Griggs v. Duke Power Company, 401 U.S. 424 (1971)

Washington v. Davis, 426 U.S. 229 (1976)

United Steelworkers v. Weber, 443 U.S. 193 (1979)

Wygant v. Jackson Board of Education, 476 U.S. 267 (1986)

Watson v. Fort Worth Bank & Trust, 487 U.S. 977 (1988)

STATUTE AT ISSUE

Title VII, 42 U.S.C.A. § 2000e-2. Unlawful employment practices

RECOMMENDED READING

Lauren Klein, Ricci v. DeStefano: *"Fanning the Flames" of Reverse Discrimination in Civil Service Selection,* 4 Duke Journal of Constitutional Law & Public Policy Sidebar 391 (2009).

Michael Newman and Faith Isenhath, *Reflections on the Supreme Court's* Ricci *Decision,* 56 Federal Lawyer 14 (2009).

Edward G. Phillips, Ricci v. DeStefano *Holds Statistical Disparities Cannot Justify Race-Based Employment Decisions Where There's Smoke but No Fire,* 45 Tennessee Bar Journal 31 (2009).

CONTRACTS

One of the fundamental rights of citizens is the right to engage in legitimate business. This right is critical to our nation's economic stability and to each individual's right to life, liberty, and the pursuit of happiness. But, as with any fundamental principle regarding the great experiment of our free market-capitalist democracy, the right to form business contracts is not without limits. For example, a business cannot contract with individuals for substandard working conditions or for wages below the federally established minimum wage. Likewise, the federal government is forbidden to pass laws that make certain business contracts illegal.

Reading the cases in this chapter, one can clearly see how the Supreme Court carefully weighs businesses' interests in having a legal climate where contracts are predictable and enforceable, against the interests of the government in regulating important public policy. For example, in the case of a business that hires workers at below minimum wage, both the business and the employee may favor freedom to contract over the interest in the government to see that people are paid fair wages. The business benefits when it hires workers cheaply, and workers may even wish to work for less than minimum wage if an employer contends that it may not be able to hire as many employees or even remain in business if forced to pay a higher wage. In this case, the Supreme Court has declared that the government has a greater inter-est of ensuring that its citizens be paid a fair wage than the aforementioned interests of either the employees or the businesses.

Over the years, there has been much conflict among governments, businesses, and private citizens as the Court strives to sort out and balance the interests of each group against the constitutional principles of life, liberty, and the pursuit of happiness.

Case Title: *Calder v. Bull*

Alternate Case Title: The "Natural Rights" Case

Legal Citation: 3 U.S. 386

Year of Decision: 1798

KEY ISSUE

Is state legislation that invalidates a prior court decision disposing of property under a will an ex post facto law that violates the Constitution?

HISTORY OF THE CASE

This case originated in a Connecticut probate court after the death of Norman Morrison. Caleb Bull and his wife and Calder and his wife were engaged in a dispute over Morrison's will, which affected how Morrison's property would be distributed.

The Court of Probate for Hartford, Connecticut, passed a decree against the will of Norman Morrison and vested a right to recover certain property in appellants Calder and his wife. The Connecticut legislature then passed a resolution of law that set aside the decree of the Court of Probate for Hartford. The effect of the resolution of law was to revise that decision of the Court of Probate for Hartford, one of its inferior courts, and to direct a new hearing of the case by the James Court of Probate. The James Court of Probate then approved the will of Norman Morrison, divested appellant Calder and his wife of the property, and declared the right of that property to be in appellees Bull and his wife. Appellants Calder and his wife claim the premises in question, in right of his wife, as heiress of N. Morrison, physician. Appellee Bull and wife claimed the property under the will of N. Morrison, the grandson.

SUMMARY OF ARGUMENTS

Appellants, Calder and his wife, contended that the so-named resolution of law of the legislature of Connecticut was an ex post facto law, prohibited by the Constitution of the United States. They further claimed that any law of the federal government or of any of the state governments contrary to the Constitution of the United States was void. Therefore, the appellants asserted that the Connecticut legislature had no power to issue the resolution granting a new hearing.

The appellees, Bull and his wife, argued that the resolution was not an ex post facto law and the Connecticut legislature had acted within the scope of its authority.

DECISION

The Court unanimously held that the legislature's action was not an "ex post facto Law" forbidden the states by Article I, Section 10. Justice Chase, writing the opinion for the Court, believed that the legislation did not impair a vested right and, therefore, was consistent with natural justice—the rules and principles that guide human conduct and are enforceable against the states even though they are not contained in the Constitution. However, the Court disagreed over the role of "natural law" in constitutional interpretation.

Justice Chase did not believe that the "omnipotence" of the legislature was absolute or without control, but he believed that its authority should not be expressly restrained by the Constitution or the fundamental law of the state. He argued that the reasons the people of the United States instituted the Constitution were for the establishment of justice, promotion of the general welfare, liberty, and the protection of their persons and property from violence. He believed that these purposes dictated the nature and terms of the social compact and legislative power, and that an act of the legislature contrary to the principles in the social compact was not a rightful exercise of legislative authority. For example, Justice Chase maintained that "natural law" prohibits "a law that destroys or impairs the lawful private contracts of citizens [or] that takes property from A. and gives it to B." He argued that private property must be protected from legislative intrusion even if the legislature were not "expressly restrained by the Constitution."

Justice Paterson wrote a concurring opinion, finding that the Connecticut legislature did nothing more than exercise its power of granting new trials as it had from the beginning. He believed that the resolution of the Connecticut legislature was not an ex post facto law within the meaning of the Constitution because the words "ex post facto," when applied to law, referred to crimes and nothing else. Thus, he believed that it referred only to penal statutes, and not this case.

Justice Iredell wrote a dissenting opinion opposing the belief that a legislative act against natural justice in itself must be void. He felt that no court should have the power to declare it so. He argued that it has been the policy of the states and the people of the United States to define legislative power precisely and to set limitations within those confines. He argued that if the federal legislature passed a law within the general scope of their constitutional power, the Court could not pronounce it void merely because it believed that the law was contrary to natural justice. He asserted that, at most, the Court could state that the act was "inconsistent with natural justice." Justice Iredell stated that if an act of Congress or of a state legislature violated the Constitution's provisions, then it was definitely void. However, he maintained that as long as the legislature pursued the authority delegated to them, their acts would be valid, since they were exercising the discretion vested in them by the people—and it is only the people to whom the legislature is responsible for the discharge of their trust.

AFTERMATH

Because the Supreme Court affirmed the actions of the probate court, Morrison's will was approved, and the property went to the Bulls. Justice Iredell disagreed with Justice Chase's proposition that legislation might be held invalid under natural law even if the legislation did not violate any specific constitutional principles or provisions, and his views have prevailed. Since the 1800s, courts have used their power to invalidate legislation, usually where specific constitutional provisions supplied the principle of invalidity.

SIGNIFICANCE

Calder demonstrated a classic debate between Justice Chase and Justice Iredell over the scope and nature of judicial power, which has proved fundamental to constitutional law. Justice Chase's opinion illustrated the belief that there is an "unwritten" Constitution consisting of principles of natural law that is enforceable against the states. Justice Iredell believed that the very existence of a written Constitution was authority against the proposition that courts can call on principles of natural justice.

RELATED CASE

Fletcher v. Peck, 10 U.S. 87 (1810)

RECOMMENDED READING

Bailyn, Bernard. *The Ideological Origins of the American Revolution.* Cambridge, Mass.: Belknap Press of Harvard University Press, 1967.

Edwin S. Corwin, *The "Higher Law" Background of American Constitutional Law,* 42 Harvard Law Review (1928).

Suzanna Sherry, *The Founder's Unwritten Constitution,* 54 University of Chicago Law Review (1987).

Case Title: *Fletcher v. Peck*

Legal Citation: 10 U.S. 87

Year of Decision: 1810

KEY ISSUE

Is a contract to convey land protected from state law by the contracts clause of the U.S. Constitution?

HISTORY OF THE CASE

This case was brought in federal Circuit Court for the District of Massachusetts as a contract action. The court ruled for the defendant, and the case was then heard by the U.S. Supreme Court, enabling it to apply both state and federal law since the case originated in federal court.

Pursuant to a Georgia legislative land grant, the original grantees of the land in question sold a portion of their land. The new buyer then resold a portion. After an election, the grant was revoked, but meanwhile the land was again resold; Peck then bought it and sold it to Fletcher, who had no notice of the revocation.

SUMMARY OF ARGUMENTS

The appellant, Robert Fletcher, argued that the title to the land sold to him by the appellee, John Peck, was impaired because the state of Georgia had no authority to sell the land. Fletcher argued that Georgia lacked authority to sell the land because the legislative act granting this power to sell was fraudulently procured, and the United States, not Georgia, held legal title.

Peck argued that the state constitution gave Georgia title to the land conveyed, and a legislative act gave Georgia all jurisdictional and territorial rights. Therefore, Georgia was legally empowered to sell the land.

DECISION

Chief Justice Marshall wrote for the majority that Georgia could not revoke its grant because of the contracts clause. A contract contains binding obligations. Under the Constitution, a law that annuls a contract between individuals violates the contracts clause. This reasoning also allows a state statute to be declared unconstitutional as part of litigation between private parties. A contract to convey land was protected from state law by the contracts clause of the Constitution.

Justice Johnson wrote a dissent, saying that the interpretation of the contracts clause espoused by Chief Justice Marshall deprived states of the power of eminent domain, the power to take private property for public use.

AFTERMATH

This was the first Supreme Court case to be decided on the obligations of the contracts clause and the first to declare a state statute unconstitutional under federal law.

SIGNIFICANCE

This case altered 19th-century constitutional law by applying the contracts provision to property. It became a major tool for state legislation to be struck down in federal courts.

RELATED CASES

Trustees of Dartmouth College v. Woodward, 17 U.S. 517 (1819)

Charles River Bridge v. Warren Bridge, 36 U.S. 420 (1837)

Home Building and Loan Association v. Braisdell, 290 U.S. 415 (1935)

RECOMMENDED READING

Magrath, Peter C. *Yazoo: Law and Politics in the New Republic: The Case of* Fletcher v. Peck. Providence, R.I.: Brown University Press, 1966.

McCloskey, Robert C. *The American Supreme Court*. Chicago: University of Chicago Press, 1960.

Robert C. Palmer, *Obligations of Contracts: Intent and Distortion,* 37 Case Western Reserve Law Review 631 (1987).

Wiecek, William M. *The Guarantee Clause of the United States Constitution*. Ithaca, N.Y.: Cornell University Press, 1972.

Case Title: *The Trustees of Dartmouth College v. Woodward*

Alternate Case Title: The Dartmouth College Case

Legal Citation: 17 U.S. 518

Year of Decision: 1819

KEY ISSUES

Is the charter of a privately funded institution a contract, and, if so, is it protected by the contracts clause of the U.S. Constitution?

HISTORY OF THE CASE

This action brought in state court requested that Dartmouth College, a corporation, turn over certain records. The case went to the Superior Court of the State of New Hampshire and then to the U.S. Supreme Court.

Prior to the American Revolution, Eleazar Wheelock sought and was granted a charter from the king of England for Dartmouth College. Under the college charter, Wheelock, as founder and president of Dartmouth, could nominate his successor. After the American Revolution, Wheelock's son John was the president of Dartmouth, and John's administration was challenged by the trustees. The dispute was taken to the state's politicians, and the New Hampshire legislature enacted several acts that purported to change the name of the college and its governing structure, among other things. However, the trustees refused to accept the charter as amended by the state legislature and brought suit. Daniel Webster argued the case for the trustees of Dartmouth College.

SUMMARY OF ARGUMENTS

The appellants, the trustees, argued that the acts enacted by the New Hampshire legislature altering the name and governing structure of Dartmouth College violated the contracts clause of the U.S. Constitution. The contracts clause states that "no state shall pass any . . . law impairing the obligation of contracts." In support of this contention, the trustees argued that the grant of corporate powers and privileges through the charter was a contract for a private purpose, and the acts of the New Hampshire legislature impaired the contract by essentially abolishing the old entity and establishing a new one.

The appellee, William H. Woodward, the secretary and treasurer of the trustees of Dartmouth, the entity established by the New Hampshire legislature, argued that the occurrence of the American Revolution changed the circumstances under which the charter was originally granted, and therefore, the original charter had become unfit for use. Woodward also argued that the charter was not the type of contract that was contemplated by the contracts clause, and even if it was, the acts did not impair the contract. Woodward also argued that Dartmouth College was a public institution, not a private charity.

DECISION

Chief Justice Marshall stated that private corporations were free from legislative interference, while public corporations did not have this protection. Private corporations were protected under the contracts clause, so legislatures were prohibited from revising or repealing their charters. Although Dartmouth had public purposes, it was a private charitable entity because private individuals founded the corporation. A public corporation is one created by public institutions for the public advantage.

The charter of a private corporation is a contract protected by the Constitution from legislative interference. The state of New Hampshire could not use legislation to put its own trustees on the college's Board of Trustees to increase its size since its charter gave the college the right to fill vacancies.

AFTERMATH

This was the first time the Court had held a corporate charter to be a contract. The decision placed corporate charters under the protection of the contracts clause. This interpretation of the contracts clause prevented legislative interference in state economic affairs.

SIGNIFICANCE

The case strengthened the power of business by giving businesses a constitutional base for appeals. Corporations could not be subject to arbitrary interference; their services were to be regarded as state functions providing goods and services that the state could not. This posed a threat to states that had no way to curb corporate abuse. Corporations used the contract clause to challenge taxation and rate regulation.

RELATED CASE

Fletcher v. Peck, 10 U.S. 87 (1810)

RECOMMENDED READING

B. A. Campbell, *John Marshall, the Virginia Political Economy, and the Dartmouth College Decision,* 19 American Journal of Legal History 40 (1975).

Friendly, Henry J. *The Dartmouth College Case and the Public-Private Penumbra.* Austin: University of Texas at Austin, 1968.

Hunting, Warren B. *The Obligations of the Contract Clause of the United States Constitution.* Westport, Conn.: Greenwood Press, 1919.

Stites, Francis N. *Private Interest and Public Gain: The Dartmouth College Case, 1819.* Amherst: University of Massachusetts Press, 1972.

Case Title: *Proprietors of the Charles River Bridge v. Proprietors of the Warren Bridge*

Alternate Case Title: The Warren Bridge Case

Legal Citation: 36 U.S. 420

Year of Decision: 1837

KEY ISSUES

Does the contracts clause distinguish between public and private contracts, and, if so, should ambiguities in public contracts be interpreted in favor of the private party or the state?

HISTORY OF THE CASE

The state of Massachusetts had granted a charter to the Charles River Bridge Co. to build a toll bridge between Boston and Charleston. The charter implied, but did not expressly say, that the state would not grant any charters for competing bridges. Later, the legislature granted a charter to another company to construct a free bridge.

The owners of the Charles River Bridge filed a bill seeking an injunction to prevent the erection of the Warren Bridge and for general relief. The Massachusetts Supreme Court dismissed the bill, and the owners of the Charles River Bridge appealed to the U.S. Supreme Court.

Early decisions of the Supreme Court interpreted the contracts clause as giving broad protection against state interference in all contracts, both private and public. In *Fletcher v. Peck* (1910), the Court noted that the language of the Constitution does not distinguish between public and private contracts.

SUMMARY OF ARGUMENTS

The Court addressed the issue of whether a charter granted by the state should be interpreted as exclusive when the charter did not explicitly state that it was exclusive. Chief Justice Taney noted earlier cases that had established that a charter is a contract binding on the state. Previous cases also established to the Court's satisfaction that a state law could work retroactively to divest vested rights so long as the law did not "impair the obligation of a contract." Taney stated that this case called for the Court to decide whether a contract to which the state was a party should be interpreted strictly according to the language it contained, or whether a court could recognize implied promises by the state.

The Court was faced with a conflict between the need for stability of contracts involving the state and the need for flexibility in cases when changing circumstances cause state contracts to result in harm to the public. If the Court decided that it would enforce the implied grant of an exclusive right to build a bridge, then the stability of public contracts would be bolstered; private parties would be able to rely on the understanding they reached with the state. If the Court ruled that implied promises would not be enforced, the state could conceivably alter bargains it had made whenever they proved inconvenient or unprofitable.

DECISION

The Court said that "any ambiguity in the terms of the contract must operate against the adventurers, and in favor of the public, and the plaintiffs can claim nothing that is not clearly given them by the act." Thus, the Court affirmed the Massachusetts Supreme Court's dismissal of the Charles River Bridge Company's claim. The decision favored flexibility over stability in public contracts.

AFTERMATH

The decision reflected the Court's intent to support a state's power over an individual's property right. The obligation of the state would now be strictly interpreted according to the language of the contract in favor of the state. The Court did not say that contracts between private parties were subject to the rule established by this decision.

SIGNIFICANCE

There developed, as a result of this case, a double standard for reviewing contracts. Private contracts enjoyed broader interpretation, which allowed for the enforcement of implied promises.

Public contracts were interpreted narrowly with a bias in favor of the state.

RELATED CASES

Fletcher v. Peck, 10 U.S. 87 (1810)

Trustees of Dartmouth College v. Woodword, 17 U.S. 518 (1819)

RECOMMENDED READING

Currie, David P. *The Constitution in the Supreme Court, 1789–1888.* Chicago: University of Chicago Press, 1985.

David P. Currie, *The Constitution in the Supreme Court: Article IV and Federal Powers 1836–1864,* 1983 Duke Law Journal 695 (1983).

Horwitz, Morton J. *The Transformation of American Law 1780–1860.* Cambridge, Mass.: Harvard University Press, 1977.

Thomas W. Merrill, *Public Contracts and the Transformation of the Constitutional Order,* 37 Case Western Reserve Law Review 597 (1987).

Case Title: *Stone v. Mississippi*

Alternate Case Title: The Police Powers Case

Legal Citation: 101 U.S. 814

Year of Decision: 1879

KEY ISSUES

Does a state legislature have the right to revoke the charter of a lottery company through exercise of its police powers against popular sentiment?

HISTORY OF THE CASE

In 1867, the Mississippi legislature granted a charter to a lottery company that was to be valid for 25 years. In 1869, the legislature passed a law that "the legislature shall never authorize any lottery," which was ratified by the people. The attorney general of Mississippi filed suit to declare the 25-year charter repealed.

SUMMARY OF ARGUMENTS

Stone argued that he was exercising his rights under his corporation's charter to operate a lottery, and these rights were not extinguished by the passage of the constitutional provision.

Mississippi agreed that Stone was complying with his charter but argued that the charter was repealed by the passage of the constitutional provision.

DECISION

Chief Justice Waite delivered the Court's opinion that state police powers create an implied term in all contracts. A legislature may not "bargain away" the ability to provide for public health, safety, and morals or "divest itself of the power to provide for them." By reading into every contract a police powers escape clause, a provision that would essentially void the contract if it impaired the public health, safety, and morals, the Court exempted state statutes affecting the public health, safety, and morals from the contracts clause prohibition. The Court considered lotteries and gambling to be included with and subject to the police powers. When determining whether a contract had been entered through the granting of a corporate charter, the Court found the state legislature had granted the company the right to conduct lotteries in return for revenue, but this alone was not enough. Rather, "whether the alleged contract exists depends on the authority of the legislature to bind the state and the people of the state in that way."

The legislation prohibiting lotteries and gambling does not conflict with the contracts clause of the Constitution. The lottery company has nothing more than a license to enjoy the privilege for the time agreed, subject to future legislation or constitutional control.

AFTERMATH

This case points out that there are differences among traditional lotteries, gift enterprises, and casino gambling. Common gambling is tolerated partly because it requires skill. Lotteries affect whole communities, while gambling only involves a few individuals. By excluding gambling from the definition of lottery, the Supreme Court gave Congress guidance when it passed anti-lottery bills.

SIGNIFICANCE

Beginning in the 1940s, the Court's contract clause interpretations demonstrated a reluctance to strike down social and economic legislation under other constitutional provisions. The Court denied every contracts clause claim presented to it between 1941 and 1977.

RELATED CASES

Manigault v. Springs, 199 U.S. 473 (1905)

Federal Communications Commission v. American Broadcasting Co., 347 U.S. 284 (1954)

City of El Paso v. Simmons, 379 U.S. 497 (1965)

RECOMMENDED READING

Robert A. Graham, *The Constitution, the Legislature, and Unfair Surprise: Toward a Reliance-Based Approach to the Contract Clause,* 92 Michigan Law Review 398 (1993).

Richard Shawn Oliphant, *Prohibiting Casinos from Advertising: The Irrational Application of 18 USC 1304,* 38 Arizona Law Review 1373 (1996).

David B. Toscano, *Forbearance Agreements: Invalid Contracts for the Surrender of Sovereignty,* 92 Columbia Law Review 426 (1992).

Case Title: *Holden v. Hardy*

Legal Citation: 169 U.S. 366

Year of Decision: 1898

KEY ISSUE

Is a Utah state law limiting the number of hours that miners and smelters can work unconstitutional under the Fourteenth Amendment or in violation of the equal protection clause?

HISTORY OF THE CASE

The Utah legislature passed a law limiting the workday in mines and smelters to eight hours. On June 20, 1896, Holden was charged with unlawfully employing John Anderson and William Hooley. Anderson was employed to work 10-hour days in Holden's mine, and Hooley was employed to work 12-hour days in Holden's smelter. Holden was found guilty on both charges and ordered to pay a fine of $50, plus costs. After an unsuccessful appeal to the Supreme Court of the State of Utah, Holden appealed to the U.S. Supreme Court.

SUMMARY OF ARGUMENTS

Holden argued that the Utah state law limiting mine and smelter workers to an eight-hour workday was unconstitutional under the Fourteenth Amendment because it deprived individuals of the right to contract freely. The plaintiff also argued that the law deprived employers and employees of the equal protection of the laws.

DECISION

Justice Brown wrote the opinion for the Court, which determined that the Utah law was not unconstitutional because it was a valid use of the state's police power to preserve the public health and safety. Brown accepted the importance of the freedom of contract but stated that the right "is itself subject to certain limitations which the State may lawfully impose . . . owing to an enormous increase in the number of occupations which are dangerous . . . as to demand special precautions for [the employees] well-being and protection."

Another important conclusion in Justice Brown's analysis was that the Court could assess the reasonableness of a statute. In this case, the court determined that there was a reasonable basis in fact to support the legislature's judgment regarding the dangers of mining. "These employments, when too long pursued, the legislature judged to be detrimental to the health of the employees, and, so long as there are reasonable grounds for believing that this is so, its decision upon this subject cannot be reviewed by the Federal courts."

AFTERMATH

A few years later, in 1905, the court ruled in *Lochner v. New York* that a New York state law setting a maximum 60-hour week for bakers was unconstitutional. The reasoning behind the Court's different rulings in two seemingly similar cases is unknown. Some believe that the Court was becoming more conservative, while others think that the Court's decisions are perfectly consistent. In both cases, the Court looked at the reasonableness of the legislation with regard to the inherent danger of the job in question.

SIGNIFICANCE

The later, seemingly contradictory ruling in *Lochner* effectively squashed the significance of *Holden*. The case interpreted *Holden* as permitting a state to set maximum hours on professions that are in some way unhealthy to workers.

RELATED CASES

Lochner v. New York, 198 U.S. 45 (1905)

Muller v. State of Oregon, 208 U.S. 412 (1908)

Bunting v. State of Oregon, 243 U.S. 426; 37 (1917)

RECOMMENDED READING

Learned Hand, *Due Process of Law and the Eight-Hour Day,* 21 Harvard Law Review 495 (1908).

Wendy E. Parment, *From* Slaughter-House *to* Lochner: *The Rise and Fall of the Constitutionalization of Public Health,* 40 American Journal of Legal History 476 (1996).

Timothy Sandefur, *The Right to Earn a Living,* 6 Chapman Law Review 207 (2003).

Case Title: *Lochner v. New York*

Alternate Case Title: The Bakeshop Case

Legal Citation: 198 U.S. 45

Year of Decision: 1905

KEY ISSUE

Does a state law that prohibits employees from working in bakeries more than 10 hours a day or 60 hours a week unconstitutionally infringe on the Fourteenth Amendment right to sell and purchase labor?

HISTORY OF THE CASE

The late 19th and early 20th centuries saw the height of the Progressive movement, which worked for reformist state legislation to improve the dismal working conditions that were a by-product of America's Industrial Revolution. The reforms included statutes regulating wages and hours, the employment of women and children, and conditions of the workplace.

The state law at issue in *Lochner v. New York* was a reformist law. Section 110 of the labor law of the state of New York provided that no employees could be required or permitted to work in bakeries more than 60 hours in a week or 10 hours a day.

Joseph Lochner owned a "biscuit, bread and cake bakery and confectionery establishment" in Utica, New York. Lochner was convicted in county court of violating the New York labor law by requiring his employee Aman Schmitter to work more than 60 hours a week. Lochner appealed his conviction to the Appellate Division of the Supreme Court, which affirmed his conviction by a vote of three to two. Lochner then appealed to the New York Court of Appeals, the highest court of the state, which also affirmed the conviction, albeit by a court divided 4-3. Lochner then sought relief from the U.S. Supreme Court.

SUMMARY OF ARGUMENTS

Lochner argued that the statute's classification violated the equal protection clause of the Fourteenth Amendment. Lochner's attorneys, Frank H. Field and Henry Weissmann, argued that the law "singles out a certain number of men employing bakers, and permits all others similarly situated, including many who are competitors in business, to work their employés as long as they choose." Lochner's attorneys argued that the law was an improper exercise of state police power because it abridged the "fundamental right to pursue occupations." The statute was not intended to protect public health, as contended by the state. Lochner's attorneys contended that the statute could not reasonably be construed as benefiting public health because "there is no danger to the employé in a first-class bakery and so far as unsanitary conditions are concerned the employé is protected by other sections of the law."

The state of New York countered by claiming that Lochner had not met his "burden of demonstrating that the statute is repugnant to the provisions of the Federal Constitution." Julius M. Mayer, the New York attorney general, argued before the Court that the statute "was a proper exercise of the police power of the State." "The unhealthful character of the baker's occupation" made necessary a statute that restricted the employees as well as the employer.

> The State . . . has a right to safeguard the citizen against his own lack of knowledge. In dealing with certain classes of men the State may properly say that . . . it shall not permit these men, when engaged in dangerous or unhealthful occupations, to work for a longer period of time each day than is found to be in the interest of the health of the person.

The state of New York simply argued that it had determined that those working as bakers needed to be protected from being forced to work potentially dangerously long hours.

DECISION

The Supreme Court held, in a 5-4 decision, that the New York law was unconstitutional, rejecting the state's argument that the statute was enacted to protect the workers's health.

The Court did not believe that a baker's occupation was unhealthy. The fact that a law relates "in a remote degree to the public health does not necessarily render the enforcement valid." Indeed, if they were to uphold this as a valid public health law, there would be no end to the degree to which the liberty of contract of employees and employers could be limited: "Some occupations are more healthy than others, but we think there are none which might not come under the power of the legislature to supervise and control the hours working therein, if the mere fact that the occupation is not absolutely and perfectly healthy is to confer that right upon the legislative department of the Government." In short, from the majority's perspective, the law was not a "health law" but merely "an illegal interference with the rights of individuals, both employers and employés, to make contracts regarding labor upon such terms as they may think best."

Justice John Marshall Harlan dissented from the majority decision and wrote an opinion that was joined by Justice Edward White and Justice William Day. Justice Harlan recognized "that there is a liberty of contract which cannot be violated" but explained "that such liberty of contract is subject to such regulations as the State may reasonably prescribe for the common good and well-being of society." Harlan believed that the test of the constitutionality of such state statutes was much more lenient than the standard used by the Court's majority.

He believed that the New York legislature could have reasonably concluded that working in bakeries more than 10 hours a day was dangerous. Justice Harlan cited contemporary treatises as authority that working conditions in bakeries were potentially unhealthy. Because Justice Harlan believed that the New York statute was a reasonable measure responding to potential health problems, he would have upheld its constitutionality.

Justice Oliver Wendell Holmes wrote a separate dissent, which filled less than two full pages in the U.S. *Reports*. While brief, the opinion is perhaps one of the most frequently cited dissenting opinions in the history of the Court. Holmes described a Constitution superior to individual ideologies and defined the proper role of the Supreme Court as primarily deferring to the choices of the majority, as expressed by state laws. The following excerpts are the most notable:

> [A] constitution is not intended to embody a particular economic theory, whether of paternalism and the organic relation of the citizen to the State or of *laissez faire*. It is made for people of fundamentally differing views, and the accident of our finding certain opinions natural and familiar or novel and even shocking ought not to conclude our judgment upon the question whether statutes embodying them conflict with the Constitution of the United States. . . .
>
> I think that the word liberty in the Fourteenth Amendment is perverted when it is held to prevent the natural outcome of a dominant opinion, unless it can be said that a rational and fair man necessarily would admit that the statute proposed would infringe fundamental principles as they have been understood by the traditions of our people and our law.

Justice Holmes would not have overturned the law that the democratically elected New York legislature deemed reasonable.

AFTERMATH

The *Lochner* decision was met by reports in the press of threatened strikes, but these never occurred. Actually, the 10-hour workday was soon achieved by many in the baking industry with unionization.

SIGNIFICANCE

The *Lochner* decision marked the peak of the Supreme Court's protection of "the liberty of contract" at the expense of state-enacted economic regulations. The Court has since abdicated its role of reviewing economic legislation, instead deferring to the judgment of state legislatures.

RELATED CASES

Holden v. Hardy, 169 U.S. 366 (1898)

Muller v. Oregon, 208 U.S. 412 (1908)

Bunting v. Oregon, 243 U.S. 426 (1917)

West Coast Hotel Co. v. Parrish, 300 U.S. 379 (1937)

RECOMMENDED READING

Bernstein, David E., Lochner v. New York: *A Centennial Retrospective*, 85 Washington University Law Quarterly 1469 (2005).

Kens, Paul. *Judicial Power and Reform Politics: The Anatomy of* Lochner v. New York. Lawrence: University Press of Kansas, 1990.

———. "Lochner v. New York: A Case of Economics, Philosophy, Politics, and the Supreme Court." Ph.D. diss., University of Texas at Austin, 1987.

Semonche, John E. *Charting the Future: The Supreme Court Responds to a Changing Society, 1890–1920.* Westport, Conn.: Greenwood Press, 1978.

Siegan, Bernard H. *Economic Liberties and the Constitution.* Chicago: University of Chicago Press, 1980.

Case Title: *Muller v. Oregon*

Legal Citation: 208 U.S. 412

Year of Decision: 1908

KEY ISSUE

Do laws that limit the work hours for women violate the U.S. Constitution?

HISTORY OF THE CASE

On February 9, 1903, the Oregon legislature passed an act that prohibited women to working in "any mechanical establishment, or factory, or laundry" for more than 10 hours a day. Curt Muller, owner of Grand Laundry in Portland, brought this suit to the Supreme Court because he was fined for allowing one of his female employees to work more than 10 hours. He was found guilty at trial, was fined $10, and the decision was affirmed by the Oregon Supreme Court. It went to the U.S. Supreme Court by writ of error, which indicated an error in law of the lower courts and sought review.

SUMMARY OF ARGUMENTS

Muller contended that the statute prevented people from making their own contracts, thereby violating the Fourteenth Amendment, which says that no state shall abridge the privileges and immunities of citizens or deny them due process. He also argued that the law did not apply equally to all people, and that it had no reasonable relationship to public health, safety, or welfare.

Oregon, represented by Louis Brandeis (later Justice Brandeis), did not present per se legal arguments but rather presented scientific evidence regarding the physiology of women and the detrimental effect of long hours on women.

DECISION

Justice Brewer delivered the opinion of the Court, which first recognized that women had equal rights of contract with men under Oregon law. It also recognized that working hour limits as applied to men were previously held unconstitutional in *Lochner v. New York* (1905), because they interfered with contractual rights. However, the Court affirmed the conviction, citing the differences between men and women as the reason for the decision. The Court held that the physical strength and reproductive role of women, as well as their dependency on men, required protection from long working hours for their own health as well as the health of future generations.

AFTERMATH

At the time, this case sent the message that women were more important to the continuation of the human race than to the labor force, especially considering that a minimum wage law for women was rejected in *Adkins v. Children's Hosp.* (1923).

SIGNIFICANCE

The limitation on maximum working hours was a signal of future events for men as well as women with the New Deal legislation, a set of social and economic reform measures used to ease the effects of the Great Depression. Sex-specific labor statutes were abolished with the Civil Rights Act of 1964, which banned discrimination in the workplace based on sex or pregnancy. However, *Muller* set a precedent for court recognition of the effect of laws on people's lives and the impact of court decisions on working people.

RELATED CASES

Lochner v. New York, 198 U.S. 45 (1905)

Bunting v. Oregon, 243 U.S. 412 (1908)

Adkins v. Children's Hosp., 261 U.S. 525 (1923)

Nebbia v. New York, 291 U.S. 502 (1934)

West Coast Hotel Co. v. Parrish, 300 U.S. 379 (1937)

RECOMMENDED READING

Ronald K. L. Collins II and Jennifer Frieser, *Looking Back on* Muller v. Oregon, Part I, 69 American Bar Association Journal 294 (1983).

——, *Looking Back on* Muller v. Oregon, Part II, 69 American Bar Association Journal 472 (1983).

Semonche, John E. *Charting the Future: The Supreme Court Responds to a Changing Society, 1890–1920.* Westport, Conn.: Greenwood Press, 1978.

Case Title: *Home Building & Loan Association v. Blaisdell*

Legal Citation: 290 U.S. 398

Year of Decision: 1934

KEY ISSUE

May the government alter existing contractual obligations in order to respond to emergency situations?

HISTORY OF THE CASE

Article I, Section 10 of the U.S. Constitution states that "no state shall pass any law impairing the obligation of contracts." The Supreme Court held that the due process clause of the Fifth Amendment extended this provision to the federal government.

During the Great Depression, the Minnesota legislature passed a statute allowing local courts to give relief from mortgage foreclosures. The severe financial and economic depression of the time had resulted in high unemployment, which created hardships for property owners who were not able to pay their mortgages. The statute allowed local courts to grant extensions to homeowners so that the banks could not foreclose on their homes. Before a court could approve an extension for a homeowner, it had to order the homeowner to pay a reasonable part of the payment due on the property. The local courts had the power to change the contracts between the homeowners and the banks in order to create a reasonable payment schedule for the homeowner. The statute was designed only to last until the end of the depression.

SUMMARY OF ARGUMENTS

Home Building & Loan argued that the statute allowing courts to interfere with private contracts violated the Constitution's statement that "no state shall pass any law impairing the obligation of contracts."

The state asserted that interference with the mortgage contracts was necessary to deal with the depression and to protect society as a whole.

DECISION

The Supreme Court upheld the Minnesota statute in order to protect vital public interests. Because the depression had created an economic emergency, modifications to such contracts were allowed as long as they were reasonable. The Court stressed that the statute would end when the economic emergency was over, and that a state had a power to protect the security of its citizens in emergency situations.

AFTERMATH

This case has not been overruled, and subsequent decisions have affirmed the idea that governments are not absolutely prohibited from modifying public or private contracts. Subsequent decisions have rendered the contracts clause ("no state shall pass any law impairing the obligation of contracts") essentially powerless.

SIGNIFICANCE

This case is often regarded as a major starting point for reading the contracts clause out of the context of the Constitution. A government is able to modify contracts in order to protect the health, welfare, and safety of its citizens.

RELATED CASES

U.S. Trust Co. v. New Jersey, 431 U.S. 1 (1977)

Allied Structural Steel Co. v. Spannaus, 438 U.S. 234 (1978)

Energy Reserves Group, Inc. v. Kansas Power and Light Co., 459 U.S. 400 (1983)

RECOMMENDED READING

Keynes, Edward, with Randall K. Miller. *The Court vs. Congress: Prayer, Busing and Abortion.* Durham, N.C.: Duke University Press, 1989.

Robert C. Palmer, *Obligations of Contracts: Intent and Distortion,* 37 Case Western Reserve Law Review 631 (summer 1987).

CRIMINAL RIGHTS

The U.S. Constitution protects individuals from government or judicial processes that may unfairly deprive a citizen of his or her liberty or freedom, but it is largely silent with respect to the rights of persons accused of crimes. However, the Sixth Amendment to the Constitution does provide specific rules regarding rights of criminal defendants. It states that an accused has a right to a speedy and public trial by an impartial jury in the state and district where the crime is alleged to have been committed, to be informed of the charges against him or her, to confront witnesses, to have access to witnesses in his or her favor, and to have counsel for his or her defense.

Criminal defendants are frequently indigent and, except in the case of many white-collar prosecutions, lack the resources of prosecutors. On that basis alone, criminal defendants are at a distinct disadvantage. Probably because of the volume of criminal cases prosecuted every day in the United States and the seriousness of the consequences, the Court has rendered many decisions that deal with the rights of the accused. Many of these cases involve extreme technicalities of the seemingly broad guarantees enumerated in the Sixth Amendment. For example, the Court has been called upon to define in detail what is meant by the "right to counsel." The Court has determined not merely that the accused must have counsel, but that counsel must be "effective." This has been further defined as meaning that an attorney must take all reasonable steps in defense of the accused, such as calling all possible witnesses and making all reasonable objections to testimony presented at trial.

Other rulings have dealt with the definition of what is a fair and impartial jury. For example, the Court has determined that not only must juries be impartial in terms of a formal process of examination and questioning of potential jurors known as "voir dire," but also that juries may not be selected from a jury pool that excludes certain groups, such as minorities or women.

While the many rulings of the Supreme Court may seem needlessly detailed for such simple principles as the right to counsel, the right to a jury trial, or the right to confront accusers, one must keep in mind that the consequences of the failure to protect these rights fully may result in the conviction and incarceration of the defendant. The constitutional philosophy is firmly rooted in the belief that "life, liberty, and the pursuit of happiness" are among the highest goals of a civil society, and anything that interferes with these principles must be scrutinized with the utmost care so that there is no chance that a person, even one guilty of a crime, may not be deprived of liberty without all constitutionally provided protections to a fair trial.

U.S. CONSTITUTION—FIFTH AMENDMENT

No person shall be held to answer for a capital, or otherwise infamous crime, unless on a presentment or in or indictment of a grand jury, except in cases arising in the land or naval forces, or in the militia, when in actual service in time of war or public danger; nor shall any person be subject for the same offense to be twice put in jeopardy of life or limb; nor shall be compelled in any criminal case to be a witness against himself, nor be deprived of life, liberty, or property, without due process of the law; nor shall private property be taken for public use, without just compensation.

U.S. Constitution—Sixth Amendment

In all criminal prosecutions, the accused shall enjoy the right to a speedy and public trial, by an impartial jury of the State and district where in the crime shall have been committed, which district shall have been previously ascertained by law, and to be informed of the nature and cause of the accusation; to be confronted with the witnesses against him; to have compulsory process for obtaining witnesses in his favor, and to have the Assistance of Counsel for his defence.

Case Title: *Weems v. United States*

Legal Citation: 217 U.S. 349

Year of Decision: 1910

Key Issue

Is 15 years' imprisonment of hard and painful labor for falsifying a public official document cruel and unusual punishment under the Eighth Amendment of the Constitution?

History of the Case

Paul Weems, acting in his capacity as a public official of the U.S. Government of the Philippine Islands, was charged in the Court of First Instance for the City of Manila with falsifying a public and official document. He was convicted and sentenced to the punishment of Cadena. The Philippine punishment of Cadena includes imprisonment of 15 years at hard and painful labor, during which the prisoner is continually chained at the wrist and ankles; payment of a fine of 4,000 pesetas; and post-release government surveillance, including compliance with certain rules of inspection and permission from authorities to change domicile for life. The Supreme Court of the Philippine Islands affirmed the decision of the lower court. The U.S. Supreme Court granted Weems's petition for certiorari.

Summary of Arguments

On appeal to the U.S. Supreme Court, Weems raised four questions, three of which had not been brought in the court below. Weems presented his argument that 15 years of hard and painful labor under a Philippine criminal code infringed upon his rights under the Philippine Island Bill of Rights forbidding the use of cruel and unusual punishment. He also argued that there was no body politic such as the U.S. Government in the Philippine Islands, that he was not properly arraigned, and that he was not present at any time during his trial.

Decision

The Supreme Court decision, as written by Justice McKenna, analyzed Weems's punishment under the Eighth Amendment. The Court showed through historical analysis how old forms of torture and barbarous conduct, such as whipping, pillory, burning, and quartering, came gradually to be considered by courts to fall within the Eighth Amendment's proscription against cruel and unusual punishment. The decision suggested that mere disproportionality might make a punishment cruel and unusual but also stated that the unique punishment there at issue, Cadena, was unconstitutional because it was unknown to Anglo-American tradition.

The analysis then focused on a comparison between the nature of the punishment and the crime committed. The Court acknowledged that the punishment of Cadena involves cruelty. The Court went further to focus on the lack of proportion between the crime and the offense, stating that the character and degree of a crime become elements in the measure of punishment. The Court then declared the Philippine statute under which the punishment was imposed unconstitutional because of the degree and kind of punishments it imposed. The Supreme Court found that 15 years' hard and painful labor for falsifying an official document was cruel and unusual punishment under the Philippine Bill of Rights; thus, the judgment was reversed and dismissed.

In his dissenting opinion, Justice White, joined by Justice Holmes, argued that the Eighth Amendment should not be read to include issues that it was not originally intended to include. The dissenters further argued that the Eighth Amendment should not be construed in such way as to limit legislative discretion to prescribe punishments for offenses in ways that are not "cruel and unusual."

AFTERMATH

The next time the Supreme Court invalidated a sentence under the Eighth Amendment was in *Solem v. Helm* (1983), when a defendant was sentenced to life without parole for six nonviolent felonies. In *Solem,* the Court held that the Eighth Amendment's prohibition on cruel and unusual punishment applies both to barbaric punishments and to sentences that are disproportionate to crimes. In that case, cruel and unusual punishment was found when a South Dakota man was sentenced to life imprisonment after receiving his seventh nonviolent felony conviction for writing a check from a fictitious bank account.

It is interesting to note that any time punishment is involved, several constitutional issues arise, such as the Eighth Amendment, the ex post facto clause, and the double jeopardy clause. However, some types of sanctions that seem like punishment are not deemed so for judicial purposes, for example, the use of civil commitments and preventive detention statutes in some states. These are not deemed punishment because they are preventive in nature, and punishment is used only for past acts of misconduct. Since these are imposed as civil penalties, the Eighth Amendment does not apply because the sanctions do not constitute punishment.

SIGNIFICANCE

This case was significant both for its treatment and application of the Eighth Amendment, as well as for its discussion of the political and legal relationship between the United States and the Philippines, which was a colony of the United States at that time, until the Philippines gained its independence after World War II.

RELATED CASES

Coker v. Georgia, 433 U.S. 584 (1977)

Solem v. Helm, 463 U.S. 349 (1983)

Thompson v. Oklahoma, 487 U.S. 815 (1988)

Kansas v. Hendricks, 521 U.S. 346 (1997)

Atkins v. Virginia, 536 U.S. 304 (2002)

Roper v. Simmons, 543 U.S. 551 (2005)

STATUTE AT ISSUE

Chapter 4 of the Penal Code of Spain—Falsification of Official and Commercial Documents and Telegraphic Despatches, § 1, Article 300

RECOMMENDED READING

Steve Grossman, *Proportionality in Non-Capital Sentencing: The Supreme Court's Tortured Approach to Cruel and Unusual Punishment,* 84 Kentucky Law Journal 107 (1995–96).

Pressly Millen, *Interpretation of the Eighth Amendment—Rummel, Solem, and the Venerable Case of* Weems v. United States, 1984 Duke Law Journal 789.

Margaret Raymond, *"No Fellow in American Legislation":* Weems v. United States *and the Doctrine of Proportionality,* 30 Vermont Law Review 251 (2006).

Case Title: *Betts v. Brady*

Alternate Case Title: The "Right to Counsel" Case

Legal Citations: 316 U.S. 455

Year of Decision: 1942

KEY ISSUES

Are a defendant's conviction and sentence a deprivation of his liberty without due process of law, in violation of the Sixth and the Fourteenth Amendments to the U.S. Constitution, when the court refuses to appoint counsel at his request?

HISTORY OF THE CASE

Smith Betts was indicted for robbery in the Circuit Court of Carroll County, Maryland. He was unable to afford counsel. Betts told the judge of his situation and requested that counsel be appointed for him. The judge refused his request, stating that this was not the practice in Carroll County unless the charge was rape or murder. Betts pleaded not guilty without waiving his right to counsel. He elected for trial without a jury. The judge found Betts guilty and imposed a sentence of eight years.

Betts filed a petition for a writ of habeas corpus with a judge of the Circuit Court for Washington County while serving his sentence. The writ was issued, the case was heard, and his contention was rejected. He filed another petition for a writ of habeas corpus, based on the same grounds as the earlier petition, with Carroll T. Bond, chief judge of the Court of Appeals of Maryland. A hearing was afforded, evidence at Betts's trial was incorporated into the record, and the cause was argued. Judge Bond granted the writ but remanded Betts to the custody of the respondent, the prison warden, Patrick J. Brady. The petitioner then applied to the U.S. Supreme Court.

SUMMARY OF ARGUMENTS

Betts argued that the Fourteenth Amendment required the appointment of counsel for indigent persons accused of crimes in state courts. He also argued that if counsel is not appointed, the prisoner is entitled to release because the court's failure to appoint counsel deprives the court of jurisdiction and renders the judgment void.

Brady argued that the appointment of counsel to an indigent person was only necessary for due process to the extent that without such appointment, the indigent defendant would not receive a fair and just hearing.

DECISION

Justice Roberts wrote the opinion for the Court, holding that the Supreme Court has jurisdiction to review the decision of the state court since it is a final disposition by the highest court of Maryland in which a judgment could be had, and that Betts's conviction and sentence was not a deprivation of his liberty without due process of law merely because of the court's refusal to appoint counsel at his request. Justice Roberts found that appointment of counsel is not a fundamental right essential to a fair trial.

Justice Roberts stated that section 237 of the Judicial Code declares the Supreme Court competent to review, upon certiorari, "any cause wherein a final judgment . . . has been rendered . . . by the highest court" of a state "in which a decision could be had" on a federal question. Justice Roberts stated that as long as a petitioner has exhausted all of his state remedies, he can appeal to the Supreme Court.

Justice Roberts found that the judgment entered by Judge Bond, the chief justice of the Court of Appeals of Maryland, complied with the requirements of section 237. Justice Roberts also found it an impermissible denial of all recourse to the Supreme Court to hold that the ability to make successive applications to courts and judges of Maryland—which is a right prisoners have— was not a final judgment. He would have held differently had the court not been the highest court of Maryland in which a judgment could be had.

Justice Roberts began his analysis of the due process by distinguishing between the Sixth Amendment due process guarantees, which apply only to trials in the federal court, and those guaranteed by the Fifth Amendment, which secure due process against invasion by the federal government and apply to state actions through the Fourteenth Amendment. He stated that the due process rules were not to be applied as a set of hard-and-fast rules but should be applied in light of other circumstances. Justice Roberts used the following test to determine when due process had been denied: If a trial was conducted in such manner that it was "shocking to the universal sense of justice" or "offensive to the common and fundamental ideas of fairness and right."

Distinguishing other cases that Betts relied on, namely, *Powell v. Alabama* (1932), Justice Roberts found the issue here to be whether in every criminal case, regardless of the circumstances, due process of law requires the state to appoint counsel. Justice Roberts decided this issue by beginning with a reference to constitutional and statutory provisions existing in the colonies and states prior to the inclusion of the Bill of Rights, and in the constitutional, legislative, and judicial history of the states to the present date. He found various constitutional provisions among the original thirteen colonies regarding the right to counsel. Justice Roberts said this background showed an attempt to do away with rules that denied representation, in whole or in part, by counsel in criminal prosecutions. In addition, he showed that the statutes in force at the time of the adoption of the Bill of Rights, the great majority of states, the people, their representatives, and their courts did not consider the appointment of counsel a fundamental right, essential to a fair trial.

Justice Roberts used this evidence to conclude that the concept of due process incorporated in the Fourteenth Amendment did not obligate the states to furnish counsel in every such case. Instead, he argued that each court had the power, if it deemed, to appoint counsel where needed in the interest of fairness. Justice Roberts added that in Maryland, if the situation had been different— if Betts had not been an able man of ordinary intelligence with a little familiarity with criminal procedure—then a refusal to appoint counsel would have resulted in a reversal of a judgment of conviction. He closed by stating that although lack of counsel in a particular case may result in a conviction lacking the fundamental fairness guaranteed by the Fourteenth Amendment, that amendment does not embody an inexonerable command that no trial for any offense can be fairly conducted and justice accorded a defendant who is not represented by counsel.

Justice Black wrote a dissenting opinion joined by Justice Murphy and Justice Douglas. Justice Black determined the petitioner's right to counsel on the basis of a narrower question than the majority proposed. He asked whether in view of the nature of the offense and the circumstances of his trial and conviction, Betts was denied the procedural protection that was his right under the federal Constitution. He noted that Betts was a farmhand, too poor to afford counsel, and was a man of little education, perhaps not of ordinary intelligence, as the majority stated.

Justice Black thought that the majority's view gave the Supreme Court too much supervisory power. He stated that earlier decisions declared the right to counsel in criminal proceedings a fundamental right, guarded from invasion by the Sixth Amendment, whose purpose was to guard against arbitrary or unjust deprivation of liberty by the federal government. Justice Black also believed that denial to the poor of the request for counsel was shocking to the "universal sense of justice" throughout this country. He insisted that no man should be deprived of counsel merely because of his poverty—doing so defeated the promise of our democratic society to provide equal justice under the law.

Aftermath

The standard established in *Betts* was overruled by *Gideon v. Wainwright*, which held that indigent defendants in state felony prosecutions have a right to the assistance of counsel. *Gideon* replaces the *Betts* balancing test with an absolute requirement declaring that no matter what the substance of the crime, a defendant is entitled to a lawyer in state and federal court.

The exception to the *Betts* decision, which required counsel to be appointed in noncapital cases when the absence of counsel would deprive the defendant of a fair hearing, was seldom used.

SIGNIFICANCE

The Fourteenth Amendment incorporation cases greatly extended the degree of supervision the Court could give to the practices of state governments, especially in the area of criminal procedure. Formerly, the Court could exercise only general oversight, but now close scrutiny became possible. *Betts* fixed the "special circumstances" test as the trigger for the provision of appointed counsel.

RELATED CASES

Gideon v. Wainwright, 372 U.S. 335 (1963)

In re Gault, 387 U.S. 1 (1967)

Argesinger v. Hamlin, 407 U.S. 25 (1972)

RECOMMENDED READING

Yale Kamisar, Betts v. Brady *Twenty Years Later: The Right to Counsel and Due Process*, 61 Michigan Law Review 219 (1962).

Case Title: *Adamson v. California*

Alternate Case Title: The State Due Process Case

Legal Citation: 332 U.S. 46

Year of Decision: 1947

KEY ISSUE

Does the Fourteenth Amendment to the U.S. Constitution require the states to apply the Fifth Amendment with regard to the privilege against self-incrimination in state criminal trials?

HISTORY OF THE CASE

Admiral Dewey N. Adamson was tried and convicted for first-degree murder in Los Angeles County, California. The conviction was based partly on the admission into evidence at trial of a portion of a pair of women's stockings found in his bedroom. The stockings found did not belong to the dead woman; however, a piece of women's stockings was found under the victim's body. The tops of the victim's stockings were not found, and the corpse was bare-legged. The California court held that the tops of the stockings were admissible in evidence because they showed Adamson's interest in women's stocking tops. This was such strong circumstantial evidence that it tended to identify the defendant as the person responsible for the crime at issue. The California Supreme Court affirmed Adamson's death sentence, and it was that judgment that was under review by the U.S. Supreme Court.

SUMMARY OF ARGUMENTS

Adamson's counsel argued that the California law permitting opposing counsel to comment on a defendant's failure to explain or deny evidence or facts in the case against him inherently violated due process guaranteed by the Fourteenth Amendment of the Constitution, in that the burden of proof was shifted to the defendant, who no longer had the presumption of innocence. Such a law as California's removes from the accused any procedural safeguards against self-incrimination. The inclusion of the stockings in evidence at trial not only was irrelevant but was used to excite and prejudice the jury and served to deny the defendant a fair trial.

The attorney general of California claimed that the state had made no shift in the burden of proof from the state to the defendant by the admission of the evidence. The right given by the statute to the court to comment upon a defendant's failure to explain or deny evidence against him violated neither the Fourteenth Amendment nor the Fifth Amendment. The attorney general also argued that the admission of the stockings found in Adamson's room was admissible evidence, and the fact that it may have been a poor reflection upon him did not mean that it was not appropriate evidence in a criminal trial.

DECISION

In a 5-4 vote, Justice Stanley Reed opposed the application of the Fifth Amendment's guarantee against self-incrimination to the states. In an opinion notable for judicial restraint, Reed spoke for a majority of the Court in continuing the view that there was a limited incorporation of federal rights in state criminal trials. He noted that the Fifth Amendment's protection from self-incrimination was not incorporated in the Fourteenth Amendment for application to state action. Thus, the states were free to abridge the privileges and immunities flowing from state citizenship. Only those rights that are so fundamental that they are "implicit in the concept of ordered liberty" are secure from state interference. Reed further argued that the courts of the states may have their own ideas as to the most efficient administration of criminal justice:

> The purpose of due process is not to protect an accused against a proper conviction but against an unfair conviction. When evidence is before a jury that threatens conviction, it does not seem unfair to require him to choose between leaving the adverse evidence unexplained and subjecting himself to impeachment through disclosure of former crimes.

Justice Felix Frankfurter wrote a concurring opinion that noted that in the period of 70 years between the incorporation of the Fourteenth Amendment in the Constitution and the beginning of the then-current membership of the Supreme Court, 43 judges reviewed that amendment, and of those 43 judges, only one ever indicated belief that the Fourteenth Amendment was a shorthand summary of the first eight amendments.

Justice Hugo Black wrote the dissent, which was joined by Justices Douglas, Murphy, and Rutledge. Justice Black refused to reaffirm the *Twining v. New Jersey* decision, which concluded that the Fourteenth Amendment protection of privileges and immunities of national citizenship did not include protection against self-incrimination, because he believed that the authors of that decision had failed to notice the intent of the framers of the Fourteenth Amendment to overturn the 1833 case of *Barron v. Baltimore*, which also held that the Fifth Amendment was inapplicable to the states. Black found that the Supreme Court had never given "full consider-

ation or exposition to this purpose." He further argued that "history conclusively demonstrates that the language of the first section of the Fourteenth Amendment, taken as a whole, was thought by those responsible for its submission to the people, and by those who opposed its submission, sufficiently explicit to guarantee that thereafter no state could deprive its citizens of the privileges and protections of the Bill of Rights." Justice Black attached 30 pages of debate and legislative history as an appendix to his dissent.

AFTERMATH

The Court has never adopted Justice Black's total incorporation approach but rather has taken a selective incorporation approach in applying nearly all the individual components of the Bill of Rights to the states. *Adamson* therefore served to keep the door of the federal courts closed to many convicted in state trials.

SIGNIFICANCE

Of the four dissenting justices—Hugo Black, Frank Murphy, William O. Douglas, Wiley Rutledge—Justices Black and Douglas continued to serve on the Court until the 1960s and were at last able to see their view prevail. In the 1964 and 1965 cases of *Malloy v. Hogan* (1964) and *Griffin v. California* (1965), the Supreme Court finally extended the privilege against self-incrimination to virtually every situation.

RELATED CASES

Barron v. Baltimore, 32 U.S. 243 (1833)

Twining v. New Jersey, 211 U.S. 78 (1908)

Palko v. Connecticut, 302 U.S. 319 (1937)

Malloy v. Hogan, 378 U.S. 1 (1964)

Griffin v. California, 380 U.S. 609 (1965)

RECOMMENDED READING

Berger, Raoul. *Government by Judiciary: The Transformation of the Fourteenth Amendment.* Cambridge, Mass.: Harvard University Press, 1977.

Cortner, Richard C. *The Supreme Court and the Second Bill of Rights: The Fourteenth Amendment and the Nationalization of Civil Liberties.* Madison: University of Wisconsin Press, 1981.

Levy, Leonard, Charles Farrman, and Stanley Morrison. *The Fourteenth Amendment and the Bill of Rights: The Incorporation Theory.* New York: Da Capo Press, 1970.

Case Title: *Robinson v. California*

Legal Citation: 370 U.S. 660

Year of Decision: 1962

KEY ISSUE

Does punishing a person for being addicted to illegal drugs violate the Eighth Amendment's protection against cruel and unusual punishment?

HISTORY OF THE CASE

Lawrence Robinson was convicted by a jury in the Municipal Court of Los Angeles and sentenced to 90 days' imprisonment under a California statute that made it a criminal offense to be addicted to narcotics. Robinson was arrested after a Los Angeles police officer observed marks, including scar tissue, discoloration, needle marks, and scabs, on his arms while he was on the streets of Los Angeles. During the trial, the officer and other examining officers testified that Robinson admitted to occasional use of narcotics. Robinson, however, denied having ever used drugs and denied being an addict. The jury was instructed that the statute made it a misdemeanor for a person either to use narcotics or to be addicted to the use of narcotics. The jury returned a verdict finding Robinson guilty of the offense.

Robinson appealed the conviction to the Appellate Department of the Los Angeles County Superior Court. The reviewing court affirmed the conviction in an unreported opinion. The Supreme Court of the United States then granted certiorari, finding jurisdiction under the issue of whether the statute, as construed by the California courts, is repugnant to the Eighth and Fourteenth Amendments of the Constitution regarding cruel and unusual punishment.

SUMMARY OF ARGUMENTS

Robinson argued that addiction to narcotics is a disease and, thus, a status. Punishing the status did not punish any act, and thus, Robinson argued that he could not be criminally punished for his disease. He also argued that punishment, of any length, for a status violates the Eighth Amendment's prohibition of cruel and unusual punishment, which is incorporated to the states through the Fourteenth Amendment.

The state of California essentially argued that its law was valid under its authority to regulate the traffic of illegal narcotics.

DECISION

Justice Potter Stewart delivered the opinion for the Court, beginning with a discussion of a state's rights to regulate narcotic drug trafficking within its borders under its police powers. Throughout the United States, these regulations take a variety of forms, including criminal sanctions for drug manufacturing, possession, sale, and purchase. States can also establish compulsory treatment for addicts, some of which may be involuntary civil commitments. The Court then noted that "the wisdom of any particular choice within the allowable spectrum is not for us to decide."

Next, the Court examined the particular California statute at issue in this case. Although the statute could have been construed to be operative only upon proof of drug use within the state, the trial court had instructed the jury that a conviction could be found absent such evidence. Thus, Robinson could have been convicted for his "status" or "chronic condition" of being addicted to narcotics. The Court, then, noted that it was impossible to determine at this point whether the conviction had been based on such a finding.

Discussing the reasonable possibility that Robinson was, in fact, convicted upon a finding of his "status" of being an addict, the Court stated "it is unlikely that any State at this moment in history would attempt to make it a criminal offense for a person to be mentally ill, or a leper, or to be afflicted with a venereal disease." Essentially, California was attempting to punish people on the basis of being in a state of illness, rather than for any specific act. Although compulsory confinement might be used to deal with such issues, the Court concluded that a law punishing such a disease "would doubtless be universally thought to be an infliction of cruel and unusual punishment in violation of the Eighth and Fourteenth Amendments." The statute in this case was deemed to fall into this category.

The Court further emphasized that although a 90-day prison sentence itself was neither cruel nor unusual in the abstract, the mandatory sentence was out of proportion to the offense. Although some addictions are acquired voluntarily, other addictions can be contracted innocently and involuntarily, such as by an infant from the moment of birth or in an addiction arising from the use of medically prescribed drugs. Accordingly, the Court held the California statute violated the Eighth and Fourteenth Amendments, and the case was reversed.

Although Justice Frankfurter was a member of the Court when this case was decided, he took no part in the decision. Justice Douglas concurred with the decision of the majority and wrote separately to address further reasons why the punishment imposed upon Robinson was cruel and unusual. He stated that "if addicts can be punished for their addiction, then the insane can also be punished for their insanity. Each has a disease and each must be treated as a sick person." He added that because an illness was being punished, the Eighth Amendment violation results from the criminal conviction of the addict, rather than from the confinement. Justice Harlan also wrote a concurring opinion, arguing that addiction alone cannot reasonably amount to anything more than a propensity to use drugs. Thus, he argued that California was punishing the mere propensity to commit a crime, and such punishment was unconstitutional.

Justice Clark wrote a dissenting opinion, arguing that California had a legitimate overriding purpose of curing less seriously addicted people to prevent further drug use. He asserted that the majority erred in concluding that hospitalization was the only treatment for narcotics addiction and that jail time was a punishment equating to a denial of due process. Justice Clark also noted that other crimes are "status" offenses that can be punished by law, such as underage drinking. Justice Clark further argued that the rehabilitation of narcotics addicts was a matter of statewide concern, and the state of California should retain control over decisions to control such behavior.

Justice White also wrote a dissenting opinion, arguing that the conviction was not for a "status" but rather for repeated or habitual use of narcotics prior to arrest. He also argued that the majority's decision had cast doubt on the ability of states to forbid drug use under threat of criminal punishment and that a final answer as to the extent of state regulation would have to wait for a later case. Further, Justice White argued that Congress and the states have a better understanding of, and are in a better position to deal with effectively, the narcotics problem in the United States, and thus, some deference should be given to them.

AFTERMATH

Subsequent to the Court's decision, *Robinson* was not followed in a 1968 ruling, *Powell v. Texas,* in which the Court, by a 5 to 4 vote, rejected the contention that a criminal conviction for chronic alcoholism was cruel and unusual. The majority thought that knowledge about alcoholism and the record in that particular case were inadequate for a wide-ranging new constitutional principle. The minority in *Powell* insisted that the *Robinson* rule should have been followed, and that "criminal penalties may not be inflicted upon a person for being in a condition he is powerless to change."

Controversy concerning whether addiction-related conduct is involuntary and entitled to be regarded as a disease has continued, but *Robinson* did establish that the cruel and unusual punishment clause of the Eighth Amendment applies to the states in appropriate cases by reason of the due process clause of the Fourteenth Amendment. *Robinson* has not been overruled, and one developing area of legal literature, regarding the treatment of homeless people, has relied heavily on the Court's decision in that case.

SIGNIFICANCE

The Court held that the California law punishing drug addiction violated the Eighth Amendment's protection against cruel and unusual punishment. The law essentially punished the "status" of addiction, which the Court compared to punishing the status of someone who had venereal disease or leprosy. Although it may seem self-evident, this case also made clear that in order for someone to commit a criminal act, an "act" must be committed. However, the opinion made clear that this decision was not aimed at the purchase, possession, or distribution of illegal drugs.

RELATED CASES

Powell v. Texas, 392 U.S. 514 (1968)

Coker v. Georgia, 433 U.S. 584 (1977)

Thompson v. Oklahoma, 487 U.S. 815 (1988)

Atkins v. Virginia, 536 U.S. 304 (2002)

Roper v. Simmons, 543 U.S. 551 (2005)

STATUTE AT ISSUE

California Health and Safety Code, § 11721 (in relevant part as the statute stood at the time of the case)

RECOMMENDED READING

Martin R. Gardner, *Rethinking* Robinson v. California *in the Wake of* Jones v. Los Angeles: *Avoiding the "Demise of the Criminal Law" by Attending to "Punishment,"* 98 Journal of Criminal Law and Criminology 429 (2008).

Jeffrey A. Rowe, *Revisiting* Robinson: *The Eighth Amendment as Constitutional Support for Theories of Criminal Responsibility,* 5 University of Maryland Law Journal of Race, Religion, Gender and Class 95 (2005).

Benno Weisberg, *When Punishing Innocent Conduct Violates the Eighth Amendment: Applying the* Robinson *Doctrine to Homelessness and Other Contextual "Crimes,"* 96 Journal of Criminal Law and Criminology 329 (2005).

Case Title: *Fay v. Noia*

Legal Citation: 372 U.S. 391

Year of Decision: 1963

KEY ISSUE

May a person obtain habeas corpus relief from an imprisonment for a conviction procured by a coerced confession obtained in violation of the Fourteenth Amendment when he or she has not availed himself or herself of the available remedies within the state judicial system?

HISTORY OF THE CASE

Charles Noia was convicted of felony murder in state court. His conviction rested on a coerced confession obtained by the police. Noia allowed the time to appeal directly to lapse and then requested federal habeas corpus review. The U.S. Supreme Court granted Noia's petition for review. Edward Fay, the prison warden, and the state objected to this. They argued that by failing to avail himself of the opportunity to appeal within the state system, Noia relinquished his right to appeal to the Supreme Court.

SUMMARY OF ARGUMENTS

Noia argued that the nature of the petition required the Supreme Court to grant jurisdiction. He thought that the circumstances that led to his conviction were such that the Court should, in the interest of justice, review his case.

Fay argued that the doctrine of abstention (in which a state is allowed to complete its administration of the case first without prejudice to federal rights interwoven in the state proceedings), which was codified in 28 U.S.C. § 2254, prevented the Court from issuing the writ of habeas corpus: Noia purposefully allowed the statute of limitation to run out and eliminated the possibility of seeking remedy in the lower courts. The state argued that federal courts should not issue the writ in a circumstance in which the defendant purposefully circumvented the state judicial system. In doing so, Fay waived his right to apply for the writ of habeas corpus.

DECISION

Justice Brennan, in writing the opinion of the Court, held that the federal courts have the power to grant relief when the state judicial system has not provided it. Noia's failure to seek state remedies did not validate the unconstitutional conduct by which the conviction was obtained. Justice Brennan relied on the notion of federal habeas corpus review as independent. He noted that rarely "has the Court predicated its deference to state procedural rules on a want of power to entertain a habeas application where a procedural default was committed by the defendant in the state courts. Typically, the Court . . . has approached the problem as an aspect of the rule requiring exhaustion of the state remedies, which is not a rule distributing power as between the state and federal courts." He also emphasized the notion that federal courts could deny relief if a petitioner deliberately failed to adjudicate his claims fully in state courts, deliberately bypassing the state court appellate procedures to be heard by the federal court.

In his dissent, Justice Harlan argued that if the habeas petitioner has violated a reasonable state rule and is, therefore, barred from state judicial review, the federal courts do not have statutory or constitutional authority to release the petitioner from detention.

AFTERMATH

This decision overruled *Darr v. Burford* (1950), in which the Court held that a state prisoner must ordinarily seek certiorari in the Supreme Court as a precondition of applying for federal habeas corpus. *Fay v. Noia* ruled that state prisoners are no longer barred from petitioning the Supreme Court after failing to file a petition in the state court system within the allotted time. The Court's rationale was that the requirement imposed by *Darr*—that the defendant proceed through the state court system and file for certiorari in the allotted time—was an unnecessary step in the processing of federal claims of those convicted of state crimes.

This case was overruled in 1992 by *Keeney v. Tamayo-Reyes.* In that opinion, written by Justice White, it was held that the *Fay* standard must be overruled in favor of a cause and prejudice standard. Justice White reasoned that in light of the decisions in the *Fay* progeny, such as *Wainright v. Sykes* and *Coleman v. Thompson,* which narrowed the ruling in *Fay,* it was necessary to implement a new, more uniform standard for petitioners seeking habeas corpus. Justice White went on to reason that the new standard served to allow state courts to correct their own errors, to allow good use of judicial economy by preventing duplicative fact finding, and to allow the use of the appropriate judicial forum.

SIGNIFICANCE

This decision empowered the federal courts to issue writs of habeas corpus regardless of what had occurred in prior state court proceedings. The sweeping language of the decision opened up to the federal court an avenue of jurisdiction in cases that were previously precluded from jurisdiction because of state procedural requirements. As noted in the decision, it marked "a return to the common-law principle that restricts contrary to fundamental law, by whatever authority imposed, could be redressed by writ of habeas corpus."

Later decisions such as *Davis v. U.S.* (1973) and *Wainright v. Sykes* (1977) limited the power of the federal court to issue writs of habeas corpus without respect to what occurred in prior state court proceedings. A defendant is now required to show cause and prejudice, meaning he or she must give reasons for the actions taken and indicate the harm done, before the federal courts will assert jurisdiction.

Fay narrowed the scope of the requirement that a petitioner exhaust state court remedies and refused to apply independent and adequate state ground doctrine to review in another proceeding. It also limited jurisdiction to lower courts where there was a deliberate bypass of state court procedures. This decision put the burden on the federal courts to determine whether the petitioner purposefully avoided the procedure of state courts—which would disentitle him or her to federal court review—or whether the defendant, because of harmless error, did not avail himself or herself of the available state remedies, in which case, federal jurisdiction could be asserted.

RELATED CASES

Ashwander v. Tennessee Valley Authority, 297 U.S. 288 (1936)

Darr v. Burford, 339 U.S. 200 (1950)

Davis v. U.S., 411 U.S. 233 (1973)

Wainright v. Sykes, 433 U.S. 72 (1977)

Reed v. Ross, 468 U.S. 1 (1984)

Coleman v. Thompson, 501 U.S. 722 (1991)

Keeney v. Tamayo-Reyes, 504 U.S. 1 (1992)

RECOMMENDED READING

Jack A. Guttenberg, *Federal Habeas Corpus, Constitutional Rights, and Procedural Forfeitures: The Delicate Balance,* 12 Hofstra Law Review 617 (1984).

Rae K. Inafuku, Coleman v. Thompson—*Sacrificing Fundamental Rights in Deference to the States: The Supreme Court's 1991 Interpretation of the Writ of Habeas Corpus,* 34 Santa Clara Law Review 625 (1994).

Maria L. Marcus, *Federal Habeas Corpus after State Court Default: A Definition of Cause and Prejudice,* 53 Fordham Law Review 663 (1985).

Kathleen Patchel, *The New Habeas,* 42 Hastings Law Journal 939 (1991).

Curtis Reitz, *Federal Habeas Corpus: Postconviction Remedy for State Prisoners,* 108 University of Pennsylvania Law Review 461 (1960).

Judith Resnik, *Tiers,* 57 Southern California Law Review 837 (1984).

Case Title: *Gideon v. Wainwright*

Legal Citation: 372 U.S. 335

Year of Decision: 1963

KEY ISSUE

Do the Sixth and Fourteenth Amendments to the U.S. Constitution require a state to provide counsel to indigent defendants in criminal prosecutions?

HISTORY OF THE CASE

Gideon was charged in Florida state court with the felony offense of breaking and entering with the intent to commit a misdemeanor. When he requested a lawyer at his trial, he was denied. The judge, in denying his request, said the state was required only to provide legal representation to those defendants charged with capital offenses. The jury at his trial convicted him, and he was sentenced to five years in state prison. Gideon then filed a habeas corpus petition, challenging the validity of his conviction and sentence. He grounded his challenge on the trial court's refusal to provide him with counsel, a right he argued was guaranteed by the Bill of Rights in the Constitution. The state supreme court denied all relief to Gideon.

SUMMARY OF ARGUMENTS

Gideon argued that the Bill of Rights as applied to the states through the Fourteenth Amendment provided him the right to counsel, which the state violated by refusing to provide him with legal representation. He, thus, felt that the conviction that resulted from his representing himself, in a trial that was inherently unfair, should be vacated.

Wainwright, the director of the Division of Corrections, argued that there was no recognized constitutional right to counsel in noncapital criminal trials, and that there were no special circumstances that would justify abandoning the state's public policy on this issue for Gideon's case.

DECISION

Justice Black, writing for the majority, overruled *Betts v. Brady* (1942) and held that the states are required by the Sixth Amendment, made applicable to the states through the Fourteenth Amendment, to provide counsel for indigent criminal defendants. In addition, he held that the state's refusal to appoint a lawyer, upon Gideon's request, violated the due process clause of the Fourteenth Amendment.

The Court noted that the facts of the *Betts* case were substantially similar to those at issue in Gideon's case. Both men were indigent criminal defendants denied the right to representation by the trial judge on the grounds that their crimes were not of the type that the state's policy allowed for representation. The Court overruled the conclusion in *Betts* that the Sixth Amendment right to counsel did not qualify as fundamental to a fair trial and, therefore, was not obligatory on the states.

Justice Black noted that 10 years before the decision in *Betts,* the Court in *Powell v. Alabama* declared that the "right to the aid of counsel is this fundamental character." Noting that although the holding of that case was limited to the facts of the case, he argued that "its conclusions about the fundamental nature of the right to counsel are unmistakable." He also noted that in *Grosjean v. American Press Co.* (1936), the Court upheld the principle that fundamental rights should be safeguarded against state action: "We concluded that certain fundamental rights, safeguarded by the first eight amendments against federal action were also safeguarded against state action by the due process of law clause of the Fourteenth Amendment, and among them the fundamental right of the accused to the aid of counsel in criminal prosecutions."

He argued that in light of the case history, even the Court in *Betts* had to concede that "one charged with crime, who is unable to obtain counsel, must be furnished counsel by the state." He contended that the ruling in this case constituted a return to old precedents that were more sound than the newly adopted ones. He said that it is an obvious truth that one cannot receive a fair criminal trial without counsel. In addition, the history of the Constitution supports the need for counsel for those tried for crimes: "From the very beginning, our state and national constitutions and laws have laid great emphasis on procedural and substantive safeguards designed to assure fair trials before impartial tribunals in which every defendant stands equal before the law."

Justice Douglas joined the Court and provided a brief history of the connection between the Bill of Rights and the Fourteenth Amendment.

Justice Clark concurred with the result of the Court. He argued that the Court's holding did no more than erase an illogical distinction between capital and noncapital offenses for the purpose of providing counsel by the state.

Justice Harlan concurred in the result but thought that *Betts* should be viewed in a light more accurate than that portrayed by the Court. He argued that *Betts,* in fact, was not a break in precedent but an extension of precedent. Harlan pointed to the specific factual circumstances in *Powell v. Alabama* and their importance to the decision that a state court had a duty to assign counsel for a capital case. Harlan contended that *Betts* extended the possibility of the existence of "special circumstances" to noncapital trials.

AFTERMATH

The Court has extended the right of counsel of defendants charged with only misdemeanor offenses, on the grounds that the brevity of sentence that a defendant faces does not negate the right of counsel. In later decisions, the Court went on to note that the nature of the charge is not the determining factor for the right of counsel but rather the character of the possible punishment—most important, the loss of liberty. These adaptations are based on the notion that the defendant who faces criminal prosecution should be on equal footing with the state that prosecutes him or her.

SIGNIFICANCE

In *Gideon,* the Court abandoned the arbitrary distinction between capital and noncapital crimes and fully incorporated the Sixth Amendment right to counsel into the Fourteenth Amendment. By designating due process as the appropriate standard by which to view abridgment of the Sixth Amendment right, the Court created a new theoretical and constitutional basis for a defendant's right to counsel in state criminal trials. Once the defendant presented the preliminary evidence of the denial of his right to counsel, the relationship with due process was presumed.

In addition, this decision acknowledged the adversarial nature of criminal proceedings. *Gideon* offers the ideal that both parties are on equal footing, and the result reached can be counted on to be accurate. Though the reality of equality among the parties in the adversarial process has not been realized, this decision creates an ideal that fairness within the criminal justice system is not a function of one's financial resources.

RELATED CASES

Powell v. Alabama, 287 U.S. 45 (1932)

Grosjean v. American Press Co., 297 U.S. 233 (1936)

Betts v. Brady, 316 U.S. 455 (1942)

Patterson v. Warden, 372 U.S. 776 (1963)

Argersinger v. Hamlin, 407 U.S. 25 (1972)

RECOMMENDED READING

Robert S. Catz and Nancy Lee Firak, *The Right to Appointed Counsel in Quasi-Criminal Cases: Towards an Effective Assistance of Counsel Standard,* 19 Harvard Civil Rights–Civil Liberties Law Review 397 (1984).

Alfredo Garcia, *The Right to Counsel under Siege: Requiem for an Endangered Right?* 29 American Criminal Law Review 35 (1991).

Richard Klein, *The Emperor* Gideon *Has No Clothes: The Empty Promise of the Constitutional Right to Effective Assistance of Counsel,* 13 Hastings Constitutional Law Quarterly 625 (1986).

Case Title: *Escobedo v. State of Illinois*

Legal Citation: 378 U.S. 478

Year of Decision: 1964

KEY ISSUE

Can the police refuse to honor a person's request for an attorney during an interrogation and then use the person's statement in judicial proceedings?

HISTORY OF THE CASE

Danny Escobedo was interrogated about the death of his brother in-law. He requested to speak with his attorney and was refused. Escobedo later implicated himself in the murder and was convicted of aiding and abetting. Escobedo appealed, arguing that the Illinois Police Department violated his Sixth Amendment right to "the assistance of Counsel" when they refused to honor his request to speak with his attorney. The Sixth Amendment guarantee, to this point, had been interpreted as operative only after the person became a suspect and became subject to judicial proceedings. In this case, the appellant was being questioned about his possible involvement in the murder of his brother-in-law. While in police custody, he requested several times to speak with his attorney; all of these requests were denied. In addition, Escobedo's attorney requested to speak with his client at the station house; all of his requests were denied. The trial court allowed Escobedo's self-incriminating statement made during this interrogation into evidence. Escobedo was convicted of murder. The Illinois Supreme Court in its original opinion held that the statement was inadmissible and reversed the conviction. At a rehearing, the Illinois Supreme Court affirmed the conviction.

SUMMARY OF ARGUMENTS

Escobedo's attorney argued that the police acted in violation of the Sixth and Fourteenth Amendments by refusing to let him speak with his attorney. At the time of his interrogation, Escobedo was "in fact" the suspect, even though he had not yet been charged with a crime. The state supreme court found that "the petitioner had become the accused, and the purpose of his interrogation was to 'get him' to confess his guilt despite his constitutional right not to do so." The state supreme court also held that the statement elicited from the defendant during this interrogation was inadmissible because "'the guiding hand of counsel' was essential to advise the petitioner of his rights in this delicate situation."

The state argued that case history supported the legitimacy of the police officers' actions in refusing to provide Escobedo with counsel. The right to an attorney was not guaranteed until the person had been formally indicted. To require legal representation at an early stage of the investigative process would impede the ability of the police to obtain information that would be helpful in resolving the situation.

DECISION

Justice Goldberg, writing for five of the justices, found that the right to counsel begins before the defendant has been indicted. It begins when the investigation is no longer a general inquiry and focuses on a particular suspect. At that time, the adversarial process begins, and the suspect should be allowed, if he wishes, to consult a legal representative. Dismissing the argument that this would make the investigative process ineffective, Justice Goldberg argued that an investigative process of any merit would not have to rely on the "citizens' abdication through unawareness of their constitutional rights."

There were three dissents in this case. Justices Harlan and Stewart relied on the *Cicenia v. La Gay* (1958) decision as binding precedent. In that case, the Court ruled the defendant did not have a constitutional right to be advised by counsel before being indicted. Justice White's dissent, which was joined by Justices Clark and Stewart, relied on *Massiah v. U.S.* (1964) to support the

argument of the state that the right to counsel begins only after indictment. He argued that the Court had made inadmissible all statements except those on which the accused expressly waives the right to counsel.

AFTERMATH

In changing the standard by which confessions were analyzed for admissibility, this decision affected the policy of police departments and district attorney's offices across the nation. This is one of a series of cases in which the Court replaced the due process analysis in determining the admissibility of confessions with an objective standard based on the Sixth Amendment right to counsel. This case extended the time at which a suspect may invoke his or her Sixth Amendment right to before the indictment stage. Escobedo found himself in trouble with the law numerous times after this decision and ultimately went to prison several years later.

SIGNIFICANCE

This case set the stage for *Miranda v. Arizona* (1966), in which the Court adopted a per se rule regarding confessions to protect suspects from the coercive atmosphere of police investigation and to protect the suspect's right against self-incrimination.

RELATED CASES

Brown v. Mississippi, 297 U.S. 278 (1936)

Cicenia v. La Gay, 357 U.S. 504 (1958)

Malloy v. Hogan, 378 U.S. 1 (1964)

Massiah v. U.S., 377 U.S. 201 (1964)

Miranda v. Arizona, 384 U.S. 436 (1966)

RECOMMENDED READING

Mark S. Bransdorfer, *Miranda Right-to-Counsel and the Fruit of the Poisonous Tree Doctrine,* 62 Indiana Law Journal 1061 (1987).

Lawrence Herman, *The Supreme Court, the Attorney General, and the Good Old Days of Police Interrogation,* 48 Ohio State Law Journal 733.

W. Brian Stack, *Criminal Procedure—Confessions—Waiver of Privilege against Self-Incrimination Held Invalid Due to Police Failure to Inform Suspect of Attorney's Attempt to Contact Him—State v. Reed*, Seton Hall Law Review 25 (1994).

Case Title: *Massiah v. United States*

Legal Citation: 377 U.S. 201

Year of Decision: 1964

KEY ISSUE

Should the Sixth Amendment's "right to counsel" protect incriminating statements made by an accused individual after he or she has already been indicted?

HISTORY OF THE CASE

The petitioner Massiah was a merchant seaman who, in 1959, was indicted under a federal narcotics law after he was caught smuggling three and a half pounds of cocaine aboard a U.S. vessel. After the indictment, Massiah retained counsel, pled not guilty, and was released on bail. While he was out on bail, a federal agent—through "surreptitious means" (a radio connection)—listened to a conversation in which Massiah made self-incriminating statements to an individual who, unbeknown to Massiah, was working undercover for the government. These statements were then used against Massiah at trial, and the jury convicted him of the narcotics offense. The court of appeals upheld this conviction.

SUMMARY OF ARGUMENTS

Massiah argued that it was "an error of constitutional dimensions" to allow the federal agent to use his self-incriminating statements at trial because the agent's use of the radio equipment to listen to Massiah's conversation with the undercover agent violated the Fourth Amendment's prohibition of unlawful governmental searches and seizures, and his Fifth and Sixth Amendment rights had been violated "by the use in evidence against him of incriminating statements which government agents had deliberately elicited from him after he had been indicted and in the absence of his retained counsel."

DECISION

The U.S. Supreme Court reversed the decision of the court of appeals and held that the government could not elicit this sort of incriminating information *after* the accused individual had been indicted.

In delivering the majority opinion, Justice Stewart focused his attention on whether the Sixth Amendment's "right to counsel" guarantee should protect an indicted individual against the government's use of such "surreptitiously" elicited statements. In examining this issue, Justice Stewart cited *Spano v. New York* (1959), in which the U.S. Supreme Court reversed a state criminal conviction because the state admitted evidence of the defendant's confession that the defendant had given after being indicted on first-degree murder charges. Because Justice Stewart agreed with the *Spano* Court's assertion that "a Constitution which guarantees a defendant the aid of counsel [at trial] could surely vouchsafe no less to an indicted defendant under [a post-indictment] interrogation by the police," he decided to widen the *Spano* holding so that it covered defendants in federal courts. Justice Stewart concluded his opinion by stating that this decision does not prevent the government from using incriminating post-indictment statements—it simply prevents them from doing so "under the circumstances here disclosed."

In his dissent, Justice White argued that the majority's ruling would exclude "relevant, reliable, and highly probative" evidence and that, at the end of the day, "the public will again be the loser." Justice White emphasized the fact that the petitioner Massiah's self-incriminating statements were voluntary, and when they were deemed inadmissible under the Sixth Amendment, the Court was overturning a law that had been upheld in "countless cases." "[Massiah]," Justice White stated, "was not questioned in what anyone could call an atmosphere of coercion. . . . There was no suggestion, or any possibility, of coercion." Thus, Justice White concluded, his incriminating statements should have been allowed into evidence.

AFTERMATH

In *Maine v. Moulton* (1985), the Supreme Court had to determine whether the *Massiah* rule should be extended to situations when the accused person—and not the government—initiates the conversation that results in incriminating statements. In his article "Criminal Procedure—Eliciting New Meaning from 'Deliberately Eliciting,'" Glenn W. Viers stated that "*Maine v. Moulton* represents a significant expansion of the Sixth Amendment guarantee of the right to counsel . . . beyond any point previously recognized and placed upon the government 'an affirmative obligation' not to act in a manner that circumvents and thereby dilutes the protections afforded by the [Constitution]."

SIGNIFICANCE

Under the *Massiah* ruling, the right to counsel attaches once formal charges have been initiated. This limits the tactics law enforcement may use when obtaining evidence, as they must do so in the presence of an attorney.

RELATED CASES

Spano v. New York, 360 U.S. 315 (1959)

Maine v. Moulton, 474 U.S. 159 (1985)

RECOMMENDED READING

W. Glenn Viers, *Criminal Procedure—Eliciting New Meaning from "Deliberately Eliciting"*— Maine v. Moulton, 21 Wake Forest Law Review 1093 (1985–86).

Case Title: *In re Gault et al.*

Legal Citation: 387 U.S. 1

Year of Decision: 1967

KEY ISSUE

Do juveniles have the right to an attorney under the Fourteenth Amendment?

HISTORY OF THE CASE

Fifteen-year-old Gerald Gault was taken into custody by the police in Arizona for allegedly having made obscene phone calls. At the time, Gault was under a six-month probation order for his participation in another boy's theft of a woman's purse. Gault was taken into custody at 10:00 A.M. on June 8, 1964, and no steps were taken to advise either his father or his mother of his detention in the county children's home. When his mother returned from work at 6:00 P.M., Gault was not home. (School was not in session.) Gault's older brother was sent to look for him at the home of a friend. He then learned that his brother was in custody.

Mrs. Gault went to the detention home and found out that the juvenile court would hold a hearing at 3:00 P.M. on the following day. The police filed a petition requesting a hearing and order regarding the care and custody of Gerald with the court on the day of the hearing. The Gaults did not receive this petition. (Indeed, although it was filed June 9, the Gaults never saw it until August 17.) At the hearing, Gerald, his mother, his older brother, and two probation officers appeared. (Gerald's father was out of town on business.) The woman who had complained of receiving the obscene phone calls was not present. No one was under oath, and there was no record made of what occurred during the hearing. Later, the juvenile judge testified that Gerald was questioned about the telephone call, and that there was some conflict about what he said. After being kept in the detention home for three days, Gerald was released and given a plain piece of paper on which one of the detention officers had written the following note:

Mrs. Gault:
  Judge McGhee has set Monday June 15, 1964 at 11 A.M. as the date and time for further Hearings on Gerald's delinquency
  /s/Flagg

On June 15, Gerald, his father and mother, and the detention officers were present before Judge McGhee. At no time did Mrs. Cook, the woman who had allegedly received the obscene phone calls, ever testify or present an affidavit to the court. One of the probation officers testified that he had talked to Mrs. Cook once on the telephone.

At the hearing, the judge referred Gerald to a juvenile delinquent facility for the period until he turned 21, until or unless he was discharged sooner. Thus, after a brief hearing, Gerald was sentenced to spend six years in the state industrial school. Had he been an adult, the maximum punishment would have been a $50 fine or two months in the county jail. There was no requirement under Arizona law that, as a juvenile, he receive any notice of the hearings or could obtain an attorney. He had no right to confront or examine the woman who complained about the phone calls. Further, there was no protection against admissions of his guilt.

Arizona law did not permit appeals in juvenile cases. Therefore, the Gaults filed a petition for a writ of habeas corpus with the Arizona Supreme Court. The writ was referred to a superior court, and on August 17, the juvenile judge was cross-examined about the basis for his actions. The superior court dismissed the writ, and the Gaults asked for a review by the Arizona Supreme Court. The Arizona Supreme Court upheld the dismissal of the writ of habeas corpus and concluded that the state juvenile system was adequate. The Gaults appealed.

SUMMARY OF ARGUMENTS

The Gaults argued that the sentence was unconstitutional because there was no requirement for a notice of hearings, there was no requirement that the parent or child be informed of the specific charges being brought, there was no right to an appeal, and the proceedings themselves were conducted without basic constitutional rights for the juvenile. These rights included the right to an attorney, the right to confront his accuser, and the privilege against self-incrimination. The Gaults also argued that the use of unsworn hearsay testimony and the failure to make a record of

the hearing made the juvenile court hearing defective.

The state and a variety of associations representing juvenile judges and juvenile courts opposed the Gaults. They argued that the nature of the juvenile justice system was intended to be informal, and that the state's intervention was based on a paternalistic regard for the best interests of a wayward or disturbed child.

DECISION

The Court held that most of the procedural due process rights afforded to adults in criminal cases should extend to juveniles under the Fourteenth Amendment. These include the right to timely notification of charges, right to counsel, right to confrontation and cross-examination of witnesses, and the right against self-incrimination. Therefore, Gault's confinement in the juvenile delinquent facility was unconstitutional on the basis of the violation of his due process rights.

Justice Abe Fortas wrote the majority opinion for Chief Justice Warren and Justices Douglas, Clark, and Brennan. Justices Black and White filed a separate concurring opinion. Justice Harlan filed an opinion that concurred in part and dissented in part. Only Justice Stewart dissented. Justice Fortas began with his decision in *Kent v. U.S.* and traced the history of the juvenile courts in the United States. In 1899, Illinois became the first state to create a juvenile court system. The idea quickly spread to every state, as well as the District of Columbia and Puerto Rico. The movement toward establishing a juvenile court system was based on the assumption that society was not concerned with whether the child was guilty or innocent but with what could be done in his or her best interests and in the best interests of the state to prevent him or her from continuing on a downward slide. The child was to be treated as essentially good and to be the object of the state's care and not treated as if he or she were under arrest or on trial.

While very high motives and enlightened impulses created the juvenile justice system, according to Justice Fortas, the results had given the justices unbridled discretion and arbitrary power. Loose procedures, heavy-handed methods, and crowded calendars often resulted in depriving juveniles of many fundamental rights to which they were entitled. Justice Fortas found that "[u]nder our Constitution, the condition of being a boy does not justify a kangaroo court." Justice Fortas was appalled that the judge made no inquiry of either Gerald's mother and father, his older brother, or his school. Had Gerald been over 18, the punishment would have been a fine ranging from five dollars to $50 or a jail sentence of not more than two months. Instead, he was sentenced to six years in a juvenile home. The idea of reaching such a tremendous decision without any ceremony, without a hearing, without the assistance of counsel, or without any legal reasoning in no way measured up to the essential standards of due process and fair treatment.

Justice Fortas noted that the parents had no time to obtain an attorney, and that they had no idea of the charges against their son. He found it particularly repugnant that, under the law of Arizona, the same juvenile officer who arrested Gerald initiated the proceedings against him and then testified against him was then charged with being the superintendent of the detention center if Gerald were sentenced. The detention officer was the only court officer present, other than the judge. There was no one present who could be said to represent the interests of the child. Further, Gerald was denied the right to confront and cross-examine his accuser. Gerald and his parents were never told that he did not have to testify or make a statement or that his statements might be used to commit him to the home for delinquent children.

The Supreme Court devoted a prolonged amount of time to the question of whether Gerald was capable of making an informed confession. His statement was made in front of the police officer who arrested him, away from his parents, without the assistance of counsel and without any notification that he had a right to be silent. This confession was never written down, signed, or submitted to the court. Justice Fortas found that there was no reason at all to find a different rule with regard to juveniles than adults. Absent a valid confession, the court must have sworn testimony by witnesses available by cross-examination in order to make any finding of guilt.

In his dissent, Justice Stewart noted that the practical consequence of this ruling was substantially to overhaul the entire system of juvenile justice in the United States.

The case was reversed and remanded.

AFTERMATH

As part of the "due process revolution" of the 1960s, *Gault* broadened the argument over extending due process requirements to the states. Contrary to Justice Stewart's concerns, the juvenile court systems continued to operate under the *Gault* decision. However, the Court did not offer clear guidelines for preventing the formation of a juvenile system that no longer afforded "special" consideration for minor defendants.

SIGNIFICANCE

The *Gault* case placed new emphasis on due process for juveniles, thereby greatly increasing the requirements to manage juvenile court cases adequately. Much debate continues over whether the *Gault* decision prompted an overemphasis on due process rather than on the issue of remedies for juvenile delinquency.

RELATED CASES

Kent v. U.S., 383 U.S. 541 (1966)

McKeiver v. Pennsylvania, 403 U.S. 528 (1971)

Goss v. Lopez, 419 U.S. 565 (1975)

RECOMMENDED READING

George, B. James. *Gault and the Juvenile Court Revolution*. Ann Arbor: Michigan Institute of Continuing Legal Education, 1968.

Kramer, Donald T., ed. *Legal Rights of Children*. Colorado Springs, Colo.: Shepard's/McGraw-Hill, 1994.

Mezey, Susan Gluck. *Children in Court: Public Policymaking and Federal Court Decisions*. Albany: State University of New York Press, 1996.

Nordin, Virginia Davis, ed. *Gault: What Now for the Juvenile Court?* Ann Arbor: Michigan Institute of Continuing Legal Education, 1968.

Case Title: *United States v. Wade*

Legal Citations: 388 U.S. 218

Year of Decision: 1967

KEY ISSUES

Does courtroom identification violate the Fifth and Sixth Amendments, such that it should be excluded from evidence, when an accused is exhibited to the witness before trial at a post-indictment lineup conducted for identification purposes, without notice to and in the absence of the accused's appointed counsel?

HISTORY OF THE CASE

Several weeks after the respondent's indictment for robbery of a federally insured bank and for conspiracy, the respondent, without notice to his appointed counsel, was placed in a lineup in which each person wore strips of tape on his face, as the robber allegedly had, and, on direction, repeated words like those the robber allegedly had used. Two bank employees identified the respondent as the robber.

At the trial, when asked whether the robber was in the courtroom, they identified the respondent. The prior lineup identifications were elicited on cross-examination. Urging that the conduct of the lineup violated his Fifth Amendment privilege against self-incrimination and his Sixth Amendment right to counsel, the respondent filed a motion for judgment of acquittal or, alternatively, for striking of the courtroom identifications. The trial court denied the motions, and the respondent was convicted. The court of appeals reversed, holding that though there was no Fifth Amendment deprivation, the absence of counsel at the lineup denied the respondent his right to counsel under the Sixth Amendment and required the grant of a new trial at which the in-court identifications of those who had made lineup identifications would be excluded. The case was then brought to the Supreme Court.

SUMMARY OF ARGUMENTS

Wade argued that it is a basic right of a fair trial to have the assistance of counsel at a lineup. It was also argued that a post-indictment lineup is a critical stage of a criminal proceeding, and many factors can change the outcome of the lineup. In addition, a suspect needs to have the right to have an attorney present to ensure there is no prejudice and to object to the factors that may affect the outcome of the trial.

The prosecutor argued that a post-indictment lineup is not a critical stage of the criminal proceeding; it is a mere preparatory step in gathering evidence, and an accused does not need counsel present. In addition, it was also argued that a post-indictment lineup is not in violation of the Fifth Amendment, because evidence is not given in a testimonial nature against the defendant.

DECISION

The Court held that the lineup did not violate the defendant's Fifth Amendment privilege against self-incrimination. Allowing a witness to look at the defendant's physical characteristics and listen to the defendant's voice differs from the defendant's giving evidence in a testimonial nature against himself, which the Fifth Amendment precludes. The Sixth Amendment, however, guaranteed the right to counsel at the accused's trial and at any critical stages of the criminal proceeding, including a post-indictment lineup.

Justice Brennan delivered the opinion of the Court and explained that the lineup is not a violation of the Fifth Amendment, because it was held that the privilege against self-incrimination only "protects an accused from being compelled to testify against himself, or otherwise provide the State with evidence of a testimonial or communicative nature." In addition, Brennan explained that the Sixth Amendment guarantee to counsel applies at all critical stages. This means that the "guarantee thus encompasses counsel's assistance whenever necessary to assure a meaningful defence." Brennan concluded, "Since it appears that there is grave potential for prejudice, intentional or not, in the pretrial lineup, which may not be capable of reconstruction at trial, and since presence of counsel itself can often avert prejudice and assure a meaningful confrontation at trial, there can be little doubt that for Wade the post indictment lineup was a critical stage of the prosecution at which he was 'as much entitled to such aid (of counsel) . . . as at trial itself.'"

AFTERMATH

Many saw this case as proof of the Court's softness on crime. When Congress passed the Crime Control and Safe Streets Act of 1968, lineup identification evidence was admitted without counsel present. Finally in *Kirby v. Illinois* (1972), the Court held that the right to counsel did not take effect until after indictment.

SIGNIFICANCE

This holding enlarged the right to counsel. Today, an accused is entitled to have an attorney present at all critical stages of a criminal proceeding, beginning after indictment.

RELATED CASES

Gilbert v. California, 388 U.S. 263 (1951)

Miranda v. Arizona, 384 U.S. 436 (1966)

Schmerber v. State of California, 384 U.S. 757 (1966)

Kirby v. Illinois, 406 U.S. 682 (1972)

RECOMMENDED READING

Bennet L. Gershman, *The Eyewitness Conundrum,* 81 New York State Bar Journal 24 (2009).

Paul Marcus, *Why the United States Supreme Court Got Some (but Not a Lot) of the Sixth Amendment Right to Counsel Analysis Right,* 21 Saint Thomas Law Review 142 (2009).

Case Title: *Duncan v. Louisiana*

Alternate Case Title: The "Right to Jury Trial" Case

Legal Citation: 391 U.S. 145

Year of Decision: 1968

KEY ISSUES

Can a state withhold a defendant's right to a trial by jury for misdemeanor offenses punishable by a maximum of two years' imprisonment under the Sixth and Fourteenth Amendments?

HISTORY OF THE CASE

Gary Duncan was convicted of simple battery in the Twenty-fifth Judicial District Court of Louisiana. Under Louisiana law, simple battery is a misdemeanor, punishable by a maximum of two years' imprisonment and a $300 fine. Duncan requested a trial by jury, but because the Louisiana Constitution granted jury trials only in cases involving capital punishment or imprisonment at hard labor, the trial judge denied the request. Duncan was convicted and sentenced to 60 days in prison and a $150 fine. He sought review from the Louisiana Supreme Court, which denied his requests, failing to find an error of law. Duncan then sought the review of the U.S. Supreme Court.

SUMMARY OF ARGUMENTS

Duncan argued that the Sixth and Fourteenth Amendments to the U.S. Constitution secured the right to jury trial in state criminal prosecutions when a sentence as long as two years may be imposed.

The state of Louisiana argued that the Constitution imposed no duty upon the states to have a jury trial in any criminal case. Louisiana also argued that if the Court held that the Fourteenth Amendment ensured a right to jury trial, the integrity of nonjury trials would be questioned. Finally, Louisiana contended that the appellant's crime did not reach the level of severity necessary for a jury trial.

DECISION

The Court held that the Sixth Amendment right to a jury trial was applicable to the states via the

Fourteenth Amendment due process clause of the U.S. Constitution.

Writing for the majority, Justice White noted the varied protections that fall under the due process clause, including the right to be compensated for property taken by the state; the rights of speech, press, and religion under the First Amendment; the right to be free of unreasonable searches and seizures under the Fourth Amendment; and various other rights guaranteed by the first eight amendments. These rights are protected against state action. To determine whether a right extended by the Fifth and Sixth Amendments with respect to federal criminal proceedings was protected against state action by the Fourteenth Amendment, he insisted on asking whether the particular criminal procedure was fundamental or necessary to the "Anglo-American regime of ordered liberty" that had developed in the United States at that time.

He answered the question of whether the state could impose criminal punishment without granting a jury trial by first analyzing the importance of the jury trial in America. He began with a review of the history of the jury trial going back to England and colonial times. He found the "structure and style" of the criminal process in America developed with and relied upon the jury trial. He concluded, "We believe that trial by jury in criminal cases is fundamental to the American scheme of justice." Thus, he maintained that the Fourteenth Amendment guaranteed a right of jury trial in all federal criminal cases under the protection of the Sixth Amendment.

Justice White also suggested that jury trials were required when the potential penalty was more than six months' imprisonment. He looked at the maximum authorized legislative penalty for simple battery in order to determine its level of severity because he recognized the need for more "objective" criteria to aid in jury trial determinations.

Justice Fortas filed a concurring opinion, in which he stated that the application of the due process clause guaranteed to states would inflict "a serious blow upon the principle of federalism." Justice Black also wrote a concurring opinion joined by Justice Douglas. Justice Harlan dissented, joined by Justice Stewart. He disagreed with the majority's approach to the case and interpretation of the due process clause, disputing the entire incorporation view of the Fourteenth Amendment. He did not see jury trials as the only fair means of trying criminal cases.

AFTERMATH

The Court subsequently added the Fifth Amendment prohibition on "double jeopardy" and the Eighth Amendment prohibition on "excessive" bail to the enumerations set out in *Duncan*. The Court held these prohibitions applicable to the states through incorporation by the Fourteenth Amendment. After *Duncan*, the potential sentence exposure, and not the sentence actually imposed, became the proper measure of an offense's severity.

SIGNIFICANCE

The Court decided in *Duncan* that the guarantees of the Bill of Rights "selectively" incorporated in the due process clause of the Fourteenth Amendment should apply to states in precisely the same manner as they applied to the federal government. *Duncan* redefined the test of *Palko v. Connecticut,* which asked whether the right was so fundamental as to be ranked "implicit in the concept of ordered liberty," to whether the right was "fundamental to the American scheme of justice."

RELATED CASES

Maxwell v. Dow, 176 U.S. 581 (1900)

District of Columbia v. Clawans, 300 U.S. 617 (1937)

Palko v. Connecticut, 302 U.S. 319 (1937)

Singer v. United States, 323 U.S. 338 (1945)

Baldwin v. New York, 399 U.S. 66 (1970)

Williams v. Florida, 399 U.S. 78 (1970)

RECOMMENDED READING

Jerold Israel, *Selective Incorporation Revisited,* 71 Georgetown Law Journal 253 (1982).

Kenneth Katkin, *Incorporation of the Criminal Procedure Amendments: The View from the States,* 84 Nebraska Law Review 397 (2005).

Note, *Trial by Jury in Criminal Cases,* 69 Columbia Law Review 419 (1969).

Case Title: *John Dalmer Benton v. State of Maryland*

Legal Citation: 395 U.S. 784

Year of Decision: 1969

KEY ISSUES

Does the due process clause of the Fourteenth Amendment prohibit a state from subjecting a person to double jeopardy?

HISTORY OF THE CASE

John Benton was convicted of burglary and acquitted of larceny in the Maryland Circuit Court. After Benton's trial, a portion of the Maryland Constitution that required jurors to declare their belief in God was held to be unconstitutional. Benton was given the option of a new trial, as the jurors in his trial were required to complete the oath. Benton chose to undergo a new trial. In the new trial, Benton was charged with both burglary and larceny and was convicted of both crimes. He appealed and brought the case to the Supreme Court, arguing that it was double jeopardy. Benton argued that he should not have been charged with larceny in the new trial since the jury had already acquitted him of the charge in the first trial.

SUMMARY OF ARGUMENTS

Benton argued that the Fifth Amendment prohibition of double jeopardy should apply to state prosecutions through the Fourteenth Amendment. He also argued that protection from double jeopardy was a fundamental right, as were all provisions of the Bill of Rights, which had been made applicable to states through the Fourteenth Amendment. Since the other provisions were applied to the states, the reasoning in *Palko v. Connecticut* should not be followed. Benton also argued that his second trial was prejudiced by the inclusion of the larceny charge. Finally, Benton claimed that he was subjected to double jeopardy because he received a greater punishment for the same offense of burglary in the second trial.

The state argued that the double jeopardy clause of the Fifth Amendment was not applicable to states through the Fourteenth Amendment. It was also argued that even if the double jeopardy clause were applicable to the states, under the circumstances of the case, the double jeopardy clause was not violated. In addition, the state did not find Benton's second case was prejudiced with the combination of the larceny and burglary charges.

DECISION

The Supreme Court held that Benton's second trial was an imposition of double jeopardy. It also held that even though there was not a provision in the state constitution for protection against double jeopardy, the double jeopardy clause was enforceable against the states through the due process clause of the Fourteenth Amendment.

Justice Marshall delivered the opinion and argued that "society's legitimate interest in punishing wrongdoers could have fully vindicated by retrying petitioner on the burglary count alone, that being the offense of which he was previously convicted." The state had no more interest in retrying an acquitted defendant than it did any other person found innocent of a crime. The Court found Benton was denied due process of the law, and the charge, therefore, must be reversed.

AFTERMATH

Ultimately, the Court overturned Benton's larceny conviction.

The Fifth Amendment's double jeopardy clause continues to bind the states from twice imposing punishment for the same crime. However, questions remain as to the limits of the clause's effects on prosecution appeals, midtrial acquittals, reversals due to prosecutorial misconduct, insanity defenses, capital punishment convictions, and other situations in which there exist opportunities for retrial.

SIGNIFICANCE

Benton overruled *Palko v. Connecticut,* making the double jeopardy clause of the Fifth Amendment applicable to the states through the Fourteenth Amendment. Though a defendant cannot be charged for the same offense twice, the conduct in question may still violate other laws and result in different charges.

RELATED CASES

Palko v. Connecticut, 302 U.S. 319 (1937)

Green v. United States, 355 U.S. 184 (1957)

Duncan v. Louisiana, 391 U.S. 145 (1968)

RECOMMENDED READING

Holmes, Burnham. *The Fifth Amendment.* Englewood Cliffs, N.J.: Silver Burdett Press, 1991.

Israel, Jerold H. *Criminal Procedure and the Constitution.* St. Paul: West, 1996.

Case Title: *Ashe v. Swenson*

Legal Citation: 397 U.S. 436

Year of Decision: 1970

KEY ISSUES

Can the state of Missouri prosecute a defendant a second time for armed robbery without violating the double jeopardy clause of the Fifth Amendment?

HISTORY OF THE CASE

Early in the morning of January 10, 1960, three or four armed men barged into the home of John Gladson and robbed six men playing poker in the basement. The men fled the scene in one of the victims' cars. Not long after the robbery, three men were arrested as they walked a short distance from where the stolen car was found. Another officer arrested Bob Fred Ashe shortly afterward, some distance away from the other men. There was confusion as to whether there had actually been three or four perpetrators of the robbery.

In the first trial, brought on behalf of one of the victims, the prosecution's witnesses were not able to identify Ashe as one of the robbers. Subsequently, he was acquitted of robbery in the first trial. Six weeks later, Ashe was brought to trial again and charged with robbery of one of the other poker players. The state had determined weaknesses in its case against Ashe in the first trial and adjusted the case to prevent the uncertainties of Ashe's participation from coming out in court during the second trial. As a result, Ashe was convicted of robbery. The Supreme Court of Missouri affirmed the conviction. Ashe then brought a habeas corpus claim, which was denied in the District Court for the Western District of Missouri. The Supreme Court granted certiorari to review the case.

SUMMARY OF ARGUMENTS

Ashe argued that the second trial violated his guarantee of protection against double jeopardy by prosecuting him twice for robbery using the same evidence and set of facts. Whereas Ashe was acquitted in the first case, he was found guilty in the second—a trial that should have never taken place.

The state argued that the second trial was different from the first trial because there were different parties involved. The state had the option to treat each robbery as a separate and independent crime, so the defendant was not technically tried twice for the same offense. The state further claimed that the Fifth Amendment was not applicable when there were multiple trials for multiple offenses.

DECISION

Applying the rule of collateral estoppel, the Court held that a second prosecution of Ashe was impermissible under the Fifth Amendment. Justice Stewart delivered the opinion.

The majority argued, "The prosecution plainly organized its case for the second trial to provide the links missing in the chain of identification evidence that was offered at the first trial." The Court explained, "One must experience a sense of uneasiness with any double-jeopardy standard that would allow the State this second chance to plug up the holes in its case." The Court held that it was a violation of the double jeopardy clause of the Fifth Amendment to prosecute the petitioner a second time for robbery. The Court stated that "when an issue of ultimate fact has once been determined by a valid and final judgment, that issue cannot again be litigated between the same parties in any future lawsuit." In addition, collateral estoppel prevents an issue from being retried after it has already been determined by a final and valid judgment. Under the circumstances, collateral estoppel can be used to reverse the conviction at the second trial, since the issue was resolved in the first trial. Even in a case involving multiple trials, the Fifth Amendment still applied to protect defendants who had "been acquitted from having to 'run the gantlet' a second time."

Chief Justice Burger dissented and argued that double jeopardy is only to be used for repeated trials of the same offense. This has been expanded to the "same evidence" test, which is applied to determine whether one case requires proof of a fact that the other does not require. Under the circumstances in this case, the second case required proof of fact—robbery of Roberts— whereas the first charge involving Knight did not. According to Burger, the Court had gone beyond the accepted rule in this case.

AFTERMATH

This case stands as rule of law.

SIGNIFICANCE

Ashe determined that a person could not be tried for the same crime twice. When there are different victims of the same offense, a state cannot prosecute the defendant more than once on the same issue without violating the double jeopardy clause of the Fifth Amendment. A defendant has a right against defending him- or herself against the same crime more than once. This helps prevent innocent people from being convicted of crimes, because if defendants must repeatedly defend themselves against a crime, there is an increased likelihood of conviction.

RELATED CASES

Hoag v. New Jersey, 396 U.S. 464 (1958)

Benton v. Maryland, 395 U.S. 784 (1969)

Waller v. Florida, 397 U.S. 387 (1970)

RECOMMENDED READING

M. C. Deason, Jr., *Rule of Collateral Estoppel Embodied in the Fifth Amendment Guaranty against Double Jeopardy,* 1 Cumberland-Samford Law Review 355 (1970).

The Due Process Roots of Criminal Collateral Estoppel, 109 Harvard Law Review 1729 (1996).

Charles W. Hendricks, *100 Years of Double Jeopardy Erosion: Criminal Collateral Estoppel Made Extinct,* 48 Drake Law Review 379 (2000).

Walter V. Schaefer, *Unresolved Issues in the Law of Double Jeopardy:* Waller *and* Ashe, 58 California Law Review 391 (1970).

Case Title: *In the Matter of Samuel Winship*

Alternate Case Title: *In re Winship*

Legal Citation: 397 U.S. 358

Year of Decision: 1970

KEY ISSUE

Does the court require proof beyond a reasonable doubt, as among the "essentials of due process and fair treatment," when a juvenile is charged with an act that would constitute a crime if committed by an adult?

HISTORY OF THE CASE

A 12-year-old boy, Samuel Winship, entered a locker and stole $112 from a woman's pocketbook. It was alleged that if Winship had been an adult, he would be charged with larceny. The judge sentenced him to 18 months in a training school, which was subject to annual extensions until his 18th birthday. The judge expressed that the proof may not establish guilt beyond a reasonable doubt. The judge relied on Section 744(b) of the New York Family Court Act that any determination is by a preponderance of evidence and rejected the appellant's contention that the Fourteenth Amendment required guilt beyond reasonable doubt. The case was brought to the Supreme Court for review.

SUMMARY OF ARGUMENTS

Winship argued that finding guilt of a juvenile on the basis of a preponderance of the evidence violates due process of law. It was also argued that a juvenile is denied equal protection of the law when the standard is less meticulous than in an adult trial.

The court of appeals relied on the issue that "a child's best interest is not necessarily, or even probably promoted if he wins in the particular inquiry which may bring him to the juvenile court." This would result in a greater number of acquittals where judicial intervention is needed. It also relied on the argument that giving juveniles the protection of proof beyond a reasonable doubt would destroy the entire juvenile process.

DECISION

Justice Brennan delivered the opinion of the Court, stating that the due process clause of the Fourteenth Amendment requires proof beyond a reasonable doubt for a juvenile act that would be a crime if an adult committed it. The Court relied on the requirement of proof beyond a reasonable doubt, which dates back to the early years of this nation. In addition, there was virtually unanimous adherence to the reasonable doubt standard in common law, which does not establish a

requirement; however, it does show a judgment about the way law should be enforced. The Court also relied on the vital role that the reasonable doubt standard plays in criminal procedure in America: "It is a prime instrument for reducing the risk of convictions resting on factual error." The Court also explained that the reasonable doubt standard must be used for the respect of the community: "It is critical that the moral force of the criminal law not be diluted by a standard of proof that leaves people in doubt whether innocent men are being condemned."

In disagreement with the court of appeals, the Court argued that the reasonable doubt standard would not disturb New York's juvenile policies, especially policies explaining that a juvenile crime is not a criminal conviction, that the juvenile is not deprived of civil rights, and that juvenile proceedings are confidential. In addition, the Court contested that intervention was in the best interest of a child when the standard of proof had not been shown. Such intervention could not take the form of the "possibility of institutional confinement on proof insufficient to convict him were he an adult." The Court concluded by explaining that "the constitutional safeguard of proof beyond a reasonable doubt is as much required during the adjudicatory stage of a delinquency proceeding as are those constitutional safeguards" such as the privilege against self-incrimination.

Justice Black dissented, arguing that the juvenile court system is different from criminal courts. Black argued that there was "no constitutional requirement of due process sufficient to overcome the legislative judgment of the States in this area." Black stated that the requirement is not in the U.S. Constitution: "Nowhere in that document is there any statement that conviction of crime requires proof of guilt beyond a reasonable doubt."

AFTERMATH

The case has not been overruled and remains good law.

SIGNIFICANCE

Winship expanded the rights and protections of minors and those rights given in the case of *In re*

Gault. This case required that juveniles be entitled to the same constitutional protections that adults have in criminal convictions.

RELATED CASES

Davis v. U.S., 160 U.S. 469 (1895)

In re Gault, 387 U.S. 1 (1967)

Cupp v. Naughten, 414 U.S. 141 (1973)

Mullaney v. Wilbur, 421 U.S. 684 (1975)

Jackson v. Virginia, 443 U.S. 307 (1979)

Sullivan v. Louisiana, 508 U.S. 275 (1993)

Apprendi v. New Jersey, 530 U.S. 466 (2000)

STATUTES AT ISSUE

New York Family Court Act, § 712, § 744(b)

RECOMMENDED READING

Edward J. Imwinkelried, *The Reach of Winship: Invalidating Evidentiary Admissibility Standards That Undermine the Prosecution's Obligation to Prove the Defendant's Guilt beyond a Reasonable Doubt,* 70 UMKC Law Review 865 (2002).

Irene Merker Rosenberg, Winship *Redux: 1970 to 1990,* 69 Texas Law Review 109 (1990).

Note, Winship *on Rough Waters: The Erosion of the Reasonable Doubt Standard,* 106 Harvard Law Review 1093 (1993).

Case Title: *Argersinger v. Hamlin*

Legal Citation: 407 U.S. 25

Year of Decision: 1972

KEY ISSUES

Do the Sixth and Fourteenth Amendments guarantee a right to counsel for defendants accused of misdemeanor crimes?

HISTORY OF THE CASE

Jon Richard Argersinger was charged with carrying a concealed weapon in Florida, a misdemeanor punishable by imprisonment up to six months, a fine, or both. At a bench trial, Argersinger was sentenced to 90 days in jail. He then filed a habeas corpus action in the Florida Supreme Court, claiming that his Sixth Amendment rights to counsel had been violated because he was indigent and not given an attorney. He argued that this resulted in a lack of sufficient defenses to the charges against him. The Florida Supreme Court, following their interpretation of *Duncan v. Louisiana* (1968), held that the right to court-appointed counsel only extends to trials for offenses punishable by more than six months in prison. Noting that 31 states have extended the right to counsel to defendants charged with crimes less serious than felonies, the U.S. Supreme Court granted certiorari.

SUMMARY OF ARGUMENTS

Argersinger argued that his right to counsel was violated when he was not given an attorney; the result was an unconstitutional conviction. Hamlin argued that the right to counsel did not extend to offenses with a sentence of less than six months.

DECISION

Relying in part on the decision in *Gideon v. Wainwright* (1963), the Court extended the right to an attorney for indigent defendants for cases involving "serious crimes" to all defendants facing possible incarceration. The decision was based on establishing fairness in all trials involving jail time.

Justice Douglas delivered the opinion of the Court.

The Court began by first stating that the Sixth Amendment has been made applicable to the states through the Fourteenth Amendment. The Court then noted that several trial rights were guaranteed to the accused, none of which was expanded or lessened by the seriousness of the offense, including the right to a public trial and to be informed of the nature and cause of the accusation. Although *Duncan* had held that the right to a jury trial could be limited to offenses punishable by more than six months in prison, the Court found no historical support for a similar limitation on the right to counsel. In common law, the right to counsel was provided for civil cases and misdemeanors but only allowed in limited circumstances for felonies. However, the Court found nothing in the language or history of the Sixth Amendment demonstrating an intention to retract the right for petty offenses. Thus, the Court rejected the argument that "since prosecutions for crimes punishable by imprisonment for less than six months may be tried without a jury, they may also be tried without a lawyer." On the contrary, the Court found that "the assistance of counsel is often a requisite to the very existence of a fair trial."

Noting that the government hires lawyers to prosecute defendants, and defendants hire lawyers to defend their own interests, the Court found that lawyers are more of a necessity than a luxury. The Court stated that they were "by no means convinced that legal and constitutional questions involved in a case that actually leads to imprisonment even for a brief period are any less complex than when a person can be sent off for six months or more." As an example, the Court discussed the vagrancy of juveniles and their need for counsel to ensure a fair trial. Counsel was deemed especially necessary when entering pleas because the accused must know exactly what he or she is doing. Also, in support of their view that counsel was necessary for fairness, the Court discussed the heavy volume of cases, which creates the risk of "assembly-line justice." The large caseloads often lead to dismissal of the charges against those with counsel, while charges against those without counsel are not dismissed. Accordingly, the Court reversed the decision of the Florida Supreme Court and held that "absent a knowing and intelligent waiver, no person may be imprisoned for any offense, whether classified as petty, misdemeanor, or felony, unless he was represented by counsel at his trial." The Court also mentioned that this holding was limited only to cases in which loss of liberty was involved, not crimes resulting in other punishments.

Chief Justice Burger wrote a concurring opinion, explaining that any deprivation of liberty is a serious matter and warrants granting the defendant counsel. He stated that laymen would have difficulty even in simple misdemeanor cases and, if they are unrepresented, appealing from a conviction after trial "is not likely to be of much help to a defendant since the die is usually cast when judgment is entered on an un-counseled trial record." In conclusion, he stated that the Court's holding "may well add large new burdens on a profession already overtaxed, but the dynamics of the profession have a way of rising to the burdens placed on it." Justice Brennan also wrote a concurring opinion, stating his view that through faculty-supervised clinical programs, "law students can be expected to make a significant contribution, quantitatively and qualitatively, to the representation of the poor in many areas, including cases reached by today's decision."

Justice Powell concurred in the Court's decision; however, he arrived at this conclusion through different reasoning. He preferred a middle ground between Florida's requirement of facing at least six months in jail in order to receive counsel and the Court's holding, stating, "I would adhere to the principle of due process that requires fundamental fairness in criminal trials, a principle which I believe encompasses the right to counsel in petty cases whenever the assistance of counsel is necessary to assure a fair trial." He considered the Court's holding as too rigid and asserted that it could be extended to all petty offenses. He stated that the Court "should be slow to fashion a new constitutional rule with consequences of such unknown dimensions, especially since it is supported neither by history nor precedent." Justice Powell was concerned that the new rule of the Court lacked details as to how it would be implemented and thought that it would have an adverse effect on the legal system by overburdening it. He would have crafted a rule giving the trial courts discretion in determining the right to counsel on a case-by-case basis and, if denying it, stating the reasons to preserve them for review.

AFTERMATH

As the Court stated in its opinion, under the rule announced in this case, all judges were put on notice that when a trial starts, no imprisonment may be imposed, even if local law permits it, unless the accused is represented by counsel. Indigent defendants are to have counsel appointed to them before the trial starts.

SIGNIFICANCE

In this case, the Court interpreted the Sixth Amendment right to counsel as applying to any person facing potential incarceration, regardless of how the offense is classified. This right does not extend to crimes without the potential for incarceration, such as some traffic offenses and other petty offenses.

RELATED CASES

Gideon v. Wainright, 372 U.S. 335 (1963)

Duncan v. Louisiana, 391 U.S. 145 (1968)

RECOMMENDED READING

Steamer, Robert J. "Argersinger v. Hamlin." In *Academic American Encyclopedia.* 1991 ed. Vol. 2, p. 152.

Case Title: *California v. Trombetta*

Legal Citation: 467 U.S. 479

Year of Decision: 1984

KEY ISSUE

Does the due process clause of the Fourteenth Amendment require a state to preserve potentially exculpatory evidence on behalf of defendants?

HISTORY OF THE CASE

This case involves two respondents whom California police stopped (in unrelated incidents) on suspicion of drunken driving. During these traffic stops, each respondent agreed to perform an "Intoxilyzer" (breathalyzer) test, and in each case, the respondent registered a blood alcohol

level higher than the legal limit—and was, thus, charged with driving under the influence of alcohol (DUI). Prior to their trials, both respondents filed a motion to suppress the results of the breathalyzer tests, claiming that the state's failure to preserve the breath samples interfered with the respondents' Fourteenth Amendment right to "obtain from the prosecution evidence that is either material to the guilt of the defendant or relevant to the punishment to be imposed." (The respondents had been unable to obtain the breath samples because the arresting police officers had followed custom and eliminated the actual breath samples at the scene; at trial, the state produced the test results in print form.) After the trial courts denied their motions to suppress and subsequently convicted the respondents, the respondents petitioned the California Court of Appeals—and that court found in their favor, ordering a new trial on the grounds that the actual breath samples would have been useful to the respondents at trial and that the arresting officers had had the ability to preserve the breath samples. The state of California then petitioned for certiorari in the California Supreme Court, and when that proved unsuccessful, they petitioned for—and were granted—certiorari in the U.S. Supreme Court.

SUMMARY OF ARGUMENTS

The respondents argued that because actual breath samples were more reliable than the Intoxilyzer printouts introduced at trial and only the state had the technology to preserve such samples, the state of California had violated their Fourteenth Amendment right to a "fundamentally fair trial."

The state of California, meanwhile, argued that, by destroying the actual breath sample, they had not violated the respondents' Fourteenth Amendment rights because the breath samples were not "material" evidence:

> This was not evidence favorable to the defense. The contrary is true. Nor would a preserved or separately collected sample yield material evidence, since reanalysis is

itself subject to error and cannot be verified. . . . [This creates] a conflict in the evidence which can be resolved but only by going back to the evidential breath test and rechecking its accuracy.

DECISION

The U.S. Supreme Court overturned the decision of the California Court of Appeals and unanimously held that the due process clause of the Fourteenth Amendment did not require the state of California to preserve actual breath samples in order to use the results of the breathalyzer test at trial.

In delivering the opinion of the Court, Justice Marshall first emphasized that one of the main purposes of the due process clause of the Fourteenth Amendment is to ensure that "criminal prosecutions . . . comport with prevailing notions of fundamental fairness." However, that being said, Justice Marshall acknowledged that this case represented the first instance in which the Court "squarely addressed the government's duty to take affirmative steps to preserve evidence on behalf of criminal defendants." The dispositive question in this case, then, seems to be whether the state's preservation of the breath samples would have had any effect on the defendants' ability to receive the sort of "fundamentally fair" trial mandated by the Fourteenth Amendment. Justice Marshall found that the State's destruction of the actual breath samples did not violate the due process clause because "a dispassionate review of the Intoxilyzer and the California testing procedures can only lead one to conclude that the chances are extremely low that preserved samples would have been exculpatory." Justice Marshall observed that the Intoxilyzer's accuracy had been carefully tested by the California Department of Health, and, therefore, "once the Intoxilyzer indicated that respondents were legally drunk, breath samples were much more likely to provide inculpatory than exculpatory evidence" (in other words, Justice Marshall found that the breath samples were generally *less reliable* than the Intoxilyzer printout). Finally, Justice Marshall noted that if the defendants were concerned about the possibility of operator error, they had the right to cross-examine the police officer who administered the test.

AFTERMATH

In her article "*California v. Trombetta*: Holding Our Breath on the Duty to Preserve," Paula B. Wasserman asserted that this case's most significant legacy would be its "threat to the ability of defendants to secure sanctions against the prosecution's failure to preserve other forms of potentially exculpatory evidence which fail to meet the Court's new test for constitutional materiality." Wasserman's prediction seemed to come true in *Arizona v. Youngblood* (1988), in which the U.S. Supreme Court held that due process protection would only be extended to that evidence that was destroyed in "bad faith."

SIGNIFICANCE

With the decisions in *Trombetta* and *Youngblood*, law enforcement agencies are not liable for destroying exculpatory or potentially exculpatory evidence unless the evidence was material to the case, was exculpatory in nature before the destruction occurred, and was no longer available through any other reasonable means. In addition, the officers must have been acting in bad faith when the evidence was destroyed.

RELATED CASES

Killian v. United States, 368 U.S. 231 (1961)

United States v. Valenzuela-Bernal, 458 U.S. 858; (1982)

Arizona v. Youngblood, 488 U.S. 51 (1988)

RECOMMENDED READING

Willis C. Moore, Arizona v. Youngblood: *Does the Criminal Defendant Lose His Right to Due Process When the State Loses Exculpatory Evidence?*, 5 Touro Law Review 309 (1988–89).

Paula B. Wasserman, California v. Trombetta: *Holding Our Breath on the Duty to Preserve*, 12 Western State University Law Review 309 (1984–85).

Case Title: *Spaziano v. Florida*

Legal Citation: 468 U.S. 477

Year of Decision: 1984

KEY ISSUE

May a judge override a jury's sentencing recommendation that a criminal defendant be sentenced to life imprisonment and, instead, impose the death penalty?

HISTORY OF THE CASE

Joseph Spaziano was indicted and tried for first-degree murder. The primary evidence against him was that of a witness who testified that Spaziano took him to a garbage dump and showed him the remains of two women Spaziano claimed to have tortured and murdered. The jury returned a verdict of guilty of first-degree murder. At the sentencing hearing, the majority of the jury recommended life imprisonment, but the trial judge imposed the death penalty.

On appeal, the Florida Supreme Court affirmed the conviction but reversed the death sentence. The judge considered part of a confidential report detailing Spaziano's previous felony convictions, as well as other charges of which Spaziano had not been convicted, when making his sentencing determination. On remand, the trial judge reaffirmed his conclusion that the crime was especially heinous, atrocious, and cruel and, again, sentenced Spaziano to die. The Supreme Court of Florida affirmed.

SUMMARY OF ARGUMENTS

Spaziano challenged the court's imposition of a sentence of death when the jury had recommended life imprisonment. The defendant argued that the Sixth Amendment's guarantee of a jury trial also guarantees a right to a jury determination of whether a convicted individual should be sentenced to death.

The state argued that the role of the jury in sentencing determinations was advisory. Further, there is no constitutional requirement that a defendant be entitled to a jury determination in capital sentencing. As such, there is no violation of Spaziano's constitutional rights in the judge's declining to follow the recommendation of the jury.

DECISION

In the opinion, written by Justice Blackmun, the Court held that the Sixth Amendment does not require jury sentencing, and it is not unconstitutional for a trial judge to override the jury recommendation and impose the death penalty so long as the result of the process is not arbitrary or discriminatory. The Court stated, "Regardless of the jury's recommendation, the trial judge is required to conduct an independent review of the evidence and to make his own findings regarding aggravating and mitigating circumstances."

On the basis of the presence of two aggravating circumstances, the Court determined that the jury override procedure did not result in arbitrary or discriminatory application of the death penalty. First, the defendant had previously been convicted of another capital felony involving the use or threat of violence against another person. Second, the trial judge found that the murder in this case was "heinous, atrocious, and cruel" on the basis of the witness's testimony regarding the condition of the bodies at the dump site and found that the defendant had "recounted his torture of the victim while she was still living."

The dissent argued that giving one government official, the judge, the power to override the decision of the jury negates the protections provided by due process of law. The dissenting justices argued that a death sentence is qualitatively different from other punishments and, as such, is worthy of additional safeguards from abuse. Further, the standards of determining what constitutes cruel and unusual punishment take into account the conscience of the community, of which a jury is a far better representation than a single judge.

AFTERMATH

The Supreme Court upheld Spaziano's death sentence, and the Supreme Court announced that sentencing decisions made by a judge rather than a jury in capital cases are not unconstitutional. That has not ended the debate on whether such power is appropriate when placed in a single individual's hands.

SIGNIFICANCE

The Supreme Court decision that jury sentencing was unnecessary and that jury recommendations in capital cases were not binding upon the judge was reaffirmed in *Harris v. Alabama* (1995). However, in *Ring v. Arizona,* a 2002 case, the Supreme Court held that defendants are entitled to have the jury determine the presence of aggravating conditions that result in an increase in their sentence. While *Spaziano* has not been overruled, and Florida's sentencing guidelines remain substantially the same to this day, some critics see no real difference between a system in which the judge decides without the advice of the jury and one in which the judge is free to disregard the advice of the jury.

RELATED CASES

Furman v. Georgia, 408 U.S. 238 (1972)

Harris v. Alabama, 513 U.S. 504 (1995)

Ring v. Arizona, 536 U.S. 584 (2002)

RECOMMENDED READING

LaTour Rey Lafferty, *Florida's Capital Sentencing Jury Override: Whom Should We Trust to Make the Ultimate Ethical Judgment?,* 23 Florida State University Law Review 463 (1995).

Latzer, Barry, ed. *Death Penalty Cases: Leading U.S. Supreme Court Cases on Capital Punishment.* New York: Butterworth-Heinemann, 2002.

John M. Richardson, *Reforming the Jury Override: Protecting Capital Defendants' Rights by Returning to the System's Original Purpose,* 94

Journal of Criminal Law and Criminology 455 (2004).

Bryan A. Stevenson, *The Ultimate Authority on the Ultimate Punishment: The Requisite Role of the Jury in Capital Sentencing,* 54 Alabama Law Review 1091 (2003).

Case Title: *Burger v. Kemp*

Legal Citation: 438 U.S. 776

Year of Decision: 1987

KEY ISSUE

Did the actions (or inactions) of Petitioner Burger's appointed attorney represent "ineffective assistance of counsel" in violation of the Sixth Amendment?

HISTORY OF THE CASE

In 1977, while stationed at Fort Stewart, Georgia, army privates Christopher Burger (petitioner) and Thomas Stevens (coindictee) stole a butcher knife from the mess hall. They called a taxi and held the knife against the body of the driver, whom they proceeded to rob and sexually assault. Eventually, they placed the driver in the trunk of the car, which they drove into a nearby pond, drowning the driver. (Apparently while Stevens threw the cab driver's radio into some bushes near the pond, Burger "opened the trunk and asked [the driver] if he was all right. [The driver] answered affirmatively. The petitioner then closed the trunk, started the automobile, and put it in gear, getting out before it entered the water.") According to a psychologist, Burger "had an IQ of 82 and functioned at the level of a 12-year-old child." Alvin Leaphart, an experienced attorney in that area, was appointed as Burger's counsel; nevertheless, at trial, a jury found Burger guilty of murder and decided to impose the death penalty (coindictee

Stevens was later convicted at a separate trial and also sentenced to death). During the trial/sentencing hearing, Burger's attorney "offered no mitigating evidence at all." Apparently, even though Burger's attorney was aware of some of his sordid family history (abusive stepfathers, one of whom exposed the petitioner to drugs and alcohol, etc.), he chose not to present evidence of it at trial.

Petitioner Burger later appealed for a federal writ of habeas corpus on the grounds that the actions of his attorney represented "ineffective assistance of counsel" under the Sixth Amendment. The petitioner first argued that there had been an impermissible conflict of interest as his attorney's partner had represented his coindictee, Thomas Stevens. Second, Burger argued that his attorney had "failed to develop and present mitigating evidence at either of the two sentencing hearings." After the federal district court found that there was "no merit" in the petitioner's claim, and the court of appeals affirmed, the U.S. Supreme Court granted certiorari.

SUMMARY OF ARGUMENTS

In his writ for federal habeas relief, Burger asserted that his Sixth Amendment right to counsel had been violated because his attorney's partner had represented the coindictee, and there had, thus, been an impermissible conflict of interests and because his attorney had not made enough of an attempt to seek out mitigating evidence.

Regarding the petitioner's first argument, the respondent claimed that allowing law partners to represent coindictees was "not uncommon" in that part of Georgia (mainly because of the rural nature of that part of the state). In response to the petitioner's second argument (that his attorney had failed to search for mitigating evidence), the respondent stated that the petitioner Burger's attorney "consulted with his client, his client's mother . . . [he] testified that he was never given any information by his client or his client's mother on which to move." In addition, the respondent argued that when considering the "totality of the circumstances, all those facts as they existed and were known to counsel at the time of trial," Burger's attorney's decision not to present certain evidence was reasonable:

The decision represented strategic choices and not incompetence.

DECISION

The U.S. Supreme Court held in a 5-4 decision that the actions of the petitioner's counsel did not violate the Sixth Amendment.

With regard to Burger's first argument—that his Sixth Amendment rights were violated when his attorney's partner represented coindictee Thomas Stevens—Justice Stevens (writing the majority opinion) determined that the *possibility* of prejudice that exists when law partners represent coindictees "is not *per se* violative of constitutional guarantees of effective assistance of counsel." Instead, the Court continued, the defendant must demonstrate that an "actual conflict of interest adversely affected his lawyer's performance." The Court concluded that there had not been an "actual conflict," as the lower courts—which were in a "far better position than [the U.S. Supreme Court]" to evaluate a charge of this kind"—found that Burger's attorney's representation had been above the constitutional "ineffective assistance" threshold.

In response to the petitioner's second argument, Justice Stevens first noted that "at both hearings, [the petitioner's attorney] offered no mitigating evidence at all." "The evidence that might have been presented," Justice Stevens continued, "would have disclosed that petitioner had an exceptionally unhappy and unstable childhood. Most of this evidence was described by petitioner's mother." However, Justice Stevens then stated as follows:

> Judicial scrutiny of counsel's performance must be highly deferential. It is all too tempting for a defendant to second-guess counsel's assistance after conviction or adverse sentence. . . . We have decided that "strategic choices made after less than complete investigation are reasonable precisely to the extent that reasonable professional judgments support the limitations on investigation. . . . Applying this standard . . . counsel's decision not to mount an all-out investigation into petitioner's background in search of mitigating circum-

stances was supported by reasonable professional judgment."

In his dissent, Justice Blackmun (joined by Justices Brennan, Marshall, and Powell) asserted that the representation of coindictees by law partners represented "actual conflicting interests," as their interests were "diametrically opposed on the issue that counsel considered to be crucial to the outcome of petitioner's case—the comparative culpability of petitioner and Stevens."

Justice Blackmun also asserted that the petitioner's counsel had failed to conduct an adequate search for mitigating evidence. Where Justice Stevens (who wrote the majority opinion) had determined that counsel's performance had not prejudiced the petitioner, Justice Blackman found that had counsel investigated that Burger's troubled childhood, that mitigating evidence might have affected the outcome of the trial:

> But for defense counsel's disinterest in developing any mitigating evidence to permit an informed decision, there is a reasonable possibility that the outcome of the sentencing hearing would have been different.

AFTERMATH

The matter of effectiveness was brought to the Supreme Court in 2003 in the case of *Wiggins v. Smith,* in which a defendant facing the death penalty claimed his counsel did not present mitigating evidence to the jury in sentencing. The Court in this case ruled in favor of the defendant, saying that an investigation into a defendant's history is key in deciding which mitigating evidence should be presented in a sentencing hearing.

RELATED CASES

Strickland v. Washington, 466 U.S. 668 (1984)

Wiggins v. Smith, 539 U.S. 510 (2003)

RECOMMENDED READING

James R. Acker, *A Different Agenda: The Supreme Court, Empirical Research Evidence, and Capital*

Punishment Decisions, 1986–1989, 27 Law and Society Review 1 (1993).

Eric T. Franzen and Perry Oei, *Effective Assistance of Counsel during Sentencing,* 1986 Army Law 52 (1986).

Case Title: *Blanton v. City of North Las Vegas*

Legal Citation: 489 U.S. 538

Year of Decision: 1989

KEY ISSUE

Does a defendant charged with driving under the influence (DUI) have a Sixth Amendment right to a jury trial?

HISTORY OF THE CASE

Blanton was charged with his first DUI offense, which at that time in the state of Nevada was punishable by a maximum prison term of six months and a fine of $1,000 (alternatively, Nevada trial courts may order the defendant to "perform 48 hours of work for the community while dressed in distinctive garb which identifies him as [a DUI offender]"). The municipal court in North Las Vegas, Nevada, decided to deny Blanton's request for a jury trial, and when Blanton appealed this decision to the Supreme Court of Nevada, that court held that the U.S. Constitution does not guarantee a jury trial for a DUI offense because the maximum sentence is six months; thus, it is not the sort of "serious" crime that is required for a jury to hear the case. Petitioner Blanton appealed the decision of the Nevada Supreme Court, and the U.S. Supreme Court granted certiorari to determine whether Blanton was entitled to a jury trial.

SUMMARY OF ARGUMENTS

Blanton argued that he was constitutionally entitled to a jury trial because the offense of DUI is *malum in se* and, thus, carries the right to a jury trial. Additionally, the statutory penalty attached to this offense—wearing clothing that identifies the individual as a DUI offender—was such a "badge of dishonor" that it should only be imposed after a jury trial.

The state of Nevada, meanwhile, argued that the bright-line rule issued in *Baldwin v. New York* (1978) (jury trials are guaranteed only in those cases when the maximal penalty is more than six months in prison) mandated that the petitioner not receive a jury trial. Concerning the "distinctive garb" that DUI offenders had to wear for 48 hours, the state argued that though such clothing is indeed "shameful," that punishment does not warrant elevating DUIs to "serious" status.

DECISION

The U.S. Supreme Court affirmed the decision of the Nevada Supreme Court and held that Blanton's DUI was not the sort of "serious" offense that required a jury trial.

Justice Marshall delivered the opinion of the Court and began his analysis by distinguishing "serious" offenses, which justify jury trials, from "petty" offenses. In *Callan v. Wilson* (1888), the Court held that the Sixth Amendment's guarantee of a speedy trial with an impartial jury did not, in fact, apply to every case:

> Except in that class or grade of offenses called "petty offenses," which, according to the common law, may be proceeded against summarily in any tribunal . . . the guarantee of an impartial jury to the accused . . . secures him the right to enjoy that mode of trial.

Eighty-two years after *Callan,* in *Baldwin v. New York,* the Court made a bright-line rule for determining what distinguished "serious" offenses from "petty" ones: "We have concluded," Justice White wrote, "that no offense can be deemed 'petty' for purposes of the right to trial by jury where imprisonment for more than six months is authorized."

Thus, in order to determine whether Blanton had the constitutional right to a jury trial,

Justice Marshall looked at the maximum prison sentence that Blanton could receive for his DUI offense under Nevada law. For first-time offenders such as Blanton, the longest possible sentence at that time (1989) was exactly six months. As the *Baldwin* Court held that "serious" offenses had prison sentences of more than six months, Justice Marshall concluded that Blanton was not entitled to a jury trial. Justice Marshall added that the Court was "unpersuaded by the fact that, instead of a prison sentence, a DUI offender [in Nevada] may be ordered to perform 48 hours of community service. . . . Even assuming the outfit [identifying the individual as a DUI offender] is the source of some embarrassment . . . such a penalty will be less embarrassing and less onerous than six months in jail." The *Blanton* decision can best be summed up this way: Given the fact that the maximum prison term for a DUI offense in Nevada was exactly six months, there was a rebuttable presumption that the petitioner Blanton was not entitled to a jury trial. That presumption could only then be overcome if the Court determined that the "additional statutory penalties, viewed in conjunction with the maximum authorized period of incarceration, are so severe that they clearly reflect a legislative determination that the offense in question is a 'serious' one." According to Justice Marshall, nothing about the Nevada statutory penalties overcame this presumption.

AFTERMATH

Since the decision, *Blanton* has been applied to many criminal offenses of all types in state and federal courts. Lower courts have, however, had difficulty with *Blanton* in determining how many "additional statutory penalties" have to be present in order to shift an offense from "petty" to "serious."

SIGNIFICANCE

This case further supported the many previous decisions determining that offenses with penalties of fewer than six months were considered "petty" and did not require a jury trial or imply the right to counsel.

RELATED CASES

Callan v. Wilson, 127 U.S. 540 (1888)

Baldwin v. New York, 399 U.S. 66 (1970)

State v. Basabe, 97 P.3d 418 (2004)

State v. Willis, 178 P.3d 480 (2008)

RECOMMENDED READING

Melissa Hartigan, *Creatures of the Common Law: The Petty Offense Doctrine and 18 U.S.C. § 19,* 59 Montana Law Review 343 (1998).

Jane W. Nall, Blanton v. City of North Las Vegas: *Gambling with Criminal Defendants' Constitutional Right to a Jury Trial,* 43 Brandeis Law Journal 303 (2004–2005).

Case Title: *Mistretta v. United States*

Legal Citation: 488 U.S. 361

Year of Decision: 1989

KEY ISSUES

Do the Federal Sentencing Guidelines, which were promulgated by the U.S. Sentencing Commission, violate the Constitution, as either an excessive delegation of legislative authority or a violation of the separation of powers, since they are implemented within the judicial branch?

HISTORY OF THE CASE

John Mistretta was indicted on three counts involving a cocaine sale in the U.S. District Court for the Western District of Missouri on December 10, 1987. Mistretta argued that the Federal Sentencing Guidelines (Guidelines) established under the Sentencing Reform Act of 1984, to which he was subject for sentencing purposes, were unconstitutional, arguing that Congress had violated the separation of powers among the three branches of

federal government by delegating excessive legislative authority to the sentencing commission, which created the Guidelines.

The district court rejected Mistretta's claims, the defendant pled guilty to one charge, and the other two charges were dismissed. He was sentenced to 18 months' imprisonment and three year's supervised release and given a fine of $1,000. Mistretta appealed to the Eighth Circuit; however, both Mistretta and the government petitioned for certiorari before the U.S. Supreme Court. The Court granted certiorari because of the mixed reception of the Guidelines: The Ninth circuit had invalidated the Guidelines on separation of powers grounds, in *Gubiensni-Ortiz v. Kanahele* (1988), and the Third Circuit had upheld them, in *United States v. Frank* (1988).

SUMMARY OF ARGUMENTS

Mistretta argued that the delegation of power to the sentencing commission in creating the Guidelines was excessive to the extent that it violated the nondelegation doctrine. He also argued that the act violated the constitutional principle of separation of powers. Additionally, he argued that federal judges should not be able to serve on the sentencing commission because their duties under the act would interfere and conflict with their duties to the judicial system.

Essentially, the federal government argued the act was a necessary solution to problems that arose under alternative sentencing forms. The government urged that the act was consistent with the constitutional principles of nondelegation and separation of powers.

DECISION

The Court began with a historical discussion about the creation of the Guidelines. Prior to the creation of the Guidelines, the federal government used an indeterminate system of sentencing for convicted offenders, which focused on rehabilitating offenders prior to releasing them back into society. Judges were given broad discretion in tailoring sentences, and a convicted offender would eventually become parole eligible. This system utilized all three branches of the federal government: Congress set the statutory penalties for crimes, judges were granted wide discretion in considering factors to determine a sentence, and correctional officers of the executive branch were allowed to release an inmate early on parole. Problems arose from disparities in sentences between similarly situated offenders, and the focus on "rehabilitation" began to be questioned. This led the U.S. Parole Board to establish customary ranges of confinement, which were endorsed by Congress. However, problems remained, and so Congress passed the Sentencing Reform Act of 1984.

The aim under the act was focused on retributive, educational, deterrent, and incapacitative goals, as opposed to rehabilitation. The act created the U.S. Sentencing Commission, which is composed of seven voting members appointed to six-year terms by the president with the consent of the Senate. The Guidelines established a mandatory range of determinate sentences for particular categories of offenses but allowed judges to depart from it if aggravating or mitigating circumstances were found and determined not to have been considered by the sentencing commission.

The Court rejected Mistretta's nondelegation argument because it deemed the act not so much a delegation of authority as an attempt by Congress to obtain assistance from the other branches, which was allowed under the "intelligible principle" test, as set forth by Chief Justice Taft in *J. W. Hampton, Jr., & Co. v. United States* (1928). In *Hampton,* the Court defined the "intelligible principle" by stating that when Congress seeks assistance from the other branches of the government, it must do so with common sense and must lay out an intelligible principle to which the party with the delegated authority must conform.

The Court held that an intelligible principle had been used and that Congress simply could not do its job without the ability to delegate authority with wide discretion. The Court also pointed out the importance of delegation when an expert body was needed, such as in creating the sentencing guidelines, to which all federal criminal offenders would be subject. The Court noted that concerns over "encroachment and

aggrandizement" have always been a part of separation of powers jurisprudence. Regarding Congress's decision to create the sentencing commission and locate it in the judicial branch, the Court stated that this decision was not unconstitutional unless it undermined the integrity of the judiciary or should be performed by another branch of government. The Court held that locating the commission within the judicial branch only acknowledged the role of the judiciary in sentencing.

Additionally, the location of the U.S. Sentencing Commission within the judiciary did not violate the separation of powers doctrine either, because, as the Court noted, it posed "no threat of undermining the integrity of the Judicial Branch or of expanding the powers of the Judiciary beyond constitutional bounds" by giving that branch legislative power. Quite memorably, the Court went on to state that the Constitution "does not forbid judges to wear two hats; it merely forbids them to wear two hats at the same time." Thus, Congress has not aggrandized the authority of the judiciary or the executive branches. Additionally, the "good cause" requirement for excluding members from the commission was viewed by the Court as an adequate safeguard to protect against granting the president too much power.

Accordingly, the majority concluded by stating that "in creating the Sentencing Commission, an unusual hybrid in structure and authority, Congress neither delegated excessive legislative power nor upset the constitutionally mandated balance of powers among the coordinate Branches." Thus, the act was deemed constitutional, and the judgment of the U.S. District Court for the Western District of Missouri was affirmed.

Justice Scalia dissented to the judgment, arguing that there was "no place within our constitutional system for an agency created by Congress to exercise no governmental power other than the making of laws." Scalia noted, "Except in a few areas constitutionally committed to the Executive Branch, the basic policy decisions governing society are to be made by the Legislature." He viewed Congress's delegation of authority as delegating its authority to make the law, which was unconstitutional, as opposed to the permissible delegation of authority to execute the law. He saw the delegation of lawmaking authority to the commission as unsupported by any legitimating theory to explain why it is not a delegation of legislative authority and, thus, was a power that Congress did not have the authority to delegate. He further claimed the majority "fails to recognize that this case is not about commingling, but about the creation of a new Branch altogether, a sort of junior-varsity Congress."

AFTERMATH

The Court's decision in this case meant that the Sentencing Reform Act of 1984 was constitutional. In later developments, the Court stated that judges may not determine facts by a preponderance of the evidence in order to find circumstances that would justify sentencing a person above the statutory prescribed limit; such facts must be proved beyond a reasonable doubt to a jury.

In *United States v. Booker* (2005) (consolidated with *United States v. Fanfan*), the Court held, as a remedial matter, that two parts of the statute had to be severed and excised: section 3553(b)(1), which *required* that sentencing courts impose a sentence within the applicable range set forth in the guidelines, and section 3742(e), which set forth standards of review on appeal and made several references to section 3553(b)(1). The severance and excision of section 3553(b)(1) meant that the U.S. Sentencing Guidelines became advisory for federal sentencing judges, instead of mandatory, as the provision had set forth. Upon abrogating section 3742(e), the Court directed appeals courts to review criminal sentences by a standard of "reasonableness," although the term was not defined.

SIGNIFICANCE

The Court upheld the Sentencing Reform Act of 1984, ruling that it did not violate the nondelegation doctrine or the separation of powers doctrine. The majority of the Court agreed that although Congress cannot generally delegate its legislative power to the executive or judicial branches, the nondelegation doctrine does not prohibit Congress from seeking assistance from the other coordinate branches. Applying the "intelligible principle" standard, the Court found that the delegation of authority to the sentencing commission was adequately tailored to satisfy that principle because Congress had outlined the work to be done by the commission.

RELATED CASES

United States v. Gaudin, 515 U.S. 506, 511 (1995)

Apprendi v. New Jersey, 530 U.S. 466 (2000)

Blakely v. Washington, 542 U.S. 296 (2004)

United States v. Booker, 543 U.S. 220 (2005)

RECOMMENDED READING

Craig Green, Booker *and* Fanfan: *The Untimely Death (and Rebirth?) of the Federal Sentencing Guidelines,* 93 Georgetown Law Journal 395 (2005).

Ronald J. Krotoszynski, *On the Danger of Wearing Two Hats:* Mistretta *and* Morrison *Revisited,* 38 William and Mary Law Review 417 (1997).

Ann Marie Tracey and Paul Fiorelli, *Throwing the Book[er] at Congress: The Constitutionality and Prognosis of the Federal Sentencing Guidelines and Congressional Control in Light of* United States v. Booker, 2005 Michigan State Law Review 1199.

Case Title: *Maryland v. Craig*

Legal Citation: 497 U.S. 836

Year of Decision: 1990

KEY ISSUE

Does a child-abuse victim's testimony via one-way closed-circuit television violate the Sixth Amendment's confrontation clause?

HISTORY OF THE CASE

The respondent Craig was charged with sexually abusing a six-year-old child under her supervision at a day-care facility she ran in Columbia, Maryland. At trial, the judge thought that forcing the six-year-old child to testify on the witness stand would result in severe emotional trauma and, thus, allowed her to testify from another room via one-way closed-circuit television (the child was examined and cross-examined by a prosecutor exactly as she would have been on the witness stand). After the testimony was given, Craig was convicted; however, the Maryland State Court of Appeals reversed the conviction, holding that before using this procedure, the trial court should have first determined that the use of two-way closed-circuit television would have caused the child witness "severe emotional trauma." On appeal, the U.S. Supreme Court granted certiorari.

SUMMARY OF ARGUMENTS

The respondent Craig argued that the use of a one-way closed-circuit television instead of live (on the witness stand) testimony violated the confrontation clause included in the Sixth Amendment, which provides that "in all criminal prosecutions, the accused shall enjoy the right . . . to be confronted with the witnesses against him."

The state of Maryland, meanwhile, asserted that the state's interest in the physical and psychological well-being of child-abuse victims should outweigh, in some cases, a defendant's Sixth Amendment right to confront his or her accuser.

DECISION

The U.S. Supreme Court held that the child's testimony did not violate the Sixth Amendment.

Delivering the opinion of the Supreme Court, Justice O'Connor wrote that the main concern of the confrontation clause is "to ensure the reliability of the evidence against a criminal defendant." However, Justice O'Connor noted, "We have never held . . . that the Confrontation Clause guarantees the defendant a face-to-face meeting with witnesses appearing before the trier of fact." Rather, O'Connor wrote, the confrontation clause "reflects a *preference*" for such face-to-face meetings.

The dispositive issue in this case, according to Justice O'Connor, was whether the state interest asserted (protecting the well-being of child-abuse victims) was actually furthered through the use of the one-way closed-circuit system. In examining this, Justice O'Connor examined "academic literature," such as the brief prepared by the American Psychological Association. This brief (1) outlined, in great detail, the severe trauma experienced by the majority of child-abuse victims; (2) suggested that children forced to deliver live testimony in front of the defendants are much more likely to be inaccurate; and (3) concluded that "whether [the state's] interest is implicated must be made case-by-case for each particular child."

Justice O'Connor held that (1) the procedure used at trial in *Craig* did not violate the Sixth Amendment's Confrontation Clause *if* live testimony would cause the child-victim severe emotional trauma, and (2) the determination of whether or not a given child would experience "severe emotional trauma" must be made on an ad hoc basis. "We think," Justice O'Connor concluded, "that the use of Maryland's special procedure, where necessary to further the important state interest in preventing trauma . . . adequately ensures the accuracy of the testimony and preserves the adversary nature of the trial."

In his dissent, Justice Scalia stated, "I have no need to defend the value of confrontation, because the Court has no authority to question it" and concluded as follows: "The Court has applied 'interest-balancing' analysis where the text of the Constitution simply does not permit it."

AFTERMATH

The validity of *Maryland v. Craig* has been questioned in the wake of *Crawford v. Washington* (2004), which held that any out-of-court statement that is "testimonial" in nature is inadmissible (unless the declarant is unavailable to testify in court, and the defendant has had a prior opportunity to cross-examine him or her). Therefore, in light of the *Crawford* decision, it will be interesting to see how the Court, if presented with facts similar to those in *Craig,* will deal with the hearsay concerns raised by child testimony delivered in such a manner.

SIGNIFICANCE

This case represents a significantly different interpretation of the confrontation clause, going against the seemingly plain language of the Sixth Amendment. The special circumstances surrounding testimony of child-abuse victims were the Court's justification for this.

RELATED CASES

Idaho v. Wright, 497 U.S. 805 (1990)

Crawford v. Washington, 541 U.S. 36 (2004)

RECOMMENDED READING

Dziech, Billie Wright, and Charles B. Schudson. *On Trial: America's Courts and Their Treatment of Sexually Abused Children.* Boston: Beacon Press, 1989.

Gail S. Goodman, *Child Witnesses and the Confrontation Clause: The American Psychological Association Brief in* Maryland v. Craig, 15 Law and Human Behavior, 13 (1991).

Perry, Nancy Walker, and Lawrence S. Wrightsman. *The Child Witness: Legal Issues and Dilemmas.* Newbury Park, Calif.: Sage, 1991.

Case Title: *Payne v. Tennessee*

Legal Citation: 501 U.S. 808

Year of Decision: 1991

KEY ISSUE

Does the Eighth Amendment, at the sentencing phase of a capital trial, preclude a sentencing judge or jury from considering testimony from a victim in the form of a Victim Impact Statement?

HISTORY OF THE CASE

On June 27, 1987, Pervis Payne entered the apartment of Charisse Christopher; her two-year-old daughter, Lacie; and her three-year-old son, Nicholas. The evidence showed that Payne had been drinking alcohol and using cocaine prior to arriving there, and he made sexual advances toward Charisse. When she resisted, Payne stabbed her 41 times with a butcher knife and stabbed Lacie and Nicholas as well. Charisse and Lacie died, but Nicholas survived the attack. Payne was convicted of two counts of first-degree murder, attempted murder, and a related charge.

During the sentencing phase of the trial, the defense presented witnesses who testified that Payne was of good character. The prosecution called Charisse Christopher's mother, who testified to the effects of the murders on Nicholas. The prosecutor argued for the death penalty and used the ongoing psychological burden on Nicholas as part of his argument. The jury sentenced Payne to death on each of the murder counts and to 30 years in prison for the attempted murder of Nicholas. The Tennessee Supreme Court affirmed, and the U.S. Supreme Court granted certiorari.

SUMMARY OF ARGUMENTS

Payne argued that the statements by the victims' family members and remarks by the prosecutor during the sentencing hearing were highly prejudicial and contrary to the Supreme Court's holdings that such evidence was not admissible. Thus, part of his argument focused on the doctrine of stare decisis, insisting that the doctrine be adhered to in this case. Payne further argued, on the basis of the Eighth Amendment, that his sentence must be set aside because the jury heard this evidence.

DECISION

In a 5-4 decision, the Court held that the Eighth Amendment erects no per se bar on the admission of victim impact evidence or prosecutorial arguments based on that evidence. The Court based its decision on the idea that the sentencing judge or jury should have the right to consider all relevant evidence that is admissible under the evidence rules used by the particular jurisdiction. The Court also took into consideration the principle that the punishment should fit the crime, and in this case, the evidence demonstrated that the murders of Charisse and Lacie Christopher and the attempted murder of Nicholas were particularly brutal. Regarding the fairness and impartiality of the trial court during the trial and sentencing phases, the Court found the decision to be justified and specifically pointed out that both aggravating and mitigating evidence was allowed during the sentencing phase.

This decision effectively overturned the holding in two prior Supreme Court cases, *Booth v. Maryland* (1987) and *South Carolina v. Gathers* (1989). In *Booth* and *Gathers*, the Court held that the Eighth Amendment prohibits a capital sentencing jury from considering "victim impact" evidence relating to the personal characteristics of the victim and the emotional impact of the crimes on the victim's family in capital cases. The Court decided that the state had the right to present evidence to counteract character evidence presented by the defendant.

Since it chose not to follow prior Supreme Court decisions, the Court addressed the doctrine of stare decisis, which is the legal principle that judges are obligated to follow precedents established by prior judicial decisions. The Court explained that this is "not an inexorable command" that must be followed at all times. Rather, the doctrine of stare decisis is a principle of policy and not a mechanical formula that must be applied in all circumstances. Turning to the facts of this case, the Court found that fairness toward the victim's rights was strong enough not to follow prior precedent. Accordingly, the Court affirmed the decision of the court of appeals, and Payne's sentence was upheld.

Justice O'Connor wrote a concurring opinion, joined by Justices White and Kennedy. She stated that "If, in a particular case, a witness' testimony or a prosecutor's remark so infects the sentencing proceedings as to render it fundamentally unfair, the defendant may seek appropriate relief under the Due Process Clause of the Fourteenth Amendment. That line was not crossed in this case." Justice O'Connor also expressed her view that both *Booth* and *Gathers* were wrongly decided because the "Eighth Amendment does not prohibit a State from choosing to admit evidence

concerning a murder victim's personal characteristics or the impact of the crime on the victim's family and community." Justice Scalia also wrote a concurring opinion, joined in part by Justices O'Connor and Kennedy, stating that he thought it was "*Booth,* and not today's decision, that compromised the fundamental values underlying the doctrine of stare decisis." Justice Souter wrote a concurring opinion as well, joined by Justice Kennedy, arguing that he, too, believed that *Booth* and *Gathers* were wrongly decided regarding information revealing the individuality of the victim and the impact of the crime on the victim's survivors.

Three justices dissented from the majority's opinion, Justices Blackmun, Marshall, and Stevens, the latter two having written separate dissenting opinions, each of which was joined by Justice Blackmun. In Justice Marshall's dissent, he argued that stare decisis should have prevented the majority from overruling a precedent that had been reaffirmed by the Court just two years earlier. He noted that during this time, no laws or facts supporting the rationale for *Booth* and *Gathers* had changed; however, Supreme Court personnel had changed during that period. Justice Stevens argued that if a defendant had murdered a victim later found to be of poor moral character, there would be no question that the evidence was irrelevant and admissible. He thought that this was analogous to the situation in the current case, stating that there is "no support whatsoever for the majority's conclusion that the prosecutor may introduce evidence that sheds no light on the defendant's guilt or moral culpability, and thus serves no purpose other than to encourage jurors to decide in favor of death rather than life on the basis of their emotions rather than their reason."

AFTERMATH

In the same year as the Court's decision in *Payne v. Tennessee* (1991), the U.S. Supreme Court heard the case of *Simon & Schuster v. New York Crime Victim's Board* (1991). In that case, a New York state law originating in 1977, known as the "Son of Sam" law, mandated that profits earned by convicts who sell their criminal stories must be turned over to the New York State Crime Victims Board, and the money then be made potentially available to victims through civil suits.

The Court held that prohibiting convicts to collect proceeds arising from selling their stories for profit was unconstitutional because the structure of this particular law violated the free speech clause of the First Amendment of the U.S. Constitution. Specifically, the rationale for the law failed to explain why the compensation money had to be only from storytelling proceeds rather than other assets owned by the convict. Thus, while *Payne* expanded the rights of victims during the time leading up to the execution of the sentence, *Simon & Schuster v. New York Crime Victim's Board* limited a victim's ability to collect restitution and other compensation.

SIGNIFICANCE

In this case, the Court recognized that victims of crimes, even in capital cases, have rights in the case against the offender. Specifically, the Court held that testimony through victim impact statements used during the sentencing phase of the trial, which can be a powerful tool to persuade or influence a judge or jury in making a sentencing decision, was admissible. This testimony was determined permissible under the Constitution, and it overruled the Supreme Court's prior decisions in *Booth v. Maryland* (1987) and *South Carolina v. Gather* (1989).

The Court further held that the sentencing judge or jury has the right to consider all relevant evidence. Additionally, the case suggested that stare decisis is not a command that must be followed at all times; rather, there are times when precedents become outdated and need to be replaced with new ones.

RELATED CASES

Booth v. Maryland, 482 U.S. 496 (1987)

South Carolina v. Gather, 490 U.S. 805 (1989)

Simon & Schuster v. New York Crime Victim's Board, 502 U.S. 105 (1991)

R. A. V. v. City of St. Paul, 505 U.S. 377 (1992)

RECOMMENDED READING

Gary Casimir, Payne v. Tennessee: *Overlooking Capital Sentencing Jurisprudence and Stare Decisis,* 19 New England Journal on Criminal and Civil Confinement (1993).

Justin D. Flamm, *Due Process on the "Unchartered Seas of Irrelevance": Limiting the Presence of Victim Impact Evidence in Capital Sentencing after* Payne v. Tennessee, 56 Washington and Lee Law Review 295 (1999).

Wayne A. Logan, *Through the Past Darkly: A Survey of the Uses and Abuses of Victim Impact Evidence in Capital Trials,* 41 Arizona Law Review 143 (1999).

Joe Frankel, Payne, *Victim Impact Statements, and Nearly Two Decades of Devolving Standards of Decency,* 12 New York City Law Review 87 (2008).

Case Title: *Sandin v. Conner*

Legal Citation: 515 U.S. 472

Year of Decision: 1995

KEY ISSUE

Does the due process clause of the Fourteenth Amendment of the Constitution extend a liberty interest to inmates punished for violating disciplinary rules while incarcerated, when the punishment results in segregation from the general prison population?

HISTORY OF THE CASE

Demont Conner was convicted of murder, robbery, and burglary and was sentenced to 30 years to life in prison. Conner was sent to the Halawa Correctional Facility, a maximum security prison located in Oahu, Hawaii. While he was incarcerated, in August 1987, a prison officer subjected

Conner to a strip search, which included an inspection of the rectal area. Conner protested against the search, allegedly using profanity and other vulgar language toward the officer. Eleven days after this event, Conner received notice that he had been charged with disciplinary infractions, including "high misconduct" for allegedly physically interfering with a correctional function. He also received a "low moderate misconduct" infraction for the language he used while "harassing" the correctional employees. These infractions carried with them punishments ranging from segregation to monetary restitution and other disciplinary sanctions.

An adjustment committee met with Conner on August 28, 1987, and refused Conner's request to present exculpating witnesses at the hearing because the witnesses were unavailable. The committee found Conner guilty of the misconduct infractions and sentenced him to 30 days of disciplinary segregation in the Special Housing Unit, from August 31, 1987, until September 29, 1987. Conner sought administrative review shortly after receiving his sentence. Nine months later, the deputy administrator expunged the high misconduct charge from Conner's disciplinary record after finding it to be unsupported by sufficient evidence.

Prior to the finding by the deputy administrator, Conner had brought this suit in the U.S. District Court for the District of Hawaii against the adjustment committee chair and other prison officials. Conner filed a civil claim under 42 U.S.C. § 1983 and asked for injunctive relief, declaratory relief, and damages for depriving him of procedural due process in the administration of the disciplinary hearing. The district court of Hawaii granted summary judgment in favor of the prison officials, and Conner then appealed to the Ninth Circuit Court of Appeals. The Ninth Circuit reversed the judgment, relying on the Court's decision in *Wolff v. McDonnell* (1974), regarding the due process rights of inmates facing disciplinary charges. The Ninth Circuit determined that a finding of substantial evidence of misconduct was required for punishment to be imposed; that meant that Conner should have been entitled to call witnesses in his favor. The state petitioned for

and was granted certiorari from the United States Supreme Court.

SUMMARY OF THE ARGUMENTS

Conner argued that the disciplinary segregation imposed on him violated his liberty interests protected by the due process clause of the Constitution. Thus, he argued, prisoners retain most of their constitutional rights while incarcerated, including the right to due process of the law. He further argued that this punishment created a hardship that he had to endure that was unlike the hardships faced by most other inmates.

Sandin and the other prison officials argued that inmates do not have the right to call witnesses at disciplinary hearings. Sandin further argued that prison inmates are not entitled to the full protection of the Constitution for disciplinary proceedings.

DECISION

The Court, in a 5-4 decision, reversed the opinion of the Ninth Circuit Court of Appeals, holding that Conner did not have a protected liberty interest, in either the Hawaii prison regulation or the due process clause, that would grant him procedural protections as set forth in *Wolff*. The decision hinged on the fact that the hearing for Conner's misconduct was within the circumstances to be expected of a person serving a long-term prison sentence. Conner's sentence to 30 days of solitary confinement for a high misconduct infraction did not impose an "atypical and significant hardship" on him in comparison to ordinary prison life.

Chief Justice Rehnquist delivered the opinion of the Court. The Court began by discussing due process rights afforded to inmates in other prisons, using prior precedents. In *Wolff*, Nebraska inmates challenged the revocation of their "good time" credits, which would have allowed statutorily created mandatory sentence reductions for good behavior, provided that the inmates had not participated in "flagrant or serious misconduct." The Court determined that the inmates had an interest in the reduction of their prison sentences, which was a liberty interest of "real substance," and developed a due process balancing test of prison management concerns with prisoners' liberty.

Two years later, the Court decided a related case, *Meachum v. Fano* (1976), in which Massachusetts inmates responsible for arson filed claims related to a transfer from a medium security prison to a less desirable, maximum security prison. The Court recognized that there are limits to the extension of due process rights concerning changes in circumstances in confinement. Also, unlike in *Wolff,* in which a state law created the right to good time credit and limited the discretion of prison officials in taking away earned good time credit, there was no law in Massachusetts to limit the discretion of prison officials when transferring inmates from one prison to another. However, certain liberty interests were protected, such as when a prisoner was to be transferred without consent to a mental hospital for mental treatment (*Vitek v. Jones* [1980]); further, "independent of any state regulation, an inmate had a liberty in being protected from the involuntary administration of psychotropic drugs" (*Washington v. Harper* [1990]).

After these decisions, the inquiry shifted from cases dealing with "mandatory" procedures to cases related to "discretionary" procedures, emphasizing that due process alone does not grant the inmates a liberty interest in freedom from governmental action that is contained in the sentence imposed. For example, *Hewitt v. Helms* (1983) dealt with inmate segregation. The Court added in *Hewitt* that the prison management's objectives were also important and that the procedural safeguards put in place in *Wolff* were unnecessary in this case. So, the inquiry began to focus primarily on the prison guidelines, particularly "whether mandatory language and substantive predicates created an enforceable expectation that the State would produce a particular outcome with respect to the prisoner's conditions of confinement." In two subsequent cases, the Court refused to find a liberty interest in discretionary transfers of inmates from one facility to a facility in another state (*Olim v. Wakinekona* [1983]) and in discretionary visitation rights (*Kentucky Dept. of Corrections v. Thompson* [1989]).

The Court then noted some of the negative effects that have been produced by the holding in *Hewitt.* First, the ruling created a "disincentive" for state prisons to codify their management procedures in an attempt to ensure uniform treatment among the inmates. As a result of this, states may avoid creation of "liberty" interests by having scarcely any regulations or by conferring standardless discretion on correctional personnel. Second, federal courts have become more involved in the daily management of prisons, contrary to several USSC opinions suggesting that federal courts should afford deference to the prison officials trying to manage the hostile environment therein. These negative effects led this Court to return to the due process principles that were established in *Wolff* and *Meachum,* discussed previously; however, the Court did not overrule *Hewitt* or any other case. The Court noted that it wanted to abandon an approach that in practice was difficult to administer and produced irregular results.

By returning to the *Wolff* standard, the Court recognized that states could create liberty interests that were protected by the due process clause under certain circumstances. However, the Court cautioned that these interests were "generally limited to freedom from restraint," which produced increased hardships on the inmate compared with the ordinary hardships of prison life. Discipline by prison officials was recognized as an ordinary response to misconduct and was "within the expected perimeters of the sentence imposed by a court of law." The Court did not accept Conner's argument that his placement in solitary confinement triggered the protections of due process. This was an issue of first impression for the USSC, and they held that the discipline Conner received was not of the sort that a state might create a liberty interest, arguing that Conner's confinement did not exceed similar forms of confinement in duration or degree of restriction. The Court reasoned that the time Conner spent in solitary confinement was not a major disruption to his confinement. Additionally, the fact that he spent time in solitary confinement did not necessarily affect his grant or denial of parole, although it was relevant for the parole board to consider. Parole boards consider many things, and inmates are afforded procedural protections at the parole hearings to explain and justify the circumstances surrounding any misconduct. The Court determined that the chance that a finding of misconduct will alter the balance in the parole board's decision is too attenuated to invoke the procedural guarantees of the due process clause. Adding to this, Conner's record regarding the charge of high misconduct had been expunged from his record prior to his parole hearing.

The Court went on to hold that "neither the Hawaii prison regulation in question, nor the Due Process Clause itself, afforded Conner a protected liberty interest that would entitle him to the procedural protections set forth in *Wolff*" (that states could create liberty interests that were protected by the due process clause under certain circumstances). Although the Court had ruled against Conner, it added: "Prisoners such as Conner, of course, retain in other protection from arbitrary state action even within the expected conditions of confinement." They may file claims based on the first, eighth, and equal protection clauses of the Fourteenth Amendment when appropriate. Inmates also may use internal prison grievance procedures and state judicial review when these remedies are available.

Justice Ginsburg, joined by Justice Stevens, dissented, stating that they would have found a "liberty" interest under the due process clause of the Fourteenth Amendment because Conner was not allowed to call witnesses, and his condition was severely altered. Although the committee's decision was reversed and the infraction expunged from Conner's record, the stigma of participating in misconduct was still attached to him. In their view, the due process afforded to inmates should be determined by the Constitution, not state codes, because, otherwise, inmates' rights would vary from state to state, with some states' granting more rights than others. Justices Ginsburg and Stevens thought that the decision by the majority provided an incentive for ruleless prison management over more controlled environments, by reducing the management's decision-making

authority. These dissenters would have remanded the case for a precisely focused determination as to whether Conner received the process that was indeed due.

Justice Breyer, joined by Justice Souter, wrote a separate dissent and would have held that Conner was deprived of "liberty" by taking into consideration the same points as the majority of the Court. As did the other dissenters, they believed that a liberty interest had been violated because of the major change in conditions, including the amount of free time and the ability to see and interact with other inmates. Breyer and Souter asserted that the prison's own disciplinary rules "cabin" the authority of prison officials to impose punishment of this type. These justices felt that the fact that a deprivation of the inmate's freedom that goes beyond the sentence imposed for the underlying offense must take place under local rules that cabin the authorities' discretionary power to impose the restraint suggests that the matter is more likely to have played an important role in the life of the inmate, which suggests that the inmate deserves due process rights. Additionally, these justices disagreed with the majority that expunging Conner's record of the infraction cured any wrong because expunging Conner's record does not restore the liberty he had already lost. These dissenters, like Justices Ginsburg and Stevens, would have agreed with the court of appeals to remand the case to the trial court level.

Aftermath

This case marked a shift by the Supreme Court away from some of its previous holdings regarding prisoners' rights. The "Atypical and Significant Hardship" test is a stringent test that makes it more difficult to establish that a prisoners' rights have been violated. Specifically, the holding made it more difficult for prisoners to bring claims against prison management and officials on constitutional grounds.

Significance

In this case, the U.S. Supreme Court established the Atypical and Significant Hardship test for determining whether a punishment for a misconduct infraction against an inmate implicates a liberty interest for purposes of due process. Under this test, if the punishment imposed upon an inmate for misconduct creates an "atypical and significant hardship" that differs "in relation to ordinary incidents of prison life," the inmate has a liberty interest that is protected by due process.

RELATED CASES

Procunier v. Martinez, 416 U.S. 396 (1974)

Wolff v. McDonnell, 418 U.S. 539 (1974)

Meachum v. Fano, 427 U.S. 215 (1976)

Vitek v. Jones, 445 U.S. 480 (1980)

Olim v. Wakinekona, 461 U.S. 238 (1983)

Turner v. Safley, 482 U.S. 78 (1987)

Kentucky Dept. of Corrections v. Thompson, 490 U.S. 454 (1989)

Washington v. Harper, 494 U.S. 210 (1990)

Muhammad v. Close, 540 U.S. 749 (2004)

Cutter v. Wilkinson, 544 U.S. 709 (2005)

STATUTES AT ISSUE

Halawa Correctional Facility—Hawaii Administrative Rule § 17-201-18(b)(2) (1983)

42 U.S.C. § 1983. Civil Action for Deprivation of Rights

RECOMMENDED READING

Donna H. Lee, *The Law of Typicality: Examining the Procedural Due Process Implications of* Sandin v. Conner, 72 Fordham Law Review 785 (2004)

Mark Adam Merolli, Sandin v. Conner's *"Atypical and Significant Hardship" Signals the Demise of State-Created Liberty Interests for Prisoners,* 15 Saint Louis University Public Law Review 93 (1995)

Scott F. Weisman, Sandin v. Conner: *Lowering the Boom on the Procedural Rights of Prisoners,* 46 American University Law Review 897 (1997)

Case Title: *Dickerson v. United States*

Legal Citation: 530 U.S. 428

Year of Decision: 2000

KEY ISSUE

Can Congress legislatively overrule the U.S. Supreme Court's decision in *Miranda v. Arizona* (1966), which established governmental requirements regarding the admissibility of statements made during custodial interrogations?

HISTORY OF THE CASE

At common law, the notion that coerced confessions are inherently untrustworthy caused the courts to rely on the test of "voluntariness" to determine whether custodial confessions were admissible as evidence. This test involved taking into consideration the "totality of the circumstances." Then, in 1966, in the historic ruling in *Miranda v. Arizona,* the Court replaced the "voluntariness" test with what came to be known as the *Miranda* warnings, holding that defendants in custodial interrogation must be informed of the right against self-incrimination prior to questioning and the right to consult an attorney before and during questioning and that the rights are understood but can be waived. Two years after the *Miranda* decision, Congress enacted 18 U.S.C. § 3501, which purported to overrule *Miranda's* warning requirement and replace it with the traditional test of "voluntariness."

Charles Thomas Dickerson was indicted for bank robbery, conspiracy to commit bank robbery, and using a firearm in the course of committing a crime of violence, all of which were federal offenses under Title 18 of the U.S. Code. When questioned by agents of the Federal Bureau of Investigation, Dickerson made incriminating statements, which he subsequently moved to suppress prior to trial because he had not received the *Miranda* warnings before being questioned.

(Dickerson admitted to being the getaway driver in multiple bank robberies.)

The federal district court granted Dickerson's motion to suppress the statements, and the government appealed to the Fourth Circuit of the U.S. District of Appeals. The Fourth Circuit reversed, holding that although Dickerson had not received the *Miranda* warnings, Congress's statute 18 U.S.C. § 3501 had been satisfied since Dickerson's statements were voluntary. The Fourth Circuit additionally held that the decision in *Miranda* was not constitutional, and therefore, Congress could set the standard for the admissibility of confessions as evidence.

Because of the importance of the decision of the Fourth Circuit of the U.S. District Court of Appeals, the U.S. Supreme Court granted certiorari.

Summary of Arguments

Dickerson argued that since he had not been given *Miranda* warnings, his statements to police were inadmissible.

The government argued that even if the *Miranda* warnings were not read, the statement was voluntary and, therefore, admissible under 18 U.S.C. § 3501, which provides that "a confession shall be admissible in evidence if it is voluntarily given."

Decision

The Court affirmed the judgment of the Fourth Circuit Court of Appeals, holding that Congress did not have the power, through 18 U.S.C. § 3501, effectively to overrule the *Miranda* warning requirements, stating that "*Miranda* announced a constitutional rule that Congress may not supersede legislatively." The Court declined to overrule *Miranda*, as well, following the rule of stare decisis. Thus, *Miranda* continues to govern the admissibility of statements made during custodial interrogations in state and federal courts.

Chief Justice Rehnquist delivered the opinion of the Court. Beginning with a historical discussion of the inherent untrustworthiness of coerced confessions derived from torture and false prom-

ises, he stated the test of voluntariness was, thus, developed by taking into consideration the "totality of the circumstances." Two constitutional bases for the requirement of voluntariness were the Fifth Amendment right against self-incrimination and the due process clause of the Fourteenth Amendment. Then, in 1966, *Miranda* was decided; it established a set of warnings required to be given to suspects by government officials prior to custodial interrogation if that testimony were to be used against the suspect at trial. Since that decision, due process is still focused upon; however, the inquiry has changed in determining the admissibility of custodial incriminating statements by establishing that a suspect must be given four warnings for a statement given during custodial interrogation to be admissible as evidence against the suspect: A suspect "has the right to remain silent, that anything he says can be used against him in a court of law, that he has the right to the presence of an attorney, and that if he cannot afford an attorney one will be appointed for him prior to any questioning if he so desires."

Two years after *Miranda* was decided, Congress enacted 18 U.S.C. § 3501, which expressly made voluntariness the criterion of admissibility, omitting the requirement of giving the *Miranda* warnings. The Court agreed with the Fourth Circuit that Congress intended to overrule *Miranda,* so the Court then addressed whether or not Congress has the constitutional authority to supersede that decision. In the case *Palermo v. United States* (1959), the Court ruled that Congress retains the authority to modify or set aside judicially created rules of evidence and procedure that are not constitutionally mandated. However, in *City of Boerne v. Flores* (1997), the Court held that Congress cannot legislatively supersede Supreme Court decisions that interpret and apply the Constitution. The issue then became whether the Court's decision in *Miranda* was merely regulating evidence in the absence of congressional authority or instating a constitutional rule. The court of appeals determined that *Miranda* did not create a constitutional rule because there are exceptions to giving the

Miranda warnings (e.g., spontaneous remarks, "public safety" exception) and because the warnings have often been referred to as "prophylactic" by the Court.

Although there was evidence to support the decision of the court of appeals, the Supreme Court disagreed with its decision. One reason the Court used was the fact that *Miranda* applied to the states, as the actual *Miranda* case derived from state court. Also, prisoners are allowed to file a habeas corpus claim, which is a claim that a person is being unconstitutionally detained, if he or she was not given the *Miranda* warnings. The *Miranda* opinion itself begins by stating that the Court wants "to give concrete constitutional guidelines for law enforcement agencies and courts to follow." Additionally, the *Miranda* opinion expressed that legislatures could take action to protect the constitutional right against self-incrimination by creating solutions that were "at least as effective in apprising accused persons of their right of silence and in assuring a continuous opportunity to exercise it."

The Court then addressed the reasoning of the court of appeals that relied on the fact that exceptions to giving the *Miranda* warnings had been created after the decision. The Court noted, however, that they had also broadened the application of the *Miranda* warnings, including the 1976 case of *Doyle v. Ohio* (the Court held that the defendant's silence in response to the *Miranda* warnings could not be used against him). The exceptions and expansions of *Miranda* suggest that "no constitutional rule is immutable," because there are various unforeseeable circumstances that may require modification of the rule.

The Court did not agree with the amicus curiae's (brief by Paul G. Cassell) contention that the increased availability of remedies under the due process clause for police misconduct supplement section 3501's protections sufficiently complied with constitutional guarantees of the Fifth Amendment right against self-incrimination. The reasoning behind this was that "§ 3501 explicitly eschews a requirement of pre-interrogation warnings in favor of an approach that looks to the administration of such warnings as only one factor in determining the voluntariness of a suspect's confession." In the Court's view, the additional remedies did not compensate for what section 3501 was lacking and, thus, were not an adequate substitute for the *Miranda* warnings.

The majority disagreed with the dissent's argument that section 3501 cannot be held unconstitutional unless the *Miranda* warnings are constitutionally required. The Court argued that it need not address that issue because in *Miranda* the totality of the circumstances test for voluntariness was deemed unfit to prevent involuntary custodial confessions from being used in the prosecution's case in chief. Section 3501 reinstated the totality test, so the Court determined that it could not be sustained unless *Miranda* were no longer considered the law. The principles of stare decisis and the fact that law enforcement practices had been adjusted to accommodate the *Miranda* requirements led the Court to conclude that it would not overrule *Miranda* without "special justification," which was lacking here. Although the Court had overruled prior precedents "when subsequent cases have undermined their doctrinal underpinnings," that had not happened here because the Court consistently reaffirmed the core of the rule "that unwarned statements could not be used as evidence in the prosecution's case in chief." The Court also expressed its view that the section 3501 totality of the circumstances test is more difficult for law enforcement officers to comply with and more difficult for courts to apply consistently than the *Miranda* warnings requirement. The Court also added that "the requirement that *Miranda* warnings be given does not, of course, dispense with the voluntariness inquiry."

Justice Scalia, joined by Justice Thomas in his dissent, argued that *Miranda* should be overruled because it was not a constitutional rule. Since it was not a constitutional rule, Congress did not violate the Constitution by disregarding it, on the basis of the decision in *Marbury v. Madison* (1803), in which the Court stated that it could only disregard duly enacted congressional statutes if they were in opposition to the

Constitution. Scalia also argued that this decision "expands" the Constitution, giving the Court immense power to create prophylactic rules that are binding upon Congress and the states. In his view, this decision was antidemocratic in nature and plainly violated the Constitution by denying this act of Congress.

Scalia further argued that the Court has "long since abandoned the notion that failure to comply with *Miranda*'s rules is itself a violation of the Constitution," in some of its decisions following that case. Scalia cited cases that made it clear that a police officer can violate *Miranda* without also violating the Constitution. See *Michigan v. Tucker* (1974) (the Court said that *Miranda*'s procedural safeguards "were not themselves rights protected by the Constitution but were instead to insure that the right against compulsory self-incrimination was protected"), *Oregon v. Hass* (1975) (defendant's statements that were voluntary could be used at trial for impeachment purposes, even though taken in violation of *Miranda*), and *New York v. Quarles* (1984) ("public safety" exception). These opinions suggest that the *Miranda* warnings are not constitutional, and, thus, the decision in *Marbury* would suggest that section 3501 could stand because it did not violate the Constitution. Scalia also addressed the importance of stare decisis; however, he saw "little harm in admitting that [the Court] made a mistake in taking away from the public the ability to decide for themselves what protections are reasonably affordable in the criminal investigatory process." In his view, this would reassure citizens that they govern themselves.

AFTERMATH

Dickerson upheld the holding in *Miranda v. Arizona* requiring that the *Miranda* warnings be read to suspects prior to custodial interrogation.

SIGNIFICANCE

The Court effectively struck down a federal statute that sought to reinstate the "totality of the circumstances" approach to determining the voluntariness of custodial interrogations at trial. However, the Court reiterated that the *Miranda* ruling and, accordingly, this ruling did not dispense with the inquiry of voluntariness regarding confessions given by suspects during custodial interrogation.

RELATED CASES

Palermo v. United States, 360 U.S. 343 (1959)

Miranda v. Arizona, 384 U.S. 436 (1966)

Michigan v. Tucker, 417 U.S. 433 (1974)

Oregon v. Hass, 420 U.S. 714 (1975)

Doyle v. Ohio, 426 U.S. 610 (1976)

New York v. Quarles, 467 U.S. 649 (1984)

City of Boerne v. Flores, 521 U.S. 507 (1997)

STATUTE AT ISSUE

18 U.S.C. § 3501—Admissibility of Confessions

RECOMMENDED READING

Daria K. Boxer, Miranda *with Precision: Why the Current Circuit Split Should Be Solved in Favor of a Uniform Requirement of an Explicit* Miranda *Warning of the Right to Have Counsel Present during Interrogation,* 37 Southwestern University Law Review 425 (2008).

Jennifer E. Laurin, *Rights Translation and Remedial Disequilibration in Constitutional Criminal Procedure,* 110 Columbia Law Review 1002 (2010).

Prentzas, G. S. Miranda *Rights: Protecting the Rights of the Accused.* New York: Rosen, 2005.

Charles D. Weisselberg, *Mourning* Miranda, 96 California Law Review 1519 (2008).

Case Title: *Ewing v. California*

Legal Citations: 538 U.S. 11

Year of Decision: 2003

KEY ISSUE

Does a sentence of 25 years to life for a repeat felon under California's three strikes rule violate the Eighth Amendment to the U.S. Constitution because the sentence was grossly disproportionate to the crime?

HISTORY OF THE CASE

On March 12, 2000, Gary Ewing was arrested and convicted of felony grand theft of personal property for stealing three golf clubs, priced at $399 each, from a pro shop in Los Angeles County. As required by the three strikes law, the prosecutor alleged that Ewing had previously been convicted of four serious or violent felonies. Ewing had an extensive criminal record at the time of his arrest, including numerous misdemeanor and felony convictions; had served nine separate terms of incarceration; and had committed most of his crimes while on probation or parole. A jury had previously convicted Ewing of first-degree robbery and three counts of residential burglary, stemming from a 1993 arrest. For that felony conviction, Ewing was sentenced to nine years and eight months in prison and was paroled in 1999, 10 months before he stole the golf clubs.

At the sentencing hearing, Ewing asked the court to reduce the conviction for grand theft, a "wobbler" under California law, meaning that the prosecutor and judge could reduce it to a less serious crime, a misdemeanor, to avoid the three strikes sentence. He also requested that the trial court dismiss the allegations of his prior serious or violent felony convictions, for purposes of avoiding a three strikes sentence. The trial judge decided that the grand theft should remain a felony and that the four prior strikes for the three burglaries and the robbery should stand. Ewing was convicted and sentenced to 25 years to life imprisonment under the three strikes law.

The California Court of Appeals affirmed the conviction, rejecting Ewing's claim that his sentence was grossly disproportionate under the Eighth Amendment. The court of appeals reasoned that enhanced sentences under the three strikes law served the legitimate goal of deterring and incapacitating repeat offenders. The Supreme Court of California denied Ewing's petition for review, and the U.S. Supreme Court granted certiorari.

SUMMARY OF ARGUMENTS

Ewing argued that his sentence of 25 years to life for stealing merchandise totaling $1,197 was grossly disproportionate and equated to cruel and unusual punishment under the Eighth Amendment.

DECISION

In a 5-4 decision, the Court upheld the sentence. Justice O'Connor, writing also for Chief Justice Rehnquist and Justice Kennedy, affirmed the trial court's decision. O'Connor argued that under the Eighth Amendment, a narrow proportionality principle applies to noncapital sentences.

The Court considered several prior cases in which it had examined lengthy sentences imposed for relatively minor crimes. In *Rummel v. Estelle* (1980), the Court upheld a sentence of life with parole under a Texas statute for a three-time offender who obtained $120.75 by false pretenses. In *Solem v. Helm* (1983), the Court struck down a life without parole sentence imposed on a defendant who had committed a seventh nonviolent felony. In a third case, *Harmelin v. Michigan* (1991), the Court upheld a life without parole sentence imposed on a first-time offender convicted of possession of more than 650 grams of cocaine.

After considering the Court's prior stances on Eighth Amendment issues, O'Connor stated that the gross disproportionality principle contained in the Eighth Amendment would require striking down only an extreme noncapital sentence. O'Connor observed that three strikes laws were created in response to public concerns about crime by focusing on offenders who pose the greatest threat to public safety and that such laws are a deliberate choice by legislatures to isolate those who have "repeatedly engaged in serious or violent criminal behavior" in order to protect public safety. Such laws serve the state's goals of incapacitation and deterrence.

In his concurrence, Justice Scalia accepted that the Eighth Amendment contained a gross disproportionality requirement but thought it could not be applied in this case. Scalia argued that because a criminal sentence can have many justifications, it is impossible to apply a proportionality requirement to noncapital sentences intelligently. Even so, Justice Scalia concurred in the judgment that Ewing's sentence was constitutional, because he believed the sentence did not violate the Eighth Amendment.

Justice Thomas argued that the Eighth Amendment contains no proportionality principle at all and, thus, concurred in the judgment.

In his dissent, Justice Stevens, joined by Justices Souter, Ginsburg, and Breyer, explained that a proportionality principle for noncapital sentences was required under the Eighth Amendment. Stevens thought it clear that "the Eighth Amendment's prohibition of 'cruel and unusual punishments' expresses a broad and basic proportionality principle that takes into account all of the justifications for penal sanctions."

Justice Breyer, with whom Justices Stevens, Souter, and Ginsburg joined, conceded that successful proportionality challenges to criminal sentences should be rare but argued that Ewing's sentence could be successfully challenged as disproportional. Breyer argued that three characteristics of a sentence bear on whether it is proportional: the length of the sentence in real time, the conduct that triggered the sentence, and the offender's criminal history. Breyer asserted although Ewing was a recidivist, his present crime was not violent, and so he should not have been sentenced as harshly as a recidivist who had committed another violent crime. Finally, the fact that Ewing's sentence would have been the same if he had been convicted of a truly violent crime such as rape or murder suggested it was too harsh a sentence for a shoplifter, even a recidivist such as Ewing.

AFTERMATH

Although the three strikes laws were created as a deterrent and a means by which the state could keep repeat offenders off the streets, statistics have shown that incidences of violent crime have actually risen since the implementation of the laws. It has even been suggested that criminals with two strikes are more likely to respond violently to police officers in an effort to avoid arrest and conviction for their third strike.

SIGNIFICANCE

This case upheld the constitutionality, under the Eighth Amendment, of three strikes laws, finding that the state's goal of protecting the public's safety generally outweighs the disproportionality between the sentences and the third strike crime.

RELATED CASES

Rummel v. Estelle, 445 U.S. 263 (1980)

Solem v. Helm, 463 U.S. 277 (1983)

Harmelin v. Michigan, 501 U.S. 957 (1991)

Lockyer v. Andrude, 538 U.S. 63 (2003)

STATUTE AT ISSUE

Penal Code of California, § 667

RECOMMENDED READING

Richard H. Andrus, *Which Crime Is It? The Role of Proportionality in Recidivist Sentencing after* Ewing v. California, 19 Brigham Young University Journal of Public Law 279 (2004).

Blake J. Delaney, *A Cruel and Unusual Application of the Proportionality Principle in Eighth Amendment Analysis*, 56 Florida Law Review 459 (2004).

Greenwood, Peter W. *Three Strikes and You're Out: Estimated Benefits and Costs of California's New Mandatory-Sentencing Law.* Santa Monica, Calif.: RAND, 1995.

Sara J. Lewis, *The Cruel and Unusual Reality of California's Three Strikes Law:* Ewing v. California *and the Narrowing of the Eighth Amendment's Proportionality Principle*, 81 Denver University Law Review 519 (2003).

Joshua R. Pater, *Struck Out Looking: Continued Confusion in Eighth Amendment Proportionality Review after* Ewing v. California, 27 Harvard Journal of Law & Public Policy 399 (2003).

Walsh, Jennifer E. *Three Strikes Laws*. Santa Barbara, Calif.: Greenwood, 2007.

INTERNET RESOURCES

FACTS—Families to Amend California's Three Strikes: http://facts1.live.radicaldesigns.org/?sub=Home&view=Default&url=/

Three Strikes and You're Out: www.threestrikes.org

Case Title: *Crawford v. Washington*

Legal Citation: 541 U.S. 36

Year of Decision: 2004

KEY ISSUES

Does the Sixth Amendment's confrontation clause prevent the use of out-of-court statements made during a police interrogation by an individual who (1) is unavailable to testify at trial and (2) has not been cross-examined by the defendant (against whom the out-of-court statements are being proffered)?

HISTORY OF THE CASE

On August 5, 1999, police arrested Michael Crawford when he stabbed Kenneth Lee, who had allegedly raped his wife (Crawford's wife was present when the stabbing occurred and was taken to the police station for questioning along with her husband). Crawford and his wife were interviewed separately. Crawford stated that he thought that Kenneth Lee had something in his hands (and, thus, acted out of self-defense), while his wife claimed that she did not see Lee carrying anything—she stated that Lee's hands had been "open."

The state of Washington charged Crawford with assault and attempted murder. At Crawford's trial, his wife did not testify because of Washington's marital privilege/spousal immunity (which is used in criminal cases to prevent any party from calling the defendant's spouse to testify against the defendant). However, in the state of Washington, this privilege is not applicable when a spouse's out-of-court statements are admissible under a hearsay exception. The state, therefore, attempted to introduce into evidence Crawford's wife's statements that Kenneth Lee had not in fact had anything in his hands.

Crawford argued that the admission of this evidence would violate the confrontation clause of the Sixth Amendment, which states, "In all criminal prosecutions, the accused shall enjoy the right . . . to be confronted with the witnesses against him." However, the trial court admitted the out-of-court statement, deeming it bore an "indicia of reliability" under *Ohio v. Robert* (1980), because (1) "she had direct knowledge as an eyewitness," (2) "she was describing recent events," and (3) "she was being questioned by a 'neutral' law enforcement officer." On appeal, the Washington Court of Appeals reversed the decision of the trial court, applying a nine-factor test to determine whether the petitioner's wife's statements contained "particularized guarantees of trustworthiness." The court of appeals found her statements untrustworthy because, among other things, (1) "the statement contradicted one she had previously given," (2) "it was made in response to specific questions," and (3) "at one point she admitted she had shut her eyes during the stabbing." The Washington Supreme Court then reversed that decision and upheld Crawford's conviction, finding that the out-of-court statements "bore guarantees of trustworthiness." The U.S. Supreme Court then granted certiorari to determine whether Crawford's Sixth Amendment rights had been violated by the use of the out-of-court statements.

SUMMARY OF ARGUMENTS

Crawford argued that the use of his wife's out-of-court statements would violate his Sixth Amendment right to confront all the witnesses against him.

The state of Washington, meanwhile, argued that Crawford's wife's tape-recorded statement could be brought in under Washington Rule of Evidence 804(b)(3)—the hearsay exception for "statements against penal interest." The state contended that this exception had been met because "[the petitioner's wife] had admitted she led petitioner to [Kenneth Lee's] apartment and thus had facilitated the assault."

DECISION

The U.S. Supreme Court reversed the decision of the Washington Supreme Court and held that the out-of-court statements had violated Crawford's Sixth Amendment right to confront his accusers. The Sixth Amendment's confrontation clause prohibits the use of out-of-court "testimonial" statements made by a witness in a criminal proceeding who (1) is unavailable to testify and (2) has not been previously cross-examined.

Justice Scalia delivered the opinion of the Court. After examining the confrontation clause's ancient origins, Justice Scalia determined that what the Sixth Amendment was really designed to protect a defendant against was the admission of *testimonial* statements made by a person who was not available for cross-examination. ("Testimonial," for Sixth Amendment purposes, refers to a statement made in the anticipation of trial.) Crawford's wife's tape-recorded statements, Justice Scalia then concluded, were as "testimonial" as anything can be: "Statements taken by police officers in the course of interrogations," he wrote, "are . . . testimonial under even a narrow standard."

AFTERMATH

Because the Court decided *Crawford v. Washington* so recently, it has not had many opportunities to refine its holding in that case. However, in *Davis v. Washington* (2006), the Court found that hearsay statements made in the context of an emergency call

to police were not "testimonial" because the out-of-court statements in this case were made "to enable police assistance to meet an ongoing emergency" and not "to establish or prove past events potentially relevant to later criminal prosecution."

SIGNIFICANCE

The *Crawford* holding essentially overturned *Ohio v. Roberts,* replacing the "indicia of reliability" standard for out-of-court statements with the more streamlined "testimonial" standard.

RELATED CASES

Ohio v. Roberts, 448 U.S. 56 (1980)

Davis v. Washington, 547 U.S. 813 (2006)

RECOMMENDED READING

Jason W. Eldridge, Crawford v. Washington: *A Small Advantage for Criminal Defense in Cases Where Prosecution Seeks to Introduce Hearsay Evidence,* 31 William Mitchell Law Review 1395 (2004–05).

Won Shin, Crawford v. Washington: *Confrontation Clause Forbids Admission of Testimonial Out-of-Court Statement without Prior Opportunity to Cross-Examine,* 40 Harvard Civil Rights–Civil Liberties Law Review 223 (2005).

Case Title: *United States v. Booker; United States v. Fanfan*

Legal Citation: 543 U.S. 220

Year of Decision: 2005

KEY ISSUES

Is the imposition of an enhanced sentence under the U.S. Federal Sentencing Guidelines based on the sentencing judge's determination of a fact (other than a prior conviction) that was not found by the jury beyond a reasonable doubt or admitted by the defendant a violation of the Sixth Amendment?

HISTORY OF THE CASE

This was a consolidated case including both *United States v. Booker* and *United States v. Fanfan*. Freddie J. Booker was arrested and charged federally with possession with intent to distribute at least 50 grams of crack cocaine, and a jury found him guilty beyond a reasonable doubt on the charges. The sentencing guidelines required the district court judge to choose a sentence between 210 and not more than 262 months in prison, based on his criminal history and the underlying offense. The judge then held a posttrial sentencing proceeding, which found by a preponderance of the evidence that Booker possessed an additional 566 grams of crack and had obstructed justice. These additional findings increased the minimum/maximum sentence to a sentence between 360 months and life imprisonment, and the trial judge imposed a 360-month sentence.

The Court of Appeals for the Seventh Circuit held that the sentence imposed by the trial judge violated the Sixth Amendment, finding that this application of the Federal Sentencing Guidelines was inconsistent with the U.S. Supreme Court's holding in *Apprendi v. New Jersey* (2000) (discussed later), which had held that facts, other than prior convictions, that increase the penalty for a crime beyond the statutorily prescribed maximum sentence must be submitted to a jury to be proven beyond a reasonable doubt. The Seventh Circuit then remanded the case with instructions either to sentence Booker within the statutory range or to hold a separate sentencing hearing before a jury. Booker then appealed to the U.S. Supreme Court and was granted certiorari.

In the other consolidated case, Duncan Fanfan was charged with and convicted of conspiracy to distribute and possess with intent to distribute at least 500 grams of cocaine, in violation of a federal law. The maximum sentence authorized by the jury under the Federal Sentencing Guidelines upon a finding of guilty by proof beyond a reasonable doubt was 78 months. The trial judge conducted a sentencing hearing and found by a preponderance of the evidence that Fanfan was responsible for larger amounts of cocaine than he had been found guilty of having by the jury and that the defendant was in charge of the criminal activity. Had these findings been applied, they would have increased the amount of time Fanfan could potentially serve under the guidelines from five to six years to 15–16 years. However, the judge decided to follow the guidelines and imposed a sentence based on the findings of the jury on Fanfan.

The government then filed a motion with the trial court to correct the sentence and was denied. Upon being denied, the government appealed to the First Circuit Court of Appeals and filed a petition for writ of certiorari with the U.S. Supreme Court. The Court granted certiorari both for the government in Fanfan's case and for Booker.

SUMMARY OF ARGUMENTS

The government set forth three arguments as to why the holding in *Blakely* should not apply to the Federal Sentencing Guidelines. One reason was that the guidelines were promulgated by a commission, as opposed to the legislature. The government also argued that *Blakely* was inconsistent with prior precedent, and pursuant to the principles of stare decisis, those prior decisions should be followed. Last, the government argued that the decision in *Blakely* conflicted with the principles of separation of powers.

DECISION

As to whether or not there was a Sixth Amendment violation, the Court held that a jury, not a judge, must determine all facts beyond a reasonable doubt that increase the sentence of a defendant in a federal criminal case over the statutory maximum limit prescribed by the Federal Sentencing Guidelines Act of 1984. This led the Court to hold, as a remedial matter, that two parts of the statute had to be severed and excised: § 3553(b)(1), which *required* that sentencing courts impose a sentence within the applicable range set forth in the guidelines, and § 3742(e), which set forth standards of review on appeal and made several references to § 3553(b)(1).

The severance and excision of § 3553(b)(1) meant that the Federal Sentencing Guidelines became advisory for federal sentencing judges, instead of mandatory, as the provision had set forth. Upon abrogating § 3742(e), the Court directed appeals courts to review criminal sentences by a standard of "reasonableness," although the term was not defined.

Justice Stevens delivered an opinion of the Court in part, answering the first question, beginning by discussing the development of Sixth Amendment jurisprudence. The Constitution protects all criminal defendants "against conviction except upon proof beyond a reasonable doubt of every fact necessary to constitute the crime with which he is charged," and it also grants criminal defendants the right to a jury trial, which must find the defendant "guilty of all the elements of the crime with which he is charged." These cases led to holdings that influenced the interpretation of modern criminal statutes, such as in *Jones v. United States* (1999), which held that since the harm to the victim during a carjacking influenced the sentencing of the defendant, it was an element of the underlying offense. The Court found that holding to be consistent with a "rule requiring jury determination of facts that raise a sentencing ceiling" under sentencing guideline schemes.

In 2000, the Court held that "other than the fact of a prior conviction, any fact that increases the penalty of a crime beyond the prescribed statutory maximum must be submitted to a jury, and proved beyond a reasonable doubt." In *Ring v. Arizona*, the Court held that "the characterization of a fact or circumstance as an 'element' or 'sentencing factor' is not determinative of the question 'who decides,' judge or jury." In 2004, the Court held that the right to have a jury find the existence of material facts is implicated whenever a judge seeks to impose a sentence that is outside the prescribed statutory range, in *Blakely v. Washington*. Part of the reason for these holdings stemmed from the fact that judges were finding additional facts that influenced sentences by a preponderance of the evidence, as opposed to the standard of evidence beyond a reasonable doubt set forth in *In re Winship*. The "beyond a reasonable doubt" standard is only triggered when the judge tries to impose a punishment *outside* of prescribed statutory range; the judge has full discretion to choose any sentence *within* the range. The Court has deemed the guidelines as mandatory and binding upon judges, as opposed to advisory, and thus, they have the "force and effect of laws."

Although the Federal Sentencing Guidelines, under 18 U.S.C. § 3553, set forth minimum and maximum ranges for sentencing purposes, § 3553(b)(1) allows judges to depart from the statutory scheme if mitigating or aggravating circumstances present were "not adequately taken into consideration by the Sentencing Commission in formulating the Guidelines." Booker was sentenced to approximately 10 years longer than the prescribed maximum sentence under the guidelines because the judge found by a preponderance of the evidence that Booker had more drugs than he had been originally charged with possessing; however, the jury did not hear about this evidence. The Court found Booker's offense to be a "run-of-the-mill drug case," which lacked any factors that were not adequately taken into consideration by the sentencing commission.

The Court then addressed three arguments set forth by the government as to why the holding in *Blakely* should not apply to the Federal Sentencing Guidelines. One reason was that the guidelines were promulgated by a commission, as opposed to the legislature. The government also argued that *Blakely* was inconsistent with prior precedent, and pursuant to the principles of stare decisis, those prior decisions should be followed. Finally, the government argued that the decision in *Blakely* conflicted with the principles of separation of powers. The Court did not find any of these arguments persuasive.

The fact that the guidelines were created by a commission rather than a legislature was deemed to lack "constitutional significance" because "regardless of whether the legal basis of the accusation is in a statute or in guidelines promulgated by an independent commission, the principles behind the jury trial are equally applicable." The argument of stare decisis was unpersuasive because none of the cases cited by the government (*United States v. Dunnigan* [1993], *United States v. Gray-*

son [1978], *Witte v. United States* [1995], and *Edwards v. United States* [1998]) was inconsistent with the Court's decision that Booker's constitutional rights had been violated. The Court then addressed the separation of powers argument, which suggested that the sentencing commission was essentially defining the elements of crimes, an inherently legislative power. The Court found no merit in this argument because *Mistretta v. U.S.* (1989) had already held that the Sentencing Reform Act of 1984 was a constitutional delegation of legislative powers. In *Mistretta,* the Court noted that the creation of the guidelines was similar to other "nonadjudicatory" activities undertaken by the judicial branch, such as the Federal Rules of Evidence. Accordingly, the Court found that Booker's sentence violated the Sixth Amendment right to have a jury find all facts beyond a reasonable doubt and reaffirmed its holding in *Apprendi,* stating that "any fact (other than a prior conviction) which is necessary to support a sentence exceeding the maximum authorized by the facts established by a plea of guilty or a jury verdict must be admitted by the defendant or proved to a jury beyond a reasonable doubt."

Justice Breyer delivered the opinion of the Court in part, addressing the second question presented in this case, dealing with the remedy: whether or to what extent the guidelines are inapplicable for purposes of severability analysis. The Court looked at legislative intent "to determine what Congress would have intended in light of the Court's constitutional holding." Although congressional intent is important, the Court noted that "sometimes severability questions (questions as to how, or whether, Congress would intend a statute to apply) can arise when a legislatively unforeseen constitutional problem requires modification of a statutory provision applied in a significant number of instances." To determine intent, the Court inquired into an evaluation of the consequences of their decision "in light of the Act's language, its history, and its basic purposes." This led to the conclusion that the constitutional requirement of a jury trial was not compatible with the Sentencing Guidelines Act as written, and thus, certain parts of the act had to be severed.

The Court reasoned that if the constitutional requirement that a jury must determine all facts beyond a reasonable doubt before a defendant's sentence could be increased beyond the statutory minimum were added to the act, it would become such that "Congress would not have intended the Act as so modified to stand." One reason was that the act referred to the judge in several instances but not to a jury. Additionally, the act made the guidelines mandatory in federal court, as opposed to advisory, inconsistently with the jury requirement set forth in Justice Stevens's majority opinion for the first issue. The Court thought the constitutional jury requirement would "destroy" the system created by the act because judges would no longer be able to rely on presentence investigation reports uncovered after trial, which are often used by judges when determining sentences. This would weaken the "tie between a sentence and an offender's real conduct," which would be inconsistent with the act's dual aim of sentencing uniformity among similarly situated offenders and having sentences reflect the offenders' "real conduct." The Court also thought that the constitutional jury requirement rule would have a negative impact on plea bargaining under the act as currently written because it would diminish uniformity by leading to "sentences that [give] greater weight" to "factors that vary from place to place, defendant to defendant, and crime to crime." An increase in prosecutorial power would also be implicated because "any factor that a prosecutor chose not to charge at a plea bargain negotiation would be placed beyond the reach of the judge entirely." These reasons led the Court to the conclusion that Congress did not take the constitutional jury trial requirement into consideration when passing the act as they did in 1984.

After determining that the entire statute need not be invalidated, the logical next step for the Court was to decide which parts to sever and excise. The Court chose to retain portions of the act that were constitutionally valid, consistently with Congress's basic intent in creating the statute and capable of functioning independently of the parts severed and excised. The Court chose to sever and excise the provision of the statute that required sentencing courts to impose a sentence within the predetermined sentencing range, 18 U.S.C. § 3553(b)(1). This provision was struck down because it made the guidelines binding on judges, thereby implicated the constitutional holding in *Apprendi,* which prohibits judges from enhancing criminal sentences beyond statutory maximums on the basis of facts not decided by a jury beyond a reasonable doubt. Therefore, without this provision, the statute falls outside the scope of *Apprendi.* They determined that the remainder of the act could function independently of this provision.

The Court conceded that the severance and excision of § 3553(b)(1) required the excision of § 3742(e), which set forth the standards of review on appeal and made several "critical" cross-references to § 3553(b)(1). The abrogation of this portion of the statute did not diminish the defendant's right to appeal under the statute because, as the Court stated, "a statute that does not explicitly set forth a standard of review may nonetheless do so implicitly." From the statutory language and structure of the act, the Court determined that the appropriate standard of review under the statute was the review for "unreasonableness." By severing and excising these two provisions, the Court believed that the act continued to retain Congress's objectives in creating the act: sentencing uniformity and proportionality, as well as allowing for individualized sentences when warranted. Although this holding effectively made the sentencing guidelines advisory, as opposed to mandatory, it left open to Congress an opportunity to develop a sentencing system that was best for the federal system, provided that it was compatible with the Constitution.

Addressing *Booker* in particular, the Court chose to affirm the judgment of the court of appeals to vacate the judgment of the district court and remand the case for resentencing. On remand, the Court directed the district court and the court of appeals to act accordingly with this opinion. The judgment of the district court against the respondent Fanfan was also remanded for further proceedings consistent with the Court's decision.

Justice Stevens wrote a dissenting opinion as to the second issue, joined by Justice Souter in whole and Scalia in part. Stevens believed it was possible to avoid the constitutional question in Booker's case without changing the guidelines because if the prosecution had submitted the actual quantity of drugs to the jury, Booker's 360-month sentence would have been within the prescribed range. He also took issue with the Court's approach to severability because it changed the traditional analysis of facial challenges. According to him, "a facial challenge may succeed if a legislative scheme is unconstitutional in all or nearly all of its applications" and in cases "in which an invalid provision or application cannot be severed from the remainder of the statute" without making the statute unworkable. Neither of those issues was present here, and Stevens saw no reason to create a third category, as he argued the Court had. Stevens also mentioned that *Blakely* rights, like jury rights, could be waived and that *Blakely* could constitutionally exist with the guidelines still in place because the word *court,* used in the statute, could be expanded to include the jury.

AFTERMATH

Prior to these cases, judges were using presentence investigation reports, usually conducted by probation officers, to find mitigating and aggravating circumstances to be considered by the judge when determining sentencing. These facts were determined by the judge by a preponderance of the evidence, as opposed to the standard of evidence beyond a reasonable doubt, and occasionally had led to sentences that were imposed beyond the maximum prescribed statutory limit. The Court stated that this decision applied to all cases on direct review and asserted that its decision retained Congress's aim of uniformity and proportionality in sentencing and that sentences reflect the defendant's "real conduct."

SIGNIFICANCE

This decision, along with a state case decided six months earlier, *Blakely v. Washington,* reaffirmed the Court's decision in *Apprendi v. New Jersey,* which had held that facts (other than prior convictions) that increase the defendant's sentence beyond the maximum statutorily prescribed sentence have to be submitted to a jury and proven beyond a reasonable doubt.

RELATED CASES

United States v. Gaudin, 515 U.S. 506, 511 (1995)

Jones v. United States, 526 U.S. 227 (1999)

Apprendi v. New Jersey, 530 U.S. 466 (2000)

Blakely v. Washington, 512 U.S. 296 (2004)

RECOMMENDED READING

Paul J. Hofer, *Immediate and Long-Term Effects of* United States v. Booker: *More Discretion, More Disparity, or Better Reasoned Sentences,* 38 Arizona State Law Journal 425 (2006).

————, United States v. Booker *as a Natural Experiment: Using Emprical Research to Inform the Federal Sentencing Policy Debate,* 6 Criminology & Public Policy 433 (2007).

DEATH PENALTY

The death penalty, also known as capital punishment, is the ultimate price that can be paid for a crime. As such, it is generally reserved for the most severe crimes and the most ruthless criminals. For centuries of civilization, the death penalty was the standard punishment for murder and treason, and other crimes, such as kidnapping or rape, also were deemed, in some jurisdictions, severe enough to warrant the death penalty.

In the United States, the death penalty has been limited to the four most heinous crimes, murder, treason, kidnapping, and rape. But, over the years, the Supreme Court has considered whether the death penalty is cruel and unusual punishment and has scrutinized the procedures and levels of proof needed to convict a defendant of a capital crime. The reason for the extreme level of scrutiny is related to the absolute nature of the punishment itself: It is permanent and irrevocable, once imposed.

Because of the extreme nature of the punishment, the Court has also looked into the defendant's state of mind. Our legal system requires that guilty defendants must have the requisite intent before they can be found guilty of a crime: That is, they must have intended to commit the crime that they committed and understand that what they did was a crime. It is thought that if a defendant did not understand, because of a mental disability, that he or she killed a person, the defendant could not be guilty of murder and, therefore, should not be subject to the punishment.

Mental disability is not the only reason a person can be found incapable of possessing the requisite intent to be found guilty of homicide. The defendant may have been influenced by factors that led to temporary insanity or incapacity or may be underage. The Court has often looked at the question of whether persons below the age of majority—juveniles—can be tried for capital crimes and be subject to the death penalty.

The Court has also scrutinized the means of execution. At present, there are five methods of execution on the books in the United States: lethal injection, lethal gas, electrocution, hanging, and firing squad. In a few states, a condemned person may choose the method of execution. In others, state law provides substitutes should the prescribed method be found unconstitutional. For example, in Oklahoma, execution is to be by lethal injection, but if that is found unconstitutional, then electrocution is specified; if that, too, is found to be unconstitutional, then firing squad is to be used. Over the years, many methods of execution have been determined to be cruel and unusual punishment and, as such, have been eliminated in states that allow the death penalty. Lethal injection has been largely recognized to be the most "humane" method of execution and is the method preferred by most states. Only Nebraska lists electrocution alone as the method of execution. Recently, electrocution has come under scrutiny when, in a few highly publicized cases, equipment failures failed to kill the condemned individual, causing unnecessary suffering.

Public opinion about the death penalty has led to broad national changes regarding its use, and many states have abolished it altogether. Part of the debate over use of the death penalty relates to the philosophy behind criminal punishment. Many argue that if the purpose of criminal penalties is rehabilitative, then the death penalty, by definition, leaves no room for rehabilitation. If the system of criminal punishment is retribution, then death is the ultimate price that a person must face when he or she commits the ultimate crimes.

U.S. CONSTITUTION—EIGHTH AMENDMENT

Excessive bail shall not be required, nor excessive fines imposed, nor cruel and unusual punishments inflicted.

U.S. CONSTITUTION— FOURTEENTH AMENDMENT

All persons born or naturalized in the United States and subject to the jurisdiction thereof, are citizens of the United States and of the State wherein they reside. No State shall make or enforce any law which shall abridge the privileges or immunities of citizens of the United States; nor shall any State deprive any person of life, liberty, or property, without due process of law; nor deny to any person within its jurisdiction the equal protection of the laws.

Case Title: *Louisiana ex rel. Francis v. Resweber*

Legal Citation: 329 U.S. 459

Year of Decision: 1947

KEY ISSUES

Did the use of the electric chair to execute Willie Francis violate the Fifth Amendment protection against double jeopardy or the Eighth Amendment protection against cruel and unusual punishment, on the basis that the first attempt at execution was unsuccessful and a second execution attempt, which was successful, was required?

HISTORY OF THE CASE

Willie Francis was convicted of murder in September 1945 and sentenced to death by electrocution. On May 3, 1946, Francis was put in the electric chair in Louisiana, prepared for execution. As a result of mechanical difficulties, the execution was unsuccessful, and Francis was returned to prison. A new execution date was set for May 9, 1946, but the execution date was stayed upon petitions to the Supreme Court of Louisiana. Francis argued that both his Fifth Amendment rights against double jeopardy and his Eighth Amendment protection against cruel and unusual punishment were violated. The state court denied the claims for relief because there was no violation of state or national law alleged in the applications. The U.S. Supreme Court granted certiorari, noting that the issue in this case lacked precedent.

SUMMARY OF ARGUMENTS

Francis argued that a second attempt to execute him would be a violation of double jeopardy because he would have received punishment for the same crime twice. Francis also argued that because he had already undergone the mental pressure of preparing to be executed, required him to do so a second time constituted cruel and unusual punishment.

DECISION

The Court held that re-executing someone does not constitute a violation of the Fifth Amendment privilege against double jeopardy. The Court also held that it did not violate the Eighth Amendment's protection against cruel and unusual punishment.

Justice Reed delivered the opinion of the Court. He began by discussing the Fifth Amendment double jeopardy issue, noting that precedent had been established that the same sovereignty could not punish an accused twice for the same crime. Even if a convicted person successfully received a reversal of the decision, there was no double jeopardy in having a new trial, as was established in *United States v. Ball* (1896). In this case, the Court deemed that retrying the execution did not constitute double jeopardy. The Court stated that when "an accident, with no suggestion of malevolence, prevents the consummation of a sentence, the state's subsequent course in the administration of its criminal law is not affected on that account by any requirement of due process under the Fourteenth Amendment."

As for the Eighth Amendment claim, the Court found nothing in the facts that would amount to cruel and unusual punishment. Francis argued that because he had already experienced the mental pressure of preparing to be executed, requiring that he experience it a second time constituted cruel and unusual punishment. Modern Anglo-American law had long recognized that unnecessary pain in executing a death is forbidden; however, *In re Kemmler* (1890) established that electrocution as a method of executing a death sentence was constitutional. Since the method of execution was deemed constitutional, the Court reasoned that "the fact that an unforeseeable accident prevented the prompt consummation of the sentence cannot, it seems to us, add an element of cruelty to a subsequent execution." The hardship faced by Francis was not deemed to have violated his due process rights, and the Court found no equal protection violation. In affirming the court of appeals and, thus, the conviction and sentence, the Court stated, "We have no right to assume that Louisiana singled out Francis for a treatment other than that which has been or would generally be applied."

Justice Burton wrote a dissenting opinion, joined by Justices Douglas, Murphy, and Rutledge, expressing his view that under these particular facts, Francis did experience cruel and unusual punishment. Therefore, he thought that the case should be remanded and certain material facts should be considered, such as the extent to which the electric current was applied to Francis on the unsuccessful attempt. He stated that it "is unthinkable that any state legislature in modern times would enact a statute expressly authorizing capital punishment by repeated applications of an electric current separated by intervals of days or hours until finally death shall result." Justice Burton asserted that this was not the intent of the Louisiana legislature and that the intent of those officials administering the execution was also irrelevant. He proposed the question "How many deliberate and intentional reapplications of electric current does it take to produce a cruel, unusual and unconstitutional punishment?" He then stated that cases such as this should be evaluated by their particular facts and that the facts here, which stated that Francis screamed in pain and complained that he could not breathe during the first attempt, made the actions unconstitutional.

AFTERMATH

In this case, the Court made clear that electrocution by itself did not constitute cruel and unusual punishment. The Court also stated that the mishandled electrocution attempt was not deliberate action of the state, and a second attempt, which was successful, did not constitute double jeopardy. Francis was electrocuted again the next year, and this time the electrocution attempt was successful.

In 2006, Allan Durand directed a documentary film about Francis entitled *Willie Francis Must Die Again*.

SIGNIFICANCE

The decision has long set precedent that electrocution is not cruel and unusual punishment under the Eighth Amendment, though use of the electric chair is in decline within the United States. In addition, the rule stands that corrections officials are not liable for inhumane conditions during imprisonment unless the conditions result from deliberate indifference to these conditions.

RELATED CASES

In re Kemmler, 136 U.S. 436 (1890)

United States v. Ball, 163 U.S. 662 (1896)

Gregg v. Georgia, 428 U.S. 153 (1976)

Jurek v. Texas, 428 U.S. 262 (1976)

Proffitt v. Florida, 428 U.S. 242 (1976)

Stanford v. Kentucky, 492 U.S. 361 (1989)

Wilson v. Seiter, 501 U.S. 294 (1991)

RECOMMENDED READING

King, Gilbert. *The Execution of Willie Francis: Race, Murder, and the Search for Justice in the American South.* New York: Basic Civitas, 2008.

Case Title: *Witherspoon v. Illinois*

Legal Citation: 391 U.S. 510

Year of Decision: 1968

KEY ISSUE

Is the elimination of potential jurors in a capital punishment case unconstitutional when based on the juror's "general objections" to the death penalty?

HISTORY OF THE CASE

In 1960, William C. Witherspoon was found guilty of murder and sentenced to death. At Witherspoon's trial, the prosecution invoked an Illinois statute that stated as follows: "In trials for murder it shall be a cause for challenge of any juror who shall, on being examined, state that he has conscientious scruples against capital punishment, or that he is opposed to the same." Because of this statute, the prosecution eliminated about half of the prospective jurors. After receiving his death sentence, the petitioner sought "postconviction relief" and was denied by the Illinois Supreme Court. On appeal, the U.S. Supreme Court granted certiorari.

SUMMARY OF ARGUMENTS

Witherspoon argued that the Illinois statute essentially stacked the deck against him by creating a jury that was "biased in favor of conviction."

The state of Illinois argued that "individuals who express serious reservations about capital punishment cannot be relied upon to vote for it even when the laws of the State and the instructions of the trial judge would make death the proper penalty."

DECISION

The U.S. Supreme Court held that a death sentence could not be carried out when potential jurors were eliminated after voicing general objections to the imposition of capital punishment.

In delivering the opinion of the Court, Justice Stewart noted that the only question to be addressed here was whether potential jurors could be eliminated for voicing general objections to the death penalty. This decision, Justice Stewart stated, "[did] not involve the right of the prosecution to challenge for cause those prospective jurors who state that their reservations about capital punishment would prevent them from making an impartial decision as to the defendant's guilt. Nor does it involve the State's assertion of a right to exclude from the jury in a capital case those who say that they could never vote to impose the death penalty." Instead, the Court focused solely on general objections, noting that "it is entirely possible . . . that even a juror who believes that capital punishment should never be inflicted and who is irrevocably committed to its abolition could nonetheless subordinate his personal views to what he perceived to be his duty to abide by his oath as a juror and to obey the law of the State."

The main problem with the Illinois statute, Justice Stewart asserted, was that by eliminating those people who had "general" objections to the death penalty, the state created a jury that was not an accurate reflection of the community at large—and, thus, as petitioner argued, the deck was stacked in favor of capital punishment. Thus, the jury was not impartial, and that circumstance violated the petitioner's Sixth Amendment right to a trial "by an impartial jury of the state and district wherein the crime shall have been committed."

In its conclusion, the Court stated, "Whatever else might be said of capital punishment, it is at least clear that its imposition by a hanging jury cannot be squared with the Constitution. The State of Illinois has stacked the deck against the petitioner. To execute this death sentence would deprive him of his life without due process of law." Accordingly, the petitioner's penalty was reversed, and the case was remanded.

Justice Douglas concurred with the majority but wrote separately to express the constitutional requirement that the jury be drawn from an impartial cross section of the community in which the trial was held. Justice Douglas argued that juries, as democratic institutions, should represent all qualified classes of people. He stated that achieving an impartial cross section of the community "certainly should not mean a selection of only those with a predisposition to impose the severest sentence or with a predisposition to impose the least one that is possible." Justice Douglas further argued that while some communities would use the death penalty, others would not, and he suggested that the accused should have the benefit of the community's principles of mercy.

In his dissent, Justice Black, joined by Justices Harlan and White, called the majority's holding a "semantic illusion" and stated that "the practical effect of the Court's new formulation of the question to be asked state juries will not produce a significantly different kind of jury from the one chosen in this case." Justice Black added that the majority's decision "[went] a long way to destroying the concept of an impartial jury as we have known it."

AFTERMATH

In 1972, the precedent established in *Witherspoon* temporarily became moot because the Supreme Court placed a moratorium on the death penalty in the United States in *Furman v. Georgia*. However, in 1976, the Supreme Court upheld the use of the death penalty in several companion cases, referred to as the "July 2nd" cases. The consolidated cases included *Gregg v. Georgia, Profitt v. Florida, Jurek v. Texas, Woodson v. North Carolina,* and *Roberts v. Louisiana*.

After the Court's decision in *Witherspoon*, those prospective jurors who were eliminated at voir dire because they would never vote to impose the death penalty were known as "Witherspoon excludables." This concept was revisited in *Lockhart v. McCree* (1986), in which the defendant argued that the removal of "Witherspoon excludables" violated his constitutional right to an impartial jury. However, the Court held that there was no constitutional violation in this case because "the Constitution does not prohibit the removal for cause . . . of prospective jurors whose opposition to the death penalty is so strong that it would prevent or substantially impair the performance of their duties as jurors at the sentencing phase of the trial."

SIGNIFICANCE

This case established the term "Witherspoon excludables," which refers to prospective jurors whose religious or conscientious reservations about the death penalty would prevent or substantially impair the performance of their duties and instructions as jurors.

RELATED CASES

Furman v. Georgia, 408 U.S. 238 (1972)

Gregg v. Georgia, 428 U.S. 153 (1976)

Roberts v. Louisiana, 428 U.S. 153 (1976)

Coker v. Georgia, 433 U.S. 584 (1977)

Lockhart v. McCree, 476 U.S. 162 (1986)

Thompson v. Oklahoma, 487 U.S. 815 (1988)

Morgan v. Illinois, 504 U.S. 719 (1992)

Atkins v. Virginia, 536 U.S. 304 (2002)

Roper v. Simmons, 543 U.S. 551 (2005)

Kennedy v. Louisiana, 554 U.S. 407 (2008)

RECOMMENDED READING

Steven C. Bennett, *Ineffective Assistance of Counsel In Voir Dire and the Admissibility of Testimony of* Witherspoon-*Excluded Veniremen in Post-Conviction Evidentiary Hearing,* 49 Louisiana Law Review 841 (1989).

Stanton D. Krauss, *The Witherspoon Doctrine at Witt's End: Death-Qualification Reexamined,* 24 American Criminal Law Review 1 (1986).

James S. Liebman, *Slow Dancing with Death: The Supreme Court and Capital Punishment, 1963–2006,* 107 Columbia Law Review 1 (2007).

Deborah L. Mahoney, *Constitutional Law: Capital Defendant's Permitted Reverse-*Witherspoon *"Life Qualifying" Questions on Voir Dire* [Morgan v. Illinois, 112 S. Ct. 2222 (1992)], 32 Washburn Law Journal 278 (1993).

Case Title: *Gregg v. Georgia*

Legal Citation: 428 U.S. 153

Year of Decision: 1976

KEY ISSUES

Would sentencing a defendant to death for armed robbery and murder under Georgia state law violate the defendant's Eighth Amendment right to be protected from "cruel and unusual punishments" and the defendant's Fourteenth Amendment right not to be deprived of his life without due process of law?

HISTORY OF THE CASE

In *Furman v. Georgia* (1972), the U.S. Supreme Court ruled, in a 5-4 decision, that existing death penalty laws were so arbitrarily and "freakishly imposed" that they qualified as cruel and unusual under the Eighth Amendment (the Supreme Court did not want to leave juries with "untrammeled discretion" to impose or withhold the death penalty). However, the *Furman* decision left states with the room to develop new statutory schemes that contained more objective standards by which capital punishment would be levied: As Phyllis A. Ewer stated in her article "Eighth Amendment: The Death Penalty," "*Furman* did not resolve the issue of whether the death penalty was unconstitutional per se."

Two years later, in 1974, Troy Leon Gregg was convicted of murder and armed robbery in a Georgia trial court for the killing (and subsequent robbing) of two men who had picked him up when they saw him hitchhiking on a Florida high-way. After being found guilty, the petitioner Gregg was then sentenced to death under the post-*Furman* "bifurcated" Georgia statutory system, under which the jury first determined the guilt of the defendant and, then, after considering mitigating and aggravating factors, decided whether or not to impose the death penalty. The "aggravating factors" the jury looked at were whether "1) the murder was committed while the offender was engaged in the commission of other capital felonies, 2) [the murder was committed] for the purposes of receiving the victims' money and automobile, or 3) the murder was 'outrageously and wantonly vile, horrible and inhuman.'" After the jury made its determination (in this case they found that the defendant had engaged in the first two aggravating factors), the Georgia Supreme Court, under the scope of the post-*Furman* statutory scheme, reviewed the sentence of death to determine whether the imposition of capital punishment would be arbitrary or disproportionate to the penalties applied in similar cases; here, the Georgia Supreme Court affirmed the petitioner Gregg's sentence. Gregg appealed to the U.S. Supreme Court; certiorari was granted.

SUMMARY OF ARGUMENTS

Gregg argued that the imposition of the death penalty in this case was "cruel and unusual punishment" in violation of the Eighth and Fourteenth Amendments, claiming that the "bifurcated" Georgia statutory system allowed arbitrary imposition of capital punishment.

DECISION

The Supreme Court affirmed the decision of the Georgia Supreme Court and held that the Georgia death penalty statutory scheme was constitutional and not in violation of the Eighth and Fourteenth Amendments.

In his plurality opinion, Justice Stevens first addressed whether or not capital punishment is per se unconstitutional. In order to support his conclusion that it was not per se unconstitutional, Justice Stevens first asserted that society had "endorsed" the death penalty for murder cases through its "legislative response to *Furman*. The legislatures of at least 35 states [had] enacted new statutes that provide for the death penalty for at least some crimes that result in the death of another person." Justice Stevens also found "social endorsement" because juries—"a . . . reliable objective index of contemporary values"— had become directly involved in the process via Georgia's new death penalty procedure. Justice Stevens then responded to the low number of jury-imposed death sentences in this way: "The relative infrequency of jury verdicts imposing the death sentence does not indicate rejection of capital punishment per se. Rather, the reluctance of juries in many cases to impose the sentence may well reflect the humane feeling that this most irrevocable of sanctions should be reserved for a small number of extreme cases."

Stevens then wrote that, in addition to "social endorsement," the constitution requires that a punishment "[comport] with the basic concept of human dignity at the core of the [Eighth] Amendment" and that "the sanction imposed cannot be so totally without penological justification that it results in the gratuitous infliction of suffering." The two main justifications, Stevens noted, for the death penalty are retribution and deterrence. Retribution, Stevens stated, "is essential in an ordered society that asks its citizens to rely on legal processes rather than self-help to vindicate their wrongs." As for the death penalty's ability to deter potential murderers, Stevens admitted that some murders would take place with or without the existence of capital punishment; however, "for many others, the death penalty undoubtedly is a significant deterrent. There are carefully contemplated murders . . . where the possible penalty of death may well enter into the cold calculus that precedes the decision to act." Stevens concluded that, on the basis of available data, it is impossible to claim that there are never situations when the use of capital punishment is wrong.

The final consideration, Stevens wrote, in determining whether the death penalty is per se unconstitutional is whether the use of capital punishment would be disproportionate in relation to the crime (murder and armed robbery) for which it

is being levied. In this case, Stevens stated, "we cannot say that the punishment is invariably disproportionate to the crime. It is an extreme sanction, suitable to the most extreme of crimes." Thus, Justice Stevens found "proportionality" between the crime of murder and the death penalty.

Having stated these reasons for why the death penalty was not "cruel and unusual punishment" for the crime of murder, Stevens then turned his attention to the Georgia statute and found that it was not "arbitrary" or "capricious" under the Eighth Amendment because "[The Georgia statute's] procedures require the jury to consider the circumstances of the crime and the criminal before it recommends sentence," and "as an important additional safeguard against arbitrariness and caprice, the Georgia statutory scheme provides for automatic appeal of all death sentences to the State's Supreme Court. . . . On their face," Stevens concluded, "these procedures seem to satisfy the concerns of *Furman*."

In his concurrence, Justice White wrote that the petitioner Gregg's assertion that there was too much discretion in the post-*Furman* system and that the government is "inevitably incompetent to administer [the death penalty] cannot be accepted as a proposition of constitutional law." "I decline," Justice White concluded, "to interfere with the manner in which Georgia has chosen to enforce such laws."

In his dissent, Justice Brennan argued that the majority erred because it based its decision to uphold the death penalty on the statutory mechanism used to determine who should receive capital punishment—and not on the extreme and final nature of the sanction itself. "Death," Brennan wrote, "is not only an unusually severe punishment, unusual in its pain, in its finality, and in its enormity, but it serves no penal purpose more effectively than a less severe punishment."

AFTERMATH

When the *Furman* decision was handed down in 1972, the Supreme Court commuted the sentences of 629 people on death row; however, in the 32 years since *Gregg*, more than 1,000 people have received capital punishment (42 in 2007 alone).

SIGNIFICANCE

The *Gregg v. Georgia* decision marked the beginning of the modern era of capital punishment. The *Gregg* ruling opened the door to the state-sponsored impositions of the death penalty that *Furman* had almost—but not quite—shut completely.

RELATED CASE

Furman v. Georgia, 408 U.S. 238 (1972)

RECOMMENDED READING

Phyllis A. Ewer, *Eighth Amendment: The Death Penalty,* 71 Journal of Criminal Law and Criminology 538 (1980).

Case Title: *Jurek v. Texas*

Legal Citation: 428 U.S. 262

Year of Decision: 1976

KEY ISSUE

Do the Texas capital sentencing procedures, which allow jury members to consider both aggravating and mitigating circumstances when making sentencing decisions, constitute "cruel and unusual punishment," in violation of the Eighth and Fourteenth Amendments?

HISTORY OF THE CASE

Although the death penalty in the United States was used prior to the 1970s, in *Furman v. Georgia* (1972), the U.S. Supreme Court ended the then-current methods of execution because its decision effectively created a de facto moratorium on capital punishment. However, some states began trying new methods of execution in attempts to retain the death penalty without violating the U.S. Constitution. Texas was one of these states.

A Texas citizen, Jerry Lane Jurek, was charged with the murder of 10-year-old Wendy Adams by choking her, strangling her, and throwing her unconscious body into a river, resulting in her drowning. After hearing Jurek's self-incriminating details of the crime, the jury returned a verdict of guilty. Under Texas law, if a defendant is found guilty of a capital offense, the trial court must conduct a separate sentencing proceeding before the same jury that found the defendant guilty.

During this proceeding, the jury heard aggravating and mitigating circumstances regarding both the character of the defendant and the crime he was found guilty of committing. The jury then answered yes to two important questions: first, whether the murder was proven beyond a reasonable doubt to have been committed deliberately with the expectation that death would result and, second, whether it was demonstrated beyond a reasonable doubt that there was a probability that Jurek would continue to commit criminal acts of violence, constituting a criminal threat to society. Following the statute, the judge sentenced Jurek to death. The Court of Criminal Appeals of Texas affirmed the decision of the trial court, and the case was appealed to the U.S. Supreme Court. Certiorari was granted to determine whether Texas's use of the death penalty violated the cruel and unusual punishment clause of the Eighth and the Fourteenth Amendments.

SUMMARY OF ARGUMENTS

Jurek challenged the constitutionality of Texas's post-*Furman* capital sentencing procedures, claiming that the arbitrariness of the system stood in violation of the *Furman* decision as the revised system accomplished nothing more than "cosmetic" changes to the law. Specifically, he argued that the second question posed to the jury in the sentencing phase, which asked whether the evidence established a probability that Jurek would commit future criminal acts of violence, constituting a continuing threat to society, was unconstitutionally vague because it is impossible for a jury to predict one's future behavior. He further argued that the imposition of the death penalty under any circumstances constitutes "cruel and unusual" punishment in violation of the Eighth and Fourteenth Amendments.

The state of Texas argued that its procedural safeguards ensured that each defendant was treated on a particularized basis and was treated in a manner consistent with the constitutional guarantee of due process. It further argued that the imposition of the death penalty itself is not cruel and unusual punishment and, thus, does not violate the Eighth Amendment of the Constitution.

DECISION

Justice Stevens authored the majority decision as the Court held that the revised Texas sentencing procedures were not cruel and unusual punishment under the Eighth Amendment. The Court's decision upheld the "revised" capital punishment statutes enacted after *Furman v. Georgia* (1972). The Court found that in Texas, while they did not specifically require inquiry into aggravating factors, the sentencing procedure essentially accomplished the equivalent by narrowing the definition of capital murder to include only five specific situations: (1) murder of a police officer or fireman; (2) murder committed in the course of a kidnapping, burglary, robbery, forcible rape, or arson; (3) murder committed for remuneration; (4) murder committed while escaping or attempting to escape from a penal institution; and (5) murder committed by a prison inmate when the victim was a prison employee.

However, Justice Stevens continued, no system of capital sentencing procedures could be held constitutional if it did not allow a jury to consider mitigating factors when making its determination whether to impose the death penalty. He argued that although the Texas statute did not explicitly address consideration of mitigating circumstances, the second question the jury was to consider, whether it was demonstrated beyond a reasonable doubt that there was a probability that Jurek would continue to commit criminal acts of violence, constituting a criminal threat to society, gave the jury an opportunity to consider reasons why the death penalty should *not* be imposed. Thus, the Court concluded that the revised Texas procedures were not arbitrary enough to trigger "cruel and unusual punishment" under the Eighth Amendment.

Concerning the petitioner Jurek's argument that the revised Texas statutory system was unconstitutionally vague because it asked jurors to predict the threat Jurek posed to society, Justice Stevens admitted that "it is . . . not easy to predict future behavior . . . however . . . the task that a Texas jury must perform in answering the [second] statutory question in issue is . . . no different from the task performed countless times each day throughout the American system of criminal justice."

Justice Stevens then concluded that the revised Texas statutory system "provided a means to promote the evenhanded, rational, and consistent imposition of death sentences under law." In his concurring opinion, Justice White similarly stated, "The Texas capital punishment statute limits the imposition of the death penalty to a narrowly defined group of the most brutal crimes and aims at limiting its imposition to similar offenses occurring under similar circumstances."

AFTERMATH

The U.S. Supreme Court's decision in *Furman* effectively created a de facto moratorium on capital punishment throughout the United States. However, the Court's decisions in *Jurek, Gregg v. Georgia* (1976), *Proffitt v. Florida* (1976), and *Roberts v. Louisiana* (1976) marked the beginning of the modern era of the death penalty in the United States. Currently, many states allow the death penalty, as do the U.S. federal government and the U.S. military. In some jurisdictions, the death penalty remains in statutes but either is limited by moratorium or used only sparingly.

SIGNIFICANCE

Jurek established the notion that a state's capital sentencing procedures must include a means by which a jury can consider mitigating factors along with aggravating factors, prefacing the Court's decisions in *Gregg, Proffitt,* and *Roberts.* Specifically, the Court in *Jurek* held that the death penalty is not a *per se* unconstitutional violation of the Eighth and Fourteenth Amendments (as in *Furman*), as long as the statutory systems meet a certain threshold of objectiveness and consistency. The particular Texas death penalty statute allowed juries to consider both aggravating and mitigating circumstances when considering the unique circumstances surrounding each case, and the defendant's character was taken into consideration. Thus, it was deemed constitutional.

RELATED CASES

Furman v. Georgia, 408 U.S. 238 (1972)

Gregg v. Georgia, 428 U.S. 153 (1976)

Proffitt v. Florida, 428 U.S. 242 (1976)

Roberts v. Louisiana, 428 U.S. 325 (1976)

Woodson v. North Carolina, 428 U.S. 280 (1976)

Coker v. Georgia, 433 U.S. 584 (1977)

Atkins v. Virginia, 536 U.S. 304 (2002)

Kennedy v. Louisiana, 554, U.S. 407 (2008)

RECOMMENDED READING

Jesse Cheng, *Frontloading Mitigation: The "Legal" and the "Human" in Death Penalty Defense,* 35 Law and Social Inquiry 39 (2010).

Brock Mehler, *The Supreme Court and State Psychiatric Examinations of Capital Defendants: Stuck Inside of* Jurek *with the Barefoot Blues Again,* 59 UMKC Law Review 107 (1990).

Thomas Regnier, *Barefoot in Quicksand: The Future of "Future Dangerousness" Predictions in Death Penalty Sentencing in the World of* Duabert *and* Kumho, 37 Akron Law Review 469 (2004).

Case Title: *Godfrey v. Georgia*

Legal Citation: 446 U.S. 420

Year of Decision: 1980

KEY ISSUES

Does a provision of Georgia's death penalty statute, which extends capital punishment to crimes deemed "outrageously or wantonly vile, horrible or inhuman," violate the Eighth and Fourteenth Amendments?

HISTORY OF THE CASE

In early September 1977, Robert Franklin Godfrey had an argument with his wife, Mildred. He threatened her with a knife, and she left the home to stay with relatives. The next day, Mildred filed assault charges against Godfrey. A few days later, she filed for divorce. Though Godfrey asked her to return several times, Mildred refused. She soon moved in with her mother, who resided in a trailer a short distance from the Godfrey home.

On September 20, 1977, during a telephone conversation, Mildred told Robert that reconciliation was impossible. She further told him that her mother supported her in that decision. In response, Godfrey took his shotgun and walked to his mother-in-law's trailer. Upon his arrival, he looked through the window and saw his wife, mother-in-law, and 11-year-old daughter inside playing a card game. He shot his wife in the head through the trailer window, walked inside the trailer, struck his daughter with the barrel of his shotgun (injuring her), and shot his mother-in-law in the head, killing her instantly. Afterward, Godfrey called the police. In a calm manner, he explained what had happened. When police officers arrived, Godfrey stated: "I've done a hideous crime . . . but I have been thinking about it for eight years. . . . I'd do it again." Godfrey was indicted on two counts of murder and one count of aggravated assault.

In 1972, the Supreme Court decided *Furman v. Georgia,* which required that each state follow federal mandates for construction of capital sentencing guidelines. In response to this decision, Georgia developed a two-part capital sentencing system, in which the jury first determined whether the defendant was guilty and then determined whether or not the death penalty should be imposed. Georgia's death penalty statute was upheld in *Gregg v. Georgia* (1976). During the sentencing phase of Godfrey's trial, the judge instructed the jury with the language of § (b)(7) of the statute. In imposing the death penalty, the jury stated that the "aggravating circumstance" that had persuaded them to levy capital punishment was that Godfrey had acted in a manner that was "outrageously or wantonly vile, horrible and inhuman." Then, as mandated by the post-*Furman* Georgia death penalty statute, the Georgia Supreme Court reviewed—and affirmed—the trial court's decision to impose capital punishment, rejecting Godfrey's assertion that § (b)(7) was "unconstitutionally vague."

SUMMARY OF ARGUMENTS

Godfrey argued that § (b)(7) of the Georgia capital sentencing statute was unconstitutionally vague.

The state argued that § (b)(7) was constitutional because it had been upheld in *Gregg*: "It is, of course, arguable that any murder involves depravity of mind. . . . But this language need not be construed in this way, and there is no reason to assume that the Supreme Court of Georgia will adopt such an open-ended construction."

DECISION

The Court overturned the decision of the Georgia Supreme Court and held that § (b)(7), as applied in this case, was unconstitutional.

In delivering the opinion of the Court, Justice Stewart noted that while § (b)(7) had been upheld in *Gregg*, "there is nothing in ["outrageously or wantonly vile, horrible and human"], standing alone, that implies any inherent restraint on the arbitrary and capricious infliction of the death sentence." Any murder, Justice Stewart argued, could be considered "vile" and/or "horrible." Where § (b)(7) could be constitutional, he continued, is if the trial court streamlined the statute for the jury so that juries were aware that "outrageously or wantonly vile" was limited to the following: The offender had to demonstrate "torture, depravity of mind, or an aggravated battery to the victim" ("depravity of mind" only included the mental state that caused the offender to commit torture/aggravated battery upon the victim, and "torture" and "aggravated battery" required evidence of severe physical abuse committed against the victim before his or her death). The constitutionality of § (b)(7) in Godfrey's case depended

upon the limits (or lack thereof) placed upon this decidedly open-ended language: "The Georgia courts," Justice Stevens concluded, "did not, however, so limit § (b)(7) in the present case." Thus, even though § (b)(7) was facially constitutional under *Gregg*, Justice Stevens reversed the decision of the Georgia Supreme Court because, when not properly limited, "outrageously or wantonly vile" could easily cover nearly every murder committed. "Petitioner's crimes cannot be said to have reflected a consciousness materially more 'depraved' than that of any person guilty of murder."

In his dissent, Justice White argued that the facts of the case easily bore a "sufficient relation to § (b)(7) to conclude that the Georgia Supreme Court responsibly . . . discharged its review function." Justice White noted that the "petitioner employed a weapon known for its disfiguring effects on targets" and that "if anything, 'vile,' 'horrible,' and 'inhuman' [were] descriptively inadequate."

AFTERMATH

The Georgia Supreme Court vacated Godfrey's death sentence and remanded the case to the trial court. The trial court had to sentence Godfrey to life in prison or resentence him to death within the limitations set by the Supreme Court's decision. The jury again sentenced Godfrey to death, but this time under § (b)(2).

The Court's holding in *Godfrey* did not alter the Georgia death penalty statute. Rather, it demanded that certain procedural safeguards—here, the limiting of the scope of broad statutory language—take place. In the aftermath of *Godfrey*, in cases such as *Beck v. Alabama* (1980) and *Adams v. Texas* (1980), the Supreme Court continued to refine the revised post-*Furman* death penalty laws it first declared constitutional in *Gregg*.

SIGNIFICANCE

The *Godfrey* decision required legislatures to use more care in defining aggravating circumstances for purposes of capital punishment sentencing.

RELATED CASES

Furman v. Georgia, 408 U.S. 238 (1972)

Gregg v. Georgia, 428 U.S. 153 (1976)

Jurek v. Texas, 428 U.S. 262 (1976)

Proffitt v. Florida, 428 U.S. 242 (1976)

Adams v. Texas, 448 U.S. 38 (1980)

Beck v. Alabama, 447 U.S. 625 (1980)

STATUTE AT ISSUE

Ga. Code Ann. Section 27-2534.1, Mitigating and Aggravating Circumstances; Death Penalty

RECOMMENDED READING

M. Kate Calvert, *Obtaining Unanimity and a Standard of Proof on the Vileness Sub-Elements with* Apprendi v. New Jersey, 13 Capital Defense Journal 1 (2000).

Death Penalty Information Center: www.death penaltyinfo.org

James S. Liebman, *Slow Dancing with Death: The Supreme Court and Capital Punishment, 1963–2006,* 107 Columbia Law Review 1 (2007).

Palmer, Louis J. *The Death Penalty: An American Citizen's Guide to Understanding Federal and State Law.* Jefferson, N.C.: McFarland, 1998.

Paternoster, Raymond, Robert Brame, and Sarah Bacon. *The Death Penalty: America's Experience with Capital Punishment.* New York: Oxford University Press, 2007.

Robert Weisberg, *Deregulating Death,* 1983 Supreme Court Review 305.

Case Title: *Enmund v. Florida*

Legal Citation: 458 U.S. 782

Year of Decision: 1982

KEY ISSUE

Is capital punishment an appropriate sentence for those convicted of felony murder, or does the punishment violate the Eighth Amendment?

HISTORY OF THE CASE

Earl Enmund was the driver of a getaway car in the robbery and murder of an elderly Florida couple, the Kerseys. Enmund sat outside in the car while his accomplices attempted to rob them. Enmund's accomplices ultimately killed the Kerseys, and both Enmund and the surviving accomplice were indicted for first-degree murder and robbery. Both were sentenced to death. The Supreme Court of Florida affirmed Enmund's death sentence, holding that even though he did not commit the murders, under Florida law, he was a "constructive aider and abettor," therefore, a "principal in first-degree murder."

SUMMARY OF ARGUMENTS

Enmund argued that since he did not actually aid in the murder, capital punishment would be "cruel and unusual" under the circumstances.

The state argued that the murders were especially heinous and cruel and, therefore, punishable by death under Florida law.

DECISION

In a 5-4 decision written by Justice White, the Court ruled that the Eighth Amendment forbids Florida to impose a death sentence on an offender who "aids and abets a felony in the course of which murder is committed by others, but who does not himself kill, attempt to kill, or intend that a killing take place or that lethal force will be employed." The Court revisited its proportionality standard and found that only about a third of American jurisdictions would permit a defendant who participated in a robbery in which a murder occurred to be sentenced to die, a fact that weighed on the side of rejecting capital punishment for the crime at issue. The Court agreed that robbery is a serious crime deserving serious punishment but determined that robbery is not a crime "so grievous an affront to humanity that the only adequate response may be the penalty of death."

Justice O'Connor, joined by Justices Burger, Powell, and Rehnquist, dissented. O'Connor stated that the majority decision "interferes with state criteria for assessing legal guilt by recasting intent as a matter of federal constitutional law." The dissent believed that matters such as intent should be left to state criminal law proceedings and not interfered with by the federal courts, as there was not an Eighth Amendment definition of intent prior to this case.

AFTERMATH

On remand to the Supreme Court of Florida, Enmund's death sentence was vacated and the case remanded to the circuit court for imposition of sentence. In *Enmund v. Florida,* Enmund challenged his conviction for robbery and first-degree murder. The Court of Appeals of Florida, Second District, overturned the convictions for robbery, stating that "a defendant could be neither convicted nor sentenced for a robbery and also for felony first degree murder for which the robbery is the underlying felony." The court of appeals certified the following question to the Supreme Court of Florida: "When a defendant is convicted of felony murder, can he be convicted of, although not sentenced for, the underlying felony?" The Supreme Court of Florida held that a person could be "convicted of and sentenced for both felony murder and the underlying felony."

SIGNIFICANCE

The Eighth Amendment prohibits sentences of death for accomplices convicted of felony murder, when the accomplices did not commit or intend to commit the murder.

RELATED CASES

Gregg v. Georgia, 428 U.S. 153 (1976)

Tison v. Arizona, 481 U.S. 137 (1987)

RECOMMENDED READING

Amnesty International: www.amnestyusa.org/death-penalty/page.do?id=1011005

Michael Antonio Brockland, *See No Evil, Hear No Evil, Speak No Evil: An Argument for a Jury Determination of the* Enmund/Tison *Culpability Factors in Capital Felony Murder Cases,* 27 Saint Louis University Public Law Review 235 (2007).

Roy Conn III, *Imposition of the Death Penalty Is Violative of the Eighth and Fourteenth Amendments Where One Neither Took Life, Attempted to Take Life, Nor Intended to Take Life:* Enmund v. Florida, 26 Howard Law Journal 1679 (1983).

Culbert, Jennifer. *Dead Certainty: The Death Penalty and the Problem of Judgment.* Stanford, Calif.: Stanford University Press, 2007.

Death Penalty Information Center: www.deathpenaltyinfo.org

Margaret Carmody Jenkins, *Intent after* Enmund v. Florida: *Not Just Another Aggravating Circumstance,* 65 Boston University Law Review 809 (1985).

David McCord, *State Death Sentencing for Felony Murder Accomplices under the* Enmund *and* Tison *Standards,* 32 Arizona State Law Journal 843 (2000).

John H. Wickert, *The Death Penalty and Vicarious Felony Murder: Nontriggerman May Not Be Executed Absent a Finding of an Intent to Kill,* 73 Journal of Criminal Law & Criminology 1553 (1982).

Case Title: *Arizona v. Rumsey*

Legal Citation: 467 U.S. 203

Year of Decision: 1984

~~~

KEY ISSUE

Does the Fifth Amendment's double jeopardy clause prevent a state from imposing the death penalty at a defendant's resentencing hearing after the life sentence initially imposed against him was set aside on appeal?

HISTORY OF THE CASE

An Arizona jury convicted Dennis Rumsey of armed robbery and first-degree murder. Under the capital sentencing statute in that state, Arizona courts conduct a two-part trial with separate guilt and penalty phases. Under this statute, if a defendant is convicted of a capital crime, then the judge—sitting without a jury—determines whether the death penalty should be imposed. The statute mandates that if the Arizona judge finds aggravating circumstances in the commission of the crime and no mitigating circumstances, then that judge must impose capital punishment. The state has the burden of proving these aggravating factors beyond a reasonable doubt. Conversely, if the judge finds that no statutory aggravating factors exist, then he or she must instead impose a life sentence.

After Rumsey was found guilty of first-degree murder, the state contended that an aggravating circumstance was present in the case. Rumsey had committed the murder in an attempt to rob his victim (he had killed for financial gain). The judge, however, determined that the "pecuniary gain" aggravating circumstance applied only to murder for hire situations and, subsequently, sentenced Rumsey to life imprisonment. The state of Arizona appealed, arguing that the trial court had erred by holding that the "pecuniary gain" aggravating circumstance did not apply to Rumsey's case. The Arizona Supreme Court, agreeing that the judge had misapplied the "pecuniary gain" standard, remanded the case for reevaluation of the aggravating/mitigating circumstances for purposes of the penalty phase. On remand, the trial court found that the "pecuniary gain" aggravating circumstance was present and subsequently imposed the death penalty against Rumsey. Under Arizona law, because capital punishment had been imposed, this decision was automatically appealed to the Arizona Supreme Court. That court held that Rumsey's death sentence violated the Fifth Amendment's double jeopardy clause, which forbids trying a defendant twice for the same crime.

SUMMARY OF ARGUMENTS

Rumsey argued that the imposition of the death penalty against him at his resentencing—after he had effectively been "acquitted" of capital punishment at his initial sentencing—violated the double jeopardy clause of the Fifth Amendment. Since the Fifth Amendment was applicable to the states through the due process clause of the Fourteenth Amendment, Arizona was bound by its mandates.

The state of Arizona, meanwhile, argued that the trial judge's erroneous ruling at the initial sentencing proceeding—and his subsequent imposition of a life sentence against Rumsey—were not the equivalent of an acquittal on the merits. During oral arguments at the U.S. Supreme Court, the counsel for the state of Arizona stated as follows:

> There is no acquittal in this case. . . . There is a decision by the trial judge to avoid any termination of proceedings on this particular point on pecuniary damage. . . . If the controlling consideration behind the Double Jeopardy Clause where there is an acquittal, is to prevent the government oppression that would come with repeated efforts to convict and to make up its deficiencies in the State's case with each new effort of reprosecution, then applying the Double Jeopardy Clause here would not accomplish that. . . . There has been no final termination factually against the State's point.

DECISION

The U.S. Supreme Court held that the double jeopardy clause prevented Arizona from imposing the death penalty on Rumsey at the resentencing hearing.

The key question, wrote Justice O'Connor, was whether the trial judge's decision during the initial sentencing proceeding to sentence Rumsey to life imprisonment—despite any legal errors he might have made—served as the functional equivalent of an acquittal on the charges. Justice O'Connor compared this case to *Bullington v. Missouri,* in which the U.S. Supreme Court held that a judge's initial imposition of a life sentence on a defendant resulted in the rejection of the death sentence—an "implied acquittal"—and, thus, when the case went back to that same judge on appeal, his decision to impose the death penalty at the resentencing hearing violated the Fifth Amendment's double jeopardy clause. "Application of the *Bullington* principle," Justice O'Connor wrote, "renders [the respondent Rumsey's] death sentence a violation of the Double Jeopardy Clause because respondent's initial sentence of life imprisonment was undoubtedly an acquittal on the merits of the central issue in the proceeding—whether death was the appropriate punishment for respondent's offense." Underlying O'Connor's opinion is the notion that, in a bifurcated death penalty procedure such as the one used in Arizona (and many other states), both the guilt *and* the sentencing phase function as individual trials, and the final decision in either part is binding for Fifth Amendment purposes—even if the judge makes a legal error. "The capital sentencing proceeding in Arizona," Justice O'Connor wrote, "[resembles] a trial. . . . The sentencer must make findings with respect to each of the statutory aggravating and mitigating circumstances, and the sentencing hearing involves the submission of evidence and the presentation of argument."

In his dissent, Justice Rehnquist argued that the trial judge's erroneous ruling did not equal an "implied acquittal" of the respondent and should not negate the fact that the state of Arizona clearly established that the "pecuniary gain" aggravating circumstance existed in this case. Justice Rehnquist stated as follows:

> The fact that, in this case, the legal error was ultimately corrected by the trial court

did not mean that the State sought to marshal the same or additional evidence against a capital defendant which had proved insufficient to prove the State's "case" against him the first time. There is no logical reason for a different result here simply because the Arizona Supreme Court remanded the case to the trial court for the purpose of correcting the legal error, particularly when the resentencing did not constitute the kind of "retrial" which the *Bullington* Court condemned.

AFTERMATH

In 2003, the U.S. Supreme Court revisited the double jeopardy clause in a capital punishment context in *Sattazahn v. Pennsylvania,* in which the defendant received a life sentence after a jury deadlock. However, when in the *Rumsey* decision the Court found that the trial judge's erroneous ruling was an "implied acquittal" on the merits, the *Sattazahn* Court held that "Double Jeopardy protections were not triggered when the jury deadlocked at petitioner's first sentencing proceeding. . . . The jury in that first proceeding was deadlocked and made no findings with respect to the alleged aggravating circumstance. That result, or nonresult, cannot fairly be called an acquittal."

SIGNIFICANCE

Once a judge has handed down a sentence of life for a crime, he or she may not later impose the death penalty for the same crime.

RELATED CASES

United States v. Wilson, 420 U.S. 332 (1975)

Bullington v. Missouri, 451 U.S. 430 (1981)

Sattazahn v. Pennsylvania, 537 U.S. 101 (2003)

RECOMMENDED READING

Robert Steinbuch, *Reforming Federal Death Penalty Procedures: Four Modest Proposals to Improve the Administration of the Ultimate Penalty,* 40 Indiana Law Review 97 (2007).

Case Title: *Strickland v. Washington*

Legal Citation: 466 U.S. 668

Year of Decision: 1984

KEY ISSUE

What merits a Sixth Amendment "ineffective assistance of counsel" claim in a death penalty case?

HISTORY OF THE CASE

During a 10-day period in September 1976, Washington committed a series of crimes including "three brutal stabbing murders, torture, kidnapping, severe assaults, attempted murders, attempted extortion, and theft." The state of Florida indicted the respondent Washington for kidnapping and murder and appointed a criminal defense lawyer to represent him. After "actively pursuing pre-trial motions and discovery," Washington's lawyer began to feel "hopelessness" about the case when he learned that his client had—against his advice—confessed to two murders. Then, again acting against the advice of his attorney, the respondent waived his right to a jury trial and pleaded guilty to all charges against him. Before sentencing, Washington's attorney spoke on the phone with his client's wife and mother but, other than that, did not seek out character witnesses. Additionally, Washington's attorney did not look for any mitigating evidence concerning his client's emotional state at the time of the murders. However, the attorney, thinking that the admission into evidence of his client's prior criminal record might further damage the case, successfully moved to exclude his "rap sheet."

At the sentencing hearing, Washington's attorney asserted that his client should be spared from capital punishment because he had expressed remorse for his deeds, he had been experiencing severe emotional disturbance at the time of the murders (a circumstance included in Florida's statutory list of mitigating circumstances), and he

was a "fundamentally good person" who "had briefly gone wrong in extremely stressful circumstances." However, the trial judge, determining that there were "insufficient mitigating circumstances . . . to outweigh the aggravating circumstances," imposed the death penalty.

Washington attempted to have his death sentence overturned on a claim of ineffective assistance of counsel under the Sixth Amendment. At the trial court, Washington's ineffective assistance of counsel claim was dismissed because the "respondent had not shown that counsel's assistance reflected any substantial . . . deficiency measurably below that of competent counsel that was likely to have affected the outcome of the sentencing proceeding." Further, the Florida trial court added that "there [was] not even the remotest chance that the outcome would have been any different." The Florida Supreme Court affirmed this decision.

Washington then filed a habeas corpus petition in federal district court, and among his numerous grounds for relief, he again claimed ineffective assistance of counsel. The district court found that "'there does not appear to be a likelihood, or even a significant possibility' that any errors of trial counsel had affected the outcome of the sentencing proceeding." On appeal, the U.S. Court of Appeals for the Fifth Circuit created a new test for addressing "ineffective assistance of counsel claims": The Sixth Amendment, the Court of Appeals stated, "accorded criminal defendants a right to 'counsel reasonably likely to render . . . reasonably effective assistance given the totality of the circumstances.'" The court of appeals then remanded the case with instructions to apply their new framework, and the state of Florida filed a petition for a writ of certiorari seeking review of the court of appeals decision. The U.S. Supreme Court granted certiorari "to consider the standards by which to judge a contention that the Constitution requires that a criminal judgment be overturned because of the actual ineffective assistance of counsel."

SUMMARY OF ARGUMENTS

Washington asserted that he had received ineffective assistance of counsel at trial because his attorney had failed (1) to move for a continuance to prepare for sentencing, (2) to request a psychiatric report, (3) to investigate and present character witnesses, (4) to seek a presentence investigation report, (5) to present meaningful arguments to the sentencing judge, and (6) to investigate the medical examiner's reports or cross-examine the medical experts.

DECISION

Creating its own two-part test, the Court held that Washington failed to establish a claim of ineffective assistance of counsel.

Justice O'Connor wrote the majority opinion. The Court created a two-part test to determine whether an ineffective assistance of counsel claim had merit. First, "the defendant must show that counsel's performance was deficient." According to the Court, this requirement demanded that counsel behaved so poorly that he or she had "[not functioned] as the 'counsel' guaranteed the defendant by the Sixth Amendment." Second, the defendant must demonstrate that his counsel's poor performance actually prevented the defendant from receiving a fair trial. In applying this test, the Court insisted that "judicial scrutiny of counsel's performance must be highly deferential . . . the defendant must overcome the presumption that, under the circumstances, the challenged action 'might be considered sound trial strategy.'" In sum, the U.S. Supreme Court determined that "[courts] must determine whether, in light of all the circumstances, the identified acts or omissions were outside the wide range of professionally competent assistance."

Turning to the facts of the case, Justice O'Connor found that Washington's claim failed to meet the "performance" and "prejudice" components of the ineffective assistance of counsel test. Regarding the performance of the respondent's attorney—who had chosen not to seek additional character evidence—Justice O'Connor stated, "Counsel's strategy choice was well within the range of professionally reasonable judgments." Then, with respect to the prejudice component of the ineffective assistance of counsel test, Justice O'Connor found that, because of the presence of "overwhelming" aggravating factors,

there was little likelihood that any of the actions taken (or not taken) by Washington's attorney would have had an effect on the trial court's ultimate conclusion.

In his dissent, Justice Marshall asserted that the reasonable performance standard, would, in practice, be so "malleable that . . . it will either have no grip at all or will yield excessive variations in the manner in which the Sixth Amendment is interpreted." Then, with respect to the prejudice component of the *Strickland* test, Justice Marshall argued that (1) it is almost impossible to determine whether a convicted defendant would have received a different judgment if defended by another lawyer and (2) every defendant—even those who are "manifestly guilty"—is entitled to a "vigorous" representation in which his or her attorney presents all relevant mitigating evidence.

AFTERMATH

In his book *Litigating in the Shadow of Death*, Welsh S. White stated: "Although *Strickland* appeared to set a low standard for attorneys representing criminal defendants, the [Supreme Court's] opinion left important questions open. In particular, it established no standards for determining when an attorney's performance falls within the acceptable 'range of reasonableness.'" In recent "ineffective assistance of counsel" cases—most notably *Wiggins v. Smith* (2003)—the Supreme Court has refined the decidedly ambiguous standard set forth in *Strickland*. For instance, in *Wiggins*, another capital murder case, the defendant's attorney "[attempted] to justify their limited investigation [into possible mitigating factors] as reflecting a tactical judgment not to present mitigating evidence at sentencing and to pursue an alternate strategy instead." The Supreme Court held that "counsel's investigation into [the defendant's] background did not reflect reasonable professional judgment. . . . The mitigating evidence counsel failed to discover and present in this case is powerful."

SIGNIFICANCE

Even though the *Strickland* decision declared that courts must be deferential to the various strategic choices made by a defense attorney, there are times—such as in *Wiggins*—when those "strategic decisions" can indeed be deemed ineffective assistance of counsel under the Sixth Amendment.

RELATED CASE

Wiggins v. Smith, 539 U.S. 510 (2003)

RECOMMENDED READING

White, Welsh S. *Litigating in the Shadow of Death.* Ann Arbor: University of Michigan Press, 2005.

Case Title: *Ford v. Wainwright*

Legal Citation: 477 U.S. 399

Year of Decision: 1986

KEY ISSUES

Does the Eighth Amendment prohibit the execution of the insane, and if so, should courts hold a hearing to determine the prisoner's mental competency?

HISTORY OF THE CASE

In 1974, Alvin Bernard Ford was convicted of murdering a police officer while robbing a Red Lobster in Ft. Lauderdale, Florida. At the age of 20, Ford was sentenced to death. At the time of his crime, trial, and sentencing, it was not suggested that he was incompetent or suffered any mental impairment. As his appeals were exhausted, Ford's behavior changed considerably. He became obsessed with the Ku Klux Klan and insisted that the Klan was trying to force him to commit suicide. He believed that members of his family were being held hostage and tortured inside the prison. He also believed that he was the only person who could save them. As

his schizophrenic delusions progressed, Ford claimed that he had fired a number of prison officials and appointed nine justices to the Florida Supreme Court and began referring to himself as Pope John Paul III. After Ford's attorneys petitioned the state to find Ford incompetent, the Florida governor appointed three psychiatrists to determine Ford's competency to be executed. This was in accordance with the requirements set out by state statute. The psychiatrists interviewed Ford collectively for 30 minutes and found that he was able to understand his punishment and why he was being punished and, therefore, was competent to be executed. Florida governor Bob Graham signed his first death warrant in November 1981.

Before Ford's second death warrant was signed, Ford's attorney requested a mental health evaluation. A psychiatrist hired by Ford's attorney found that Ford was not competent to be executed because he had "no understanding of why he was being executed, made no connection between the homicide of which he had been convicted and the death penalty, and indeed sincerely believed that he would not be executed because he owned the prisons and could control the Governor through mind waves." With just 14 hours before Ford's scheduled execution in December 1982, Ford's attorney invoked Fla. Stat. §922.07. Under this law, the governor must review individual, independent psychiatric assessments to determine a prisoner's competency for execution. In order to be mentally competent for execution, a prisoner must be able to understand the nature of the death penalty and the reasons why it was imposed on him or her. The 11th Circuit granted a stay of execution. Three psychiatrists evaluated Ford and determined that he did comprehend his sentence despite three separate and different diagnoses. During this evaluation, Ford's attorneys were present but were instructed not to ask questions or present any information about their client's behavior or mental state.

As outlined in the statute, the governor must render a final decision. He signed a second death warrant for Ford's execution in April 1984 without explanation. Again, the 11th

Circuit granted a stay just 14 hours short of his execution. Ford's counsel filed a petition in the U.S. District Court for the Southern District of Florida, seeking an evidentiary hearing on Ford's mental capacity. The petition was denied without a hearing, and the court of appeals affirmed. Ford named Louie Wainwright, the secretary of the Department of Corrections in Florida, in his lawsuit against the state. The U.S. Supreme Court decided to review this case under its discretion.

SUMMARY OF ARGUMENTS

Ford argued that it would be cruel and unusual punishment to execute an insane person. Ford further claimed that Florida's procedures for determining sanity violated his Fourteenth Amendment right to due process.

Wainwright argued that Florida's procedure determining mental capacity was adequate. The three psychiatrists who evaluated Ford all found that he was able to understand the punishment and why he was being punished, and it was in the governor's power to find Ford competent to stand execution and sign the second death warrant.

DECISION

The Court determined that executing the insane did not serve any penological goals and was a violation of the Eighth Amendment. The Court also held that Florida's procedures for determining competency were inadequate.

The opinion, written by Justice Marshall, took a close look at the evolving standards of the Eighth Amendment as consistent with those of a maturing society. Marshall looked at historical information and found that society, throughout time, has been opposed to acts branded as barbaric. In early English and American common law, the execution of insane was considered "savage and inhuman."

The Supreme Court first determined that the execution of an insane prisoner violated the Eighth Amendment protection against cruel and unusual punishment. By looking at common law principles, the Court concluded that the Eighth Amendment was intended to protect against this punishment because the practice was not permitted at the time the Bill of Rights was drafted.

The Court reviewed the process in which Governor Graham made his decision to reissue Ford's death warrant. His decision was based on the conclusions of the three psychiatrists he had selected, whom Ford's attorney was not allowed to question and who spent a total of 30 minutes with Ford. Ford's attorney attempted to submit additional evidence to prove that Ford lacked the required mental capacity to be executed, but Governor Graham did not indicate whether he considered this material when he made his decision.

The mere fact that Ford was unable to provide any additional evidence to show his mental incapacity gave the court pause. It is a long-standing tradition that in cases when someone faces execution, the decision maker should have all relevant and available information to make sure the right decision is reached. Because of this, the Court found Florida's procedure determining mental capacity to be inadequate. The Court thought that Ford had the right to be heard and was denied that right when his lawyer was not allowed to advocate for him.

Florida's competency determinations were left solely to the executive branch. The governor had the ability to sign death warrants on the recommendation of a panel of psychiatrists appointed by the state. The Court held that a proper judicial hearing, in which full procedural rights would be afforded, including the right to have counsel and to cross-examine witnesses, was necessary to determine competency.

AFTERMATH

After the Court issued its decision, Ford was removed from death row and transferred to Florida State Hospital for further evaluation. Nevertheless, his sanity was never determined. In 1989, a trial was conducted, during which Ford was found competent for execution. The 11th Circuit Court of Appeals did not render its final decision, however, as Ford died of natural causes on February 28, 1991.

SIGNIFICANCE

This case provided stricter guidelines for determining requisite mental competency for capital punishment eligibility. Any procedure used to determine a prisoner's mental capacity for execution must provide the decision maker with all relevant information and give the prisoner an opportunity to advocate for himself and to be heard. The Supreme Court concluded, following common law practices, that the Eighth Amendment prohibits the state from subjecting an insane prisoner to the death penalty.

RELATED CASES

Schriro v. Smith, 546 U.S. 6 (2005)

Panetti v. Quarterman, 551 U.S. 930 (2007)

STATUTE AT ISSUE

Fla. Stat., chapter 922, Execution, § 922.07. Proceedings when person under sentence of death appears to be insane

RECOMMENDED READING

Death Penalty Information Center: www.death penaltyinfo.org/mental-illness-and-death-penalty

David S. Friedman, *The Supreme Court's Narrow Majority to Narrow the Death Penalty,* 28 American Bar Association Human Rights 4 (2001).

M. E. Grenander Department of Special Collections and Archives: library.albany.edu/speccoll/findaids/apap159.htm

National Center for State Courts: www.ncsconline.org/wc/CourTopics/FAQs.asp?topic=Cap Pun#FAQ1084

Robert F. Schopp, *Wake Up and Die Right: The Rationale, Standard, and Jurisprudential Significance of the Competency to Face Execution Requirement,* 51 Louisiana Law Review 995 (1991).

Caryn Tamber, *U.S. Court of Appeals, 4th Circuit Rules Man Is Competent Enough to Die, Daily Record* (Baltimore, Md.), March 13, 2006.

Case Title: *Turner v. Murray*

Legal Citation: 476 U.S. 28

Year of Decision: 1986

KEY ISSUE

Does the judge in a capital murder case (in which the defendant and the victim are of different races) have a constitutional obligation to ask potential jurors questions specifically intended to gather information about their racial biases?

HISTORY OF THE CASE

In 1978, Turner (an African-American male) murdered the owner of a jewelry store (a white male) during the course of a robbery in Southampton County, Virginia. Before the voir dire phase of Turner's capital murder trial—which was conducted in Northampton County, Virginia, some 80 miles away from the crime scene—Turner's attorney gave the judge a list of proposed questions to ask the potential jurors. Among them was the following: "The defendant . . . is a member of the Negro race. The victim . . . was a white Caucasian. Will these facts prejudice you against [Turner] or affect your ability to render a fair and impartial verdict based solely on the evidence?" However, the trial judge did not ask this question (though he did ask the prospective jurors whether any of them were aware of any reason why they would be unable "to render a fair and impartial verdict," to which they all responded, "no").

After receiving the death sentence, Turner appealed to the Virginia Supreme Court on multiple grounds. Among them was that the trial judge "deprived him of his constitutional right to a fair and impartial jury by refusing to question prospective jurors on racial prejudice." The Virginia Supreme Court upheld Turner's death sentence, and Turner then sought, and was denied, habeas relief in both federal district court and the U.S. Court of Appeals for the Fourth Circuit. The U.S.

Supreme Court then granted certiorari to review the Fourth Circuit's decision that "petitioner was not constitutionally entitled to have potential jurors questioned concerning racial prejudice."

SUMMARY OF ARGUMENTS

Turner argued that because of the "substantial likelihood of racial prejudice in this kind of case," the trial judge should be constitutionally required to ask potential jurors whether the victim's race would have an effect on their ability to render an impartial verdict. At oral argument, the counsel for Turner stated as follows:

> What often happens in capital cases is that the jury considers in some way or another the relative worth of the life of the defendant against the relative worth of the life of the man he killed, and it is unfortunately the case that . . . when the blacks are the victims . . . the death penalty does not get applied. . . . All that we are asking in this case is that black capital defendants have the right to be sure that inadmissible influences such as race not be allowed to decide who lives and who dies.

The state of Virginia, meanwhile, argued that the trial judge satisfied his constitutional obligations when he asked the jurors "whether any of them were aware of any reason why they would be unable to render a 'fair and impartial verdict.'" The state also pointed out that when Turner's attorney requested that the judge read the "racial bias" question, "the petitioner's attorney made no proffer to the court of any reasons why the question should be asked."

DECISION

The U.S. Supreme Court reversed the decision of the Fourth Circuit and held that "a defendant accused of an interracial capital crime is entitled to have prospective jurors informed of the victim's race and questioned on the issue of racial bias."

In delivering the opinion of the Court, Justice White offered the Fourth Circuit's description of the key issue in this case: "whether, under all of the circumstances presented, there was a constitution-

ally significant likelihood that, absent questioning about racial prejudice, the jurors would not be indifferent as [they stand] unsworne." Justice White observed that the Virginia death penalty statute gave the jurors a broad range of discretion, as it allowed them to consider how much weight to give to any aggravating or mitigating factors presented at trial. Because of this, Justice White thought that the power given to juries by the Virginia death penalty statute created "a unique opportunity for racial prejudice to operate, but remain undetected."

"On the facts of this case," Justice White stated,

> a juror who believes that blacks are . . . morally inferior might well be influenced by that belief in deciding whether [the petitioner Turner's] crime involved the aggravating factors specified under Virginia law. . . . More subtle, less consciously held racial attitudes could also influence a juror's decision in this case. Fear of blacks, which could easily be stirred up by the violent facts of [this] crime, might incline a juror to favor the death penalty.

Justice White concluded his opinion by offering two arguments in favor of this voir dire requirement. First, Justice White asserted, the rule was "minimally intrusive," as the trial judge "[retained] discretion as to the form and number of questions on the subject, including the decision whether to question the [prospective jurors] individually or collectively." Second, the decision to remand this case so that this rule could be applied did not affect the verdict rendered at the guilt phase of the proceeding: "Our judgment in this case," Justice White wrote, "is that there was an unacceptable risk of racial prejudice infecting the *capital sentencing proceeding.*"

In his dissent, Justice Powell argued that the Court's new rule presumed the existence of racial prejudice in the jury—even though no evidence had been brought forth to prove that it had somehow affected the outcome of the trial. Justice Powell stated as follows:

> Nothing in this record suggests that racial bias played any role in the jurors' delibera-

tions. . . . From *voir dire* through the close of trial, no circumstance suggests that the trial judge's refusal to inquire particularly into racial bias posed "an impermissible threat to the fair trial guaranteed by due process."

Justice Powell concluded his dissent by asserting that the mandatory inclusion of such questioning would unnecessarily place racial issues at the center of such a trial, thus distracting jurors from the actual merits of the case at hand.

AFTERMATH

After this case was remanded, Willie Lloyd Turner's death sentence was upheld. After spending 15 years on death row and being scheduled for execution some six times (and receiving five stays of execution), he was put to death on May 25, 1995, by lethal injection.

SIGNIFICANCE

Defendants involved in an interracial crime are entitled under the Sixth and Fourteenth Amendments to question potential jury members about racial bias. If a court does not allow such questioning, subsequent death penalties are vacated.

RELATED CASES

McCleskey v. Kemp, 481 U.S. 279 (1987)

Morgan v. Illinois, 504 U.S. 719 (1992)

RECOMMENDED READING

Brewer, Thomas W., "Race and Jurors' Receptivity to Mitigation in Capital Cases: The Effect of Jurors', Defendants', and Victims' Race in Combination," *Law and Human Behavior* 28, no. 5 (2004): 529–545.

Case Title: *McCleskey v. Kemp*

Legal Citations: 481 U.S. 279; 107 S. Ct. 1756

Year of Decision: 1987

KEY ISSUES

Does a statistical study showing that black defendants convicted of murdering white victims were disproportionately given the death penalty necessitate a finding that the capital punishment system is unconstitutional?

HISTORY OF THE CASE

Warren McCleskey was a black man convicted of two counts of armed robbery and one count of murder in the Superior Court of Fulton County, Georgia. The date of the conviction was October 12, 1978. McCleskey's conviction arose out of the murder of a white police officer that occurred during the course of a robbery of a furniture store. At the sentencing hearing, the jury was asked to consider imposing the death penalty, as it could do only if it found that the murder was accompanied by one of the statutory aggravating circumstances set forth in the Georgia Code Annotated, § 17-10-30(c). This statute also required the jury to consider whether there was any mitigating evidence that would weigh in favor of McCleskey. The jury did find that the robbery constituted an aggravating circumstance, and McCleskey did not present any mitigating evidence. McCleskey was sentenced to death.

On appeal to the Georgia Supreme Court, the court affirmed the conviction and the sentence. The U.S. Supreme Court denied McCleskey's writ of certiorari. After seeking post-conviction relief in state courts, McCleskey eventually field a writ of habeas corpus in the U.S. District Court for the Northern District of Georgia. In his petition, McCleskey claimed that the Georgia capital sentencing process was unconstitutional in that it violated the Eighth and Fourteenth Amendments to the U.S. Constitution. In support of this claim, McCleskey offered a statistical study authored by Professors David Baldus, Charles Pulaski, and George Woodworth (which was known as the "Baldus study"). The study was based upon an analysis of more than 2,000 murder cases that occurred in Georgia during the 1970s and purported to show a disparity in the imposition of the death penalty based upon the race of the murder victim as well as the race of the defendant. The study showed that black defendants convicted of murdering white victims had the highest chance of receiving the death penalty.

The district court held an evidentiary hearing and closely considered the Baldus study but denied McCleskey's claim for relief. On appeal to the U.S. Court of Appeals for the 11th Circuit, the court again considered the constitutional arguments raised by the Baldus study but held that even if the study was accurate, it was insufficient to show a violation of either the Eighth or Fourteenth Amendment. The U.S. Supreme Court then granted McCleskey's petition for certiorari.

SUMMARY OF ARGUMENTS

McCleskey first presented his claim that the Georgia capital punishment statute violated the equal protection clause of the Fourteenth Amendment to the U.S. Constitution because of the evidence that the race of the defendant and the race of the victim resulted in the disproportionate imposition of the death penalty. McCleskey also argued that the Georgia capital punishment system as a whole violated the Eighth Amendment's prohibition against cruel and unusual punishment.

DECISION

The Court found that the death penalty, as applied in this case, was not disproportionate within any recognized meaning of the Eighth Amendment.

In a decision written by Justice Powell, the Court began its analysis by looking at McCleskey's equal protection claims under the Fourteenth Amendment. The Court emphasized that the defendant had the burden of proving that purposeful discrimination occurred and that this discrimination existed in his particular case. The Court acknowledged that it had accepted statistical studies as proof of intent to discriminate, but only in limited circumstances. Because McCleskey offered no specific evidence that racial discrimination played a role in the imposition of the death penalty in his particular case, his equal protection argument failed. Neither could McCleskey show that the Georgia legislature acted with discrimina-

tory intent when enacting its capital punishment sentencing system.

In ruling upon McCleskey's Eighth Amendment claim, the court summarized the evolution of its jurisprudence on the death penalty, extensively discussing the cases of *Furman v. Georgia* (1972) and *Gregg v. Georgia* (1976). The opinion noted that the Court has recognized a constitutionally permissible range of discretion when courts impose the death penalty.

The majority opinion did discuss the Baldus study at length but found that the conclusions embodied in the study were best presented to a state's legislature, which has the responsibility for determining the appropriate punishment for particular crimes.

In dissent, Justice Brennan, joined by Justice Marshall, declared his belief that the death penalty was in all cases unconstitutional as a violation of the Eighth Amendment's prohibition against cruel and unusual punishment. As for the Baldus study, Justice Brennan believed that it showed a significant chance that race played a role in determining whether McCleskey was sentenced to death.

AFTERMATH

McCleskey continued to appeal his conviction and again had his case heard on different grounds before the Supreme Court in the case of *McCleskey v. Zant* (1991). He was executed in September 1991.

SIGNIFICANCE

McCleskey was but one of several death penalty cases of the 1970s and 1980s that struggled to define the acceptable parameters of how the death penalty could be applied by the states. Some commentators consider the *McCleskey* case to have been the last major challenge to the death penalty at the Supreme Court level.

RELATED CASES

Furman v. Georgia, 408 U.S. 238 (1972)

Gregg v. Georgia, 428 U.S. 153 (1976)

McCleskey v. Zant, 499 U.S. 467 (1991)

RECOMMENDED READING

Biko Agozino, *How Scientific Is Criminal Justice? A Methodological Critique of Research on* McCleskey v. Kemp *and Other Capital Cases*, 17 National Black Law Journal 84 (2003).

Baldus, David C., George Woodworth and Charles A. Pulaski, Jr. *Equal Justice and the Death Penalty: A Legal and Empirical Analysis*. Boston: Northeastern University Press, 1990.

Steven Graines and Justin Wyatt, *The Rehnquist Court, Legal Process Theory, and* McCleskey v. Kemp, 28 American Journal of Criminal Law 1 (2000).

Randall Kennedy, McCleskey v. Kemp: *Race, Capital Punishment, and the Supreme Court*, 101 Harvard Law Review 1388 (1988).

Evan Tsen Lee and Ashutosh Bhagwat, *The McCleskey Puzzle: Remedying Prosecutorial Discrimination against Black Victims in Capital Sentencing*, 1998 The Supreme Court Review 145.

Case Title: *Thompson v. Oklahoma*

Legal Citation: 487 U.S. 815

Year of Decision: 1988

KEY ISSUE

Does a state's execution of a person for a crime committed at the age of 15 constitute "cruel and unusual punishment" under the Eighth Amendment of the Constitution?

HISTORY OF THE CASE

When William Wayne Thompson was 15 and a child under Oklahoma law, he and three older people brutally murdered Thompson's brother-in-law, Charles Keene. Before Thompson's trial, the state of Oklahoma filed a request that the District Court of Grady County certify Thompson as an "adult," which was granted. Thompson appealed his adult certification all the way up to the Oklahoma Court of Criminal Appeals, which affirmed the certification. The evidence at trial was overwhelming against the defendants, and all four men were convicted of the murder and sentenced to death. Thompson appealed his sentence, claiming that his age when the crime was committed would make his execution cruel and unusual punishment. The court of criminal appeals upheld his punishment as constitutional. From this judgment, Thompson appealed to the U.S. Supreme Court.

SUMMARY OF THE ARGUMENTS

Thompson argued that the execution of any person who committed a crime before reaching the age of 18 would be cruel and unusual and, therefore, prohibited by the Eighth Amendment.

Oklahoma argued that the age at the time a crime was committed should only be presented as a mitigating circumstance and not bar imposition of the death penalty in cases involving juveniles. The state also argued that the minimum age of execution should be left to the discretion of state legislatures, which may examine supporting data and define the age of criminal culpability accordingly.

DECISION

The Court, in a plurality opinion by Justice Stevens and a concurrence by Justice O'Connor, overturned the Oklahoma Court of Criminal Appeals and held that Thompson's execution did violate the Constitution's prohibition of cruel and unusual punishment.

Writing for a four-justice plurality, Justice Stevens first noted that the term "cruel and unusual punishment" is not defined by the Eighth Amendment and that, therefore, judges deciding its meaning must be guided by society's "evolving standards of decency." Justice Stevens asserted that such standards could be determined by looking at the actions of state legislatures and the sentences returned by juries in murder trials. Justice Stevens pointed out that Oklahoma's legislature had specifically restricted the rights of persons under the age of 16 to engage in certain activities.

In addition, Oklahoma's criminal laws distinguished 15-year-olds as "children" and prosecuted them in juvenile, as opposed to adult, court. Similar restrictions and distinctions exist, in various forms, in every state. Such uniformity in legislative treatment of 15-year-olds indicates that our society views them as incapable of acting as adults do, motivated by full consideration of the consequences of their actions. Moreover, Justice Stevens noted that juries almost never sentence 15-year-old offenders to death, indicating society's general rejection of this punishment. These facts reinforce and justify the conclusion that it is U.S. society's generally held belief that children are and should be punished differently than adults for the same acts. In addition, the views expressed by the American Bar Association and the American Legal Institute, along with the standards of other countries sharing the Anglo-American legal heritage, both argued in favor of limiting the punishment of minor offenders. With the weight of all this evidence, Justice Stevens concluded that social opposition was significant enough to label the execution of a 15-year-old offender cruel and unusual.

In her concurrence, Justice O'Connor agreed with the plurality that examining society's evolving standards of decency is the proper inquiry to determine the meaning of cruel and unusual. However, she was unsure whether the existence of a national consensus against executing 15-year-old offenders could be inferred from the plurality's evidence. Justice O'Connor noted that 19 states, Oklahoma included, had legislation that allowed 15-year-old offenders to be certified as adults in certain criminal prosecutions, thereby rendering them punishable as adults. But in none of those states did the legislature expressly set a minimum age for an offender to be death eligible. It was, therefore, quite possible that each of these legislatures did not consider the possibility that one so young when he or she committed a crime would be executed. This lack of explicit consideration, especially given a possible national consensus against such an execution, rendered the execution unacceptable.

Justice Scalia dissented. He argued that the federal government and a majority of the states that use the death penalty allowed for the possibility that offenders as young as Mr. Thompson be sentenced to death. He also noted a legislative trend toward lowering the age at which people could be certified as adult, which spoke against a national rejection of executing juvenile offenders.

AFTERMATH

In 2005, the court declared in *Roper v. Simmons* that it was cruel and unusual punishment to execute anyone who was under the age of 18 at the time the crime was committed.

SIGNIFICANCE

The prohibition on executing a 15-year-old offender set out in *Thompson* established the minimum age for execution for nearly two decades.

RELATED CASES

Gregg v. Georgia, 428 U.S. 153 (1976)

Roper v. Simmons, 543 U.S. 551 (2005)

STATUTE AT ISSUE

Oklahoma Stat., tit. 10 § 1101(1) (Supp. 1987), 1112(b) (1981)

RECOMMENDED READING

Katherine H. Federle, *Emancipation and Execution: Transferring Children to Criminal Court in Capital Cases,* 1996 Wisconsin Law Review 447.

Joseph L. Hoffmann, *On the Perils of Line-Drawing: Juveniles and the Death Penalty,* 40 Hastings Law Journal 229 (1989).

Victor L. Streib, *Executing Juvenile Offenders: The Ultimate Denial of Juvenile Justice,* 14 Stanford Law & Policy Review 121 (2003).

Case Title: *Penry v. Lynaugh*

Legal Citation: 492 U.S. 302

Year of Decision: 1989

KEY ISSUE

Does the Eighth Amendment prohibit the execution of mentally challenged defendants upon conviction?

HISTORY OF THE CASE

On October 25, 1979, Pamela Carpenter was raped, beaten, and stabbed with a pair of scissors in her home. Before she died, she was able to describe her assailant, leading police to John Penry, who was on parole from a previous rape conviction. At a competency hearing, it was determined that Penry was mentally challenged and had the mental age of a six-and-a-half-year-old. However, the jury found Penry competent to stand trial.

At trial, the jury rejected Penry's insanity defense and found him guilty of capital murder. During the sentencing hearing, the jury was asked to consider three "special issues"; if they unanimously answered "yes" to all three, the trial court had to sentence Penry to death; otherwise, Penry would have been sentenced to life imprisonment. The jury answered yes to all three issues, and Penry was sentenced to death despite the defense's objections to the jury's inability to consider aggravating and mitigating circumstances and the argument that executing the mentally challenged would amount to cruel and unusual punishment under the Eighth Amendment.

The Texas Court of Criminal Appeals affirmed Penry's conviction and sentence. On appeal, the U.S. Supreme Court granted certiorari.

SUMMARY OF ARGUMENTS

Penry argued that his sentence violated the Eighth Amendment because executing a mentally challenged person constituted cruel and unusual punishment because mentally challenged people do not possess the level of moral culpability to justify imposition of the death sentence. He further argued that the emerging national consensus opposed executing the mentally challenged.

Penry further argued that the trial court failed to instruct the jury on how to weigh mitigating factors when addressing the three special issues. Because they were limited to these three questions, Penry argued that the jury could not fully consider and give effect to the mitigating evidence of his mental retardation and abused childhood when it made its sentencing decision. He argued that this evidence had relevance to his moral culpability beyond the scope of the special issues and that the jury was unable to express a reasoned moral response to determine whether the death penalty was appropriate in this particular case.

The state of Texas argued that there was insufficient evidence about the existence of a national consensus against executing the mentally challenged. The state further argued that there are adequate procedural safeguards that protect the interests of mentally challenged persons.

DECISION

The Court began by discussing whether granting Penry the relief he sought would create a "new rule," because, if so, and subject to few exceptions (if it places certain kinds of primary, private, individual conduct beyond the power of the criminal lawmaking authority to proscribe any rules prohibiting a certain punishment for a class of defendants because of their status or offense), the rule could not be applied or announced in cases on collateral review. Essentially, a "new rule" is created if the result was not dictated by precedent in existence when the defendant's conviction became final. Penry sought a rule that when juries are given jury instructions, they be told to consider relevant mitigating evidence regarding whether a defendant should be subject to death. The Court concluded that this is not a new rule because it did not impose any new obligations on the state of Texas, and other relevant precedent made clear that a state could not prevent the sentencer from considering mitigating evidence against imposition of the death penalty.

The Court next addressed the jury instructions regarding aggravating and mitigating evidence regarding Penry's sentence, stating that "in the absence of instructions informing the jury that it could consider and give effect to the mitigating evidence of Penry's mental retardation and abused background by declining to impose the death penalty, we conclude that the jury was not provided with a vehicle for expressing its 'reasoned moral response' to that evidence in rendering its sentencing decision." The Court expressed concern that it did not want to risk having the death penalty imposed in a case that may call for a less severe penalty because that would be incompatible with the demands of the Eighth and Fourteenth Amendments.

Specifically, the three questions asked to the jurors were Did Penry act deliberately when he murdered Pamela Carpenter? Is there a probability that he will be dangerous in the future? And did he act unreasonably in response to provocation? The Court thought that a reasonable juror could answer yes to all three of these and still feel that the defendant deserved a less severe penalty because of mitigating factors. Thus, the jury was deprived of taking into account all relevant evidence regarding the defendant's moral culpability when determining his sentence. Accordingly, the Court held that mitigating evidence regarding the defendant's mental status should have been allowed when sentencing was determined.

Addressing Penry's claim that executing a mentally challenged person would constitute cruel and unusual punishment, the Court stated that if it ruled that way, it would create a "new rule." However, "such a rule would fall under the first exception to the general rule of nonretroactivity and would be applicable to defendants on collateral review." The Court then turned to the merits of Penry's claim, taking into consideration whether evolving standards of decency are opposed to the execution of mentally challenged persons. The Court looked at objective evidence, noting that only two state statutes prohibited the execution of the mentally challenged and that 14 other states banned capital punishment completely. However, the Court ruled that there was insufficient evidence of a national consensus for it to conclude that the Eighth Amendment categorically prohibited it.

The Court held that evidence of mental retardation can be considered a mitigating factor that might diminish the defendant's culpability, but it could not conclude that all mentally challenged persons lacked the cognitive and moral capacity to act with a degree of culpability capable of

receiving the death penalty. The Court noted that studies had shown that those suffering mental deficiencies vary tremendously in their abilities, and some are capable of learning and improving their mental capabilities. The Court rejected Penry's claim that his mental age was determined to be that of a seven-year-old, because there was no finding by the trial judge or jury regarding Penry's mental age, and the idea of mental age was inherently problematic. Accordingly, the Court reversed Penry's sentence because the jury was not informed that it could consider mitigating factors regarding Penry's mental status and affirmed the lower court's decision that the Eighth Amendment did not prohibit the execution of persons who had mental deficiencies.

Justice Brennan wrote an opinion, joined by Justice Marshall, in which he concurred that mitigating evidence should have been taken into consideration during the sentencing phase of Penry's trial. However, Justice Brennan dissented in part, arguing that the Eighth Amendment prohibits the execution of mentally challenged persons who lack moral culpability. He further argued that the goals of punishment (deterrence, retribution, etc.) were inapplicable as to mentally challenged persons and, thus, punishing them was a purposeless imposition of pain and suffering. Justice Stevens also wrote an opinion in which he concurred in part and dissented in part, joined by Justice Blackmun. Like Justice Brennan, he agreed that mitigating circumstances should be considered upon imposition of a sentence in a capital case, but he disagreed with the majority's view that retroactivity of the law applied to capital cases. He also argued that execution of those suffering from mental retardation was unconstitutional.

Justice Scalia, too, wrote an opinion, in which he concurred in part and dissented in part, joined by Justices White and Kennedy, as well as Chief Justice Rehnquist. Justice Scalia agreed with the majority's view that the Eighth Amendment did not prohibit execution of mentally challenged persons. However, he disagreed with the majority that Penry's sentence was unconstitutional because the jury was not permitted to consider mitigating factors regarding his mental condition and background of abuse. He stated that the Court had never held that the Constitution requires the consideration of mitigating evidence, and he suggested that these considerations produce unpredictable sentences.

AFTERMATH

The Court again addressed the issue of whether sentencing a mentally challenged person to death constituted cruel and unusual punishment in *Atkins v. Virginia* (2002). Fifteen years had passed since its decision in *Penry*, and the Court noted that evolving standards of decency warranted reconsideration of the issue. The Court held that a national consensus against executing mentally challenged persons had emerged and, thus, held that such an execution violated the Eighth Amendment of the Constitution. The Court also noted that serious concern had arisen as to whether retribution and deterrence of capital crimes apply to mentally challenged offenders because of their lessened culpability.

SIGNIFICANCE

In this controversial decision, the U.S. Supreme Court held that the Eighth Amendment does not prohibit the use of the death penalty for mentally challenged persons. The Court further held that the jury in John Penry's rape and murder trial was improperly instructed because it was not allowed to consider certain mitigating factors regarding Penry's mental deficiencies when determining his sentence.

RELATED CASES

Furman v. Georgia, 408 U.S. 238 (1972)

Coker v. Georgia, 433 U.S. 584 (1977)

Thompson v. Oklahoma, 487 U.S. 815 (1988)

Atkins v. Virginia, 536 U.S. 304 (2002)

Roper v. Simmons, 543 U.S. 551 (2005)

Kennedy v. Louisiana, 554 U.S. 407 (2008)

RECOMMENDED READING

Lyn Entzeroth, *Putting the Mentally Challenged Criminal Defendant to Death: Charting the Development of a National Consensus to Exempt the Mentally Challenged from the Death Penalty*, 52 Alabama Law Review 911 (2001).

Lyndsey Sloan, *Evolving Standards of Decency: The Evolution of a National Consensus Granting the Mentally Challenged Sanctuary*, 31 Capital University Law Review 351 (2003).

Peggy M. Tobolowsky, *The Road to* Atkins *and Beyond in Texas: The Tale of One Mentally Challenged Capital Offender*, 59 Baylor Law Review 735 (2007).

———, *Texas and the Mentally Challenged Capital Offender*, 30 Thurgood Marshall Law Review 39 (2004).

Case Name: *Stanford v. Kentucky* and *Wilkins v. Missouri*

Legal Citation: 492 U.S. 391

Year of Decision: 1989

KEY ISSUE

Does the execution of a person for a crime committed at age 16 or 17 violate the cruel and unusual punishment prohibition in the Eighth Amendment?

HISTORY OF THE CASE

The petitioner Stanford was 17 years and four months old when he and an accomplice repeatedly raped and then killed Barbel Poore while robbing a gas station. After he was arrested, Stanford was certified to stand trial as an adult pursuant to Kentucky law because of the severity of his crime and the inability of the juvenile system to treat his past instances of delinquency adequately. He was convicted of murder, first-degree sodomy, first-degree robbery, and receiving stolen property. He was sentenced to death and 45 years in prison. The Kentucky Supreme Court affirmed.

The petitioner Wilkins, when he was 16 years and six months old, robbed a convenience store and, in the process, stabbed Nancy Allen to death. "Relying on the 'viciousness, force and violence' of the alleged crime, petitioner's maturity, and the failure of the juvenile justice system to rehabilitate him after previous delinquent acts, the juvenile court" certified Wilkins as an adult for trial. He pled guilty to charges of first-degree murder, armed criminal action, and carrying a concealed weapon and was sentenced to death. The Missouri Supreme Court affirmed the sentence, rejecting the Eighth Amendment argument.

SUMMARY OF ARGUMENTS

Both petitioners argued that their executions would violate the "evolving standards of decency that mark the progress of a maturing society," which is an accepted judicial test for what constitutes cruel and unusual punishment. The petitioners found these evolving standards in the actual practices of states allowing for execution of 16- and 17-year-old offenders. Specifically, these states had executed far fewer such offenders compared to offenders 18 and older. Additionally, the petitioners pointed to a recently enacted federal statute permitting execution for certain drug offenses but limiting its application to offenders 18 and older.

DECISION

Justice Scalia delivered the opinion of the Court. Accepting "evolving [*American*] standards of decency" as the only standard for determining cruel and unusual punishment under which petitioners might prevail, Justice Scalia decided that American society had not conclusively demonstrated a consensus rejection of executing juvenile offenders.

First, of the 37 states that allowed execution, Justice Scalia noted that only 15 precluded the possibility of executing 16-year-old offenders, and only 12 precluded executing 17-year-old offenders. Second, looking to one narrow federal drug law ignores the fact that many general federal laws carrying the death penalty allow for 16- and 17-year-old offenders to be certified as adults for

trial and, thereby, become death eligible. Thus, federal law provides no basis for finding a consensus against executing juvenile offenders.

Finally, while conceding that in practice far fewer juvenile offenders have been executed than adults, Justice Scalia discounted the importance of such statistics with respect to the issue in question. While the statistics showed that prosecutors and juries rarely sought to impose the death penalty on 16- and 17-year-old offenders, the fact that sometimes such sentences were imposed indicated that there was not a categorical rejection of juvenile execution. In a portion of his opinion not joined by Justice O'Connor and, thus, not representing a majority of the Court, Justice Scalia went on to reject arguments that sought to set the minimum age for offenders to be death eligible at 18 that were based either on state statutes setting the age of 18 for other age-based classifications (such as those granting the right to vote, drive, or drink alcohol) or on indicia other than enacted laws and their application (such as public opinion polls; the views of special interest groups, professional organizations, or other nations; and/or socioscientific data about the mental development of 16- and 17-year-olds).

Justice O'Connor refused to join in certain parts of Justice Scalia's opinion because she believed that, in certain circumstances, the considerations mentioned served a recognizable role and should not be categorically excluded.

Writing in dissent, Justice Brennan believed that killing someone for a crime committed under the age of 18 constituted cruel and unusual punishment. This conclusion followed from a broader consideration than that engaged in by Justice Scalia, which was explicitly limited to legislative enactments and applications thereof. While Justice Brennan believed that even Justice Scalia's limited consideration of the question should conclude execution of juvenile offenders to be unconstitutional, his Eighth Amendment analysis asked two additional questions. First, was there "disproportion between the punishment imposed and the defendant's blameworthiness?" Noting the societal and legislative recognition that juveniles are, as a general class, less blameworthy than adults, Justice Brennan answered this question in the affirmative. Second, did the punishment serve either of the principal purposes of the death penalty, retribution or deterrence? Because the retributive effect of punishment depends heavily on the defendant's possessing a sufficient degree of culpability, which juveniles generally lack, the retributive effect of executing juveniles was small. Similarly, because a punishment's deterrent effect requires a sufficient degree of foresight and judgment, which again juveniles generally lack, the deterrent effect was similarly small. Thus, the execution of juvenile offenders served no true constitutionally valid purpose.

AFTERMATH

This case, along with *Thompson v. Oklahoma* (1988), decided one year earlier, set, for a time, the minimum age of eligibility for the death penalty at 16 years old. However, the 2005 case of *Roper v. Simmons* (2005) held it unconstitutional to execute anyone who was under the age of 18 at the time the crime was committed.

SIGNIFICANCE

This decision expanded the reach of capital punishment. It was nearly 16 years before the Supreme Court again addressed the constitutionality of the minimum age for imposing the death penalty in *Roper*.

RELATED CASES

In re Gault, 387 U.S. 1 (1967)

In re Winship, 397 U.S. 358 (1970)

Thompson v. Oklahoma, 487 U.S. 815 (1988)

Roper v. Simmons, 543 U.S. 551 (2005)

RECOMMENDED READING

James R. Acker, *Dual and Unusual: Competing Views of Death Penalty Adjudication,* 26 Criminal Law Bulletin 123 (1990).

Jeffery Fagan and Valerie West, *The Decline of the Juvenile Death Penalty: Scientific Evidence of*

Evolving Norms, 95 Journal of Criminal Law & Criminology 427 (2005).

Kenneth E. Gewerth and Clifford K. Dorne, *Imposing the Death Penalty on Juvenile Murderers: A Constitutional Assessment,* 75 Judicature 6 (1991).

Case Title: *Blystone v. Pennsylvania*

Legal Citation: 494 U.S. 299

Year of Decision: 1990

KEY ISSUE

Does a state death penalty statute violate the Eighth Amendment if it requires a mandatory death sentence when a jury unanimously finds that aggravated circumstances outweigh any mitigating factors in a death penalty eligible case?

HISTORY OF THE CASE

In September 1983, Scott Wayne Blystone was driving on a Pennsylvania road and picked up a hitchhiker with the intent of robbing him. Shortly afterward, Blystone pulled out his revolver, stopped the car, and ordered the hitchhiker onto a nearby field. After removing $13 from the hitchhiker's wallet, Blystone shot him six times in the back of the head.

Blystone was charged with first-degree murder, robbery, criminal conspiracy to commit homicide, and criminal conspiracy to commit robbery. He was eligible for the death penalty under Pennsylvania state law. Under the Pennsylvania capital punishment system, Blystone had a two-part trial with separate guilt and sentencing phases. During the guilt phase, the jury convicted Blystone on all charges. During the sentencing phase—in which Pennsylvania law required the jury to impose the death penalty if they found more aggravating factors than mitigating factors—the jury found as an aggravating factor that Blystone had "committed a killing while in the perpetration of a felony," and seeing no mitigating circumstances, the jury was then obligated to impose capital punishment. On automatic appeal, the Supreme Court of Pennsylvania affirmed the decision of the lower court. The Supreme Court of the United States then granted certiorari.

SUMMARY OF ARGUMENTS

Blystone challenged the Pennsylvania capital sentencing statute as it was applied to his case, alleging that his Eighth Amendment rights had been violated because the mandatory imposition of the death penalty precluded the jury from evaluating the weight of the aggravating circumstance and that the mandatory imposition of the death penalty also "limited the jury's consideration of unenumerated mitigating circumstances."

The state of Pennsylvania, meanwhile, argued that its death penalty statute was constitutional because it did not require the jury to impose capital punishment until two thresholds had been passed (the first, that the defendant committed first-degree murder; the second, that the "aggravating circumstance" had been established beyond a reasonable doubt) and the statute also allowed the jury to consider "all relevant mitigating evidence in making the decision as to whether or not to impose the death penalty."

DECISION

The Court held that the Pennsylvania death penalty statute did not violate the Eighth Amendment of the Constitution.

In delivering the opinion of the Court, Justice Rehnquist first noted that statutes mandating that the jury impose the death penalty in the finding of aggravating circumstances (or, conversely, in the absence of certain mitigating circumstances) had been examined previously—and struck down if they mandated the imposition of capital punishment without allowing the "particularized consideration of relevant aspects of the character and record of each convicted defendant." The Pennsylvania statute, Rehnquist observed, seemed facially constitutional (unlike the statutes in *Woodson v. North Carolina* [1976] and *Lockett v.*

Ohio [1978]) because it "[provided] a jury with a nonexclusive list of mitigating factors which may be taken into account—including a 'catchall' category."

Regarding Blystone's first "unconstitutional as applied" argument (the mandatory imposition of the death penalty under the Pennsylvania statute violated the Eighth Amendment as it precluded the jury from evaluating the weight of the aggravating circumstance), Justice Rehnquist stated that "the presence of aggravating circumstances serves the purpose of limiting the class of death-eligible defendants, and the Eighth Amendment does not require that [they] be . . . weighed by a jury." Then, with respect to Blystone's second "unconstitutional as applied" argument (the statute violated the Eighth Amendment because it did not allow the jury to consider "unenumerated" mitigating circumstances), Justice Rehnquist stated that, at Blystone's trial, the judge informed the jury that it could consider any mitigating factor that seemed relevant to the case. The jury, Justice Rehnquist noted, was in fact instructed that "it was entitled to consider 'any other mitigating matter concerning the character or record of the defendant, or the circumstances of his offense.'"

In his dissent, Justice Brennan argued that because the Pennsylvania capital sentencing statute required that the jury impose death when it found more aggravating than mitigating factors, the jury was, thus, unable to make an independent judgment—and the statute should have been deemed unconstitutional. Justice Brennan then concluded his dissent with the following statement: "Even if I did not believe the Pennsylvania statute unconstitutionally deprives the jury of discretion to impose a life sentence, I would vacate [Blystone's] sentence. I adhere to my belief that the death penalty is in all circumstances cruel and unusual punishment."

AFTERMATH

In *Furman v. Georgia* (1972), the Supreme Court held that the existing death penalty laws were so "arbitrary" and "capricious" that they violated the Eighth Amendment. In response to this ruling, many states—including Pennsylvania—enacted capital sentencing statutes that employed what the legislatures of those states considered to be highly objective standards so that the death penalty would be consistently applied to specific fact patterns.

In the wake of decisions such as *Blystone,* the Supreme Court seemed willing to uphold death penalty laws as long as they employed a standardized, rational procedure (such as the mandatory imposition of the death penalty where aggravating factors outnumbered mitigating factors) and that they allowed the trier of fact to consider *all* relevant mitigating factors. *Blystone* seems to stand for the proposition that, as long as these two criteria are satisfied in the eyes of the Supreme Court, a state's death penalty statute will probably be upheld.

SIGNIFICANCE

Under *Blystone,* the Constitution does not require that juries consider aggravating circumstances when the death penalty is a possible sentence. Accordingly, it is at the discretion of the states to require such factors in a jury's decision to render the death penalty as a sentence.

RELATED CASES

Furman v. Georgia, 408 U.S. 238 (1972)

Woodson v. North Carolina, 428 U.S. 280 (1976)

Lockett v. Ohio, 438 U.S. 586 (1978)

Odle v. Vasquez, 754 F.Supp. 749 (1990)

STATUTE AT ISSUE

42 Pa.C.S.A. § 9711. Sentencing procedure for murder of the first degree

RECOMMENDED READING

David Barron, *I Did Not Want to Kill Him but Thought I Had to: In Light of Penry II's Interpretation of* Blystone, *Why the Constitution Requires Jury Instructions on How to Give Effect to Relevant Mitigating Evidence in Capital Cases,* 11 Journal of Law and Policy, 207 (2002).

Capital Punishment, 37 Georgetown Law Journal Annual Review of Criminal Procedure 764 (2008).

Jeffrey L. Kirchmeier, *Aggravating and Mitigating Factors: The Paradox of Today's Arbitrary and Mandatory Capital Punishment Scheme,* 6 William & Mary Bill of Rights 345 (1998).

Sandra Shultz Newman, Eric Rayz, and Scott Eric Friedman, *Capital Sentencing: The Effect of Adding Aggravators to Death Penalty Statutes in Pennsylvania,* 65 University of Pittsburgh Law Review 457 (2004).

Case Title: *Atkins v. Virginia*

Legal Citation: 536 U.S. 304

Year of Decision: 2002

KEY ISSUE

Is the execution of mentally retarded persons "cruel and unusual punishment," prohibited by the Eighth Amendment?

HISTORY OF THE CASE

Daryl Renard Atkins was convicted of abduction, armed robbery, and capital murder and was sentenced to death. On August 16, 1996, Atkins and William Jones, both armed with semiautomatic weapons, abducted Airman Michael Nesbitt, robbed him, drove him to an ATM, forced him to withdraw money, and then took him to an isolated location, where he was shot eight times at close range. At the penalty phase of the trial, the state proved two aggravating circumstances: future dangerousness and "vileness of the offense." The defense relied on the testimony of Dr. Evan Nelson, a forensic psychologist, who had evaluated Atkins before the trial and concluded that he was "mildly mentally retarded." The jury sentenced Atkins to death, and the Supreme Court of Virginia affirmed.

SUMMARY OF ARGUMENTS

Atkins argued that he could not be sentenced to death because he was mentally retarded.

DECISION

The Court held that execution of mentally retarded persons violated the Eighth Amendment.

In a 6-3 decision, Justice John Paul Stevens wrote that the meaning of the Eighth Amendment must be drawn from "the evolving standards of decency that mark the progress of a maturing society." At the time of this decision, 18 states had determined that the execution of the mentally retarded was cruel and unusual and, thus, deemed illegal. Justice Stevens focused not on the number of states that shared this opinion but on the consistency of the direction of change. "Given the well-known fact that anti-crime legislation is far more popular than legislation providing protections for persons guilty of violent crime," he stated, "the large number of states prohibiting the execution of mentally retarded persons (and the complete absence of states passing legislation reinstating the power to conduct such executions) provides powerful evidence that today our society views mentally retarded offenders as categorically less culpable than the average criminal."

In addition, unless it could be shown that executing mentally retarded persons promoted the goals of retribution and deterrence, doing so was nothing more than "purposeless and needless imposition of pain and suffering," which the Eighth Amendment forbids. Justice Stevens concluded that the Eighth Amendment prohibited executing the mentally retarded under the "evolving standards of decency" test, in which punishments are evaluated to determine whether they are cruel and unusual.

AFTERMATH

In 2005, a jury found that Atkins's newly reported IQ score of 70 qualified him for execution under Virginia law. The IQ increase was attributed to Atkins's constant involvement in litigation of his case and abstention from alcohol and drugs. His execution was scheduled for December 2005 but was later stayed.

In 2008, Atkins's intelligence was again called into question. This time, Atkins's codefendant, William Jones, was unable to testify because of allegations of prosecutorial misconduct. Atkins's death penalty sentence was subsequently reduced to life in prison. Though prosecutors appealed the decision, the Virginia Supreme Court upheld Atkins's commuted sentence.

SIGNIFICANCE

The Supreme Court decision in *Atkins* reversed death penalty sentences in dozens of capital punishment cases across the United States. Defendants who have intellectual disabilities convicted of crimes eligible for capital punishment are now exempt from death penalty sentences. However, it is left up to the states to define mental retardation for purposes of the holding.

RELATED CASE

Penry v. Lynaugh, 492 U.S. 302 (1989)

RECOMMENDED READING

Alexis Krulish Dowling, *Post-*Atkins *Problems with Enforcing the Supreme Court's Ban on Executing the Mentally Retarded,* 33 Seton Hall Law Review 773 (2003).

Case Title: *Roper v. Simmons*

Legal Citation: 543 U.S. 551

Year of Decision: 2005

KEY ISSUE

Does the execution of minors violate the prohibition of "cruel and unusual punishment" found in the Eighth Amendment?

HISTORY OF THE CASE

In 1993, in the state of Missouri, the then 17-year-old Christopher Simmons and two friends, Charles Benjamin and John Tessmer, planned to murder

Shirley Crook by breaking into her house, tying her up, and throwing her off a bridge. Simmons was a junior in high school at the time of the events, and the record indicates that he believed they would not be punished for the crime because they were minors. Tessmer changed his mind, but the other two broke into Crook's home, bound her hands, covered her eyes, and then drove her to a state park and tossed her off a bridge.

Police were tipped off that Simmons was bragging about the murder at high school, and he was arrested. He waived his rights and eventually confessed to the chilling crime, and his accomplice, Tessmer, who was initially charged with conspiracy, had his charge dropped in return for testimony against Simmons. It was then discovered that although Simmons and his cohort were unaware of whose home they had broken into, he recognized Crook from a prior vehicle accident the two had had, and this confirmed his resolve to murder her. He was charged with burglary, kidnapping, stealing, and murder in the first degree. The jury returned a guilty verdict and, after considering a number of mitigating factors, still recommended a death sentence. On appeal, the Missouri Supreme Court affirmed.

However, prior to the Supreme Court's decision in this case, that Court held that the Eighth Amendment prohibits the execution of a mentally retarded person in *Atkins v. Virginia* (2002). Simmons then filed a new petition for state postconviction relief based on the fact that the *Atkins* decision contained reasoning that could potentially be used to persuade a court that juveniles also should not be subject to the death penalty. The Missouri Supreme Court agreed, holding that evolving standards of decency in the United States suggest that subjecting juveniles to death does in fact violate the Eighth Amendment. That court then set aside Simmons's death sentence in favor of life imprisonment without the possibility of release. The state of Missouri appealed to the U.S. Supreme Court and certiorari was granted.

SUMMARY OF ARGUMENTS

Simmons argued that since the Court considered the nation's evolving standards of decency as the basis for its decision in *Atkins,* the same analysis should apply to whether or not the Eighth Amendment prohibits the execution of minors because it constitutes cruel and unusual punishment.

The state of Missouri argued that the state should be allowed to treat Simmons as an adult and thus eligible for the death penalty upon a conviction for murder, because of the severity of the offense and because of the state law that defined *adult* as "a person seventeen years of age or older."

DECISION

In a 5-4 decision, Justice Anthony Kennedy reasoned that under the "evolving standards of decency" test, it would be cruel and unusual punishment to execute a person who was under the age of 18 at the time of the murder. Kennedy looked at the number of states that prohibit the juvenile death penalty—30. He also considered that in the 20 states that do not expressly prohibit the juvenile death penalty, it is used infrequently. The majority stated, "Capital punishment must be limited to those offenders who commit 'a narrow category of the most serious crimes' and whose extreme culpability makes them 'the most deserving of execution.'"

The Court distinguished juveniles under the age of 18 from "the worst offenders," who are adults subject to the death penalty, in three ways: First, scientific studies have shown that juveniles exhibit a lack of maturity and responsibility; second, juveniles are more vulnerable to negative influences and outside pressures; and, third, juveniles have not fully developed their personality traits and character. These characteristics diminish culpability and, thus, lessen the justifications for the death penalty. The Court also considered the fact that the United States was the only country in the world that continued to sanction the death penalty for juveniles. Accordingly, the Court held that the imposition of death upon a person under the age of 18 violated the cruel and unusual punishment portion of the Eighth Amendment.

Justice Stevens agreed with the majority's opinion and wrote a concurring opinion, joined by Justice Ginsburg, stressing the importance of evolving standards of decency when construing the Constitution. Justice O'Connor wrote a dissenting opinion, arguing that the Court's ruling in *Stanford v. Kentucky* (1989) should have been followed. In that case, the Court relied upon contemporary standards of decency in reaching its conclusion that children over the age of 15 but under the age of 18 could be subjected to the death penalty. Justice O'Connor argued that evidence of contrary contemporary standards of decency had not emerged to substantiate the majority's opinion. She also argued that the record failed to demonstrate that jurors were incapable of assessing the defendant's maturity and mitigating characteristics of being a youth.

Justice Scalia also wrote a dissenting opinion and was joined by Chief Justice Rehnquist and Justice Thomas. He urged that the Court was imposing its own moral standard on the nation. He argued that the meaning of the Constitution should not be determined by the subjective views of the members of the Court and other like-minded foreign courts and legislatures. Justice Scalia went on to note that the number of offenders under the age of 18 subject to the death penalty had held steady or slightly increased since *Stanford,* thus discrediting the majority's argument that the national consensus had changed since the decision in that case. In questioning the existence of a "national consensus" against imposing the death penalty on children under the age of 18, Justice Scalia stated that "all the Court has done today, to borrow from another context, is to look over the heads of the crowd and pick out its friends."

Aftermath

The Court's decision in this case effectively overruled *Stanford v. Kentucky,* which had upheld the use of the death penalty for offenders of at least age 16 at the time of the crime. However, in 2003, the Kentucky governor Paul Patton commuted Stanford's death sentence.

The Court's decision in this case was met with some criticism, particularly from those who argued that any person, including juveniles, should be treated as an adult for purposes of punishment when the crimes were heinous, such as first-degree murder. One case in particular, which drew national recognition, was the "Beltway Sniper" case. In that case, a 17-year-old boy, Lee Boyd Malvo, was involved in many shooting attacks on individuals in 2002 in the Washington, D.C., Metropolitan Area, and evaded authorities for quite some time. Malvo was eventually apprehended; however, he was not eligible for the death penalty because he was only 17 when the crimes were committed and, thus, not eligible under the Court's decision in *Roper.*

Significance

The Court's decision in this case made it clear throughout the nation that children under the age of 18 could not be sentenced to death, regardless of the crime committed, because execution would constitute a violation of the cruel and unusual punishment clause of the Eighth Amendment. Of key importance in the Court's decision-making process was the "national consensus" determined to exist by the Court that the nation as a whole disapproved of such executions, as evidenced by the fact that 30 states had already passed laws disallowing the death penalties for persons under the age of 18. Foreign courts and legislatures that held the same view of such executions also influenced the Court.

Related Cases

Coker v. Georgia, 433 U.S. 584 (1977)

Thompson v. Oklahoma, 487 U.S. 815 (1988)

Stanford v. Kentucky, 492 U.S. 361 (1989)

Atkins v. Virginia, 536 U.S. 304 (2002)

Kennedy v. Louisiana, 554 U.S. 407 (2008)

Recommended Reading

Tamar R. Birckhead, *The Age of the Child: Interrogating Juveniles after* Roper v. Simmons, 65 Washington and Lee Law Review 385 (2008).

Erin H. Flynn, *Dismantling the Felony-Murder Rule: Juvenile Deterrence and Retribution post–* Roper v. Simmons, 156 University of Pennsylvania Law Review 1049 (2008).

Janine D. Garlitz, *The Abolition of the Juvenile Death Penalty in* Roper v. Simmons, 30 Nova Law Review 473 (2006).

Catherine B. Pober, *The Eighth Amendment's Proscription against Cruel and Unusual Punishments Requires a Categorical Rejection of the Death Penalty as Imposed on Juvenile Offenders under the Age of Eighteen:* Roper v. Simmons, 44 Duquesne Law Review 121 (2005).

Case Title: *Brown v. Sanders*

Legal Citation: 546 U.S. 212

Year of Decision: 2006

KEY ISSUE

Should a death sentence stand when a state supreme court invalidates two of the four special aggravating circumstances considered by the jury during sentencing?

HISTORY OF THE CASE

Ronald Sanders and a companion broke into the home of Dale Boender and his girlfriend, Janice Allen. Sanders bound and blindfolded Boender and Allen and struck both victims on the head with a blunt object. Allen died of the blow. Sanders was convicted of first-degree murder, attempted murder, robbery, burglary, and attempted robbery.

The jury found four special circumstances under California law, each of which independently rendered Sanders eligible for the death penalty. During the penalty phase, the jury was instructed to consider a list of sentencing factors relating to Sanders's background and the nature of the crimes. The jury sentenced Sanders to death. On appeal, the California Supreme Court invalidated two of the four special circumstances found by the jury but affirmed the sentence. The Ninth Circuit Court of Appeals overturned Sanders's sentence.

SUMMARY OF ARGUMENTS

Sanders argued that the jury's consideration of invalid special circumstances rendered his death sentence unconstitutional under the Eighth Amendment. Inclusion of the invalid circumstances was not a harmless error but one that unfairly led to the jury's imposition of the death penalty at sentencing. The Ninth Circuit was correct in determining that the jury should not have received instructions on the invalid special circumstances.

Jill Brown, warden for the state, argued that Sanders's case was not prejudiced by the invalid special circumstances presented to the jury. In California, a "nonweighing" state, aggravating circumstances are less significant in the sentencing process. The jury considers more than just special circumstances when determining the appropriate sentence. Inclusion of invalid special circumstances was a harmless error, and therefore, Sanders's sentence should be upheld.

DECISION

In a 5-4 decision, the Court upheld the sentence and established a new rule: Invalidated sentencing factors made a sentence unconstitutional if they added aggravating weight to the jury's weighing process, "unless one of the other sentencing factors enables the sentencer to give aggravating weight to the same facts and circumstances." In California, the sentencer is instructed to weigh aggravation against mitigation and can only consider evidence in aggravation if the evidence falls within a statutorily defined factor.

In this case, all of the aggravating facts and circumstances that were considered under the invalidated factors were also properly considered under one of the valid factors. Thus, the invalidated factors did not "skew" the sentence, and no constitutional violation occurred.

AFTERMATH

The decision resulted in upholding the death sentence for the petitioner by agreeing with the district court's determination that the invalid special circumstances did not prejudice its decision that the valid special circumstances warranted a sentence of death.

SIGNIFICANCE

This decision established a firm standard for dealing with special circumstances in sentencing. If jury instructions required the jury to examine the existence of special circumstances and weigh them in determining the sentence imposed, the court need not necessarily find that if some were found invalid on appeal, the whole sentencing trial had to be retried. Rather, it could decide if the invalid special circumstances were of sufficient weight to influence the remaining valid circumstances. This had a result of giving courts more authority to settle sentencing issues without lengthy rehearings.

RELATED CASES

Zant v. Stephens, 462 U.S. 862 (1983)

Stringer v. Black, 503 U.S. 222 (1992)

Tuilaepa v. California, 512 U.S. 967 (1994)

RECOMMENDED READING

Eighth Amendment—Death Penalty—Consideration of Invalid Sentencing, 120 Harvard Law Review 134 (2006).

Nicholas Fromhertz, *Assuming Too Much: An Analysis of* Brown v. Sanders, 43 San Diego Law Review 401 (2006).

Stephen Hornbuckle, *Capital Sentencing Procedure: A Lethal Oddity in the Supreme Court's Case Law,* 73 Texas Law Review 441 (1994).

Ryan J. Miller, *A Death Sentence May Be Constitutional Despite a Determination That Two of Four Special Circumstances Found by the Jury Were Invalid:* Brown v. Sanders, 45 Duquesne Law Review 343 (2007).

Case Title: *Oregon v. Guzek*

Legal Citation: 546 U.S. 517

Year of Decision: 2006

KEY ISSUES

Do the Eighth and Fourteenth Amendments to the U.S. Constitution grant a defendant facing the death penalty a constitutional right at sentencing to present new evidence that is inconsistent with his or her prior conviction and sheds no light on the manner in which the crime was committed?

HISTORY OF THE CASE

Randy Guzek was convicted of murder and sentenced to death for the murder of a woman during a burglary. Evidence was presented at trial that Guzek's two associates pointed to him as the ringleader, and a jury found Guzek guilty. Guzek was sentenced to death, and he appealed the decision, attacking the constitutionality of Oregon's death penalty scheme, among other arguments. On appeal, the Oregon Supreme Court affirmed his conviction but vacated the sentence, ruling that the death sentence violated the Eighth Amendment because the jury "must be given the full range of authority to consider and act on mitigating evidence that the federal Constitution requires." The court remanded the case back to the trial court for a new sentencing trial.

On remand, Guzek was again sentenced to death. He appealed, and the Oregon Supreme Court again vacated the sentence, ruling that "victim impact" evidence presented by the state during the sentencing was not relevant; thus, Guzek's death sentence was unconstitutional. The case was remanded for a third sentencing trial.

At the third sentencing trial, Guzek was again sentenced to death. On appeal, the Oregon Supreme Court found that the trial judge failed to instruct the jury that life in prison without the possibility of parole was an available alternative sentence to the death penalty. Once again, Guzek's sentence was vacated and remanded for a new sentencing trial. The court, to avoid further errors at his next sentencing, also addressed the exclusion of alibi evidence that Guzek had sought to admit. This alibi evidence comprised transcripts of testimony by his mother and grandfather, stating that he was with them at the time of the murder. The Oregon Supreme Court ruled that Guzek had a right to present this alibi evidence at his upcoming death penalty sentencing. The state of Oregon then petitioned the U.S. Supreme Court for review.

SUMMARY OF ARGUMENTS

Guzek first presented a motion asking the Supreme Court to dismiss his claim for lack of jurisdiction over a state law. Guzek then argued that he had a constitutional right under the Eighth Amendment to present new evidence showing that he was not at the scene of the crime at a sentencing trial.

The state argued that the Eighth Amendment did not grant a defendant the right to his legal culpability or guilt at the penalty stage. The state further argued that there was no alternative Oregon state law allowing for admitting alibi evidence at the penalty phase. The state contended that the penalty phase was simply used for deciding the appropriate penalty for the defendant's crime and did not allow for a redetermination of the defendant's guilt.

DECISION

In an 8-0 decision (Justice Alito did not participate), the Supreme Court, in a decision written by Justice Breyer, held that the Court had jurisdiction "to review state court determinations that rest upon federal law" and that Guzek's sentence was based on legal conclusions established in relevant part upon federal law. The Court then went on to discuss whether Guzek had a constitutional right to introduce evidence at sentencing that was not only new but also inconsistent with his prior conviction. The Court held that there is nothing in either the Eighth or the Fourteenth Amendments that provides a right of this type for a capital defendant.

The Court summarized its prior cases discussing a constitutional right to present evidence. The Court had decided in *Lockett v. Ohio* (1978) that at sentencing a defendant may not be precluded from presenting evidence of a mitigating factor of any aspect of the defendant's character or any circumstance of the offense. However, the Court here distinguished Guzek's alibi evidence as evidence to show whether he had even committed the crime, not the way the crime was committed; thus,

Guzek's evidence was not sentence related. The Court also stated that in the prior case, evidence that was allowed was not inconsistent with the jury's finding of guilt, as Guzek's evidence was.

The Court then discussed its prior plurality decision in *Franklin v. Lynaugh* (1988), in which it made clear that the Court had not interpreted the Eighth Amendment to provide a capital defendant with a right to produce at sentencing evidence to cast doubt upon his guilt of the crime. The Court held that the states are permitted by the U.S. Constitution to limit such evidence as Guzek was attempting to present to evidence that had already been presented at trial. The Court further ruled that the Eighth Amendment did not create a right to introduce evidence of innocence in a defendant's death penalty sentencing phase if it had not been introduced in the trial phase.

In a concurring opinion, Justice Scalia, joined by Justice Thomas, argued that the Court should eliminate all doubt as to the legitimacy of Eighth Amendment claims regarding presenting new evidence at trial. He stated that the Court should make it clear that any claim that the amount of residual doubt evidence presented in the guilt phase of the trial was insufficient to satisfy the compelling need for innocence-related evidence was meritless under the Court's holding.

AFTERMATH

Guzek prevented future defendants from fighting a death sentence by using the argument that they were not responsible for the crime unless the court decided to allow such evidence at the penalty stage. This ruling encouraged defendants to ensure all evidence of innocence was presented at trial since they did not have a guaranteed right to present such evidence at a later time.

SIGNIFICANCE

This case set limits on the evidence that a defendant could submit during the penalty phase of the trial. The Supreme Court found that residual doubt evidence concerned whether the defendant committed the crime, an issue the jury had already resolved. While the Court did not find that a defendant could not offer residual doubt evidence during the penalty phase of the trial, the Court did find that there was not an absolute right to have such evidence included. Instead, the states could decide for themselves which evidence was relevant.

RELATED CASES

Lockett v. Ohio, 438 U.S. 586, 604 (1978)

Green v. Georgia, 442 U.S. 95 (1979)

Franklin v. Lynaugh, 487 U.S. 164, 173, n. 6 (1988)

RECOMMENDED READING

Kenneth C. Haas, *The Emerging Death Penalty Jurisprudence of the Roberts Court,* 6 Pierce L Rev 3 (2008).

James S. Liebman, *Slow Dancing with Death: The Supreme Court and Capital Punishment, 1963–2006,* 107 Colum L Rev 1 (2007).

Victor Streib, *The State of Criminal Justice,* 22 WTR Crim Just 30 (2008).

Case Title: *Kennedy v. Louisiana*

Legal Citation: 554 U.S. 407

Year of Decision: 2008

KEY ISSUE

Does the imposition of the death penalty for those convicted of child rape when the rape did not and was not intended to result in the death of the child violate the Eighth Amendment's protection against cruel and unusual punishment?

HISTORY OF THE CASE

This case involved the violent rape of an eight-year-old girl by her stepfather, Patrick Kennedy. At 9:18 A.M. on Monday, March 2, 1998, Kennedy called 911 to report that his stepdaughter, referred to in this case as "L. H.," had been raped

that morning while she was near the garage of her home. Kennedy claimed that he heard L. H. screaming, and so he ran outside, finding that L. H. was on the ground and that two neighborhood boys had committed the rape. When the police arrived, they found L. H. wrapped in a blood-stained blanket. Kennedy had used water and a cloth to wipe blood from the victim, which later prevented the collection of a reliable DNA sample.

L. H. was then taken to the Children's Hospital, and testimony from an expert in pediatric forensic medicine stated that L. H.'s injuries were the worst he had ever seen from a sexual assault in his experience. From the time of the injuries and up until a few weeks after the event, both Kennedy and L. H. maintained that two boys from the neighborhood had raped L. H. However, L. H. reportedly told one family member that Kennedy had raped her. Eight days after the crime had been committed, Kennedy was arrested on the basis of evidence that suggested that the crime had occurred in L. H.'s bedroom, not outside where L. H. and Kennedy claimed the events had occurred. Further evidence showed that Kennedy had informed his employer he could not work that day and had called a colleague and carpet cleaning service in an attempt to remove the bloodstains from the carpet, all of which took place before 8 A.M. L. H. later admitted to her mother that Kennedy had, in fact, been her assailant.

Kennedy was charged with aggravated rape, and the Louisiana statute made this crime punishable by death. The trial began in August, and L. H., who was then 13 years old, testified against Kennedy, identifying him as her attacker. Kennedy was convicted and, after evidence of another sexual molestation surfaced, was sentenced to death. The Supreme Court of Louisiana affirmed this, noting that the federal government and 14 states allowed the death penalty for nonhomicide crimes. The U.S. Supreme Court granted certiorari.

SUMMARY OF ARGUMENTS

Kennedy argued that the death penalty was not a proportionate punishment for the crime of rape and that Louisiana's law allowing the death penalty for rape of minors violated the Eighth Amendment.

DECISION

The Court held that imposing the death penalty for offenders convicted of child rape violated the Eighth Amendment because it constituted cruel and unusual punishment. This decision was narrowly construed as to include only those cases in which the crime did not, and was not intended to, result in the death of the victim.

Justice Kennedy delivered the opinion of the Court.

The Court began by stating that all states are subject to the Eighth Amendment through the Fourteenth Amendment. In discussing the scope of the Eighth Amendment, the Court referenced *Atkins v. Virginia* (2002), which established that the amendment prohibits "all excessive punishments, as well as cruel and unusual punishments that may or may not be excessive." The Eighth Amendment is also guided by a general principle that punishments be proportionate to sentences. The death penalty as a consequence for committing a crime does not inherently violate the Eighth Amendment; however, not all crimes can be punished by the death penalty. The Court then turned to whether Louisiana's child rape law, which provided for possible death by execution, was permissible under the Eighth Amendment.

The Court focused on current societal norms and changes in the law since its decision in *Furman v. Georgia* (1972), which temporarily suspended the death penalty throughout the United States, to determine whether a national consensus existed on the issue. In general, the Court has attempted to confine the instances in which the death penalty can be used. The Court has held that the death penalty cannot be used against juveniles, mentally retarded individuals, or offenders who rape an adult in which no death occurs or was intended to occur. To gain a better understanding of national sentiment toward the death penalty for child rape, the Court also explored objective criteria, such as the number of current states with laws similar to that of Louisiana. Since the Court's decision in *Furman*, six states reenacted varying capital rape provisions, all of which

were eventually shot down. Louisiana was one of these states. However, it reintroduced the death penalty for the aggravated rape of a child in 1995, essentially making rape of a child a strict liability offense because mistake of age was not allowed as a defense. Five other states followed Louisiana's lead with varying legislation that essentially addressed the same issues. On the basis of these findings, the Court concluded that "the evidence of a national consensus with respect to the death penalty for child rapists, as with respect to juveniles, mentally retarded offenders, and vicarious felony murderers, shows divided opinion but, on balance, an opinion against it."

The Court also looked at a number of death sentences for child rape, finding statistics that confirmed a social consensus against the death penalty for the crime of child rape. According to those statistics, no person in the United States had been executed for the rape of a child or adult since 1964. The state then argued that *Coker v. Georgia* (1977), in which the death penalty for adult rape was held to be unconstitutional, did not apply to cases involving children. However, the Court held that although *Coker* did not address child rape, some of the same reasoning used there applied to this case. For instance, as in *Coker*, this case involved a rape in which no life was taken. The Court found that fact to be a compelling reason as to why the death penalty was disproportionate to the crime of rape, even though rape is a reprehensible crime. Thus, the Court held that the only nonhomicide crimes in which the death penalty can be imposed are crimes against the state.

The Court further reasoned that allowing this type of legislation would make death penalty standards "indefinite and obscure." The Court additionally looked at the further impact on the victim's life, including court appearances and testimony, and found that using the child to advocate the death of the perpetrator "forces a moral choice on the child, who is not of mature age to make that choice." The Court also noted that children's testimony is often unreliable and can be induced, and thus, there is a risk of wrongful conviction in some of these cases. The Court expressed concern that, since these crimes usually involve family members, the number of unreported incidents might increase if the death penalty were allowed because the child might fear that a family member would be sentenced to death. Further reasoning suggested that prohibiting the death penalty when death of the child did not result created an incentive for the offender not to take the victim's life. On the basis of the previous discussion, the Court held that "a death sentence for one who raped but did not kill a child, and who did not intend to assist another in killing the child, is unconstitutional under the Eighth and Fourteenth Amendments." Accordingly, the judgment of the Supreme Court of Louisiana was reversed, and the case was remanded for further proceedings.

Justice Alito wrote a dissenting opinion in which he disagreed with the Court's justifications of a national consensus and its independent judgment. As for the majority's reference to a "national consensus," Justice Alito argued that this claim was flawed because dicta in *Coker* suggested such legislation would be struck down and "has stunted consideration of the question whether the death penalty for the targeted offense of raping a young child is consistent with prevailing standards of decency." He asserted that "the *Coker* dicta gave state legislators a strong incentive not to push for the enactment of new capital child-rape laws even though these legislators and their constituents may have believed that the laws would be appropriate and desirable." Thus, legislatures' failure to enact child-rape laws could not be viewed as evidence of a national consensus against such a punishment. As for the majority's "independent judgment," Justice Alito stated that "the Court has provided no coherent explanation for today's decision" because the Court's policy arguments did not answer whether using the death penalty for these crimes constituted cruel and unusual punishment.

AFTERMATH

The decision in this case received heavy criticism and was even discussed during the 2008 presidential campaigns of President Barack Obama and his opponent, Senator John McCain. Both President Obama and Senator McCain expressed discontent with the decision, as did many media outlets and legal scholars.

SIGNIFICANCE

This case limited state power in implementing the death penalty for crimes that do not result in the victim's death, which is now limited to crimes against the state. Of these crimes against the state, several were explicitly mentioned, including treason, espionage, terrorism, and drug kingpin activity.

RELATED CASES

Coker v. Georgia, 433 U.S. 584 (1977)

Thompson v. Oklahoma, 487 U.S. 815 (1988)

Atkins v. Virginia, 536 U.S. 304 (2002)

Roper v. Simmons, 543 U.S. 551 (2005)

RECOMMENDED READING

Benjamin J. Flickinger, Kennedy v. Louisiana: *The United States Supreme Court Erroneously Finds a National Consensus against the Use of the Death Penalty for the Crime of Child Rape*, 42 Creighton Law Review 655 (2009).

Kelly J. Minor, *Prohibiting the Death Penalty for the Rape of a Child While Overlooking Wrongful Execution*: Kennedy v. Louisiana, 54 South Dakota Law Review 300 (2009).